Economic Decisions for Consumers

Economic Decisions for Consumers

Don R. Leet
California State University, Fresno

Joann Driggers
Mount San Antonio College

Wadsworth Publishing Co.
Belmont, California
A Division of Wadsworth, Inc.

Economics Editor: Bob Podstepny
Developmental Editor: Sheryl Fullerton
Production: Del Mar Associates
Designer: Louis Neiheisel
Editorial Supervisor: Jackie Estrada
Copy Editor: Andrea Matyas
Illustrators: Karl Nicholason, John Odam
Technical Illustrators: Richard Carter, Kim Fraley

Photo Credits
Cover: William Call, Steve Dunn, Godlis, Vernon Gerety, Jerri Booth. 22: Gordon Menzie/Photophile; 26, 57, 58, 99, 143, 148, 165, 169, 178-181, 187, 248, 282, 418, 462, 473: William Call; 75, 294: Godlis; 88, 115, 171: Steve Dunn; 234: Jackie Estrada; 311: Courtesy of NASA; 312: Courtesy of Edmund Scientific; 316: Leonard Rhodes/Photophile; 330, 354, 385: Vernon Gerety; 407: Wide World Photos; 426: Jerri Booth.

© 1983 by Wadsworth, Inc. All rights reserved. No part of this book may be reproduced, stored in a retrieval system, or transcribed, in any form or by any means, electronic, mechanical, photocopying, recording, or otherwise, without the prior written permission of the publisher, Wadsworth Publishing Company, Belmont, California 94002, a division of Wadsworth, Inc.

Printed in the United States of America

3 4 5 6 7 8 9 10—87 86 85 84

ISBN 0-534-01061-X

Library of Congress Cataloging in Publication Data

Leet, Don R
 Economic Decisions for Consumers

 Includes index.
 1. Consumer education. I. Driggers, Joann.
II. Title.
TX335.L43 1982   640.73   82-13590
ISBN 0-534-01207-8

Preface

In this decade Americans have seen record-high interest rates, unemployment, and continuing inflation. This has caused havoc with consumer earning and spending, to say nothing of goals and dreams. Perhaps your search for a way to cope with one or more of these problems has caused you to enroll in this course. As a consumer, you can be assured that there are many things you can do to improve your economic situation. We hope that after reading this text you will make better, more-informed economic decisions.

The Plan of the Book

We begin our quest for improving your economic decision-making skills by introducing some basic economic concepts in Chapter 1. Chapter 2 deals with the forces that influence consumers choices, values, and goals. It also introduces a decision-making model that is applied throughout the book. The next few chapters explore the factors that affect consumers' spending decisions, including stages in the individual and family life cycles, career choices, advertising, consumer protection agencies and legislation, budgeting and spending patterns, inflation, and the use of credit. In Chapter 9 we introduce the process of comparison buying and apply it to clothing and household textiles and durables. Chapters 10 through 17 apply the decision-making skills developed earlier in the text. These later chapters cover the important consumer topics of food, energy, transportation, housing, health care, taxes, investments, life insurance, and retirement.

Special Features

Neighborhood Capsules After the introductory chapter, all chapters begin with a story about how consumers confront a specific problem that will be addressed in the chapter. We hope that you will find these vignettes interesting and relevant to the topic at hand. You may even recognize a problem that you have faced. The Neighborhood Capsules often end without resolving the problem or with some loose ends that are drawn together in the "Neighborhood Revisited" sections, which also contain some questions that tie the neighborhood problem to the content of the chapter. As the title indicates, these are consumer-oriented problems that could occur down the street from where you live—in your own neighborhood.

Did you know that... Every chapter includes a list of interesting facts or concepts that are explored in the chapter and that are unknown to most consumers. By perusing this list you will get some idea of the information contained in the body of the chapter.

Introductions and Summaries Each chapter begins with an overview that explains how the topics and subtopics of the chapter fit into a cohesive whole. The summaries tie up loose ends and stress the major topics within the chapter. We believe that it is important to have both an overview and a complete summary of each chapter so that students will have an overall grasp of the chapter. These parts of the chapter will be especially helpful in reviewing for examinations.

Chapter Boxes There is a wealth of material that can enrich a course that focuses on the many economic decisions facing consumers. Some of this material involves applying concepts and strategies to the specific personal problems that a consumer may encounter. In a number of chapters we have provided worksheets for the reader to enter real-world data and to try some of the strategies for better decision making suggested in the text. These interactive boxes should make the chapter material come alive and be of more relevance in the day-to-day world of the student-consumer. Other boxes provide asides or additional detail that may not be crucial to a particular section but that add depth and breadth of knowledge. These enrichment boxes were fun to write, and we hope that they are interesting asides to the reader. They may also serve to open discussion in the classroom. Many enrichment boxes are followed by discussion questions that try to involve the reader in applying the boxed material.

End-of-Chapter Materials Each chapter ends with Key Terms, Questions, Projects, and Suggested Readings. All of the key terms are in bold type when they first appear in the chapter, and all are defined in the glossary. The questions and projects were selected to emphasize the most important point of the chapter and to allow the student to apply the concepts presented. The reading list serves the dual purpose of documenting specific citations within the chapter and of providing articles and books from which a student can gather data and additional information about subjects mentioned within the chapter.

Appendixes We have included three informational appendixes because we believe our textbook should be helpful whenever you confront a real-world consumer problem. Appendix I lists many of the most common consumer complaints and suggests the relevant local, state, and federal agencies to contact. Appendixes II and III provide a directory of these agencies.

Glossary All of the boldfaced words in the text are collected and defined in the glossary. If you are unsure of the meaning of any key term, you can always find it defined in the glossary at the back of the book.

Acknowledgments

We are indebted to many people who have helped us in completing our book. Our first debt of gratitude must go to our families and friends, who have shown us support and consideration throughout the long and sometimes tedious process of creating a viable manuscript. Secondly, we must single out Jerri Booth, Shirley Pennell, Sue Ann Landers, Vickie Leet, and Ingrid Matenge for typing parts of the manuscript. Most of the photographs were done expressly for our book by Vernon Gerety or Jerri Booth and they deserve our appreciation for work above and beyond the call of duty. The staff at Wadsworth also deserve kudos. We thank them all, from Steve Rutter and Marshall Aronson, who first pointed out the need for this book, to Sheryl Fullerton who shepherded our phrases into a flock of logically consistent chapters with lots of "for examples." Of course the quality of the manuscript owes a great deal to the helpful reviews we received from Joseph E. Barr, Framingham State College; Howard K. Boone, Monterey Peninsula College; Genevieve H. Cory, Canada College; Joseph L. Craycraft, University of Cincinnati; Joanne R. Dempsey, Bradley University; Judy Farris, South Dakota State University; Vickie L. Hampton, University of Texas, Austin; Hilda Jo Jennings, Northern Arizona University; John Neal, Lake Sumter Community College; Clifford Pew, Gavilan College; Shirley Schecter, Queens College of the City University of New York; Peter R. Senn, Wright College; Elsie Takeguchi, Sacramento City College; and June Varner, Ohio University.

Professor Driggers would like to offer a special thank you for help, for love, and for understanding to George and Jo Portlock, Larry Redinger, and JoAnn Crist.

Professor Leet would like to offer special thanks to his colleagues Loy Bilderback, James Echols, James Garrett, Mary Littwin, Henry Placenti, and Izumi Taniguchi at California State University, Fresno, for their help during the project. I also want to acknowledge the technical/legal assistance that my brother, James L. Leet, Esq., rendered above and beyond the call of brotherly duty. Finally, I want to thank my wife Vickie and my children Sara, Megan, and Andrew for their special support and understanding.

Contents

1 Life in Consumer America: Survival of the Fittest—1

The Need for Consumer Education 4
What Is Consumer Economics? 5
The Rewards of Good Decision Making 6
The Age of High Mass Consumption 6
Factors in Consumption Patterns 8
Income 8
Time 9
Tastes: Consumer Preferences Revealed 10
Prices 11
Consuming: Past, Present, and Future 11
Past and Present Consumption Patterns 12
Future Consumption Patterns 13

2 Decision Making: Learning to Choose—17

Scarcity: The Mother of Decisions 20
Opportunity Costs 20
Benefits, Too 21
Consuming: More Than Just Buying 22
Values and the Consumer 23
Sources of Values 24
Value Systems and Conflicts 26
Clarifying Values 26
Goals: Values in Action 27
Setting Goals 27
Evaluating Goals 27
Constraints and Restrictions on Decision Making 29
Parents and Family 29
Advisors and Interested Parties 30
Social Customs 30
Advertising, Big Business, Big Government, and Consumer Sovereignty 31
The Consumer Decision-Making Model 33

3 Life Cycles and the Consumer—39

Income: Not Just a Paycheck 42
Level of Income: Facts and Factors 44
Education: Benefits and Costs 44
Supply and Demand 45
Age 46
Demography 46
Sex 46
Race 47
Geographic Location 49
Two-Income Households 49
The Changing American Family 52
Past Marriage and Family Patterns 52
Today's Marriage and Family Patterns 52
Types of Households 53
Single-Person Households 53
Married-Couple Households and the Family Life Cycle 54
Special Problems in the Family Life Cycle 57
Divorce 57
Single Parents 58

vii

Changing Family Roles: Money and Time   58
Work Roles   58
Housework   59
Childcare   62
Career and Job Decisions   62
Leisure Time   63
Retirement   64

Advertising: Information or Manipulation?—69

The Birth of the Advertising Industry   72
Who Are the Major Advertisers?   73
Types of Advertising   76
Informative Advertising   78
Puffery Advertising: A Lot of Hot Air   79
Deceptive Advertising: An Attempt to Mislead the Consumer   82
The Benefits of Advertising   86
Information: More Than You Ever Wanted to Know   86
Advertising and Competition: Lower Prices   87
Brand Names and Quality Control   87
Positive Side Effects of Advertising   89
How to Obtain Information: Just the Facts   89

5 Consumer Protection and Redress: Doing unto Others as They Do unto You—95

Caveat Emptor: An Outdated Concept   98
The Informed Consumer: An Ounce of Prevention   98
The Beginning of Protective Legislation   99
Weights and Measures: Information   99
Food Safety: Protection   100
The Modern Consumer Protection Movement   102
Increasing Consumer Awareness   102
Presidential Support for Consumers   103
The Costs and Benefits of Government Regulation   104
Costs May Outweigh Benefits   105
Regulations Provide Safety   106
Cost-Benefit Analysis   106
Types and Levels of Consumer Protection   106
Federal Protection   108
State and Local Protection   111
Private-Sector Activity   111
Consumer Rights and Responsibilities   116
Enforcing Your Rights: A Practical Problem   116
The Local Level: The Place to Voice Your Problem   117
The Manufacturer   119
State and Federal Agencies   119
The Courts and Legal Assistance   119
Consumer Protection in the 1980s   123

6 Budgeting: Getting in Control—127

The Need for Budgeting 130
Income and Expenses 131
Designing Your Budget 133
The Budgeting Process: How One Family Manages 136
Net Worth 140
Money and Emotions 141
Collective Money Management Techniques 142
Paying Bills 144

7 Inflation: The Declining Dollar—149

Defining and Measuring Inflation: The Consumer Price Index 152
The History of Inflation in Recent Times 155
Demand-Pull Inflation 156
Cost-Push Inflation 157
Hyperinflation 158
Productivity: The Real Enemy of Inflation 158

Inflation: Winners and Losers 160
The Government 160
Businesses 161
Individuals 162
Fighting Inflation: The Personal Side 165
Personal Investments 165
An Overall Personal Plan 167
Rules for Inflation-Wise Consumers 169
Fighting Inflation: A Society-Wide View 171
Politics 171
Special-Interest Groups 172
Consumer Co-Ops 173

8 Credit: Buy Now, Pay More Later—179

An Overview of Credit: How Big? How Much? How Important? 182
The Benefits of Credit 183
Synchronizing Income with Expenses 184
Forced Savings 185
Emergency Fund 186
Inflation and Credit 186
Recordkeeping, Identification, and the Cashless Society 187
Costs of Consumer Credit 187
The Risk of Insolvency 187
Budget Commitment and Flexibility 188
Limited Choice and Higher Costs 188
Finance Charges 188
The Cost of Open-End Credit 191
The Hidden Costs of Credit 196
Sources of Credit 196
Commercial Banks: Full-Service Institutions 196
Consumer Finance Companies 198

Credit Unions 198
Retail Outlets 198
Savings and Loan Associations 198
Family and Friends 199
Life Insurance 200
Pawnbrokers 200
Applying for Credit 200
The Three C's: What Creditors Are Looking For 201
The Creditor's Decision to Accept or Deny Applications 203
The Equal Credit Opportunity Act 203
Credit Without Discrimination 203
What to Do If You Are Denied Credit 204
Fair Credit Billing Act 205
Correcting Billing Errors 205
Stopping Payment for Defective Goods or Services 206
Reporting Lost or Stolen Credit Cards 207
How Much Credit Equals Too Much Debt? 207
Some Guidelines for Establishing Credit Limits 207
Credit Counseling 210
Dealing with Bill Collectors 210
Wage Garnishment 210
Bankruptcy: The Last Resort 211

Review Your Budget 225
Investigate Options 225
Narrow Your Choice 227
Make a Choice 227
Evaluate Your Choice 227
Accept Responsibility of Ownership 227
The Buying Process: Textiles 228
Determine What You Need 228
Review Your Budget 230
Investigate Options 230
Narrow Your Choice and Choose 236
Evaluate Your Choice 238
Accept Responsibility of Ownership 238
The Buying Process: Household Durables 239
Determine What You Need 239
Review Your Budget 240
Investigate Options 242
Narrow Your Choice 244
Make a Choice 244
Evaluate Your Choice 245
Accept Responsibility of Ownership 245

9 Comparison Buying in Fashionable America: Textiles and Household Durables—217

Fashion, Style, and Fads 220
Influences on Fashion 222
Fashion Dictators? 223
The Buying Process 223
Determine What You Need 224

10 Food: More Than a Matter of Taste—249

Food for Thought, Fuel, and Fat 252
Factors That Affect Calorie Needs 252
Factors That Affect Food Choices 252
Guides to Good Nutrition 254
Government Labeling 256
Nutritional Labeling 257
Fair Packaging and Labeling Act 258
Need for Other Kinds of Labeling 259
Safety and Quality 260
Meat Inspection and Grading 260
The Rest of Your Diet 260

Codes: Prices and Dates 262
Universal Product Code 262
Unit Pricing 262
Fresh, Aged, or Stale? 264
Hazards to Food Safety 265
Pesticide Residue 266
Food Additives 267
Costs and Benefits of Safety 269
Back to Nature: Health Foods and Vitamins 270
Natural and Organic Food 271
Dietary Supplements 272
Getting Good Nutrition at Reasonable Prices 272
Planning, Spending, Eating–and Decision Making 273
Convenience Foods 277

11 Energy: Conservation Pays—283

Energy: How Much, What, Who? 287
Energy and Transportation 289
The Automobile 290
Other Forms of Personal Transportation 294
Mass Transit 295
Ridesharing: A Personal Alternative to Mass Transit 297
Energy Use in the Home 299
Measuring Home Energy Use 299
Saving Energy in the Home 303
Energy and Your Future 310

12 The Automobile: Wheels and Deals—317

Basic Automobile Decisions 320
The Costs of Automobile Ownership and Operation 322
Fixed Costs 322
Variable Costs 325
Evaluating Costs 327
Shopping for a Car 330
New Car Buying Strategies 330
Leasing a New Car 332
Buying a Used Car 334
Automobile Repairs 337
Automobile Warranties 337
Auto Service Contracts 339
Selecting a Mechanic 340
Automobile Insurance 342
The Basic Insurance Package 342
Looking for Auto Insurance 345
No-Fault Insurance 348

13 Housing: Home Sweet Home—355

To Rent or to Buy? 358
Advantages of Renting 358
Disadvantages of Renting 359

Advantages of Buying 359
Disadvantages of Buying 359
The First Step: Identifying Your Needs 361
The Second Step: Estimating How Much You Can Afford 361
The Third Step: Exploring Housing Options 364
Single-Family Homes 364
Multiunit Housing Complexes 364
Mobile Homes 365
New or Old? 366
Whether Renting or Buying: Investigate 366
The Fourth Step: Choosing Your Housing 368
Renting 370
Buying a Home 374
The Fifth Step: Moving 389
The Sixth Step: Evaluating Your Choice 390
Renting 390
Buying 391
The Seventh Step: Accepting Responsibility 391

14 Health Care: What Happens When You Get Sick in Consumer America—395

Health Care in the United States 398
The Cost of Health Care 402
The Demand for Health Care 404
Medicare: Aid for the Elderly 406
Medicaid: Health Care for the Poor 407
The Supply of Medical Care 407
Physicians 407
Increasing the Supply of Health-Care Personnel 408
Hospitals 410
Health System Agencies: The Consumer Counterattack 412

The New Jersey Hospital Cost Containment Plan 413
Prescription Drugs 414
Generic Drugs: A Bargain for the Consumer 415
Over-the-Counter Drugs 416
Health Insurance: Private Plans 416
Basic Coverage 419
Major Medical-Expense Insurance 420
Disability Income Protection 421
Dental-Expense Insurance 422
The Health Maintenance Organization 422
Alternative Health-Care Systems: Is There a Better Way? 423
Staying Healthy: The Best Way to Avoid the High Cost of Health Care 424

15 Government Services and Taxation: Paying Your Fair Share—431

The Government: An Overview 434
Providing Goods and Services 434
Transferring Income 435
Taxation 436
The Principles of Taxation 438
Progressive, Proportional, and Regressive Taxes 438
The Federal Budget and Income Tax 441
Federal Income Tax 442
Marginal and Average Tax Rates 445

Understanding the Federal Income Tax 447
An Overview of Tax Calculations 447
Exclusions 448
Deductions 449
Exemptions 452
Tax Credits 452
Seeking Tax Advice: Professional Tax Preparers 453
The Dreaded Tax Audit 454
The Overall Tax Burden: Is It Fair? 456

16 Saving and Investing: Is a Penny Saved a Penny Earned?—463

The Vocabulary of Investment and Personal Finance 466
Yield 466
Risk 467
Capital Gains (and Losses) 467
Liquidity 468
Inflation Hedges 468
Information, Transaction, and Management Costs 468
Tax Status and Investment Strategies 469
Investment Tradeoffs 469
Types of Investments: Creating an Investment Portfolio 471
Savings Accounts 471
Certificates of Deposit 473
Government Securities 475
Money-Market Mutual Funds 477
The Stock Market 477
Equity Mutual Funds 479
Real Estate 483
Human Capital 484
Comparing Various Investments 485

17 Planning for Your Future: Insurance, Retirement, and Beyond—491

Life Insurance 494
Types of Insurance Companies 495
Four Ways to Buy Life Insurance 496
Term Insurance 499
Cash-Value Insurance Policies 501
Which Form of Insurance Is Best for You? 505
How Much Life Insurance Do You Need? 506
The Cost of Life Insurance 512
Retirement 513
Social Security and Retirement Income 514
Company Pension Plans 517
Personal Pension Plans: IRA and Keogh 519
Making a Will 519
Funeral and Burial Arrangements 521

Appendix I
Seeking Help for Consumer Problems 526

Appendix II
Directory of Federal Consumer Agencies 529

Appendix III
Directory of State Consumer Agencies 533

Glossary—538

Index—554

Did You Know That...

- the average score of seventeen-year-olds in a national consumer education test was only 57 percent?

- the average American household loses about $700 per year from some form of consumer fraud?

- consumer economics is really closer to Aristotle's idea of what economics ought to be?

- the economic gains of being an intelligent decision maker are tax free?

- families living below the poverty line today have a higher level of living than the average American family did in 1900?

- the real cost of an item equals its price in time as well as in money?

- American consumers spend almost as much on transportation as they do on food?

- necessities such as food, clothing, and shelter have been taking a declining portion of consumers' budgets since the beginning of the twentieth century?

1 Life in Consumer America: Survival of the Fittest

The Need for Consumer Education
The Age of High Mass Consumption
Factors in Consumption Patterns
Consuming: Past, Present, and Future

There is an old saying that you cannot know where you are going unless you know where you have been. In other words, you need a sense of perspective before you can evaluate your own position. Your role in Consumer America is no exception to this general rule. In this chapter, we introduce you to the ever-changing world of the modern American consumer. We begin with the rationale for studying consumer economics—after all, your time is valuable and you should be informed early about the benefits as well as the costs of this course. Then we explore the phenomenon of economic growth, the process by which a society moves from a bare existence for most of its members to a situation in which even the poor are participating in a world of high mass consumption. The next section examines those factors that determine our consumption activity: income, time, tastes, and prices. Given these underlying determinants of consumption, we are better able to understand our past and present consumption patterns, and we can make some predictions about future trends. We conclude the chapter with a section on the importance of your developing personal decision-making skills as an aid in controlling your future.

The Need for Consumer Education

Have you ever bought something that you really didn't need or even want? Has one of your appliances ever broken down the week *after* the warranty expired? Or, have you ever had an appliance break down and then discover that the problem was *not* covered by the warranty? Do you think chemical additives in your food, drink, or clothing are harming you? Are you paying higher taxes than other people with similar incomes?

Most consumers would answer yes to some or all of these questions. Perhaps experiences with life in Consumer America have led you to take a college-level course in consumer economics, or you may be basically satisfied with your consuming ability. But should you be?

A recent study completed for the U.S. Office of Education concluded that "The greatest area of difficulty in general knowledge areas of adults appears to be consumer economics. Almost 30 percent (34.9 million) of American adults fall into the lowest level of competency, while another one-third (some 39 million) adult Americans function with difficulty" (Wilcox, 1979, p. 29). For teenagers, the test results are not any more optimistic. The average score of seventeen-year-old students on the Consumer Skills Test was only 57 percent. According to Roy Forbes, director of the National Assessment of Educational Progress (NAEP), which created the test, "There is evidence that the seventeen-year-olds really are not very well prepared for their future consumer responsibilities" (NAEP *Newsletter*, 1979). The report on teenagers went on to cite personal finance, consumer protection and behavior, economics, and energy as particularly troublesome areas for teenage consumers. Box 1-1 contains sample questions that appeared on the test.

If a large proportion of American consumers cannot pass a test designed by well-meaning consumer educators, how are they to protect themselves against firms that engage in fraudulent practices? Short weights and measures (selling fifteen ounces of hamburger and charging for a pound) or charging for ten gallons of gasoline when pumping only nine have been estimated to cost the consumer as much as $10 billion per year. Other forms of consumer fraud may cost an additional $40 billion (Spillman, 1976). Ignorance may be bliss, but it is also very expensive. And few people can afford it.

Sometimes statistics can be rather boring and impersonal, such as those that show the $50 billion lost by consumers every year. If this seems mind boggling, divide it by the number of American households—like yours—and you get an understandable figure. The average American household loses almost $700 every year from consumer fraud—$700 that may be saved by studying consumer economics.

It would be incorrect, however, to assume that the number-one problem facing consumers today is identifying and punishing businesses whose major goal is to defraud the public. Although the amount of consumer loss through fraud and deception is high, it is certainly no larger than the estimates of the annual cost of shoplifting—an activity that victimizes businesses (and fellow consumers). The vast majority of consumers never engage in shoplifting; so too, the vast majority of businesses do not attempt to cheat their customers. It would also be incorrect to point an accusing finger at government and lay the blame for consumer ignorance, fraud, and high prices on its doorstep. Nevertheless, because most consumers receive their formal education at public expense, a poor consumer education program in the schools, coupled with a lackadaisical approach to enforcing consumer

> **BOX 1-1**
> ## Sample Questions from Consumer Skills Tests
>
> Which of the following statements about financing an automobile are correct and which are incorrect?
>
> | | Correct | Incorrect | I don't know |
> |---|---|---|---|
> | | *Percent responding†* | | |
> | A. The lending institution can repossess your car and sell it to another buyer if you fail to keep up your payments. | 85.7* | 9.5 | 4.8 |
> | B. If a repossessed car is sold for less than you owe the lender, you are personally liable for the difference. | 32.2* | 42.3 | 25.1 |
> | C. If you are in a situation in which you can't make your car payment, it is wise to turn the car over to the lender. | 46.8 | 34.7* | 18.2 |
> | D. If the dealer is lending you the money, you must buy credit life insurance. | 15.5 | 48.0* | 36.1 |
> | E. If you intend to have car insurance, you must use the insurance company suggested by the lender. | 9.2 | 82.4* | 7.9 |
> | F. The dealer usually provides finance arrangements; therefore it is not necessary to investigate other possible sources for a loan. | 18.0 | 70.3* | 11.2 |
> | G. By signing a contract that includes a "confession of judgment," you are liable for all court costs if you default. | 51.8* | 11.7 | 36.1 |
>
> *Right answer.
> †Figures may not total 100 percent because nonresponses are not included.
> SOURCE: National Assessment of Educational Progress, *Newsletter*, 7 (June 1979), 4.

legislation, may lead to an increase in consumer misfortunes in the marketplace. Some observers have also noted that some government regulations, such as those governing automobile emissions and safety standards, push up prices and restrict consumer choice, thus lowering the level of consumer satisfaction.

If one were to identify the root of most consumer problems, it would not be an unsavory character selling stolen goods on a street corner. Neither would it be an overly zealous government bureaucrat creating regulations for the joy of it. Most consumer problems result from poorly made decisions based on insufficient or inaccurate information obtained in an unsystematic way. In other words, the fault often lies not in our stars but in ourselves. The responsibility for making more satisfying choices and thus becoming a better consumer cannot be shifted to someone else. Because you are the ultimate beneficiary, it is only right that you take charge and assume the role of a rational, knowledgeable decision maker. Studying consumer economics can help you achieve this goal.

WHAT IS CONSUMER ECONOMICS?

To the famous Greek philosopher Aristotle (384–322 B.C.), the term "consumer economics" would have belonged in what some comedians call "the department of redundancy department." Translated literally from its Greek origins, the word *economics* means management of the household. Thus, according to the early Greeks, all economics was consumer economics.

In modern times, the study of economics encompasses more than household management. In fact, there was a time when few economists bothered to study the household because household behavior had already been described by making a few assumptions. There seemed little need to clutter up a neat theory with messy, real-world behavior. However, those times are past. Today, consumer economics is a legitimate field of study for economists, home economists, and business professors alike.

In order to understand the discipline of consumer economics, you must first appreciate its two components: consumerism and economics. **Consumerism** is a movement whose goal is to ensure that individuals who buy and use products and services get fair value. **Economics** is not a social movement, but a field of study that looks at how people and societies cope with the fundamental problem of satisfying their unlimited wants with limited resources. Economists' attempts to cope with this dilemma have led some people to offer a shortcut definition of economics as the "science of choice."

Consumer economics, like economics itself, can be seen as the study of choice but with a more limited scope. Whereas economics deals with the problem of unlimited wants and limited resources on both a society (macro) and an individual (micro) level, consumer economics deals with the wants-versus-resources problem in the area of personal consumption. Consumer economics is personal economics, and in that sense is closer to the original Greek meaning of the term. And because it involves choice, we can then say that it is the study of personal economic decision making.

This does not mean that consumer economics is not concerned with the entire economy. It is, but usually only insofar as the behavior of the economy in general affects a particular consumer. Thus, when we talk about inflation in consumer economics, we are less concerned with the causes of inflation than with strategies for consumers to cope with inflation. Consumer economics does not try to move mountains; instead we try to make consumers better able to survive in those mountains.

THE REWARDS OF GOOD DECISION MAKING

One of the best ways to ensure your continued survival as a consumer is to develop and sharpen your decision-making skills. This requires some hard work and practice. An important question to consider at the outset of the course is whether the benefits of improving your decision-making skills and knowledge of consumer economics exceed the monetary and time costs involved. E. Scott Maynes (1969), chairman of the Department of Consumer Economics at Cornell University, lists five advantages to effective consumer decision making:

1. It increases your purchasing power by helping you select the least expensive product of equal quality.
2. The money saved in this process is untaxed and, therefore, understates the true saving because an equivalent amount of additional income earned would be subject to federal and state income taxes.
3. Decision-making skills can be learned by anyone; thus, greater purchasing power does not depend on someone getting a better job or having an unusual skill.
4. Good decision makers are less likely to become the victims of fraud or deception; thus they will not have to bear an equal share of the $50 billion consumer loss caused by fraud.
5. The actions of good decision makers have a social payoff because those firms that offer better goods on better terms will be rewarded with business, whereas less efficient competitors will disappear. This serves as an incentive for all firms to offer more value to their customers.

As you can see, there are significant rewards for improving your decision-making skills. Chapter 2 explores the decision-making process in greater detail and provides a model that will be applied throughout the text. But why do consumers have so many decisions to make? To fully understand the need for good decision-making skills today, we need a historical perspective about the development of our modern American economy.

The Age of High Mass Consumption

In 1960 Professor W. W. Rostow wrote *The Stages of Economic Growth,* in which he proposed five stages that societies pass through in reaching a high level of living:

1. Tradition.
2. Preconditions for takeoff.
3. Takeoff.
4. Drive to maturity.
5. Age of high mass consumption.

Table 1-1. Levels of Living in the United States 1900–1970

Percentages of families with:	Among all families 1900	Among poor families 1970
Flush toilets	15	92
Running water	24	99
Central heating	1	58
One or fewer occupants per room	48	96
Electricity	3	99
Refrigeration	18	99
Automobiles	1	41

SOURCE: Stanley Lebergott, *The American Economy: Income, Wealth, and Want* (Princeton, N.J.: Princeton University Press, 1976), p. 8. Copyright © 1976 by Princeton University Press. Reprinted by permission of Princeton University Press.

In all of these stages, consumption is the primary reason for production. But in the first stage, tradition, the society has great difficulty producing enough goods and services to ensure the survival of its members. Such a society is what economists call a **traditional economy;** it has very little need for individual decision making. The fundamental economic questions of what to produce, how to produce, and then how to distribute the final products are determined by age-old customs (tradition). If you were to be magically transported to one of these societies and you asked some members why they produce a particular product or why they choose a particular occupation, they would simply answer that it has always been done this way or that their parents were in the occupation and trained them for it. In short, it is *traditional* to do things a certain way or to enter a particular occupation. In such a society, individual decision making is highly limited, and for good reason. In a tradition economy, there is little margin for error. One mistake could lead to starvation.

In the second and third stages of economic growth, the society increases its output and does not consume everything directly. Some resources are put aside and invested in better methods of production so that, in the long run, more can be produced. This increase in investment, coupled with new, more productive ways of doing things, creates more consumer goods, job opportunities, purchasing power, and choices. Once this process becomes self-perpetuating, the economy "takes off" in Rostow's words. The "takeoff" analogy derives from the similarity of this process to an aircraft that begins from a dead stop, gradually builds speed on the runway, and then suddenly becomes airborne. Once an economy takes off, it never returns to an earlier stage.

According to Rostow, the United States economy took off around 1850. From 1850 until 1900, the economy was in its "drive to maturity" stage. Increasing the number and share of producer goods in total output characterized this stage. Many of today's industrial giants, such as Exxon, U.S. Steel, and Westinghouse, were formed during this period.

The United States entered the age of high mass consumption in the early twentieth century—an age characterized by rising incomes and general affluence. You may not believe that your situation is "affluent," but a historical comparison may change your perspective. Data from the U.S. Census illustrate just how far we have come in this century. Table 1-1, for instance, compares the consumption levels of certifiably "poor" families in the United States in 1970 with those of all American families in 1900. Note that in every category the poor family of 1970 was objectively better off—that is, had a higher level of living—than the average American family at the turn of the century. For example, in the United States in 1970, 99 percent of all poor families had running water, whereas in 1900, three out of four American families did not. In 1900, only an elite 1 percent had central heating, but by 1970 a majority (58 percent) of poor families had it. Electricity, refrigeration, living space, flush toilets, and automobiles are only a few of the categories in which the poorest of our society today can claim they are better off than the average family a few generations ago.

If even the poorest families in our society today are demonstrably better off than their more affluent ancestors, why do we have the nagging suspicion that we are no better off and perhaps worse off than previous generations? Part of the answer lies in the wants-versus-resources dilemma cited earlier. Consumers living in the age of high mass consumption have exhibited a massive escalation in their wants. Whereas in 1900 central heating might have been viewed as a luxury, today it is seen as something everyone deserves. Consumers' wants tend to multiply as rapidly as the resources they use to satisfy those wants. This problem highlights the importance of becoming an efficient decision maker so that you can stretch your resources and get the most satisfaction from them. To become a better decision maker, you need to understand the factors underlying your consumption pattern.

Factors in Consumption Patterns

Several forces exert strong influences on your consumption activity. These factors have an impact on individual consumers' decisions and thus help to shape our society-wide consumption pattern. These factors include income, time, tastes, and prices.

INCOME

Income is the primary determinant of individual buying power in the marketplace. In a **market economy**—one in which the type and amount of goods produced are essentially determined by the demand for them—your income level equals the strength of your voice. If you have high income, whenever you speak, the market listens. If, on the other hand, your income is small relative to that of other consumers, you do not have much influence on what gets produced.

As your income increases relative to that of other consumers, your particular consumption pattern gains added weight in the society's economy. But something else happens as your income rises: your consumption pattern changes. For example, if your income were to double over the next five years, would you buy twice as much food? Not likely, but you would spend more money on food because you would switch from less expensive foods (hamburger) to more expensive foods (steaks). Although you would spend more on food, the expense would probably be a smaller part of your income. The fact that food requires a smaller proportion of your budget as your income rises was first suggested by Ernst Engel, a nineteenth-century Prussian statistician. His observation has been shown to be accurate under so many different conditions that it is now known as **Engel's law.** Figure 1-1 shows three Engel curves for food based on American household behavior. As (a) shows, the value of food consumed at home rises as income goes up, but it rises much more slowly than income. Thus we can confirm Engel's nineteenth-century hypothesis by looking at the behavior of American consumers.

Food is a **normal good;** that is, we buy more of it as income rises. However, as Engel's law indicates, food's share in our household budget tends to decline as our incomes rise. There are other normal goods, sometimes called **ultrasuperior goods,** whose share in our total budget actually becomes larger as our incomes rise. Ultrasuperior goods are sometimes referred to as ''luxury goods'' because people with low incomes generally don't buy them. Restaurant meals, new cars, private education, foreign travel, and medical care are among these goods. Figure 1-1 (b) shows an Engel curve for restaurant meals, a good that takes a larger proportion of consumer budgets as incomes rise.

Goods purchased less often at higher incomes, such as chicken wings in Figure 1-1 (c), are called **inferior goods;** as consumers' incomes rise, a smaller amount is actually spent on these goods.

To generalize from these observations, we can say that as consumers' incomes rise, their budgets will allow for more normal and, especially, ultrasuperior goods. Automobiles, medical care, and recreation grow in relative importance, while food and clothing decline. On the other hand, if consumers' incomes fall, inferior goods command a larger proportion of consumer budgets.

Figure 1-1. Engel curves for (a) normal, (b) ultrasuperior, and (c) inferior goods.

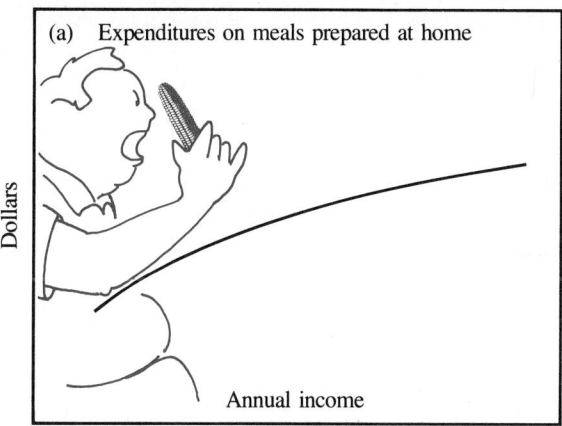

TIME

Time is also an important part of expenditures. As your income rises, so does the value of your time. In all societies there are, of course, the same number of hours in the day. But in highly productive, high-income societies, those hours are more precious because there are so many ways to use one's time.

For example, consider two consumers. One is a highly skilled, highly paid management consultant. The other is a semiskilled worker in an automobile assembly plant. Whose time is more valuable? Because the management consultant is paid more for his or her time, he or she obviously earns a considerably higher income. But perhaps it is less obvious that the consultant's buying habits are affected by this difference—by what we call **time costs.**

All consumers are affected by time costs, but some are less aware of it than others. Have you ever waited for an hour in a doctor's office? Did that increase the cost of your visit? Of course it did—you had to give up something in order to see the doctor. You gave up time as well as money. While you waited, you did not do something else you may have wanted or needed to do, such as working to earn money or getting a new tire for your car. Who is more likely to be willing to wait the extra hour—the consultant or the assembly-line worker? Who has less to lose by waiting? The one with the lower time cost.

Whenever you have to give up something, you experience what economists call **opportunity costs.** In the case of a visit to your doctor, the opportunity cost is the money you pay for service *plus* the value of your waiting time. If the consultant has to give up an hour's work on a consulting job, then the total cost of the trip is the doctor's fee, say $25, plus the lost earnings, $100. Whenever you have to wait, visualize yourself as a taxicab driver with the meter running. A highly paid driver has a meter that runs faster and costs more per hour. An unemployed cab driver has a meter that does not run at all.

In general then, as incomes rise, time becomes more precious and it becomes more important for consumers to add the cost of their time to the monetary cost of an item. Fast-food restaurants have boomed while food prepared at home has become much less important in consumer budgets because of

Figure 1-2. The total cost of an item is equal to its monetary cost plus its time cost.

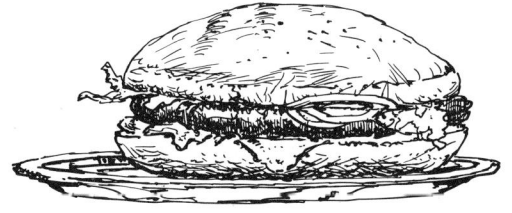

Homemade burger =
cost of hamburger + bun ($.50)
+ preparation and cleanup time (20 minutes)

Big Mac = cost ($1.29) + waiting time (5 minutes)

---

the time-cost factor (see Figure 1-2). Convenience food markets such as Seven-Eleven and the AM-PM Minimarts prosper in spite of their higher food prices because they offer quicker service, better hours, and more convenient locations than supermarkets. These characteristics help lower a consumer's time costs and, thus, the total cost of the loaf of bread he or she needs tomorrow morning.

TASTES: CONSUMER PREFERENCES REVEALED

Taste, or preference, is another variable that influences consumer purchasing of items such as clothing, transportation, personal care, recreation, and sometimes even housing and food. However, though it is fairly easy to show that specific items within any of these categories rise or fall with a change in preference, it is harder to prove that a new allocation of the consumer dollar among these categories is the result of taste. For example, it is fairly easy to see how a change in personal care, such as in men's hairstyles, can wreak havoc with the old-fashioned barbershop and create a boom for "hair stylists." It is much more difficult to quantify the effect of this hairstyle change on the proportion of the consumer dollar spent on other nonpersonal care items such as transportation or recreation. Nevertheless, such changes in taste do occur, and they affect your expenditures in a variety of areas.

An example of how a change in consumer tastes can affect other sectors might be found in the disappearance of the hat from the American male's wardrobe. Just a generation ago, no self-respecting man would have admitted to not owning a hat. Hats came in all styles, shapes, and sizes, and cost considerably more than a pair of shoes. Nevertheless, consumers began to abandon the hat in the late 1950s, and by 1970 a man with a hat was rare. This taste change freed some income to be spent elsewhere. We don't know where this income went. But if most of it went into shoes, ties, or other apparel, our statistics would show no change. If, however, the consumer bought more gasoline as a result of spending less on hats, a shift among the categories would have taken place. Transportation would have gained while clothing lost (transportation +1, clothing −1).

It is sometimes difficult to measure the impact of shifting tastes on consumer expenditure patterns; it is even harder to *predict* changes in taste. In the 1960s, wine with a meal was rare in most American households, but by the 1980s, it was commonplace. In addition to developing a taste for the fruit of the vine, consumers exhibited a distinct preference for white wine. This change in preference caught many winemakers by surprise and resulted in a frantic attempt by the growers to shift production away from varieties that produce hearty red wine to those that produce white. The causes of these changes in taste have never been fully explained, but they had a real impact on what was produced and consumed.

PRICES

Certainly, income, time costs, and tastes influence what we buy and how we act, but the impact of prices on our behavior is always given star billing by economists. Economists argue that as the price of an item rises, consumers find it worthwhile to buy less of it and to substitute other items when it is practical to do so. The relationship between a change in the price of a good and the subsequent change in the amount demanded by consumers is obvious and so common that the relationship has come to be called the **law of demand.** The law of demand holds that consumers will buy more at lower prices than at higher prices. Sometimes the association between price and quantity demanded is called an ''inverse relationship'' because the two variables always change in the opposite direction. As one goes up, the other goes down.

If you compare the energy-related behavior of consumers in 1970 with that of today, you have an excellent real-world application of the law of demand. In 1970, the price of a barrel of oil was $1.80, and leaded regular gasoline cost 36 cents per gallon. In 1974, oil rose suddenly to $11.65 per barrel, and gasoline went to 52 cents per gallon. The energy crisis was born. Since 1974, energy prices have continued to rise, and many consumers remain outraged at the price hikes and complain to anyone who will listen. This may help them psychologically, but in economic terms the best remedy is to react to the higher prices by cutting back on their use of oil and oil-related products. This means driving less, insulating more, buying smaller, more fuel efficient cars, turning thermostats down in the winter to save fuel oil or natural gas, and keeping air conditioners off in the summer to save electricity. All these actions are in keeping with the law of demand.

Keeping the price constant but lowering the quality of an item has the same effect as raising the price. If a firm holds the price of its chocolate bars constant but begins to use imitation chocolate in the production process, or if it begins to shrink the size of the bar to cut costs, the quality of the product has changed and so, too, has the real price.

Good decision makers always try to avoid higher prices whether they come in the form of bigger price tags or lower quality. However, this bargain-hunting attitude can be successfully implemented only when consumers have good information. As Professor Maynes (1969) has written:

> The importance of consumer ignorance in explaining variations in prices and quality of products sold in the marketplace can scarcely be overemphasized. If consumers were capable of obtaining complete and valid price and quality information about all variants of the products they were interested in, relatively little price and quality variation would remain. (p. 101)

Professor Maynes does not doubt the importance of the law of demand; his argument is that consumers often have difficulty judging the quality of an item because they lack good information. If you think about it, this makes sense. People do occasionally confuse price with quality. For example, if one set of automobile tires costs twice as much as another, many consumers infer that the more expensive set is better. They may feel more ''secure'' when riding on tires that cost $100 rather than $50. But did they make a good decision? Are they really getting more for their money? One of the principal functions of consumer economics is to help you answer such questions so that you will be a more informed, rational, and efficient consumer.

Consuming: Past, Present, and Future

Consumer consumption patterns reflect income, time costs, tastes, and the prices of various goods. As these underlying variables change, so do buying patterns. We can get some idea of the magnitude of future changes by looking at consumption patterns of the past and present.

PAST AND PRESENT CONSUMPTION PATTERNS

What do you spend most of your money on? What is the biggest single item in an average consumer's budget? If you guessed "shelter," you are correct. Expenditures for shelter, which include the cost of housing and household operations such as heating and lighting, account for about 30 cents of every consumer dollar spent on goods and services today. The other two **necessities,** food and clothing, account for another 30 cents of the consumer dollar. This leaves consumers about 40 cents of every after-tax dollar to spend on nonnecessities. As Figure 1-3 shows, necessities have taken a smaller share of the average consumer's dollar throughout the twentieth century. By the same token, consumers have **discretionary income**—buying power that does not have to be spent on necessities. In 1909, more than 80 cents of the consumer dollar went for food, clothing, or shelter, and only 20 cents was discretionary. By 1950, the proportion claimed by necessities had fallen to 68 cents, and by 1980 necessities took less than 60 cents of every consumption dollar. The age of high mass consumption has also been one of increasing discretion as consumers have been given the opportunity to pick and choose among an even wider variety of goods and services.

Table 1-2 indicates the winners and losers among the consumption categories that compete for the consumer dollar. Some, such as medical care and transportation, have risen rapidly in importance over this century. Both take a larger chunk out of our budgets today than one of the necessities—clothing. And, if present trends continue, it may not be long before our transportation costs exceed our food bills. Other expenditures, such as recreation and personal business expenditures, have grown in importance as we have acquired more leisure time and income to use and invest.

One key to the changes in the consumption pattern of the typical American consumer is the rise in overall income level. Table 1-1 alludes to this by showing that, in absolute terms, even those who today qualify as poverty stricken have a level of consumption that compares favorably to that of the average American in 1900. This comparison would be even

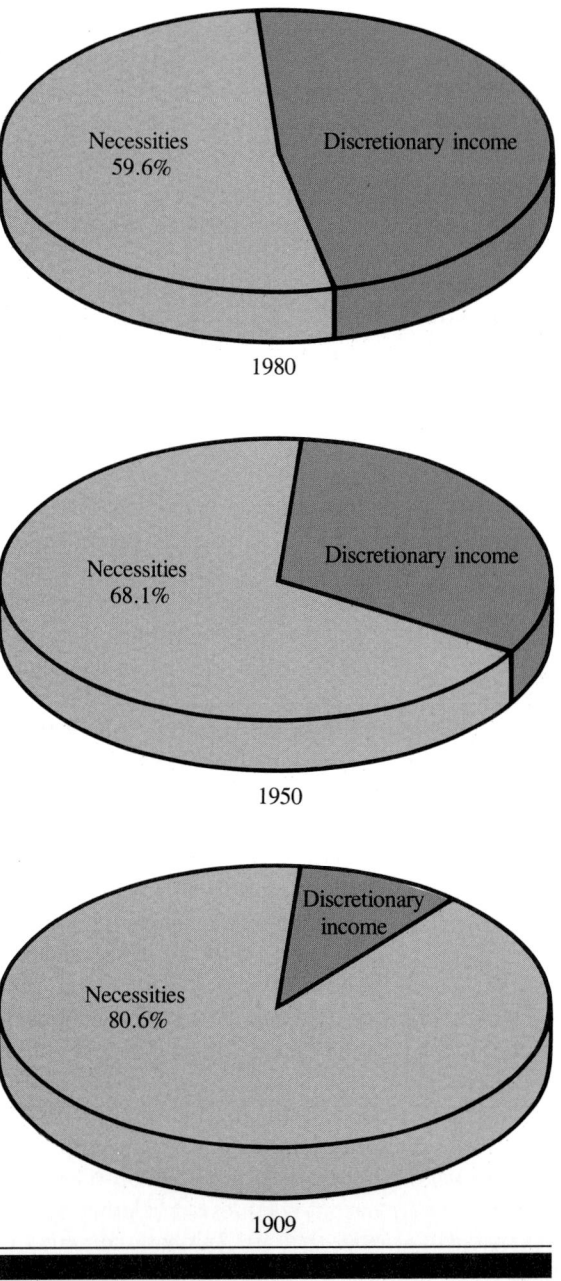

Figure 1-3. The share of necessities in consumers' expenditures. Necessities include food, clothing, and housing.

Table 1-2. Expenditures as a Percentage of Consumption

	1909		1950		1980	
Food	34.0		30.3		21.7	
Clothing	13.9	80.6	12.3	68.1	7.9	59.6
Shelter	32.7		26.5		30.0	
Transportation	5.2		13.2		14.3	
Medical care	2.7		4.7		9.8	
Recreation	3.0		5.8		6.8	
Personal business	3.0		3.4		5.0	
Private education	1.4		0.9		1.6	
Personal care	0.9		1.3		1.4	
Religious activities	2.8		1.2		1.3	

SOURCES: U.S. Bureau of the Census, *Historical Statistics of the United States* (Washington, D.C.: U.S. Government Printing Office, 1960); and *Survey of Current Business* (September 1981).

---

more graphic if the sizes of the three consumption pies in Figure 1-3 reflected per capita consumption expenditures in those years. In 1909, the average American consumer spent $318 on personal consumption; in 1950, the figure rose to $1,260; and by 1980, it had risen to $7,468. This amounts to a 23-fold rise in per capita consumption expenditures from 1909 to 1980. Of course, we must also account for price-level changes, because a 1909 dollar could buy more than a 1980 dollar. But even after accounting for the fact that a 1909 dollar could buy 6.7 times more than a 1980 dollar, American consumers in 1980 had 3.5 times more buying power than their 1909 counterparts. They could purchase the equivalent of $1,114 worth of 1909 goods and services, even after allowing for the impact of inflation.

FUTURE CONSUMPTION PATTERNS

In this century, we have witnessed an unparalleled rise in consumer purchasing power and a decrease in the proportion of our budgets devoted to the necessities. As a result, late-twentieth-century consumers have more decisions to make about how to spend their income than any generation before. On the other hand, storm clouds are appearing on the horizon. In the 1970s, consumer incomes began to rise more slowly, energy costs rose dramatically, and the productivity of the labor force actually declined in some sectors. Some observers have turned pessimistic about the ability of our economy to continue to grow at the historical rates. As Ronald Stampfl, professor of consumer science and business at the University of Wisconsin, wrote:

> It would appear that the productivity gains of an earlier industrialized economy are now behind us. The economic pie of our industrial age seems to have all but stopped growing. American consumers are being forced to confront the economic, political and social imperatives of the Post-Industrial age. Unfortunately, they have not much more than an outmoded set of Industrial-Age values to guide them in their marketplace behavior. (1981, p. 4)

American consumers enter the last two decades of the twentieth century with more buying power than they have ever possessed, but also with a greater sense of uncertainty about how long it will last. The combination of income and uncertainty highlights the need for developing good decision-making skills. In the case of transportation, for example, Table 1-2 documents the high priority American consumers have placed on getting themselves from point A to point B. The American love affair with the automobile, coupled with the rising costs of caring for the creature, means that we now spend almost as much on transportation as on food, compared with only one-seventh as much in 1909. Will this trend continue? The answer is far from clear. But what we do know is that consumers must now decide not only what kind of car to buy, whether new or used, and so on, but also whether to buy one at all. And how does buying a car affect other decisions: where to live, where to work, what to forego to have the right car? As the complexity of our economic system grows and our choices as consumers increase, we have to become better at being critical decision makers.

Summary

This chapter has had two major foci: first, we have tried to give a general picture of where American consumers are today. In the broad historical view, the American consumer belongs to one of the richest, most powerful groups ever to walk the earth. As Rostow indicated, Americans were the first to enter the age of high mass consumption and are in no collective rush to leave it. On the other hand, for a group that is so used to consuming on a massive scale, our national tests indicate a surprisingly high proportion of consumer ignorance. Studies on the dollar costs of consumer fraud verify the need for more and better consumer education. The second focus is a more micro or personally oriented one. The key here is to be alert to those factors that influence consumer behavior. Income, time, tastes, and prices are variables that exercise a major influence on our individual and collective consumption patterns. As our incomes rise, we tend to spend a smaller proportion of our budget on necessities such as food and a larger proportion on discretionary categories such as recreation and transportation. This emphasizes the importance of choice and personal decision making as we find ourselves surrounded by ways to spend our discretionary income. As for the future, if the pessimists are right and our incomes stop rising at their historical rates, personal decision making will be even more crucial as consumers struggle to improve their level of living by getting more satisfaction from a limited income. Chapter 2 explores the elements of decision making and should help you to make better choices.

KEY TERMS

consumer economics
consumerism
discretionary income
economics
Engel's law

inferior good
law of demand
market economy
necessities
normal good
opportunity cost

tastes
time costs
traditional economy
ultrasuperior good

QUESTIONS

1. The Sentry Insurance Company recently commissioned Louis Harris to survey public attitudes on consumer issues. Harris found that 92 percent of those polled favored additional support for consumer education. What are the major society-wide benefits to be obtained from better consumer decision making? What are the major personal benefits?

2. According to Rostow, what are the five stages of economic growth? Which stage is a subsistence economy most likely to be in? Which stage is the American economy in now?

3. According to the text, what are the four variables that exert strong influences on consumption patterns?

4. How do we define a normal good? Give some examples.

5. Which item takes the largest share of the average consumer's budget today? Has this always been the most important expenditure?

6. What is discretionary income? Do consumers have more or less discretionary income today than in 1950? In 1909? What areas have grown in importance over these periods? Why?

7. Define the law of demand and give an example of its application to a real-world situation.

PROJECTS

1. Administer your own mini-consumer skills test using the questions in Box 1-1. Find at least five consumers willing to answer the questions. Does your mini-survey indicate a general need for more consumer education?

2. When the energy crisis first sent the price of gasoline over the 50 cents-per-gallon mark, Shell Oil began a campaign to educate consumers on the gas-saving advantages of driving slower. They used an example similar to this one: If two consumers own identical cars and both want to travel 300 miles from city A to city B, they may choose to travel 50 miles per hour or 60 miles per hour. At 50 miles per hour, their cars average 20 miles per gallon, whereas at 60 miles per hour, they get only 15 miles per gallon. The fuel savings from going slower and conserving would equal 5 gallons. At the time, the value of this fuel saving equaled $2.50. Despite this saving, people continued to go much faster than 50 miles per hour. Why? Did the fuel saver give anything up? (Hint: What is the time cost of following the Shell Oil Company's advice?)

Would the time cost be different for a retired person than for a truck driver? Have you ever noticed this time-cost difference reflected in the highway driving of these two groups?

3. No two consumers have identical consumption patterns, partly because our incomes, time costs, and tastes are so diverse.

  a. Given the following tasks:
  - laundry
  - housecleaning
  - preparing lunch
  - making clothes
  - childcare
  - cashing a check
  - repairing a leaky faucet

  Evaluate the likelihood that members of the following groups will do these tasks for themselves:
  - management consultant
  - banker
  - student
  - homemaker
  - physician
  - retired plumber

  b. Are your predictions about the decisions of these people based on your estimates of income, time costs, and tastes? Explain how these factors might affect their choices.

REFERENCES AND READINGS

Greyser, Stephen A. *Consumerism at the Crossroads.* Green Bay, Wis.: Sentry Insurance Company, 1978.

Lebergott, Stanley. *The American Economy.* Princeton, N.J.: Princeton University Press, 1976.

Lee, Susan, and Passell, Peter. *A New Economic View of American History.* New York: W. W. Norton, 1979.

Leet, Don R., and Shaw, John A. *Economics: Concepts, Themes, Applications.* Belmont, Calif.: Wadsworth, 1980.

Maynes, E. Scott. "The Payoff for Intelligent Consumer Decision-Making." *Journal of Home Economics,* February 1969.

National Assessment of Educational Progress. *Newsletter,* June 1979.

Rostow, Walt Whitman. *The Stages of Economic Growth: A Non-Communist Manifesto.* Cambridge: Cambridge University Press, 1960.

Spillman, Nancy Z., ed. *Consumers: A Personal Planning Reader.* St. Paul, Minn.: West Publishing, 1976.

Stampfl, Ronald W. "Consumer Values in Transition." *Forum,* Spring/Summer 1981.

U.S. Bureau of the Census. *Historical Statistics of the United States.* Washington, D.C.: U.S. Government Printing Office, 1960.

Wilcox, Suzanne Dale. "The Educated Consumer: An Analysis of Curriculum Needs in Consumer Education." U.S. Office of Education, 30 October 1979.

Did You Know That...

- *learning how to make better decisions is at the heart of consumer economics?*

- *scarcity is the reason that decisions have to be made? If there was more than enough of everything, we wouldn't need good decision-making skills.*

- *there are some basic rules of good decision making that you can learn and then apply in many different situations?*

- *conspicuous consumption is an activity that many people engage in to make themselves happier, and yet if everyone consumes conspicuously, no one achieves more satisfaction?*

- *goals represent your values in action, and once you set your goals there are a number of ways to evaluate your progress in meeting them?*

- *family, friends, customs, advertising, and economic institutions all restrict our choices?*

Decision Making: Learning to Choose

Scarcity: The Mother of Decisions
Consuming: More Than Just Buying
Values and the Consumer
Goals: Values in Action
Constraints and Restrictions on Decision Making
The Consumer Decision-Making Model

Neighborhood CAPSULE
A Big Decision

Sally was frustrated. She had set a mental time limit for declaring her college major: the first semester of her junior year. And here it was, and she still didn't know what she was going to major in. The time constraint seemed to make sense to her when she was a freshman. She hadn't had enough information at that time to make an intelligent choice. And she didn't want people to think that she couldn't make up her mind. That was one stereotype that she didn't need to carry with her.

In her freshman year, college seemed like a smorgasbord of classes with a strange Chinese-dinner twist. Although there were hundreds of courses to choose from, she could only choose a limited number from social sciences, humanities, and natural sciences. One from column A, two from column B, and so forth. While Sally was contemplating the Chinese-dinner analogy, Alice, her roommate, noticed the blank stare from across the lunch table and tried to snap Sally out of it.

"Where are you?" Alice asked in a peremptory tone. "You seemed so far away. Were you thinking about Ken?" Alice was always a little curious about other people's relationships.

"Ken?" Sally responded vaguely. "Oh, no." She decided that at that moment he was in the outer reaches of her memory bank. She was working on a much more important topic.

"Well, what then?" Alice continued, eager to get inside that 3.5 GPA brain.

"Oh, I'm just a little depressed, that's all."

"A little depressed about what?" Alice went on. By this time she was getting a little annoyed, and she took it out on her tuna sandwich.

As Alice began munching, Sally explained: "Here I am at the beginning of my junior year and I still don't know what I'm going to major in. I mean, it's O.K. to be undeclared in your freshman or even your sophomore year, but not in your *junior* year."

"Well I can tell you what part of your problem is," Alice opened. "You're too good at studying."

"What does that mean?" Sally wanted to know.

"It means that normal students get signals about what to do by looking at their grades. We see what we're good at and what we're not good at. Take me, for example. I always do well in the humanities, but I never do well in the sciences. And math is practically impossible. I get a queasy feeling in my stomach every time I think about that math class I had to endure for my general education requirement. But you do well in just about everything, so you don't get any signals—no red lights. For you everything is go."

Sally was about to interrupt, but Alice was just beginning to get into her lecture.

"And I'll tell you something else. You've got to figure out what *you* think is important. Not what your parents think or what Ken thinks or . . ."

"Or even what Alice thinks." Sally couldn't resist the quip, but Alice took it good naturedly.

"Yes, or even what I think. Be your own person. Figure out what's important to you and set some long-term goals. Then draw some standards that give you something to shoot for in the short run. If you are achieving your standards, then you can be pretty sure that you're on your way to your goals."

Sally was a little surprised at this monologue. It made a lot more sense than some others Alice had delivered on topics such as reincarnation, dieting, and speed reading.

"Where did you get this strategy, Alice?"

"It's right here in Chapter 2!"

James Duesenberry (1960), former chairman of the Harvard Economics Department, once wrote, "Economics is all about how people make choices. Sociology is all about why people don't have any choices to make." If that is the case, then consumer economics is all about how individuals can make better choices.

Good decision makers are made, not born. You must learn and practice decision-making skills if you are to cope with the hundreds of decisions that you will make in a lifetime. Decisions come in all sizes and shapes. Some, such as choosing a career or getting married, occur only infrequently. Some, such as having children or getting a college degree, are irreversible. Other choices are important but occur frequently enough to allow for some learning and reevaluation to take place. Buying a car or a house and making an investment are examples of these kinds of decisions. Then, there are the more frequently made decisions of food shopping or obtaining credit. Life in Consumer America is riddled with decisions.

This chapter develops some tools for dealing with our world of decisions. We begin where we left off in Chapter 1, acknowledging that there is at least one major fact of life—you don't get something for nothing. Opportunity cost is involved in all major decisions. But there are benefits, too. Comparing costs and benefits can help you go a long way toward making your life in Consumer America a little easier. Then we look at consumption itself and discuss its objective: to increase happiness. This leads us to the question of values: what they are, where they come from, and how you can clarify your own. After discussing values clarification, we will discuss goals and standards and will follow with a discussion of some constraints on the decision-making process. Finally, we will present our decision-making model and apply it to a consumer problem.

Scarcity: The Mother of Decisions

Everyone knows that we have to make choices in all areas of our lives. We can't be two places at once; neither can we have our cake and eat it, too, as the old saying goes. The reason for this fact of life is that our resources are limited, whereas the possible uses of those resources are unlimited. Money is an obvious example. At this moment, you have a limited amount of money. What could you do with that resource? "Spend it," you say. But spend it on what? A new album, lunch, a moped, a textbook (good choice), a gift, shoes—what? There is a whole range of choices open to you. You have to *decide* the best use of your money at this time, based on your wants, needs, and goals.

Money, then, is a **scarce resource,** that is, it is limited; you only have so much of it. An example of an opposite of a scarce resource is air. You can take in as much air as you like and no one will be very concerned. You never think about what to do with the air in your room because it is not scarce. Air is what economists call a **free good**—it is there for the asking. It is a "good" because we like to use it, and it is free because it is so abundant that there is no cost.

OPPORTUNITY COSTS

All scarce resources have costs associated with them. The cost is often expressed as a money cost. For example, if a new stereo system costs $800, you must give up $800 to get the stereophonic sound that you want. But the $800 does not represent the real cost of the system. The only way to evaluate the real cost is to know what else you might have done with that money. You could have gone on a vacation, added significantly to your wardrobe, or simply let the money draw interest in the bank for a year. Of these alternatives let us say that the vacation is your next best choice. Economists say that you gave up the opportunity to take a vacation in order to buy a stereo. The opportunity cost of the stereo decision is the vacation because opportunity cost is the value of what you must give up in order to get something else. Opportunity costs are often referred to as **tradeoffs** because they involve trading one thing for another. Our example involves a tradeoff between buying a stereo and taking a vacation. It is incorrect to say that the opportunity cost of the stereo is the vacation *plus* the clothes you didn't buy *plus* the lost bank account interest because the alternatives are mutually exclusive. Once you decide to do one of them, you can't do the others.

Opportunity costs are involved in every decision you make. Money is a fairly good measure of opportunity cost, as long as consumers understand the alternative uses of their money. If, on the other hand, consumers buy goods and services randomly, without thinking about alternatives, money does not serve as an accurate yardstick of the lost opportunities (opportunity cost).

The concepts of scarcity and opportunity cost are not tied to money alone, however. They apply in any situation in which there is too little of something valuable to go around. Take the age-old problem of the university grading system. Some professors still grade their students using a method known to students as the dreaded "curve." The curve represents the statistical concept of a normal distribution, which shows that if class talent is distributed randomly, most students will be average (and earn a C), whereas the number above and below average (B and D, respectively) should be equal, as should the number of A and F students. Thus, in a class of this sort there are fewer A's than students who want to get A's. If this class is composed completely of students who could earn a grade of B or better in an objectively graded class (that is, without curve grading), the opportunity cost of earning a good grade is higher than in an objectively graded class. Students have to give up more to get a high grade because they have to work harder to put themselves on the high side of the curve. The opportunity cost of such a class is considerably higher, and a rational consumer of higher education would be well advised to think twice before enrolling in a course with such grading policies.

The example of the college grading system also implies another measure of opportunity cost—time. As we mentioned in Chapter 1, a person's time is also a valuable resource. Suppose, for example, that a good, but not great, student enrolls in the curve-graded class. Assume that the student takes four other classes and works parttime. This consumer-student will have significant time problems by the end of the term. Eventually, a choice situation may evolve: In order to get a B, the student must run the risk of not studying for two other classes or cutting out the parttime job. The opportunity cost of the first class turns out to be very high. And that's where the importance of decision making becomes clear.

As a consumer—whether of education, tenspeed bicycles, or food—you need to be aware of the total cost of your decisions. The explicit money cost plus the implicit time cost should both be included in your opportunity-cost calculation. If you underestimate these costs, your decisions will be based on faulty information and may lead to mistakes. These errors in judgment can be avoided if you develop good consumer decision-making skills and use them.

Understanding opportunity costs is an important first step in the process of learning to be a good decision maker, but you also need to be able to value the benefits of a choice. Once you can measure the costs and the benefits, you are well on your way to making a rational decision.

BENEFITS, TOO

Cost is not the only element of decision making to consider. Benefits of a particular action must also play a role. The consumer-student in the curve-grading example may be choosing wisely in taking such a time-consuming, high-cost class if the end result is favorable. Perhaps the professor is an outstanding teacher; or maybe the class will produce countless benefits, such as a course in consumer economics. If, after talking to other students, sitting in on the class a few times, and seeing the professor during office hours, the student estimates that the benefits outweigh the costs, taking the course is an intelligent, rational decision. But it is not rational to take on four other classes and a parttime job! In general, to be a good decision maker you should remember these principles:

1. Your time and income are limited and *both* are valuable.
2. Total cost equals explicit (money) cost plus implicit (time) cost.
3. Decisions should be made only after weighing both the costs and benefits of alternative actions.

These basic principles form the core of the decision-making process. But before you can apply these principles to your personal situation, you must clarify your own wants and needs. This means examining your consumer lifestyle, the values that support it, and the forces that influence it. The remainder of this chapter helps you to do this and then to apply what you've learned to a full-fledged consumer decision-making model. But first, we need to clarify your view of consumption. Is more consumption always better than less, or are you concerned with the impact your consumption habits have on the world around you?

Consuming: More Than Just Buying

Until recently, economists and most other people assumed, without necessarily saying so, that more is always better than less, bigger is always better than smaller, and too much is never enough. Most economists do believe that people are happier if they are able to consume more. However, this is a judgment that they, when challenged, justify on the basis of observation: Would someone who just bought a modest two-bedroom home be willing to trade it for a larger, more comfortable one at no additional cost? Most would do so quickly and without hesitation. Thus, more is better seems to be based on reality.

But E. F. Schumacher, who wrote *Small Is Beautiful: Economics As If People Mattered* (1973), posed a new question. Would the family that moved to a larger house be *happier* there? How long would this happiness last? Would it change if someone built a bigger, more luxurious house across the street? The answers are far from obvious.

The elusive connection between more material possessions and human satisfaction has been the subject of a long debate. Many church leaders, political leaders, and humanists have argued against the view that more possessions bring greater happiness. Even Karl Marx, the intellectual founder of the communist movement, wrote pessimistically about the issue: "A house may be large or small; as long as surrounding houses are equally small it satisfies all social demands for a dwelling. But if a palace rises beside the little house, the little house shrinks into a hut" (1933).

Thorstein Veblen (1899), founder of the Institutionalist School of economic thought, was also fascinated by the transitory happiness that consumption brings. He coined the term **conspicuous consumption** to represent his observation that an individual's satisfaction from a good or service often depends on the number of goods and services consumed by other people. In other words, having more than you used to have is not enough. The important question is whether you have more than your neighbor. Conspicuous consumption leads people to buy goods

Sometimes we buy things not so much because we want and need them but because they represent the fact that we have reached a certain status in our society. By owning, using, and displaying a variety of expensive consumer items, we let others know that we have been successful enough to afford these luxury products. When it comes to leisure activities, for example, many individuals purchase the most expensive and prestigious recreational equipment even if they only use their tennis racquet, bicycle, or skis a few times a year. This pattern is part of what Veblen has termed "conspicuous consumption."

or services because of the status associated with them rather than for a specific need. Suppose, for example, that your family has a good-running, but aging, family car. Let us further suppose that your next-door neighbor buys a beautiful new car. Suddenly your old car looks shabby and your family begins to wish they had a better one. Within a week or two your family buys a new car that is even more expensive than your neighbor's. You have engaged in conspicuous consumption, sometimes known as "keeping up with the Joneses." You don't *need* a new car, but you don't want your neighbors to think that you can't afford one. Neither do you want to appear to be less-successful members of society.

Is conspicuous consumption "bad"? This is a question of **values,** that is, learned beliefs that arouse strong emotional, as well as intellectual, responses when challenged. If your values include a high regard for individuality and concern about wasting society's resources, you may dislike conspicuous consumption because it leads to a society of spendthrift conformity. This negative opinion is an outgrowth of your values and is often referred to as a **value judgment.** If, however, your values include a dislike for being different, you may want to practice conspicuous consumption and demonstrate by your consumption patterns that you do, indeed, belong to a group. In either case, if you understand and appreciate your values, your consumption patterns are more likely to lead you to a higher level of satisfaction. If you don't—if your consumer decisions are not built on known, well-defined values—you are not likely to be satisfied—or happy. Thus the next section tries to help you clarify your values so you can set goals that will guide you in your consumer decision making.

Values and the Consumer

As we have implied, there are two reasons to examine values at this point in our study. First, you cannot make a logically consistent set of decisions without first knowing what is important to you—without understanding your values. Second, you need a better perspective on the values of other consumers. We live in a multicultural society in which different people have different values. What might appear to be bizarre, uneconomic behavior to you may, in fact, be quite rational given another person's value structure. A good motto is: Be slow to judge others, but regularly recheck your own value network.

Ronald Stampfl (1981), professor of Business and Consumer Science at the University of Wisconsin, has identified sets of values that underlie what he calls industrial-age, transitional, and post-industrial-age consumption patterns.

Here is an exhibit of the two value clusters most opposed to one another, industrial-age and post-industrial-age:

Industrial-age consumer values	Post-industrial-age consumer values
Consuming as much as possible is desirable.	Consuming only as much as necessary is desirable.
Disposable products are desirable.	Recycling is important.
Convenience is more important than cost.	Foregoing convenience if cost-benefit ratio is low is desirable.
Fashion and style are unrelated to function and are relatively important.	Functional changes are more important than style or fashion.
Ownership is important.	Leasing is as acceptable as owning.
Economic growth and the quantity of goods and services in the marketplace are important.	Economic stability and the quality of goods and services are important.
Concern for social or environmental cost of products is not important.	Conservation is important.
Consumer movement has limited impact and is unimportant.	Consumer movement has great impact and is important.

According to Professor Stampfl, American consumers who have **industrial-age values** reached adulthood between 1920 and 1960, when consumers believed that "more was better, natural resources were all but inexhaustible, convenience was to be expected and that every American was entitled to all the *things* which constituted the good life." Consumers with **post-industrial-age values** will reach adulthood sometime after 1990, and they will be confronted by an era characterized by "inflation, materials shortages, pollution problems, energy crisis and unprecedented governmental regulation of the marketplace." In between these two eras are consumers with **transitional-age values,** who reached or will reach adulthood between 1960 and 1990. These consumers have been taught the industrial-age values but intellectually are moving toward post-industrial-age values. This change may lead to a conflict between

---

BOX 2-1

What Type of Consumer Are You?

Place an X on the continuum that best represents your values—what you *believe*. Then reread the test and place a circle at a point that represents your *behavior* as a consumer.

I consume as much as I want, and I feel that more is generally better than less.	....	I consume only as much as I need, and I feel that more is not necessarily better.
When I am finished with a product or a package, I throw it in the trash.	....	When I am finished with a product, I try to pass it on to someone else who can use it. When I am finished with a package (bottle, can), I try to recycle it.
I always try to buy products and shop in stores that provide the most convenience for me.	....	I try to assess the cost of "convenience" when making product or store choices.
When I see a new model of a product I already own, I am anxious to trade in my old model.	....	When I see a new model of a product I already own, I don't care to have it unless it truly performs its function better than my old model.
I'd prefer to own my own home, car, appliances, tools, recreational vehicles, and so forth rather than lease (rent) them.	....	As long as I can use a nice home, car, appliances, tools, recreational vehicles, and so forth, it doesn't matter to me whether I own, lease, or rent them.
I believe that government regulations to protect the environment and workers are a waste of my money if they increase the price I must pay for a product.	....	I believe that the government should fully protect the environment and the workplace even if I must pay more for the products I buy.
I believe that a good economy is continually growing and producing an increasing quantity of goods and services.	....	I believe that a good economy is stable (low inflation and unemployment) and provides a high quality of life for its citizens, rather than an increasing quantity of goods and services.
I believe that the consumer movement is a threat to jobs and adds unnecessary costs to products.	....	I believe that the consumer movement is an important force in protecting the rights of consumers in the marketplace and is, therefore, justified.

Analysis: If marks fall predominantly on the left-hand side of the test, you have industrial-age consumer values and behavior. If there is no real pattern or if most marks fall in the center, you are a transitional consumer. If the X's and circles are far apart, some conflict exists between what you believe and what you do. To check your accuracy, ask someone who knows you well to fill out his or her perception of your consumption pattern on this scale. The result could prove interesting.

SOURCE: Ronald W. Stampfl, "What Type of Consumer Are You?" © 1981 J.C.Penney Company, Inc., Consumer Education Services, *Forum* (Spring/Summer 1981), pp. 3–5.

---

consumption patterns and beliefs—between what consumers want and what consumers believe they ought to want. Box 2-1 contains Dr. Stampfl's test designed to help you identify into which camp your consumption values fall.

SOURCES OF VALUES

As we said earlier, values are strongly held beliefs that tend to arouse strong emotional, physical, and intellectual responses when they are challenged. But where do we get our values? Generally speaking, the family is the most important transmitter of values. Often this transmission is more a product of osmosis than of conscious, well-planned instruction. As a child, you see and interact with your parents, and this contact tends to build a certain value framework that you plug all of your future experiences into.

Using Professor Stampfl's framework, a lack of respect for the environment is an example of an industrial-age value that can easily be transmitted from parent to child. For example, when driving their children somewhere, parents can (and often do) litter the highways with garbage hurled from their cars and pickup trucks. They don't feel obliged to deposit trash in proper receptacles. Their children in turn feel no compunction about littering the playground with candy wrappers and empty soda bottles. After all, they learned by observing their parents.

On a more positive note, young consumers can and do learn values such as honesty and consumer responsibility by observing their parents' behavior. At the checkout stand in a local market, for example, if a customer receives too much change or if the checker charges too little for an item, a responsible consumer calls this to the worker's attention. Such behavior reinforces the values of honesty and responsibility. It teaches young consumers by actions as well as by words.

After the family, the peer group generally exerts the greatest influence. Peer friends and acquaintances can affect the clothes you wear, the activities you engage in, and even your manner of speech. By now you can probably be objective enough to see the group influence on your values and your consumer behavior. But just in case you don't see the connection, think about the last article of clothing you bought, the last item related to sports you bought, or even the last novel you bought. Was your purchase influenced by a friend's opinion, either implicitly or explicitly? Did his or her values concerning beauty or competition or entertainment influence your values and thus your decision-making process? You would be a rare consumer if they played no role at all. And as long as you are aware of the influences that other consumers' values have on you and your consumption pattern, you are still in control of the decision-making process.

A third influential group consists of the people you admire or may wish to emulate. Their influence

Peers can affect consumer choices by influencing our clothes purchases, hairstyles, recreational activities, and so on.

can vary greatly, but certainly rock music stars, athletes, comedians, and other media people affect our values far more than many of them realize. The punk-rock and new-wave musicians of the early 1980s demonstrated a distinct affinity for the bizarre by dyeing their hair strange colors and wearing clothes studded with razor blades and zippers. These values were quickly assimilated by some groups of young consumers, who then purchased the most outlandish array of jewelry and clothing. A backlash against the values displayed on television has been gathering momentum among a coalition of groups sometimes labeled "the moral majority." These people believe that the values they wish to instill in their children are undermined by television programs that seem to emphasize sex and violence. The real impact of television is still disputed, but according to the Surgeon General's Advisory Committee on Television and Social Behavior, violence, defined as "the overt expression of physical force against others or self, or the compelling of action against one's will on pain of being of hurt or killed," is the dominant theme of American television. Moreover, the frequency of violence in children's programs is six times greater than adult programs.

VALUE SYSTEMS AND CONFLICTS

An individual's values are generally quite complex and sometimes at odds with one another. The importance and sanctity of motherhood, for example, has been an important value in many societies, including our own. Anyone who challenges the importance or value of mothers had better be ready to defend that challenge against a storm of protest. Likewise, most of us accept the democratic value as stated by the founders of our republic, that "all men are created equal." In the early 1960s, Betty Friedan's book *The Feminine Mystique* (1963) openly questioned whether adherence to the traditional motherhood value conflicted with the democratic value that all people, men *and* women, are created equal. Out of this controversy, the most recent debate about an Equal Rights Amendment was born, with all of its subsequent emotional, intellectual, and sometimes physical conflict.

Clarifying our own values and acting on them can sometimes put us into conflict with traditional societal values.

CLARIFYING VALUES

It is obvious that the values of a society, as well as those of an individual, can conflict, leaving one in a quandary. Resolving these conflicts and avoiding others can be achieved by frequently reviewing, evaluating, and revising one's values. The process of search and choice that helps you understand your values is called **values clarification.** It can take the form of a frank discussion with a counselor, a clergyman, or a good friend who can give you some insight into how your values have grown or changed. Or you can perform your own values clarification by reviewing your answers to the consumer values quiz in Box 2-1. You might even keep a record of your opinions over time to see how your underlying values and your explicit consumer behavior have changed.

Many consumers are just too busy with their day-to-day activities to bother with the process of rechecking their values. The danger here is that in a comparatively short time, such consumers may discover that they are not enjoying their work or their lifestyle. They may feel trapped or hooked into a set of roles that are not fulfilling. This is the stuff of which personal crises are made. You may read about the most extreme cases in the newspaper—"Mother of Five Abandons Children"—or you may hear of it in the proverbial story about the husband who goes out to get a pack of cigarettes and never returns to his family or his job. But the more common result of ignoring one's value structure is mental depression and a general state of unhappiness or boredom. If your lifestyle has not changed significantly over the past few years but your personal satisfaction index has plummeted, it is a good bet that your values have changed.

Part of this change could be the result of entering a new life cycle, of moving from adolescence to single adulthood, or of moving from being newly married to being a new parent. Chapter 3 discusses this process in detail. It could also be that your family, your peer group, or the media have led you to challenge and change values. Whatever the reason, the effect is the same—you no longer hold the same values you once did. You no longer give a high priority to those beliefs that you once held sacred. And because your decision-making ability is founded on the assumption that you *know* what you believe and what you want, your decisions about using your money, your time, and your energy will be haphazard. These decisions will not be satisfying or bring you happiness—the ultimate goal of all consumer behavior.

Even if you have a good grasp of your value structure, you will have difficulty in actualizing these values unless you set some goals for yourself based on these values. The next section outlines the goal-setting process and shows you how to measure your progress in achieving these goals.

Goals: Values in Action

Values are fairly abstract. They are not directly obtainable through a specific action. You cannot achieve a value. Goals, on the other hand, are specific and tangible. A **goal** is a result or an achievement toward which effort is directed. Values are the bases for goals. They are not the specific things sought, but they give meaning to the immediate objective. The goals that you pursue should reflect the values that you hold. If your external goals are not based on your internal values system, they will tend to be aimless and confused.

SETTING GOALS

As we discussed earlier, you must first clarify your values before you can expect to be a rational decision maker. Suppose, for example, that one of your most important values is to be independent. But this value does not specify how you will become independent. It could, however, lead you to a specific goal, such as getting a good job. Such a job and its high income would certainly make you independent. But what kind of job can you (should you) get? You may need to break this overall goal into subgoals. For example, you might decide that the most likely avenue to a good career is a college degree. Thus, your subgoal is to get a higher education. The subgoal of that might be to get an electrical engineering degree.

We usually have many goals and subgoals, but given the ever-present problem of scarcity, we cannot work toward all of them at once. It is therefore necessary to choose a few that seem most important at a specific time and direct our resources toward achieving them by ranking goals in order of importance. In electing to pursue a particular goal or subgoal, keep in mind that this selection has an opportunity cost associated with it. The opportunity cost is the value of the next-most-preferred goal that must be postponed while you try to accomplish the higher-priority goal.

For example, if you decide to pursue an electrical engineering degree, you may have to give up another important goal, such as becoming an accomplished pianist. Or if you decide to get married and have a family, you must realize that this will have an impact on your career goals. By ranking your goals in order of importance you can clarify your immediate course of action and thus simplify daily decision making.

It is important to set goals that are consistent with your values and to reevaluate those goals in light of the changes in your value system. For example, if being economically independent isn't so important any more, the career goal may not be either. Another part of evaluation involves considering whether these goals meet your values. For example, perhaps a college degree will not ensure a good career. Finally, you should realize that values and goals are interrelated and sometimes conflict. A strongly career-oriented person must adopt a different style of consumption and production from someone who places more emphasis on current income and employment. Getting ready for a good career may mean years of lowered consumption while you continue your studies. This describes the pattern of anyone who wants to practice medicine, for example. On the other hand, those who have both a strong need for immediate gratification and a strong desire for economic independence at a young age may be heading for a value clash and a mixed-up set of goals.

EVALUATING GOALS

You should review your goals and subgoals on a regular basis. It is becoming commonplace for firms to set up plans for the short run, the long run, and the very long run. The same should be true for households. They need to plan for the future. Can you imagine what you will be doing in one year? In five years? In ten years? If you have little or no idea, you are running the risk of drifting.

This is not to say that you, like the Soviet Union, must have a five-year plan with specific targets that cannot be changed. But a little bit of planning review now can lead you to a more efficient allocation of your time in the future. And remember, your plans can change. You wouldn't want a seventeen-year-old running your life, would you? Then why stick to a decision that you made when you were seventeen?

In the sections that follow we will provide you with some tools to help you in your attempt to achieve your goals. First, we will discuss the establishment of standards—the most important technique in helping you discover how close you are to achieving your goals. Then we will discuss three other tools—the sunset clause, zero-based budgeting, and sunk costs—that can help you in the goal-setting and evaluation process.

Tool Number 1: Standards. Once you have clarified your values and ranked your goals, you need to have some road signs to tell you how close you are to achieving those goals. These progress measures can be called **standards.** Standards are qualitative or quantitative measures of performance or achievement. In our career-oriented example, finishing one year of college might be a reasonable standard by which to gauge your progress toward the goal of economic independence. Finishing that year of education with better-than-average grades would give a quantitative, as well as a qualitative, index. Standards allow you to see, on a regular basis, your success (or lack of it) in attaining an overall goal.

Standards vary from person to person. As a general rule, it is good to stretch yourself somewhat, but not too much. In other words, don't set a standard that is so low and easy to reach that it invites sloth, but don't set the standard so high that you invite continual frustration. Studies show that people do their best work when they are a bit uneasy about the likelihood of success. In such situations, they are just a bit on edge and get a small surge of adrenalin. If your standards for achievement are set at this level, you are challenging yourself in a coherent way. If your standards do not engender any stressful periods, you are probably not expecting enough from yourself. If you find yourself habitually nervous, perhaps you are setting your sights too high. The answer, then, may be to proceed at a slower pace toward your goal or, possibly, to reevaluate the goal itself with the realization that it may be unattainable.

Tool Number 2: The Sunset Clause. The **sunset clause** is a planning rule from government that states that any new agency or department will be terminated at the end of a specified period unless it can be proven that it should be kept. The sunset clause puts the burden of proof on the agency to prove its worth or else face automatic extinction. It is too bad that consumers haven't used this principle with respect to their values and goals. If a given value is simply cluttering up your life, supplying guilt and pain but little else, you should be able to purge it automatically.

Tool Number 3: Zero-Based Budgeting. **Zero-based budgeting** has great potential for evaluating goals. The concept was first applied to budget requests for government agencies. The argument was that, when making a budget request for the coming year, many agencies simply start from last year's budget and add on the costs of additional programs, with some adjustment for inflation. Under the zero-based budgeting concept, all funds requested must be justified as if they had never been funded in the past. We could apply this concept to our goal-setting and goal-fulfillment behavior if we realize that each goal requires us to spend some of our resources (both time and money) on it. Under the zero-based scheme, we do not spend any more time or money on that goal in the coming year unless we can still justify the goal in light of our values.

Tool Number 4: Sunk Costs. A major objection to a zero-base in goal setting comes from the fear of admitting that one is wrong. You may, for example, spend quite a bit of your time and resources pursuing the goal of an advanced degree, say a doctorate in history. Let us assume that your goal is to teach history at the college level and that a doctorate is essential. If new information comes to you that there are almost no openings in the history field now and there will be fewer in the future, your likelihood of success is nil. Should you continue to pursue your education in history? No. Some people, however, would argue that because you have already invested so much you ought to continue. Continuing to pursue the unattainable simply because you are already devoting resources to the goal runs directly counter to zero-based budgeting. Economists argue that you should ignore

Decision Making: Learning to Choose   29

One social constraint on the consumer decisions we make is parental opinions and attitudes.

past costs and look only at future costs and benefits. Past costs are called **sunk costs;** they are fixed and cannot be changed. They should be ignored in all current decisions. Zero-based bugeting, by ignoring such costs, is a superior method for allocating resources.

The principle of sunk costs is exemplified in our culture by two mottoes: "Let bygones be bygones" and "Don't throw good money after bad." Have you ever heard someone say, "I can't get rid of that car, it cost me too much to fix it"? Was he aware of the doctrine of sunk costs?

Sunk costs apply to past decisions, whether they relate to consumer goods purchased or to goals you set and spent time pursuing. It is uneconomical and just plain inefficient to throw good money after bad. Let bygones be bygones in your role as a goal setter, as well as in your role as consumer.

Constraints and Restrictions on Decision Making

Now that you can define your values, set goals to achieve them, and use measurable standards to evaluate your progress—all while maintaining a planning process that continues to reevaluate your actions in terms of sunset clauses, zero-based budgets, and sunk costs—you are almost ready to review the rational decision maker's model. First, though, perhaps you should know about the social constraints that lead sociologists to argue that people have no choices to make.

PARENTS AND FAMILY

Because your family of orientation (your parents and siblings) plays an enormous role in shaping your values, goals, and standards, it also affects the decisions you make. We all must evaluate and judge for ourselves whether to accept parental advice and constraints that are always well intentioned but may not be in keeping with our own lifestyles.

For example, parents frequently place a high value on security and stability. They like to see that their children share this value and demonstrate this sharing by setting goals and establishing standards that reinforce the commonality of values. Thus, parental advice often takes a form that opposes risk taking: "Don't buy a motorcycle, you might get hurt." "Put your money in the bank where it is insured, don't buy speculative stock." "Get a house and settle down, don't keep renting." All of this advice is offered with the best intentions, and all is an attempt to influence your decisions. But following advice does not help you become a better decision maker, because it does not reflect your values, goals, and standards. In the case of the motorcycle, perhaps you are willing to trade an increased risk of bodily injury for a less expensive form of transportation. That might not be an acceptable tradeoff for your parents, but it is not their decision to make—provided, of course, that you are paying for the transportation. Similar analyses can be made for your investment behavior or your decision to rent an apartment rather than buy a house. In both of these cases, parents' advice is based on their values and goals, which they assume are yours. On the other hand, for most sons and daughters, parental respect is an important value. If that respect is damaged by the decision to buy a motorcycle, for example, the opportunity cost of the motorcycle rises accordingly.

ADVISORS AND INTERESTED PARTIES

Back when saddle shoes, beach-party movies, bobby sox, and the young Pat Boone were popular, one of the topical questions of the day involved decision making after marriage: Should the husband be the boss or should family decisions be shared equally? In the eighties, when divorce, single-parent families, feminism, and the two-income family are common, the question of decision-making supremacy may seem simplistic. Nevertheless, it points out an important factor in decision making: many of your choices will be *joint* ones. Because they may affect your spouse, your children, or your roommate, your particular values, goals, and standards must often be tempered by those of your partners in this decision. A corporation president has a board of directors who affect and are affected by the president's decisions; so too, do most people have a board of directors.

Your board of interested parties should have some input into your decision, and they should be consulted before any major change in policy. The number of people to consult and the weight you give to their advice depends on a variety of factors. Obviously, the once-traditional American family (husband, wife, and 1.8 children) has a different process for handling decisions from that of a divorced mother with three children or a retired couple or two college students sharing an apartment. In each of these situations, the decision of any one person will be conditioned by the views of the other parties involved. If you must make an important decision, such as where and when to spend your family vacation, you will do well to consult those involved, ponder their opinions, and try to achieve some agreement. If no consensus emerges, you must either postpone the decision or allow someone to take the initiative (and the chief responsibility) for the action.

Conferences may limit your options and slow the decision-making process. Because your time and that of your partners is valuable, a quick cost-benefit analysis about the expected outcome of such sessions is in order *before* you ask for a committee meeting. You should also be forewarned about expecting too much from these meetings. Nevertheless, if they are run sincerely, they can go a long way toward removing some significant barriers to your actions.

SOCIAL CUSTOMS

At an exclusive restaurant in Southern California, the owner (who is also the maître d') has one rule that must be strictly followed if you are to eat there: You must *not* wear a necktie. If some unsuspecting diner comes in with a tie on, the owner takes out a pair of scissors and cuts it in half! This is done in the spirit of good-natured fun, and some people suspect that it is a gimmick for entertainment value. Nonetheless, it does work. The point of this anecdote is that social custom constrains the range of your choices. You cannot do whatever you want to do, partly because society conditions you either directly or indirectly to act in certain ways. This social conditioning is called **custom**.

Customs are built on a society's values, goals, and standards. They change slowly, and most of us remain subject to them all our lives. In your role as a consumer, custom affects you in many ways. For example, do you think you would buy as many gifts for other people if it weren't for the custom of gift giving? Christmas, birthdays, weddings, and baby showers all spark us to look for the right present. Custom also often dictates the kind of food we eat as well as the quantities of food we prepare on traditional holidays such as New Year's, Easter, Thanksgiving, and Christmas. The gifts you give, the food you eat, the holidays you celebrate, and even how you celebrate these holidays are just some of the ways that custom restricts your range of choices.

Customs are not necessarily bad or economically inefficient. Neither does following them condemn you to a life of mindless conformity. In fact, because decisions take time and involve search costs, social customs can sometimes be real time savers in decision making by helping you to decide what to do in certain situations and thus helping you to economize on your scarce resources. As customs break down, the time costs of decisions can actually go up. For example, in the 1950s it was fairly commonplace for a male going to a senior prom to rent a texedo. He had two choices—a white tuxedo or a black tuxedo. Today the choices and styles of apparel are so numerous that they are almost mind boggling. The same problem holds true for many social gatherings. As the types of acceptable social attire widen, the amount of time spent trying to choose the most appropriate thing to wear also increases. Did you ever try to shorten this period of uncertainty (what shall I wear?) by calling a few friends to find out what they were going to wear? This is a perfect example of looking for a custom to help eliminate uncertainty and lower the time cost. Did you ever buy something to wear because it was appropriate for that special occasion? This is an example of how custom conditions consumption.

One drawback of using customs to eliminate time costs is that they sometimes lead us to *perceive* fewer choices than actually exist, thus limiting our decision-making ability. A good example is the traditional wedding in which the division of expenses and responsibility for the wedding are well established by long-standing customs. The rules of "who pays for what" have undoubtedly stood the test of time and have prevented many interfamily arguments, but in many cases the traditional rules do not make good economic sense. For example, in most American weddings the bride's parents are expected to pay most of the expenses. But suppose the bride's family is not well-to-do, whereas the groom's family is much better off. Custom dictates that the bride's family pay for the wedding regardless of its financial situation. This custom may have made more sense in medieval Europe, when it was considered helpful to have a son-in-law and burdensome to have an unwed daughter. But in twentieth-century America, it makes better economic sense for the bride's parents to break with custom and ask for financial help from the groom's parents.

ADVERTISING, BIG BUSINESS, BIG GOVERNMENT, AND CONSUMER SOVEREIGNTY

There is no doubt that many of our decisions are influenced by customs, friends, and family. But with the advent of large, multinational corporations that use sophisticated marketing strategies and of government regulatory agencies staffed by seemingly endless rows of bureaucrats, many observers argue that consumer choice is so severely restricted that it is practically nonexistent. The argument that consumers have no real choices to make strikes at the heart of the

---

BOX 2-2

Custom and Your Career

Custom can play a role in your life as a producer as well as your life as a consumer. The choices that you perceive for potential careers, for example, have a strong element of custom in them. One of the strongest and most obvious restrictions on career choice has been based on sex. Women, in particular, have had their range of careers narrowed significantly by custom—even discrimination can become a custom if it is the standard practice.

---

doctrine of consumer sovereignty—one of the basic tenets of consumer economics. The theory of **consumer sovereignty** holds that consumers rule a market economy because they have the ultimate power to determine what gets produced and which firms survive in the marketplace. Supporters of the consumer-sovereignty doctrine often liken the American economy to a polling booth, where dollars equal votes and the candidates (products) that get the largest share of the votes (dollars) survive and prosper. However, unlike a modern political democracy, the economy need not adhere to the "one person, one vote" rule or recognize any age minimum for the electorate. In a market economy, whoever has money can vote, and he or she can vote for foreign candidates by buying a Japanese car or a French wine. The result of such actions, according to the doctrine of consumer sovereignty, is that success or failure of firms and their products ultimately depends on their acceptance by consumers.

Some critics of consumer sovereignty point to the advertising industry as an example of the flimsy nature of consumer power. We will discuss advertising in greater detail in Chapter 4, but regarding consumer decision making we should note that advertising has two influences: information and persuasion. In 1982, American firms spent over $60 billion in advertising their products. This total includes everything from the cost of grocery store ads in newspapers (information) to the cost of putting a fictitious grocery clerk in front of a small mountain of toilet tissue for a television commercial (persuasion). The success of these advertisements is just as difficult to gauge as their usefulness. Their object, however, is quite simple. It is to get you, the consumer, to buy their products. In the case of grocery store ads, the device is generally a full page of prices, although some chain stores are running noninformational ads such as, "We have the lowest prices in town." Toilet tissue manufacturers never mention price. They obviously believe that consumers will react more favorably toward their product after watching adults clustered around a store display compulsively squeezing rolls of tissue. Before you scoff at their logic, you should be aware that Mr. Whipple's "squeezably soft" Charmin is the leading seller. But is its success caused by an illusion or is it simply a better product than its rivals?

Other real-world objections to the doctrine of consumer sovereignty are based on the sheer size and influence of institutions such as the federal government and large corporations. Indeed, it is nearly impossible to read a newspaper or watch the nightly news and *not* see some reference to a major corporate merger or to a government regulation that affects our lives. Harvard economist John Kenneth Galbraith and other prominent scholars have argued that the rise of multinational corporations and the coming of big government has effectively ended the era of consumer sovereignty. They use a number of examples to support their view that corporate and governmental behavior seriously restricts the consumer's ability to make meaningful decisions, but the automobile is one of their favorites because it combines government regulation with large corporate production and mass marketing. According to these critics, consumers' transportation needs have been transformed into a desire for the private automobile, produced by General Motors, fueled by Exxon, and regulated by the Environmental Protection Agency (EPA). These same institutions collaborated on the catalytic converter, a piece of equipment whose personal costs are apparent but whose short-run benefits are elusive. GM makes *all* of them, Exxon sells unleaded fuel for many of them, and the EPA requires them on almost every car. The critics ask, "Where is consumer sovereignty here?"

BOX 2-3

Decidophobia (Dē-sī-dō-fō-bē-ə)

Do you suffer from decidophobia? This disease affects most consumers at some point in their lives and can become a chronic illness if it is not caught early enough. Decidophobia is a fear of making decisions. It was first isolated by Walter Kaufmann, who reported on it in his book *Without Guilt and Justice: From Decidophobia to Autonomy* (1973). This social disease strikes people who are afraid of being responsible for themselves. They crave a life without choice and will go to great lengths to avoid making a decision.

Check the following list to see whether you have any of the symptoms of decidophobia:

1. *Drifting*—You generally leave things to chance or you simply go along with the crowd. The status quo is fine as far as you are concerned.
2. *Pedantry*—You get involved in more minute questions or distinctions so that you don't have to grapple with the larger, more important questions.
3. *Blind allegiance*—You belong to an organization that allows you to follow along, to "belong" without having to make your own choices.
4. *Manicheanism*—You tend to see most issues as black and white. One side is all right, the other all wrong. Decisions tend to make themselves.
5. *Marriage*—You use your spouse as a scapegoat because you basically go along. You lean completely on your partner and deny responsibility when something turns out badly.

The answer to that question lies in the bigger picture. Of course, in a complex modern economy where "bigness" is often associated with "badness," there are many examples of restrictions on consumer choice. (If there weren't, we wouldn't be including a section on it here.) But there are also many examples of the power of the consumer. Ford Motor Company's failure in the 1950s to convince the American public to buy a new car called the Edsel cost the company over $250 million. The huge losses and near bankruptcy of the Chrysler Corporation in 1980 were prompted by its slowness in introducing smaller, more fuel-efficient cars. Market shares and market success require more than big advertising budgets. Billy Beer, introduced in 1978 to capitalize on Billy Carter's well-known penchant for the brew, was produced, packaged, and promoted in one of the slickest ad campaigns ever. It was such a colossal failure that by 1980 the cans were collectors' items.

In our opinion, the reports of the death of consumer sovereignty have been exaggerated. There are serious restrictions on your freedom of choice, but they do not amount to a straitjacket of regulations and advertisements that force you to buy products you don't want, don't need, and can't get to work. Consumers may not be sovereign, but they aren't corpses either.

Consumer education can further bolster consumer sovereignty by providing consumers with some perspective on their crucial role in a market economy. Part of this educational process should include the fundamentals of consumer decision making. In the next section we will present a decision-making model that we will use throughout the remainder of the text. Study it well; the path to consumer sovereignty is easier to follow if you develop your decision-making skills early.

The Consumer Decision-Making Model

As we said at the beginning of this chapter, scarcity is the mother of decisions. If we did not live in a world where our wants exceed our resources, we would not have to be good decision makers. However, given that our resources are scarce, good decision-making skills help us to stretch those resources and thus to get greater personal satisfaction out of the choices we make. Reaching our highest level of satisfaction entails learning about and using cost-benefit analysis so that we can evaluate alternative choices and rank them on the basis of their expected net benefit. In this way, higher-valued alternatives will always be selected before lower-valued ones.

Choices do not take place in a vacuum. Your choices are conditioned by your values and goals, as well as by those of others. Your decisions are also limited by the social and institutional constraints mentioned in the last section. Nevertheless, choices do exist. And if you are to be a better consumer, you

No matter how much a product is promoted and advertised, if consumers don't want the product, it will not succeed.

should begin by studying a formal decision-making model. Throughout the remainder of this text we will apply this model wherever possible to clarify a choice-making situation.

Our seven-step decision making model is summarized here, followed by an example to demonstrate how it might be used:

1. Define the problem and outline some potential solutions.
2. Determine how your values, goals, and standards may limit your choice.
3. Seek advice and collect information on the alternatives.
4. Weigh the costs and benefits of alternatives; include time as well as money costs.
5. Make a choice.
6. Evaluate and periodically review all major decisions.
7. Be responsible for your decisions.

You are now prepared to use what you have read in this chapter in the context of this model. Perhaps the easiest way for you to pull all of that information together and put it into the model is to apply it to a common major consumer decision such as providing yourself with transportation.

In Step 1, you need to define the problem. Let us suppose that you are moving away from home and are going to college for the first time. You move into an off-campus apartment less than two miles from campus, but you have an off-campus parttime job on the other side of town. You will be commuting from home to school to work to home, five days a week. You need some form of transportation. After a brief brainstorming session, you identify several potential solutions: buy a bus pass, a bicycle, a car, or a motorcycle or rely on hitchhiking. You also have the option of finding another solution. You don't want to be close-minded. (See Box 2-4 for a representation of this and the other stages of decision making.)

In Step 2 you must clarify your values, goals, and standards concerning transportation. For example, if your values coincide with those of the post-industrial consumer, you will be concerned with how your decision affects the environment and what affect it may have on your health and the health of others. If, on the other hand, you have industrial-age values, you will be more concerned with personal convenience and ownership. These value clusters play a major part in evaluating the benefits of alternative modes of transportation. In addition, there are other values that may be important to this decision but that do not fit into the industrial or post-industrial-age value clusters. For example, you may be concerned with your personal safety. This would lead you to rule out more dangerous forms of transportation such as hitchhiking. Motorcycles would also get low marks from risk averters. Even bus riding is less appealing if you have to wait for a bus or walk home from the busstop late at night.

In Step 3, you seek input from knowledgeable sources. This may include talking to friends and acquaintances who may have already faced this situation and made a decision. It may also involve collecting some basic price information on the alternate forms of transportation, in addition to making an estimate of how much you can afford to pay for transportation. This process can be fairly long and involved or fairly brief. Remember, there are costs involved in finding information. For an important decision such as finding basic transportation, higher search costs seem to be justified. In less important situations, such as deciding what to have for dinner or where to open a bank account, shorter searches are needed. You can spend too much time gathering information and fall into the "pedantry" decidophobia category (see Box 2-3).

Once you make a good estimate of how much you can afford to pay for transportation and of the costs of the alternatives, you need to bring all of this information together in a cost-benefit decision matrix (Step 4). These cost-benefit calculations should incude both the explicit monetary costs and the implicit time costs of all viable alternatives. Do not lose sight of the opportunity cost principle. Spending more money (or time) on transportation means spending less money (or time) on another area. If you decide to buy a car, you may not be able to afford a vacation. If you choose to buy a bicycle, you may spend more time commuting and therefore have less time to study.

Once you have established the advantages and disadvantages of your potential solutions, it is time to choose an alternative. In our example, hitchhiking is the least expensive in money terms, but it has significant time costs and is the least safe. If you are a 100 percent post-industrial-age consumer, the bus and the bicycle get high marks because they are more socially responsible from an ecological point of view. The motorcycle falls somewhere between the bicycle and the car in money cost, but its safety ratings is low and its cost in human energy is significantly higher than that of a car.

Now it's time for Step 5—making a decision. If you have followed the procedure up to this point, one alternative should clearly be superior to the others. If there is no perfect solution, you have two options: Select the "least bad" alternative or postpone a decision until you have more information. Both are viable options and should be considered if no clear choice emerges. But let us assume for the sake of our example that you choose to purchase a car. It offers the lowest time costs and more personal safety, and it fits well with your industrial-age values of convenience and ownership. The increased cost means that you will not be able to take a skiing holiday, but that tradeoff seems worth making, given the alternatives. You have made a rational decision, but, of course, this decision is only the beginning. Now you have to

BOX 2-4
An Example of the Decision-Making Model

1. Identify the problem.

   I need to decide what kind of transportation to use:

2. Determine which values, goals, and standards affect the problem:
   a. Money.
   b. Time.
   c. Safety.
   d. Ecology.
   e. Privacy.
   f. Ownership.
   g. Other.

3. Collect information:
   a. Books.
   b. Magazines.
   c. Telephone.
   d. Personal interviews.
   e. ?

4. Weigh costs and benefits of alternatives:

Values	Hitchhiking	Bicycle	Car	Bus	Motorcycle
Money	+ +	+ +	- -	+	-
Time	- -	-	+ +	-	+
Safety	- - -	-	+	+	-
Ecology	+	+ +	- -	+	-
Privacy	- -	+	+ +	-	+
Ownership	-	+	+	-	+
Other					

5. Make a choice.

6. Periodically evaluate and review.

7. Assume responsibility.

decide what kind of car to buy, whether to get a new or used one, and so on. We will return to this decision when we discuss transportation in Chapter 12.

Once you get your car, you continue on your decision-making road by evaluating and periodically reviewing it. The experience you gain from your decisions should be used to better make future decisions. You may discover, for example, that you don't use the car very much or that you underestimated the cost of owning the car. Gasoline prices and insurance costs, for example, have a way of exploding. Or your values, goals, or standards change; as a result, you may become dissatisfied with your decision. If this happens, you need to determine the cause of your dissatisfaction so that future decisions can lead to happier consequences.

The seventh point could simply be labeled "responsibility." You must take responsibility for your actions. Otherwise, it is too easy to fall into decidophobia or to blame others for your mistakes. Decidophobia causes rootless and luckless consumers to fall prey to the unscrupulous people, who undoubtedly account for a large portion of consumer fraud. If you believe that you made the right decision but are not enjoying the fruits of your labor because you feel cheated, take action. Chapter 5 outlines some major courses of action. And you can use this model to help you decide whether redress is worth fighting for. Throughout the text we highlight this framework and suggest ways to use it in your multifaceted career as an American consumer.

Summary

If there is a key chapter in this text, this is it. We have brought together the threads of the decision-making process in a way that we hope will be useful in the following chapters and for all your future major consumer decisions. Scarcity creates the need for decisions, and the attempt to maximize one's satisfaction while minimizing one's resource expenditure makes rational consumer decision making necessary. Understanding the reason for the scarcity dilemma is fairly easy, but learning to cope with it through good decision-making habits is not. Decision making is a skill that must be applied in order to be learned well. The following chapters refer to our decision-making model and use it to help you determine the most efficient course of consumer action. Keep in mind, however, that decisions are not made in a vacuum. As we have seen in this chapter, decisions are conditioned by personal values and goals. And they are constrained by a number of society-wide factors. Nevertheless, we are more in tune with Professor Duesenberry's comment about economics (it is all about how people make choices) than we are with his comment about sociology (it is all about how people have no choices to make).

Neighborhood REVISITED

1. Did Sally incur any opportunity cost by waiting until her junior year to declare her major? Did she benefit by waiting?

2. If Sally's values are basically those of an industrial-age consumer and if she values her future financial independence highly, set up some goals and standards that might suit her.

3. Given a rough outline of Sally's values, goals, and standards, what academic majors would be good choices? Which, in your opinion, would be poor choices? Explain.

KEY TERMS

conspicuous consumption
consumer sovereignty
custom
free good
goal
industrial-age values

post-industrial-age values
scarce resource
standards
sunk costs
sunset clause
tradeoffs

transitional-age values
value judgment
values
values clarification
zero-based budgeting

QUESTIONS

1. Opportunity costs are involved in almost all decisions consumers make. Use your understanding of this concept to explain the following behavior:
   a. Consumers often patronize the local convenience store even though it has higher prices and a more limited selection than the local supermarket.
   b. Most people choose Friday and Saturday to have a night on the town.
   c. People with active, physically demanding jobs are more likely to consume regular beer, whereas those with more sedentary occupations choose light beer.
   d. Television stations run public-service programs on Sunday morning rather than during prime time.
   e. Consumers take longer to decide where to live than where to bank.

2. If we lived in a place where all goods were abundant, would the concepts of scarcity and opportunity cost exist? Would decision making be important?

3. Does an increase in consumption lead to greater happiness? Give examples from your own experience in which it has and has not.

4. What is conspicuous consumption? Have you ever engaged in it? Could the boom in designer jeans have been accelerated by conspicuous consumption? Can you think of other possible examples?

5. Take three important goals and measure your progress by a standard. Are you closer to meeting some goals than others? Do your standards result in stressful periods? Should they?

6. Have you ever heard someone say, "I can't quit now, I have too much invested"? This might relate to a business, a career, or a personal relationship. What kind of advice might you give such a person based on your knowledge of zero-based budgeting, sunset clauses, and the principle of sunk costs?

7. Consumer sovereignty is an important assumption behind consumer decision-making theory. In general, are consumers sovereign in the American marketplace? How can consumer education increase the level of consumer sovereignty?

8. Can you think of a recent purchase of yours that was a product of social custom? Of advertising? Of peer group pressure?

PROJECTS

1. Take Professor Stampfl's values clarification test (Box 2-1) and then administer it to a friend. Discuss your results. Does the test accurately measure your values?

2. List three important goals that you have set for yourself. Then identify the values underlying these goals. Do any of these values conflict with each other? Can you prioritize your values or your goals? Explain your ranking.

3. Put some flesh on the decision-making model presented at the end of the chapter by selecting another real-world problem you are facing and proceeding through the steps outlined. Briefly evaluate the outcome.

REFERENCES AND READINGS

Duesenberry, James S. "Comment," in Universities–National Bureau Committee for Economic Research, *Demographic and Economic Change in Developed Countries.* Princeton: Princeton University Press, 1960.

Friedan, Betty. *The Feminine Mystique.* New York: Dell, 1963.

Gilder, George. "Galbraithian Truth and Fallacy." *Forbes,* 12 November 1979.

Hayek, F. A. "The Non Sequitur of the Dependence Effect." *Southern Economic Journal,* April 1961.

Kaufmann, Walter. *Without Guilt and Justice: From Decidophobia to Autonomy.* New York: Peter H. Wyden, 1973.

Marx, Karl. "Wage-Labor and Capital," in *Selected Works,* vol. 1. New York: International Publishers, 1933.

Maynes, E. Scott. *Decision-making for Consumers.* New York: Macmillan, 1976.

Mermelstein, David, ed. *Economics: Mainstream Readings and Radical Critiques.* New York: Random House, 1972.

Paolucci, Beatrice, et al. *Family Decision Making: An Ecosystem Approach.* New York: Wiley, 1977.

Schumacher, E. F. *Small Is Beautiful: Economics as If People Mattered.* New York: Harper & Row, 1973.

Stampfl, Ronald W. "Consumer Values in Transition." *Forum,* Spring/Summer 1981.

"Values and Decision Making." *Home Economics Research Abstract,* No. 6. Washington, D.C.: Family Relations and Child Development, American Home Economics Association, 1968.

Veblen, Thorstein. *The Theory of the Leisure Class: An Economic Study of Institutions.* New York: Macmillan, 1899.

Did You Know That...

- the biggest cost of employment is the time you give up in order to work?

- one-third of America's current population is a result of the "baby boom"?

- the average pay that women receive relative to men has actually dropped over the last two decades?

- over 45 percent of the married women with children under the age of six are in the work force?

- two-fifths of the single adults in America are women over age fifty-five?

- two of every three marriages do not end in divorce?

- two of every five single-parent families live in poverty?

- husbands spend the same amount of time on household tasks, regardless of the employment status of wives?

Life Cycles and the Consumer

Income: Not Just a Paycheck
Level of Income: Facts and Factors
The Changing American Family
Types of Households
Special Problems in the Family Life Cycle
Changing Family Roles: Money and Time

Neighborhood CAPSULE

Debbie and Ralph had had this discussion before. "We've got to have more money to do the things we want to do!" Ralph said for the second time. "It's so depressing. I have my college degree, and I seem to have little to show for it!"

"I've really given this some thought," Debbie responded, "and I think I'd like to go back to work. The children are older now, and . . ."

"But Amy is only three and a half," Ralph exclaimed, "and Christofer is just ready for school . . ."

"That's my point! They are old enough to do without me during the day. The bank is hiring management trainees and I understand that they have a new policy of promoting women."

"You're thinking of a full-time job? I had no idea . . ."

"Well, I really have been feeling stale lately. You come home from work and it seems that your day was so exciting—but mine is pretty boring. I liked working when we were first married. I know it will be different now that we have Amy and Chris, but we really could use the extra money."

"Well, do you think we'd come out ahead, with clothes, babysitting . . .? We'd need to replace that old station wagon with something more reliable. Who would take care of the kids? You know, with the extra money we could take a vacation!"

"If I could get the time off from work. I'd need more help from you around the house, of course."

"Oh, sure, no problem. I could help cook dinner and watch the kids a little bit."

"Yes, plus I was thinking that you could be in charge of the vacuuming and dusting, as well as of bathing the children at night."

"Gee, Hon, I don't know. At night I'm really beat when I get home and . . ."

"Oh, and I wouldn't be, is that what you're saying?"

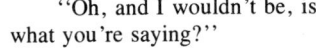

Economic Decisions for Consumers

Decision making doesn't take place in a vacuum. Who we are—our age, sex, education, income—all affect the process and the results. In addition, most of us do not make decisions alone; 96 percent of us marry, and most of us have children. Family decisions change as a family grows up. Just as individuals go through a **life cycle** (that is, a series of identifiable stages that occur in a certain order from infancy through old age, as shown in Figure 3-1), so does a family. Decisions made during adolescence or during the early stages of the family life cycle stay

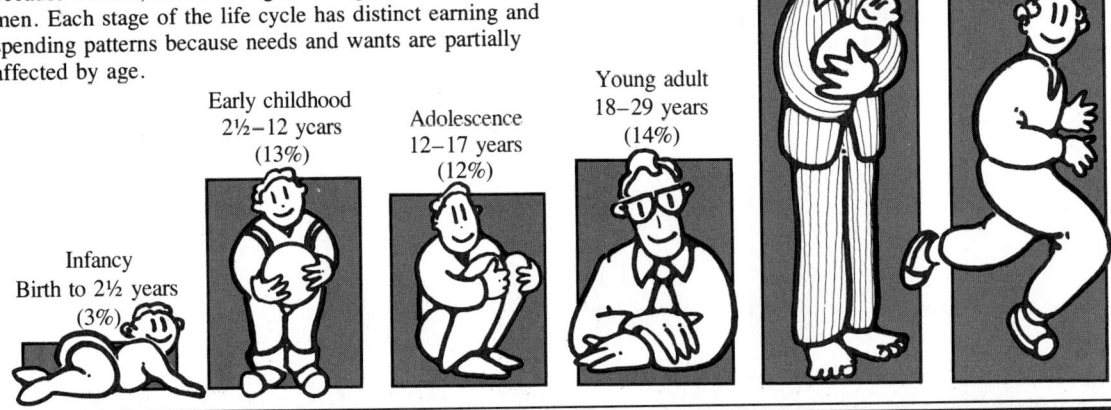

Figure 3-1. The individual life cycle begins with infancy and early childhood and progresses to the stages of adolescence, middle-aged adulthood, and older adulthood. The ages on the figure are approximate because people do not all develop at the same rate. Percentages are based on a 75 year lifespan, although this, too, varies, particularly because women, on the average, live eight years longer than men. Each stage of the life cycle has distinct earning and spending patterns because needs and wants are partially affected by age.

with us for a long time and become increasingly difficult and expensive to change. Moreover, neither individuals nor families can meet their economic goals without considering the impact of decisions about careers, marriage, parenthood, and use of time that are made throughout the life cycle.

In this chapter we look at these factors as they affect us as consumers. In a sense, we are providing a context for much of what you will read about later in the book. Knowing what factors affect income, looking at the family and the family life cycle, and thinking about how we spend our time all provide us with more information to use in decision making. Specifically, if we know how these forces and factors operate, we can better know what to anticipate, how to judge what happens to us, and how to make decisions, rather than feeling as though someone or something else is controlling us. In addition, understanding these topics will be important when we get to other chapters, particularly those on budgeting, credit, transportation, and health care.

We begin this chapter with the basics of income—how we get it, how much we get, what factors affect our level of income, and how second incomes make a difference. Then we move to the family—its life cycle and how it affects consumer needs and decisions. From there we go on to time away from work. Although that may not seem part of consumer decision making, it definitely is part of personal economics because we spend 7 percent of our incomes, as well as much of our time, on recreation.

Income: Not Just a Paycheck

The most obvious form of income is **labor income,** that is, the wage or salary paid to an individual, plus benefits such as pensions, medical and dental insurance, life insurance, paid vacation and sick days, and employers' Social Security contributions. That is what we normally think of as income, but each job or career also has **psychic income**—the feelings of satisfaction, status, or prestige gained from it or the pleasure of working in certain surroundings. In interviewing college students for her book *The Case Against College,* Caroline Bird (1975) found that most were hoping for ''interesting work'' in which they could ''help others'' or make a contribution to society. They wanted their jobs to be rewarding as well as to provide a decent income.

> **BOX 3-1**
>
> **Lifetime Goals**
>
> In his 1973 classic on time management, *How to Get Control of Your Time and Your Life,* Alan Lakein recommends setting lifetime goals in order to establish the balance you prefer between personal, family, social, career, financial, community, and spiritual goals. He recommends the following exercise to help you match your use of time with your priorities. You will need several pieces of paper, a pen or a pencil, and a watch or a clock.
>
> 1. Label the first paper "lifetime goals." Take *two minutes* to list as many of your goals as you can think of. Nothing is too far-out or outrageous to include. You are not required to reach these goals, so include everything that comes to mind.
> 2. Take a minute or so to review the list to see that it is complete.
> 3. Label a second paper "five-year goals." Take *two minutes* to list all the things you would like to do in the next five years. This list will probably be more specific than the first one.
> 4. Take a minute to review the second list, and be sure to include whatever else comes to mind.
> 5. Label a third paper "my last six months." For a different perspective, consider what you would do if you only had six months to live. Assume that matters relating to your death, such as a will, a funeral, and so forth, are all taken care of. How would you spend your time? What would your goals be?
> 6. Spend a few minutes reviewing all three lists to make additions and clarifications.
> 7. Evaluate your results. Some people find that all three lists are similar—that lists 2 and 3 are extensions or elaborations of list 1. Other people find that list 3 is radically different from lists 1 and 2. There is no "correct" result, just an opportunity to learn about yourself. Ask yourself:
>   a. What goals are on all three lists?
>   b. What goals are on only one list?
>   c. What do these results seem to indicate about my priorities?
> 8. Identify goal conflicts. Decide what is most important to you *at this time.* Your lists probably include more goals than you have time to accomplish, which creates goal conflicts. You may have to give up one goal (earning money) for another goal (going to school). Recognize that both can be equally important to you but that you may not be able to give them equal time at this point.
> 9. Set priorities:
>   a. Select three goals from list 1 that are most important to you. Label them in order of importance from 1 to 3.
>   b. Take the other two lists and number the three most important goals on each.
> 10. Keep these priorities in mind as you spend your time.
>
> SOURCE: Reprinted with permission from *How to Get Control of Your Time and Life* by Alan Lakein, copyright 1973. Published by David McKay Co., Inc.

The amount of psychic income that you want—and get—is determined in part by your values and standards. When you evaluate this aspect of a job, you have to look at psychic costs and benefits. For example, you have to weigh all the things you have to put up with—a long commute, disagreeable coworkers, a gloomy office, a restrictive dress code—against the things that make you feel good—your enjoyment in doing the work, the feeling of contributing, the freedom to set your own work hours. If you accept a different job at the same pay, the psychic income from your current job is negative or not enough. But if you stay on the job even with a cut in pay, the psychic income is positive.

As we saw in Chapter 2, time is a scarce resource that has to be spent wisely. When we spend a large portion of it to get labor income, we cannot use that same time for other purposes. Many people feel that they do not have enough time for everything they want to do. Time is a finite resource—168 hours per week—so the way we spend it is critical. If we do not work for income, we have more time, but we have less money. When we work for income, we often need to buy services that we can do but no longer have time to do, such as cleaning, gardening, childcare, laundry, or cooking. Other chores or skills, such as carpentry, sewing, car repair, or fruit and vegetable canning, are even more time consuming; if you do not have the money to pay for them, you may have to take the time to do them yourself, or you may have to do without them entirely. When we take the time to save money and do home repairs and maintenance chores ourselves, we engage in what is called **nonmarket home production,** which causes us to give up not only time that we could be working for income but time that we could be using for leisure. This is called **leisure foregone;** if we give up income for leisure, it is income foregone.

Values and goals play an important part in making decisions about time and money. Some people choose a career or job that requires no overtime, has little additional responsibility, or has a short work week, so they can pursue hobbies and outside interests or perform more service tasks (gardening and cleaning, for example) themselves. Others may find the psychic income from their jobs so great that they are willing to work long hours and buy most of the services mentioned here. The important thing is to match your use of time with the priorities in your life. Box 3-1 shows you a way to begin to do this.

Level of Income: Facts and Factors

If you're so smart, why aren't you rich? This epithet has been hurled at more than one professor and it has a grain of truth to it. Intelligence—and by implication, education—do not automatically bring you fame and fortune. There are many factors that determine your income and consequently your ability to consume. In this section we outline these factors beginning with education. Although your education level is strongly correlated with your income, other variables beyond your direct control can also affect your earnings potential. The impersonal forces of supply and demand, along with your age, sex, race, and geographic location, can also play a role in your income. By understanding the importance of these influences you can often adjust your goals, thus increasing your chances of personal success.

Table 3-1 Annual Money Earnings by Education, Age, and Sex

Earner categories	Mean earnings*	Percent of mean
All individuals	16,318	100.0
By education		
Elementary	10,411	63.8
Some high school	12,983	79.5
High school graduate	14,295	87.6
Some college	16,356	100.2
College graduate	23,384	143.3
Postgraduate	26,367	161.2
By age		
18–24	10,264	62.9
25–34	15,446	94.7
35–44	18,517	113.5
45–54	18,399	112.8
55–64	17,662	108.2
65 and over	14,310	87.7
By sex		
Female	11,964	73.3
Male	19,992	122.5

*Full-time, year-round earnings of workers over 18.
SOURCE: U.S Bureau of the Census, "Money Income of Families and Persons in the United States: 1979," *Current Population Reports,* Series P-60, No. 129 (Washington, D.C.: U.S. Government Printing Office, 1981).

EDUCATION: BENEFITS AND COSTS

Occupation, of course, determines labor income; training and education determine occupation. Although the gap in lifetime earnings between high school and college graduates has narrowed in recent years, college graduates still make more (see Table 3-1). This doesn't mean that schooling by itself makes money. It might be that only bright, goal-oriented people obtain college degrees and that they would make more money anyway. But an education does provide you with **human capital,** that is, training or skills that allow you to perform certain services you could not otherwise do. You can increase your human capital by acquiring more skills or education, which makes you more valuable in the labor market.

Beside providing increased income, more education provides more job security. Generally, high school dropouts have unemployment rates four times higher than those of college graduates. Specifically, in early 1979, when the national unemployment rate was 7.5 percent, the rate among college graduates was 2.4 percent. Young people are particularly affected by a poor job market. In 1976, high school graduates ages twenty through twenty-four had an unemployment rate of 14.1 percent, whereas for college graduates of the same ages it was 6.1 percent. The additional education made these young people more employable. The U.S. Bureau of Labor Statistics predicts that by 1985, 18.1 percent of all jobs will be reserved for college graduates (*Changing Times,* 1979).

More education may mean more income and better job security, but it also costs money and personal energy. For example, estimates of the direct costs of becoming a doctor (eight years of tuition, fees, and books) range from $40,000 to $60,000. This does not include room and board, even though it probably is necessary to move away from home to attend school; neither does it include long-distance travel between school and home for visits. One reason then that a doctor achieves a high income is that he or she is willing to invest the time, the money, and the effort in training.

Another cost of education is the lost labor income. Because it is usually not possible to work full time while in school, students have to give up income—and perhaps forego other uses of their time. This opportunity cost is the highest cost incurred for education.

A third, nonmonetary cost of investing in human capital is personal energy. Many people may not have the interest, abilities, or motivation to complete long-term training. Most educational programs contain a few courses that may be dull or distasteful to a specific student. Some courses may be too rigorous and require remedial training or additional effort. When all the monetary and nonmonetary costs are balanced, education may cost too much for some people. Fortunately, however, formal training is not the only answer. Neither is it the answer for everyone. You can learn on your own by reading and studying or through on-the-job training.

SUPPLY AND DEMAND

We have generalized that education can increase income, but the choice of occupation actually determines income. Some occupations are more in demand at some times than at others, which affects job availability and salaries. If few qualified individuals are available for an occupation, salaries in that field tend to rise. When other people become aware of the rise in salaries, they may enter the occupation, eventually leading to a surplus of job seekers, particularly if other factors contribute to a decline in demand. If a surplus exists, employers can offer relatively lower salaries.

During the late 1950s and early 1960s, for example, demand for elementary and secondary teachers was great because of the large number of post-World War II "baby boom" children entering school. Teachers' salaries rose faster than inflation, and young people flocked to teaching. By the late 1970s, school enrollments were decreasing, schools were closing, and teachers were faced with possible layoffs, reassignments, and little prospect of cost-of-living raises.

Certainly one aspect of evaluating a career is to compare the amount of money you will make in that career with your needs and your preferred lifestyle. Although it is difficult to predict with certainty what the supply and demand conditions will be for a given occupation, estimates are available. The *Occupational Outlook Handbook* of the U.S. Department of Labor gives some guidance on the future of a wide variety of occupations, such as personnel management, retail buying, police science, auto mechanics, computer programming, and many others. Look for this publication in your school library or placement office.

AGE

Although you cannot do much about your age, it affects your income throughout your lifetime. When you are first employed, you are inexperienced and may need on-the-job training. As your skills and knowledge grow, thus increasing your **mental human capital,** your productivity and value to your employer also increase, which is reflected in a higher income that usually peaks between the ages of forty-five and fifty-five.

An exception to this is the person who develops **physical human capital.** Baseball players, ditch diggers, or welders find that their reflexes, strength, and senses begin to deteriorate after age thirty or thirty-five. This means that they are less useful and productive for an employer, so their incomes peak earlier. The gradual rise and leveling off or decreasing of an individual's income as he or she gets older is called an **age earning curve.** Figure 3-2 compares the age earning curve for someone who has mental human capital with someone who has physical human capital.

But this is not the whole picture. At this time, older people have (on the average) less education than younger ones because each successive generation in America is better educated than the one before. As we saw earlier, those who have more human capital usually earn more. But remember, there must be a demand for workers in your particular field when you are finished training. Even if you are the best in your chosen career, if that skill is not needed by anyone, you will not be paid to use it.

DEMOGRAPHY

Demography—the number of people of certain ages in a population—also affects income. In the United States, individuals born between 1946 and 1964 are identified as members of the post-World War II "baby boom." This particular group of people—one-third of our present population—has special employment problems identified by Landon Y. Jones in *Great Expectations* (1980). As a result of their large numbers, these people face stiff competition for jobs and have found lower salaries as a result. A larger proportion of this generation than of any previous generation has completed college, yet they can anticipate smaller raises, fewer promotions, and a flatter age earning curve. For example, from 1969 to 1977, men age fifty-five to sixty-four experienced income increases of 17.6 percent, and men thirty-five to forty-four saw increases of 10.4 percent, while wages for male workers twenty-five to thirty-four rose only 2.6 percent. The college-educated felt the competition most severely. They often accepted lower salaries than they had anticipated and settled for less than "college-level" positions. By the end of the 1970s, these young adults had "effectively lost about ten years' income growth" relative to that of the previous generation. Partially as a result of the low wages of the baby boom, the median family income for all occupations rose only 10 percent during the 1970s, as compared to 38 percent in the 1950s and 39 percent in the 1960s (Ehrbar, 1980).

SEX

An individual's sex also affects labor income. The fact that women earn less money is apparent in Table 3-1. We will not explore the reasons in depth, but we would like to mention some of them. Women entered the work force in unprecedented numbers in the 1960s and the 1970s, often with few marketable skills. At the time, there was a large demand for workers in the expanding clerical and service fields. This made job hunting easier, but these jobs are low-paying and often dead-end positions. Because so many women were grouped in these low-paying positions, the average pay for women dropped from 72 percent of men's pay in 1956 to 59 percent by 1980.

During the same period, small numbers of men and women began to enter occupations more commonly held by the opposite sex. We are no longer surprised to find male bank tellers, nurses, phone operators, or flight attendants; neither is it strange to find female truck drivers, mail carriers, bank officers, or physicians. These options for both sexes have been supported by the women's liberation movement and the Civil Rights Act of 1964. It is important to note, however, that there is still a significant difference between the salaries paid to men and women in *identical* fields with virtually the same training and experience.

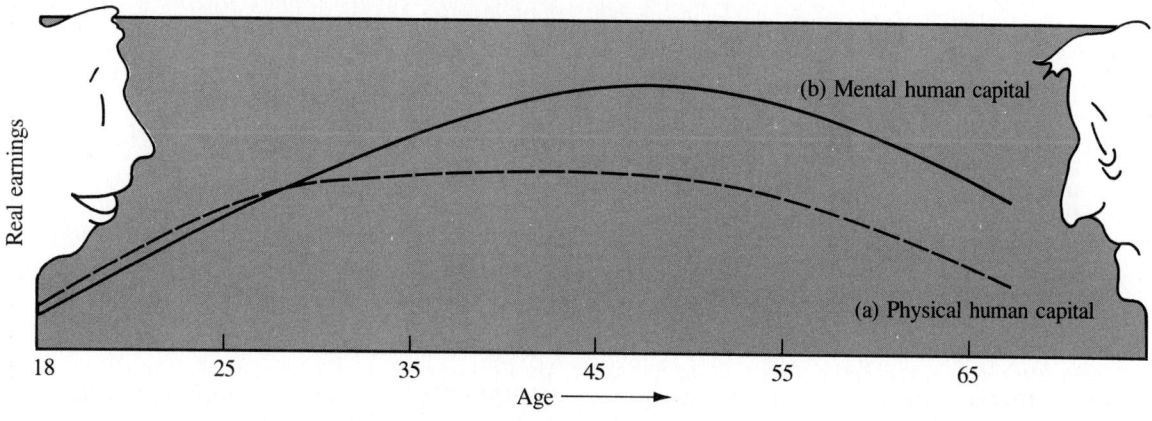

Figure 3-2. Age earning curve and human capital. Lifetime earnings partially depend on human capital. Earnings are lowest when people start to work and peak in mid-adult years. Those who use primarily physical human capital (a) may find that their earnings peak between ages 30 and 35, when they are most productive. Those who use primarily mental human capital (b) may start with a lower income while gaining education or training but find that income peaks between ages 45 and 55. Income for both types of individuals gradually decreases from the peak until retirement, around age 65.

Discrimination exists in an even more subtle form. In fields in which women predominate in a job classification, the wage scale is often lower. Efforts are now being directed to rectify this situation in the traditional women's occupations (those in which 70 percent or more of the work force is female). The goal is *equal pay for comparable work*. Consider, for example, the pay scale of two city government positions in a California suburb in 1981. Both positions require a bachelor's degree. The senior librarian position is traditionally held by a woman, is supervisory, and pays approximately $1,950 a month. The senior chemist at the sewage treatment plant has comparable skills and responsibilities, is traditionally male, and makes approximately $2,450 a month. The $500-a-month difference can, of course, dramatically affect how individuals and families live.

It is important to remember that equal pay for comparable work has costs and benefits. In 1980, the Supreme Court refused to hear an appeal of a case that upheld the right of Denver, Colorado to pay city hospital nurses less than it paid park maintenance workers. The judge in the case said the adjustment of salaries would "disrupt the economic system of the United States and its way of life." If equal pay for comparable work were mandated by government, great amounts of research and discussion would ensue to set new standards that would then have to be enforced. These research and enforcement costs as well as the higher pay scales, when required, would be passed on to taxpayers and consumers in the form of higher prices for goods and services. The benefits would include increased income for some families and individuals. Even this brief explanation of the tradeoffs involved in this decision shows why this is one of the most controversial issues of the 1980s.

RACE

Another factor that affects income but that you cannot control is racial background. Generally, nonwhites, such as blacks, Hispanics, and American Indians, make less money than whites. For example, in 1980,

> **BOX 3-2**
>
> ## Is Discrimination the Cause of Differences in Incomes?
>
> Racial and sexual job discrimination have often been cited as major factors in determining the comparatively lower earnings of blacks, Hispanics, and women. However, not all commentators agree that current job discrimination explains the black-white or female-male income gap. George Gilder (1982), citing the work of a respected black economist, Thomas Sowell (1980), presents some interesting arguments. According to Gilder, part of the reason black income is only 60 percent of white income is that the average age of the black population is twenty-two as compared to twenty-nine for whites. Since younger workers tend to make less than older workers, part of the income difference could be explained by age differences. Geography can also play a role in explaining the black-white earnings gap. Almost 50 percent of all blacks live in the South, a region that has the lowest average salaries, although not necessarily the lowest real income. The average income of blacks in New York is 33 percent higher than blacks in Atlanta, and almost two and one-half times higher than blacks in Mississippi. Gilder's final point is that black men are two times more likely than white men to be single. Since single men of all races work 20 percent fewer hours than married men and earn less than 60 percent as much money as men who are husbands, the marital status of black men also helps explain the lower income.
>
> Gilder also attacks the sexual discrimination explanation for the male-female earnings gap. He argues that much of the income difference can be explained by female labor force behavior. For example, women between twenty-five and fifty-nine are eleven times more likely than men to voluntarily leave their job, and the average woman spends only eight months on a job versus three years for a man. He is willing to accept the argument that women get paid less partly because they are concentrated in a few occupations. But he does not believe in the equal pay for comparable work remedy. He argues that equal pay for equal work is a principle that applies nowhere, not even among men. Truck drivers and plumbers (male and female) often earn more than historians and librarians, regardless of gender. If there is a job bias in our economy, according to Gilder, it is that most workers want "indoor work with no heavy lifting, but only women nearly always get it, thus driving down their pay."

blacks, our largest minority (11 percent of the population), averaged 60 percent the income of whites. Unemployment rates for minorities are usually two to three times higher than for whites, which contributes to their lower average income. As is the case for women, despite the many complex socioeconomic causes for this situation, the most important are lack of training and discrimination. (For a dissenting view, see Box 3-2.)

Studies indicate that members of minority groups with good educational credentials, work experience, and strong motivation are experiencing gains in professional, managerial, and skilled jobs. The problem for many members of minorities is affording the education. Generally, the higher the family income, the greater the probability that young people of all racial backgrounds will seek training beyond high school, because they can better afford the direct costs of tuition and books, as well as the opportunity cost of little or no income. Because of proportionately lower family incomes, children of minority families are less likely to receive job training beyond high school.

The second factor, discrimination, has been under federal regulation since the passage of the Civil Rights Act of 1964. Title VII of that act outlawed discrimination on the basis of race, color, sex, religion, or national origin in areas of hiring, pay, and promotion. During the 1970s the Equal Employment Opportunity Commission, responsible for the enforcement of the Civil Rights Act, was given the power to initiate lawsuits on behalf of people who experience discrimination in the job market. Companies who bypassed individuals for raises or promotions were required to compensate them with cash payments and promotions. These cases have led to greater occupational upgrading for minorities in clerical, technical, and service jobs in government and education. Much slower expansion of job opportunities has occurred in the corporate world, especially in management (National Urban League, 1980).

The goal of equal economic opportunity for minorities and women continues to be elusive. It is particularly endangered by work layoffs during recessions, such as the one we experienced in 1981–1982, when relatively new employees hired under the affirmative-action guidelines (standards to correct previous discrimination) were laid off because of lack of seniority. In addition, the continuation of affirmative action programs depends on money to enforce federal laws. In light of changing political and economic attitudes and budget cutting at all levels of government, the future of these programs is in doubt.

GEOGRAPHIC LOCATION

Besides education, age, sex, and race, your geographic choice of residence determines your **real income,** the amount of goods and services you can purchase with your labor income. For example, a $1,500-a-month labor income yields a lower real income in San Francisco and Honolulu than it does in Atlanta or Spokane, primarily because of differences in the cost of housing. The cost of living varies by regions because of differences in taxes, weather, union influences, and historic trends. For this reason, it is important to apply the decision-making process when evaluating jobs in various geographic regions. Your cost-benefit analysis should consider costs of food, housing, utilities, and transportation, as well as salary and psychic income.

TWO-INCOME HOUSEHOLDS

Another important determinant of income is the number of people in a family who earn labor income. The most common form the American family takes today is one in which both husband and wife are employed. In 45 percent of households both partners are employed, and in an additional 15 percent of families *more* than two members are employed; thus, a total of 60 percent of the households in America have two or more paychecks to budget and spend. In most families, the wife contributes the second paycheck. In other cases, the husband joins his wife in the work force after completing his education. Occasionally, one or more children are employed and contribute to household expenses. This trend toward having more than one breadwinner has contributed greatly to the **level of living,** that is, the lifestyles and types of possessions that the income levels of American families allow. As you can see in Figure 3-3, despite the low pay that many women received, by 1980 over half of those between the ages of sixteen and sixty-five were employed, three-fourths of them at full-time jobs. The most dramatic change in the female work force has been the increase in the number of working mothers, particularly those with children under age six (Figure 3-4). In 1950, almost 12 percent of married women with children under six and 28 percent of married women with children age six to seventeen were in the labor force. In 1980, those figures had risen to 43 percent and 59 percent, respectively.

Some of the factors that led to this shift in the composition of the labor force include:

1. *The availability of jobs in a growing economy.* In the 1960s, the job market expanded to fulfill the demands of government-sponsored social services and the Vietnam War. This growth continued in the 1970s, primarily in jobs traditionally dominated by women, such as clerical positions in banks, government, and schools, and service positions in restaurants, retail sales, and personal care.

2. *Better birth control.* This gave women more choice about whether and when to have children. A Rand study in 1977 "decisively linked the decline in the birth rate of the 1960s and 1970s to the availability of jobs, rather than to the Pill" (Bird, 1979, p. 292). Although birth control is not the cause of increased employment, it does allow women to plan for education and careers.

3. *Rising college enrollments.* In 1958, women made up 35 percent of the college population. In the last half of the 1970s, college after college across the nation reported that enrollments were composed of more women than men for the first time in history.

50   Economic Decisions for Consumers

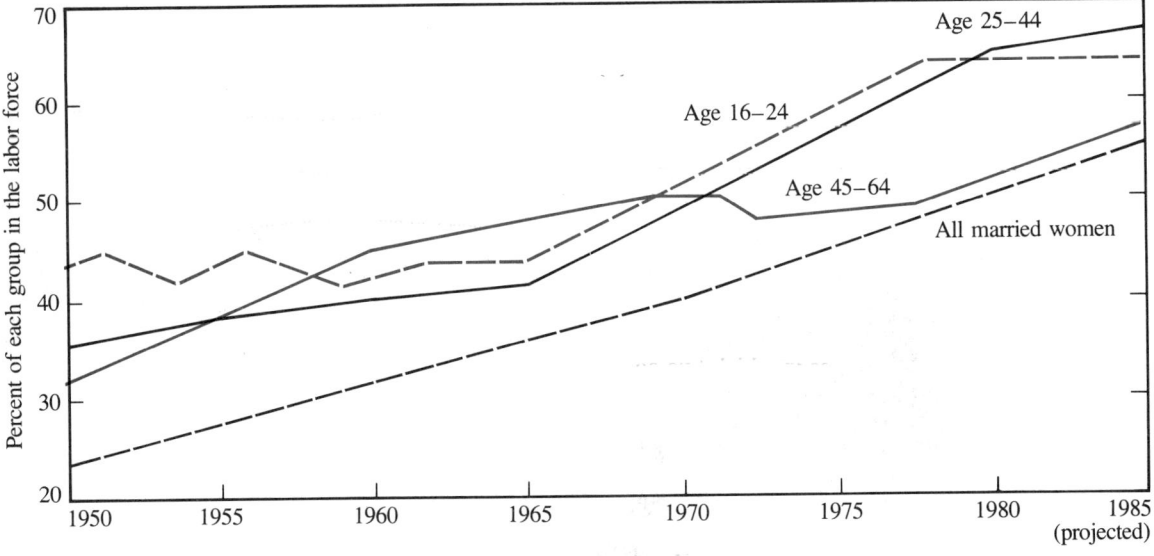

Figure 3-3. The dramatic increases in the number of women of all ages on the work force, particularly in the number of married women (dotted line). The graph compares the number of working women by age group. The broken line represents ages 16–24, the solid line represents ages 25–44, and the dash-dot line represents ages 45–64.

SOURCE: U.S. Bureau of Labor Statistics.

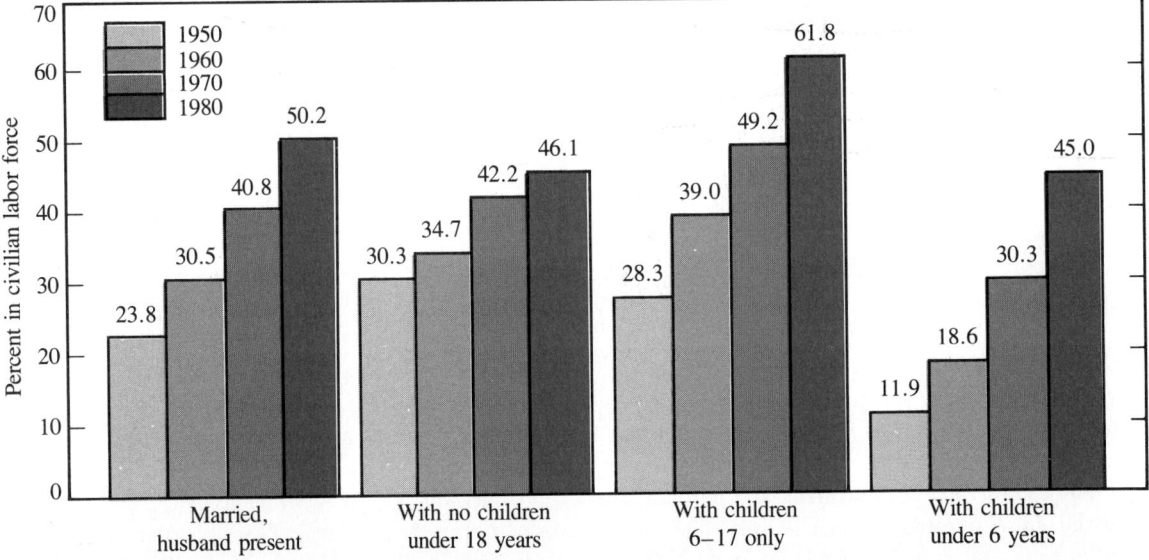

Figure 3-4. Labor force participation rates of married women with husband present, by presence and age of children, 1950–1980.

SOURCE: U.S. Bureau of the Census and U.S. Bureau of Labor Statistics.

These female graduates set out, diplomas in hand, to meet the challenges of the world of work. Seven out of eight young female college graduates are in the work force today (Gazzardi, 1979).

4. *Economic and social pressures.* Nearly two-thirds of all working women in 1979 were single, widowed, divorced, separated, or had husbands who earned less than $10,000 that year. Often, a wife's earnings raise a family out of poverty. On the average, working married women contribute more than one-fourth of the total family income. For families in which the wife is employed full-time, the median contribution is two-fifths of the total income.

5. *Rising inflation.* High inflation and high unemployment in 1974–1975 and again in 1979–1981 combined to make bill paying very difficult for the average family. In those families in which two adults worked, the level of living was at least protected and there was the possibility that it might rise. The second paycheck also served as security; about half the unemployed husbands in the country had wives who were working, which meant that, in many cases, the family could still make house and car payments and continue with insurance coverage.

What does the second income usually buy? For many families, it is the source of money for a second car. The next biggest spending difference between one- and two-income households is in spending on housing—particularly furniture, household appliances, and housewares. Additionally, employed women increase their spending on clothes for all members of the family.

Up to this point, we have discussed the economic benefits of having two incomes. As you have probably guessed, nonmonetary factors also affect the choice to work for labor income. Box 3-3 provides the beginning of a cost-benefit analysis of two incomes. It is not meant to be complete. Are there additional costs or benefits of two incomes that you can think of?

Managing two careers and a household is a tough job. Most of us do not have parents in this situation to serve as role models or examples, so we have few guidelines. Dual-earning couples consistently report having excessive stress as well as a lack of time, particularly when both earners are concerned with career advancement. To survive these pressures, couples can benefit by applying the decision-making process described in Chapter 2 to identify and solve problems, by being flexible when looking for alternatives, and by remembering that tradeoffs are inevita-

---

BOX 3-3

Cost-Benefit Analysis of Two Incomes

The decision to spend time in acquiring labor income rather than in nonmarket home production involves a series of tradeoffs. Here is the beginning of a list of monetary and nonmonetary costs and benefits of entering the labor force. Can you think of more?

Benefits

MONETARY

More money to buy more or better shelter, household goods, transportation, and clothing.

Health and life insurance.

Pension plan or Social Security.

Family security in case of illness, unemployment of spouse, death, or divorce.

NONMONETARY

Self-fulfillment, good feelings about using abilities and skills.

Family members become more self-sufficient.

Costs

MONETARY

Increased need for transportation.

Increased wardrobe needs.

Increased need to buy services: childcare, housekeeping, and so forth.

Move to higher tax bracket.

Miscellaneous: dues, lunches, office gifts.

NONMONETARY

Having children later or having fewer children.

Less personal leisure time.

Less family time.

Guilt feelings over not being available for spouse or children.

Family members will need to share household tasks.

Increased stress caused by demands for time.

ble because time and energy are scarce resources.

So far, we have studied the many factors that affect an individual's level of income. Now let us look at the social and economic factors that affect how that income is spent. We will look at the changes in the structure of the American family over the last two centuries and how they have affected the way families obtain necessities (such as food, clothing, and shelter) and protection during emergencies.

The Changing American Family

The **nuclear family**, defined as a husband, a wife, and any dependent children, is one of a number of social groups that influence individual consumer decisions. Under normal circumstances, it is the first group an individual belongs to and the group an individual belongs to for the longest time. Approximately three-fourths of the nation's population currently lives in nuclear families, which are usually responsible for providing their members with food, clothing, shelter, other consumer goods, and protection during emergencies. Ideally, we are born into a family and remain with it during infancy, childhood, and, generally, adolescence. As we get older, we leave our nuclear family to live alone or to marry.

In this section, we briefly look at the economic functions of the family, both in the past and now. This gives us a basis for examining the economic needs and decisions a family makes through its life cycle. Understanding these concepts gives us, as family members and consumers, more information to help us in making decisions to reach our financial goals.

PAST MARRIAGE AND FAMILY PATTERNS

In the marriage pattern of the lower and middle classes of eighteenth- and nineteenth-century Europe, a man could not marry until he had permission from the community leaders to build a house or a cottage. In this home-production economy, productive property, such as a loom, carpentry tools, or bakery ovens, was mandatory. Men needed to show their ability to manage a productive enterprise, which indicated their capacity to support a family, before marriage was allowed. The oldest son, who inherited his father's farm or business, was lucky. Women also had a financial contribution: a dowry of farm animals or household goods. When times were prosperous or the population small because of low birth rates and high death rates, more people could marry. When times were hard, people had to wait longer—sometimes forever.

At the same time in America, land was plentiful and there was no limit on the number of businesses allowed in a community. Most families lived in rural communities, and marriage was encouraged. Despite the well-known myth, few **extended families**—those with three generations living together—existed per se because most people did not live long enough to be grandparents. On the other hand, aunts, uncles, sisters, brothers, or cousins might live very near each other. These blood relatives gave time and money to help during emergencies such as fire, illness, drought, and death. In effect, they provided protection, insurance, and welfare for each other.

As technology increased in the late nineteenth century, fewer people were needed to produce a given amount of food on the farms. Technology simultaneously created new jobs in the cities and caused people to move from the farms to be near developing factories and businesses. As people relocated, they could no longer rely on their extended families; the nuclear family had to shoulder a greater responsibility for the economic welfare of its members.

TODAY'S MARRIAGE AND FAMILY PATTERNS

Today "a major task of families is to prudently manage energy so all families exist above the level of mere survival'' (Paulucci et al., 1977). This energy includes the skills and strengths of family members to provide and produce goods and services for the family such as food, clothing, shelter, and transportation. Families today usually purchase several forms of insurance to protect themselves in cases of accident, fire, theft, and death. This protection works in conjunction with government programs such as Social Security, unemployment insurance, and welfare. In addition, both spouses are likely to be employed today in order to meet their obligations.

Perhaps as a result of increasing monetary and opportunity costs, a higher standard of living, and higher educational levels of women, family size has been decreasing. Following World War II, American fertility rates rose until they peaked at 3.8 births per

Figure 3-5. U.S. total fertility rate, 1940–1980. This figure shows the postwar baby boom in graphic format. At the end of World War II (1945), American women were averaging a little over two children; by the late 1950s, this average had risen to almost four children per woman. Then in the 1960s and 1970s, the fertility rate fell to less than two. This is the baby boom and bust.

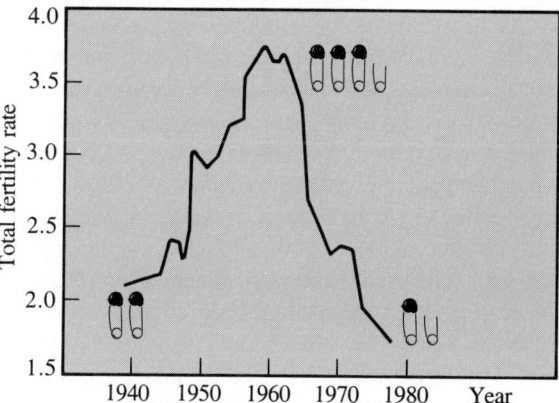

SOURCE: Adapted with the permission of the Population Council from "The Conflict Between Aspirations and Resources," by Richard A. Easterlin, *Population and Development Review* 2, nos. 3 and 4 (September-December 1976), p. 418.

Figure 3-6. Living arrangements of households, 1960, 1970, and 1980.

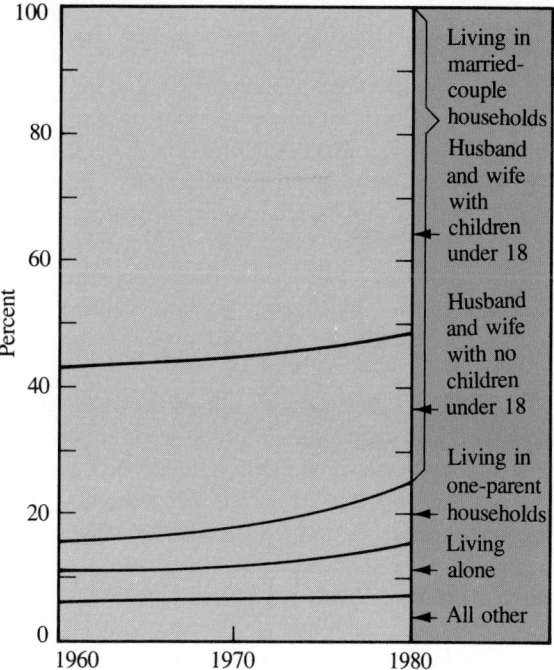

SOURCE: U.S. Bureau of the Census.

woman in 1957. In 1962, the birth rate started its steep descent to its present level of 1.8 births per woman (see Figure 3-5). Families are having fewer children or, in some cases, no children.

If women's current intentions are carried through, a lower birth rate will be maintained for some time. Consider the result of a U.S. census taken in 1967 and again in 1980. Of wives from the ages of eighteen to thirty-four in 1967, 3 percent wanted to remain childless and 37 percent wanted no more than one or two children. Thirteen years later, of wives in the same age group, 6 percent planned to remain childless and 61 percent wanted either one or two children.

Types of Households

The U.S. Bureau of the Census identifies three basic types of households: those consisting of married couples with or without children, of one parent living with one or more children, or of people living alone. The remainder ("all other" category) includes nonrelated individuals of the same or opposite sex who live together. Some of these situations are roommate arrangements in dormitories, sororities, fraternities, or apartments. Other households include couples who are living together as husband and wife (cohabitants) but who are not married.

SINGLE-PERSON HOUSEHOLDS

As you can see in Figure 3-6, there has been a marked increase in single-person households, which now total 12 million. Part of the reason is that more young adults are marrying later and living alone first. Adults also form single-person households after marital separation, divorce, or the death of a spouse. Because of the death of their husbands, two of every five persons living alone are women over age fifty-five, who form the largest age-sex group of single-person households.

Single people are, of course, totally responsible for their resources. They can decide how best to use their labor income, and they can choose the amount of nonmarket home production and leisure time they wish. But they must also support themselves and accept all household responsibilities, including establishing an independent household; purchasing furniture, appliances, and automobiles; and buying clothing, household linens, and consumer services such as repairs, household maintenance, recreation, and entertainment. Some adults may have a financial obligation to children of a previous marriage, or they may have to meet the challenge of living on limited resources, as is often the case for widows. Whatever their situation, they do it all on their own.

People are increasingly willing to live together as husband and wife without a formal wedding ceremony. The number of cohabiting unmarried persons has doubled over the last decade and exceeds 2 million. Although this may seem like an easy way out, or seem to provide more freedom, it does not necessarily eliminate the costs and obligations of marriage. This was dramatically demonstrated by the Marvin vs. Marvin case involving the well-known movie actor Lee Marvin. When they separated, Michelle Marvin asserted that she should share the assets Lee Marvin had accumulated during the six years they lived together because she gave up her career to care for him and their home. This case established the right of nonmarried people to sue for community property, a right that exists in at least thirty-one states. Recognizing the legal factors involved, many unmarried cohabitants now write contracts to establish who owns what in case of separation.

MARRIED-COUPLE HOUSEHOLDS AND THE FAMILY LIFE CYCLE

Seventy-five percent of us now live in nuclear families, and we compose approximately half of the 60 million households in America. Changes in the last fifty years in family composition, in the standard of living, and in the roles of individual family members, particularly those related to work both at home or in the labor force, have affected consumer decision making and spending patterns. As family members interact with the society around them, their goals and values change, which influences personal, economic, and social behavior. For example, most couples who married fifteen or twenty years ago expected to follow the marriage pattern of their parents, with the man as the wage earner and the woman as the housewife. Many of these couples expected to live as well as their parents lived, but their standards conflicted with the reality of high inflation when prices rose faster than wages, making their economic goals difficult to reach. Simultaneously, it became easier for women to work outside the home because of changes in the society around them, such as the women's liberation movement, the increased availability of jobs, and access to the Pill. In the process of evaluating the possibility of employment for the woman, couples found that their individual values had changed. Sometimes, the newer value system of one spouse matched that of the other spouse, but other times it did not. Conflicts arose between spouses over the economic role the wife should fill, and unresolved conflicts occasionally resulted in divorce. In this section, we explore these issues as we identify the stages of the family life cycle and relate them to family composition; to decisions about family roles, economic goals, and spending; and to the economic effect of divorce and single-parenting on families.

Despite all the changes in family composition, Americans believe in marriage. As we have already noted, 96 percent of all men and 97 percent of all women marry at some point and begin the five stages of the **family life cycle** (Figure 3-7):

1. Starting out, without children.
2. Becoming a young family with children of preschool age.
3. Going through the early middle years with children of school age.
4. Launching children leaving home.
5. Enjoying later years and retirement.

Even with rising divorce rates, two of every three marriages remain intact. Some marriages go through all five stages, but others may experience only stages one and five if the couple has no children. The family life cycle may be disrupted by separation, divorce, or death. Divorced parents may begin

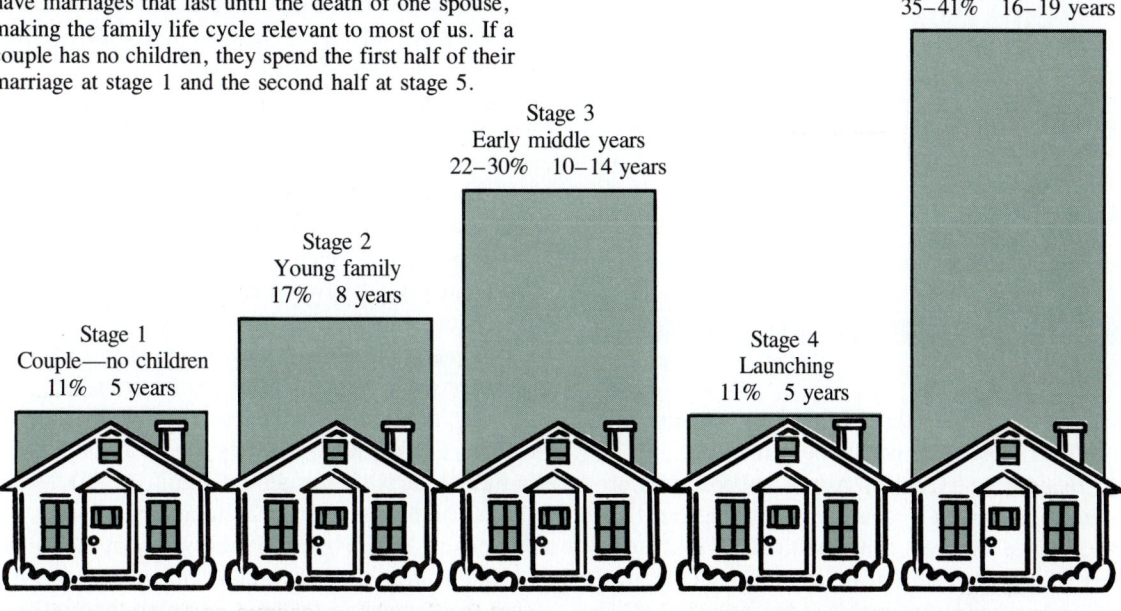

Figure 3-7. The five stages of the family life cycle, indicating the approximate years spent at each stage for an average couple with two or three children, married forty-six years. Currently, two of every three couples have marriages that last until the death of one spouse, making the family life cycle relevant to most of us. If a couple has no children, they spend the first half of their marriage at stage 1 and the second half at stage 5.

another family life cycle when they remarry. If both partners bring children from previous marriages, they form **blended** or **reconstituted families.** Let us look now at the five stages and the economic decisions that go with them.

Couples Without Children. Young couples find that more goals are formed related to career and income, family composition, and standard of living during the first five years of marriage than at any later period (Deacon and Firebaugh, 1975). It is a time to shift from dependency on parents to responsibility for self and consideration of the welfare of a spouse. Decisions at this stage relate to the anticipated level of income and use of resources such as skills and time. Will both partners have full-time labor income jobs? How will decisions be made about job transfers, especially in dual-earner families? Are children desired? If so, how many? Will the woman's career be interrupted or terminated when she has a child? How will the parenting responsibilities be distributed? All of these decisions are not entirely economic, but they affect family income.

Young Families. Having children has always been viewed as one of the major functions—and obligations—of marriage. Becoming a parent can, however, involve conscious decision making, a process during which a couple discusses the pros and cons and realizes that having children implies a long-term commitment to create a positive economic, social, and moral environment for new family members.

There can be great joy in watching a child grow to adulthood. It can be ego-gratifying to know that one is responsible for that growth. Although these benefits are difficult to put into monetary terms, many of the costs are easier to quantify. The total direct average cost of raising a child born in 1979 until age eighteen is estimated to be $134,414, considering an annual inflation rate of 8 percent. This does not in-

Table 3-2. Cost of Raising One Child

Budget item	1960's Child	1979's Child
Food	$ 8,766	$ 36,645
Clothing	3,662	12,129
Housing	10,467	41,121
Medical care	1,602	6,703
Education	520	2,288
Transportation	5,267	20,355
Other costs	3,990	15,173
Totals	$34,274	$134,414

SOURCE: Reprinted from *U.S. News & World Report*, November 23, 1981. Copyright 1981, U.S. News & World Report, Inc.

clude a college education. Table 3-2 compares these costs with those for a person born in 1960.

Besides the monetary cost of children, the opportunity costs must be considered. Parents must give up their time to raise a child, particularly in the early years. If a parent chooses to stay home to care for a child rather than to be employed for, say, $14,000 a year, the opportunity cost of that child can be quite dramatic. For a child born in 1980 the opportunity cost of a wife's time was estimated to be $45,355 (Espenshade, 1980). In addition to the actual income loss, there is growing recognition that responsibility for childcare, which rests primarily with women, is a significant barrier to equal opportunity for advancement.

The young family stage merges two stages of the individual life cycle. The parents' adult needs, as well as the children's needs (special clothing, furniture, toys), must be met. Young families who often have a low or moderate income level feel these heavy demands on their budgets. Some families must choose between having children or purchasing a house, particularly because many families have only one income when children are infants. Growing family size increases spending for housing (shelter, furnishings, and utilities) and medical care. In order to keep budgets balanced, families usually reduce spending for clothing, recreation, and education, and may have to forego savings. These decisions are not made easily and may require difficult adjustments because couples become accustomed to a more generous spending pattern when they have smaller families. Young people beginning a marriage are sometimes finishing their educations and beginning careers. All of these goals are more difficult to achieve if a child is born soon after marriage or before marriage.

Early Middle Years. This stage of the family life cycle covers the time from when the youngest child starts school until he or she leaves home. By this stage, many family goals have been set and some have been reached, such as home ownership, career success, and financial stability. The percentage of income spent for housing and furnishings often declines because many families occupy homes they have owned for a few years. These are the years for Brownies, soccer games, and braces. Gail Sheehy, in *Passages* (1976), describes this period as having an "in-turned focus on raising children" (p. 43).

As children begin to mature and pass into adolescence, they begin to have money of their own to spend as they wish. Families with adolescents increase their spending for food, clothing, and recreation (records, movies, stereo equipment, sports). One of the highest expenses for this period is vocational training and education for maturing children. Parents themselves may decide to go back to school. Sometimes these same families are responsible for the care or partial support of grandparents. Even though these families may be at their peak of lifetime earnings, all of these simultaneous expenses can create a budgeting burden.

Launching Children. As children reach adulthood and can support themselves and move out to their own residences, the family gains new stability. This can be an exciting time for spouses, who now have more time together and more money to spend on themselves. Women can anticipate living with their husbands for an average of thirteen years beyond the time when their last child leaves home (Barber, 1981).

Sometimes this period is called the "empty nest" stage, referring to the decreased need for the woman to "mother" her children. Recent research indicates that this loss can have a negative effect on

When families reach the retirement stage, consumer decision making becomes more oriented toward hobbies and other leisure activities.

fathers as well as mothers (Barber, 1981). Also relevant to this stage is the potential need to house an adult child who returns home, often after a divorce and perhaps with children of his or her own.

The Later Years: Retirement. During this last stage, people face uncertainties in income and health and the eventual death of their spouse and themselves. Because of their reluctance to face these inevitable changes, some people enter this stage with inadequate planning for savings, investments, insurance, and protection of assets with a will. These issues are discussed in Chapters 16 and 17.

Retirement from employment changes established income and thus spending patterns. Money management is especially important if senior citizens depend on fixed incomes during a period of rising prices. Careful planning for this stage should begin earlier, at the young family stage, for example, to establish income from pension plans, Social Security, and investments. Most families find that their needs for housing and transportation have been met, so major expenses at this stage include travel, health care, and funerals.

This is a time to relax and maintain a slower pace, enjoying hobbies and the company of friends and relatives. For many, it is a time to fulfill long-held goals for travel and recreation. Unfortunately, there may be too much leisure time for those who have few outside interests or hobbies.

The later years pose a special problem for women. There are over one-third more elderly women in America than there are elderly men, and more than half of these women are widowed or divorced. This is the situation for only one-fourth of the elderly men. The reasons for this difference include the shorter life expectancy of men, the fact that wives are usually younger than husbands, and the fact that when widowers remarry, they often choose wives younger than themselves. The result is that many women spend their last years living alone, often on a poverty-level income. Decision making and planning in anticipation of this possibility can help ease the financial difficulties and make the later years a time for self-fulfillment.

Special Problems in the Family Life Cycle

The family life cycle, as we have viewed it so far, applies to couples who remain married until the death of one partner. As we have noted, this is the case for the majority of marriages, but certainly not all. We will now look at the special economic circumstances that affect consumer decision making in families involved in divorce.

DIVORCE

During the 1970s, the rising divorce rate was often cited as proof that the American family was dead. As we have seen, however, it was just gradually changing its composition. Divorce not only disrupts family composition, it also affects income and consumer decision making. The reasons for these trends have much to do with a changing society and its attitudes toward divorce.

During the 1950s and early 1960s, changes were made in the law to eliminate the need to prove adultery, cruelty, desertion, fraud, insanity, or criminal acts in order to obtain a divorce. ''Irreconcilable differences'' is now an adequate reason for divorce in many states. Besides increasing the acceptable reasons for divorce, it has also decreased the need for lengthy court battles, simultaneously decreasing legal costs. In addition, women have more education and marketable skills than in previous generations. Their greater economic independence has given them the option to leave an unsatisfactory marriage. And as more people seek divorce as a way out of an unfortunate situation, the stigma attached to it has disappeared. Today, divorce is so common that the continuing pool of divorced adults comprises 10 percent of the population between the ages of twenty-four and fifty-four (Jones, 1980).

This does not mean that divorce should be taken lightly. It is costly, both financially and emotionally. But it is a way to rectify what has turned out to be a bad decision. Remember, too, that although families are disrupted by divorce today, they were separated by death in previous times. As a result of improved medical care, more families have two parents today than in colonial times.

SINGLE PARENTS

The prevalence of divorce has complicated economic relationships within the family. The children of a divorced couple may receive child support from a parent who is now a part of a second family that must now do without part of his or her income. This is difficult at best, and probably plays a part in the fact that, after one year, only 25 percent of parents without custody send child support, even if they are ordered by a court to do so.

The number of single-parent families has risen in the last decade. In 1970, one of every nine families with children under eighteen was maintained by a single parent. By 1979, that figure had risen to one of every five and had not yet leveled off (Johnson, 1980). Both divorce and birth out of wedlock are the main factors in this dramatic increase. Divorce generally means a loss of the wage earner, a decrease in income level for both partners, and establishment of a second household. The increased housing and transportation costs, coupled with lack of child support payments, account for the fact that two of every five single-parent families have incomes below the poverty level, compared to one in sixteen for two-parent families. Single-parent families compose about ten

Single parents are faced not only with greater responsibilities but also with greater expenses, less income, and more consumer decisions.

percent of all households, and 90 percent are headed by women.

Changing Family Roles: Money and Time

We have noted changes in family composition and level of living, particularly as a result of increases in the numbers of dual-earner families. Concurrently, there have been changes in roles for men and women, both within families and within society as a whole. All of these changes are, of course, interrelated. These changing behavior patterns have involved Americans in controversies ranging from who should open the car door to which partner is responsible for birth control. The consumer issues that are affected include money management, buying decisions, and career and job choices, as well as management of household tasks and leisure time. We will briefly look now at how the Industrial Revolution defined work, created housework, and established values and standards related to household management that are still held today. We will see how twentieth-century technology has given us a new phenomenon—leisure time—and how its availability can affect our economic and physical well-being.

WORK ROLES

Before the Industrial Revolution it was necessary to work twelve to fourteen hours a day, seven days a week to eke out a living on a farm or in a factory. By the early twentieth century, a typical work week dropped to fifty or fifty-five hours, and many workers had weekends free because more goods could be produced in less time by fewer people. Specialization of family responsibilities developed. Men were employed outside the home on a specific job that provided money to purchase goods such as food, furniture, a house, clothing, and if the family was lucky, an automobile.

Women's specialty was the home, and they provided services such as childcare, housekeeping, cooking, laundry, and shopping. Many young women worked for a few years in their teens while they waited for a marriage proposal, and then they married and had children. Although it was possible to be an unmarried housewife, the majority of housewives were married women. Ann Oakley wrote a perceptive analysis of the development of housewifery as an economically dependent occupation in *Woman's Work* (1974). She pointed out that the housewife's work was not and is not appreciated for the time and energy it involves because housewives receive no salary for it. Because "work" was a place where people went, and a "job" a thing they did in exchange for money, the nonmarket home production performed by housewives was not work. In addition, because no money was paid for housework, housework was not valued. (See Box 3-4 for an analysis of the dollar value of housework.)

Today women are most often employed outside the home. Media coverage and the general "feel" of what is happening on the family scene reflect the American public's changing notion of what is appropriate sex-role behavior for women and men. More and more people are endorsing the need for equal division of labor at home because they recognize that a personal or a family decision to work more and have more income is also a decision to have less leisure time.

HOUSEWORK

Several researchers have found that a full-time homemaker in the traditional pattern spends about eight hours a day, seven days a week on housework—nonmarket home production. This in-

---

BOX 3-4

Dollar Value of Housework

How much is a housewife worth? The answer to this question is important to life insurance companies faced with setting a monetary value on the loss of a wife and mother. The answer is also important to women during the dissolution of a marriage. Michael Minton, an attorney specializing in divorce law, has worked on the subject for the past six years. His theory is that the specific duties a housewife performs have an objective economic value; that is, if the wife is not there to do them, the husband has to hire someone else.

Minton consulted economists, job counselors, employment agencies, and others. He came up with a detailed chart that lists exactly how the average housewife with two young children spends her time—how many hours she spends on each function and how much that time is worth:

Job performed	Hours/week	Rate/hour	Value/week
Food buyer	7.0	$ 5.75	$ 40.25
Nurse	2.0	7.14	14.28
Tutor	2.0	6.43	12.86
Waitress	2.5	3.41	8.53
Seamstress	1.0	3.75	3.75
Laundress	5.9	3.10	18.29
Chauffeur	3.5	5.50	19.25
Gardener	2.3	5.00	11.50
Family counselor	7.0	25.00	175.00
Maintenance	1.7	4.90	8.33
Child care	168.0	1.00	168.00
Cleaning woman	7.5	3.21	24.00
Housekeeper	10.0	4.75	47.50
Cook	13.1	4.75	62.23
Errand runner	3.5	3.79	13.27
Budget manager	4.0	6.43	25.72
Decorator	1.0	32.00	32.00
Caterer	1.5	7.71	11.57
Dishwasher	6.2	3.10	19.22
Dietician	1.2	6.80	8.16
Secretary	2.0	5.00	10.00
Maid/hostess	3.0	20.00	60.00
Weekly value:			$793.79
Yearly value:			$41,277.08

SOURCE: Beverly Stephen, "Dollar Value of Housework," *Los Angeles Times*, August 14, 1980. Reprinted by permission of Tribune Company Syndicate, Inc.

Figure 3-8. How the man in the house shares the work.

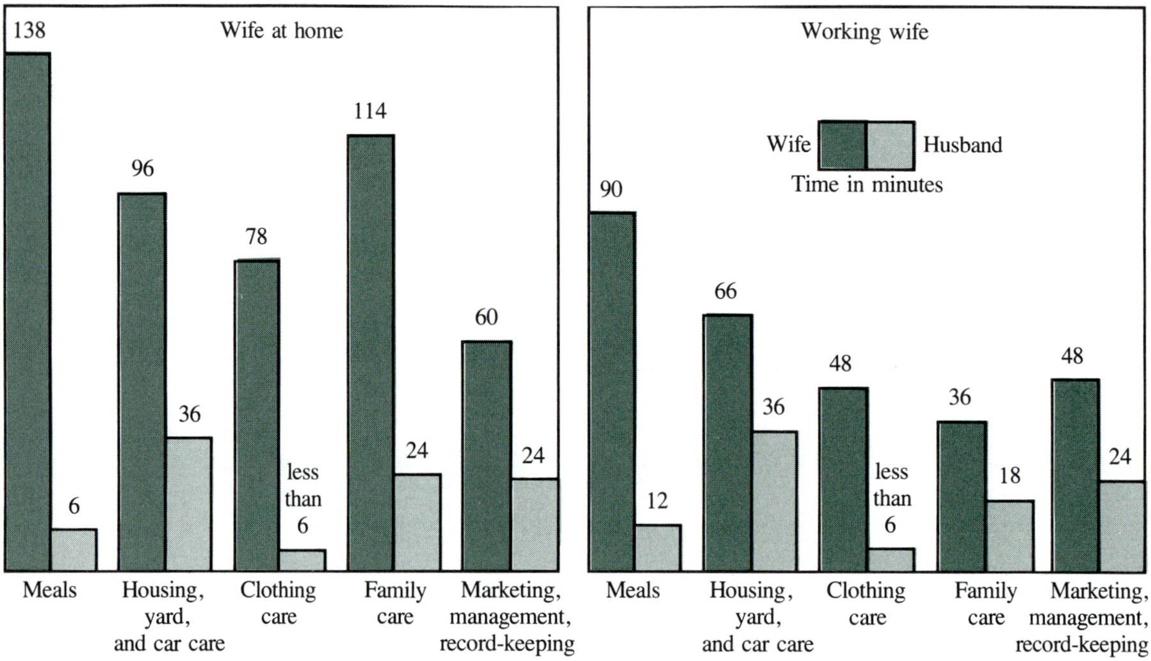

Wife at home (Time in minutes)
- Meals: Wife 138, Husband 6
- Housing, yard, and car care: Wife 96, Husband 36
- Clothing care: Wife 78, Husband less than 6
- Family care: Wife 114, Husband 24
- Marketing, management, record-keeping: Wife 60, Husband 24

Working wife (Time in minutes)
- Meals: Wife 90, Husband 12
- Housing, yard, and car care: Wife 66, Husband 36
- Clothing care: Wife 48, Husband less than 6
- Family care: Wife 36, Husband 18
- Marketing, management, record-keeping: Wife 48, Husband 24

SOURCE: From *Making It Together as a Two-Career Couple* by Marjorie Hansen Shaevitz and Morton H. Shaevitz. Copyright © 1979 by Marjorie Hansen Shaevitz and Morton H. Shaevitz. Reprinted by permission of Houghton Mifflin Company.

---

cludes childcare, meal preparation, family shopping, cleaning, laundry, and outside errands. A woman working parttime devotes approximately seven hours daily to these tasks, whereas a wife employed full-time spends five hours daily. The home production of these goods and services is a direct contribution to the family level of living. Although the tasks have changed, a 1973 comparison with a study done in 1917 shows that the time necessary for housework has not (Walker, 1973).

The amount of time spent by husbands on household tasks averages one and a half hours daily, whether the wife is employed or not (see Figure 3-8). Tasks are still sex-stratified. Husbands tend to accept responsibility for tasks that can be deferred to a convenient time, such as car maintenance, yard work, or bill paying. Husbands may also do grocery shopping, childcare, and meal preparation. However, the major responsibility is still the wife's. As one woman put it, "If the husband cooks dinner, the wife makes the shopping list, buys the food, defrosts the meat, keeps the kids entertained while he cooks, and then she cleans up afterward. That's called making dinner" (*Los Angeles Times,* June 15, 1980).

We do not wish to blame men or to imply that men refuse to help out. Deeply instilled role patterns are slow to change. Often, women desire to be all things to all people: they try to do the cooking, cleaning, and chores of the housekeeper as well as be a loving wife. In short, some try to be "superwomen." Both women and men need to think over priorities and challenge their rigid thinking about standards. Families need to determine what is desirable, appropriate, and manageable. Box 3-5 gives some suggestions to help couples set priorities and improve their time management.

BOX 3-5

Time Management and Household Tasks

Because the dual-earner family pattern is likely to continue during this decade, it is important that couples reassess the division of household tasks in terms of income, time, interests, skills, and physical capabilities in order to maximize life for all family members. It is a five-step process:

1. *Look for time wasters*. Check those that apply to you.
   - _____ Lack of objectives, priorities, and deadlines.
   - _____ Attempting to do too much at once, and underestimating the time it takes to do it.
   - _____ Involvement in routine and detail that should be delegated to others.
   - _____ Indecision and procrastination.
   - _____ Failure to set up clear lines of responsibility and authority for a job.
   - _____ Lack of or unclear communication and instruction.
   - _____ Lack of standards and progress reports.
   - _____ Crisis situations for which no plans are possible.
   - _____ Cluttered desk or work areas and personal disorganization.
   - _____ Telephone interruptions.
   - _____ Visitors dropping in unexpectedly.
   - _____ Meetings, both scheduled and unscheduled (including coffee klatsches).
   - _____ Inability to say no.
   - _____ Fatigue.
2. *Set priorities*. Alan Lakein, in *How to Get Control of Your Time and Your Life* (1973), suggests setting priorities for daily tasks by deciding whether tasks are: A's—highly important, must-do; B's—important but postponable; or C's—unimportant. By doing more A's and fewer C's, you may have a greater feeling of accomplishment (although the A tasks may be more difficult or less enjoyable than the C's).
3. *Reevaluate your standards*. Time is wasted if standards for a specific task are unclear or inappropriate (too weak or too strict, for example). You need to identify standards for tasks that seem to take too long or for tasks you do often, and then reevaluate them.
   a. Identify standards
      Draw a horizontal line on a piece of paper and write standards along the continuum to describe the task you are evaluating. For example, to evaluate your housekeeping, you might write:

Sloppy, disorganized	Moderately neat	Neat, well organized

      Mark where you think you are on this continuum.
   b. Reevaluate standards
      Are you satisfied with your standards? Or should you change them? For example, valid reasons for wanting a neater, cleaner house might be: to have a comfortable, attractive home where family members can enjoy living—disorder is inefficient, upsetting, fatiguing, embarrassing; to set a good example for children; to have a healthier, safer home—filth breeds bugs and germs, junk can be a fire hazard or can cause accidents; or to save money—grit wears out carpets and furnishings, redecorating costs a lot. Valid reasons for being less neat night be to save time and energy for more important matters, or to provide a more comfortable, relaxed atmosphere. For best results, involve other family members in your evaluation. Have them use the same rating continuum you used to see whether their standards agree with yours.

      By talking over the problems of differing standards and expectations you can often work out compromises, strengthen your relationships, and make your home a happier place for everyone. Such a discussion—if it is done calmly and cooperatively, and not as a blaming confrontation—can help all family members see what their responsibilities are for the smooth functioning and operating of your home.

(Continued on p. 62)

4. *Assign responsibilities.* Once you have identified time wasters, set priorities, and reevaluated standards, you are ready to assign responsibilities.
   a. Identify the tasks that must be done to reach your goals.
   b. Decide how often a task should be done—daily, weekly, monthly, yearly.
   c. Decide, based on interests, abilities, and time, who will do the task.

   You may want to have a rotating schedule of responsibilities rather than having everyone do the same job all the time. Don't forget to include children of all ages in your plan—each according to his abilities.
5. *Work smarter–not harder.*
   a. Save time for a purpose. Having your A-priority goals in mind will help.
   b. Plan your schedule first thing in the morning and set priorities for the day. Make a daily to-do list and tick off important items first.
   c. Eliminate nonessentials; practice "intelligent neglect" of C-priority items, and then don't waste time feeling guilty about what you don't get done.
   d. Plan to eliminate tasks in the future: replace "ironables" with permapress fabrics, light-colored floor coverings with darker colors, and so forth.
   e. Set deadlines to help avoid procrastination; break down a dreaded task into smaller, more manageable tasks.
   f. Use odd moments; put waiting time to good use; refer to your to-do list and ask "What is the best use of my time right now?"
   g. Delegate everything you possibly can to others.
   h. Give yourself time off as a special reward when you have accomplished important tasks.
   i. Remind yourself that there is always enough time for the important things.

   Making good use of time does not mean constantly trying to beat the clock or filling every waking moment with purposeful activity. Rest, relaxation, time to do nothing or to think or meditate are important, too.

SOURCE: Adapted from "Today's Homemaker" by Dorothy Wenck, Cooperative Extension, Orange County, California.

CHILDCARE

Childcare poses a special challenge to two-career families and single-parent families. Although attitudes toward working wives have gone from slight disapproval in the 1950s to sanctioned approval in the 1970s, considerable prejudice still remains about turning over the continuity of childcare, especially of preschoolers, to anyone besides the mother. No conclusive scientific or sociological evidence exists to prove that young children need their biologic mothers around them all the time or that mothers are better parents than fathers. Nonetheless, an employed mother who entrusts her child to a babysitter or to a day-care center may feel at least a twinge of guilt. Such guilt is unnecessary because most experts today agree that it is not the quantity of time spent on parenting but the quality that counts.

CAREER AND JOB DECISIONS

Job advancement is another area in which decisions about time need to be made. Part of the role of the traditional wife is to further her husband's career. Sociologist Jessie Bernard in her book *The Future of Marriage* (1972) points out that in a traditional marriage the wife gives a husband status, helps in his career, and provides him with unpaid help to care for his home and children. Bernard asserts that women have no such support system and that in fact being a wife and mother ordinarily holds a woman back in the workplace. For example, because of commitments to husband and children, women are more likely than men to take time off from work to tend a sick child, are less available for out-of-town business trips, and often do not have time beyond the average work week to spend on extra job duties or entertainment. Single adults of both sexes face similar difficulties because they lack the services such as household care, bookkeeping and banking, entertainment, and errand running provided by a traditional wife.

To meet the challenge of combining a successful career with an involved family life, some new time-management role patterns are developing. Some two-career families decide to be less concerned about career advancement than families of the more traditional pattern and choose to turn down promotions and transfers that might result in a poor career move for the other partner. In other marriages, the woman's career may take precedence over the man's, and the man chooses more family involvement over career involvement. A third option is for both partners to choose jobs that allow for greater autonomy and flexibility of time schedules. Other options include remaining childless or maintaining separate residences in different geographic locations. Needless to say, these changes in marriage roles and in use of time involve far more than just a change in attitudes and behavior within the home. They call for sweeping reforms and changes on the part of employers, city planners, childcare providers, and society as a whole.

LEISURE TIME

Time not committed to income production or nonmarket home production is **leisure time.** Your time-management decisions determine how much leisure you have. Here, we want to discuss the role that leisure time plays in your mental, physical, and emotional health because being healthy is essential to earning and spending. Leisure time used to refresh the mind, body, and spirit is **recreation.** The pressures of job and family can be put in perspective during moments of physical activity or quiet solitude, allowing us to be more effective members of family and society. An important part of recreation is exercise to help maintain proper weight and muscle tone and, at the same time, to reduce stress. Time spent for activity and play gives a pleasurable alternative to work.

Besides maintaining physical health, sports and hobbies provide an opportunity to develop our abilities and personalities. Recreation allows people who become narrowed by their jobs an opportunity to express themselves. For example, a computer programmer might choose to spend leisure time gardening or playing tennis. A carpenter might choose to collect stamps or practice yoga. As you can see, what is work to one person might be recreation to another. True recreation involves a free choice of activity, whether it be fishing, photography, dancing, sewing, or soccer. Such acitvities provide opportunities for relaxation, self-expression, and fullfillment.

Families can use leisure time not only as an opportunity for recreation and relaxation but as a chance to interact and to strengthen relationships.

Many jobs involve routine, rigid work, much of which is done in isolation. Leisure time allows for a break in this seclusion. It might be spent interacting in club or fraternal organizations or, more informally, in visiting with friends and family. It can provide us with personal support systems as well as a chance to get in touch with ourselves.

Some people "never have time" for recreation or leisure. In many cases **Parkinson's law** comes into play: Work expands to fit the time allowed. We need to remember that the counterpart of increased work time, whether market or nonmarket production, is decreased leisure time. Leisure foregone is the greatest cost of employment, particularly to wives, mothers, and those living alone, because these people are responsible for personal, family, and household care in addition to employment responsibilities. A positive attitude toward time management needs to be applied in order to achieve a balance and allow for leisure time in busy schedules.

RETIREMENT

Retirement provides full-time leisure, a time to be used however one wishes. The concept of retirement from work was born during the Depression as a way to create jobs for younger workers. For example, in 1900 three out of four males over age sixty-five were still working, compared to one out of five today. Thanks to exercise, improved diet, and modern medicine, older Americans are healthier and more vigorous than ever before, which makes them physically able to enjoy retirement.

Workers who retire today at age sixty-five can expect an average of fourteen years of retirement. By the year 2000, this figure is expected to increase to an average of twenty-five years. Because of increased health, economic need, and changing Social Security regulations, many people choose to postpone retirement, take part-time jobs, or start new businesses of their own. All of these factors emphasize the need to apply the decision-making process to the use of leisure time during retirement. Retirement planning should map out the entire scope of this new phase of life and should focus on skills, values, and economic and psychic needs. One may choose to continue spending time in one's original field, such as sales, medicine, or accounting. On the other hand, this may be the time to explore a totally new field. In either case, one's skills might be used to earn money or may be given freely as a volunteer. The joy of retirement is that one's work is self-assigned, making it truly leisure.

Summary

Most of us live much of our lives as members of at least one family. As a result, many of our consumer decisions are made jointly with family members. Key decisions regarding career, family composition, and family size can determine, to a great extent, the quantity of money and leisure time we have.

The career people choose is a major factor in their present and future level of living. Generally, the more education one has, the higher one's salary and the greater one's job security. Other factors that affect individual income are age, sex, race, and location of residence. Family income depends on the earning capabilities of family members and on the number of members earning labor income.

A family is responsible for the economic welfare of its members. The ability to meet this responsibility often depends on family composition, size, family life-cycle stage, and income level. In recent years there has been a marked increase of single-parent families, as well as of households composed of one individual. A third trend has been a decreasing birth rate, resulting in smaller families and a greater number of childless families.

Family spending patterns are a reflection of family composition, the stage of the family life cycle, the family income level, the number of family members who work, and values, goals, and standards. Any changes in these variables can cause changes in spending patterns.

We are constrained by time as well as money. When we choose to spend our time earning income, we automatically decrease the time available for nonmarket home production or for leisure. The goal for individuals and families is to manage this time to allow for necessary household tasks and recreation. The challenge is to develop an equitable distribution of tasks so that all family members have sufficient leisure.

Neighborhood REVISITED

The kitchen was quiet for a minute as Ralph and Debbie thought about the implications of Debbie's returning to work. Debbie broke the silence.

"It seems to me that we really need more information before we decide if I should go back to work. Maybe I should try a parttime job at first to gradually get back into the swing of managing a career and a home."

"OK, I see what you're saying," Ralph replied. "Let's make a list of all the options and try to investigate the consequences of each option."

Parttime work for Debbie
- retail clerk
- bank teller
- waitress
- self-employed salesperson

Full-time work for Debbie
- same as for parttime
- bank management trainee

Parttime work for Ralph
- swim instructor—YMCA
- newspaper delivery driver
- waiter

After looking at the employment options, Debbie and Ralph decided that Debbie should go to the bank to investigate parttime work. They then made a list of consequences or changes that would occur if Debbie worked.
- more money
- less time at home for Debbie
- replacing older car
- spending money for childcare
- Amy would get to go to preschool
- expanding Debbie's wardrobe
- increased transportation costs
- house not cleaned as often
- less home baking and cooking
- perhaps a higher food bill
- less leisure time for Ralph
- increased savings
- possible vacation for family

Debbie and Ralph also decided to talk with their two-income friends to gain insight into the time pressures and changed spending patterns that result. In the event that Debbie does go to work, the family planned to reevaluate the impact of two incomes within six months. At that time they would decide whether Debbie should continue working, and if so, whether she should look for a full-time job.

1. What consequences of Debbie's working parttime were overlooked by Debbie and Ralph?
2. How would the cost-benefit analysis of parttime employment for Debbie differ from that of full-time employment?

KEY TERMS

age earning curve
blended (reconstituted) family
demography
extended families
family life cycle
human capital
labor income

leisure foregone
leisure time
level of living
life cycle
mental human capital
nonmarket home production
nuclear family

Parkinson's law
physical human capital
psychic income
real income
recreation

QUESTIONS

1. What is the difference between a nuclear family and an extended family?

2. What are the stages of the individual life cycle? Of the family life cycle?

3. There are differences in salaries between men and women who have similar education and experience. Why is this so? What has been done to rectify this situation?

4. What are the arguments involved in the demand for "equal pay for equal work"?

5. Do you think there is a strong correlation between the time and money costs of an education and the salaries earned? Why?

6. What specific suggestions appear in the text to improve time management? Which ones are particularly relevant for you?

7. From your own experience, identify some of the major expenses for each stage in the individual and family life cycles.

PROJECTS

1. Following the directions in Box 3-1, list your lifetime goals, your five-year goals, and your six-month goals. Evaluate them and assign priorities to them.

2. Choose a career that interests you and predict how it would affect your social life, personal satisfaction, leisure time, and general life cycle.

3. Interview couples at different stages of the life cycle to learn what financial and time pressures they feel and what they are doing about them. Try to select families who have no children, one or two children, and several children.

4. If you are currently married or have a roommate, make a record of how each person in the family spends his or her leisure and nonmarket production time. Analyze the record to see whether this time is being used to maximize the home environment for each family member.

5. Do a cost-benefit analysis for yourself concerning one or more of the following decisions:
   a. Marriage.
   b. Parenthood.
   c. Investment in career training.
   d. Joining the work force.
   e. Changing your career.
   f. Retirement.

Be sure to include monetary and nonmonetary factors and consider the impact of your decisions on family members, roommates, and close friends.

REFERENCES AND READINGS

Barber, Clifton E. "Parental Responses to the Empty-Nest Transition." *Journal of Home Economics,* Summer 1981.

Bernard, Jessie. *The Future of Marriage.* New York: World, 1972.

Bird, Caroline. *The Case Against College.* New York: David McKay, 1975.

Bird, Caroline. *The Two-Paycheck Marriage.* New York: Rawson, Wade, 1979.

Deacon, Ruth E., and Firebaugh, Francille M. *Family Resource Management.* Boston: Allyn & Bacon, 1975.

"Does College Really Matter?" *Changing Times,* November 1979.

Easterlin, Richard A. *Birth and Fortune.* New York: Basic Books, 1980.

Ehrbar, A. F. "The Upbeat Outlook for Family Incomes." *Fortune,* February 25, 1980.

Espenshade, Thomas J. "Raising a Child Can Now Cost $85,000." *Intercom,* September 1980.

Fabe, Marilyn, and Wikler, Norma. *Up Against the Clock.* New York: Random House, 1980.

Gilder, George. *Wealth and Poverty.* New York: Bantam, 1982.

Greiff, Barrie S., and Munter, Preston K. *Tradeoffs: Executive, Family and Organizational Life.* New York: New American Library, 1980.

Guzzardi, Walter. "Demography's Good News for the Eighties." *Fortune,* November 5, 1979.

Hall, Francine S., and Hall, Douglas T. *The Two-Career Couple.* Reading, Mass.: Addison-Wesley, 1979.

Jones, Landon Y. *Great Expectations.* New York: Coward, McCann and Geoghegan, 1980.

Johnson, Beverly L. "Single-Parent Families." *Family Economics Review,* Summer/Fall 1980.

Lakein, Alan. *How to Get Control of Your Time and Your Life.* New York: Peter H. Wyden, 1973.

Moore, Joan W., and Pachon, Harry. *Mexican Americans.* Englewood Cliffs, N.J.: Prentice-Hall, 1976.

National Urban League. *The State of Black America 1980.* New York: The National Urban League, 1980.

Oakley, Ann. *Woman's Work.* New York: Pantheon Books, 1974.

Paolucci, Beatrice; Hall, Olive A. and Axinn, Nancy. *Family Decision Making: An Ecosystem Approach.* New York: Wiley, 1977.

Shaevitz, Marjorie Hansen, and Shaevitz, Morton H. *Making It Together as a Two-Career Couple.* Boston: Houghton Mifflin, 1980.

Sheehy, Gail. *Passages.* New York: Dutton, 1976.

Sowell, Thomas. *Markets and Minorities.* London: Basil Blackwell, 1980.

U.S. Bureau of Labor Statistics. *Occupational Outlook Handbook.* Washington, D.C.: U.S. Government Printing Office, published annually.

U.S. Bureau of the Census. *Social Indicators III.* Washington, D.C.: U.S. Government Printing Office, 1980.

Waite, Linda J. "U.S. Women at Work." *"Population Bulletin,* May 1981.

Walker, Kathryn E. "Household Work Time: Its Implication for Family Decisions." *Journal of Home Economics,* October 1973.

Walker, Kathryn E., and Gauger, William H. *The Dollar Value of Housework.* Ithaca, N.Y.: Cornell University Press, 1980.

Weinstein, Grace W. *Life Plans: Looking Forward to Retirement.* New York: Holt, Rinehart, and Winston, 1979.

Did You Know That...

- *firms spend over $55 billion each year to advertise their products to consumers? This amounts to an advertising budget of $250 for every consumer in America.*

- *advertising can actually result in lower prices to the consumer by providing valuable information and by stimulating competition among firms in an industry?*

- *a few firms spend almost half of their sales revenues on advertising?*

- *the average American sees 20,000 television commercials a year during the 1,300 hours he or she watches the tube?*

- *there are half a dozen federal agencies that have some jurisdiction over advertising practices, but the Federal Trade Commission is the one with the broadest powers? The FTC can require a firm to pay for corrective advertising if false or misleading claims have been made.*

- *you have three working days from the time you sign a door-to-door sales contract if you want to cancel your order?*

- *it is illegal for a firm to advertise a product at a very low price with the intention of attracting consumers, exposing the faults of the item, and then getting the consumer to buy a different, more expensive model?*

- *some studies show that firms that advertise heavily have a greater investment in their reputation and thus are more likely to provide high-quality products?*

Advertising: Information or Manipulation?

The Birth of the Advertising Industry
Who Are the Major Advertisers?
Types of Advertising
The Benefits of Advertising
How to Obtain Information: Just the Facts

Neighborhood CAPSULE
A Day at the Fair

The weather was perfect and the attitude of the group matched it as they crowded into the county fairgrounds. Fun, games, amusements, famous entertainers, and a general day of frolic were all ahead for the Bilderback family. As they wandered down the midway, they were attracted by a large crowd surrounding a stand where a man was sawing a frozen steak in half with a kitchen knife.

"Yes sir, ladies and gentlemen, this here knife is an absolute revelation. The only knife made in America of pure, genuine, 100 percent surgical steel. Why, you could leave this knife on your back porch, let it be rained upon, spat upon, stepped upon, and even soiled by your cat (laughter), and it would still shine right up and be sharp as ever.

"Notice how, even after cutting that frozen meat in half, it can still slice tomatoes so thin that they only have one side." He proceeded to slice a tomato very thin, and then he held it up so you could see right through it. "After all," he went on, "how do you think restaurants make one tomato last through a whole lunchtime crowd of hamburger lovers?" The crowd loved him.

"This knife is not available in any store. You can't get it through the mail. Nosiree, your only chance to obtain this marvelous invention is here and now. Not at $15.95 or even $12.95, but at only $9.95 per knife or three for $20.00. And in this day of inflation, where can you get such a bargain? I have only a *limited* supply of these, but for those of you who see the value in this right *now,* I will also throw in, *free of charge,* this plastic juicer."

He then produced a small green plastic cylinder, which he jammed into an orange. With what appeared to be a gentle squeeze, the orange gushed. He filled a glass with juice

and drank from it as the hot, thirsty crowd wet their lips.

"And that's not all. For you first brave souls, I will also give you a handy paring knife made of the same 100 percent surgical steel." He then produced the knife and skinned a potato in seconds, made roses from radishes, and made a beautiful carrot garnish. To almost everyone in the crowd it was apparent that he or she had stumbled onto a bargain. How lucky could one be?

"What if I don't like it?" said a skeptical voice in the audience.

"I will be here all during the fair and I'll buy it back, if one of your neighbors doesn't beat me to it." (Laughter and good will were heaped on him by the crowd.)

At the end of the presentation many knives were bought. But oddly enough, he had enough left over to sell more and more.

As we noted in Chapter 1, the American economy has passed through various stages of development. In the earliest years, most of our labor force was on the farm. Consumer products as we know them today were almost nonexistent, because most products were produced in the home. The biggest household expenditure was for the family stove, which often served the dual purpose of cooking and heating. As our economy industrialized, people moved off the farm and into the cities to work for wages. Because urban workers could not produce their own goods and services, they exchanged their labor income for a variety of products. By the end of the nineteenth century, the United States was on the brink of an era that Walt Rostow (1960) termed "the age of high mass consumption." An important part of this age was the birth and growth of the advertising industry.

This chapter focuses on advertising and related informational media that are an important part of one's everyday experience in Consumer America. As you saw in Chapter 2, good decisions are impossible without good information. Advertising at its best can provide this crucial input. At its worst, advertising can distort your decision-making process by giving you false or misleading information that could lead you to make a poor choice. But as you may already suspect, most advertising is neither all good nor all bad. There are some real benefits that can be attributed to advertising, along with some genuine costs to society as well as individuals. On the benefit side, by providing consumers with information, advertising can promote competition among producers and thus help create lower prices for consumers. It is also true that firms that produce many brands and advertise heavily are investing in their name. This means they must keep product quality or risk tarnishing their reputation. Procter & Gamble's swift action in removing Rely tampons from the marketplace as soon as danger to the consumer was suggested can be seen as an example of a large advertiser trying to protect its reputation and that of its other consumer-oriented products. Advertising also has some beneficial side-effects such as providing subsidies to other informational media such as television, radio, magazines, and newspapers. The negative aspects of advertising hinge on its ability to produce informational confusion among consumers so that their decision-making ability is impaired and they buy what they are told to buy. According to this view, firms advertise to create wants in the consumer rather than to satisfy consumer needs that already exist. Advertising can also be used to keep potential competitors out of a market by making it expensive to get the consumer's attention. Small firms may find it impossible to spend millions of dollars just to become well enough known for consumers to try their product. If smaller firms are intimidated by the huge advertising budgets of their larger rivals, advertising becomes a barrier to competition that results in higher prices.

In this chapter we explore these pros and cons of advertising in greater detail, but our emphasis is not on deciding the merits of advertising. Instead, we want you to be able to distinguish information from manipulation. Then, you can feed the information provided by advertising into your decision-making process and get more satisfaction out of your expenditures.

The first part of this chapter describes the development of the advertising industry and the firms that use it. The middle sections analyze the major types of advertisements and give you some ways to recognize them. The next sections deal with the consumer benefits of advertising, and the final section extends the consumers' search for information from advertising to other readily available sources.

The Birth of the Advertising Industry

High mass consumption was accompanied by assembly-line production (for example, in automobile production) and by grand distribution networks such as department stores and supermarkets. Consumers' needs were being met by the market system. An important part of that system was (and still is) *information*. Producers needed to let consumers know what they were willing to produce and consumers wanted to know what was available and at what price. The time was ripe for the birth of the advertising industry.

Figure 4-1 illustrates the growth of advertising in the United States since 1880. You can see a gradual but steady growth in expenditures from 1880 to about 1930. This coincides with the entrance of the American economy into Rostow's age of high mass consumption. The 1930s show a decline because of the Depression, which was encountered during the decade when unemployment rates soared to 25 percent and almost all industries experienced a decline in sales. Beginning in the 1940s and continuing to the present, we have seen a veritable explosion in advertising in the United States. In 1940, advertisers were spending about $2 billion; by 1980 they were spending $55 billion—more than twenty-five times as much. Of course, consumer prices also rose between 1940 and 1980, so the increase in the real buying

Figure 4-1. Advertising expenditures in the United States, 1880–1980.

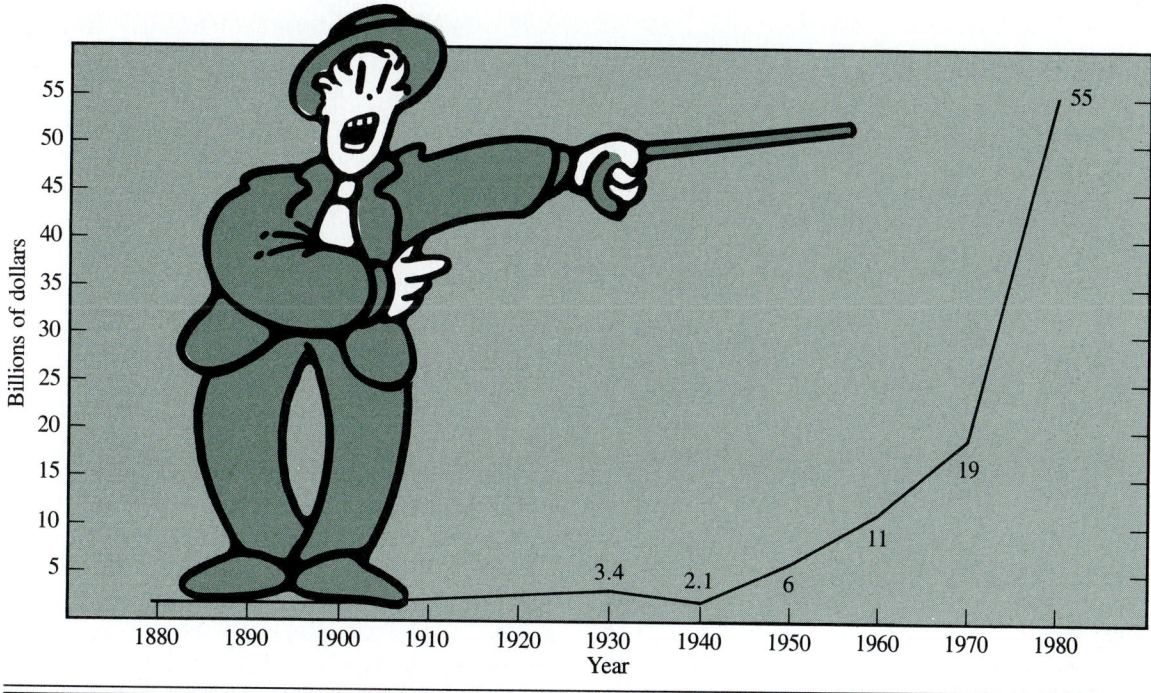

power of the advertising expenditures was not equal to $50 billion. We will discuss the impact of inflation in greater detail in Chapter 7 because it is an important issue in almost every consumer decision. But for now we will just mention that consumer prices rose about 600 percent between 1940 and 1980. Nevertheless, even when the 1980 dollars are adjusted for their loss in buying power, advertising expenditures rose more than four-fold between 1940 and 1980.

Because advertising is part of the cost of doing business, it is included in the price of the product. This means that in 1980, an average consumer contributed $250 to firms' advertising expenditures by buying their products. Thus, a typical four-person American household pays for $1,000 worth of advertising annually through their purchases. In essence, these dollars pay for a vast information service that many consumers may not be using to their best advantage. Think about it. If you were paying $1,000 a year to subscribe to a buying information service, you would be very concerned with its usefulness. However, many consumers seem to take advertising for granted. They don't realize that it can supply helpful information that can be incorporated into their decisions. On the other hand, advertising can also send misleading signals that consumers should ignore or avoid. Throughout this chapter we want to help you distinguish between these two so that advertising is an aid, not a hindrance, in your decision-making process. The next section gets you started by profiling the typical advertisers. Then we discuss the rationale for advertising, the types of ads, and finally, how you can benefit from advertisements.

Who Are the Major Advertisers?

Table 4-1 lists the top thirty advertisers in 1980. Take a look at the list and see how many names are familiar to you. Some of these companies, called **retailers** because they sell *directly* to the consumer, are well known. Sears, K-Mart, and J.C. Penney are good

Table 4-1. The Top Thirty Advertisers in 1980

Advertiser	Millions of advertising dollars
1. Procter & Gamble	$649.6
2. Sears, Roebuck	599.6
3. General Foods	410.0
4. Philip Morris	364.6
5. K-Mart	319.3
6. General Motors	316.0
7. R. J. Reynolds	298.5
8. Ford Motor	280.0
9. American Telephone & Telegraph	259.2
10. Warner-Lambert	235.2
11. Gulf & Western	233.8
12. Pepsi	233.4
13. Colgate-Palmolive	225.0
14. McDonald's	207.0
15. Ralston Purina	206.8
16. American Home Products	197.0
17. Bristol-Myers	196.3
18. Mobil	194.8
19. Esmark	189.9
20. Coca-Cola	184.2
21. Anheuser-Busch	181.3
22. Johnson & Johnson	177.0
23. Beatrice Foods	175.0
24. U.S. Government	173.0
25. General Mills	171.1
26. Heublein	170.0
27. RCA	164.3
28. Unilever	158.3
29. General Electric	156.2
30. Seagram	152.0

SOURCE: Reprinted with permission from the September 10, 1981 issue of *Advertising Age*. Copyright 1981 by Crain Communications, Inc.

examples of retail firms. Other firms may be less familiar because they are **wholesalers,** that is, they sell only in bulk to firms that either retail their products or use them to produce other goods to be sold to the consumer. Another reason you may have difficulty recognizing such firms as Esmark, Gulf & Western, Norton Simon, or Unilever is that many of these unfamiliar corporations own a number of better known and better advertised firms. For example, Esmark owns Playtex, STP, and Swift Meats; Gulf & Western owns Paramount Pictures, Madison Square Garden, and Simon & Schuster Publishers. Although Norton Simon, Unilever, and American Home Products are not exactly household words, very few consumers have not heard of Hunt's catsup and Wesson oil made by Norton Simon, Close-up toothpaste produced by Unilever, or Anacin sold by a subsidiary of American Home Products.

Most consumers have only a vague appreciation of the huge sums of money spent on advertising. A thirty-second television commercial can cost over $1 million to produce, and many times that to show on prime-time TV during the regular season. Why does Procter & Gamble spend over half a billion dollars on such tactics? This may seem especially odd when you realize that in 1980 the ad budget was greater than the profits distributed to their shareholders. Why don't the shareholders unite, throw the advertising maniacs out, and double their dividends? At least part of the reason lies in the basic belief that advertising increases sales and gives the firm a competitive edge in the marketplace. It may cost $200,000 to buy a thirty-second spot during the Super Bowl, but if a company can reach 40 million households in that time period, it's cheaper than using the U.S. mail system.

Clearly, there is more to advertising than simply trying to give consumers what they need. The objective of a profit-making firm's advertising is to benefit the corporation first. Often this means satisfying the consumer; thus both parties are better off with the advertising expenditures. It may seem odd that the advertising of some products actually competes with other products made by the same company. Procter & Gamble produces half a dozen detergents, from Ivory Snow to Tide and Oxydol, all heavily advertised. It also produces Mr. Clean and Spic and Span—products familiar to all soap-opera watchers. But Procter & Gamble is not alone in its intracorporate competitiveness. Minute Maid and Snow Crop orange juice are both made by Coca-Cola; Home Pride bread, Wonder bread, and Profile bread are products of International Telephone & Telegraph; Swanson and Pepperidge Farm soups are owned by Campbell's Soup; Blue Bonnet and Fleischmann's margarines are

Advertising is ubiquitous in our lives. We cannot walk down the street without encountering ads on billboards, storefronts, and even vehicles such as taxis, trucks, and buses.

trade names used by Standard Brands; and General Foods advertises a wide variety of its coffees: Maxim, Maxwell House, Sanka, Yuban, and Brim.

Critics of advertising say that this proliferation of brands and the heavy use of advertising is a way of limiting competition. After all, there is only so much space on supermarket shelves. If General Foods heavily advertises five different brands of coffee, there is less shelf space for products of other firms. And the fact that there are so many brands gives the appearance of competition, when, in fact, only a few firms produce most brands. On the other hand, multi-product firms are quick to point out that consumers' tastes differ. Not everyone likes the same coffee blend; by producing a variety of brands, firms are able to increase sales (and profits) by responding to demand in the marketplace. And how else do consumers learn about different blends unless the firm gives them distinctive names and then informs consumers about their availability?

This debate cannot be resolved here. For our purposes, a more important question is one of cost. Who pays how much to whom?

Table 4-2 shows the advertising expenditures of representatives of the top one hundred firms as a percentage of their total sales. From a consumer's perspective, this table shows how much of each sales dollar goes to pay for the advertising budget. As you can see, many firms spend little in percentage terms. The oil, automobile, airline, and retail chain store companies spend less than 2 percent of their sales revenues on advertising. So for every dollar spent in airfare, for instance, only 2 cents is the result of advertising. But some companies, especially those dealing with personal care items such as cosmetics, spend relatively large amounts on ads. In 1979, Noxell, the makers of Noxema, spent 22.3 percent of their revenues on advertising. If you spent $2 on a jar of Noxema, 44.6 cents went for advertising! Drug companies such as Miles Laboratories (Alka-Seltzer) and Sterling Drug (Bayer Aspirin) also spent over 10 percent of your dollar to buy advertising, and major gum, candy, and toy companies—Wrigley, Mars, and Mattel—spent between 7 and 8.5 percent of their revenues to tell the public about their products. If you have ever watched professional football on television, it comes as no surprise to you to find that beer companies also have significant expenditures on advertising. Joseph Schlitz and Anheuser-Busch (Budweiser-Michelob) spent over $50 million trying to convince the American public that their beers are among the finest brewed anywhere in the world. But for every six-pack sold, 5 percent of the revenue went toward advertising, not ingredients.

Table 4-2. Advertising Expenditures as a Percentage of Total Sales for Firms Selected from the Top 100 Advertisers

Ad rank	Company	Advertising	Sales	Advertising as percent of sales
Airlines				
73	UAL	$50,624,437	$3,890,296,000	1.3
84	Trans World	37,500,000	3,695,000,000	1.0
Appliances, TV, radio				
21	RCA	140,000,000	6,644,500,000	2.1
31	General Electric	121,294,400	19,653,800,000	0.6
Automobiles				
4	General Motors	266,346,000	63,221,100,000	0.4
6	Ford	210,000,000	42,784,100,000	0.5
Drugs				
51	Sterling Drug	78,000,000	724,595,001	10.8
63	Miles Laboratory	62,258,000	536,983,000	11.6
Food				
3	General Foods	340,000,000	5,472,500,000	6.2
14	General Mills	170,000,000	3,745,000,000	4.5
19	Norton Simon	144,591,000	2,428,797,000	6.0
23	McDonald's	136,803,000	4,575,000,000	3.0
Gum and candy				
67	Mars	60,180,000	837,400,000	7.2
83	Wrigley	37,771,852	445,639,000	8.5
Oil				
16	Mobile	163,043,300	37,331,000,000	0.4
88	Exxon	38,752,500	64,886,000,000	0.6
Photographic equipment				
44	Eastman-Kodak	86,071,700	7,012,923,000	1.2
71	Polaroid	52,752,500	1,376,590,000	3.8

SOURCE: Reprinted with permission from the September 6, 1981 issue of *Advertising Age,* Copyright 1981 by Crain Communications, Inc.

Types of Advertising

As consumers, we are constantly exposed to advertising—while we're walking, driving, riding a bus, looking at a magazine or newspaper, even in our homes while watching TV. In fact, according to the most recent surveys, the average American logs 1,300 viewing hours each year from the age of two on. This is more time than he or she spends in school. This means that a viewer sees 20,000 commercials a year. TV and other forms of advertising, then, create a situation that calls for consumers to know about and be prepared for this overwhelming amount of information. If we allow ourselves to be manipulated or persuaded to buy without thinking, we abandon our role as careful and conscious decision makers responsible for their choices. However, by analyzing advertisements, we can learn to use the information and disregard the rest, including the emotional or false

Ad rank	Company	Advertising	Sales	Advertising as percent of sales
Retail chain stores				
2	Sears, Roebuck	417,934,900	17,946,000,000	1.9
5	K-Mart	250,000,000	11,695,549,000	2.1
27	J. C. Penney	125,000,000	10,845,000,000	1.2
Soaps, cleansers				
1	Procter & Gamble	554,000,000	9,329,306,000	5.9
18	Unilever	145,000,000	1,812,000,000	8.0
29	Colgate-Palmolive	122,500,000	4,312,054,000	2.8
Soft drinks				
16	Pepsi	156,000,000	4,300,006,000	3.6
22	Coca-Cola	136,805,300	4,337,900,000	3.2
Telephone service and equipment				
13	American Telephone & Telegraph	172,822,100	40,933,356,000	0.4
Tobacco				
6	Philip Morris	236,851,000	6,632,463,000	3.6
12	R. J. Reynolds	182,596,300	6,622,100,000	2.8
Toiletries, cosmetics				
7	Warner-Lambert	211,000,000	2,878,496,000	7.3
9	Bristol-Myers	192,850,000	2,450,429,000	7.8
38	Gillette	99,000,000	1,710,471,000	5.8
91	Noxell	34,902,400	156,408,000	22.3
96	Alberto-Culver	32,391,872	172,537,684	18.1
Beer				
34	Anheuser-Busch	116,599,000	2,701,611,000	4.3
68	Joseph Schlitz Brewing	58,213,000	1,083,272,000	5.4
Toys				
88	Mattel	35,629,600	493,563,000	7.2

and deceptive advertising that accomplishes a company's sales goals at the expense of our own.

In this section and the ones that follow, we present the major categories of advertising as outlined by the Federal Trade Commission (FTC). The FTC is the federal agency with the major responsibility for policing national advertising campaigns and ensuring that false or misleading claims are stopped. The FTC is not the only agency that regulates advertising. On the federal level, the Food and Drug Administration (FDA), the Federal Communication Commission (FCC), the U.S. Postal Service, and even the Securities and Exchange Commission (SEC) all have a hand in overseeing the advertising practices of some firms. Consumer protection agencies in various states and their respective attorney generals are also involved in advertising at the local level. And in recent years, the FTC has come under fire from those who oppose government regulation in the economy. Nevertheless, it is the FTC that continues to be the most prominent government agency involved in advertising and national consumer protection matters.

The FTC classification for ads is based on the ad's content. They list ads as being "informative," "puffing," or "deceptive." We will adopt this framework for broad categories of ads, but it will be useful to break some of them down into more specific types so that you can see the kinds of appeals that producers make.

INFORMATIVE ADVERTISING

An **informative advertisement** provides the consumer with specific, understandable, and verifiable claims about the product or service. For a consumer, one of the most important pieces of information contained in any informational ad is the price. It is very important that the consumer know ahead of time just how much a good or a service will cost. Otherwise, the cost-benefit step in our decision-making framework becomes a "guesstimate," or one is required to spend additional time searching for price information. Given the importance of price information, it seems odd that this particular item is often missing from the promotional pitch. Retail store ads are a notable exception. They frequently give specific price and product information. Even here, however, the modern trend seems to be to advertise the noninformative slogan "We have the lowest prices in town."

It is true that national advertising of brands is often unable to mention specific price information because prices vary with different retailers. A pair of Levi's jeans, for instance, may sell for quite different prices, even in the same town. Even the price of an orange is affected by transportation costs, store overhead, and seasonal variation. So there are times when even the most avid consumer advocate has to admit that specific price information is not possible. Nevertheless, if advertising is to serve a valuable service to consumers, advertisers have an obligation to try to inform, and not simply persuade, the public about their product.

Besides telling price, informational ads can describe nutritional content, shrinkage resistance, fabric composition, or practical tips on how to use the product. Recipe ads are informational because they tell the public how to prepare and use the product or how to combine it with other ingredients to fix a meal. Recent utility- and oil-company-sponsored energy ads are also examples of informational advertising. They actually inform the consumer about conserving energy. Changing the filter in your furnace, closing the drapes at night, and checking the air pressure in your tires are all tips on how to be more energy efficient and how to save money, too.

Informational advertising is the most valuable kind for consumer decision-making because it lessens the time that consumers must spend searching for information. It also aids consumers by specifying more clearly the costs and benefits associated with the good or service involved. This makes the cost-benefit calculation easier and more accurate in our decision-making model. And finally, informational ads are valuable because they give the consumer more options. A greater variety of options leads to more competition, better service, lower prices, and, ultimately, greater consumer satisfaction.

A small proportion of all ads are purely informational. Most contain some fluff, if only to retain consumer interest. The key to classifying and then

---

INTRODUCING... The New Leetwood

- Seats six people under 150 pounds or four people under 120 pounds and one person over 175 pounds or three people over 225 pounds.
- Free spare tire.
- Bumpers front and rear.
- XL-94002 super power cigarette lighter.
- DuroPlast leatherette semi-plush seat covers and arm rests.
- Two sets of keys with every car.
- Semi-pro pseudo disk brakes, front and rear.
- 3-speed semi-automatic Zarbo transmission including reverse and park.
- All new Driggers JA2207 2-cylinder direct drive cast iron power unit.
- Super high beam flourescent head lamps yielding 97.865 lumens.
- Ultra-grip two-season tires with one nylon cord construction to yield semi-long wearing tread life.
- 12 cubic inch capacity chrome-like two-knob ash tray.
- Three thousand four hundred twenty-seven cubic centimeter trunk space with a four-watt electric blue light and reostat power control switch.
- Six-speed dual angstrom windshield wiper system with "Power-Kleen" 18-inch blades.
- Nontinted "EzVu" windows all around.
- AM-FM 6-channel Luigi sound system with two 3-inch Armondo speakers.

Some ads are *too* informative.

analyzing an advertisement is looking at the major thrust of the ad. If you know a good deal more after seeing it than you did before, the ad was informational. If, on the other hand, your knowledge was only minimally increased or if you were misled, then the ad falls into another category.

PUFFERY ADVERTISING: A LOT OF HOT AIR

Puffery is an advertising category the FTC uses to describe ads that supply little or no constructive information about the product. After you read or hear a puffing ad, you do not know much more than you did before. Price information is always left out, and the claims in favor of using this product are laudatory but vague and not easily tested. There are many forms of puffery, but all aim to *persuade* rather than to inform. The advertiser wants the consumer to buy the product based on some mythical, unverifiable, emotional belief rather than on hard, empirical evidence. The forms of puffery—testimonial, institutional, emotional, comparative, and truth to convey falsehood—are the most common advertising techniques. They can be combined in any number of ways to achieve the goal of getting you to buy or, in some cases, of trying to short circuit your decision-making process.

Testimonial Ads: Trust Me. A **testimonial ad** is a positive recommendation about a good or a service. As consumers, we often ask our friends or relatives about the merits of a particular restaurant, movie, or appliance they have tried; we ask for opinions that we can weigh, and then we come to our own conclusions. The difference between testimonials and recommendations is that testimonial ads are *always* favorable. They glow with superlatives about the quality of the service or the longevity of the product or the whiteness of the wash. They are never balanced or objective, so it is important to weigh them carefully—and skeptically—when we use them as part of the information we need to make a decision.

Testimonials come in two varieties: celebrity endorsements and "typical consumer" endorsements. Celebrity endorsements are by far the older and more traditional type of advertisement. In your experience you must have seen or heard thousands of such ads from people such as Joe Namath for a famous panty hose company or Bill Cosby for Jell-O. All of these ads are puffery in the sense that they provide no specific verifiable claims. They amount to the classic line "Trust me, would I steer you wrong?"

In one of the most successful testimonial ads ever run, the late John Wayne made a pitch in his cowboy outfit for a bank in southern California. Millions of dollars were deposited in that bank because "the Duke" said it was all right. On the other hand, Pat Boone was sued when it was discovered that the acne remedy he and his family recommended simply did not work. And Karl Malden, the spokesman for American Express, was taken to court by an irate consumer when she did not get an instant refund when her traveler's checks were stolen in Latin America. Even former Olympic hero Bruce Jenner was taken to task over his sponsorship of Wheaties breakfast cereal. The argument was that he did not eat them. The rules as laid out by the FTC state that the person giving the testimonial must use the product at least some of the time. Jenner was subsequently cleared when it was shown that he was a Wheaties consumer.

Partly because of some of the problems with the FTC rules and partly because of consumer skepticism about the sincerity of famous folk, advertisers have turned to common people to give an "honest" evaluation of their products. Sometimes this takes the form of unsolicited letters to the manufacturer, which are followed up and then reenacted for the television ad campaign. You have surely seen the all-American mother who got those dirty socks clean even though they were covered with grease, or the watch that kept on ticking after it had been inadvertently left in a tire for six months, or the family that owned twelve Pintos because Pintos are such good cars. These ordinary testimonials may also be contrived by an advertising firm that tests hundreds of consumers with hidden cameras and then produces honest testimonials: "My headache is gone," "I didn't think he would like stuffing instead of potatoes," "It *is* cleaner," "My hands are younger looking," and so forth.

Institutional Ads. Someone once said that no politician could lose by including patriotism, motherhood, and sports in a speech. This appeal to some of the underlying values of most Americans has been adopted by corporate advertisers as well. An **institutional ad** associates the product with ideas and institutions that are not only familiar but also very dear to the vast majority of the consuming public. The Chevrolet Motor Division of General Motors, for instance, did this very effectively with its ad campaign a few years ago. The lyric to the jingle was "Baseball, hot dogs, apple pie, and Chevrolet." The spring campaign showed a large Fourth of July family gathering, the centerpiece of which was a shiny Chevrolet. These pleasant and culturally valued associations may dispose a consumer to buy the product that is associated with them. If this is the case, the ads have succeeded in short circuiting the consumer's decision-making process.

The nature of institutional advertising often promotes **stereotyping,** that is, a subtle form of discrimination that identifies people with certain roles and thereby restricts their behavior and image, both individually and as a group. Have you ever noticed how the elderly are depicted in television commercials? Old people wait for phone calls, care for their dentures, and find it unbelievable that lemonade can actually be made from a mix. They rarely drive a car or drink Coca-Cola, and they seldom wash their hair. According to a study done at the University of Maryland, children's images of older people are a product of their television watching. Children reported that old people are sick, sad, tired, dirty, ugly, wrinkled, crippled, and do not have teeth. When asked how they will be when they are old, the children denied that they will ever grow old (Adler, 1980). Such stereotypes are part and parcel of institutional puffery because an institutional ad must rely on the common conceptions and feelings of the masses. This means that such ads unwillingly reinforce these ideas and thus in some cases help to foster discrimination. For an interesting pictorial review of how ads have treated sex, race, health, diet, and even alcohol, read Robert Atwan's *Edsels, Luckies & Frigidaires* (1979).

Emotional Ads. An **emotional ad** is one whose major focus is to persuade a consumer to buy a product because it will satisfy a psychological rather than a physiological need. Thus, a producer of scotch whisky might stress that only a few consumers will be able to appreciate the exquisite taste of a limited bottling of their aged scotch. They intimate that if you buy the product, you are among the elite. They appeal to your self-image, your ego.

All consumers carry emotional baggage with them. Advertisers that use emotional ads attempt to open this psychological bag and play on various parts of it. Advertising firms employ staffs of psychologists, sociologists, and social psychologists, who apply their knowledge of human behavior and emotions to create a profitable ad campaign. Guilt and fear are two old standbys that can be highly effective tools in convincing consumers to pay more. For example, an ad asks, "Does your family deserve the best?" or "When was the last time you called home?" Vanity is another emotion that cosmetics and vitamin manufacturers have used for decades. Even the federal government (the twenty-fourth largest U.S. advertiser) uses some psychological ploys when it promises adventure to Navy recruits or status to Marine recruits ("The Marines are looking for a few good men"). Taken as a whole, emotionally based puffery ads can make consumers feel dissatisfied, insecure, or downright miserable, unless of course they rectify the situation by doing as they are told. A better solution is to use one's consumer skills to see through the ad and block the response. But not everyone has the benefit of such a course (see Box 4-1).

Comparative Ads. Advertisers have for a long time used **comparative advertising** to compare their brand to the imaginary "Brand X," an unnamed (and clearly inferior) competitor. Only recently, however, has Brand X disappeared, to be replaced by actual brand-name competition. Now we can see for ourselves that extra-strength Anacin has twice the pain reliever of its two major competitors, Bufferin and Bayer. Of course, what they never mention is that the pain reliever is "acetylsalicylic acid," commonly called aspirin. And they never mention the price. Often it would be cheaper to take two tablets of aspirin rather than one tablet of extra-strength Anacin.

> **BOX 4-1**
>
> ## Kids and the Tube
>
> It was Saturday morning in the Clemo household and Sara, eight, Megan Ann, five, and Andrew, two, were gathered before their color television set watching early-morning cartoons. The attention of the two smaller children occasionally wandered, but generally their eyes were riveted on the electronic marvel in their living room. Practically every show was interspersed with short, incisive, and often entertaining tidbits about the wondrous world of cereal, snack foods, candy, and soft drinks. Characters similar to their cartoon "friends" slyly tempted the children to try sugar-frosted this, or sweet, crispy that. By the time their parents awoke and herded the children to the breakfast table, it was obvious that a meal of juice, eggs, and bacon was not at the top of their list.
>
> "Why don't we ever have anything good to eat?" asked Sara, who was the most articulate spokesperson in the group. "We never get chocolate-covered Sugar Sparkles," she went on.
>
> "I like Tony the Tiger," Megan Ann interrupted, affirming her loyalty to the cartoon huckster most closely associated with one of those sugar-based confections labeled "cereal" by its producers.
>
> "Me, too. Mmm, good," burbled the youngest Clemo, Andrew.
>
> "Don't you want me to make you bacon and eggs?" asked Vickie, their mother.
>
> "No!" was the resounding chorus as the children wiggled and jiggled in their seats. "We want Tony! We want Tony!" was the watchword of the day.
>
> "All right, all right, we'll buy some of that at the store next time. I promise," said the weary homemaker. And so she did.
>
> 1. A study conducted by Scott Ward at the Harvard School of Business discovered that attention to commercials was greatest among younger children. He found that the percentage of mothers "usually yielding to a child's purchase influence attempts" (for children ages five to seven) was:
>   - breakfast cereals   88%
>   - snack foods   52%
>   - candy   40%
>   - soft drinks   38%
>
>   Do these percentages seem correct in your experience? Are they alarming?
> 2. Is this a far-fetched example? Have you ever witnessed a scene in which the children requested (or perhaps demanded) an advertised brand?
> 3. Should TV advertising aimed at children be more closely regulated than other forms of advertising? Why or why not?

The failure to mention price is what turns comparative advertising into puffery. Some comparative advertising could be classified as informative if useful price comparisons were made, but that has proved hazardous in some cases. Bristol-Myers used one of the earliest comparative advertising blitzes to introduce Datril, a nonaspirin pain reliever (acetaminophen), which competed with the number-one seller, Tylenol. Datril's manufacturer decided to undercut Tylenol's price and advertise the price difference. After the ad campaign was set, the commercials made, and time and space purchased, Tylenol cut its price dramatically. The result was a misleading ad campaign in which Datril claimed to be just as effective (true) and cheaper (true when the commercials were made, but false when they were run). The makers of Tylenol sued Bristol-Myers and all the newspapers, magazines, and networks involved, creating a messy situation that almost brought back Brand X. It was a warning to other competitors, who rarely advertise comparative prices, to avoid doing what Datril did unless they are sure that there will be no retaliation.

Truth to Convey Falsehood. When advertisers tell the truth but make it sound as if they have a competitive edge when in fact they don't, they are using **truth to convey falsehood.** For example, the government regulates many industries and often does not allow firms to charge different prices. Interest rates that banks offer on savings accounts are set by law and cannot be raised by an individual bank. This does not stop them, however, from advertising that they have the "highest interest rates in town." This is true, but so do most of the other banks. In the past, airlines often advertised that they had the lowest fare between two cities, when, in reality, all air carriers were regulated so that prices were uniform. With the national deregulation of airlines, ads about fares have greater informational content—provided that airlines continue to advertise their prices.

Another example of truth to convey falsehood occurs in automobile advertising when the manufacturer advertises the fact that a car or pickup can go farther on a tank of gas than its competitor can go. The cruising range is higher because the gas tank is bigger, not because the car gets better mileage. The oil industry is not immune to this type of advertising either. Back when oil companies aggressively tried to lure customers from a competitor's brand to their own, Shell Oil Company made a television commercial in which two cars with identical amounts of gasoline drove around an auto race track. They erected a paper barrier on the track to indicate where the first car ran out of gas and where the second car dramatically crashed through because it had fueled with Shell gasoline, which contained the high-mileage additive called platformate. What they didn't say was that almost all gasoline sold in the United States contained a similar additive. Shell told the truth but conveyed a false impression about its competitive advantage.

DECEPTIVE ADVERTISING: AN ATTEMPT TO MISLEAD THE CONSUMER

Truth to convey falsehood and all other forms of puffery have their faults, but none involve outright lying. Whereas puffery-style advertising tries to gently direct (or misdirect) the consumer's attention—to blur his or her vision a bit—**deceptive advertising** is a conscious attempt to deceive and mislead the consumer. In less serious cases, firms exceed the bounds of acceptable puffery and stray into an area in which, according to the FTC, the average consumer cannot separate fact from fiction. In more extreme cases, outright fraud may be involved if the firm tries to gyp the consumer. In cases of fraud, legal action involving fines or imprisonment may be imposed on the offender. Box 4-2 lists some of the commonly used phrases in deceptive advertising. In the sections that follow, we describe some of the more common forms of deception that involve these catch phrases: false claims, free goods, now or never, contests, and bait and switch.

False Claims. In the latter part of the nineteenth century it was common to see individuals peddling medicinal tonics that promised to cure ills from rheumatism and arthritis to cancer. With the founding of the Food and Drug Administration in 1906 and the Federal Trade Commission in 1914, such claims had to be substantiated. Quack remedies were gradually removed from the highways and byways of the American economy, but false claims have not entirely disappeared. A few years ago Chevron Oil Company showed a car with a plastic bag attached to its exhaust pipe to catch pollutants. Chevron contended that one of their new fuel additives, F-310, was responsible for the lower level of pollutants in the car's exhaust. As it turned out, however, the miracle additive did not produce fewer pollutants and Chevron was misleading the public by implying that it did. Geritol was another well-known name that indulged in false claims. For years Geritol was advertised as a cure for "iron deficiency anemia" or "tired blood." What the advertising didn't report was that almost no one in the United States suffered from the malady and, further, that it was not caused by a lack of iron in the diet. Geritol finally removed the ads after a decade of litigation with the FTC.

The Federal Trade Commission has been reprimanded by some consumer advocates for being too slow to act and too lenient when it does pursue false claims. Partly as a response to this charge, the FTC has demanded **corrective advertising** as part of the retribution for wrongdoing. Three cases of corrective advertising have involved Profile diet bread, Ocean Spray cranberry juice, and Listerine mouthwash. Profile claimed that its bread has fewer calories per slice, which is true, but the reason is that the slices are thinner. There is no difference in the caloric count of the loaf itself. Profile was required to advertise the discrepancy and thus inform consumers of its misleading claim. Ocean Spray advertised that its cran-

> **BOX 4-2**
>
> ## The Watchwords of Deceptive Advertising
>
> The Department of Justice of the State of California developed the following list of gimmicks that characterize deceptive advertising. If you hear these words, be careful—you may be cheated.
>
> 1. **"You have won a *free* gift."** You will usually end up paying more than the gift is worth.
> 2. **"I am *not a salesman*,"** or **"I'm the advertising manager."** No matter what he tells you, a person who tries to get money from you, or your name on a contract, is a salesman.
> 3. **"Only a *few people* are getting this *special deal*."** You can be sure that the company is selling to you at or above the regular price.
> 4. **"This is your last chance—I will not be in the neighborhood again."** Before you spend a lot of money on anything, think it over; compare prices elsewhere. Don't be rushed.
> 5. **"This low-priced advertised special is not for you—you want the expensive one."** If the salesman tells you that what he advertised is not good, he may be using the bait and switch technique. Walk away and have nothing more to do with him.
> 6. **"Not only do you get these books, but *you also get . . .*"** Be careful when a person sells you more than one thing. You may not want or need all of the items he is selling.
> 7. **"It will *only cost* you the price of *one package of cigarettes a day*."** One package of cigarettes a day on a three-year contract can be over $500.
> 8. **"This is a great item—it is *guaranteed for life*."** In most cases, if the company goes out of business, if you can't find the company, or if it is not reliable, your guarantee is worthless. If you read a guarantee carefully, you will often find that it is filled with things the company will *not* do rather than things the company *will* do.
> 9. **"I am in a contest—one more order and I will win."** Most of these sales pitches are phony. Do not buy from anyone unless you want what the person is selling and you want to pay the amount he is charging.

berry juice gives the consumer more energy than orange juice. What does this mean? It means that cranberry juice has more *calories,* a fact that the FTC made the company advertise correctively. The Listerine case was more blatant because for years the company had claimed that Listerine kills germs by the millions and prevents colds and flu. These claims are false, and a portion of the advertising had to be devoted to correcting a false image that still lingers in the minds of many consumers.

Free Goods. As you know, economists are fond of saying that there is no such thing as a free lunch. All goods and services must be paid for by someone. In the early 1900s you could go to the local bar at lunchtime, buy a beer, and get a sandwich "free." That was the proverbial free lunch, but of course the price of the beer covered the meal, too, so it really wasn't free. Today, some firms pretend to give the consumers certain goods or service "free" if they purchase their product. Strange as this may seem, some consumers still believe they are getting something for nothing.

The free-goods sales strategy is common among door-to-door salespeople, in late-night television ads, among county fair hucksters, and in record- or book-of-the-month clubs. You must have seen the record club ads that offer you ten records or tapes for $1.00. The only obligation is that you join the record club and agree to buy a certain number of monthly selections at the regular "low" prices. As with the free-lunch cost included in the price of the beer, the free-album or free-tape cost is included in the price of the "low" regular price of the additional records you must buy to fulfill the agreement. This pitch is not illegal. All of the conditions are advertised, but many consumers do not take the time to see them. The advertiser preys on the consumer's desire for a bargain, and it must work some of the time because "free goods" continue to be offered. This technique is often combined with the following high-pressure sales idea—it's now or never.

Now or Never: A Once-in-a-Lifetime Offer. Often used in conjunction with the "free goods" technique, the now-or-never offer generally tries to get the consumer to act on impulse, to forget the old adage "look before you leap," and to think only that "he who hesitates is lost." This kind of advertising is especially deceptive because it preys on people's fear of being bad consumers, of missing an opportunity to save money and stretch their budget. Door-to-door salespeople have been known to use this technique effectively to push a consumer from a "let me think it over" position to a "where do I sign" view. The situation can almost be stereotyped—the salesperson looks perplexed at the consumer's unwillingness to immediately sign up for a set of encyclopedias, a life insurance policy, or a new car. Then suddenly, an idea occurs to the salesperson, and he or she offers to lower the price or throw in some "free" goods, but only if the consumer agrees to buy *right away*. Of course, no reputable firm withdraws a legitimate offer to sell if you refuse to commit yourself on the spot. After all, the heart of the decision-making process is evaluation. It is often difficult to rationally evaluate your options while the salesperson is staring at you with a once-in-a-lifetime deal.

The now-or-never pressure is even more difficult to escape when the sales pitch is made in your own home. A consumer can walk out of an automobile showroom or a furniture store; it is often more difficult and intimidating to get a salesperson to leave your home. Recognizing this difficulty, the Federal Trade Commission has placed a three-day **cooling-off provision** on door-to-door sales of $25 or more. If you sign an installment contract after talking with a door-to-door salesperson, you have three business days to change your mind and void the contract. You can cancel the contract either by sending a written notice to the seller within three days or by completing and returning the form that the salesperson is legally bound to give you at the time of purchase. Notice, however, that this law applies only when you are to repay the debt in installments, that is, when credit is

Door-to-door salesmen have perfected techniques for getting consumers to commit themselves to major purchases.

involved. Door-to-door sales such as Avon and Amway, in which the consumer orders and pays on delivery, are not included.

Contests: Everyone Is a Winner. Another scheme to gyp and defraud consumers is the contest in which everyone is a winner. The contest could be carried out by mail, by telephone, or sometimes in person. In some cases, you never even enter the contest—you are informed by mail or telephone that you have won a prize and all you need to do is come to the store and pick it up. In other schemes, you may be asked a series of questions that then result in your winning a "valuable gift," you may be asked to answer a survey that earns you a "valuable gift," or you may be asked to fill in a coupon with your name and address and later learn that you have won a "valuable gift." All of these roads lead to the same place—to a merchant's place of business—where you will be given the op-

> **BOX 4-3**
>
> ## Advocacy Advertising: Politics and Economics
>
> **Advocacy advertising** is advertising by a firm, an industry, or a group of individuals that seeks to change public opinion in their favor on a local or national issue. As political decisions become more important in the economy, the number of advocacy ads has grown. The recent attempt of the Savings and Loan Foundation to get people to support a tax break on savings accounts is a good example of advocacy advertising. In the first six months of 1981, the Foundation spent $4.5 million on ads that stated the industry's case for creating a tax exemption on interest from savings accounts. The magazine and newspaper ads included ballots that people could deposit at their local savings and loan associations or mail to the Foundation's Washington office. They had hoped to collect 1 million coupons to help convince Congress to enact the necessary legislation. By June they had received 5.2 million responses, and the House Ways and Means Committee, the committee that makes recommendations on such laws, was seriously considering such an exemption.
>
> As Michael Stevenson, president of the Savings and Loan Foundation said, "We feel that because we're the only ones who went public on this and for this, it's one in the win column for us" *(Wall Street Journal,* June 25, 1981, p. 27).
>
> 1. Most industries have national organizations almost all competitors join. Have you seen any advocacy ads from banks, homebuilders, real estate agencies, or insurance companies? What issues would the associations be interested in? Would they tend to agree or disagree?
> 2. On national issues, small firms need to unite under a national association to have an impact on public opinion. But large national corporations often take out advocacy ads on their own. Have you seen any ads in which an individual firm does this?
> 3. In local disputes, firms and unions will sometimes use an advocacy ad. Why?
> 4. Do advocacy ads ever use puffery techniques? Give some examples.

portunity to spend your money to buy something to go along with your prize. A common prize is a sitting at a photography studio and an 8″ x 10″ photograph. Once you go in, you discover that several poses are taken, and then a magnificent array of photos are available for you to purchase. If children are involved, especially grandchildren, it is often nearly impossible to walk away from the offer with your single "free" photograph. Photographers are not the only contest runners; dance studios, health clubs, stereo firms, sewing machine shops, solar firms, and cookware and meat companies have all been known to use these schemes.

Bait and Switch. **Bait and switch** is one of the oldest and most successful ways to defraud consumers. However, it is an illegal tactic that is punishable by fine or imprisonment under federal law. Like many other forms of deception, bait and switch involves the consumer's natural urge to get a bargain—to get something of value for a low price. The low-priced item is the "bait." It lures the "fish" (consumer) by its appealing low price and apparent high quality. Once the consumer has been attracted to the store, the sales staff tries to get him or her hooked on another, more expensive model. This is called "the switch." During the switch, the salesperson carefully and forcefully convinces the prospective buyer that the advertised bait is inadequate for his or her needs. Instead, the consumer should buy (switch to) a more expensive model. In a variation of this sales technique, the merchant is supposedly out of the advertised item but sells the consumer a much better model at a slightly higher price. Home appliances such as washers, dryers, vacuum cleaners, and sewing machines are the favorites of bait-and-switch artists because they are expensive enough to provide the salesperson with a commission on each sale, and they are complicated enough to make it difficult for the consumer to compare quality and performance of different models at the time of sale.

The best defense against bait and switch is a strong background in consumer education and a history of dealing with longstanding, reputable businesses. However, even a reputable firm can be found guilty of this technique. In the 1970s, Sears, Roebuck & Company was said to have practiced this time-honored technique in some of its stores. The original complaint alleged that a Sears ad offered a $58 sewing machine that could do buttonholes and zig-zag stitches, and could operate in reverse. But if a customer tried to buy the machine, a salesman said that the machine really could not perform as well as advertised and that it was noisy, lacked a standard guarantee, and required a lengthy wait for delivery. A more expensive model was then suggested—a classic example of bait and switch.

It is important to realize that not all merchants are on the wrong side of the law. Most are decent, law-abiding citizens who abhor the techniques described under the "false claims" section. We now explore the positive side of advertising to see how advertising may benefit the consumer and the economy.

The Benefits of Advertising

A few years ago when X-rated movies were the objects of some local district attorneys' scorn and filmmakers were periodically hauled into court for producing pornographic acts on celluloid and distributing them to the public as "art," the Supreme Court was asked to weigh the Constitutional guarantees of free speech versus the public's right to decency. The judges, after considerable discussion, research, and viewing of the films, handed down a doctrine that generally absolved the filmmakers of any wrongdoing as long as they could demonstrate that the films had some potential redeeming social value. In other words, was there anything in the film that provided some benefit to society? A similar question might be put to the advertising community.

Consumers are perpetually bombarded with ads that run the gamut from impugning our ability to select the correct after-shave to intimating that our temperaments and bodily functions can both be improved by using a laxative. Are there any socially redeeming qualities to advertising?

INFORMATION: MORE THAN YOU EVER WANTED TO KNOW

The initial defense of advertising has been made and will continue to be made on the basis of the consumer's need for information. In other words, advertising alerts consumers to the availability of a particular product. As one advertising executive put it, familiarizing the consumer with a product "is the absolutely basic value created in advertising, the one underlying all the others" (Commanor and Wilson, 1979, p. 472).

A more traditional view of the producer-consumer dichotomy argues that if someone were to build a better mousetrap, the world would beat a path to his or her door. We know that is not true in our economy today. A new consumer product has to have tremendous promotion and field study before it will ever be allowed on the store shelf, because an unwanted product could mean large losses for a firm.

Of course, this analysis should not lead you to conclude that massive advertising outlays and a skilled public relations campaign automatically result in a profitable product. On the contrary, the American marketplace is littered with new, improved brands that never made it or that were profitable for awhile and have since been discontinued. Ipana toothpaste, Billy Beer, Super Suds, Old Gold cigarettes, Studebaker automobiles, and Micrin mouthwash are just a few of the thousands that have disappeared from Consumer America despite heavy advertising. Advertising may be a necessary, but certainly not a sufficient, condition to ensure success among consumers.

Supporters of advertising as an informational medium are not terribly concerned with the FTC's categories. The advertising message may provide some useful information regarding product charac-

> **BOX 4-4**
>
> ## Advertising and Brand-Name Identification
>
> "I have a cut, Mommy. Can I have a Band-Aid?"
>
> This request is honored in millions of homes throughout America. Very few children, or adults for that matter, ask for "adhesive plastic bandage strips." This is an example of a marketing executive's dream—succeeding so completely that even the competition is willing to accept your brand's name as the ideal. There are a number of products that have so overwhelmed the competition that their trade name has become the accepted term for all products of that type. Many of us ask for a Kleenex when we mean a tissue, Jell-O when we want a gelatin dessert, or Vaseline when referring to petroleum jelly. Some product names actually become verbs, as in the phrase "Xerox it" rather than "photocopy it." This kind of success is not the result of advertising alone, but it is seldom achieved without advertising.

teristics and price, or it may simply call attention to the existence of the product, or it may even be entertaining. The point, as far as these supporters are concerned, is that you the consumer become aware of their product. If they make the product a household word, they consider their job successfully completed. See Box 4-4 for some examples of successful brand-name and item identification.

ADVERTISING AND COMPETITION: LOWER PRICES

Some studies have shown that advertising can at times result in greater competition among firms and can lower prices for consumers. This seems to be especially true when the public is dealing with a professional group whose services are fairly standardized but who for one reason or another have avoided advertising in the past. Physicians, pharmacists, lawyers, and dentists are included in these groups, but the original discovery of the correlation between advertising and *lower* prices was reported by Professor Lee Benham (1972) in his article "The Effect of Advertising on the Price of Eyeglasses." According to Benham, those states that prohibited opticians from advertising had significantly higher prices than those in areas where advertising was permitted. In fact, the average pair of glasses cost more than twice as much in the restrictive states.

Since Professor Benham's pioneering study, the FTC has conducted more studies to determine the effect of advertising on the cost and quality of eyeglasses and examinations provided by optometrists. The FTC reported that the average cost of an eye examination and glasses in cities with the fewest restrictions on advertising was $71.91 compared to $94.58 in the most restrictive cities. The FTC report concluded that:

1. The existence of advertising and commercial practice by some optometrists in a market does not result in a lowering of the quality of examinations available to consumers.
2. The existence of price advertising and commercial practice by some optometrists does result in lower prices. The prices of both less thorough and more thorough eye examinations and eyeglasses were significantly lower in the least restrictive cities than in the most restrictive cities (*Consumers' Research Magazine,* April 1981).

Given the results of its investigation on eye examinations, the FTC has fought to eliminate bans on most professional advertising. Professional associations such as the American Medical Association (AMA) and the American Bar Association (ABA) attempted to limit this avenue of competition because abuses might creep in. The possibility that a physician or a lawyer would appear in a television commercial to drum up new business was, to the AMA and the ABA, unprofessional at best and unprofitable at worst. Nevertheless, the ban on professional advertising has been overturned and as a result it is one area in which you can expect to receive more informational advertising in the near future.

BRAND NAMES AND QUALITY CONTROL

Poet Gertrude Stein wrote, "A rose is a rose is a rose." And Romeo said, "A rose by any other name

Highly advertised designer jeans may cost more, but consumers are willing to pay extra for the "prestige" and for the quality guaranteed by the manufacturers.

would smell as sweet." But many consumers simply do not believe this—and show it in their behavior. They continue to buy nationally advertised brands when similar lower-priced products are conveniently located on the adjoining shelf of the local supermarket. Despite its higher price, the heavily advertised brand of peaches or pudding often outsells its lesser-known counterpart by as much as ten to one. Is it collective brainwashing that prevents the consumer from buying the nonadvertised product, or is it something else? Advocates of brand names frequently argue that it is something else, namely, quality assurance.

If a firm spends millions of dollars on advertising its products, it is doing more than simply informing the consumer about a particular product. It is investing in a reputation. Multiproduct firms such as General Motors, General Electric, and Procter & Gamble are well aware that their advertising does more than sell cars or toasters or shampoo—it says something about their company. Once they put their brand on an item they are implicitly saying that their reputation stands behind it. Consumers are aware of the unwritten guarantee of brand names and are often willing to pay a premium price for the uniform quality and performance implied by large advertising budgets and well-known companies.

A large advertising investment must be safeguarded, and one way to do so is to produce a good product and then stand behind it. Nothing can be more damaging than a bad reputation or a company "trading on its name." Procter & Gamble's handling of the Rely tampon problem is a good example of how a large advertiser with a good reputation for quality deals with a potentially damaging situation. In 1980, reports of a new disease called toxic shock syndrome began to appear in the news media. This disease seemed to strike women who used tampons, especially Procter & Gamble's brand, Rely. Although the evidence linking toxic shock syndrome to Rely tampons was far from conclusive, Procter & Gamble elected to voluntarily remove them from the marketplace rather than run the risk of harming anyone and ruining their reputation. If Rely tampons had been produced by a small manufacturer, the chances are slim that they would have voluntarily been recalled. A smaller firm would have been bankrupted by such an incident, and it would have had a considerably smaller advertising investment in its reputation to protect.

The ability to discriminate among competitors on the basis of brand names is considered a luxury that socialistic countries often decide to avoid. However, even the Soviet Union is beginning to change in this regard. They have begun to require labeling of some consumer products so that the particular factory of origin is obvious. Their reasoning is similar to that of the supporters of brand-name advertising. Brand labeling is a defense against shoddy workmanship. Imagine one Russian saying to another, "I only buy vodka made by People's Factory Number 5. I know it's of good quality."

POSITIVE SIDE EFFECTS OF ADVERTISING

Sometimes an economic transaction has an unintended impact on third parties. Such **spillover effects,** sometimes called **externalities,** can be either positive or negative. In the case of advertising, one of the positive spillovers is the support it gives to the media: radio, television, newspapers, and magazines. None of these media could survive as we know them today without their advertising revenues. Advertisers, who provide over two-thirds of the gross revenues of newspapers and magazines, use the media to inform the public about their products. Indirectly, however, such expenditures allow the press to gather general news and to produce special stories that inform, entertain, and enlighten the public. Advertising is thus a classic example of a good that entails significant spillover benefits.

How to Obtain Information: Just the Facts

Given that advertising revenues support our newspeople, where can we as consumers get straight talk? One way is by reading some of the major consumer-oriented magazines in your library or by subscribing to them yourself. Two that accept no advertising and threaten to sue companies that use their names in promotional literature are *Consumer Reports* and *Consumers' Research Magazine*. Both were founded before World War II and produce an annual buyer's guide in addition to a monthly magazine. Consumer products are purchased and rated in competitive tests by experts. The ratings are then published, giving consumers objective data on the relative strengths and weaknesses of a particular good. These magazines are especially helpful for expensive items that consumers purchase infrequently—items such as clothes dryers, automobiles, and room air conditioners. But even here, you may find that you disagree with the "experts." For years, *Consumer Reports* rated the Volkswagen sedan an unsafe car that should not be purchased. However, millions were sold, not out of ignorance, but because the other features of the VW bug—mileage, performance, durability, and price—outweighed the safety factor. As with all information, only you can be the final judge. But at least with *Consumer Reports* or *Consumers' Research Magazine* you know that potential advertising revenue loss (or gain) is never a factor in the ratings.

There are other consumer-oriented periodicals such as *Money, Changing Times,* and *Consumer's Digest* that contain good consumer information. Periodicals such as *Better Homes and Gardens, Family Circle,* and *Sunset* that focus on family living frequently have articles on consumer topics such as energy, food, banking, appliances, and personal inflation strategies, among others. You might also look more closely at your local media for sources of consumer information. It is a rare local newspaper that does not contain at least one consumer column, and many local television and radio stations are hopping the consumer bandwagon by featuring syndicated consumer advocates.

There are many sources of consumer information that do not directly relate to advertising. Nationally oriented consumer magazines, buying guides, general periodicals, and local media are only a few. You may also rely on the experiences of friends, relatives, and even casual acquaintances to fill in some gaps in your knowledge about particular brands or products. It is a common practice to ask someone who has just bought a new appliance or a car, "How do you like it?" This natural inquiry is not simply idle curiosity; it is a request for information that can be used in a later decision.

Of course, as we stressed in step 2 of our decision-making model, options must always be conditioned by personal values and goals. If you ask someone's opinion and his or her values do not coincide with yours, the opinion should be weighted accordingly. In the Volkswagen example, one of the reasons that consumers continued to buy VW bugs despite their dismal ratings in *Consumer Reports* was that the values held by the rating experts were different from those held by the consumers. The experts clearly valued safety above all else. And crash tests showed that the lightweight, compact, rear-engine Volkswagen was no match for the heavier, full-size, front-engine V-8s produced in Detroit. But consumers by the millions were not as concerned with safety as with security, dependability, and economy—values that the magazine gave secondary consideration.

Similar examples can be drawn from conversations about most consumer items. A family that values convenience may be happy with a huge frost-free refrigerator-freezer because it stores large amounts of food and dispenses water and ice right through the door. Their neighbor will not be as satisfied with the same product if he or she does not value convenience as much. For example, a post-industrial-age consumer, to use terminology from Chapter 2, is more concerned with the impact such an appliance has on energy use, and he or she might be happier with a smaller, less resource-intensive unit. In this case, the information received from the convenience-minded consumers would not lead to a wise decision by their post-industrial-age neighbors.

Aside from accounting for possible differences in value orientations, you must also consider the cost of seeking information in your decision-making process. As you know, the cost of anything equals the explicit monetary cost plus the implicit time costs. Sometimes you can get a tradeoff between these two kinds of costs when you consider information costs. For example, if you pay for a subscription to a consumer magazine, you save time by not having to go to the library to read it, but the dollar cost is, of course, higher. If you realize that getting information involves both explicit and implicit costs, you also know that it is possible to spend too much time or money obtaining information about a purchase. In general, the information costs you are willing to incur should be directly proportional to the amount of income you spend on the item. In other words, you should be more willing to spend time and money on gathering information about getting a place to live than you do on buying a pair of pants because the impact on your budget of a bad choice in homes is more devastating than the impact of buying the wrong apparel. As our cost-benefit rule suggested, limited resources should be spent on the highest-benefit items first. It is interesting to note here that most consumer magazines have the same opinion about how much space to devote to various consumer items. They spend more time on big-ticket items such as cars, stereos, and refrigerators than they do on toothbrushes or clothing.

Goods and services that you purchase frequently, such as gasoline, food, and clothing, have fairly low information costs if you pay attention to the feedback you get after consuming them. For such repeat-purchase items, there is little need to spend much time or money on obtaining information for the early steps of the decision-making framework. The key to good decision making with these items is in step 6—review and evaluation. This is where you allow your experience to provide information. For example, suppose you plan to purchase a cake mix. Perhaps you normally purchase a certain brand, but you see that the store has a sale on a competitor that you never tried before. The overall cost of either mix is small, but the sale difference amounts to perhaps 10 percent of the price. Because this is a repeat-purchase item that takes a small proportion of your budget, it does not justify a lengthy information search about the merits of the less-expensive brand. A quick cost-benefit analysis will probably lead you to choose the sale item because it is cheaper. Once you have tried it, you should mentally review and evaluate it in step 6 of our model. If it is as good as your old brand, you have widened your choices by obtaining some experience-based information at little cost. If you judge it to be inferior to your old brand, you still have more information, and you can buy it again if you want to bake a cake for someone with less finicky tastes.

Summary

The consumer's search for information is an integral part of the decision-making process. The advertising industry has grown, at least partly, because it is able to fill this need. Firms spend over $55 billion each year to advertise and inform consumers about their products. And, as you saw in this chapter, some of the information provided is of real service to consumers who need input before making a decision. Advertising has benefits other than simply providing information. Ads promote competition and thus lower retail prices. They create an image of product quality that firms are so loathe to lose that they act in responsible ways by removing potentially harmful products long before they are required to do so. And advertising revenues subsidize much of the news and entertainment media. On the other hand, advertising can also manipulate consumers or even mislead and deceive them. Such advertising can be an unproductive but harmless expenditure, or it can be fraudulent activity punishable by fine or imprisonment. Fraudulent advertising, puffery, and deception are the objects of much criticism by those who see advertising's major goal to be informational.

Advertising is not the only form of product information. Consumer demand for information is large enough to have stimulated a number of groups to supply it. Magazines, newspapers, and radio and television media furnish the consumer with information on a regular basis. Of course, this information network extends beyond the media—to friends, family members, and acquaintances. But the search for information also has a significant opportunity cost and should not be extended to the point where the cost is greater than the benefit.

The Bilderback family rushed in to take advantage of the bargain price (three knives plus the bonus for $20). After a few weeks, however, the blades dulled and tarnished, the handle came off the paring knife when it was cleaned in the dishwasher, and the juicer could never be made to produce a glassful of orange juice.

1. What forms of false advertising did the knife salesman use?
2. What kinds of logical or emotional techniques did he use?
3. Was puffery involved?
4. What recourse do the consumers of the knife have? Will the various forms of recourse produce results?
5. Have you ever had a similar experience?

KEY TERMS

advocacy advertising
bait and switch
comparative advertising
cooling-off provision
corrective advertising
deceptive advertising
emotional advertisement
informative advertisment
institutional advertisement
puffery
retailers
spillover effects (externalities)
stereotyping
testimonial advertisement
truth to convey falsehood
wholesalers

QUESTIONS

1. Trace the growth in advertising revenues in the United States from 1880 to 1980. How do you explain advertising's early growth, its decline in the 1930s, and its subsequent boom?
2. List and then briefly explain three ways that advertising can benefit consumers. Give some real-world examples.
3. Which advertising medium gets the greatest share of the advertising dollar?
4. What are the three major categories of advertising as developed by the Federal Trade Commission? Classify the following ads by the FTC category you think they fall into:
   a. Grocery store ads for weekly shopping.
   b. A ridiculously low advertised price for a new color television.
   c. A famous baseball player's television ad extolling the virtues of a new yogurt.
   d. An ad for a brand of muffin in which the mother is criticized for buying a cheaper substitute.
   e. A television commercial in which several headache remedies are shown side by side, but only one has more pain reliever.
5. If you agree to buy a set of encyclopedias from a door-to-door salesperson, how long is the cooling-off period during which you can cancel the sale? How would you exercise this right?
6. Explain the bait-and-switch advertising technique. How can you recognize it? What would you do if a person tried to use it with you?
7. Is there any reason to assume that name brands are of better quality than unadvertised brands? Explain.
8. Rate the following in order of the time you would be willing to spend on seeking information about them (first, the item you are most willing to spend time researching): automobile, toothpaste, aspirin, denim jeans, blender, ball point pen, physician, potatoes.
   a. Why did you choose to rank them in a specific order? Did the price of the good play a role?
   b. Beside each item, list where you would seek information. Was advertising one of your sources? Why or why not?
   c. Would you really spend much time in selecting these items or would you just shop out of habit or by brand name? Which items fall into this category and why?

PROJECTS

1. Select three advertisements for similar goods or services. If ads are from magazines, newspapers, and so forth, include the original or a photocopy in your paper. If you select ads from television or radio, include a brief description of the ad with your paper. Give the following analysis for each of the advertisements:
   a. What is the ad trying to sell?
   b. Which FTC category does the ad fit under most appropriately?
   c. Who placed the ad? Who is the ad aimed at (audience)?
   d. What response is the ad seeking from the audience? Does the ad affect your emotions?
   e. What kinds of information are provided for the consumer? Of what value is the ad to the consumer? Is the information credible?
   f. Does the ad appear deceptive in any way? Does it use puffery?
   g. Does the ad promote stereotypes? Explain.
   h. What is your overall reaction to the ad? Would you buy the product?
   i. Of the three advertisements, which do you prefer? Why?
2. Select two categories of consumer goods and gather information on them from *Consumer Reports, Consumers' Research, Changing Times,* and *Moneysworth.* Compare these evaluations. How do they differ? Next, find some advertisements of specific brand names and see how they differ from the "objective" evaluations of the consumer-oriented magazines.
3. Look in your local newspaper for a likely bait-and-switch advertisement. Pose as a shopper and go to the merchant with this in mind. Give a brief report on your experience.
4. Have you ever been gypped or defrauded by advertising techniques? One way to obtain such an experience is to tour the sales booths at your county fair. A fine report could be made on such a trip.
5. Write to the manufacturers of a product and ask them to substantiate their claims. For example, if the advertisement alludes to a "clinical study," get the details of when, where, why, how, and who. Firms' addresses are available from the product package or at the local library. Evaluate the reply. Do the data really support the claims?

REFERENCES AND READINGS

Adler, Richard P. *The Effects of Television Advertising on Children.* Lexington, Mass.: D. C. Heath, 1980.

"Advocacy Advertising." *Wall Street Journal,* June 25, 1981.

Atwan, Robert, et al. *Edsels, Luckies & Frigidaires.* New York: Dell, 1979.

Benham, Lee. "The Effect of Advertising on the Price of Eyeglasses." *Journal of Law and Economics,* October 1972.

Brozen, Yale, editor. *Advertising and Society.* New York: New York University Press, 1974.

Commanor, William S., and Wilson, Thomas A. "Advertising and Competition: A Survey." *Journal of Economic Literature,* June 1979.

Federal Trade Commission. *Hearings on Advertising.* Washington, D.C.: U.S. Government Printing Office, 1971.

"How Advertising Affects Price and Quality." *Consumers' Research,* April 1981.

Leffler, Keith B. "Persuasion or Information: The Economics of Prescription Drug Advertising." *Journal of Law and Economics,* April 1981.

Packard, Vance. *The Hidden Persuaders.* New York: David McKay, 1957.

Palda, Kristian. *The Measurement of Cumulative Advertising Effects.* Englewood Cliffs, N.J.: Prentice-Hall, 1964.

Preston, Ivan. *The Great American Blow-Up.* Madison: University of Wisconsin Press, 1975.

Rostow, Walt. *The Stages of Economic Growth: A Non-Communist Manifesto.* Cambridge: Cambridge University Press, 1960.

Scherer, F. M. *Industrial Market Structure and Economic Performance.* Chicago: Rand McNally, 1970.

Skinner, Stanley. *The Advertisement Book.* Evanston Ill.: McDougall, Littell, 1976.

Telser, L. G. "Advertising and Cigarettes." *Journal of Political Economy,* October 1962.

Ward, Scott. *Effects of Television Advertising on Children.* Cambridge, Mass.: Marketing Service Institute, 1971.

Weiss, Ann E. *The School on Madison Avenue.* New York: E. P. Dutton, 1980.

Did You Know That...

- consumer protection regulations date back to early Greek and Roman law?

- muckraking journalists are responsible for creating public awareness of the need for pure food and drug laws?

- before 1938 drugs were not tested for safety before marketing?

- most accidents with consumer products are caused by consumer error or recklessness rather than faulty product manufacture or design?

- the government pays travel expenses for some consumers who present testimony at public hearings?

- the Better Business Bureau is organized by business people to benefit business, not consumers?

- there is a Federal Information Center to help answer consumer questions or put you in touch with experts that can?

- since the advent of advertising by attorneys, the price of legal assistance has decreased?

5 Consumer Protection and Redress: Doing unto Others as They Do unto You

Caveat Emptor: An Outdated Concept
The Informed Consumer: An Ounce of Prevention
The Beginning of Protective Legislation
The Modern Consumer Protection Movement
The Costs and Benefits of Government Regulation
Types and Levels of Consumer Protection
Consumer Rights and Responsibilities
Enforcing Your Rights: A Practical Problem
Consumer Protection in the 1980s

Neighborhood CAPSULE
William Mahoney and the Need for Consumer Protection

(*Note:* This neighborhood capsule is based on an actual event.)

It was very late on a cold February night when William Mahoney left the movie theater. He had been there almost all day desperately seeking some escape from the grim realities of his world. But now, the projectors were still and he was on his way back to his wife, Betty, and their four children. Somewhere along the way he made a decision and went into a drugstore to make a purchase. As he left, he opened the package and began to eat rat poison. By 2:00 A.M. William had reached home and had told his wife. She called the police, who came and took him to the hospital. As the police carried him into the street, a letter dropped from his pocket. It had been sent to William by a Chicago firm that had sold him a used television—a television that broke the day after it was delivered. The letter threatened William with legal action if he did not pay for the set. The letter was dated Tuesday, and William had until Saturday, the day he died, to pay.

William's wages had been garnisheed before, although there were no judgments against him when he died. On that other occasion a stranger had come to the door and left a bedspread. "Just sign here, please," the good-natured delivery boy had said. "It's for your neighbor, and I need a receipt for my boss." Shortly thereafter William's pay was garnisheed for the $34 bedspread.

William Mahoney owed about $700 at the time of his death. Part of this was for an expensive religious medal he bought for his wife. It was later valued at fifty cents. Given these circumstances, the fear that more garnishments might anger his employer and cost him his job, and knowing that the reduction in his salary would mean great hardship to his family, William took the only escape route he could think of.

As we noted in Chapters 1 and 3, American lifestyles have changed dramatically in this century. The simple life of the eighteenth-century farm family has gone the way of the dodo bird. We eat prepackaged, preprocessed, roasted, toasted, freeze-dried, preservatives-added-for-freshness food. We drink low-calorie liquids containing nonnutritive sweeteners that, according to some studies, cause cancer. Our medicine chests are generally crammed with an assortment of over-the-counter and prescription drugs whose ingredients and their side effects test the understanding even of physicians. Our normal life routine so depends on energy that an oil shortage or an electrical blackout would give us problems ranging in severity from not being able to get to work to sleeping in a cold, unheated waterbed. And, of course, we pay for our wide range of consumer goods with a financial system so complex that it can only be managed by computer.

Given this exceedingly complex level of living, it is little wonder that consumers seek, need, and expect help. This chapter explores the help available to consumers. It begins with the historical progression of consumer legislation from primarily providing information to providing protection and safety. It shows the transition from consumers having total responsibility for their economic and physical well-being in the marketplace to the sharing of that responsibility by industry. This chapter also provides specific suggestions for seeking help with consumer complaints, including information about consumer rights and the responsibilities that accompany those rights. Included are procedures for complaint handling beginning at the local level, progressing to state and federal agencies, and concluding with small claims court.

The authors recognize that the vast majority of business people are reputable and want to provide the best possible goods and services. However, some unscrupulous business people do exist, and mistakes do happen. In that light, this chapter offers solutions to those situations.

Caveat Emptor: An Outdated Concept

People have been involved in the exchange of goods since prehistoric times. With the passing of centuries, buyers and sellers have become more skillful at exchanging goods. **Caveat emptor** is a Latin phrase that means ''let the buyer beware.'' It means that the buyer must be cautious and is responsible for not getting cheated. According to this doctrine, if you happen to buy something that breaks after a few uses or that turns out to be less than you expected, you should not expect any sympathy from the merchant or society. In the classic caveat emptor scenario, a visitor to New York (or Paris or Chicago) is approached by a street vendor selling $400 watches for $50. Obviously, these watches have been obtained illegally, but the prospective consumer is caught up in the idea of getting such a bargain. A few days later, the consumer finds out that the watch is a cheap imitation of a more expensive brand and is not even worth $10. Most of us would blame and want to punish the seller, but the buyer's greed is also at fault. The buyer who fails to beware has little recourse. There is simply no way to report the fraud without incriminating the buyer as well as the seller.

The caveat emptor doctrine resulted from increased specialization and technology compounded by a complex marketing system. As technology advanced and individuals became more mobile, the likelihood that purchased goods were produced by a stranger rather than a friend or a relative increased. In the nineteenth century the roots of our mass-marketing and distribution system began to develop as railroads were built, mail order chain stores were founded, and department stores opened in downtowns across the nation. According to anthropologist Marvin Harris (1981), the social relationship between producers and consumers is a major factor that determines whether a product is well made and safe. A man is not likely to chisel a blunt arrowhead for himself; neither is a woman likely to weave her own basket out of rotted straw. In contrast, when the product has been made by a stranger and sold by another stranger, as is typical in industrial societies, the buyer indeed must be wary. In this impersonal relationship, caution is often not enough.

The Informed Consumer: An Ounce of Prevention

Of course, it has never been good business to continually bilk the public, especially if there are competitors. Consumers will then *vote* for the competitors by buying *their* products. The decision to buy from one producer rather than from another, however, depends on knowledge of the existence of a better-quality or lower-priced good or service. In societies less complex than ours, sufficient information can be acquired through personal experi-

No matter what type of product a consumer is thinking of buying, he or she is usually confronted with an incredible array of brands and models to choose from.

ence with a product. Consider a society in which the diet is simply rice, fresh fruit, and occasional bits of chicken; in which food is cooked in an iron pot over an open fire; in which transportation is by foot or ox cart; in which clothes are simple flat fabrics wrapped around the body and houses are made of bamboo. Members of this society can easily judge the quality of the few consumer goods they purchase.

In contrast, the number of consumer goods in our society seems to approach infinity, and their complexity can be overwhelming. In our complex environment a cautious attitude is not adequate protection against consumer disappointment or fraud. Product information is essential to decide whether an item should be purchased and, if so, with what features and from whom.

Additionally, an ignorant or misinformed consumer is of concern to a legitimate business and to society as a whole. Ignorant consumers do not follow rational, logical rules of consumption. They fall prey to criminals who pretend to offer goods or services that are comparable with those available from reputable local businesses. Such fraud tarnishes the reputations of businesses in general and literally steals money from the honest firms. If money is spent on a cheap watch that breaks after one winding or a religious medal that turns out to be worthless, it cannot be spent for legitimate goods at reputable businesses. As a result, it is in the interest of consumers, businesses and governments alike to inform and protect consumers.

The Beginning of Protective Legislation

Societies have for a long time had to deal with the problem of short-weighting and adulterated food. The standardization of measures for ale, wine, and corn in England was set forth by King John in the Magna Carta (A.D. 1215). In an earlier era, Greek and Roman law specifically prohibited selling wine that had been diluted with water; offenses were punishable by death. Even in Colonial America, consumer protection was an issue. Records of the Massachusetts Bay Colony indicate that in 1630, Nicholas Knopf was sentenced to pay a fine or be whipped in the town square for selling "a water of no worth nor value" as a cure for scurvy (a vitamin C deficiency disease).

It is clear from this brief digression into history that government involvement in consumer protection is not just a twentieth-century phenomenon. In the next few sections we outline the early role that our federal government played in establishing weights and measures, and the beginnings of its more recent attempts to regulate food and drugs.

WEIGHTS AND MEASURES: INFORMATION

In its broadest form, consumer protection as a part of economic activity has been a governmental responsibility since the earliest days of our country. The Constitution of the United States gave Congress the power "To regulate Commerce with foreign Nations, and among the several States" and to "fix the Standard of Weights and Measures." Congress provides national **weights and measures standards** that are used today in buying and selling goods, in judging environmental quality, and in ensuring consumer and product safety. It provides consumers with product information necessary for comparison shopping and decision making.

Despite its power to do so, Congress has never enacted an all-inclusive weights-and-measures law but has chosen instead to occasionally pass laws that regulate specific products. The responsibility for comprehensive weights-and-measures legislation has instead rested with state governments, which are responsible for inspecting businesses and policing the laws.

As consumers, we often take weights and measures for granted. But in reality they are among the most important protections that consumers have, because they provide information as well as protection in the form of inspection and penalties for violations. If no one periodically inspected gasoline pumps, how long would it be before some stations altered the rate at which gasoline flows through the nozzle? How long before a liter bottle of cola contained less than a liter? Even with inspections it is estimated that consumers in the United States lose $6–$10 billion per year because of short-weights or counts, as the expense of hiring more inspectors to check more products more frequently is prohibitive.

Historically, weights and measures standards were initiated by the business community because producers were concerned about the marketing of short-weight goods. In the dairy industry, for example, one dairy was cited for selling milk by the gallon in a container that could not hold a gallon of liquid. A toothpick manufacturer put 400 toothpicks in boxes labeled 750. A butcher sold meat by the pound, but in his store a pound equaled only 14½ ounces. In all of these cases, not only were customers cheated but the firms' competitors were injured by unfair competition. Misinformed consumers, seeking to stretch their budgets, bought these "cheaper" products and the legitimate firms lost customers.

FOOD SAFETY: PROTECTION

Until the late nineteenth century, American consumer protection resulted incidentally from government intervention as it established standardized weights and measures. As 1900 approached, the dangers of consuming grew apace with urbanization and industrialization. When families left their farms and moved to the city, fewer and fewer people could raise their own food. As a consequence, a large wholesale and retail food industry blossomed. Development of refrigeration and the use of preservatives led for the first time to national food distribution. Names such as Armour, Heinz, and Swift grew to be household words. These companies were instrumental in supplying the urban consumer with the staples of life.

Unknown to the consumer, however, conditions in some food processing and packaging companies were dusty, dirty, and germ ridden. In the absence of standards, sick workers often handled food in a filthy environment. Worse yet, food products were not always what they seemed to be. For example, rancid butter was disguised by using flavorings or was extended by oleomargarine, wheat flour was mixed with flour from cheaper grains, and diseased swine and cattle were slaughtered and sold for human consumption. Much of this adulteration was not visible, so some producers represented the food as high quality but sold it for lower than market prices.

Not surprisingly, the earliest pressure for regulation came from farmers whose markets were invaded by these inferior products. In states where farming was a major industry, farmers caused the creation of state departments of agriculture. Food chemists in these departments organized the National Association of State Dairy and Food Departments and began lobbying for regulations against adulterated food and farm products. Many reformers, particularly Dr. Harvey W. Wiley (then chief chemist for the United States Department of Agriculture), added their voices to the call for a Pure Food and Drug Act.

The proposed regulations had little support until the publication of Upton Sinclair's *The Jungle* in 1906. The work was an exposé of the deplorable conditions in the Chicago meatpacking houses at the turn of the century. Sinclair described, for example, the problems that the meatpackers had with rats. The meatpackers solved the problem by placing poisoned bread around the plant to kill the rodents. That seemed fine except that the employees threw the dead rats and poisoned bread into the vats where sausage and salami were being made. Those same vats also contained a few employees who had accidentally fallen in! It was clear from Sinclair's study that the federal government needed to protect consumers' physical safety as well as their economic well-being.

The Jungle shocked the Congress and President Theodore Roosevelt into taking some action to specifically ensure the safety of consumers. Before this time, consumer protection had been a side effect of

> **BOX 5-1**
>
> **The Roots of Consumer Protection**
>
> We have reproduced below the first general prohibition in the United States against all forms of food adulteration. This Massachusetts law, passed in 1785, shows early concern for legislating consumer protection.
>
> **An Act against selling unwholesome Provisions.**
>
> *WHEREAS* some evilly disposed persons, from motives of avarice and filthy lucre, have been induced to sell diseased, corrupted, contagious or unwholesome provisions, to the great nuisance of public health and peace:
>
> Be it therefore enacted by the Senate and House of Representatives, in General Court assembled, and by the authority of the same, That if any person shall sell any such diseased, corrupted, contagious or unwholesome provisions, whether for meat or drink, knowing the same without making it known to the buyer, and being thereof convicted before the Justices of the General Sessions of the Peace, in the county where such offence shall be committed, or the Justices of the Supreme Judicial Court, he shall be punished by fine, imprisonment, standing in the pillory, and binding to the good behaviour, or one or more of these punishments, to be inflicted according to the degree and aggravation of the offence.
>
> [This act passed *March* 8, 1785.]
>
> SOURCE: "The U.S. Food and Drug Law: How It Came, How It Works," FDA 79-1054 (1979).

government regulations, rather than its main purpose. The resulting action was the Pure Food and Drug Act of 1906, which established the Pure Food and Drug Administration. The Meat Inspection Act was passed in the same year, to specifically rectify the problems described in *The Jungle*.

Public opinion played a strong role in the passage of these first two acts of consumer protection. Credit for public awareness goes to "muckraking" journalists of the time, whose major themes included the purity and safety of foods and drugs. Muckrakers worked for mass-market, inexpensive magazines that specialized in exposing fraud and corruption in business and politics. This early push for protective legislation should be viewed within a larger social, intellectual, and political development of the time—progressivism. In its broadest form, the progressive spirit was seen as a struggle of "the people" against special-interest groups.

In 1914, the Federal Trade Commission Act was passed and the Federal Trade Commission (FTC) was created. Although its prime function was to help maintain competition and prevent monopolies, it was also given responsibility for policing unfair or deceptive trade practices. In 1938, this latter function was interpreted and amended to include advertising.

Vigorous consumer protection activity died with the onset of World War I and the business orientation of the 1920s. In the interim, court cases had limited the powers of the FDA so much that by the 1930s it played only a minor role in consumer affairs. Once again, it took the publication of a book—in this case, two books—to inspire a major outcry against firms that marketed unsafe products. Arthur Kallet and F. J. Schlink's book *100,000,000 Guinea Pigs* (1932) pointed out that many goods came to the market untested and untried. If they were harmful, the public found out the hard way. Ruth de Forest Lamb's

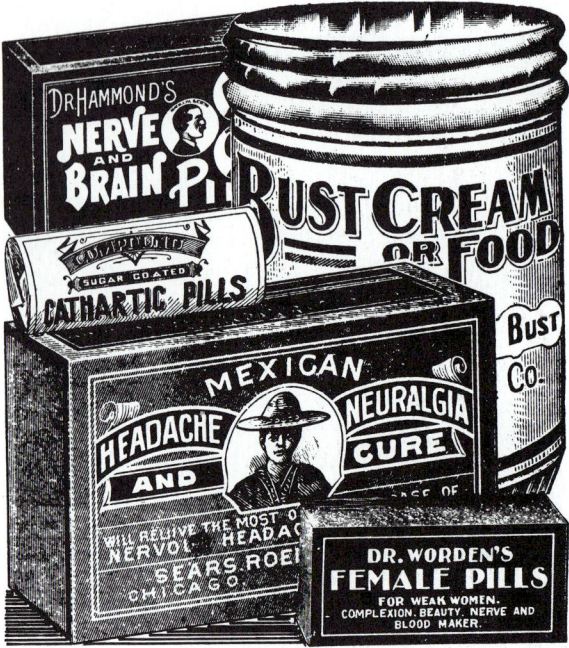

The proliferation of products claiming to treat and cure a wide variety of human ailments eventually led to the creation of a federal agency, the FDA, to regulate production and sale of such patent medicines.

American Chambre of Horrors (1936) described cases of horrible disfigurements, blindness, poisoning, and death caused by some unregulated drugs and cosmetics.

Corrective legislation was proposed and public hearings were held, but there were strong objections from the patent-drug industry. Business in general opposed the advertising regulations contained in the proposed bill. In 1938, a compromise was made, and the latter issue was resolved. A separate bill, the Wheeler-Lea amendment to the Federal Trade Act, assigned responsibility for regulating advertising to the more lenient Federal Trade Commission rather than to the FDA.

A tragedy was the final impetus necessary to force passage of a strengthened Pure Food and Drug law. A new liquid sulfa drug called Elixir Sulfanilamide came on the market in 1938. Sulfa drugs were called wonder drugs in those days because they cured so many serious diseases. This particular drug, however, had never been tested for safety, and over a hundred people died from using it. When it was learned that the 1906 law allowed the FDA to act only after the fact, a great deal of public pressure was generated.

Shortly after this tragedy the Food, Drug, and Cosmetic Act was passed, and on June 30, 1938 the modern Food and Drug Administration was created to enforce the law. The new law included regulation of cosmetics and medical devices, as well as food and drugs. Major provisions were that: new drugs be proven safe before marketing, the definition of food adulteration be expanded, and the FDA be given the power to prevent the sale of products found hazardous.

The Modern Consumer Protection Movement

Interest in consumer protection was a casualty of World War II. During the late 1940s through the 1950s, the only consistent voice of consumer interests was *Consumer Reports* (Nader, 1965), a magazine published by Consumers Union, a private nonprofit organization that is discussed later in this chapter.

INCREASING CONSUMER AWARENESS

In the 1960s, Americans began to develop a greater awareness and a willingness to question existing conditions and to make changes in all areas of their lives. From Rachel Carson's *The Silent Spring* (1962), which alerted us to the dangers of pesticides and other forms of environmental pollution, to Ralph Nader's investigation of the automobile industry, *Unsafe at Any Speed* (1965), consumers were awakened to specific threats to human health and safety.

The consumer movement found support from legislators as well as from ordinary citizens. As a result of hearings on the prescription drug industry held by Senator Estes Kefauver's Antitrust and Monopoly Subcommittee, Americans learned that they had narrowly missed another tragedy. Thalidomide, a drug that produced birth defects when taken by pregnant women, had been approved for mass marketing in the United States. Luckily, slow production and the persistence of a Food and Drug Administration employee kept thalidomide off the market in the United States until reports of children born without limbs surfaced in Europe and triggered a ban of the product in the United States. Public emotion created by the issue caused a demand for drug amendments to require more stringent testing. The amendments became law in 1962.

In the opinions of many consumer activists, the "breakthrough" issue that brought consumer protection permanently to the front page was auto safety. Between 1962 and 1964 Congress passed three auto safety bills as a result of Congressional hearings held between 1956 and 1964. Public attention focused again on this issue with the publication of *Unsafe at Any Speed,* resulting in demand for additional safety regulations.

These auto safety laws, coupled with the drug amendments, indicated a trend toward providing consumers with protection as well as information. Consumers need information for comparative shopping and prudent decision making. **Informative legislation** requires that businesses supply consumers with product specifics. In contrast, **protective legislation** forces producers to alter the features or quality of their product or in some cases to discontinue its production altogether. It is based on the principle that consumers are unable or unwilling to rationally choose a specific product. An example of informative legislation is the Federal Cigarette Labeling and Advertising Act of 1966. It requires this statement on cigarette packages and advertisements: "Warning: The Surgeon General Has Determined that Cigarette Smoking Is Dangerous to Your Health." Protective legislation might take the form of banning the sale of cigarettes.

PRESIDENTIAL SUPPORT FOR CONSUMERS

The successful passage of legislation often depends on the position taken on the issue by the President. The first presidential support for consumer issues came from President John F. Kennedy. In the first Consumer Bill of Rights to Congress in 1962, he outlined four consumer rights: (1) the right to safety, (2) the right to be informed, (3) the right to choose, and (4) the right to be heard. A significant result of Kennedy's speech and Lyndon Johnson's support for consumer issues was the creation of the office of Special Assistant to the President for Consumer Affairs in 1964. This position was created to expand and institutionalize consumers' "right to be heard." It was President Johnson who was first during this period to adopt a set of legislative consumer protection proposals and actively work toward their passage.

By 1965, consumer protection was high on public and government agendas. Spurred by the increasing availability of complex consumer goods, the introduction of bank credit cards, and the rise of computerized billing, Congress responded with consumer legislation. The most notable was the Consumer Credit Protection Act, commonly called the Truth-in-Lending Act, which requires full disclosure to consumers of all interest costs and terms when borrowing. At a time when involvement in the Vietnam War was being questioned and the poverty and civil rights issues were becoming subject to tension, support of consumer protection was good politics. Furthermore, the costs of consumer protection were extremely low for government compared to the costs of other legislation of the period, such as pollution control or social programs such as Medicare and low-cost housing. As a result, this was a strong consumer period. More than twice as many federal consumer protection laws were passed between 1965 and 1980 than in the previous hundred years.

The 1970s saw the passage of the Equal Credit Opportunity Act and the Fair Credit Reporting Act (both discussed in Chapter 8), the expansion of food and textile labeling laws, and in 1973, the creation of the Consumer Product Safety Commission (CPSC). This federal agency has authority to set standards for a wide variety of products, and it has the power to ban any consumer product outright if it feels it is hazardous to consumers. Also in the 1970s, the use of **recalls**—the power to eliminate hazardous products from the market—was used extensively by the CPSC as well as by the FDA, the FTC, and the Environmental Protection Agency (EPA), which is responsible for policing the Clean Air Act.

By the end of the decade, consumers had suffered through two energy crises and double-digit inflation, and soaring interest rates showed many Americans for the first time what it is like to live with scarce resources. Consumers began to reevaluate their spending and to look critically at government spending as well. Inflation and a tax cut were major issues

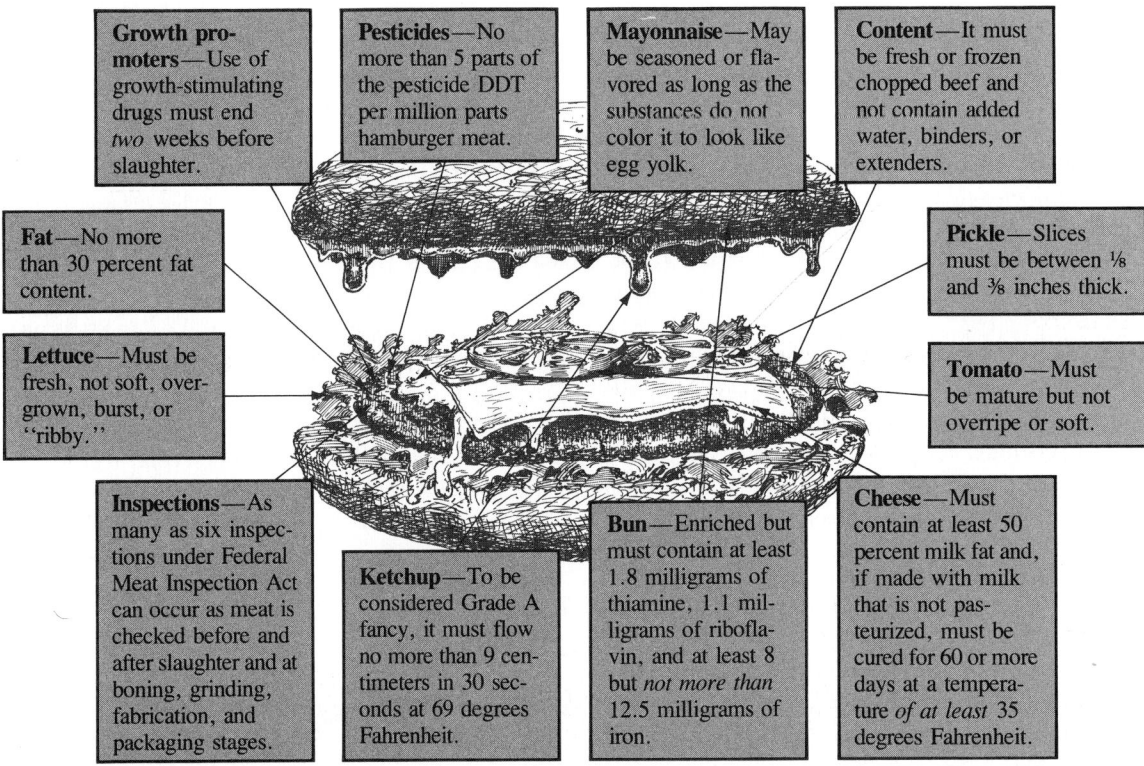

Figure 5-1. The hamburger. staple of the quick, inexpensive meal, is the subject of 41,000 federal and state regulations, many of those stemming from 200 laws and 111,000 precedent-setting court cases. Together, they add an estimated 8 to 11 cents per pound to the cost of hamburger. This illustration gives just a sampling of the rules and regulations governing the burger you buy at the corner sandwich stand.

Growth promoters—Use of growth-stimulating drugs must end *two* weeks before slaughter.

Pesticides—No more than 5 parts of the pesticide DDT per million parts hamburger meat.

Mayonnaise—May be seasoned or flavored as long as the substances do not color it to look like egg yolk.

Content—It must be fresh or frozen chopped beef and not contain added water, binders, or extenders.

Fat—No more than 30 percent fat content.

Pickle—Slices must be between ⅛ and ⅜ inches thick.

Lettuce—Must be fresh, not soft, overgrown, burst, or "ribby."

Tomato—Must be mature but not overripe or soft.

Inspections—As many as six inspections under Federal Meat Inspection Act can occur as meat is checked before and after slaughter and at boning, grinding, fabrication, and packaging stages.

Ketchup—To be considered Grade A fancy, it must flow no more than 9 centimeters in 30 seconds at 69 degrees Fahrenheit.

Bun—Enriched but must contain at least 1.8 milligrams of thiamine, 1.1 milligrams of riboflavin, and at least 8 but *not more than* 12.5 milligrams of iron.

Cheese—Must contain at least 50 percent milk fat and, if made with milk that is not pasteurized, must be cured for 60 or more days at a temperature *of at least* 35 degrees Fahrenheit.

SOURCE: From *Micro-economics* by Ralph T. Byrns and Gerald W. Stone. Copyright © 1982 Scott, Foresman and Company. Reprinted by permission.

in the political campaigns that elected President Ronald Reagan and fellow conservative legislators in 1980.

The Costs and Benefits of Government Regulation

We have described the tremendous increase in consumer information and protective legislation in the past twenty years. Not everyone, however, agrees that increased federal regulation and consumer information or protection are worth the benefits we get from them. Murray L. Weidenbaum (1980), the first chairman of President Reagan's Council of Economic Advisors, once estimated that if the *direct* and *indirect* costs of the fifty-five federal regulatory agencies that deal with consumer activities were to be totaled for one year, the bill would amount to $96 billion—$4.5 billion for government to actually run the agencies and $91.5 billion for private firms and individuals to comply with the regulations. According to Weidenbaum, the average house is $2,000 more expensive, the average hospital bill is $22 larger, and the price of hamburger is 7 cents higher per pound because of regulations (see Figure 5-1).

COSTS MAY OUTWEIGH BENEFITS

Consumers pay for government costs with tax dollars and for industry costs with purchasing dollars. Examples of business regulations that increase costs are housing insulation standards, detailed hospital billing procedures necessary for Medicare, and strict regulations on fat and water content of hamburger, which include labeling and record keeping. The general activities required by regulations include product development and testing to meet government standards, consumer and business surveys, public hearings, and enforcement. These regulations may prevent consumers, particularly those with low incomes, from purchasing some products because of their higher cost.

Besides increasing product costs, regulations often restrict product design. Automobiles underwent many design changes in the last decade to incorporate required safety and pollution-control standards. More recently, home appliance design has been affected by 1981 energy-efficiency standards to the point that new appliances may not look or perform as consumers expect them to (*Consumers' Research,* 1981). These standards are planned to become more stringent in 1986. For example, refrigerators may have increased insulation but proportionately smaller usable interior space. New automatic clothes washers will achieve energy efficiency by using less hot water in wash cycles and by eliminating warm-rinse cycles. Changes to increase efficiency in electric ranges, room air conditioners, and freezers will be forthcoming. The initial cost of these changes, which individual consumers may or may not want, will be passed on to those who purchase new appliances. The result may be that families choose to keep and repair older appliances or completely do without items. These standards represent an example of government regulations that have been criticized by industry and consumers in both substance and impact.

Economists such as Murray L. Weidenbaum and Rose and Milton Friedman worry about the lack of choice that regulation creates as well as the cost increases. The Friedmans, in their book *Free to Choose* (1980), attack federal regulation on this ground. Besides being forced to change current products, businesses must channel their resources away from product development in order to comply with regulations. Thus they have fewer resources and less flexibility to meet changing consumer needs and demands. The red tape and bureaucracy can slow down or totally discourage the introduction of new products.

For example, the Food and Drug Administration standards for new drugs are so strict that a company must do extensive testing before it can bring a drug to the market. When one drug firm wanted to put a skeletal-muscle relaxant on the market, the documentation for safety and effectiveness consisted of 456 volumes, weighed more than a ton, and would have stood higher than an eight-story building. Such red tape, these experts argue, has hindered innovations in the United States, whereas in other countries new drugs find their way to market much more quickly. At this moment, a major asthma remedy, an epilepsy drug, and a dozen heart drugs used in Europe are banned in the United States pending further testing. This extensive testing may cost some Americans suffering, pain, and perhaps even their lives. The issue is one of choice and economic freedom for businesses to offer products in a competitive market and for consumers to choose based on rational decision-making and product information.

The Friedmans, Weidenbaum, and others are even more critical of the more recent federal regulatory agencies such as the Consumer Product Safety Commission (CPSC) and the Occupational Safety and Health Administration (OSHA), which sets and enforces job safety and health standards for workers in private businesses. In his PBS film series, Milton Friedman showed CPSC personnel shooting cap pistols and registering decibel levels as one example of useless regulation. Others have mentioned the OSHA regulation that makes oval toilet seats illegal in the workplace (the horseshoe-shape seat is more sanitary) as another example of federal regulation that goes too far and costs too much relative to the costs and benefits received by the public. Critics believe that these are trivial matters that have a limited negative effect on a small number of people and show poor judgment and misplaced priorities on the part of CPSC and OSHA.

Finally, on the matter of product safety, we must note that accidents are most often caused by consumer errors or recklessness rather than inherent faulty product design. For example, mattresses are required to be flame retardant because people fall asleep while smoking in bed—not because the mattresses are inherently dangerous. "Zero-risk," or the total elimination of risk, cannot be achieved by product design or by government intervention. Consumers themselves must accept some responsibility for their own safety.

REGULATIONS PROVIDE SAFETY

In defense of existing regulatory bodies, consumer advocates remind us that consumer protection legislation reduces suffering and saves lives. The CPSC, for example, estimates that its actions save approximately 300 lives a year (Kirkland, 1981). Their regulations have practically eliminated crib deaths caused by strangling. The regulatory agency ruled that all cribs manufactured after 1975 must have bars closer together so that infants cannot put their heads through, get caught, and perhaps strangle. Before 1975, not one manufacturer had used the idea on a voluntary basis, partly because it costs more. Here is an example of an improved design that consumers may have wanted but that no producer felt confident enough to offer because it increases the consumer's cost.

The automobile industry also resisted safety change, claiming that safety features do not appreciably add to the salability of their cars and only increase prices. The government finally intervened to require model changes, not just for appearance, but to make cars safer during a collision. These changes included not only the addition of seatbelts but redesigned dashboard, bumpers, and seats.

COST-BENEFIT ANALYSIS

We have seen that some consumer legislation provides information that allows people to make rational point-of-purchase decisions. Other consumer legislation provides protection when consumers are unable to evaluate the quality of a product such as a prescription drug on their own. The result in most cases is economic saving and physical well-being and safety. The debate between those who see increased regulation as a terrible injustice and those who feel it is necessary will undoubtedly continue. In the final analysis, you and the political community as a whole will decide whether to increase, decrease, or maintain regulation at current levels.

An **economic impact statement** might be one way to judge the merits of a proposed agency or regulation.

Such a statement weighs the social costs of the agency or regulations against the expected social benefits. In the case of the baby crib regulation, *all* babies using cribs marketed before 1975 were in danger of death by strangulation. There seems little doubt that the saving of innocent lives far outweighs the costs. What parent wouldn't pay a few extra dollars for the elimination of this hazard? In the case of the OSHA regulation on oval toilet seats, the costs of collecting data, identifying hazards, setting standards, publicizing regulations, and prosecuting those who fail to comply do not seem worth the benefits of increased sanitation. When social costs exceed their benefits, there is **overregulation.**

As consumers we are required to ultimately bear the cost of governmentally mandated programs to clean the air and water, increase product safety, and provide us with product information. We pay with increased taxes, increased product costs, and often with decreased freedom of choice. A decision to support consumer information and protection should be made only after carefully comparing the costs to the benefits for society as a whole.

Types and Levels of Consumer Protection

As a result of legislation at the federal, state, and local levels, there are hundreds of agencies and thousands of regulations that give consumers information and protection when they make buying decisions. Of course, passing a law does not guarantee information or improved safety; it is only the first step in the process. Consumer advocates often cite three factors that result in consumer legislation that provides less protection than anticipated: inadequate enforcement, insufficient budget allotments, and a close relationship between regulators and business that is detrimental to

> **BOX 5-2**
>
> **A Wolf in Sheep's Clothing:
> The Uses and Abuses of Consumerism**
>
> Consumer economics in general and consumerism in particular are sometimes used to camouflage special-interest legislation. At the outset, let us disabuse you of the notion that consumerism generally means getting more laws passed to protect the defenseless consumer against the all-powerful, ruthless producer. In general, our economic system could not function unless there was a basic harmony of interest between consumers and producers. Nevertheless, there are times when the profit motive masquerades as consumerism.
>
> A specific example of false consumerism was cited in the film *The Incredible Bread Machine*. In the 1950s, two inexpensive brands of whiskey dominated the California market—Ten High produced by Hiram Walker Distillery and Four Roses made by Schenley. Schenley hired Arthur Samish, a well-known California lobbyist, to develop a scheme to knock out the competition from Hiram Walker. Samish discovered that there was one major difference between the two brands: Ten High was aged only three years before being bottled, whereas Four Roses was aged four years. Now you might expect an advertising campaign to alert consumers to the difference in the whiskeys' ages. No, that would have been expensive and possibly futile because the whiskey buyers cared more about price than quality. So what could Samish do?
>
> Samish had a "consumer protection" bill introduced into the California legislature to prohibit the sale of three-year-old whiskeys in the state. According to Samish, the consumers were being robbed by the producers of Ten High, who aged their whiskey for only three years and then charged almost as much as for four-year-old whiskeys (meaning Four Roses). The bill passed both houses, was vetoed by the governor, but then was passed over his veto by both houses. Ten High was knocked out of the competitive market and Four Roses became the best seller in California. It was a triumph for Samish and Schenley Corporation, but was consumerism served or slighted?

consumer interests. Enforcement procedures should clearly outline the consequences for noncompliance, whether a fine, withdrawal of a business license, or removal of the product from the market until the violation is corrected. Adequate money must be allotted for the inspection and prosecution of violators. Critics of consumer legislation point out that these ideal conditions do not usually exist.

The Geritol case mentioned in Chapter 4 is often cited by consumer advocates as an example of inadequate enforcement complicated by a "pro-business" attitude. In 1962, the FTC issued a complaint against the makers of Geritol, the J. B. Williams Company, for false advertising. The company made no changes in its advertising, so finally in 1965 the FTC issued a cease and desist order that formally required the Williams Company to change its ads. The order was challenged by Williams but affirmed by the U.S. Court of Appeals in 1967. In 1969, the FTC found that the Williams Company was still violating the law, but it did not ask the Justice Department to take action until the end of that year. It took the FTC over eight years to stop one business from advertising falsely.

Besides indicating inadequate and tardy enforcement of the law, critics of governmental agencies often point to the fact that agency regulators are often former employees of the industries they oversee. Certainly this increases their understanding of the industry, but could it result in a bias toward the manufacturer rather than the consumer? Consumer advocates think so and thus have often criticized this close association between regulator and industry. Their fear is that the regulator can too easily lose sight of his or her primary concern—the consumer's interest.

Since the Geritol case and the rise of the consumer movement in the 1960s, pressure has been applied to federal and state agencies to set priorities

108 Economic Decisions for Consumers

So many government agencies and bureaus are involved in consumer protection that dealing with them may be a frightening prospect to the individual consumer.

and to increase consumer participation in policy decision making. Consumers have also begun to recognize their responsibility to actively participate in their own protection by being informed, by choosing safe products, and by reporting hazardous ones to appropriate agencies by telephone, by letter, or in person at public hearings.

Public hearings regarding consumer and industry reactions to a proposed or current regulation are usually held in major cities across the nation. Participating in public hearings away from home can place a strain on a family budget. In order to encourage and facilitate consumer participation, a few federal agencies now provide reimbursement for expenses incurred when participating in agency and court proceedings. Potential recipients of these funds must usually show that they represent a group that would be substantially affected by the proceedings, would not otherwise be adequately represented, and could not be represented without financial assistance. A goal of consumer advocates today is to pass federal and state legislation to sustain and advance reimbursement and tax credit policies for individual consumers who participate in public hearings. The reasoning is that travel costs for lawyers, public relations personnel, and researchers for industry are passed on to consumers in the price of goods and services, that government specialists are paid for by taxes, but that consumers do not have such support or such representation.

In order to facilitate your problem solving and increase your feedback to consumer agencies, we will now identify channels of communication available to you at the federal, state, and local levels—commonly called the **public sector**—as well as in the **private** or **business sector.** You should be aware, however, that many government agencies can only act on behalf of large numbers of consumers and will not be able to force a company to replace a product or refund money to one individual—no matter how strong the case.

FEDERAL PROTECTION

At the federal level, forty agencies and 400 bureaus and subagencies are responsible for running almost 1,000 consumer programs. We will briefly identify seven major agencies here and include a description of each agency's responsibility. Appendix I contains a more complete list.

Federal Information Center. The FIC helps consumers find needed information or the right federal, state, or local agency to help with problems. They can be reached only by telephone, but they have toll-free phone numbers and are located in major cities throughout the United States. Check Appendix I for the number closest to you or order a free copy of ''Federal Information Centers,'' publication 637H, from Consumer Information Center, Department Z, Pueblo, Colorado 81009, for the complete national list.

Consumer Product Safety Commission. The CPSC protects consumers against unreasonable risks from consumer products used in and around the home, in schools, and in recreation areas, and it assists consumers in evaluating product safety. The CPSC develops uniform safety standards for consumer products, it promotes research, and it investigates product-related deaths, injuries, and illnesses. The CPSC has the authority to ban hazardous products, set mandatory safety standards, and seek court action to have products declared hazardous.

By law, a manufacturer that learns about a defect must notify CPSC. If necessary, CPSC may order a recall. Most recalls are voluntary, with manufacturers offering either repair, replacement, or refund. Occasionally, CPSC takes a manufacturer to court to obtain a recall.

It has authority to administer the Hazardous Substance Act, the Child Protection and Toy Safety Act, the Poison Packaging Act, the Flammable Fabrics Act, and the Refrigerator Safety Act.

CPSC has a toll-free hotline to take reports from consumers about product-safety hazards and to provide information on product recalls. The Commission provides sample copies of approximately 200 fact sheets and pamphlets on most products used in and around the home. These consumer information-education materials cover fire safety, electrical safety, poison prevention, toy safety, recreation equipment safety, power equipment safety, and household structure safety. Write to: Director, Office of Communications, Consumer Product Safety Commission, Washington, D.C. 20207. Call 800-638-8326, 800-492-8363 (in Maryland), or 800-638-8333 (in Puerto Rico, the Virgin Islands, Alaska, and Hawaii).

Environmental Protection Agency. The EPA is charged by Congress to protect the nation's land, air, and water systems. Under a mandate of national environmental laws, the EPA's programs focus on air, noise, radiation, water quality, drinking water, solid waste, hazardous waste, toxic substances, and pesticides. It establishes and monitors pollution requirements, tests automobiles for gas mileage performance, and publishes a booklet that lists EPA mileage figures. The EPA also conducts studies on the effectiveness of water purifiers and sets standards for home and farm use of pesticides.

Many of this agency's programs include Congressional mandates to develop and enforce regulations, to provide technical assistance, to provide information and grants, and to require public participation in its decision-making processes. The EPA is highly decentralized; its ten regional offices work closely with state agencies to implement environmental laws.

The EPA's goal is to achieve a compatible balance between human activities and the natural systems that support and nurture life. Write to: Consumer Complaints, Public Information Center (PM-215), Environmental Protection Agency, Washington, D.C. 20460. Call: 202-755-0707.

Food and Drug Administration. The FDA assures that all food, other than meat and poultry, food additives, and cosmetics are safe, pure and wholesome, and honestly and informatively packaged and labeled. It also assures that drugs and medical devices are properly labeled, safe, and effective for intended use. If these products do not meet FDA standards, they cannot be marketed in the United States. The FDA determines whether a drug should be a prescription drug, obtainable only with a doctor's order, or a drug sold over the counter, readily available in any quantity to anyone.

Unsanitary or mislabeled food, drugs, or cosmetics or injuries or adverse reactions caused by food, drugs, or cosmetics should be reported to the FDA, which will investigate and take corrective action as necessary. The FDA is particularly interested in seeing the container or the food, cosmetic, or drug that has caused the problem because the product can then be traced to its location of manufacture or packaging. Write to: Director, Consumer Affairs and Information, Food and Drug Administration, Department of Health and Welfare, 5600 Fishers Lane, Rockville, Md. 20856. Call: 301-443-3170.

Federal Trade Commission. The FTC is responsible for preventing the use of unfair, false, or deceptive advertisements of consumer products. This includes television, radio, and printed ads. This agency enforces laws related to the use of credit: the Truth-in-Lending Act, the Fair Credit Reporting Act, and the Fair Debt Collection Practices Act, which we will discuss in detail in Chapter 8. It administers the Magnuson-Moss Warranty Act, explained later in this chapter, plus the Textile Labeling Law and the Energy Efficiency Ratings (EER) for major household appliances, discussed in Chapters 9 and 11 respectively. Although the FTC does not investigate individual complaints, it can act when it receives a large number of specific advertising complaints involving substantial consumer harm. Write to: Office of the Secretary, Federal Trade Commission, Washington, D.C. 20580. Call: 202-523-3598.

National Highway Traffic Safety Administration. The NHTSA works to reduce highway deaths, injuries, and property losses by writing and enforcing Federal Motor Vehicle Safety Standards (FMVSS) for vehicles and vehicle equipment. NHTSA investigates reports of safety-related defects and substantial equipment failures, and it enforces laws requiring recall and remedy.

Recalls may be done voluntarily by a manufacturer when it discovers a safety problem through its own testing or from other sources. Recalls may also be ordered by NHTSA when a vehicle or its equipment has a safety-related defect, when the manufacturer fails to comply with FMVSS, and when the problem is common to a group of vehicles or items of equipment of the same make, model, and year.

Whether a recall is voluntary or ordered by NHTSA, the manufacturer must supply NHTSA with information on how the recall will be conducted and what actions will be taken. Manufacturers must also notify all owners by mail, and the defect must be corrected at no charge.

NHTSA establishes average fuel economy standards for manufacturers of passenger cars and light trucks. It does not have jurisdiction over actual gas mileage performance of individual vehicles. Write to: Administrator, National Highway Traffic Safety Administration, Department of Transportation, Washington, D.C. 20590. Call: 800-424-9393; 202-426-0123 (in Washington, D.C.).

U.S. Department of Agriculture. The USDA supervises the Food Safety and Quality Service (FSQS) Agency, which assures that meat and poultry—and products made from them—are safe, wholesome, and truthfully labeled. In packing, housing, and processing plants, the FSQS inspects meat and poultry products for sanitation, accurate labeling, and proper use

Recalls of vehicles may be ordered by the National Highway Traffic Safety Administration when potentially hazardous defects are found in a specific make or model.

of food additives. The FSQS also monitors meat and poultry to detect potentially hazardous residues above the levels set by the FDA. In the case of suspected food poisoning from meat or poultry, the FSQS recommends contacting a doctor or a local public health authority who will contact USDA's Meatborne Hazard Control Center.

The FSQS also provides voluntary grading services and develops grade standards for meat, poultry, eggs, dairy products, and fresh or processed fruits and vegetables. In addition, egg products are inspected for freshness and quality. The FSQS investigates individual complaints concerning the freshness and quality of egg products and the grading of dairy products, eggs, poultry, or meat. Write to: Meat and Poultry Inspection, Food Safety and Quality Service, Department of Agriculture, Washington, D.C. 20250. Call: 202-447-3473.

The Food and Nutrition Service (FNS) of the USDA administers programs that make food assistance, including food stamps and the National School Lunch and School Breakfast Programs, available to the needy.

USDA also serves as the national office for the U.S. Cooperative Extension System, a three-way partnership including the state land-grant universities, the Department of Agriculture, and the county government. Extension home economists provide information on new and useful ideas for homemaking and family living. Their educational programs focus on family-related concerns such as food and nutrition; housing; consumer education on use of money, credit, and other resources; development of healthy human and family relationships; and clothing for function, utility, and economy. Look under "County Government" for Extension System or write to: Department of Agriculture, Washington, D.C. 20250. Call: 202-447-4111.

STATE AND LOCAL PROTECTION

There is also a great deal of consumer protection at the state and local levels. State and local governments generally have the freedom to establish laws that are more stringent than federal laws. As a result, many state laws have served as models or pilot cases for national legislation. State and local governments are responsible for: setting standards for marketing behavior in the areas of advertising, labeling, and weights and measures; defining fraud; health and sanitation in public and institutional eating and medical facilities; and contract rights of both buyers and sellers. These laws can be enforced locally by city or county officials or by the state attorney general's office.

In addition, each state has a collection of commissions, boards, and departments that regulate the operation of specific professional or occupational services. Their purpose is to maintain standards by protecting the public from incompetence and fraud. These state boards either license or register professions and occupations such as those of doctors, nurses, accountants, attorneys, funeral directors, plumbers, and collection agents. To be licensed, a professional must have a certain amount of education and experience and must pass a test that measures qualifications. Registrants do not have a test to pass but are simply granted a legal right to do business under the laws and regulations that apply to their trade.

State boards set licensing standards; set rules and regulations; prepare and conduct examinations; issue, deny, or revoke licenses; bring disciplinary actions; and handle consumer complaints. Let us say that you have a complaint against an accountant. First, you would check your local phone book under state government offices or professional listings in order to contact the licensing board. After hearing your complaint, the board would conduct an investigation. If necessary, the board would take disciplinary action against the licensee in the form of probation, license suspension, or license revocation. Many boards also have consumer education materials to help you to select a professional or a tradesperson.

In addition to licensing and registering boards, there are state and local consumer affairs offices to provide further assistance. Local consumer offices can be particularly helpful because they can be easily contacted by phone or in person. These offices will either help you with a problem directly or refer you to the proper agency for assistance.

PRIVATE-SECTOR ACTIVITY

Private industry has played an important role in consumer protection in the past fifty years. Some organizations in the private sector, or business world, are primarily interested in consumers. These organizations may offer information, assistance with complaints, or actual protection from faulty products.

Better Business Bureau. Perhaps the best-known nongovernment organization related to consumer problems is the Better Business Bureau (BBB). Originally organized in New York in 1911 to combat "badvertising" and business dishonesty, this group has branches in most major cities. The bureaus are organized locally, are totally sponsored by private businesses, and collect membership dues; therefore, they must be careful not to antagonize members lest they withdraw their support. The BBB has no policing authority and depends on voluntary compliance and peer pressure from other businesses. Thus, it is not always effective, particularly in communities in which membership is small.

In response to consumerism, the BBB has increased its arbitration program (a panel of business and consumer representatives who hear both sides of the problem and recommend a solution) to include the areas of auto repair, dry cleaning, home improvement, television repair, and household appliances. Arbitration is a way for people to settle a dispute by having an impartial person or board decide the outcome of the dispute. In arbitration, parties are bound by the decision, and it can be enforced by the courts. Do not enter arbitration lightly, because you must follow the decision that is made. You will find the BBB in the white pages of your phone directory.

Seals and Ratings. Consumers are increasingly concerned about how well the products they buy work. In some cases, the presence of a seal indicates that the product has met certain standards of performance. Perhaps best known is the UL seal, which stands for a nonprofit testing organization, Underwriters' Laboratories. This seal applies only to the electrical parts of the appliance to which it is attached, usually the cord. For gas appliances such as ranges, clothes dryers, and outdoor grills, the Blue Star indicates that the product has met defined standards for safety, durability, and performance.

The National Association of Furniture Manufacturers Seal of Integrity may be attached to any manufacturer's furniture that meets the minimum warranty. This furniture is supposed to be free from defects in workmanship, material, and construction for a reasonable period of time, but not less than twelve months from the date of delivery to the customer. Other types of seals (see Figure 5-2) exist for a variety of electrical or gas, steel or aluminum products. They indicate that a product meets the industry standards.

The newest rating, EER, available on eight major household appliances, including air conditioners and refrigerators, stands for Energy Efficiency Rating. It is useful in evaluating the cost of using major appliances. Details of the EER are discussed in Chapter 11.

Another seal that indicates the level of confidence that a third party has in a product is the so-called seal of approval. *Good Housekeeping* magazine and *Parents* magazine have both issued seals for approved products. Many consumer educators are skeptical of these seals for several reasons. First, the only products that qualify for such seals are those that advertise in the magazines. This generally means that a company buys a minimum of two-thirds of a page of advertising per year at an approximate cost of $20,000. Second, the standards for testing the product are seldom revealed. Third, there is a basic conflict of interest because the higher the standards for testing, the smaller the number of potential advertisers, which lowers the potential gross income. Finally, neither magazine will disclose the number of cases in which replacements or refunds are made to consumers, in effect refusing to be accountable for their guarantees of quality.

Warranties. The private sector has another device—a **warranty**—to reassure consumers regarding the future performance of products. A warranty, in simple terms, is a guarantee that a product is in working order and that it will give good service for a reasonable period of time. Most of us are familiar with statements such as "money back guaranty" or "lifetime guaranty." These statements are virtually worthless. Whose lifetime do they mean? The product's? The consumer's? Is the guarantee transferable if you sell the product?

The Magnuson-Moss Warranty Act of 1975 was established to eliminate such confusion. It provides comparison-shopping information by setting regulations for warranty provisions, and it leaves the decision to offer or not to offer a written warranty to the manufacturer. It does require that any product that costs $15 or more and that offers a written warranty must provide the following information:

1. Name and address of warrantor.
2. What is covered and for how much.
3. Procedure for placing a claim.
4. Procedure for settling disputes over the claim.
5. Warranty duration.

This act also prevents manufacturers from requiring that the buyer of the product use it in conjunction with a specific brand-name product or service. For example, the maker of a washing machine cannot require you to use only Tide detergent for the warranty to be effective.

Consumer Protection and Redress: Doing unto Others as They Do unto You   113

Figure 5.2 What is in a seal? Many different companies manufacture the same appliance, equipment, or merchandise you buy. It is often difficult to make a wise decision as to which brand you want to purchase. One way to decide is to see if the product has a seal. This seal means the product meets specified standards, regardless of its cost, that are important to you, the buyer, but that you cannot easily measure or verify yourself. The seal should be one of the criteria you use to decide which product to buy.

The seal	What it means	Where to find it
Air-Conditioning and Refrigeration Institute "Sound Certification" Seal	Equipment has been sound rated according to stringent industry-wide standards.	Found on outdoor condenser units of "split" cooling systems and on "single package" systems.
American Gas Association Certification Seal	Products have been tested by A.G.A. and conform to standards of the U.S.A. Standards Institute. They are factory inspected at least once a year to insure continued conformity.	Found on gas appliances and/or accessories such as clothes dryers and ranges.
American Institute of Laundering Certification Seal	Products have passed original and periodic A.I.L. tests for color and sunfastness, shrinkage, fiber strength, launderability of zippers, buttons and snaps, appearance after laundering and other tests related to product performance during or after laundering.	Found on labels attached to ready-made merchandise such as bedding, clothing, and draperies.
Architectural Aluminum Manufacturers Association Certification Seal	Products have passed tests for such factors as air infiltration, windload, strength of members, and water resistance.	Found on prime windows, sliding glass doors, and aluminum combination storm windows and doors.
Association of Home Appliance Manufacturers Certification Seal	Name plate capacity ratings on products have been tested according to nationally recognized standards.	Found on portable electric heaters, room air conditioners, humidifiers, dehumidifiers, refrigerators, freezers, and home laundry appliances.
Better Light Better Sight Bureau "Seal of Approval"	Lamps have met a set of conditions including the "Lighting Performance Recommendations for Portable Study Lamps" of the Illuminating Engineering Society, standards of mechanical and electrical safety.	Found on study lamps.
"Steelmark" Seal	Products are made of steel and have the qualities of steel.	Found on anything made of steel such as washers, dryers, manicure scissors, mobile homes.
Underwriters' Laboratories Inc. Certification Seal	Products have passed original and laboratory tests and periodic examination according to U.L. standards for safety.	Found on all equipment, appliances, and materials that could be fire, electric, or accident hazards or used to stop the spread of fire.

SOURCE: "What's in a Seal?" *What's New in Home Economics*, September 1974, p. 87.

There are two types of written or **expressed warranties:** full warranties and limited warranties. The difference between the two lies in consumers' rights regarding repairs or replacement.

Under a **full warranty,** the warrantor must fix the product within a reasonable time without any charge. In fact, the warrantor must pay for incidental expenses (food, lodging, rental fees) caused by unreasonable delays. Let us say that you buy a heating system that does not function properly, despite many repairs. If you needed to move to a hotel because of extreme cold weather while the heater is being repaired, the cost of your lodging may be covered by the warranty. (Refer to Chapter 12 for a discussion of automobile warranties.)

The Magnuson-Moss Act gives the FTC the power to limit the number of unsuccessful repair attempts possible under a full warranty. If repeated attempts at repair are futile, consumers can choose between replacement or refund. Replacement must be free. If the consumer opts for a refund, the warrantor can deduct a sum for depreciation, that is, the warrantor can subtract a reasonable amount of money based on the actual use of the product.

All rights given to consumers by full warranties can be transferred to the new owner if the product is sold during the warranty period.

If a warranty does not include free repair or replacement and compensation for inconvenience, it is a **limited warranty.** This limited status must be explicitly stated, along with all other conditions or exceptions. For example, if the motor on a power lawnmower burns out within one month of purchase, a limited warranty might indicate that the consumer pay for the labor to repair it but that the parts be replaced free.

So far we have discussed expressed warranties—those guarantees explained on product labels, in instruction booklets, or in advertisements. Products also carry **implied warranties.** This means that the manufacturer implicitly states that the product is usable and will not fall apart or break down under normal use. This implied protection can often last beyond the limited-warranty period. Twenty-five states have some explicit provisions for implied warranty protection. Every state except Louisiana has adopted Section 2-719 of the Uniform Commercial Code, which states, "where circumstances cause an exclusive or limited remedy (warranty) to fail of its essential purpose, remedy may be had as provided in this Act." For example, let us say that you buy a raft that does not have a warranty. When you take it home and pump it with air, it does not stay inflated. The implied warranty protects you and guarantees replacement or refund.

The Uniform Commercial Code, which governs sales of items in the United States, includes two categories of implied warranties: one of merchantability and the other of fitness. An *implied warranty of merchantability* arises every time a merchant sells a good that he or she specializes in. Retailers of waterbeds give an implied warranty of merchantability whenever they sell a waterbed, but an individual who sells a waterbed through an advertisement in the newspaper does not.

Products that are merchantable are "fit for the ordinary purpose for which such goods are used." They must do what they are created to do. Examples of nonmerchantable goods include inflatable air mattresses that do not remain inflated, clothes dryers that do not get hot, flame-proof fabrics that burn, and electric lawnmowers that give a shock when turned on. The implied warranty of merchantability places absolute liability for product safety on the merchant.

There is also an *implied warranty of fitness* whenever a seller, merchant or nonmerchant, knows the particular purpose for which a buyer will use the product. This warranty of fitness takes effect when the seller knows that the buyer relied on the seller's skills or judgment to select suitable products. For example, let us say that you need a room air conditioner. You take the measurements of your kitchen or family room and purchase an air conditioner on the advice of the salesperson. When you get it home and install it, however, you find that it does not have the power to cool the room adequately. Under the implied warranty of fitness, the product is returnable.

A contract can include both a warranty for merchantability and a warranty for fitness. For example, a seller recommends a particular food blender knowing that a customer wishes to mix beverages, chop foods, and crush ice. The buyer, relying on the seller's

Items purchased at flea markets, garage sales, swap meets, and other such events rarely come with warranties; if a product proves defective or unsatisfactory, the buyer may not even be able to locate the seller, much less return or exchange the product.

judgment, purchases the blender and then finds that the blender mixes and chops but will not crush ice. The seller has met the warranty for merchantability but has breached the warranty of fitness for the buyer's particular purpose.

Consumers should study warranties and instructions carefully before choosing products, in order to avoid disappointment later. Obviously, full warranty provides more recourse than limited warranty, but limited warranties are far more common.

Recalls. Sometimes, product defects are not easily or immediately observable by consumers, even though the defect may pose a safety hazard. When such is the case, the product is recalled. No doubt you are or have been the owner of a recalled product. If you don't think so, it might interest you to know that in 1979 alone, the Consumer Product Safety Commission recalled 53 million products, including electric hair dryers that expelled asbestos and baby cribs that could strangle infants. In the same year, the National Highway Traffic Safety Administration reported recalls of 9 million cars, trucks, and motorcycles and 2 million items of vehicle equipment such as jacks and fuel filters (*Changing Times,* 1980).

If a recall becomes necessary, the CPSC issues a press release giving details of the hazard and including the number of people likely to be affected. The notice is then picked up at the discretion of media personnel and included in radio and television newscasts and in the newspaper. Companies that make the unsafe or defective products also have a responsibility to alert the public to the problem. They often create advertisements offering a refund or an exchange. In the case of automobile recalls, the NHTSA sends written notification to every owner. Despite these efforts, CPSC and NHTSA estimate that only half of the products are returned for repair of replacement.

Consumer Publications. Product information is essential for rational decision making. There are two private-sector organizations in the United States that publish objective product information. The largest of these nonprofit organizations is Consumers Union. It was chartered in 1936 in the state of New York, and it publishes *Consumer Reports.* Since the magazine's inception, it has included articles on the merits and relative costs of consumer goods ranging from toys to breakfast cereals to video cassette recorders. *Consumer Reports* contains no advertising, is available by subscription or on the newsstands, and includes advice on purchasing services such as legal assistance, home insulation, and medical care. Products featured for review are purchased by Consumers Union in the open market and tested in their own laboratory and research facility. CU is particularly known for annual testing of automobiles. At year's end, Consumers Union publishes a *Buying Guide,* with summaries of product test results.

Consumers' Research is published by Consumers' Research, Inc., founded in 1929. It contains general consumer information and advice, as well as product test results. *Consumers' Research* often borrows samples of large, expensive items from manufacturers for testing, and it requires a signed statement from the manufacturer that the items were selected at random. *Consumers' Research Annual Guide,* published in October, contains product test results and comparison shopping advice.

Consumer Rights and Responsibilities

Although consumers are quick to point out the shortcomings of the business world and complain loudly if their rights have been violated, they often ignore their own responsibilities. A supermarket chain in Los Angeles recently experimented with this issue. It purposely shortchanged twenty customers and gave twenty customers too much change. Can you predict which group reported the error more often? Most of the people who were shortchanged noticed the error, whereas only a few of those who received too much change "noticed." This example reminds us that consumers have the responsibility to see that they do not cheat merchants, just as the merchants have the responsibility to see that they do not cheat consumers. Without consumer responsibilities, consumer rights are worthless.

As we mentioned earlier in the chapter, President John F. Kennedy presented the first Consumer Bill of Rights to Congress in 1962. With these consumer rights come corresponding consumer responsibilities, as you can see in the following list. In the social relationship between buyer and seller, you, as the buyer, need to use the decision-making process. It is the fundamental tool for consuming and the ultimate antidote for caveat emptor.

1. The right to safety:
   a. Examine the safety features of merchandise before buying.
   b. Study warranties and labels.
   c. Read and follow care or use labels carefully and in detail.
   d. Use the merchandise with reasonable caution and care.
   e. Contact the appropriate seller, manufacturer, agency, or legislator if a product proves unsafe.
2. The right to be informed:
   a. Collect accurate information about goods and services.
   b. Study or evaluate product-performance claims carefully.
   c. Question retailers about products, and pursue answers if necessary.
   d. Expand your understanding of the American marketing system.
   e. Let the appropriate manufacturers, legislators, or policymakers know that you need specific information.
3. The right to choose:
   a. Understand consumer motivation and persuasive selling techniques.
   b. Expand your perception of alternatives.
   c. Apply the decision-making process to the selection of goods and services.
   d. Compare the cost of time, money, and other resources necessary to obtain a product.
   e. Assume personal responsibility for your choice.
4. The right to be heard:
   a. Assertively state your rights when you find dangers or poor quality of goods or services.
   b. Be familiar with consumer protection agencies and know how to get redress.
   c. Inform merchants about poor selling techniques or practices, and praise good ones.
   d. Actively support changes in laws and policies when necessary.
   e. Suggest improvements to manufacturers.

Enforcing Your Rights: A Practical Problem

Even with government and private regulation and personal acceptance of responsibilities, problems still arise for consumers. You may take the appropriate steps to avoid a problem, yet your car brakes may squeal, the picture on your television may roll, a toy may break on its first use, or your microwave oven may not work. Before you do anything else, find out whether the problem is a simple one. For example, check to see that the item is plugged into the wall socket or that it is turned on and properly adjusted. (A high percentage of "repairs" involve only these basics!) Check care labels, warranties, instruction books, and the like.

If these first-line remedies fail and you are sure that a problem exists, you have two choices: to be passive or to be active. The passive choice means that you choose to ignore the problem. In some cases, this may be defensible if you determine through the decision-making process that the costs of asserting your rights are greater than the benefits. Your costs

Consumer Protection and Redress: Doing unto Others as They Do unto You   117

Asserting your rights as a consumer may not be easy.

are time, money, and possibly some personal unpleasantness. Your benefits are a product that works and perhaps some personal satisfaction in receiving redress. You have to decide whether to be passive, but this text can lower the costs of pursuing the active solution because you will *know* what to do. You will spend less time on the problem, and you will be more efficient and, presumably, more successful.

If you decide to respond actively to the problem, what should you do next?

1. *Identify the problem*. Prepare yourself to clearly and concisely describe the problem to a stranger. When stating your complaint, be factual, specific, and as brief as possible. Do not be sarcastic or emotional.

2. *Explain what you expect the firm to do about it*. Do you want the product replaced or would you settle for a repair? Or do you want your money back?

3. *Support your request*. Supply proof of purchase and warranty, and include receipts, charge slips, canceled checks, service invoices, hang tags, and any other documents to support the accuracy of your request. Make copies of these documents to show to the business firm or manufacturer, but save the originals for your records. Keep in mind that some stores will not make adjustments or give cash refunds without a sales receipt.

To provide an example of this process, let us assume that you buy a waterbed that begins to leak. You should:

1. *Identify the problem:* "I recently purchased a waterbed, style H349. After one week of use, the water bag had sprung a leak."

2. *Explain what you expect:* "I have decided that I would like a different style—one that is stronger. I would like to exchange this waterbed for style H549 and apply the credit toward that purchase."

3. *Support your request with proof:* "I have the sales charge slip and the one-year warranty that promises repair or replacement."

Now that you have accomplished this, where do you go to complain?

THE LOCAL LEVEL: THE PLACE TO VOICE YOUR PROBLEM

Start the complaint procedure at the local level. Go back to or telephone the business or individual that sold the service or product and explain why you are displeased. More than likely, the problem will be solved right there. Occasionally, a salesperson may not have the authority to help you. Simply ask the clerk to tell you who does have the authority and talk with that person. Nearly every business of any size has a person or office set up to handle consumer complaints.

If you cannot get satisfaction by telephone or in person, your next step is to write to the merchant or dealer with whom you have the problem. This indicates that you are a serious complainer, and it provides a record for purposes of legal action if necessary

Figure 5-3 A Sample letter of complaint.

Your Address
Your city, state, ZIP
Date

Appropriate Person
Company Name
Street Address
City, State, ZIP

Dear Sir or Madam:

The purpose of this letter is to inform you of my dissatisfaction with (name the product with serial number or the service performed) that I purchased (state the date and location of the purchase).

My complaint concerns (state the reasons for your complaint). In order to solve the problem, I (state what you have already done). Because the problem still exists, I would like (state the specific action you desire for satisfaction).

I look forward to your reply and a resolution to my complaint, and I will allow two weeks before referring it to the appropriate consumer agency. Write to me at the above address or contact me by phone at (your home and office phone numbers).

Sincerely,

Your name

Enclosures: (Include copies, <u>not</u> originals, of all related records)

SOURCE: Adapted from "You Can Do A Lot—About Complaints," Department of Consumer Affairs, State of California.

---

later. A sample complaint letter is provided in Figure 5-3. Your letter should include:

1. Your name, address, and home and work phone numbers.
2. The name of the product with serial number or the unsatisfactory service that was performed.
3. The date and location of purchase.
4. The reason for the complaint.
5. What you have already done.
6. A request for action within a reasonable time.
7. Copies of all documents.

Keep a copy of this letter for your records.

THE MANUFACTURER

If for some reason you do not get satisfactory action at the retail level, the next step is to write to the manufacturer of the product in care of the consumer relations department. Names and addresses of manufacturing firms can be found on product hang tags or warranties. If not, go to a school library or a public library and look up the address in *Thomas' Register of Manufacturers* or *Standard and Poor's Register of Corporations*. Your letter should follow the format shown in Figure 5-3 and should include a description of the efforts you have already made to remedy the problem.

To facilitate consumer disputes, industries have organized consumer action panels (CAPs). CAPs consist of members from a specific industry plus consumer representatives. Their purpose is to mediate disputes between consumers and dealers or manufacturers. If your problem has not been solved by a local dealer or manufacturer, write to the appropriate CAP for assistance. Here is a list of names and addresses of some of these panels:

Carpet and Rug Industry
Consumer Action Panel (CRICAP)
Box 1568
Dalton, Georgia 30720

Furniture Industry
Consumer Action Panel (FICAP)
P.O. Box 851
High Point, North Carolina 27261

Major Appliance
Consumer Action Panel (MACAP)
20 N. Wacker Drive, Room 1514
Chicago, Illinois 60606

The National Association
of Furniture Manufacturers
8401 Connecticut Avenue
Suite 911
Washington, D.C. 20015

STATE AND FEDERAL AGENCIES

If efforts to resolve the problem at the local level fail, assistance is available from state agencies. Many states have departments of consumer affairs, which are involved in legislation, research, advertisement substantiation, and protective lawsuits. Such agencies also provide consumer education and can refer you to the proper state or federal agency for your problem. Some maintain branch offices at locations throughout the state. Many have assembled directories that contain names and addresses of complaint-handling agencies. Ask to see it at your local consumer affairs office or at the public library.

As mentioned earlier, there are dozens of licensing or registering commissions in each state. One of their functions is to resolve consumer complaints. Each agency is responsible for the honest and orderly conduct of professionals or tradespersons such as architects, auto mechanics, or insurance agents. In order to register a complaint, locate the proper agency either through a local consumer affairs office or in the telephone book. You should find a complete list under "Consumer Complaint and Protection Coordinators of the State of (Your State)." When filing a complaint, write a letter stating all the facts as shown in Figure 5-3.

Numerous federal agencies deal with consumer issues. Sometimes a single issue may be shared by more than one agency or office. Appendix I provides a list to help you identify the agency most germane to your problem. An indispensable free source of information is the *Consumer's Resource Handbook,* which may be obtained by writing to the Consumer Information Center, Department 532G, Pueblo, Colorado 81009. It has guidelines for making complaints and it lists federal services as well as addresses and phone numbers of regional offices. It also includes a directory of state and local consumer affairs and protection offices.

If your search for help is not successful, we recommend one of two specific federal agencies to guide you through the maze. Federal Information Centers (FICs) have been organized to answer questions or put individuals in touch with experts who can. FICs are operated by the General Services Administration and are located in key cities across the country. You can find them in the *Consumer's Resource Handbook* or Appendix I of this text.

THE COURTS AND LEGAL ASSISTANCE

If you have a complaint that you have not been able to resolve through other channels, it may be necessary to get legal advice or to take legal action. Legal advice is available from attorneys, from legal clinics, or through prepaid legal plans. It is, however, a rare individual who files a lawsuit for his rights as a consumer; the costs of attorney and filing fees are too high. The most practical alternative is small claims court, which was created to provide low-cost litigation—a landlord-tenant dispute over a security deposit, for example.

Legal Assistance. The fear of high costs for legal advice often keeps people from pursuing their rights. One popular lower-cost alternative is the **legal clinic.** In this setup, several lawyers share office space and equipment. They standardize procedures and forms, select common case types (uncontested divorces, traffic citations, or the like) and try to conduct a high-volume business in these categories. Highly trained paraprofessionals assist the lawyers in routine work that does not involve actual law practice, such as completing forms or filing forms with the court. All of these adaptations allow the attorneys to reduce fees by 25 percent to 50 percent below what a regular law firm might charge. As you might expect, legal clinics usually do not take cases involving extensive litigation.

The availability and visibility of legal clinics has increased tremendously in the last five years, largely because of two Supreme Court decisions. In 1975, the Supreme Court ruled that lawyers' associations should not be allowed to dictate "minimum fee schedules." For example, all the lawyers in a geographic region cannot decide to charge less than $500 for an uncontested divorce. In the 1977 case of *Bates vs. State Bar of Arizona,* the U.S. Supreme Court ruled that lawyers' rights to advertise were guaranteed in the Constitution (right to free speech). Since then, lawyers have begun to be more price competitive and consumers have begun to comparison shop for legal services on the basis of price as well as quality. As a result, prices for services have declined. Today, consumers can find lawyers and legal clinics described in the yellow pages of telephone directories, as well as in newspapers and television advertisements.

Perhaps a second reason that legal clinics are becoming more common is that the number of lawyers has doubled in the last decade. Each year, 30,000 lawyers are admitted to the bar, but only about 16,000 positions open annually in law offices and public service. The strong competition has made lawyers more innovative and service oriented. Besides creating clinics, lawyers have developed two new alternatives to benefit consumers: prepaid legal plans and advice by telephone.

Prepaid legal plans function much like medical insurance and are available through some employers. Often, the sponsors of these plans are labor unions, credit unions, business organizations, and school systems. Most plans cover everyday legal problems such as wills and estates, divorces and separations, and consumer debt. The plans stipulate what services are offered, whether the lawyer will be from the legal staff of the employer, and whether the employee is free to choose his or her own attorney. Fees for the plan are typically $8 to $10 per month for family coverage. They depend on the nature and amount of services offered, how many members of the group actually use the services, and how the lawyers are chosen. If staff lawyers from the place of employment are used, expenses are less than if a private attorney is consulted.

The future of prepaid legal plans remains to be seen. However, if more legal clinics are established and the cost of routine legal advice decreases, perhaps the need for these protection plans will diminish. More information about prepaid legal plans as well as legal clinic locations is available from the National Resource Center for Consumers of Legal Services, 1302 18th Street N.W., Washington, D.C. 20036, or from the American Prepaid Legal Services Institute, 1155 E. 60th Street, Chicago, Illinois 60637.

In an effort to encourage consumers to seek legal advice as soon as a problem arises rather than waiting until a formal lawsuit is filed against them, many bar associations now sponsor a service commonly called Tele-law. For a small fee ($10 to $15) billed to a bank credit card, consumers can call and briefly speak to an attorney to seek advice. Or they can call and listen to free recorded messages on consumer topics such as auto repair, landlord-tenant problems, credit, and the like.

An alternative source of assistance for some

Consumers who seek assistance in handling problems with landlords, utility companies, creditors, or merchants can choose from a number of services that vary in expertise and cost, remembering that high cost does not guarantee a high level of expertise.

people is Legal Aid and Legal Services. These programs are financed by federal, state, or local funding to provide legal assistance to people who cannot afford to hire private lawyers. There are more than 1,000 of these offices around the country, staffed by lawyers, paralegals (people who have taken courses in legal assistance), and law students. All offer free legal services to those who meet the financial eligibility requirements based on income and family size that are set by each office. Some people are often considered automatically eligible—those living on fixed incomes (Social Security Disability, Supplemental Security Income, general welfare, Aid to Families with Dependent Children, unemployment, and some retirement incomes).

Eligibility is usually determined as soon as you contact the office because problems often require immediate help. These offices give legal assistance with problems such as landlord-tenant disputes; credit problems; problems with utilities; and family issues such as divorce and adoption. They also work on cases involving Social Security, welfare, unemployment, and workers' compensation. For more information, look under "Legal Aid" or "Legal Services" in your local phone book, or phone your local consumer office or courthouse. Even if you have doubts about your eligibility for free legal assistance, it is worthwhile to contact an office to see whether you are eligible. If you are not eligible or if the offices involved cannot help with your problem for some other reason, they will try to refer you to other sources of help.

Small Claims Court. After pursuing all complaint channels and perhaps seeking legal advice, you may decide to file a legal claim. **Small claims court** was established in all states to provide a simple, economical system for individuals to obtain help in cases involving small amounts of money, usually under $1,500. It has many advantages, including a small filing fee (less than $20), informal atmosphere, no need to be represented by an attorney, and prompt settlement of the issue. Recently, some courts have scheduled evening and weekend sessions to better accommodate the needs of working people. The two major problems cited with respect to small claims

BOX 5-3
The Consumer and Small Claims Court

Using Small Claims Court

1. *Identify your opponent (the defendant)*. Use the legal name of the business, which can usually be found on certificates or licenses posted to be visible to the public.

2. *Send a warning letter to the defendant*. This may encourage a quick settlement without going to court. State your claim unemotionally. Include dates, dollar amounts, and how much you expect to be paid. Indicate that you will go to court if there is no reply within a certain time—say fourteen days. Send the letter by certified mail so you will have a receipt.

3. *Find the court*. It may be listed in the phone directory under "Small Claims Court" or under the name of the parent court—usually a city or county civil or trial court.

4. *File a claim*. Be prepared to give your name and address, the defendant's name and address, a short description of the problem, and how much, in dollars, you expect to receive. After paying the filing fee and the summons fee (less than $20), the clerk will schedule a hearing, most often within two or three weeks. The clerk is your best source of up-to-date information on how to use the court.

5. *Notify the defendant*. The court will make the first attempt to notify the defendant, usually by certified mail. If this is unsuccessful, you can have the notice delivered by a marshal or a sheriff.

6. *Gather the evidence*. Gather as much evidence to support your claim as possible. Include contracts, warranty statements, receipts, canceled checks, repair estimates, correspondence, and photographs showing the problem. If the evidence is verbal rather than written, take a witness with you. If your witness will not come voluntarily, the court can order (subpoena) him or her to appear.

7. *Consider settling out of court*. When the defendant realizes that you are serious, he or she may decide to settle out of court. If so, write down the terms of the settlement on paper. Each of you should sign it, date it, and keep a copy.

8. *Present your case*. Typically, both the plaintiff (you) and the defendant will be sworn to tell the truth. Then each presents his or her side of the case, including all documents and witnesses. The judge may choose to ask questions during the procedure. Then each party can ask questions or challenge the other's evidence. The judge may immediately announce the decision, or he or she may choose to notify each party by mail within a few days.

9. *Winning by default*. If the defendant does not appear, the judge will still ask to hear your evidence. If he or she is convinced by your testimony, he or she may award a "default" judgment, and you win the case.

Collecting a Small Claims Judgment

It is common for successful plaintiffs to have trouble collecting their judgments, that is, the money. If you do have trouble, contact the small claims clerk and ask what steps you can follow to collect. Some possible actions follow:

1. *Revocation of a business license*. After giving a business seven days to pay the judgment, call and say that you expect to receive a check in five days. If you do not receive it, say that you will take a copy of the judgment to the business license bureau and ask them to revoke the license. This procedure is usually effective. If not, use one of the other techniques described here.

2. *Garnishment of wages*. If the defendant is employed and you know where, you can request that the sheriff or marshal arrange to have deductions made from the defendant's wages. This procedure, called garnishment, has some restrictions, but the clerk can help you with it.

3. *Deductions from bank accounts*. For a fee, a sheriff or a marshal can take the money owed to you from the defendant's savings or checking account. You must first find out which bank the defendant uses (if you paid by check, look at the back of the canceled check for the bank name). The sheriff's fee for this service can also be collected from the defendant's account.

4. *Liens on real estate*. You can put a lien, or claim, on any real estate the defendant owns. When there is a lien on property, it cannot be sold until the debt is paid off. Again, check with the clerk for details.

court are the difficulty in collecting your judgment if you win and the possibility that the defendant will ask to have the case transferred to a civil court where you, the plaintiff, will also need an attorney. In Box 5-3 we have outlined the entire process of pursuing a complaint in small claims court. It is essentially an easy process, but it requires planning on your part to build your case and gather proof of your claim.

Consumer Protection in the 1980s

As we have noted, the direction of consumer protection often depends on the position taken by the U.S. President. Ronald Reagan fulfilled campaign promises with federal budget-cutting and tax-slashing victories in 1981 and 1982. The Reagan administration has proposed abolishing the Consumer Product Safety Commission and has obtained large budget cuts for the Federal Trade Commission, the Environmental Protection Agency, the Food and Drug Administration, and other federal consumer agencies. Reagan's goal is to diminish federal taxes, regulations, and social services and to transfer these responsibilities to state governments and private businesses. Whether this shift in economic policy will provide more or less information and protection for consumers remains to be seen. It does indicate that Congress will probably not enact any new consumer protection legislation in the next few years. These new trends mean that consumers need to have knowledge of their rights and need to be alert to the features of existing protective legislation. Consumers must also accept the responsibilities that correspond to their four consumer rights and must exercise these rights and responsibilities to ensure continuing information and protection.

Summary

We have briefly shown the transition of consumer legislation from providing information to giving consumers protection. At the same time we have looked at some of the public-sector agencies and regulations that give us this information and protection. We have seen that the private sector also provides agencies, seals and ratings, warranties, and publications that can be useful to consumers.

Consumers have a responsibility to seek out and use product information and to apply the decision-making model in order to avoid disappointment in consumer choices. Despite all this, consumers still encounter problems with products and services. As a result, they must return to the place of purchase and request assistance. In cases in which this is ineffective, consumers need to contact local, state, or federal consumer affairs agencies or they may need to file a claim in small claims court.

Neighborhood REVISITED

1. William Mahoney died on February 6, 1960. What consumer agencies available today might have helped? What private agencies could he have turned to?

2. Does this sad story bolster the case for government regulation to protect the consumer, or would you agree with George Stigler (1980), a University of Chicago economist, who commented on this story by saying, "I assume this tragic tale is true—what shall we do? My basic answer to this painful problem is: In order to preserve the dignity and freedom of the individual in my society, I shall if I must pay the price of having some fail wholly to meet the challenge of freedom. I find it odd that a society which once a generation will send most of its young men against enemy bullets to defend freedom, will capitulate to a small handful of citizens unequal to its challenge."

KEY TERMS

caveat emptor
economic impact statement
expressed warranty
fraud
full warranty
implied warranty
informative legislation
legal clinic
limited warranty
overregulation
private (business) sector
protective legislation
public sector
recalls
small claims court
warranty
weights and measures standards

QUESTIONS

1. What are the two types of consumer legislation? Give examples of each.

2. What are the two types of expressed warranties and what are their features?

3. What are the four consumer rights identified by John F. Kennedy? What consumer responsibilities accompany each right?

4. What reasons can you give for being easily taken in by deceptive manufacturers and dishonest sellers?

5. What seal of approval or rating do you trust? Why?

6. Considering both costs and benefits, do you think it is valuable to have and enforce weights-and-measures laws? Defend your opinion.

7. What did you do the last time you were dissatisfied with the performance of a relatively new purchase? What would you do now if you had the same experience?

8. What position has the President of the United States taken concerning consumer protection in the last two or three years?

9. What sources of information do you generally use when choosing a product?

10. What consumer services do you want and expect from your local government?

11. Do you think the federal government should financially assist private citizens so that they can testify at hearings or special meetings that represent a consumer viewpoint? Does the government help business in any way when they testify? Why or why not?

12. It has been said that if a person is an intelligent and alert consumer, he or she does not need help from the government in consumer matters. Do you agree? Why or why not?

13. Economist George Stigler (1980) once said, "No method of displaying one's public spiritedness is more popular than to notice a small problem and pass a law. It combines ease, the warmth of benevolence, and a suitable disrespect for a less enlightened era . . . [but] I urge you to attempt the more difficult task of exercising your critical intelligence in an appraisal of the comfortable wishfulness of contemporary policy." Does this statement fit the history of the consumer protection movement? Have we sometimes simply passed laws to end problems?

PROJECTS

1. Have you ever used small claims court? If so, share your experience with the class. If not, visit small claims court and report the court decisions. What caused the judge to decide the cases the way he or she did?

2. Locate the consumer affairs office and the Better Business Bureau in your community. Investigate the specific services each one can provide for you. What procedure do they follow if you have a consumer problem?

3. Call your closest Legal Aid office to determine the level of income individuals and families must have to be eligible for free legal assistance.

4. Conduct a survey to determine how much confidence people have in brand names and seals of approval.

5. Conduct a survey of local attorneys and legal clinics to compare available services and costs.

REFERENCES AND READINGS

"The American Consumer." *Current History,* May 1981.

"The Appliance Revolution." *Consumers' Research,* February 1981.

Best, Arthur. *When Consumers Complain.* New York: Columbia University Press, 1981.

Carson, Rachael. *The Silent Spring.* New York: Houghton Mifflin, 1962.

Eisenberger, Kenneth. *The Expert Consumer.* Englewood Cliffs, N.J.: Prentice-Hall, 1977.

Feinman, Jeffrey. *The Purple Pages.* New York: Hawthorn Books, 1979.

Fornell, Claes. "Increasing the Organizational Influence of Corporate Consumer Affairs Departments." *Journal of Consumer Affairs,* Winter 1981.

Friedman, Milton, and Friedman, Rose. *Free to Choose.* New York: Harcourt Brace Jovanovich, 1980.

George, Richard. *The New Consumer Survival Kit.* Boston: Little, Brown, 1978.

Green, Mark, and Waitzman, Norman. "Cost, Benefit, and Class." *Working Papers for a New Society,* May/June 1980.

Guzzardi, Walter, Jr. "The Mindless Pursuit of Safety." *Fortune,* April 9, 1979.

Harris, Marvin. "Why It's Not the Same Old America." *Psychology Today,* 1981.

Horowitz, David. *Fight Back and Don't Get Ripped Off.* New York: Harper & Row, 1979.

Kallet, Arthur, and Schlink, F. J. *100,000,000 Guinea Pigs.* New York: Vanguard Press, 1932.

Kirkland, Richard I., Jr. "Hazardous Times for Product-Safety Cars." *Fortune,* June 15, 1981.

Laczniak, Gene R., and Curley, Anne. "Public Participation in Rulemaking by the Federal Trade Commission: A Survey of Some Recent Experiences." *Journal of Consumer Affairs,* Summer 1981.

Lamb, Ruth de Forest. *American Chamber of Horrors.* New York: Farrar & Rinehart, 1936.

Nader, Ralph. *Unsafe at Any Speed.* New York: Simon & Schuster, 1965.

Newman, Stephen A., and Kramer, Nancy. *Getting What You Deserve.* Garden City, N.Y.: Doubleday, 1979.

"Paying Less for a Lawyer." *Consumer Reports,* September 1979.

"Recalls." *Changing Times,* October 1980.

"The Role of the Small-Claims Court." *Consumer Reports,* November 1979.

Rosenbloom, Joseph. *Consumer Complaint Guide.* New York: Collier Macmillan, 1979.

Shuptine, F. Kelly, and Moore, Ellen M. "Even After the Magnuson-Moss Act of 1975, Warranties Are Still Not Easy to Understand." *Journal of Consumer Affairs,* Winter 1980.

Stigler, George. "The Government of the Economy." In Robert C. Puth, ed. *Current Issues in the American Economy.* Lexington, Mass.: D.C. Heath, 1980.

Striker, John M., and Shapiro, Andrew O. *Power Plays.* New York: Rawson, Wade, 1979.

Weidenbaum, Murray. "Time to Control Runaway Regulation." In Robert C. Puth, ed. *Current Issues in the American Economy.* Lexington, Mass.: D.C. Heath, 1980.

Did You Know That...

- *a budget can help you get the things you really want?*
- *money management can help you control both your money and your life?*
- *food and housing account for over half of household spending?*
- *emergencies can and should be anticipated?*
- *money is a major source of arguments among couples, rivaled only by sex?*
- *spending helps people fulfill emotional as well as physical needs?*
- *traditional ways of handling money within a family are usually not effective in two-income families?*

6

Budgeting: Getting in Control

The Need for Budgeting
Income and Expenses
Designing Your Budget
The Budgeting Process: How One Family Manages
Net Worth
Money and Emotions
Collective Money Management Techniques
Paying Bills

Neighborhood CAPSULE
The Lost Vacation

"I just can't believe it," Bob explained to his wife Cathy. "This is the third time Gary and Sue have canceled at the last minute."

"I'm not really surprised," Cathy said. "They just don't seem to plan ahead."

Cathy and Bob Tate and Sue and Gary Gallagher are neighbors and friends. Over the last two years they have planned two skiing trips together, as well as a week at the beach. However, when the time approached to make a deposit on rentals or to plan food purchases, and so forth, Sue and Gary always changed their minds. Each time they didn't have their share of the deposit and just generally didn't have enough money for the trip.

"The children are really going to be disappointed," Bob continued. "You know, Sue and Gary make more money than we do, yet they never seem to have anything or do anything."

"I know what you're saying, Bob, but I disagree with you to some extent. It seems that they are always buying some gadget or trinket, and they eat out a lot. Neither one seems to have much resistance to salespeople either. Remember the time we went to the swapmeet? It seemed like they bought everything in sight! Their money seems to just dribble away."

"We used to be a little bit like that," noted Bob. "I guess the big change came when you quit work to have Jennifer. Remember how we sat down for the first time to decide how we wanted to spend our money?"

"Yes, I do. And I also remember how hard it was to follow our plan. Remember how unrealistic it was? We've really learned a lot!"

Cathy and Bob Tate are actually using the process of **money management**—a system of planning for spending based on expected income. The tool used for money management is called a **budget,** or spending plan, so the process is often called budgeting. The purpose of budgeting is to help people individually or as a household to achieve their goals. It cannot guarantee increased income, but it can ensure greater satisfaction with the results of spending. Budgeting is a direct application of the decision-making process discussed in Chapter 2.

This chapter provides you with the knowledge and skills necessary to plan a personal budget. You will need to analyze your goals and values, look at alternative uses for your money, and make decisions about priorities. You will then be prepared for the last half of this text, which deals with the purchase of consumer goods and services.

This chapter focuses on the reasons why money management is important in your life. We look at the spending patterns of average American families, which can be used as guides for personal budgeting. We include a five-step process for budgeting, and we apply the process directly to the needs of our neighborhood family, the Tates. We conclude with an explanation of net worth and a discussion of the emotional and practical aspects of budgeting.

Many factors affect budgetary decisions, including the external factors of advertising, social customs, and family background and personal factors such as income level, family composition, and stage in the life cycle. We discussed these factors in Chapters 2 and 3. We learned at that time that we could control income level by our career choice and by our decision to use time for income production or leisure. Inflation and use of credit also affect our economic choices, so they are discussed in later chapters.

The Need for Budgeting

It takes money to get most of the things we want. Unfortunately, most of us do not seem to have enough money for all the things we want now. This is part of the scarcity we discussed in Chapters 1 and 2. One of us was discussing this fact of life with an eight-year-old niece, Lisa Michelle. Lisa was in a toy store trying to decide which toy to buy with her $2. I was explaining that the choice is limited because $2 isn't very much money. Lisa suggested that we just go get more money. When asked where we would go to get it, she replied, "to the grocery store or bank." How simple it all seemed!

Most adults recognize, of course, that money is a scarce resource. If we choose to totally ignore the fact that we have a limited income, the result may be serious family arguments, loss of job performance caused by anxiety about overdue bills, divorce, or any number of serious consequences. That's why money management is essential.

There are five basic reasons for budgeting your money:

1. *It helps you get what you really want.* It is very easy to spend money on items that will not supply much satisfaction. The American marketplace gives us an endless array of products. Unfortunately, many of our purchases end up unused in closets, basements, or garages. If you have a plan, however, you can apply the decision-making process rather than purchase haphazardly. Planning allows you to look at all of the options, consider what and when to buy, and make a rational choice. Planning provides you with an opportunity to express your own opinions and define your own lifestyle. For example, let us say that you like to travel, but cannot afford it. You could investigate sites that are close to home, inexpensive motels, or house-sharing, and begin to set aside small amounts for the trip.

2. *It prevents you from spending beyond your income.* No matter how high one's income is, choices still need to be made, especially as income increases. Mass media can sometimes effectively create needs and wants where none exist. So there never is enough money to "buy it all." You need to apply the decision-making process, determine what your income is, decide what your goals are, and then set priorities. This requires compromise and even sacrifice. Nevertheless, it is always best to make these decisions *before* spending money or signing a contract.

3. *It can help you maintain a harmonious home.* Studies repeatedly show that a major problem for households is failure to agree on a spending plan. Often when counselors investigate a specific family's problems, they find that individual family members do not talk about their desires or wants. These problems can reach such proportions that they are often listed as a prime cause for divorce. Decisions about spending and

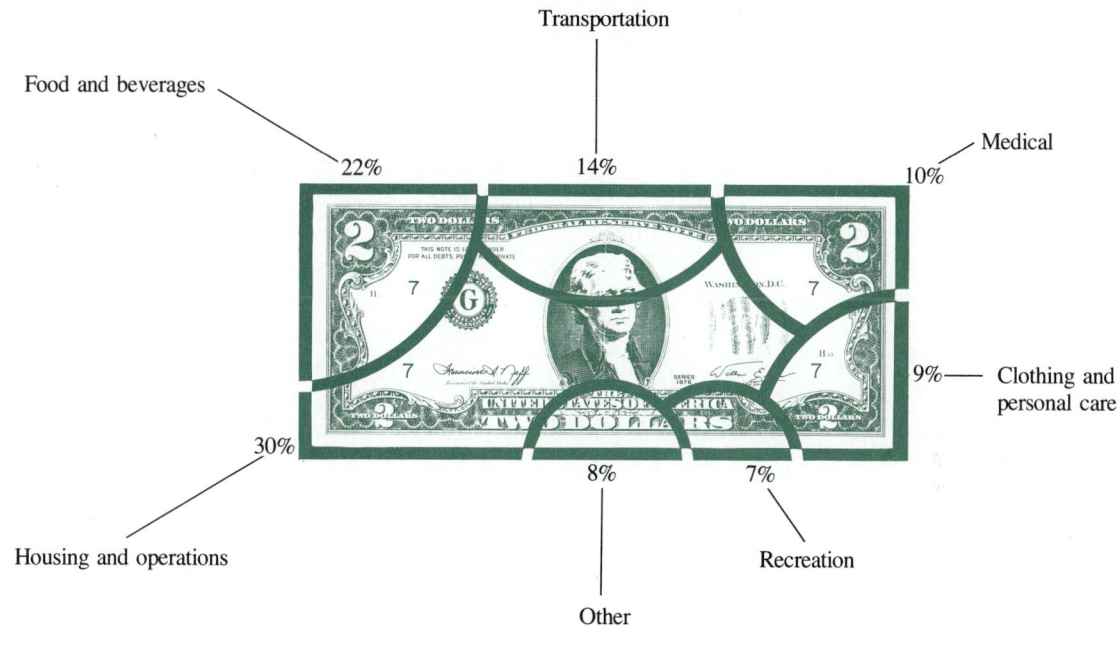

Figure 6-1. An average American family's budget for after-tax (disposable) income.

SOURCE: U.S. Bureau of Economic analysis and *Survey of Current Business,* March 1982.

saving for the future need to be a joint effort of all members of the household, based on values, goals, and standards.

4. *It can help keep track of expenditures.* Checking periodically to evaluate progress toward your goals is a part of planning that also helps in future planning. Budget records can also assist you in computing taxes and may minimize your tax bill. Such records are also useful when questions arise regarding warranties or product performance.

5. *It puts you in control and helps you stay there.* When consumers do not have enough money to pay cash for an item, they often borrow. The cost of borrowing, that is, the interest charges, diminishes the amount of money available to a family. Too much debt can be disastrous. A system of disciplined spending is the key to avoiding financial disaster. Money management helps you control not only your money but your life as well.

These five reasons for managing money make using a budget worth the effort. By using a budget, a household can make rational economic decisions that reflect its values and help it achieve its goals. In this chapter, we will roll up our sleeves and learn how to budget.

Income and Expenses

It is useful to use budgets for the "average American family" as a guide for planning a budget. Figure 6-1 shows how the average family spends its **net,** or **disposable income.** Net income is commonly called take-home pay. Notice that there are no categories for Social Security or income taxes because this money is primarily beyond the decision-making power of a household and usually is deducted before you get your paycheck.

Food and housing, the two largest budget categories, account for over half of household spending. Included in the food category is all food, regardless of whether it is eaten in or out of the home. Alcoholic

Table 6-1. Annual Budgets for a Four-Person Urban Family at Three Levels of Living, Autumn 1980

Component	Lower		Intermediate		Higher	
Total budget	$14,044		$23,134		$34,409	
Total family consumption	11,243		16,969		23,266	
Food	4,321	30.8%	5,571	24.1%	7,024	20.4%
Housing	2,608	18.6	5,106	22.1	7,747	22.5
Transportation	1,160	8.2	2,116	9.1	2,751	8.0
Clothing	907	6.4	1,292	5.6	1,888	5.5
Personal care	352	2.5	471	2.0	668	1.9
Medical care	1,298	9.2	1,303	5.6	1,359	3.9
Other family consumption	597	4.2	1,109	4.8	1,829	5.3
Other items	583	4.2	957	4.1	1,610	4.7
Social Security and disability	881	6.3	1,427	6.2	1,608	4.7
Personal income taxes	1,337	9.5	3,781	16.3	7,924	23.0

SOURCE: *Family Economics Review* (Fall 1981).

beverages and tobacco are also under this category. Housing and operations categories include rents or mortgages; utilities such as gas, electric, and telephone; furniture and appliances; household supplies; and purchased household services such as a maid or a gardener.

The next largest expense, transportation, includes both personal and public transportation. Because of the cost of energy, the percentage of money spent in this category has risen over the last decade. The remaining categories include clothing and personal care, medical care, and recreation. The "other" category includes items such as savings, education, gifts, and contributions. Of all of these, medical expenses put the most pressure on family budgets. We will see why in Chapter 13.

Charts such as Figure 6-1 are useful only as guidelines. Differences in spending patterns occur according to the individual's or the family's stage of the life cycle, its size, and its geographic location, which involves both climate variations and setting, whether urban or rural. The most obvious difference in spending patterns, however, relates to the household income level. Table 6-1 illustrates how much money was necessary for an imaginary family of four to live at a low, a medium, or a high level in autumn 1980. In this data, **gross income** is used—the grand total of wages before deductions.

Perhaps the two categories that change most noticeably from the low-budget level to the intermediate- or high-budget level are food and housing. As incomes rise, families spend a smaller percentage of their money on food and a larger portion on housing. This is not too surprising. Although our appetite for more expensive food may increase with income, our stomach capacity does not. But our desire for larger and better-located housing generally outpaces the growth of our income.

Two less obvious differences are in medical care and taxes. Notice the impact of medical costs on a low budget. The dollar cost is similar to that of the intermediate- and high-budget families, but as a percentage of the total, low-income families spend twice as much on medical care. And finally, notice that personal income taxes increase both in absolute amounts and as percentages as income increases. This is in part caused by our **progressive income tax** system—the more you make, the greater the percentage of your income that goes for taxes.

Now that you know how "average" families

spend their incomes, you are ready to learn the specifics of money management. Keep in mind, however, that you need to tailor your budget to your family size, your life cycle, your goals, and your values.

Designing Your Budget

Planning a budget involves matching future income to future expenditures. As with other decisions, before making a budget you need to gather information. You need to know how your money is spent now, and you need an accurate estimate of your income. You can then evaluate your spending to see how it is or is not helping you reach your goals. The simplest way to begin is to *record for one month* how you and your family spend your money. Keep paper and pencil handy for each member to jot down daily how much money he or she spends. Keep a running total for each day, and round the amounts to the nearest dollar for simplicity.

Grouping expenses into general categories simplifies record keeping. The food category, for example, can include the grocery bill, food eaten out, pet food, and alcoholic beverages. Transportation expenses include car payments, gasoline and oil costs, car maintenance and repair costs, and public transportation expenses.

Worksheet 6-1 shows a form that you can use to group and record daily totals. As you look at your own spending, you will gain insight to enable you to personalize the form by adding categories such as "vacation," "emergency fund," "child support," and so forth.

Next, *estimate your income* for a year. Those who earn a salary can refer to paycheck stubs to estimate income for the next twelve months. A second source of this information is last year's income tax return. Be realistic and do not include overtime, because it is not guaranteed. Be sure to account for recent raises, if appropriate. Add other cash income you expect, such as bonuses, veteran's benefits, Social Security payments, rents, investments, and interest on savings. Include money from all members of the household who depend on the unit for support. All of these figures should be added together and divided by twelve for a monthly budget, or by twenty-four for a bimonthly budget.

Now you are ready to evaluate your current spending pattern and to decide how you want to spend for the next twelve months. All family members should be involved so that their personal goals become known and contribute direction to the family's life. If all members are included in the decisions and involved in establishing goals, then all can be expected to cooperate to reach them.

When the family meets together, each member should be informed of the result of the spending record in an uncritical manner. This is not a time to chastise a member of the family for past spending, because it cannot be altered anyway. This is the time for family members to share their short-term and long-term goals. Every person should number his or her goals in order of importance. The family can then separate unrealistic dreams from goals and establish a budget to reach goals by following the five steps outlined below and in Worksheet 6-2.

1. *Record income* information that was previously gathered.

2. *Calculate fixed expenses.* The spending record helps you distinguish fixed expenses from flexible ones. **Fixed expenses are large, regular, and predictable.** They are fixed because you commit yourself to paying them in a contract or agreement. They include rent or mortgage, insurance, installment payments, taxes, church contributions or tithes, and regular savings for family goals. Utilities are included here because you have agreed to pay for the service, and, with the exception of a phone, you would probably not consider eliminating them. However, the amount of these bills may vary monthly or seasonally. Some fixed expenses are due on a quarterly, a semiannual, or an annual basis, so they may not be reflected in the monthly spending record. It is necessary to set aside a portion of each paycheck to have enough money to meet bills without straining other budget categories or without borrowing. For example, an auto insurance payment of $300 may be due twice a year. By setting aside $50 each month or $25 every two weeks in a special account, you will be sure to have the money and you can stay within your budget. Checking and charge-card records, as well as previous tax returns, are a source of this information.

3. *Create an emergency fund.* Murphy's law says that if something can go wrong, it will. It is

WORKSHEET 6-1
Monthly Spending Record

Family Income and Expenses for the Month of _____ 19 ___

Date	Income	Food	Clothing & laundry	Housing (rent)	Household expenses	Utilities (gas, water, etc.)	Transportation	Insurance	Medical	Education	Recreation	Other	Savings
1													
2													
3													
4													
5													
6													
7													
8													
9													
10													
11													
12													
13													
14													
15													
16													
17													
18													
19													
20													
21													
22													
23													
24													
25													
26													
27													
28													
29													
30													
31													
Amount spent													
Amount planned													

SOURCE: From Home Economics Instructional Materials Center, Texas Tech University.

WORKSHEET 6-2
Budgeting

Step 1: Calculate income.

Income from jobs _____

Income from other sources _____

Total: _____

Step 2: Calculate fixed expenses.

House payment or rent _____
Insurance
   auto _____
   health _____
   household _____
   life _____
   mortgage _____
Installments
   _____ _____
   _____ _____
Utilities
   electric _____
   gas _____
   phone _____
   water _____
Savings _____
Other
   _____ _____
   _____ _____

Step 3: Calculate emergency fund, _____

Step 4: Calculate flexibile living expenses.

Food and beverages _____
Clothing and personal care _____
Household expenses _____
Transportation _____
Entertainment, recreation _____
Gifts, contributions _____
Other
_____ _____
_____ _____
_____ _____

Step 5: Compare income to expenses.

Total all expenses _____

Compare to income _____

Readjust if necessary!

---

normal for households to have unexpected expenses such as those for illness or accident, unemployment, or the need to repair a car or a broken appliance. Even more common is that all of these things happen at once! This is the most important step of the plan, yet most people skip it. Families who declare bankruptcy or lose their homes because of financial crisis often indicate that it was a "little emergency" that pushed them over the brink.

The amount of money you should set aside for an **emergency fund** depends upon the regularity of your employment, your job security, and your general income level. At minimum, a couple should have two months' income saved above and beyond savings accounts set aside for a specific goal. If your employment is sporadic, as is the case with construction, or has predictable periods of unemployment, as in teaching, then you may need to set more aside. Two

---

> **BOX 6-1**
>
> **Emergency Fund**
>
> **How Much?**
> Your emergency fund should be enough to allow you and your family to withstand unemployment for approximately six months. Generally *two to three times your monthly net income* will be adequate. Consider:
>
> 1. Sources of support available to you, such as unemployment insurance, food stamps, or sick pay.
> 2. Income from more than one salary.
> 3. Sources of income other than salary.
> 4. Possible cut-backs in the family budget.
> 5. Current debt load.
> 6. Frequency or likelihood of unemployment.
> 7. Plans for purchase of big-ticket items in the future.
>
> **How to Save**
>
> 1. Treat your emergency fund as a fixed expense.
> 2. Have money deducted from your paycheck rather than making the decision every payday.
> 3. Deposit windfall money such as tax refunds, bonuses, overtime pay, and the like.
> 4. Deposit the money earned from a pay raise rather than changing your budget.
> 5. Save "loose money" at the end of the day—all the quarters, or single dollar bills—and watch them add up.
> 6. Have a "Rediscover Home Week"—spend no money on recreation, eating out, and so forth during the week and deposit the savings.

months' income may seem like a lot of money, but just begin to save as much as you can. Box 6-1 provides suggestions on how to reach this goal. After you have established your full emergency fund, do not touch that amount, except for unexpected problems. When you do withdraw funds, they should be replaced as soon as possible.

4. *Calculate flexible expenses.* **Flexible expenses** include food, clothing, gasoline, routine medical care, entertainment, education, and household expenses. They are considered flexible because consumers can control how much they spend, even to the point of choosing not to spend at all. Some of these expenses are paid for by **discretionary income,** the portion of income that is left after fixed expenses are paid and basic necessities purchased. Use your one-month spending record to determine the average amounts you spend on these items.

5. *Compare income with expenses.* You and your family are now ready to compare expenditures with income. Total the monthly averages of the fixed expenses, the emergency fund, and flexible expenses, and compare them with your monthly income. If money is left over, it can be allocated to any goal or category you choose. However, if total expenses exceed income, you must adjust your budget. This is the time to make priority decisions. What can be changed? Which goals should the family strive for now and which ones should be postponed? Is a vacation more important than weekends at the movies? Is it worth giving up new carpeting to get a new car? Your income is limited, and so your family cannot have everything they want. This planning process involves compromise and requires sacrifices, but it results in satisfaction in reaching family goals.

The Budgeting Process: How One Family Manages

Now that you are familiar with the budgeting process, it will be helpful to look at how one family applies and individualizes this process. Remember Bob and Cathy Tate—those folks in the Neighborhood Capsule, who seemed to have such a workable and realistic budget? Their experiences can be helpful to you, so let's take a closer look at how they created their plan.

Bob and Cathy have been married for eight years. Bob, thirty, is a policeman, and Cathy, twenty-eight, is a housewife. They have two children, ages six and four. They have always enjoyed family vacations, camping or at the beach. But in the last few years, vacations have become more difficult to manage, because of rising costs and increasing family needs as the children grow older. So Bob and Cathy sat down to discuss the situation. They realized that they needed more income to achieve all of their goals. They decided that Cathy should return to work. She began to sell cosmetics parttime, and her business

Sometimes budgeting requires setting aside specific monthly amounts to be used for future goals, such as a new car, a vacation, or a down payment on a house.

gradually grew. Although Bob's parents live close by and enjoy babysitting their grandchildren, Bob is sometimes responsible for childcare.

Cathy and Bob decided that they want to buy a new car and also have a special family vacation. This meant that they needed a new budget to accommodate these two goals. Before making their plan, they gathered the information they needed, which included last year's tax return, current check stubs, and receipts. They also kept a record of their spending for flexible expenses to get an up-to-date idea of where their money was going. Cathy and Bob then followed the five steps we have outlined. First they calculated their income:

Net income from Bob's job	$17,880
Net income from Cathy's job	3,000
Income from savings	310
Total	$21,190
Divide by 12—	
monthly budget	$ 1,765

Bob and Cathy have owned their house for two years. It is a fifteen-year-old, three-bedroom house, with one and a half baths. It is their second house. The first was a mobile home that they owned for three years. They reevaluate their insurance needs yearly and of course are prepared for the possibility that property taxes will increase. They look forward to paying off their television in two months and have one year of payments left on the car. They save $25 each month in order to accumulate a down payment for a second car. When the first car is paid off, they intend to buy a new car and keep the older one. In the meantime, Cathy and Bob share rides with each other and with friends. They choose to view utilities as fixed expenses and have installed conservation devices such as a water-heater blanket, a water-saving bag in the toilet tank, and water restrictors in the shower. Their house was insulated to the recommended level by the previous owner. They have then calculated their fixed expenses as:

House payment	$ 475
Insurance	
auto	35
health (deducted from gross pay)	—
household (fire and theft)	20
life	20
mortgage	18
Installments	
car payment	160
furniture	30
Taxes on the house	35
Utilities	
electric	50
gas	40
phone	25
water, trash	25
Savings	25
Vacation savings	40
Auto license	10
	$1,008

Cathy and Bob have had an emergency fund since they first got married:

Currently in the emergency fund	$3,175
Monthly allotments to the fund	50

At that time, Cathy was working full-time and they were able to set aside over $100 each month. They have used this fund many times for minor repairs and accidents. It was especially helpful after their second child was born. They had saved enough money for basic medical and baby expenses not covered by insurance, but then Cathy needed unexpected surgery. The $50 is used for household or major appliance repairs or emergency medical expenses if necessary during the month. If no emergencies occur, the money is saved in the account for that purpose.

Their spending record provided Bob and Cathy with an estimate of their current spending for flexible items. The family eats out once a week, usually at a coffee shop. They enjoy family movies, and they usually set aside at least one night each month for Bob and Cathy to go out alone. Bob's mother usually babysits the children on those evenings as well as during the day when Cathy is working. Bob babysits on the nights that Cathy works. Their flexible living expenses are:

Food and beverages	$340
Clothing and personal care	75
Household	
laundry and dry cleaning	15
household supplies & maintenance	25
Transportation	
gasoline	90
maintenance, minor repair	25
Entertainment	50
Routine medical	15
Gifts, contributions	30
Childcare	20
	$685

After calculating their expenses and income, the Tates were pleased to see that they were not spending beyond their income. In following Step 5 they found:

Total fixed expenses	$1,008
Total emergency fund	50
Total flexible expenses	685
Total monthly budget	$1,743
Total monthly income	1,765
	$22 left over

They found that $22 was left unaccounted for and they view this as a cushion, or slight protection, against inflation. They realize that this is not an adequate amount to balance the effects of inflation, but they hope that Cathy's business will continue to grow. But just in case that doesn't happen, Cathy plans to see what other parttime jobs are available in the area. With these things in mind, they looked closely at their budget for areas that could be adjusted to accommodate their vacation and second-car goals.

Cathy and Bob first set their goals. They determined that they wanted $1,000 for the vacation in ten months. They also wanted $1,200 for the car down payment in twelve months, which would be added to the $1,500 they had already set aside for this purpose.

Their first priority was the car. They calculated how their current savings budget compared to their new goals:

Current budget

Car	$25 × 12 months	$300
Vacation	$40 × 10 months	400
		$700

Amounts desired for new goals

Car	$1,200
Vacation	1,000
	$2,200
	$1,500 short

Next Cathy and Bob looked at their flexible expenses—those they could personally control (Worksheet 6-3). Cathy decided that with a little more planning and by using less meat she could cut the food budget by $10. This wasn't much, but she considers herself a careful planner; by conserving on paper goods and cleaning supplies the family could save another $5. The Tates decided to go to the movies less often and to buy less expensive clothing and gifts. They also agreed that Cathy would plan more cosmetics parties in the evening so Bob could babysit. Although this would give the family less time together, it would allow for more saving. These changes amounted to $60.

Next, they looked at fixed expenses. The only expenditure they felt they could change was utilities.

WORKSHEET 6-3
Cathy and Bob Tate's Budget

Step 1: Calculate income: Total: **$1,765**

Step 2: Calculate fixed expenses.

House payment	475
Insurance	
auto	35
health	deducted from gross
household	20
life	20
mortgage	18
Installments	
CAR Payment	160
furniture	30
Utilities	
electric	50
gas	40
phone	25
water	25
Savings	
Car down Payment	25
vacation	40
Other	
auto license	10
taxes on house	35

Step 3: Calculate emergency fund.   50

Step 4: Calculate flexible living expenses.

Food and beverages	340
Clothing and personal care	75
Household expenses	40
Transportation	115
Entertainment, recreation	50
Routine medical	15
Gifts and contributions	30
Childcare	20

Step 5: Compare income to expenses.

Total all expenses.   **$1,743**

Compare to income.   **$1,765**

They were doing their best with everything except the phone. By making long-distance calls on weekends and by writing letters more often, they felt they could save $5. The furniture would be paid off in two months and that would free another $30. The total changes amounted to $65 currently and $95 later. They calculated their savings:

$$\begin{aligned} \$65 \times 2 \text{ months} &= \$130 \\ \$95 \times 10 \text{ months} &= \underline{950} \\ & \$1{,}080 \end{aligned}$$

Although this was $420 short of their goal, the Tates were pleased with the result. They felt that they could still have an enjoyable vacation even though it might not be as long as they hoped. They also recognized that they could live with this budget because it was flexible and allowed for emergencies. Therefore, they felt optimistic that they might even be able to save more and come closer to their goal.

The budget categories used by the Tates were personalized for their needs. You can create a plan for yourself to include your own needs and goals. For example, perhaps vacations aren't important to you at all. Maybe you would rather accumulate a down payment for your first house or save up for a new TV. In either case, if you don't actually set money aside for your goals, you may never reach them.

Spending plans can be personalized in other ways, such as giving a separate clothing budget to each family member. Another good idea is to include a category of personal choice, or "mad money." This would be a small percentage of a budget (1–3 percent) but would allow each family member to spend without explaining or accounting to anyone else.

Inflation has caused havoc in family budgets over the last decade. Chapter 7 discusses this topic in detail, but we must mention it here. When prices rise faster than wages, families must reduce their spending. Family goals should be clarified and prioritized in terms of values. Then families can reduce or eliminate spending for items that do not give them maximum satisfaction.

Net Worth

Comparing actual spending to the budget you planned is one way to evaluate your financial position. It indicates your immediate progress but does not account for past spending patterns. For this you need a net worth statement, which shows the relationship between your **assets** and your **liabilities.** An asset is something you own, whereas a liability is something you owe. The mathematical difference between assets and liabilities is **net worth.** In other words, net worth is what would be left if everything you own were sold and the money was used to pay your debts.

An annual accounting of net worth will help you or your family keep track of your financial progress. Worksheet 6-4 is an example of a net worth statement. When using this form, record only the current cash value of each item. To find the cash value of a life insurance policy, locate the value table printed on the policy itself. Figures in the table are for each $1,000 of the face value (total amount of insurance) for each year of the policy's duration. The cash value of annuities can be determined the same way.

Young people often have a low net worth or even a negative net worth. If this is the case, do not be discouraged. Young people are in the process of obtaining education and establishing a career, and they can usually anticipate higher future income. As individuals and families move through the life cycle, their net worth steadily increases. When retirement approaches and income slows or stops completely, net worth usually begins to fall as accumulated assets are used to pay for living expenses.

Once you have computed your net worth, you will want to consider questions that the figures raise. Is your money helping you reach your goals? Is your emergency fund large enough to pay your bills for two or three months if you cannot work? Were your debts created to buy assets or to cover ordinary living expenses? What adjustments should you make in your spending to be sure you reach long-term goals five, ten, or twenty-five years from now? The net worth statement should be used to give focus to your budget. It should be updated annually to evaluate your progress.

Now you know what steps are involved in creating a spending plan. You may even have begun one. But a budget does not guarantee that you can manage your money successfully. The plan has to be followed consistently and revised when necessary. And that

WORKSHEET 6-4
Net Worth Statement

Assets	Liabilities
Cash on hand	Unpaid bills
checking account _____	charge accounts _____
savings account _____	utilities _____
Investments	other _____
savings bonds _____	Installment loans—secured
stocks and bonds _____	automobile _____
mutual funds _____	other _____
cash value of life insurance _____	Installment loans—unsecured _____
cash value of annuities _____	Mortgage loans _____
Home and property _____	Education loans _____
Automobile _____	Other _____
Personal property (cameras, jewelry, and so forth) _____	Total liabilities _____
Total assets _____	Net worth = Assets minus liabilities

means regular family discussions about the way the budget is working. It means periodic reevaluation whenever there are changes in household income, family size, or family goals.

Money and Emotions

Throughout our budget discussion we have stressed the need for joint decision making. It is important to work these problems out together because money is a major source of arguments among couples, rivaled only by sex. Families that argue about money matters report that members do not feel free to communicate their opinions or desires. When we remember the contribution of both partners in labor and nonmarket home production, it is understandable that both partners want to be included in decisions. Older children and teenagers can also be involved in decisions related to the problem of scarcity, and they understand the need for tradeoffs.

It is important to realize that money discussions can be sensitive and can elicit strong emotional reactions, because spending often fulfills emotional as well as physical needs. Differences in values often become noisily apparent in budgeting discussions. People who pause to examine their own values will find it easier to cooperatively plan within the household. For example, we are all familiar with the individual who achieves status through spending. "Keeping up with the Joneses" can quickly put a hole in your budget. If this seems to be a problem, ask yourself if it is really *your* values that are creating your desire for a jacuzzi or a Caribbean cruise.

Sometimes individuals spend money to "get even" with others in the family. Consider the young wife who buys a new dress because her husband stayed out late after work without calling her. To retaliate, the husband buys a new fishing rod. Both of these people use money to express anger. This does

In some families, the person in charge of the purse strings can become a Mr. Scrooge, using money to exert power over other family members.

not solve their problem; it creates a new, budgetary problem.

If one family member handles the money and withholds information regarding income or expenditures, he or she is using money to exert control. Other signs of this are the requirement that he or she be asked, even begged, for money or that he or she ridicules the wants and needs of other family members. Money can represent power to control decisions, lifestyles, and life itself. Such a situation leads to resentment, lack of cooperation, and perhaps even rebellion.

All of these attitudes and habits can sabotage family planning sessions and spending plans. They should be consciously avoided and eliminated. Being aware of these potential problems is part of the solution. Open and free discussions of individual needs, goals, values, and feelings should be encouraged in your family.

Collective Money Management Techniques

Even when everyone in a family is convinced that a plan is desirable and when everyone honestly wishes to cooperate, some partners cannot get through step one—determining income. They cannot agree how much of their income should be shared with the household and how much should be kept separate. Most of us grew up in a one-income family. We learned to handle money decisions within our families, so we tend to do as our parents did. Now that more and more two-income families exist, we need to devise new options.

We would like to present four methods that can be used to manage money collectively (Shaevitz and Shaevitz, 1980). One of these methods or a variation of it may help make you more comfortable with both the sharing of money and the sharing and delegating of power. The method you choose should clearly outline the financial responsibility of each family member and should be agreeable to him or her.

In the first option, *proportional contributions*, households determine their basic necessities and then each individual contributes to basic expenses in proportion to his or her income. Let us say that a family needs $1,500 each month. If one member makes $1,500 and one makes $500, they would contribute $1,125 (3/4) and $375 (3/4), respectively. There is a degree of fairness in this method because both partners contribute to household maintenance, while both have a degree of freedom to spend as they wish. The obvious disadvantage is that the partner with the smaller income has less freedom because he or she has less money. This system is quite unfair if one partner makes little or no money.

A second option is to *split household expenses evenly*. In other words, if expenses are $1,600 per month, each contributes $800. Each person keeps separate checking and separate savings accounts. The advantages here are that each person contributes equally and each shares equally in any benefits derived from this system. Individuals would personally benefit from a raise; their income would increase but their contribution wouldn't. This method can be adapted easily to accommodate more than two people. It can be especially suitable for unrelated people sharing a household and has often been adopted by college students living away from home. Disadvantages exist with this system when there is a big difference in income; one individual ends up with considerably less discretionary income after contributing to the household.

In the third collective money management technique, household members *pool their income*. Under this arrangement all money is placed in joint savings and joint checking accounts. No one is

There are a number of ways in which a couple can share household expenses while keeping personal expenses separate.

penalized for earning less money, because all share equally. There is no distinction between contributions of time (household tasks) or money. All work is considered worthwhile regardless of where it is done (inside or outside of the household) and without reference to the amount of money earned. This is one of the simplest methods and fits the traditional marriage pattern.

Pooling requires considerable trust and cooperation because both parties have access to all the money. This may be a real disadvantage if they do not agree about the distribution of the money. Also, there is no money specifically available for independent use. It would be almost impossible to put money aside for a special purpose without the other partner knowing about it.

In the fourth option, couples pool most of their money but also create two small "independent fund" accounts. This system is similar to pooling but with one distinct characteristic: each party has a specific amount of money available to spend as he or she wishes. The amount can be large or small, equal or unequal, but it is free from the influence or review of the other person.

> **BOX 6-2**
> ## Paying the Bills: Get Organized!
>
> **Work Center**
> First you need a work center with
> 1. A place for writing.
> 2. A place for supplies.
> 3. A place for storing financial records.
>
> You need a desk, a drawer, and a small portable file box.
>
> **Work System**
> 1. Have a definite place for incoming bills, notices, and so forth.
> 2. Stock this location with appropriate supplies:
>   - checkbook
>   - account book
>   - address book
>   - writing supplies
>   - postage
> 3. Create a filing system with accordian files or manila folders for:
>   - budget and financial records
>   - salary statements
>   - bills and debt notices with dates of payment
>   - sales slips, receipts, guarantees for major purchases
>   - canceled checks and bank statements
>   - investment records, including bankbooks
>   - income tax records
>   - property records, including insurance records
>   - automobile records, including insurance records
>   - credit card numbers and addresses in case of loss
>   - life insurance records
>   - employment records
> 4. Obtain a safe deposit box for valuable papers:
>   - stocks, bonds, negotiable securities
>   - property records—deeds, mortgages, and so forth
>   - record of insurance policies
>   - birth certificate, passport
>   - marriage certificate, divorce papers
>   - discharge papers from the armed forces
>   - auto titles
>   - wills, trust agreements
>   - household inventory

To control money you will need a plan or system. Discuss these four systems with your partner(s) before choosing one. You may find that you will create a totally different system from the ones presented here. What is important is that you talk over the advantages and disadvantages and find something that works for all of you. Consider how you feel, for example, about giving equal spending power to your partner(s). How will you feel about consulting your partner(s) *before* purchasing, rather than after the fact? Experiment with a system and then evaluate and revise when necessary, to the satisfaction of all family members.

Paying Bills

Once you create a system, someone has to run it—you need to decide how the bills will get paid and who will pay them. Perhaps the person who most enjoys doing it should be appointed. Some people prefer to organize and control financial matters, whereas others feel uncomfortable with this task. Or one party may be very good at keeping up-to-date records and bank statements. Don't forget to consider the time this individual spends in other household duties so as not to overload him or her.

Or you might decide to pay bills together. The advantage of sitting down once or twice a month to pay bills and discuss financial matters is that there are no "unknowns" for either partner. Each knows where the money is going and how much is left.

If no one really enjoys the details of record keeping and bill paying, and doing it together seems tedious or unnecessary, one partner could take over the job for a specified time. After that, the task would rotate to the other partner. This way each partner is familiar with the task and knows generally what the financial picture is, but isn't always responsible for it. In any event, both partners need to know and understand all the details of family business matters and to be able to assume full responsibility for management and record keeping if the need arises. Many widows have bemoaned the fact that they "knew nothing" about managing the family finances and as a result went through a difficult or costly adjustment period after their husband's death.

Box 6-2 provides some practical advice on how to set up a record-keeping system.

Summary

Achieving consumer spending that provides maximum satisfaction depends on having a budget based on family goals and values. Budgeting is a direct application of the decision-making process. In this case, the "problem" is to create a budget that considers each person's needs, wants, and goals and that is realistically based on anticipated income. The next step is to gather information such as spending records, tax returns, and check stubs. Then the family weighs alternatives and prioritizes goals; analyzes current spending patterns and identifies financial commitments that result in fixed expenses. The family can then decide to readjust spending in areas they choose and select a method of managing money collectively, if appropriate. Budgeting also includes periodic evaluation of financial progress by using a net worth statement. Finally, it is important to realize that the decisions and discussions involved in creating and implementing the plan may become emotional, but all feelings should be listened to and fairly considered.

Neighborhood REVISITED

1. If you were Cathy or Bob Tate, how would you have readjusted their budget? Why would you have made those decisions?

2. Plan a budget for Sue and Gary Gallagher based on the information below. Use Worksheet 6-5 on page 146.

Sue and Gary would like to create a budget. Because they don't really have a system, they decide to keep a daily record of their spending for one month. They total their spending and record totals on a budget worksheet.

Gary is a salesman. He does a lot of driving and pays for gasoline himself. One car is leased for him by his company. The other car was serviced this month. The Gallaghers usually owe about $200–$300 at the department store, so they pay something each month on the balance. This month they decide to pay for everything in cash or by check so that they can get a better idea of where their money is going. Even though they try to record all their spending, they can only account for $1,930 out of $1,975. Next month their car insurance is due. It is a semiannual premium of $278. They have a total of $675 in the bank.

Sue and Gary don't feel that they are staying even, let alone getting ahead. Sue earns some money babysitting and typing reports at home but feels that she is doing as much work now as she can handle. She doesn't want to go to work outside her home. The children are now four and seven years old, and she thinks they're too young to have a working mother.

The Gallaghers would like to increase their savings so they can feel more secure. They want to take a camping vacation next summer and can use the tent, sleeping bags, and other equipment they already own. Their furniture will be paid for in three months and the stereo in nine months. They've recently been looking at a portable TV; they think a second TV would really be convenient.

Considering the Gallaghers' lifestyle, income goals, and spending habits, help them create a realistic plan that they could follow to help them achieve their goals. Use the following outline and using their spending record for reference.

If you were the Gallaghers:
1. What is the first thing you would do to plan a budget?
2. How would you pay for the car insurance next month?
3. Would you establish an emergency fund? If so, how?
4. The Gallaghers are considering buying a television. If so, how should they fit this into their budget? How about the vacation?
5. What changes would you make in the Gallaghers' budget? How would you make these decisions? Record your adjustments on their spending record.

WORKSHEET 6-5
Spending Record

	Sue and Gary Gallagher	Your adjustments
Step 1: Calculate income.		
Income from jobs	$1,850	_____
Income from other sources	125	_____
Total:	1,975	_____
Step 2: Calculate fixed expenses.		
House payment or rent	570	_____
Insurance		
auto	0	_____
health (covered at work)	0	_____
household (included in house payment)	0	_____
life	25	_____
mortgage (included in house payment)	0	_____
Installments		
car payment	190	_____
department store	65	_____
furniture	30	_____
Utilities		
electric	55	_____
gas	40	_____
phone	50	_____
water	25	_____
Savings	25	_____
Other	25	_____
Step 3: Calculate emergency fund.	0	_____
Step 4: Calculate flexibile living expenses.		
Food and beverages	385	_____
Clothing and personal care	120	_____
Household expenses	55	_____
Transportation	175	_____
Entertainment, recreation	60	_____
Gifts, contributions	20	_____
Routine medical	10	_____
Other	15	_____
Step 5: Compare income to expenses.		
Total all expenses	1,930	_____
Compare to income	1,975	_____
Readjust if necessary.		

KEY TERMS

assets	emergency fund	gross income	net (disposable) income
budget	fixed expenses	liabilities	net worth
discretionary income	flexible expenses	money management	progressive income tax

QUESTIONS

1. List five reasons for using a budget.

2. Why is it helpful to look at spending patterns of the "average American family"?

3. Planning a budget involves matching future income to future expenditures. What information must be gathered before a budget can be made? Where can families get this information?

4. What factors should be considered for families when determining the size of an emergency fund? How much should your emergency fund be?

5. What is the purpose of a net worth statement?

6. Consider the four methods presented in the text for managing money collectively. Which one do you prefer and why? Ask your spouse or a close friend the same question. Is there a conflict of opinion? How could a compromise be reached?

7. Should children be included in budget planning sessions? If so, at what age? How should teenagers be involved in planning the budget?

8. Some partners, most often wives, do not know how much money their spouse makes. What kind of problems could develop as a result?

9. What should a young person who plans to marry know about a prospective spouse's attitudes and values about money and budgeting? Explain your answer.

10. What are some of the reasons that individuals and families cannot follow a spending plan?

11. What are some common emergencies that might happen to a family to require them to dip into savings? Are all of these really unexpected?

PROJECTS

1. Keep a record of all the spending you or your family does for an entire month. Analyze each budget category to see whether you are spending more or less than you thought. What changes would you recommend to increase the satisfaction you get from your spending?

2. Using the format presented in the chapter, create a spending plan for yourself. Follow it for two months, and then revise it when necessary.

3. Plan a budget for Brian Morris based on the following information and what you know about average family spending:

Brian Morris, age 21, recently moved from New York to southern California. His sister has lived in Anaheim for three years, and now Brian lives with her and her husband. He pays them $200 per month for room and board. Brian worked as a sales clerk for awhile, and then he got a job at a gas station. He wasn't really sure what he wanted to do, but he knew an education was important if he wanted a decent job.

Brian decided to enroll full-time at the local community college. He knew this would mean working fewer hours, so he wasn't sure he could afford it. He investigated loans, grants, and parttime jobs.

The financial aid office helped Brian get a $2,000 loan for the year. It also helped him find a job on campus. He works fifteen hours each week for $3.90 an hour, or about $235 per month. His gas station job pays him another $300 each month.

His budget is quite simple. He paid for his first semester fees and books from savings. He still has $520, but he tries not to use that money except for emergencies.

REFERENCES AND READINGS

"A Guide to Budgeting for the Family." U.S. Department of Agriculture Home and Garden Bulletin No. 108, Washington D.C.: U.S. Government Printing Office, 1980.

Hefferan, Colien. "Retirement Income." *Family Economics Review,* Winter 1981.

Jolly, Desmond A. "Low Income Life-Styles and the Consumption of Durable Goods: Implications for Consumer Educators." *Illinois Teacher of Home Economics,* May/June 1978.

"News You Can Use in Your Personal Planning." *U.S. News & World Report,* July 11, 1977.

"The 1976 *Family Circle* Survey on Working Wives." *Family Circle,* November 1976.

Shaevitz, Marjorie Hansen, and Shaevitz, Morton H. *Making It Together as a Two-Career Couple.* Boston: Houghton Mifflin, 1980.

Wright, Lois A. "Families in Debt." *Journal of Home Economics,* January 1978.

Did You Know That...

- an increase in the price of only one commodity is not inflation?

- the chief measure of inflation, the Consumer Price Index, contains the monthly retail prices of 400 commonly purchased items in eighty-five urban areas throughout the U.S.?

- by dividing your current income by the price index you can find out how much real buying power you have?

- if inflation averages 10 percent for the next two decades, a hamburger will cost $12 by the year 2001?

- U.S. consumers save a smaller percentage of their after-tax income than consumers save in any other nation?

- the biggest winner in the inflationary spiral is the federal government?

- there are ways to insulate your income and investments from inflation?

- recent economic research indicates that higher- rather than lower-income groups suffer more from inflation?

- there are inflationary and deflationary time cycles for many items, so by timing your buying during the year you can significantly increase your buying power?

7

Inflation: The Declining Dollar

Defining and Measuring Inflation: The Consumer Price Index
The History of Inflation in Recent Times
Inflation: Winners and Losers
Fighting Inflation: The Personal Side
Fighting Inflation: A Society-Wide View

Neighborhood CAPSULE
Inflation and the Tooth Fairy

"David, stop playing with that tooth and eat your lunch," Lydia Carpenter called from the kitchen as she continued to put away some groceries. She was a bit testy today, with some justification. Despite her skill at applying good consumer buying habits, inflation was taking its toll on her food budget. She was in the process of peeling off three layers of price stickers on a jar of mustard to satisfy her curiosity about how much it cost when it was first placed on the grocer's shelf, when David yelled, "It's out, Mom. It's come out."

"What are you talking about?" came the reply as Lydia came out of the storage area.

"It's my tooth. Look."

Sure enough, five-year-old David was proudly displaying a baby tooth—the first he had ever lost.

"I guess this means that the tooth fairy is going to visit us, right Mom?"

The tooth fairy had never visited the Carpenter house before because she had never been invited; David had no brothers or sisters and no teeth had been placed under any pillow in the house. Lydia knew what she must do: Find out what the going rate was for teeth.

"Have any of your friends had a visit from the tooth fairy?" Lydia asked cleverly.

"Oh, sure," came the reply. "Susie got a dollar when she lost her tooth."

"Think about getting a quarter," Lydia said, recalling her morning brush with inflation at the supermarket. Don't tell me the tooth fairy's price has gone up that much. Just a few years before, she recalled, the tooth fairy used to bring her a dime.

Why, a dollar in those days would get you into the movies, pay for a couple of candy bars, and still allow you to stuff yourself on popcorn. Occasionally there was even enough left over to buy a comic book on the way home.

"Mom, are you all right?" David asked. His mother seemed to have drifted off.

"Oh sure, I was just thinking." And so she continued to ponder the worth of a modern dollar. Today a dollar buys a box of crayons or a coloring book, but not both. And the box is small, none of those interesting colors, just the standard red, blue, and yellow variety.

"Does a dollar buy something big?" David wanted to know. "Can I get a catcher's mitt or a soccer ball?"

Lydia didn't want to explain the vagaries of inflation and the fall in the value of the dollar. She simply shook her head and said, "We'll see. The tooth fairy hasn't brought the dollar yet." In her heart she knew that the tooth fairy would bring David a dollar. And she also knew that it wouldn't buy very much.

When the Susan B. Anthony dollar was first introduced in 1979, the American public almost unanimously rejected it. Public outrage focused on its size, color, and general similarity to a quarter. Many people claimed to have confused the two coins and to have suffered economic loss in the process. During the uproar one pundit remarked, "I don't see what everyone is so upset about. Given the current rate of inflation, the Susan B. will soon be worth only 25 cents anyway." Indeed, the rapid rise in prices in the 1970s and early 1980s brought a host of problems to the Federal Reserve System, the controllers of the American money supply. Public indignation over the Susan B. Anthony dollar was quickly followed by another monetary problem—the near disappearance of the American penny. Inflation was also the culprit for the demise of this once-proud coin. Disheartened by the penny's lack of buying power, American consumers simply refused to carry and exchange it, which led to a penny shortage.

If the disappearance of the penny were the most serious consequence of inflation, we would hardly devote a chapter to the topic. However, as you are plainly aware, **inflation,** a sustained rise in the average level of prices, has far more serious consequences for the American consumer. In fact, during the 1980 presidential election, voters claimed that the most important issue was not unemployment or national defense but what to do about the high and seemingly ever-rising cost of living. Consumers' budgets—and patience—were stretched to the limit; they wanted an end to rising prices.

After reading this chapter you will not be able to singlehandedly stem the tide of rising prices. On the other hand, you should be able to succeed where many others have failed; you should be better equipped to handle inflation. In order to succeed in your battle against rising prices, you must follow the first rule of any good strategist—"Know Your Enemy." The first section of this chapter helps you to know your enemy by introducing you to the chief descriptive tool of inflation, the Consumer Price Index. After explaining what inflation is, we go on to discuss some of the causes of inflation as well as some potential society-wide remedies. But the heart of this chapter is devoted to helping you plan a personal strategy for dealing with inflation. This plan involves investments, shopping habits, and consumer activities that help you to avoid the ravages of inflation. The object here is to move you from the "loser" category to the "winner" category. Not all of our suggestions will apply to your circumstances today. But, as we discussed in Chapter 3, some suggestions that may seem irrelevant now could be helpful in a few years as you move through the life cycle. One point that is always relevant, however, is the use of our decision-making model to identify, evaluate, and then assist you in making some important choices about the inflationary strategy that suits you best.

Defining and Measuring Inflation: The Consumer Price Index

Mohammad Ali, three-time heavyweight boxing champion, fondly described his boxing prowess with the statement, "I float like a butterfly and sting like a bee." This description might also apply with equal strength to inflation, which seems to float harmlessly until consumers enter the marketplace and are almost always stung in a vulnerable area—their pocketbooks. Misunderstandings about inflation add to our frustrations and have to be cleared up before we can begin to fight it.

The most common mistake that consumers make with regard to inflation is identifying the rise in the price of a particular commodity as "inflation." Inflation is not that simple. An increase in the price of new cars, for example, does not signal a rise in the general level of prices, just as a nation's commissioning of a new submarine does not signal the appearance of a world-class navy. We have to look at the larger picture, at what is happening to prices in *general*. If other prices were falling while the price of cars were rising, the general level of prices would not be rising and the economy would not be experiencing inflation.

Because consumers can't possibly look at all prices, a government agency, the Bureau of Labor Statistics (BLS), monitors inflation. To discover the general level of prices the bureau has developed several measuring devices, called **indexes.** An index is a number used to characterize a set of data. In the case of a price index, the value of the index is determined by the average prices of a bundle of goods and services that the Bureau of Labor Statistics considers typical of all prices in the economy.

The most commonly used index is the Consumer Price Index for Urban Consumers, generally called the **Consumer Price Index (CPI).** Data for the CPI are gathered monthly from eighty-five urban areas in the United States—retail prices for a market basket of 400 items commonly purchased by 80 percent of American consumers. In a given year, the Bureau collects about 1,500,000 price quotations on such common goods as food, housing, fuels, and clothing

BOX 7-1
A Page from the Consumer Price Index

Here is a section from the Consumer Price Index for nonfood expenditures in the average U.S. city. As you can see, the Bureau of Labor Statistics keeps price data on a wide variety of goods and services, from cold remedies to pet supplies.

1. In January 1982, how much money did consumers have to pay to obtain the equivalent of $100 worth of medical services in 1967?
2. What was the percentage increase in the cost of eyeglasses from the Index base year of 1977 to January 1982?
3. Can you find an example of a price decline between December and January?

Group and item	Other index base	Dec. 1981	Jan. 1982
Medical care		310.5	312.9
Medical care commodities		195.3	196.3
Prescription drugs		181.8	182.1
Anti-infective drugs	12/77	137.8	138.2
Tranquilizers and sedatives	12/77	144.8	145.4
Circulatories and diuretics	12/77	131.9	132.2
Hormones, diabetic drugs, biologicals, and prescription medical supplies	12/77	164.6	165.6
Pain and symptom control drugs	12/77	145.9	147.3
Supplements, cough and cold preparations, and respiratory agents	12/77	138.1	138.8
Nonprescription drugs and medical supplies	12/77	139.2	139.9
Eyeglasses	12/77	128.4	128.3
Internal and respiratory over-the-counter drugs		221.3	223.7
Nonprescription medical equipment and supplies	12/77	134.6	135.9
Medical care services		335.8	338.7
Professional services		290.0	292.0
Physicians' services		313.0	315.5
Dental services		273.9	275.8
Other professional services	12/77	140.3	140.3
Other medical care services		391.7	395.2
Hospital and other medical services	12/77	162.7	165.6
Hospital room		519.5	526.8
Other hospital and medical care services	12/77	159.6	162.2
Entertainment		228.2	229.7
Entertainment commodities		232.0	232.9
Reading materials	12/77	139.6	142.9
Newspapers		267.7	270.5
Magazines, periodicals, and books	12/77	143.5	149.0
Sporting goods and equipment	12/77	130.0	129.5
Sport vehicles	12/77	132.1	NA
Indoor and warm weather sport equipment	12/77	119.9	120.1
Bicycles		195.9	196.4
Other sporting goods and equipment	12/77	126.2	125.3
Toys, hobbies, and other entertainment	12/77	132.0	132.2
Toys, hobbies, and music equipment	12/77	130.1	130.8
Photographic supplies and equipment	12/77	125.2	125.2
Pet supplies and expense	12/77	140.2	139.7
Entertainment services		223.0	225.5
Fees for participant sports	12/77	137.6	139.6
Admissions	12/77	129.7	131.2
Other entertainment services	12/77	123.7	124.2

*1967 = 100, unless otherwise noted.

and on consumer goods and services sold throughout the nation. The cost of these items is then totaled and divided by their cost in a preselected **base year** (base period). By comparing the cost of the same market basket of goods and services for two base periods, the BLS is able to make some general statements about the rise in prices over this period.

For example, if the average cost of an identical market basket of goods and services was $30 in 1967 (the base year) and $45 in 1972, the price of the basket rose by one-half, or 50 percent, over this period. The CPI summarizes price changes since the base year by arbitrarily assigning the base year a value of 100. In our example, the Consumer Price Index would equal 100 in 1967 and 150 (50 percent higher) in 1972. In May 1981, the CPI was 269.4, using 1967 as the base year. This means that it took $269.40 in 1981 to buy what $100 purchased in 1967.

Movements of the Consumer Price Index are usually expressed in percentages. Thus, you will sometimes read that "consumer prices rose 1.1 percent for the month of February." The 1.1 percent monthly inflation rate is simply the index number for the most recent month, February, minus the value of the CPI for January, divided by the value of the January index. In arithmetic terms we have:

$$235.8 \text{ (February CPI)}$$
$$-233.2 \text{ (January CPI)}$$
$$2.6$$

$$\frac{2.6}{233.2} = 0.011$$

$$0.011 \times 100 = 1.1 \text{ percent change}$$

Sometimes the monthly rate is converted into an annual estimate. It is common (but incorrect) for the news media to simply multiply the monthly rate by 12 to estimate the annual change in prices. This shortcut does little harm if the inflation rate is below 1 percent per month, but with higher rates the error can be significant. For example, if a 3 percent monthly rise in prices were to continue throughout the year, the annual rate would be closer to 42.5 percent rather than the 36 percent suggested by the simplistic "twelve times the monthly rate" answer.

A more serious problem for many consumers occurs when they confuse annual rates and monthly rates. Whenever the monthly CPI data are reported, these trends are hypothetically annualized. Thus, our 1.1 percent monthly figure becomes 14 percent on an annualized basis. Don't be fooled into thinking that prices rose 14 percent during the previous month. Inflation is hard enough without making it appear worse. A 14 percent *monthly* rate would cause a price level to be almost five times higher at the end of the year than at the beginning.

You can use the CPI for a variety of purposes, but one of its most important functions is to help you distinguish between nominal dollars and real dollars. **Nominal dollars** are measured by their face value. **Real dollars** are nominal dollars adjusted for inflation. The real value of dollars equals the quantity of goods and services that they will buy in a certain year. For example, a $100 bill printed in 1967 had a nominal value of $100, and, if it was still in circulation in May of 1981, it still had a nominal or "face value" of $100. But in *real terms* its purchasing power had declined over this period because of inflation. In 1967, that $100 bill could have bought more goods and services than it bought in 1981. The Consumer Price Index allows us to measure this change in the real value of money. To do this for any period, we divide current nominal dollars by the price index. Using our previous example, an index of 269.4 in 1981 tells us that a 1981 dollar would be worth about 37 percent (100 ÷ 269.4 = .37) of its 1967 purchasing power. To return to our $100 bill example, a $100 bill in 1981 bought only $37 worth of the goods and services it could have purchased in 1967.

Before you go running off to the library to measure your real income by getting the latest Consumer Price Index figures, we should warn you that there are a number of problems with using the CPI. In the first place, many people mistakenly believe that the CPI is a cost-of-living index. It is not. For one thing, the Consumer Price Index does not include income or sales tax. A second problem is that the index assumes that consumers always buy the same proportion of goods in their market basket. Real consumers do not always buy the same mixture of goods and services. The current CPI market-basket mixture is based on a nationwide survey of consumer spending habits conducted in 1972 and 1973—an era when gasoline was cheap and the V-8 engine was king. Today, the Sunday drive in a full-size car with eight cylinders has been replaced by jogging or bicycling, which are considerably less expensive. Eating habits have also changed. As beef and veal have become more expensive, we are eating more chicken and fish. These adjustments are made by consumers to help them avoid some of the burdens of higher prices, but the CPI has difficulty in taking these adjustments into account.

Another problem with using the CPI as a measure of inflation is that sometimes a price change reflects a change in the quality of an item. If a new color television costs $25 more than last year's model but has a better picture, only part of the higher price should be included in the inflation rate. Yale economist Richard Ruggles argues that if the dramatic quality changes in American goods and services had been fully taken into account, prices would have fallen steadily from 1949 to 1966, whereas the CPI

> **BOX 7-2**
>
> ## Inflation and You: The Case of the $12 Hamburger
>
> The power of inflation rates, like interest rates or population growth rates, is easy to underestimate. For example, if the price of a hamburger were to rise by 10 percent per year, how many years would it take for the price to double? Because a doubling would equal a 100-percent increase, most students are inclined to divide 100 by the inflation rate (10 percent) and arrive at an answer of 10 years. This is wrong because in each succeeding year the 10 percent price increase is added to the increase for the previous year. This is known as **compounding,** and it makes it difficult to come up with the right answer to our question. Fortunately, there is a simple arithmetic rule for solving the question of how long it would take for something to double if it is growing at a specified rate compounded annually. It is called **the rule of 70.** Divide 70 by the inflation rate and you will discover the number of years it takes to double the price level. In our case, 70 ÷ 10 = 7 years to double the price of a hamburger. If 1980 is the base year, by 1987 the price will double, by 1994 it will double again, and by 2001, it will double again.
>
> In tabular form, here is what it might cost you to go to McDonald's if prices rise at 10 percent per year.
>
> | Year | Hamburger | Small fries | Medium Coke | Total |
> |------|-----------|-------------|-------------|-------|
> | 1980 | $ 1.50 | $ .45 | $ .50 | = $ 2.45 |
> | 1987 | $ 3.00 | $ .90 | $1.00 | = $ 4.90 |
> | 1994 | $ 6.00 | $1.80 | $2.00 | = $ 9.80 |
> | 2001 | $12.00 | $3.60 | $4.00 | = $18.90 |
>
> By the end of the twentieth century, you could be lucky to get back some change from a $20 bill for a modest lunch.

showed a price rise of 36 percent. Although all economists concede that prices have risen since 1966, they must agree with Ruggles that price changes are not adequately adjusted to show improvements in quality (Meadows, 1978).

A final element of controversy surrounding the Consumer Price Index concerns the way it incorporates the price of housing into the inflation rate. In 1982 the Bureau of Labor Statistics tried to correct some of the upward bias in the CPI by using a "rental equivalence" measure of housing costs rather than the older approach, which relied on estimates of new home prices and mortgage rates. While the new method has its critics who claim that using rents is simply a way of reducing the inflation rate through statistical manipulation, most economists believe the new method will produce a better estimate of the inflation rate.

If the Consumer Price Index has difficulty in accurately measuring the change in the purchasing power of our money, no other price index is without its problems either. The one that most economists prefer, the Gross National Product Implicit Price Deflator, called the **GNP deflator,** was created by the Department of Commerce. The major purpose of this index is to convert the nominal value of *all* final goods and services produced in the United States into real value. This means that it covers many more goods and services than the CPI but excludes the prices of imports—a real drawback when so much of what we buy is produced in other countries. Another problem with this index is the time lag involved in creating it. Much of the underlying calculations depend on data from the Bureau of Labor Statistics (and the CPI) and from reports of sales in hundreds of industries. As a result, there are no monthly reports of the deflator—only quarterly reports that often must be revised two or three times. This means that the CPI remains our number-one monitor of inflation. But what causes the CPI to gyrate?

The History of Inflation in Recent Times

In spite of the fact that the Consumer Price Index is not a perfect yardstick of inflation, it is still the best

Figure 7-1. Percent change in the Consumer Price Index, 1948 to 1981. Average annual inflation rates for blocks of years are also indicated.

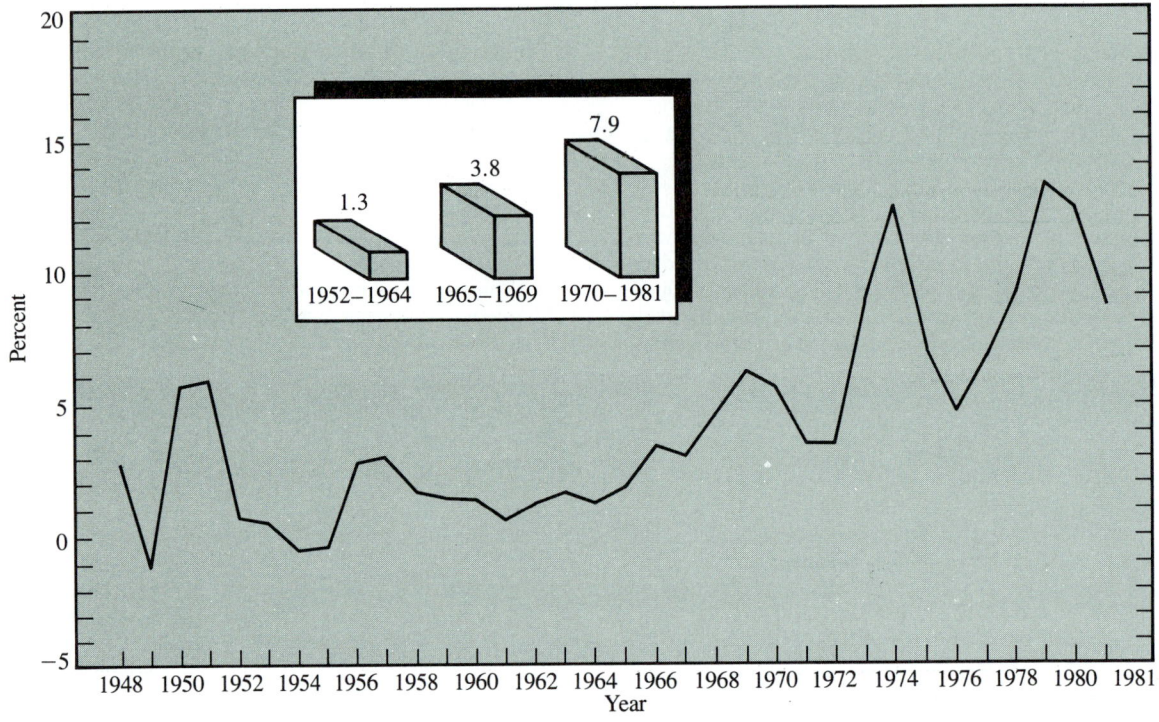

SOURCE: Department of Labor, Bureau of Labor Statistics.

estimate of the historical movement of prices. By looking at price trends over time you can get a better understanding of our current inflation.

Figure 7-1 shows the course of the CPI from 1948 to 1981. As you can see, inflation of more than 5 percent per year was fairly rare before 1970. And such "high" rates were generally associated with periods of war. World War II inflation (at the far left-hand portion of the figure), the Korean War inflation during 1950–1952, and the Vietnam War inflation from 1968 to 1970 were all associated with armed conflicts. Between wars the inflation rates were generally well below 5 percent. During the periods when we actually had a decrease in the overall level of prices, we experienced **deflation.** But since 1970, inflation rates of less than 5 percent per year have been the *exception* rather than the rule. From 1970 to 1981 the inflation rate averaged 7.9 percent versus a 1.3 percent rate from 1952 to 1964. Peace time no longer means stable prices.

DEMAND-PULL INFLATION

Why have wars generally been associated with inflation? The answer lies in what the government does during a war. It demands more engines of destruction and more people to run them, and it often winds up paying for them with newly created money. If increased government demands for goods and services are not offset by a decrease in the demands of the private sector, a classic case of "too much money

> **BOX 7-3**
>
> ## Gresham's Law:
> ## Bad Money Drives Out Good
>
> **Monetarism,** a school of modern economic thought that sees the increase in the money supply as the only cause for inflation, claims that the inflationary spiral of the twentieth century can largely be explained by the willingness of governments, particularly the United States government, to keep printing and spending more and more money. Monetarists believe that as new money is put into circulation, the value of money declines. Certainly there is some validity to this view. Imagine that our nation's money supply magically doubled overnight so when you wake up tomorrow you have $2 for every one you have today! This sounds great until you realize that everyone has the same good fortune. When people begin to spend this new-found wealth, they will soon discover that prices are on the upswing and that the real value of their money really hasn't changed much at all.
>
> The relationship between inflation and the money supply is not simply a twentieth-century phenomenon. In the Middle Ages, European sovereigns were often tempted to meddle with the money supply to increase their buying power. One way to do so was to call in old coins, melt them down, extract some of the gold or silver, and then mint new coins of equal nominal value but with less gold or silver content. The result was a larger money supply followed by inflation and a decline in the value of money. As the purchasing power of money declined, so did the consumer's faith in money. In response, Sir Thomas Gresham, a sixteenth-century financial adviser to Queen Elizabeth I, formulated one of the earliest economic laws. In arguing against tampering with the money supply he simply said, "Bad money drives out good." The newly minted, lower-value money would be used and the older, higher-value money would be hoarded and driven out of circulation.
>
> A similar phenomenon occurred recently in the United States. Until 1965, all coins worth 10 cents or more were 90 percent silver. After 1965, the silver content was replaced by nonprecious metals. Gresham's law would predict that pre-1965 coins would be driven from circulation, and they were. In fact, the value of those coins today varies from fifteen to twenty-five times their face value. Some smart gasoline station owners recently offered to sell gas at pre-1965 prices if their customers would pay in pre-1965 silver coins. The going price was 15 cents per gallon. This seemed like a bargain to consumers until they realized that the price of five gallons, three silver quarters, was worth over $15. The dealers were selling gas at about $3 per gallon!

chasing too few goods'' exists. This is sometimes called **demand-pull inflation** because increases in demand pull the prices of products ever upward. This is essentially what happened in the United States during the Korean and Vietnam conflicts.

COST-PUSH INFLATION

On the other hand, most economists agree that inflation can also be caused by a rise in the general cost of doing business. (For a dissenting view, see Box 7-3.) This is called **cost-push inflation.** The quadrupling of oil prices during the 1973–1974 period is often indicated as the major culprit in that inflationary period. Energy is such a vital part of our economy that any sudden shift in price tends to boost the Consumer Price Index unless other prices fall dramatically—a highly unlikely event. Thus, the rise in oil prices reverberates throughout the economy and brings inflation with it. The Iranian hostage crisis in 1979 and 1980 and the subsequent oil cutoff also set off a similar cost-push inflation.

Cost-push and demand-pull factors often interact with each other. A demand-pull inflation, for example, carries the seeds of inflationary discontent among workers whose multiyear contracts were signed before inflation gathered a full head of steam. Thus, when it is time to sign new contracts, the workers' unions may be expecting even worse inflation and thus make large wage demands. If this is a general phenomenon and if businesses give in to these demands, the cost of doing business rises and we have cost-push inflation.

Consumers' decisions are also intertwined with the inflation rate. If consumers are convinced that inflation is going to get worse, it makes good sense for them to alter their buying habits to avoid further price increases. They may decide to "buy now" rather than save and buy later at presumably inflated prices. Chapter 9 discusses the use of credit in more detail, but we should point out here that by using someone else's money during an inflationary spiral you gain in two ways: First, you get to enjoy the item now, at a lower price than would be possible if you postponed your purchase; second, you get to repay the borrowed money with less-valuable future dollars. Thus an inflationary strategy generally leads you to accelerate your purchases during the inflationary upswing. Unfortunately, acting on your **inflationary expectations** can fuel the inflation by injecting greater demand into the overall economy. This makes it even more difficult to bring the rate of inflation under control. Ironically, by acting rationally and accelerating your purchases to make yourself better off, you may make society as a whole worse off.

HYPERINFLATION

In some nations in the past, inflation rates accelerated to such an extent that money became almost worthless. Germany after World War I, Hungary in the 1940s, and Brazil in the early 1960s all had inflation rates of 1000 percent per month! When inflation approaches these rates, it takes bushels of currency to buy a loaf of bread. Workers want to be paid daily, or hourly if possible, and the fabric of the economy wears away. Such situations are called **hyperinflation,** and they are clearly the stuff of which political revolutions are made.

PRODUCTIVITY:
THE REAL ENEMY OF INFLATION

Because all economists agree that one basic form of inflation involves too much money chasing too few goods, one suggested remedy is increasing the production of goods and services without using more resources. The best way to do so is to increase the **productivity** of those resources—making them produce more with the same amount of input. For example, increasing labor productivity in the automobile industry means producing more cars per hour without increasing the work force. In the steel industry, increases in labor productivity would lead to greater steel production with the same labor force or a reduction in the work force with no reduction in output. In short, labor productivity means increasing the real value of what a worker produces without making that worker stay longer hours or work harder.

Labor productivity is the value of output that can be produced by one worker, and if a worker's productivity increases, given the same amount of time and effort, the worker is able to produce more.

If labor productivity increases in the economy as a whole, there will be more goods and services available for everyone to consume. This rise in the level of production can slow the inflationary spiral by reversing the order of demand-pull inflation from "too much money chasing too few goods" to "many more goods looking to be caught." This changeover would allow all of us to enjoy higher consumption patterns with less inflation.

It may surprise you to learn that the American economy has a very good track record with regard to productivity. As Figure 7-2 shows, output per hour of labor rose at an annual rate of 2.8 percent from 1940 to 1970. But since 1970, the rate of productivity advance has been a measly 0.82 percent. This abrupt slowing of productivity advance has done much to worsen our inflation problem. If the economic pie doesn't grow at the same rate that the consuming population and our aspirations continue to increase, we are all going to have smaller slices of economic pie.

Part of the answer could lie in reducing our level of expectations—settling for less. We discussed this alternative in Chapter 2 when we reviewed Ronald Stampfl's ideas on post-industrial-age values. Despite Professor Stampfl's arguments for a transition to post-industrialism, few of today's consumers view this as a long-run solution to our economic problems. A second and generally more preferred course of action is to take steps to increase the productivity of our labor force. One way to do so is to improve the way we produce, that is, improve our technology.

Figure 7-2. Productivity of the U.S. labor force. Base year: 1967 = 100.

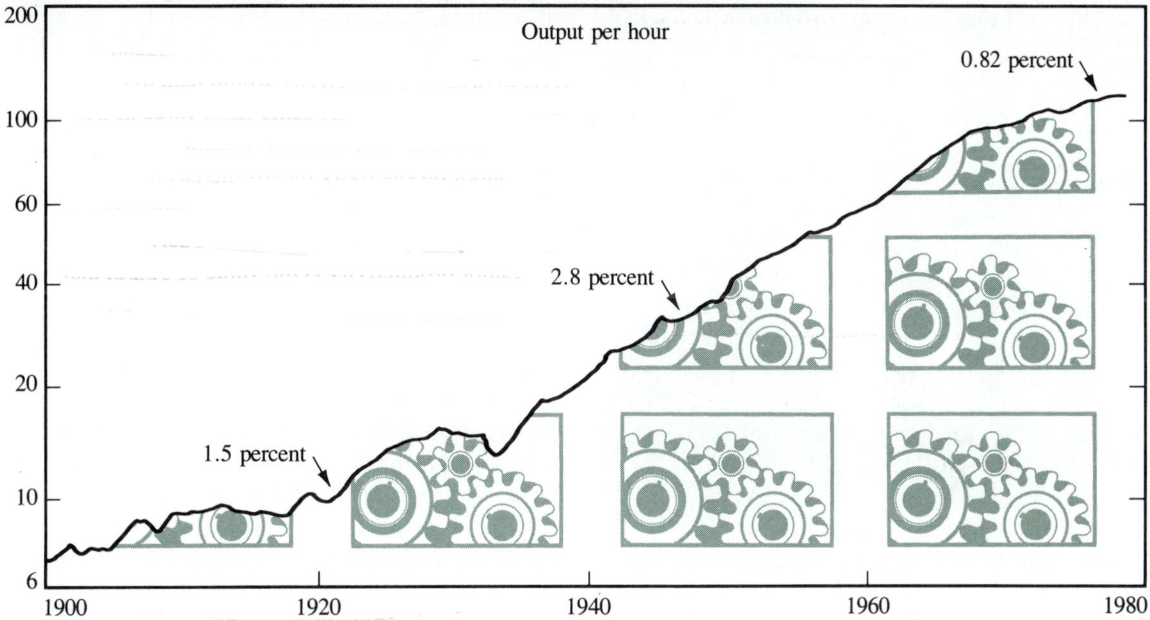

SOURCE: *1981 Historical Chartbook*, Board of Governors of the Federal Reserve System (Washington, D.C.: U.S. Government Printing Office, 1982).

Technology can be defined as society's pool of useful knowledge. It is useful in the sense that it can be applied to the production process and it can help workers to produce more. Technology has two components: research and implementation. Today, American spending on research and development is at a postwar low. We are utilizing less than 2½ percent of our national income on research and development activity, and only 25 percent of that small sum is spent on basic research, the kind of "think tank" activity that results in major breakthroughs such as the invention of the transistor or solar cells.

Implementation is also at a dangerously low level. In order to put new technology to work, we must build new plants and buy new equipment. This is called **investment.** Of all the major industrialized nations, only the United Kingdom spends a smaller fraction of its income on investment than we spend. Part of the problem here rests with consumers, because our investment capability is closely linked to our savings rate. Without a large pool of savings, banks simply do not have the money to lend to firms that want to modernize their old factories or build new, more efficient ones. Japanese consumers save 20 percent of their take-home pay, West Germans save 15 percent, and Canadians save an average of 11 percent. Americans save only about 5 percent of their take-home pay—a dismal showing that has hampered the economy's ability to finance new investments.

When a low savings rate is coupled with a modest level of investment and a declining research budget, the results are bound to be lower productivity, lower income for workers, and, ironically, an even smaller pool of savings. If we can turn this equation around, we can also reverse the dismal trend. If by becoming better consumers we can learn to maintain our current lifestyles with smaller expenditures, we can save more. This increases the funds available for investment, which in turn can lead to greater investment, productivity, and economic growth in the fu-

In recent years, Uncle Sam has been the biggest borrower of loanable funds. During inflationary times, this borrowing pattern may temporarily benefit the government, but not the general public.

ture. This is certainly part of the long-run solution to our inflationary ills.

We must also be concerned with our short-run problem of coping with inflation on a personal basis. Inflation does not treat everyone equally. Some groups actually benefit from inflation whereas others are clearly big losers. In reviewing the winners and losers outlined in the next section, you should be able to enhance your inflationary perspective and sharpen your decision-making skills so that you move from the losing toward the winning categories.

Inflation: Winners and Losers

At first glance it might seem that no one gains from inflation because by its very nature inflation eats away at the value of a given quantity of money and quietly destroys people's willingness to accept money (see Box 7-2). Those who win against inflation are those who have more buying power at the end of an inflationary spiral than at the beginning. In general, the biggest losers are those whose incomes are fixed in nominal dollar terms. Retired persons whose pensions are not adjusted for inflation or those whose incomes and net worth values do not rise as fast as the general rise in prices are in this category. To be more specific, retirees, creditors, savers, and people with large dollar balances generally lose during an inflationary period, whereas debtors and those whose incomes are automatically adjusted for inflation gain.

THE GOVERNMENT

The biggest debtor in the American economy is the federal government, and as such it is the number-one beneficiary of the American inflationary spiral. On the other hand, the people and institutions who bought government bonds have been among the biggest losers in the recent inflation. The government gains in two ways from inflation. First, whenever someone buys a government bond, he or she gives up the use of that money in return for the assurance of getting his or her money back plus some extra money (interest) to compensate for lending that buying power to the government. The lender loses, however, if the principal plus the interest paid back to the bondholder in nominal dollars does not equal the real dollars (buying power) of the original loan. This happens if the rate of inflation is greater than the interest rate. The lender's loss is, of course, the borrower's gain. Second, the government gains from inflation through the tax system, which takes part of the nominal dollar interest in the form of income tax. As the bottom line in Figure 7-3 illustrates, from 1965 to 1977 the real return to U.S. bondholders was negative when taxes and inflation were both taken into account. Since that time, yields on Treasury bills have risen considerably, but U.S. Savings Bonds have remained such a poor investment that in 1980 the Federal Trade Commission began an investigation into the advertising of such bonds on the grounds that the ads were false and misleading! We will discuss these investments in more detail in Chapter 16, but as far as savings bonds are concerned, you would do well to remember the old saying "Let the buyer beware."

Aside from gains from possibly defrauding small bondholders, the federal government also gains through the progressive income tax system. As we mentioned in Chapter 6, a **progressive income tax** takes a larger percentage of your income as your in-

Figure 7-3. Yields on Treasury bills discounted for taxes and inflation.

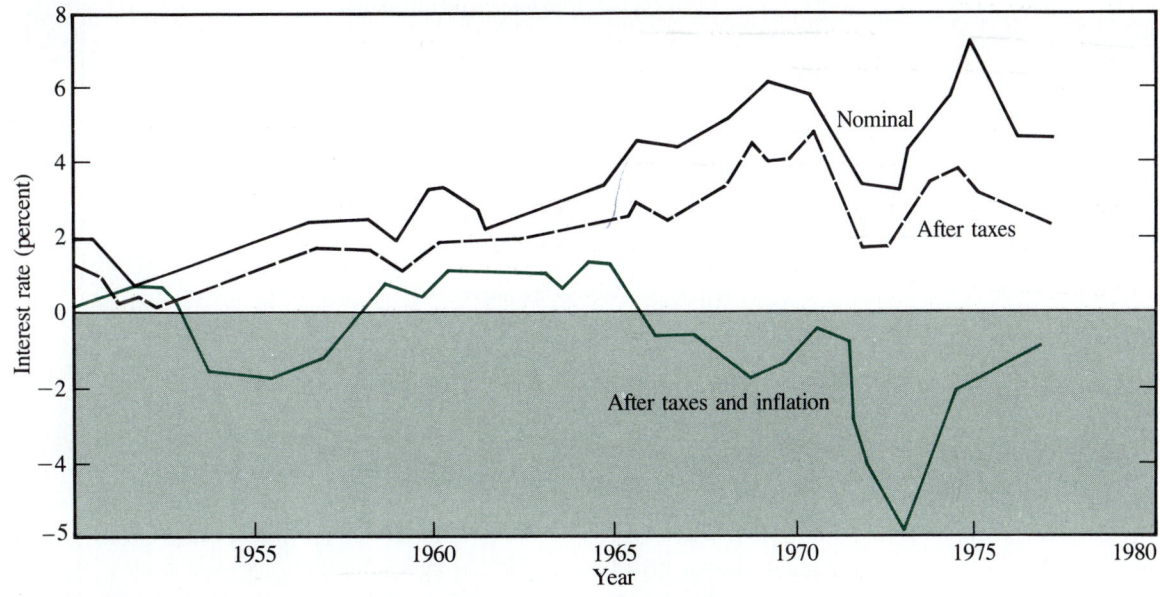

SOURCE: Jack Beebe, *Business and Financial Letter*, September 23, 1977, with permission of the Federal Reserve Bank of San Francisco.

come rises. The original idea behind the progressive tax was that someone earning $30,000 per year should be able to pay a higher percentage in income tax than someone earning $15,000 annually. Most Americans agreed with the idea, but this was before serious inflation set in. As Figure 7-4 illustrates, keeping up with inflation may swell your before-tax income, but under a progressive income tax system a higher income puts you in a higher tax bracket. A family earning $15,000 in 1970 would have paid $2,228 in federal income and Social Security taxes and would have had $12,772 in purchasing power. But in 1981, in order to have the same after-tax purchasing power ($27,179), the same household needed an income of $34,402 because it would have owed $7,223 in taxes. Although the household's nominal money income had to double just to maintain purchasing power, the government was able to beat inflation because its tax revenues tripled. If inflation rates and tax laws don't change, the same household will have to earn $87,708 in 1990 just to maintain its 1970 real income.

BUSINESSES

Government is not the only beneficiary of inflation. Private enterprise has been known to take advantage of the upward drift in prices in a number of ways. Companies that tend to have large inventories can be the sudden recipients of inflationary gifts called **windfall profits.** The oil companies experienced two such episodes in the 1970s. In 1973–1974, when OPEC quadrupled the price of crude oil, the oil companies' storage tanks and oil fields suddenly contained a commodity whose price had risen fourfold almost overnight. In the latter part of the decade, during the Iranian crisis, similar price hikes were obtained and the profits of the petroleum companies rose dramatically. This is only one of a number of possible examples that indicate how inflation can serve as profit insurance for companies. If the price of a firm's product keeps pace with inflation, a firm can be fairly sure that whatever it buys now will fetch a higher dollar price in the future.

Inflation has also been accused of serving as a

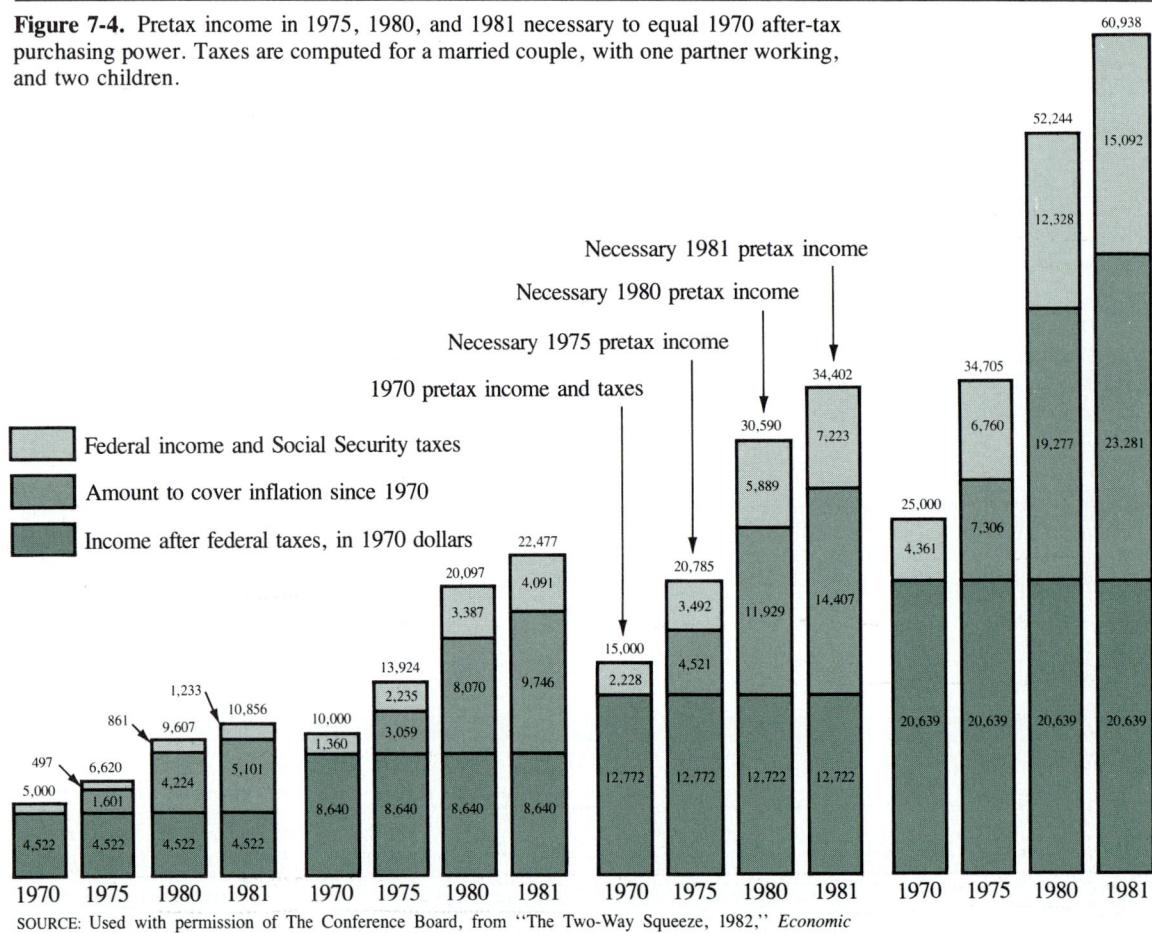

Figure 7-4. Pretax income in 1975, 1980, and 1981 necessary to equal 1970 after-tax purchasing power. Taxes are computed for a married couple, with one partner working, and two children.

SOURCE: Used with permission of The Conference Board, from "The Two-Way Squeeze, 1982," *Economic Roadmaps*, April 1982.

scapegoat for companies that want to raise prices in order to boost profits but fear that such a self-serving approach might produce an adverse consumer reaction. Such firms can simply argue that inflationary pressures forced them to raise their prices. John Case in his book *Understanding Inflation* (1981) cites Kodak as an example of a firm that was looking for an excuse to raise prices. In 1980 the Hunt brothers, through speculation, had driven the price of silver up to $50 a troy ounce from the previous year's average of $14. Because silver is a prime ingredient of photographic film, Kodak raised its prices an average of 27 percent, but on some products such as x-ray film, Kodak almost doubled its price. After the Hunts'

silver speculation failed, the price of silver returned to the $14 level, but Kodak reduced its prices very little. X-ray film was reduced by 20 percent and the price of 35mm motion-picture film was cut from $70.20 a roll to $61.70, but before the price hike, movie film had sold for $42.50 a roll. Kodak's first-quarter earnings were 10 percent higher than in the previous year.

INDIVIDUALS

Have any individuals gained during an inflation? You probably will not find many people who claim to gain by inflation, so taking a poll will not help you answer the question. It's a bit like asking people who have just come back from gambling in Atlantic City or Las

Table 7-1. Who's Ahead in Real Pay, 1977–1978

	Average weekly pay before taxes	Gain in pay, 1977-1978	Change in real pay—allowing for higher prices, taxes*		Average weekly pay before taxes	Gain in pay, 1977-1978	Change in real pay—allowing for higher prices, taxes*
Those ahead . . .							
Farm operators	$230.38	$49.23	+$21.45	Shoe-factory workers	140.91	8.14	− 3.87
Tire-factory workers	372.22	58.68	+ 19.17	Machinery workers			
Metal-can makers	368.94	57.06	+ 18.02	(nonelectrical)	305.86	24.64	− 4.18
Steelworkers	412.16	60.01	+ 16.61	Veterans on full disability	211.48	13.58	− 4.23
Metal miners	364.04	54.94	+ 16.52	Lumber workers	227.48	16.68	− 4.70
Petroleum-refinery workers	411.65	44.00	+ 3.55	Metal-product workers	277.62	20.58	− 4.74
Bank clerks	155.73	9.73	+ 2.92	Sporting-goods workers	176.33	11.75	− 4.76
Aluminum workers	399.81	41.72	+ 2.48	Rubber workers,			
Oil, gas-field workers	388.07	40.07	+ 1.99	except tires	221.40	15.99	− 4.85
Aircraft workers	355.91	33.31	+ .38	Chemical workers	305.95	22.37	− 6.03
Laundry workers	132.86	11.41	+ .18	Furniture workers	194.57	11.91	− 6.05
. . . and behind				Meatpackers	309.33	22.71	− 6.06
Social Security pensioners	$ 58.62	$ 3.47	−$ 1.49	Electric, gas-company			
Construction workers	328.99	29.72	− 1.97	workers	329.80	24.56	− 6.09
Wholesale-trade workers	239.68	20.89	− 2.10	Food processors	241.80	16.12	− 6.16
Clothing workers	146.52	10.78	− 2.12	Electrical-equipment			
Auto workers	395.60	35.74	− 2.13	workers	249.48	16.13	− 6.68
Retired federal workers	163.62	12.70	− 2.36	Printing and publishing			
Retail clerks	133.42	8.84	− 2.50	workers	255.46	15.95	− 7.20
Leather-goods workers	148.40	10.39	− 3.16	Schoolteachers	282.10	14.77	− 10.08
Local bus drivers	286.86	23.12	− 3.54	Federal-government			
Instrument workers	247.28	19.72	− 3.58	workers	348.65	18.17	− 11.58
Paper-mill workers	296.24	24.18	− 3.68	Cigarette-factory workers	288.79	9.69	− 14.82
Textile workers	182.78	13.45	− 3.82	Telephone workers	311.24	9.40	− 16.77

*After federal income and Social Security taxes and adjustment for the rise in consumer prices. Assumes a family of four for tax purposes, except for retired federal workers, who are assumed to be married couples.

Note: Latest available weekly pay, usually December 1978. Farm operators often include family members instead of individual workers.

SOURCE: J. H. Moore, "Inflation and the Burden of Taxation" (National Federation of Independent Business, *Public Policy Discussion Series*, 1979).

Vegas whether they won more than they lost. Their stories seldom reflect the economic realities of the situation. To get the real facts, you need an impartial observer.

Wages, Taxes, and Inflation. John Moore (1979), a professor at the University of Miami, conducted a study of the impact of inflation and taxes on workers' buying power. He classified workers by their occupations and analyzed their gains in wages after adjusting for higher prices and higher taxes. The results are presented in Table 7-1. As you can see from the table, some workers were able to beat inflation, but the majority simply could not. Of those who were able to stay ahead, most belonged to strong labor unions in the steel, mining, rubber, or oil industries. The biggest losers were government employees such as school teachers and civil servants.

Cost of Living Adjustments. The primary method that some unions use to keep their members ahead of inflation is the automatic **cost-of-living adjustment** (COLA) written into their contracts. A COLA clause (sometimes called an escalator clause) usually ties the hourly wage to some index of inflation such as the Consumer Price Index. Thus, as the CPI rises, hourly wages increase. In 1948, the United Auto Workers got the first labor contract that included a COLA. From 1948 to 1965, COLA clauses began to catch on, but even in 1965 only 26 percent of all union employees were covered by such agreements. However, with the beginning of the Vietnam War inflation, unions began to look for a way to preserve the increases in buying power that they had won at the negotiating table. The COLA appeared to be of significant help, and by 1981 almost 60 percent of all union workers had a COLA in their contracts.

The COLA that all unions prefer is an adjustment that rises in lockstep with the rise in the CPI. Thus, if the union wage for a sheet-metal worker was $8 per hour in January and the CPI rose 10 percent by December, the sheet-metal worker would receive 10 percent more ($8.80) by Christmas. Very few unions have COLAs that operate this way. Most allow the workers to take on only a portion of the increase in the CPI, and many COLAs are "capped," which means that there is a maximum allowable wage increase under the contract no matter how much the CPI rises. If you read about a dispute over an uncapped COLA, you should realize that the argument is not about a stale soft drink. Rather, the union and management representatives are at odds over removing the ceiling on these automatic wage adjustments. The Council of Economic Advisors estimated that current COLA clauses add about 1 percent to the national inflation rate. They are good insurance for individuals covered by them, but they are bad news for inflation fighters.

Union members are not the only people who have tried to insulate their incomes from the ravages of inflation. Social Security recipients, retired government workers and military personnel, and even people on welfare all receive automatic income adjustments for inflation. In fact, according to the 1981 federal budget, 42 percent of all government outlays will go to programs in which the recipients' benefits are indexed to rise with inflation. In July 1980, for example, all Social Security recipients received a 14.3 percent increase in their benefits because the CPI had risen a similar amount in the first six months of that year. However, because many economists believe that the CPI actually overstates inflation, any individual whose income rises in unison with the CPI actually gains some buying power. In the case of wage adjustments, as with COLAs, this slight gain is probably wiped out by the additional taxes that are owed on the increase. The real income of our $8.80-per-hour sheet-metal worker's take-home pay in December was probably less than it was in January because of income taxes. However, for a recipient of Social Security or for a welfare recipient, the increase in payments triggered by a rise in the CPI is not negated by taxes because these payments are tax free. Adjustments such as these led Joseph T. Minarik (1979), an economist at the Brookings Institution, to argue that those with lower incomes are not harmed as much by inflation as those with higher incomes because the poor tend to receive more untaxed subsidies that are indexed to rise with inflation. Of course this position has not gone unchallenged. Others have argued that the rise in the prices of necessities has been more rapid than the rise in the prices of luxuries. This argument, called "the four-necessities theory," states that food, fuel, housing, and health care are the four most important commodities and that the prices of these goods have risen much more rapidly than the CPI in general. As a result, the poor have suffered more from inflation than any other group (Nulty, 1979). The four-necessities theory is not highly regarded among most impartial observers because the index seems flawed. For example, why isn't clothing included as a necessity? Some critics argue that to include clothing would not support the theory because prices of apparel have not risen as rapidly as the CPI. And the food component of the necessities index includes not only basic food items but sirloin steaks and restaurant dinners as well (Case, 1981).

Fringe Benefits. If poor consumers are not suffering more than other consumers, it is partly because of their nontaxed benefits. Food stamp allotments and rent subsidies are automatically increased because of

Inflation: The Declining Dollar

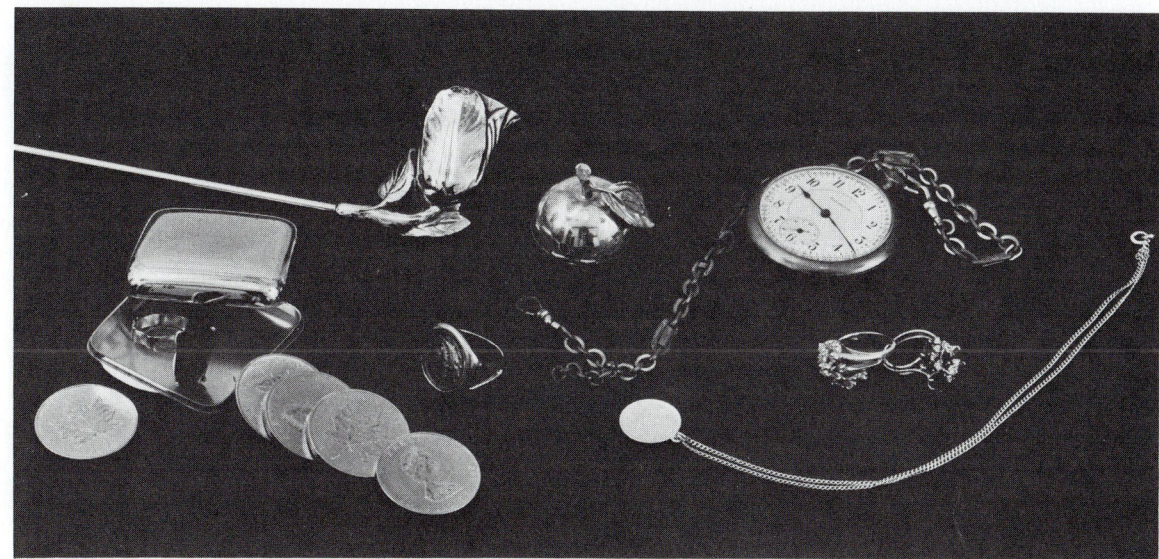

Collectibles of various kinds have always been a standard hedge against inflation.

inflation. The nonpoor can learn a lesson here. If a worker can get his or her employer to pay for something he or she wants, the worker gets what amounts to tax-free income. It is unlikely that workers would accept a food allotment from their employers, but they do accept free dental plans and hospitalization plans. Employer contributions to the employee that do not directly involve salaries are called **fringe benefits**. By increasing their fringe benefits, employees are able to obtain more goods and services without incurring additional income tax obligations. Fringe benefits have become an important part of most labor negotiations, and before you accept employment you should inquire about them just as you would ask about the salary. The United Auto Workers, who pioneered the COLA clause, was also among the first unions to see the importance of fringe benefits. At General Motors, for example, the annual cost of the fringe-benefit package exceeds the amount paid for steel. It is not unusual for fringe benefits to add 25 to 30 percent to the cost of labor.

Fighting Inflation: The Personal Side

As the last section showed, individuals have developed a number of novel methods to preserve their paychecks from inflation. Collective bargaining, COLA clauses, and more emphasis on fringe benefits are three common tactics used in this battle. But the inflation war extends far beyond the workplace. Hard-won gains in pay can be quickly squandered in the marketplace by consumers who forget to use their decision-making skills. In this section, we emphasize those strategies that are relevant to your investing and spending habits as they relate to inflation. It is not an exhaustive discussion of either investing or spending because both will be dealt with in later chapters. Nevertheless, if you are to move from the losing to the winning category in your bout with inflation, you need some guidelines. We expand on the investment discussion in Chapters 15–17 and on consumer buying strategies in Chapters 9–14.

PERSONAL INVESTMENTS

Telling other people what to do with their money has become a major occupation. Newspapers, magazines, and books are filled with information from so-called "experts" on how you can harness the forces of inflation, invest wisely, and become a millionaire. "Buy gold," say some financial wizards. "No, buy land," say the real-estate buffs. "Nonsense," says a third expert, "Buy diamonds." The chorus goes on and on. Who should you believe?

Table 7-2. Inflation Hedges, Compound Annual Rate of Return

Hedge item	10 years Increase	Rank	5 years Increase	Rank	1 year Increase	Rank
Gold	31.6%	1	28.4%	3	104.0%	1
Oil	31.6	2	17.7	7	92.4	2
Silver	23.7	3	27.3	4	76.8	3
U.S. stamps	21.8	4	31.0	2	43.2	4
Chinese ceramics	18.8	5	38.7	1	13.1	11
Rare books	16.1	6	12.7	10	14.0	10
U.S. coins	16.0	7	21.9	5	25.3	5
Diamonds	15.1	8	18.3	6	25.0	6
Old Masters paintings	13.4	9	15.2	8	17.4	7
U.S. farmland	12.6	10	13.4	9	14.3	9
Residential housing	10.2	11	11.6	11	10.4	13
Consumer Price Index	7.7	12	8.9	12	14.5	8

SOURCE: *Wall Street Journal*, July 28, 1980. Reprinted by permission of *Wall Street Journal*.
© Dow Jones & Company, Inc. 1980. All rights reserved.

The first point to remember is that there is no absolutely safe method to avoid inflation through investment. All investments entail some risk, and as a general rule the higher the potential return, the greater the risk. Having read this, you should go back to our decision-making model and decide how much of a return you want to make on your investment and how much risk you are willing to accept. There is a tradeoff here between risk and return. No financial expert can solve this dilemma for you, although a good adviser can categorize the riskiness of various ventures.

Once you have established your goals, you need to collect and process information on alternative investments. This is where Table 7-2 may come in handy. It presents some of the most successful inflation hedges of the last decade. Of course, there is no guarantee that these investments will do as well in the 1980s as they did in the 1970s, but given this information no one can mislead you about the performance of one of these investments.

Over the 1970 to 1979 period, the top-rated inflation hedge was gold, which rose at a compound annual rate of 31.6 percent while the CPI rose at 7.7 percent. Perhaps this explains the success of the experts who recommend buying precious metals such as gold or silver. In addition to precious metals, oil, stamps, Chinese ceramics, rare books, and old coins all rose more than twice as fast as the CPI over this period. Some investments did not do much better than the CPI. Residential housing and U.S. farmland are two investments that did not show the same spectacular gains exhibited by precious metals. Nevertheless, they did outpace inflation, and given the spectacular fluctuations in the prices of gold and silver over this period, housing and farmland could be your preferred investment if you want to limit your risk.

As Box 7-4 points out with respect to diamonds, information is not free. Many investments require the services of an expert whose fees will eventually be deducted from your net gain (or added to your loss, if you are unfortunate). Once you have selected an investment alternative, you will want to follow along the lines of the decision-making model presented in Chapter 2 and evaluate your decision by monitoring your investment. If you don't cope well with uncertainty, some experts suggest that you set up specific criteria for selling your investment. For example, if it rises in value (appreciates) by a certain percentage (say, 50 percent) or falls by a certain percentage

> **BOX 7-4**
>
> ## Are Diamonds a Girl's Best Friend?
>
> Well before the American divorce rate cracked the 40 percent level, a song titled "Diamonds Are a Girl's Best Friend" was popular. The argument was that women could be more sure of the value of their jewelry than of the value and constancy of their spouse. But before you go to your local jeweler to pick out a diamond pendant or ring, you should know something about the diamond market. In the first place, diamond prices are tightly controlled by South Africa's DeBeers Consolidated Mines Ltd., which markets 80 percent of the world's diamonds. They have such significant market power that they virtually set the price for their product. If they choose to mine and market more diamonds, they will undoubtedly have to lower the price and thus jeopardize your investment. The second problem is storing and appraising diamonds. Here there is no substitute for expert advice and management, and the investor will have to pay a premium for both. Fees for appraisal start at $80 for a one-carat stone, according to the Gemological Institute of America. The diamond transaction itself has significant costs, with sales commissions ranging from 10 to 15 percent both when you buy and when you sell. If you pay a 15 percent commission when you buy the diamonds and 15 percent when you sell them, they must rise in value (appreciate) over 30 percent before you can recoup your initial investment. Such increases are seldom seen in less than a year's time, so plan on holding onto these stones for quite awhile. But before you get ready to enjoy them, remember that investment-grade diamonds should never be placed in a setting. To get a maximum return, you must simply leave them in a safe place and hope for the best. This will probably deflate their value to you as a consumer good because one of the major enjoyments of owning diamonds comes from displaying them to friends and acquaintances.

(perhaps 25 percent), you automatically sell. You may never be a big winner under this rule, but you will never be a big loser. And adopting such a rule economizes on your time, a resource that is certainly valuable.

AN OVERALL PERSONAL PLAN

If inflation has become an important component in deciding where to invest and what to invest in, it has added an even more important dimension to our day-to-day lives. Every day we find ourselves confronted with higher prices, smaller quantities, and diminished quality. The all-pervading nature of inflation makes good consumer decision-making skills a necessity. By making these skills part of your daily routine, you will be able to lessen the impact of rising prices on your budget.

Shopping Habits and Relative Prices. There are certain battle-tried techniques that may help you to cope with inflation. One of the most useful is a general awareness of the importance of *relative* as opposed to absolute price changes. In an inflationary period most prices rise, but some rise faster than others. Thus, you can lessen inflation's impact on your buying power by adjusting your shopping practices: substitute items whose prices have risen relatively little for items whose prices have increased greatly.

Table 7-3 presents data that appear in the Consumer Price Index on the cost of various foods. As you can see from the table, food costs rose 8.9 percent from January 1979 to January 1980. However, a smart shopper need not have experienced the full impact of food inflation. As you look down the list of foods, notice that some, such as poultry, rose relatively slowly (a 3.6 percent annual increase), while others actually *decreased*. Pork and fresh vegetables were actually cheaper in 1980 than they were in 1979. On the other hand, the prices of beef and veal rose more rapidly than the food index and thus were relatively more expensive to purchase. By using the decision-making model and adjusting your buying habits, you can avoid part of the increase in the high cost of consuming.

Table 7-3. Changes in Food Costs

Foods	January 1979 (base period)	January 1980	Percentage increases 1979–1980
Cereals	100.0	111.0	11.0
Beef and veal	100.0	116.2	16.2
Ground beef	100.0	115.1	15.1
Pork	100.0	91.0	−9.0
Poultry	100.0	103.6	3.6
Fish	100.0	109.0	9.0
Dairy	100.0	111.0	11.0
Fresh fruits	100.0	111.2	11.2
Fresh vegetables	100.0	92.7	−7.3
Processed fruits	100.0	107.4	7.4
Processed vegetables	100.0	105.2	5.2
Overall food index	100.0	108.9	8.9

SOURCE: U.S. Department of Labor, Bureau of Labor Statistics, *Monthly Labor Review*, April 1980.

As we mentioned earlier in this chapter, the Consumer Price Index does not take changes in consumer behavior into account, because the index is based on the purchase of a fixed market basket of the same goods and services in the same proportions each month. Good consumer decision makers do not behave the way that the CPI assumes they behave. They alter their buying habits to take relative price changes into account. Nevertheless, many people continue to incorrectly refer to changes in the CPI as changes in the cost of living. These people are obviously ignoring changes in consumer spending patterns that are an integral part of trying to avoid shouldering the entire burden of inflation. We will cover food buying in greater detail in Chapter 10. The point here is that by being a price-conscious consumer, you may be able to cut the real cost of inflation by as much as one-third.

Timing and Buying. The question of when you buy can sometimes be as important as what you buy. There are certain cycles to consumer buying, as anyone who has ever been to a department store after Christmas already knows. If you have ever gone into a clothing store on a chilly March day and seen swimsuits on sale, you have some idea about the importance of timing to retailers. They are on a fairly rigid schedule for much of their merchandise, and anything that is unsold by a certain date must be disposed of. This is when smart shoppers can sometimes pick up bargains by anticipating the end-of-season sales. Chapter 9 mentions some of the most common goods that regularly appear in a regular price–sale price cycle.

Of course, there are some drawbacks to a wait-for-the-bargains plan. You may buy something that is at the very end of its fashion cycle. This is explained in greater detail in Chapter 9, but it amounts to buying a good that is perfectly functional but no longer the latest model. This may be unimportant for an appliance, but it may make quite a difference to you in clothing. A second problem with waiting for the sales and then pouncing on low prices is that the quantities of goods will be limited, and you will not have the range of selections that you might prefer. You may be forced to use your valuable time to hunt for what you want in various stores. This tradeoff of shopping time and higher prices is very real. But if your major objective is to find lower prices, you will have to invest some time to find them.

RULES FOR INFLATION-WISE CONSUMERS

In addition to timing your purchases to coincide with downturns in traditional buying periods, there are other rules that smart buyers follow:

1. *Budget your income*. Chapter 6 covers this topic. Although it is a difficult task for consumers, the time you spend budgeting will pay off.

2. *Shop with a list*. If you know just what you want, you will be less likely to stroll aimlessly along the aisles of a store and engage in impulse buying. Store managers know how to make products more seductive. Mood music, large shopping baskets, and locating the most frequently purchased consumer items (such as bread, eggs, and milk) at the rear of the store are all calculated to encourage buying. A list helps you to resist temptations.

3. *Compare prices and quality*. The appearance of generic (nontrademarked) goods offers you an opportunity to avoid inflation brought on by higher advertising costs. Chapter 14 lists a number of generic drugs that may be used in place of their more expensive and better-known competitors. Try them.

4. *Buy used goods*. You can often save substantially by purchasing good used consumer durable goods such as washing machines, refrigerators, automobiles, and microwave ovens. Community bulletin boards, classified ads, and friends in your neighborhood may be good leads to bargains.

5. *Avoid door-to-door salespeople*. There are genuine disadvantages to shopping in your home. In general, home-shopping prices are higher and you often don't have sufficient time to consider the offer. The best advice is to simply shut the door. But as we said in Chapter 5, if you do sign a contract, the law states that you have three days to cancel the order.

6. *Buy larger quantities*. This tip has two parts. First, you will generally save by buying the so-called economy packs, although even here you must beware of quirks in pricing in which the unit cost may be higher for a larger size if there is a sale on a smaller size. Second, shop for and stock up on "specials." A little time spent on setting up a household storage area can pay big dividends in your fight against inflation.

7. *Minimize your cash*. Keeping money in your pocket or in a noninterest-bearing checking account maximizes your exposure to inflation. As prices rise,

The advent of aisles full of "generic" foods and products in big supermarkets is a sign that consumers are willing to forgo familiar brand names in order to get the most for their food dollars.

the buying power of that money deteriorates. If that money is not earning any interest, it is losing its value at the rate of inflation. Remember, inflation is to cash what kryptonite is to Superman. Inflation makes money weak and helpless. Thus, the more money you hold today in liquid form, the less buying power you will have tomorrow.

8. *Do it yourself*. The costs of many services have escalated to the point where it may benefit you to do the job yourself. A number of simple jobs such as changing your car's motor oil, installing light fixtures, repairing leaky faucets, and putting up wallpaper are fairly simple to learn and can save you money. It will probably take you longer to do them than it would take a professional, but the real question is, how many hours would you have to work at your job to earn enough after-tax income to pay a professional? If you are in the 50-percent tax bracket, you have to earn $200 for every $100 you owe for services. Inflation plus the progressive income tax have done a great deal to encourage the do-it-yourself movement.

> **BOX 7-5**
>
> ## Barter: Trade Rather Than Pay
>
> Trading merchandise for merchandise is the simplest form of bartering. Determination of barter value depends on the age and condition of the product, its resale price, and the ease of resale. Bartering can help you decrease the impact of depreciation because you can get rid of what you don't want before it is valueless and get something else in return.
>
> Service-for-service barter is more complex. First, decide on a service you can supply, then make a list of all the people who might use your service. Make a second list of all the services you pay for, and do some matchmaking with the first list. For example, perhaps you can exchange your accounting skills for interior-design advice. The fixed dollar value of service-for-service exchange is often difficult to establish, so the criterion used for negotiation should be mutual satisfaction.
>
> ### Making the Contact
> Bulletin boards at school, at work, or in the supermarket are excellent trading posts. Local newspapers' classified sections can also be used. Place your ad in the "Merchandise for Sale" section or in the section that lists services you wish to obtain, for example, the "Photography" section if you want to barter to have some wedding pictures taken.
>
> ### Negotiating the Deal
> Be prepared to be flexible. Keep in mind that each person is getting something he or she wants. Do not commit yourself to something that seems unfair, but do be willing to give in a little. With practice, your skills at bartering will increase along with your spending power.
>
> ### Formalized Barter
> There are some organized barter exchanges to help you get in touch with others interested in bartering. They require a membership fee for participation. A few are listed here:
>
> 1. The Learning Exchange (P.O. Box 920, Evanston, Illinois 60204) is a telephone referral service that puts prospective students and teachers in touch with one another. It is a nonprofit organization. Its $15 yearly membership fee includes a quarterly newsletter and catalog update.
>
> 2. The Vacation Exchange Club (350 Broadway, New York, New York 10013 and Box 4529, Honolulu, Hawaii 96813) is a house-swapping organization. Membership entitles you to two directories a year: You can be a listed subscriber ($15) and have your home listed in either the February or April directory, or you can be an unlisted subscriber ($12) and receive both directories.
>
> 3. American Barter Systems (202 Westchester Avenue, White Plains, New York 10601) charges a one-time fee of $200 to join its network and annual dues of $100. Members trade with other members for goods and services; no money changes hands—it's a credit system.
>
> 4. Barter Communique is your best source of information on barter clubs and exchanges. It contains useful articles on barter and related subjects such as tax implications. A subscription costs $20. Write to *Barter Communique,* the National Newspaper of the Barter Industry, Full Circle Marketing Corporation, P.O. Box 2527, Sarasota, Florida 33578.
>
> ### Tax Implications
> The Internal Revenue Service may not appear to be concerned about whether you trade your used refrigerator for a used color television, but they are. This concern has become more pronounced in recent years because of the loss of income taxes that results from extensive bartering. Barter exchanges that give you buying power *are* taxable. For specific questions, consult an accountant or an attorney (whose services you've just bartered, of course).

9. *Barter.* Another way to try to minimize the ravages of inflation on your buying power is to engage in **barter,** which is an exchange of goods or services between two parties in which money is not used. It is essentially a swap. You probably engaged in barter as a child. Remember when you traded cards and swapped marbles? Today, many Americans are resorting to barter because it gives them more spend-

ing power and it's fun. For example, you might trade your old stereo for a used bicycle, or if you enjoy repairing engines, you could trade this skill for legal assistance from an attorney. Almost anything can be bartered, from time to talent to merchandise. See Box 7-5 for more details on how to enter the barter economy.

Fighting Inflation: A Society-Wide View

You can do quite a bit to limit the ravages of inflation on your personal budget by following the tips outlined earlier. By being a better decision maker you will help defuse some of the cost-push inflation forces by making it difficult for firms to simply pass along their cost increases in the form of higher prices. If consumers are price conscious, they will reward the more efficient, lower-cost firms with new business while penalizing the cost-push inflation strategy practiced by the less-efficient firms. This kind of consumer behavior can help to police the marketplace and hold back cost-push inflationary forces.

The decisions of individual consumers are also important in checking demand-pull inflation. As we stated earlier, demand-pull inflation occurs when the demand for goods and services in the economy exceeds what the economy can produce. This leads to a situation in which "too much money is chasing too few goods." The result is an increase in the price of those goods—inflation. If we as consumers can budget our income so as to save more and buy less, we can do our part to lessen demand-pull inflation. We can also have the added comfort of knowing that our savings can serve as a pool for future investments in new technology that can increase productivity, thereby creating more goods for everyone. As a spokesperson for the Securities Industry Association said in hearings before the Senate Finance Committee in May 1981, "Personal saving is an essential link to corporate capital formation. A low level of savings precludes a high level of capital investment and severely limits productivity gains."

POLITICS

We should not ignore the consumer's role in the political economy of inflation, however. Inflation can be propagated and sustained by misguided govern-

Many goods and services can be found at low prices at flea markets and swap meets because dealers specializing in factory seconds, refurbished used goods, and homemade items have a low overhead and no advertising costs.

ment policies. In your role as an active member of a representative democracy, you will be presented with a number of political choices that will affect the entire economy. Many of these choices will be made in the voting booth, so you should have a basic grasp of the fundamentals of good inflationary strategy.

Political candidates frequently condemn inflation, but we all need to support those who have a genuine grasp of the complexities of the situation. This means that you should not vote for those who offer a quick-fix solution. For example, in periods of strong demand-pull inflation such as we experienced during the Vietnam War, a tax increase was the economically correct solution. It may sound bad to lose an additional $300 to $400 each year to higher taxes, but you should ask yourself: What does this mean for the overall welfare of the society? In a demand-pull inflation, taxes must be increased or government expenditures must be cut in order to avoid a situation in which "too much money is chasing too few goods." Neither of these alternatives is very appealing to politicians who are accustomed to

> **BOX 7-6**
>
> ## A Politician's View of Inflation
>
> According to some authorities, one of the reasons that inflation has proved so difficult to contain in the United States has been the vested interest most politicians have in its continuance. As Irwin Kellner, senior vice-president and economist of the Manufacturers Hanover Trust Company wrote in the company's *Economic Report* (1981):
>
>> One group with an interest in inflation is our elected officials. Under inflation, politicians can make more promises than they know will be kept in real terms. This is because they can promise to spend certain amounts of dollars on various projects, benefits etc., knowing that by the time they are spent, these dollars will not buy what their constituents think they will. In addition, thanks to our "progressive" tax structure, inflation pushes people into higher tax brackets, increasing the revenues that Washington (and some states) gets from income taxes. This, too, benefits politicians, for it gives them more money to spend. On the local scene, politicians benefit additionally from inflation because higher prices on goods and services mean more sales taxes will be collected without there necessarily being an expansion in the real volume of transactions.
>
> We might add to this the charge that inflation allows politicians to give us illusory tax cuts so that it appears that they are giving consumers a break when in reality they are only returning some of the additional tax money they received because of inflation.
>
> On the other hand, politicians do not have a great deal of power to control inflation. The nation's money supply is regulated by the Federal Reserve Board (Fed), which is a semiautonomous agency whose members serve fourteen-year terms. The Fed establishes monetary policy. Even the size of the federal budget, as you will see in Chapter 15, is largely predetermined by programs that were enacted decades ago. Social Security, military pensions, health care, and farm-support programs are not easily changed. Thus, there is not much a Congressman or a Senator can do except promise to do his or her best.

getting elected by promising their constituents *more*, not less (see Box 7-6). Nevertheless, you should realize by now that we can't cure inflation by throwing money at it. As economists are fond of saying, "There ain't no such thing as a free lunch." The politicians who promise the most are often elected, but that doesn't mean that they will deliver on those promises. Beware of the free lunch; you often wind up paying a lot more for your dinner.

SPECIAL-INTEREST GROUPS

Special-interest groups are certain segments of society that appeal to the government for special help. The members of these groups often have a common occupation or industry, and they have a paid staff in Washington to look out for their interests. These staff members are called **lobbyists**, and they try to convince our elected officials of the merits of their employers' special interests. The special-interest group could be the U.S. sugar-beet growers, who want to restrict the amount of foreign sugar that we import. Or it could be the U.S. automakers and autoworkers, who press for higher trade barriers on imported automobiles. Or it could be the dairy farmers, who want the government to guarantee a certain price for butter and then guarantee to buy all the butter that remains unsold at that price.

There is nothing inherently bad about special-interest groups. They are an integral part of the American political process. However, because consumers' interests are so diverse, it is difficult for them to form such groups to counterbalance the power of the sugar lobby or the dairy lobby. A dairy farmer might be willing to make a tax-deductible $1,000 contribution to the dairy lobby because the expected return to the farmer from the new farm-support legislation is many times this amount. A consumer, on the other hand, may wind up paying 25 cents a pound more for butter and $5 more in taxes to support the program. Will consumers write in about this issue? The odds are all in the lobbyist's favor.

There are a few lobbyist groups that seek to represent consumers. These groups help combat the special-interest cost-push inflation by commissioning studies on the impact of special-interest legislation, by testifying before Congress, by informing their members of pending legislation, and by organizing consumer resistance. If you are interested in supporting their work in combating some narrow special-

> **BOX 7-7**
>
> **Consumer Lobbies**
>
> Common Cause
> 2030 M Street N.W.
> Washington, D.C. 20036
> 202-833-1200
> National nonpartisan public affairs lobbying organization concerned mainly with government reform and accountability.
>
> Consumer Federation of America (CFA)
> 1012 14th Street N.W., Suite 901
> Washington, D.C. 20005
> 202-387-6121
> A federation of 225 national, state, and local nonprofit groups that advocates consumer interests before Congress, the executive branch, regulatory agencies, and the courts on food, energy, credit, banking, and health issues. Publishes monthly newsletter, *CFA News* ($24 per year).
>
> National Consumers League
> 1522 K Street N.W., Suite 406
> Washington, D.C. 20005
> 202-797-7600
> The nation's oldest consumer organization; sponsors consumer education programs and lobbies for consumer rights in a variety of areas. Publishes bimonthly newsletter, *The Bulletin* ($15 per year to members).
>
> Public Interest Research Group Clearinghouse
> 1346 Connecticut Avenue N.W.
> Washington, D.C. 20036
> 202-833-3934
> Brings attention to many vital issues through state public-interest research groups (PIRGs) by lobbying, researching, and organizing. Inspired by Ralph Nader, PIRG projects range from energy to scholastic testing reform. Publishes bimonthly newsletter, *Of the People* ($5 per year to individuals, $12 to organizations).
>
> Public Citizen
> P.O. Box 19404
> Washington, D.C. 20036
> 202-293-9142
> Promotes consumer interests in many areas, such as marketing safe drugs and products, tax reform, congressional accountability, and a consumer-oriented energy policy. Publishes quarterly *Public Citizen* newspaper, which is free to members ($15 per year). Other publications that deal with consumer issues are: *The Congress Watcher* ($5 for 6 issues per year); *Critical Mass Energy Journal* ($10 for 12 issues per year); and *People and Taxes* ($7.50 for 12 issues per year).
>
> Volunteer: The National Center for Citizen Involvement
> 1119 19th Street
> Arlington, Virginia 22307
> 703-276-0542
> Stimulates and strengthens citizen volunteer involvement. Publishes quarterly *Voluntary Action Leadership* ($9 per year) and two bimonthly newsletters: *Volunteering,* on advocacy, and *Newsline,* on program activities (both are free on a trial basis).
>
> Washington Center for the Study of Services
> 1518 K Street N.W., Fourth Floor
> Washington, D.C. 20005
> 202-347-9612
> Provides technical assistance to groups that wish to develop surveys of quality or price of local service establishments. Also specializes in developing, printing, and distributing materials at low cost to low-income consumers. Publishes quarterly, *Washington Consumers Checkbook,* which contains evaluation of Washington, D.C.-area service establishments such as auto repair shops, hospitals, and food stores ($16 per year; discount for quantity orders).

interest groups, write to them for further information. All of them are listed in the U.S. Office of Consumer Affairs, *People Power: What Committees Are Doing to Counter Inflation* (1980). Information on selected groups is provided in Box 7-7.

CONSUMER CO-OPS

A **consumer co-operative** is an organization whose major goal is to benefit its members by organizing their buying power. A co-op can be a small organization formed and run by a few consumers, or it can be a

In some food co-ops, individuals take responsibility for buying foods in quantity in order to keep unit costs down for all members.

multimillion-dollar business with thousands of members and a paid staff. The difference between a co-op and a business firm is that a co-op does not try to earn a profit. The cost advantages of buying in bulk are passed along to the co-op members in the form of lower prices or refunds on their purchases.

Many areas of consumer spending are likely candidates for co-operatives. There are health co-operatives such as the Kaiser-Permanente Group, which we will discuss in Chapter 14; auto co-ops such as Cooperative Auto of Ann Arbor, Michigan; and housing co-ops such as Jubilee Housing, Inc. of Washington, D.C. But the spending category in which consumer co-operatives have been most successful has been groceries.

A food co-op enables its members to buy products at the wholesale price, thereby eliminating an important but costly link in the farm-to-consumer food chain. Many food co-ops have been organized around the country, and they vary in size and complexity. Some are simply food-buying clubs whose members take turns collecting orders and then purchasing food from wholesalers. Other co-ops involve full-scale supermarkets and multistate warehouse systems. Of course, there are drawbacks as well as advantages to co-ops. Co-ops are seldom as convenient, either because of their location or their more restrictive store hours. There is sometimes a membership fee, and there is often a requirement that members contribute some time to help run the co-op. Finally, few co-ops are able to present the variety either in brands or in merchandise that a large, modern supermarket routinely stocks.

The U.S. Congress encouraged the development

of consumer co-operatives by establishing the National Consumer Cooperative Bank in 1978. Public Law 93-351 states the Congressional rationale for the bank:

> The Congress finds that user-owned cooperatives are a proven method for broadening ownership and control of the economic organizations, increasing the number of market participants, narrowing price spreads, raising the quality of goods and services available to their membership and building bridges between producers and consumers and their members and patrons. The Congress also finds that consumer and other types of self-help cooperatives have been hampered in their formation and growth by lack of access to adequate cooperative credit facilities and lack of technical assistance. Therefore, the Congress finds a need for the establishment of a National Consumer Cooperative Bank which will make available necessary financial and technical assistance to cooperative self-help endeavors as a means of strengthening the nation's economy.

The bank's initial capital for loans consisted of $300 million from the U.S. Treasury, but it has authorization from Congress to borrow $3 billion from other sources so that it can assist co-operatives throughout the nation. If you are interested in forming a co-op, you can write to the NCCB at 2001 S Street N.W., Washington, D.C. 20009, or you can call (toll free) 800-424-2481.

Summary

There is no indication that the inflation rate will fall below 5 percent in the near future. If we predict a steady 7 percent rise in the Consumer Price Index, prices will double every decade. A home that sold for $100,000 in 1970 would cost $800,000 by the year 2000. A hot dog that cost 50 cents in 1970 would cost $4 by the end of the century. Clearly, this kind of change will have an impact on your life. It is nearly impossible to be a good decision maker without taking inflation into account.

In this chapter we have tried to give you the broad outlines of the nature of inflation and its causes and consequences, both from a societal and a personal viewpoint. It is obvious that no single consumer can stop the inflationary spiral. On the other hand, by practicing good decision making, by taking an active part in the political process, and by supporting the anti-inflationary forces in our economy, there is much that individuals can do to slow the rate of inflation. If you incorporate some of the suggestions of this chapter into your day-to-day affairs, you should be able to stretch your buying power and make the budgeting process discussed in Chapter 6 a bit easier. Chapter 8 discusses the use of credit and the impact that credit has on your buying power.

Neighborhood REVISITED

1. When you were losing your baby teeth, what was the standard tooth-fairy payment? How much is it today? Compared to other prices, has this change matched the overall rate of inflation?

2. Is the rise in the cost of tooth-fairy payments inflation? Why or why not?

3. If Mrs. Carpenter had saved her dimes in a piggy bank, how valuable would they be today? Would she have gained or lost buying power?

KEY TERMS

barter
base year (period)
compounding
consumer co-operatives
Consumer Price Index (CPI)
cost of living adjustment (COLA)
cost-push inflation
deflation
demand-pull inflation
fringe benefits

GNP deflator
hyperinflation
indexes
inflation
inflationary expectations
investment
lobbyist

monetarism
National Consumer Cooperative Bank
nominal dollars
productivity
progressive income tax
real dollars
rule of 70
special-interest group
technology
windfall profits

QUESTIONS

1. Define inflation and discuss its impact on the following groups: retired people; college students; oil refinery workers; children; welfare recipients.

2. What is the most widely used measure of inflation in the U.S. economy? What are its strengths and weaknesses?

3. Since the end of World War II, has inflation always been a major problem in the American economy? What were the major causes of inflation from 1948 to 1980?

4. Why doesn't the Consumer Price Index measure your personal cost of living?

5. Are politicians and the federal government two of the biggest winners during an inflationary period? Explain.

6. What is a COLA clause? How effective are such clauses at protecting a worker's income from inflation? Do COLAs have any negative effects on the overall rate of inflation?

7. If you were asked to lecture on the topic "How to Avoid the High Cost of Living," what suggestions would you make? Can anything be done?

8. Tilford Gaines, senior vice-president of Manufacturers Hanover Trust, once wrote: "There is nothing at all novel about what needs doing if inflation is to be restrained and avoided. All that is necessary is that the public authorities themselves adopt programs aimed at limiting the total of demand upon the economy to what the economy is able to produce without inflation." Do you agree? Is he speaking of demand-pull or cost-push inflation?

PROJECTS

1. Are there any consumer co-ops in your community? If there are, interview one of the members. What are the benefits and costs of such an organization?

2. Get a copy of the Consumer Price Index and chart the cost changes of a few major items over the last ten years. Has there been a pattern in absolute prices? In relative prices?

3. Deflate today's dollar by the CPI base year. How much is today's nominal dollar worth in real terms?

4. Make up a list of ten items and conduct your own market-basket survey each week for one month. Which items have increased the most? Have any decreased?

5. Survey your friends and relatives for inflation-fighting ideas. Have they come up with any not mentioned in the chapter?

REFERENCES AND READINGS

"Beef up Your Job to Beat Inflation." *Changing Times,* November 1979.

Board of Governors of the Federal Reserve System. *1980 Historical Chart Book.* Washington, D.C.: Federal Reserve Board, 1980.

Case, John. *Understanding Inflation.* New York: William Morrow, 1981.

Consumers Opposed to Inflation in the Necessities. *Citizen Inflation Action Handbook.* Washington, D.C.: COIN, 1979.

Dobson, Steven W. "Inflation: The Role of Market Structure." Federal Reserve Bank of Dallas *Review,* June 1977.

Federal Reserve Bank of San Francisco. "Educated Consumers." *Weekly Letter,* October 10, 1980.

Federal Reserve Bank of San Francisco. "Revising the Yardstick." *Weekly Letter,* November 13, 1981.

Hayes, Linda Snyder. "How Americans Turned Into Spendthrifts." *Fortune,* April 7, 1980.

"How to Survive Inflation." *U.S. News & World Report,* April 7, 1980.

It Makes Good Cents: Money, Inflation & You. United California Bank, 1980.

Irwin Keller. "The Politics of Inflation." *Economic Report,* June 1981.

Meadows, Edward. "Our Flawed Inflation Indexes." *Fortune,* April 24, 1978.

Minarik, Joseph J. "Who Wins, Who Loses From Inflation." *Challenge,* January/February, 1979.

Minarik, Joseph J. "Necessities Inflation Once Again." *Challenge,* January/February, 1981.

Moore, John H. "Inflation and the Burden of Taxation." National Federation of Independent Business, *Public Policy Discussion* Series, 1979.

Nulty, Leslie Ellen. "How Inflation Hits the Majority." *Challenge,* January/February 1979.

Okun, Arthur M. "An Efficient Strategy to Combat Inflation." *The Brookings Bulletin,* Spring 1979.

Schwenk, Frankie N. "Two Measures of Inflation: The Consumer Price Index and the Personal Consumption Expenditure Implicit Price Deflator." *Family Economics Review,* Winter 1981.

"The U.S. Productivity Crisis." *Newsweek,* September 8, 1980.

U.S. Department of Labor. *The Consumer Price Index: Concepts and Content Over the Years.* Washington, D.C.: U.S. Government Printing Office, 1978.

U.S. Office of Consumer Affairs. *People Power: What Communities Are Doing to Counter Inflation.* Washington, D.C.: U.S. Government Printing Office, 1980.

Zalusky, John. "Cost-of-Living Clauses: Always Playing Catch-Up." *The AFL-CIO American Federationist,* August 1980.

Did You Know That...

- about one-third of all retail sales in the United States are rung up with the help of some form of credit?

- more than 75 percent of American families have at least one credit card?

- The Truth in Lending Act requires all lenders to disclose both the absolute cost (finance charge) and the relative cost (annual percentage rate) in writing to a prospective borrower *before* an agreement is signed?

- credit-card accounts with identical interest rates can have widely different finance charges, depending on their accounting methods?

- if you are denied credit, you have the right to know why?

- if you receive damaged goods or poor-quality services purchased with a credit card, you can often get a refund from your credit-card company?

- in a typical year, more than 200,000 Americans file for bankruptcy, and even after filing bankruptcy a consumer is allowed to keep a certain amount of property?

8 Credit: Buy Now, Pay More Later

An Overview of Credit: How Big? How Much? How Important?

The Benefits of Credit

Costs of Consumer Credit

Sources of Credit

Applying for Credit

The Equal Credit Opportunity Act

The Fair Credit Billing Act

How Much Credit Equals Too Much Debt?

Bankruptcy: The Last Resort

Neighborhood CAPSULE

Seeking Credit for the First Time

Barbara Chang had just graduated from high school and had begun working full time as a telephone operator. She planned on keeping her job and attending night classes at her local community college.

It was payday, and Barbara had received her first paycheck. On her way home from work she decided to stop by Stern's department store to see whether she could get a new coat. Sure enough, she found just what she was looking for, but the only problem was that the coat cost $160 and her paycheck was $148.58. Besides, Barbara had other expenses, and she didn't want to spend all of her hard-earned money on a coat.

The salesperson was very helpful and suggested that Barbara open a charge account. "Just fill out a credit application and wait a few days for it to be processed. Meanwhile, I'll hold the coat for you." It sounded simple enough and Barbara filled out the application.

After waiting for three days without getting a reply, Barbara called the store to find out what was holding up the process. She was looking forward to getting her new coat that week. When she finally got someone who could answer her question, he said, "We're sorry Ms. Chang, but Stern's is unable to open a credit account for you at this time."

Barbara was so embarrassed that it was all she could do to say thank you and hang up.

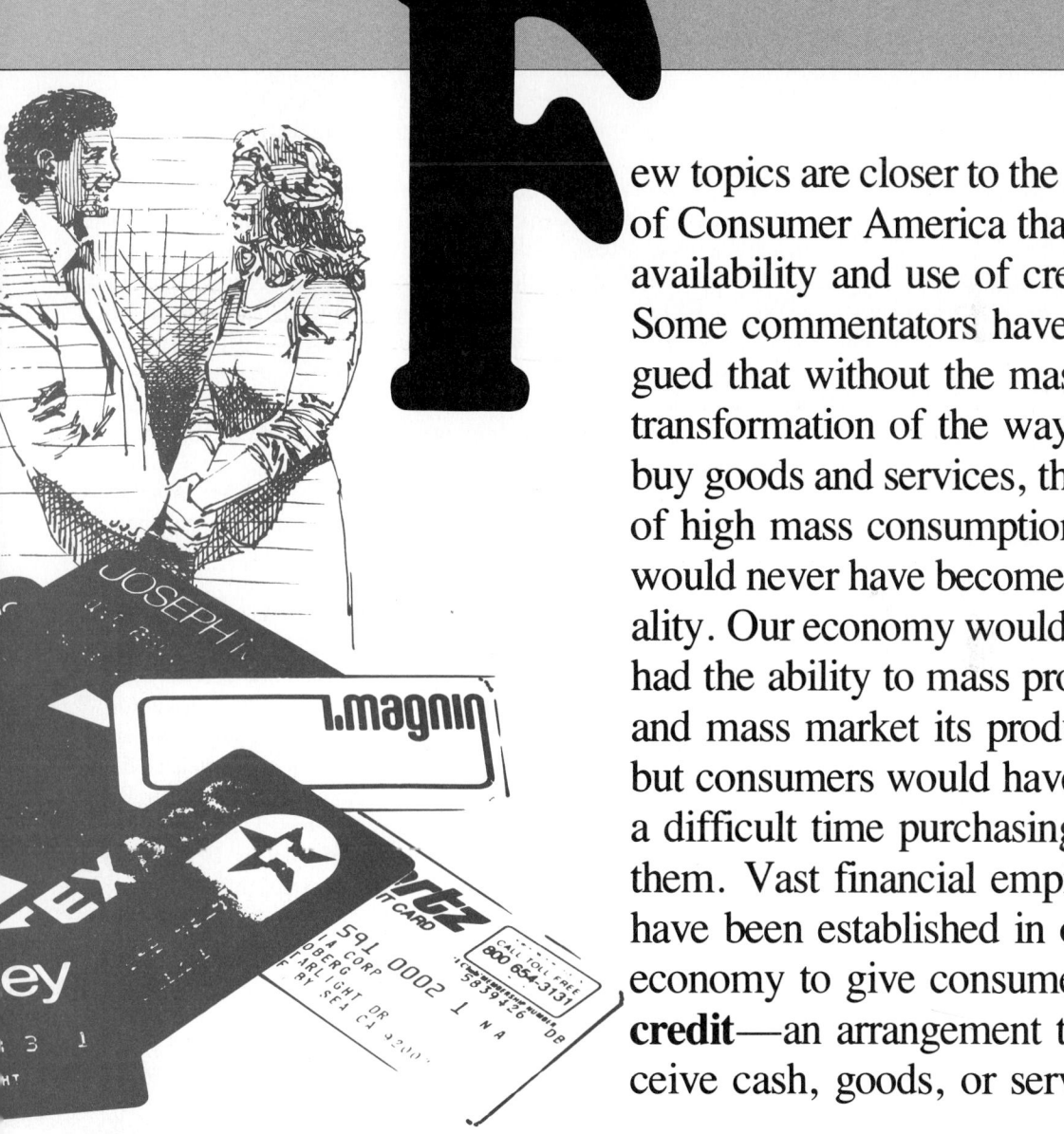

Few topics are closer to the heart of Consumer America than the availability and use of credit. Some commentators have argued that without the massive transformation of the way we buy goods and services, the age of high mass consumption would never have become a reality. Our economy would have had the ability to mass produce and mass market its products, but consumers would have had a difficult time purchasing them. Vast financial empires have been established in our economy to give consumers **credit**—an arrangement to receive cash, goods, or services in the present and pay for them in the future. Debt—the amount of money a consumer owes as a result of using credit—has become a way of life for most Americans. In this chapter we deal at some length with the hows and whys of credit in twentieth-century America.

Before we begin, we should point out that we are not dealing with all types of loans or consumer debts. We are primarily concerned with consumer credit as it pertains to borrowing for noninvestment purposes. Installment debt and credit-card charges are two examples of noninvestment borrowing. We are not talking about borrowing money to invest in the stock market or to buy a home, because these purchases should produce a return in excess of the original purchase price and as such are not relevant here. We will deal with home mortgages and investment loans in Chapters 13 and 16. The primary objective of consumer credit is the enjoyment we receive from consumption, not the increased income we get from wise investments.

After reading this chapter you should have a better understanding of your credit rights and responsibilities, so that when you face credit problems, you will be in a better position to make informed decisions. To improve your credit decision-making skills, we have designed this chapter to cover specific problems as well as general topics. We begin with an overview of the role of credit in the American economy. Then we present some information on the benefits and costs of credit, so that when you come to the cost-benefit step of the decision-making model, you will be able to weigh all the factors *before* you make a choice. After the cost-benefit sections, we outline some of the major sources of credit, the application process, and steps to take if you have a credit problem. Finally, we offer some guidelines on self-disciplined credit limits and on how to work your way out of credit problems, including using the last resort—personal bankruptcy.

An Overview of Credit: How Big? How Much? How Important?

In the not-so-distant past, "debt" was one of those four-letter words that was not used in public. Consumers were taught to be wary of debt and to avoid it at all costs. The maxim that first appeared in Shakespeare's *Hamlet,* "Neither a borrower, nor a lender be," was repeated and learned at a very tender age, and for good reason. In Colonial America, people were sent to debtor's prison if they were unable to pay their debts. Today, of course, these penalties have been erased, but the collective human memory has historical roots, and there are still some people who avoid debt out of fear of what might happen to them if they are unable to repay it. Consumer surveys continue to reveal a dread of credit among the general public. For example, a study conducted by the Survey Research Center at the University of Michigan showed that only a little over 50 percent of the American public give their unqualified approval to **installment (closed-end) credit,** that is, borrowing a certain amount of money and then repaying the debt with interest in equal monthly payments (installments) over a specific time period. This is especially interesting in light of the finding that at any given moment, slightly over half of all American households are repaying an installment debt.

Despite their protests to the contrary, Americans are using the vast credit network of banks, finance companies, credit unions, and other financial institutions to help them obtain goods and services in the present rather than in the future. As Figure 8-1 illustrates, consumer installment debt has been rising rapidly over the last twenty years. As you can see, the absolute volume of debt has risen from around $40 billion in 1959 to over $300 billion today. The burden of this debt on the average consumer's budget has also grown, as the percentages in Figure 8-1 show. In 1959, consumer debt represented 11.7 percent of after-tax (disposable) income, but by 1980 debt was over 17 percent of consumer disposable income. As a nation of consumers, we were collectively going deeper and deeper into debt.

The rise in the amount of consumer installment debt and in the ratio of this debt to consumer income has led some credit executives to speak out on the subject. Patricia Patterson (1981), legal counsel for the American Express Corporation, said recently, "Credit can be sinister. Adults are like kids with their nose pressed up against the candy store window. You have to realize you have to stay within your means."

Figure 8-1. Outstanding consumer installment debt and the percent of consumers' disposable income, 1959–1980.

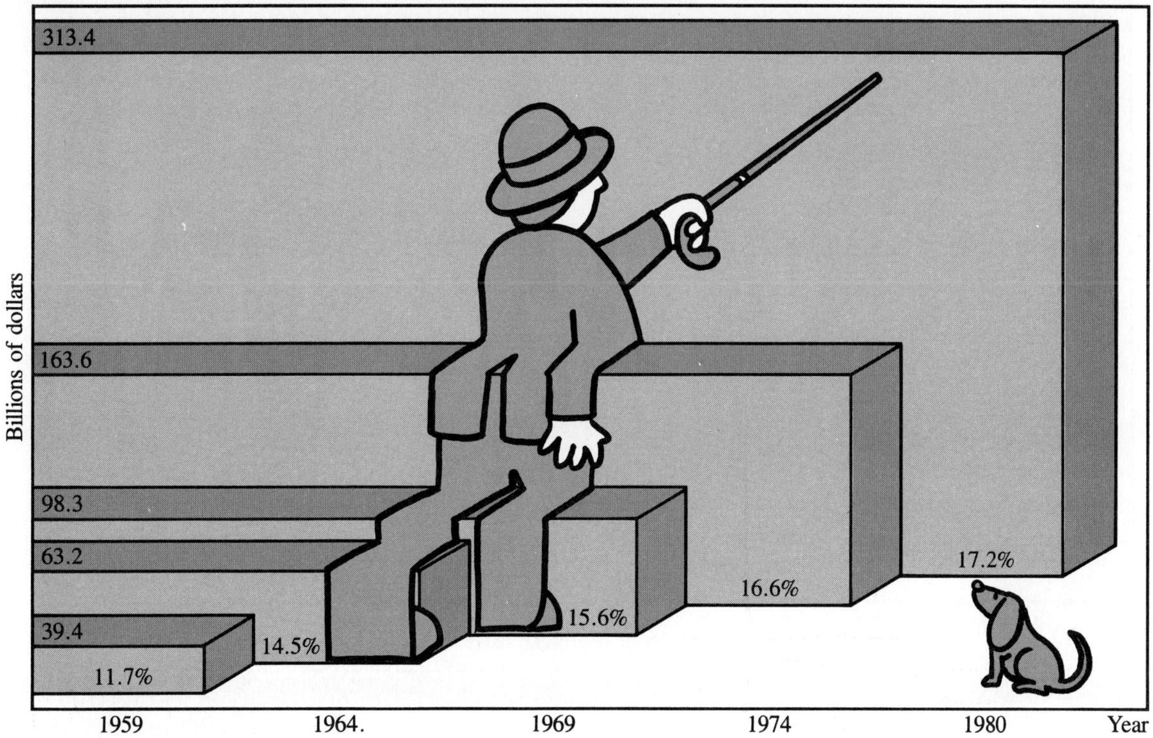

Year	Billions of dollars	Percent
1959	39.4	11.7%
1964	63.2	14.5%
1969	98.3	15.6%
1974	163.6	16.6%
1980	313.4	17.2%

SOURCE: *Economic Report of the President* (Washington, D.C.: U.S. Government Printing Office, 1981).

Of course, it is difficult to heed this advice when at every turn consumers are being bombarded with invitations to join in the charge of the credit brigade. Today there are over 115 million MasterCards and VISA cards in circulation. Many consumers have both. Millions of additional charge cards have been issued by department stores and other retailers. The J.C. Penney Company, for example, issued its first card in the late 1950s. By 1980, Penney's had over 30 million charge-card customers whose credit purchases accounted for over 40 percent of their retail sales. Nationwide, three out of every ten retail sales dollars are rung up with the help of credit. The pressure on the seller to provide credit, and on the consumer to use credit, has been growing over the years.

Before you turn in your credit cards and swear off installment credit forever, you ought to learn about the benefits of credit. There can be good sound reasons for seeking and obtaining credit. In the next section we will explore some of the more important ones.

The Benefits of Credit

Credit, like many other modern inventions, is neither all bad nor all good. And, if credit is used judiciously, you can be ahead of the game by seeking and obtaining it.

The benefits of credit depend on a consumer's lifestyle, values, and needs. Few consumers will consider all of the following advantages relevant to their personal circumstances, and not all forms of credit offer all of these benefits. Nevertheless, these advan-

Figure 8-2. Example of a life-cycle income and expenditure pattern.

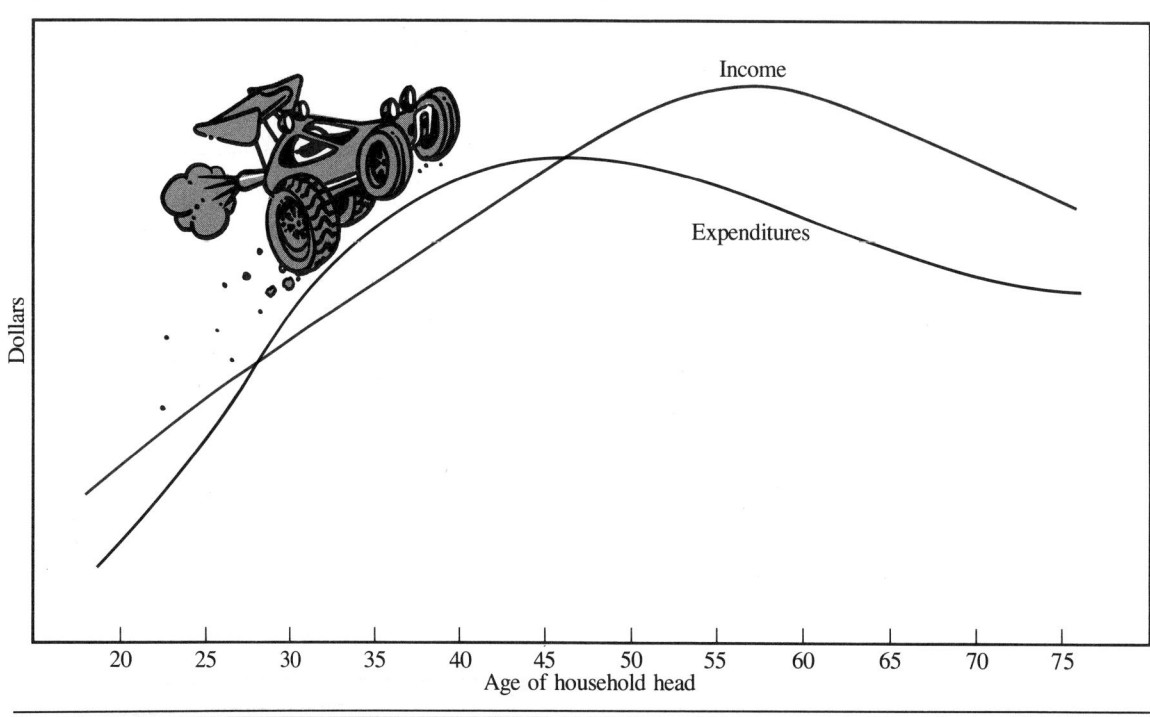

tages are legitimate reasons for seeking and obtaining credit. Whenever credit appears to be one of the potential solutions to a consumer problem you have identified, you would do well to review these benefits to see whether credit can indeed be of some help. But you do not want to ignore the costs of consumer credit, either. We consider this topic in the section that follows our discussion of benefits.

SYNCHRONIZING INCOME WITH EXPENSES

Contrary to popular belief, few Americans are paid on an hourly or a daily basis. People may *earn* their incomes hourly or daily, but the shortest pay periods are generally once a week, twice a month, or sometimes once a month. A monthly paycheck does not always allow consumers to meet daily expenses or to take advantage of clearance sales or bargains. Credit can be a dollar stretcher because it gives the consumer sufficient buying power to purchase items when they are discounted for a limited time.

We can apply this principle to the consumer's life cycle mentioned in Chapter 3. A household's income is generally low in the early years and then builds as workers age and gain experience. For most occupations, late middle age is the time of peak earnings. Yet the need for income to support a household is often highest when the household is producing and nurturing children. Figure 8-2 illustrates one typical pattern of lifetime income and expenditures. Notice that in the earliest stage, expenditures of young households exceed income, and couples have to draw on their savings to make up the difference. During the family formation years, expenses continue to rise more rapidly than income. In fact, income may actually decline if the wife or the husband decides to leave the workforce for a while to rear the children. During this stage, credit can play a crucial role in helping households to cope with their needs. As the children grow up and establish households of their own, the life-cycle expenditure pattern levels off, and may even decline. Meanwhile, the household is in its peak earning years. Both spouses may be working,

> **BOX 8-1**
>
> ## A Consolidation Loan and Emergency Credit
>
> A **bill consolidation loan** combines several debts into one by providing the borrower with enough money to pay them off. Bill consolidation loans are a typical form of emergency credit. Finance companies often advertise their ability to get you out of debt by lending you enough money to pay off all your small bills and thus consolidate your debt into one big payment. This new debt is generally spread over a longer period, so that your monthly payment is smaller than the sum of all your previous debt payments. Remember, though, that even magicians cannot make something vanish—they can only make you *think* it disappeared. The same is true for finance-company loan officers—you may think they have lowered your indebtedness, but in reality they have only restructured your payments. You will be paying more, over a longer period of time—frequently at higher interest rates. Nevertheless, if an emergency occurs, you may need this help.
>
> A consolidation loan may help you if you have overextended yourself and you simply cannot pay your bills on time. However, this does not mean that you can continue to use credit instead of cash to buy goods and services.
>
> A consolidation loan may help you if:
>
> 1. You are living in a multi-income household and one of the wage earners loses his or her job. The sudden decline in monthly income prevents you from supporting your current short-term debt. A consolidation loan could lower the monthly payment.
> 2. You are chronically late in paying your bills. Your income does not allow you to pay all your creditors every month. Some are threatening to take you to court.
>
> In both of these circumstances you must do two things. First, determine whether you can meet the new lower, but longer, monthly debt-repayment scheme. Second, avoid taking on any new debts until either your income rises or you have repaid the consolidation loan. If you cannot meet these two requirements, there is no value to using the consolidation loan as a form of emergency credit.

and surplus income can then be used to repay old debts and establish a savings pool for the retirement years.

Credit allows consumers some leeway in matching their needs for goods and services to their ability to pay for these commodities with current income. Of course, the economic problem is always important. Most consumers do have insatiable wants and limited resources; nevertheless, the burden of the economic problem is generally more severe for the younger families. For them, the judicious use of credit can become an asset rather than a liability. The wise use of credit can help a family over the inevitable hump of rising expenses and lagging income.

FORCED SAVINGS

Because many consumers find it difficult to set up a budget and save money, credit purchases can be a source of forced saving. Consumer researchers have found that many people borrow money to purchase something—a set of encyclopedias, for example—even though they have enough money in their savings account to purchase it outright. And because the interest rate on the loan is generally greater than the interest rate on savings, it seems illogical to choose to lose the difference. Why do consumers do this? The answer given most frequently is that they fear that they simply wouldn't have the stamina to build their savings back to their previous levels. However, they would make room in their budgets to pay off the encyclopedia loan. This amounts to being forced to save after the fact. It is the same reason that some families shop in stores that give trading stamps. They know that the prices are somewhat higher, but the stamps are a form of forced saving that can later be cashed in for a home appliance or another good. Obviously, planned savings are preferable to forced savings, but forced savings are better than no savings at all.

EMERGENCY FUND

In Chapter 6 we stressed the importance of having an emergency fund of ready cash to use if something goes wrong. If you are sick for a long time or lose your job, you may be forced into a financial bind. Credit should not be used in place of this emergency fund, but it can be used to reinforce your savings. A good credit rating and a few closely supervised credit cards can help a household that is temporarily in distress. We cannot, however, overemphasize the importance of knowing the difference between a real emergency and a simple desire to consume more. Like the little boy who cried wolf once too often, if you use your credit in nonemergency situations, no one will be around to bail you out of a real emergency. If consumers exhaust their financial resources by transforming all their wants into needs and then paying for them with credit, they mortgage their future earning power. This can lead to financial disaster if something unexpected happens.

INFLATION AND CREDIT

In the late 1970s and early 1980s, inflation reached such a high rate that it became advantageous for some consumers to buy on credit. You may recall from Chapter 7 that inflation is a rise in the general level of prices, or a fall in the purchasing power of money. If the rate of inflation is higher than the interest rate and if your income is rising with the general rise in prices, it may make good sense to borrow to buy something you really want, because the loan's *real* rate of interest (corrected for inflation) will be negative. In effect, you will be borrowing at a negative rate of interest, because the money you use to pay off the loan in the future will be worth less than the money you borrow today. This is a highly unusual circumstance, because creditors want some reward for giving you the use of their money. Nevertheless, it can happen.

Suppose, for example, that you want to buy a new piano that costs $2000. If the annual inflation rate is 10 percent and if the piano's price can be expected to rise as rapidly as the general price level, the piano would cost $2200 if you bought it next year. However, if you could find someone to lend you $2000 for one year at 5 percent interest, you would pay negative interest, because the $2100 you would repay at the end of the year ($2000 principal plus $100 interest) would have less buying power than the money you borrowed at the beginning. In essence, at a 5 percent annual interest rate on $2000, you are giving the lender $100 for the use of that money. But if inflation is reducing the value of money by 10 percent per year, that $2000 principal loses $200 worth of buying power during the year. The $100 you pay in interest makes up for some of the loss in purchasing power, but the lender still loses $100 in our example. Because $100 is 5 percent of the original loan, the real interest rate is a minus 5 percent. You get the piano *and* save money by financing it.

The real interest rate on any loan can be calculated by subtracting the annual inflation rate from the nominal rate stated in the contract. A 5 percent nominal rate becomes a minus 5 percent when the inflation rate is 10 percent. Lenders, of course, are also aware of the real rate of interest, and they try to take it into account. But sometimes they miscalculate. A good example of this is the interest rates on thirty-year mortgages that were written in the 1960s. These mortgages often included a 6 percent, 7 percent, or 8 percent interest rate. If inflation was 2 percent, a 7-percent mortgage amounted to a real interest rate of 5 percent. But if inflation reaches 10 percent, the real rate becomes a minus 3 percent. Such miscalculations have benefited the consumers who received these mortgages, but they have certainly harmed the lenders. As a result, almost all interest rates are adjusted for inflation, and because lenders are uncertain about future inflation rates, it is difficult to get them to lend money for thirty years at a fixed rate. We will discuss this problem in more detail in Chapter 13, "Housing: Home Sweet Home."

Adjusting the nominal interest rate for the effects of inflation will give you better information *before* you decide to borrow. However, we should warn you that including the real rate of interest in your personal decision-making process may cause you to miscalcu-

It is often much easier to get merchants to accept credit cards than to accept personal checks, especially when traveling.

late your budget unless two conditions hold. First, your income must be expected to rise at least as fast as the general rise in prices. If your income lags behind the inflation rate, the real burden of the debt does not fall as rapidly as our earlier calculations suggested. Second, the price of whatever you are planning to buy must also be expected to rise with inflation. For example, if you had obtained a low-interest loan in 1980 to buy a home computer but in the next year the price *fell* 25 percent, it would have been less expensive to postpone getting it. If you cannot be sure that your income will rise or if the price of the prospective purchase is likely to fall, it is not a good idea to use credit to buy it.

RECORDKEEPING, IDENTIFICATION, AND THE CASHLESS SOCIETY

Credit cards have three advantages that normal installment credit does not: They provide recordkeeping and identification and they minimize cash transactions. Consumers make hundreds of transactions every month; purchasing food, buying gasoline, and paying rent are only a few of them. Many people find it advantageous to have a record of these transactions. Checking accounts can help, but so can credit cards. Every month the credit-card company sends a statement showing where you made a credit purchase and how much you paid. You also receive a receipt from the merchant when you make the purchase. Receipts from the merchant have a way of disappearing, but the monthly statement can provide a valuable record of your purchases that can help you in establishing your budget and in preparing your tax return or other records of expenses.

When you make a purchase by check, merchants frequently ask for some form of identification and some assurance that you are a good credit risk. Properly validated and up-to-date credit cards can provide this assurance. Credit cards can also limit the need to carry large amounts of cash, because you can use them in place of cash. And in many hotels, banks, and airports, you can use them to obtain a cash advance. The use of credit cards has become so commonplace in hotels and motels that it is difficult to check in without presenting one. Hotel keepers often run a blank charge on your card to ensure that you don't leave without paying for the room.

Costs of Consumer Credit

Now that we have outlined many of the benefits of obtaining credit, let us look at the other side of the coin—the costs of credit to the consumer. As we mentioned in Chapter 1, only by weighing the costs and benefits of a particular action can we come to a rational decision. Credit is no exception to the decision-making rule.

THE RISK OF INSOLVENCY

Whenever you apply for or use credit to purchase something, you should always keep this question in mind: "Can I afford it?" In this world of choices, decisions about what to buy can be so overwhelming that people don't pay enough attention to *how* they'll pay. This can become a real problem when a consumer discovers that, after paying his creditors at the beginning of the month, there simply is not enough income to buy even the bare necessities. If what a person owes exceeds what he makes and if there is no way to pay off his debts, he ends up in a condition

Maintaining one's balance on the credit tightrope can be difficult.

called financial insolvency. We will discuss this problem in greater detail later in this chapter, because it is a serious and common one.

BUDGET COMMITMENT AND FLEXIBILITY

Warning signs do appear well before a consumer becomes financially insolvent. One of these warning signs is the degree of flexibility in the monthly budget. As consumers take on more installment debt, they begin to notice that they just don't have as much discretionary income as they once had. Have you ever heard yourself or someone else say, "Oh, we would like to do that, but it's the end of the month and we just can't afford it"? This kind of statement should be like a smoke alarm going off in the middle of the night—it should alert all the members of the household to the danger of impending bankruptcy. Loss of flexibility means that the household in question is walking a tightrope—one false move, one tiny slip could cause disaster. As a rule of thumb, if more than 20 percent of after-tax income is being spent to pay off installment debt, a consumer is on that tightrope and could be in danger of falling off.

LIMITED CHOICE AND HIGHER COSTS

Credit can also limit your options in deciding where to shop. This limitation is not as applicable to universal charge cards such as VISA or MasterCard, but it may apply to individual store accounts, if you get locked into shopping at stores that have already given you a credit account. Of course, you may be able to take advantage of special sales and bargains at those stores, but you also may be *less* likely to shop around. No one store has a monopoly on bargains. Hitching your credit wagon to a few retailers can limit your choice, and the result may be that you pay more for goods and services.

The problem of paying more is especially applicable to those with lower incomes who may use credit as a form of forced saving. Some merchants even advertise "easy credit" to entice the unwary. In general, if a retailer is advertising his or her willingness to offer loans, it generally means that the prices of both the merchandise and the loans are higher than those of competitors.

FINANCE CHARGES

In the final analysis, you get credit by promising to pay in the future for something you receive in the present. For this service, the lender charges a fee to cover the costs of maintaining the credit staff, obtaining the money, providing for the losses on unpaid loans, and earning a profit for the company. The fee that you pay for the convenience of obtaining credit is called a **finance charge**.

The finance charge is the total dollar amount you pay to use credit. It includes interest on the money borrowed, service charges for processing the loan, and even insurance premiums, if they are credit related and required by the lender. Under the Truth in Lending provisions of the Consumer Credit Protection Act of 1968, a creditor must tell the borrower, in writing and before any agreement is signed, the exact amount of the finance charge in dollars and cents.

In addition to informing the prospective borrower of the exact amount of the finance charge, the lender must also convert this charge to an **annual percentage rate (APR)**. The APR is the percentage cost or relative cost of credit per year. The higher the APR, the greater the cost of the loan to the consumer.

Table 8-1. Monthly Payments, Finance Charges, and Total Cost of a $2000 Loan for Various Repayment Periods and Annual Percentage Rates

Annual percentage rate (APR)	Length of loan	Monthly payment	Total finance charge	Total cost
12%	1 year	$177.70	$132.40	$2132.40
12	2 years	94.15	259.60	2259.60
12	3 years	66.43	391.48	2391.48
15	1 year	180.52	166.24	2166.24
15	2 years	96.98	327.52	2327.52
15	3 years	69.34	496.24	2496.24
18	1 year	183.36	200.32	2200.32
18	2 years	99.84	396.16	2396.16
18	3 years	72.30	602.80	2602.80
22	1 year	187.18	246.16	2246.16
22	2 years	103.75	490.00	2490.00
22	3 years	76.38	749.68	2749.68

The APRs for two loans of equal amounts from different lenders can vary depending on the size of the service charges, the interest rate, or even the method of structuring the repayment. But the most important point to remember is that when you are shopping for a loan, always compare finance charges and annual percentage rates.

Table 8-1 reinforces the idea that consumers can save money by comparing finance charges and APRs. It illustrates the total costs of a $2000 loan for various interest rates and time periods. As you can see, the shorter the loan period, the smaller the finance charge. This makes sense, because the charge is calculated to compensate the lender for giving up the buying power of that money for a period of time. The longer the loan period, the greater the finance charge. For example, an 18 percent loan incurs a $200.32 finance charge on $2000 repaid in one year, but it incurs a $602.80 finance charge if extended for three years. Finance charges are always lower on shorter-term loans when APRs are equal. Another advantage of a shorter-term loan is that if you choose to prepay the loan, the finance charge is less. For further details on how finance charges are computed on early payoffs, see Box 8-2.

The finance charge also varies with the size of the APR. The higher the APR, the greater the finance charge. According to Table 8-1, a $2000 loan for two years at 12 percent interest would cost the borrower $259.60 in finance charges. At 22 percent interest, the same loan's finance charge would almost double.

When looking at the APR and the associated finance charges in Table 8-1 you should notice another interesting feature of installment loans—the amount of the finance charge is *not* equal to the annual percentage rate times the size of the loan. For example, in line 1 of the table, the finance charge for a $2000 loan at 12 percent APR, repayable in twelve monthly installments, is not $240 (12 percent of $2000); it is only $132.40. The reason for the difference is that the consumer does not have the use of the $2000 for the entire year. Because the loan begins to be repaid the month after it was given, the consumer has the full amount for only one month. Thereafter, the payment begins to pay the interest *and* reduce the principal on which the interest is calculated.

A shortcut method of converting the finance charge to an annual percentage rate for a monthly installment loan is to multiply the finance charge by 24, and then divide the answer by the value of the

> **BOX 8-2**
>
> ## The Rule of 78: What Happens If You Pay a Loan Off Early?
>
> The finance charge on a loan is smaller than you would suspect if you were to simply multiply the APR by the principal for only one month and then make monthly payments that would reduce the principal and pay the finance charge in equal amounts. The fact is, a larger portion of your monthly payment goes to pay interest in the early months of your loan than in later months. If you decide to pay off the loan early, your creditor will have to calculate how much of a finance charge you still owe.
>
> On a one-year loan, creditors generally use the **rule of 78.** That is, they assign 78 parts to a finance charge for a twelve-month loan based on the fact that $1 + 2 + 3 \ldots + 11 + 12 = 78$. The first month, you pay 12/78 of the finance charge. The second month, you pay 11/78 of the finance charge, and so on, until the twelfth month, when you pay only 1/78 of the total finance charge. The rule of 78 means that you will pay considerably more interest in the early months of your loan. For example, according to the rule, if you pay a twelve-month loan off in six months, you owe 57/78 of the finance charge: $(12 + 11 + 10 + 9 + 8 + 7) \div 78$, or about 73 percent. Common sense would argue that you owe only 50 percent of the finance charge, because six months is half of the loan period. Using the rule of 78 and the information on the first loan in Table 8-1, you can see that if you decided to pay off your 12 percent loan after six months, you would have to pay $96.65 in finance charges (.73 × $132.40), not the $61.20 you might think you are supposed to pay.
>
> For loans of two or three years, the rule of 78 does not apply because there are twenty-four or thirty-six payments instead of twelve. But the basic principle of charging a higher proportion of the finance charge earlier in the loan period does apply. For loans of twenty-four monthly installments, most financial institutions use the rule of 300, because $1 + 2 + 3 + 4 \ldots + 23 + 24 = 300$.
>
> For thirty-six monthly installments, the rule of 666 applies, because $1 + 2 + 3 + 4 \ldots + 35 + 36 = 666$. If you choose to repay a three-year installment loan at the end of two months, you would owe 71/666 of the finance charge $(35 + 36 \div 666)$ in addition to the principal. Thus, on a three-year $2000 loan with an APR of 18 percent, you would owe a finance charge of $64.26 if you choose to pay off the loan in two months (71/666 or 10.66 percent of $602.80). (See line 9 of Table 8-1 to verify this calculation.)
>
> Using Table 8-1 and the rule of 78, calculate how much you would owe in finance charges if you chose to pay off a twelve-month, 22 percent, $2000 loan in six months. How much would you owe if the creditor prorated the finance charge equally for all months?
>
> Which rule would a creditor use to estimate the finance charge owed on an early payoff for a two-year loan that was to be repaid in twenty-four monthly installments?

loan times the number of payments plus 1. This gives you an approximate APR. The formula is:

$$\frac{24F}{L(n + 1)}$$

where: F = the finance charge
L = the value of the loan (the principal)
n = the total number of monthly payments

For example, if you were to get a $500 loan that was to be repaid in twelve equal monthly installments and the finance charge was $100, you would pay $50 per month, or $600. This might seem like an APR of 20 percent, because $100 is 20 percent of $500. But if you put these numbers into the formula you discover that:

$$\frac{24 \times 100}{500 (12 + 1)} = \frac{2400}{6500} = 36.9\% \text{ interest}$$

So the APR is almost double what it appears to be if you simply divide the finance charge by the amount of the loan. The cause for the difference,

Families with revolving charge accounts may fall into the pattern of charging as much each month as they pay back; with finance charges added, their balance slowly creeps up each month.

again, is that the borrower does not have the use of the $500 for an entire year—he or she has the use of the entire $500 for only the first month. Thereafter, part of the principal is paid back. On the average, for an installment loan the borrower has the use of only one-half of the loan over the life of the contract. We will return to this phenomenon later when we discuss borrowing from friends and relatives.

THE COST OF OPEN-END CREDIT

The preceding discussion works well in determining the cost of closed-end, or installment, loans—that is, loans that are set up to be repaid in set amounts at constant intervals over a fixed period of time. But a growing portion of consumer debt now takes the form of what was once called revolving charges or **revolving credit** and is now universally termed **open-end credit**. Whereas installment loans are one-shot deals with a clear end in sight, open-end credit can be used over and over as long as the consumer does not exceed a prearranged borrowing limit. Open-end credit includes bank credit cards, department-store charge plates, and check-overdraft accounts that allow you to write checks for more than your actual balance in the bank.

Truth in lending applies to open-end credit just as it does to installment credit. But in addition to clearly detailing their finance charge and the annual percentage rate, these creditors must also tell you: (a) when finance charges begin on your account and (b) the method of calculating the finance charge. The first requirements tell you how much time you have to pay your bill *before* a finance charge is levied. Some creditors, for example, may give you thirty days to pay your balance before imposing a finance charge. However, this free ride is rapidly becoming extinct, because it amounts to an interest-free loan from the creditor to the consumer that, in times of high inflation and high interest rates, are extremely costly to the lender.

Methods of Calculating Finance Charges. The method of calculating the finance charge can also affect the cost of credit to the consumer. The three most common methods are adjusted balance, previous balance, and average daily balance.

Under the **adjusted balance method,** creditors add finance charges only after subtracting all payments made during the billing period. This amounts to giving the consumers up to 30 days of free credit if they pay off their bills every month. To see how the adjusted balance method works let us assume that a consumer owes $500 on a credit card on which the interest charge is 1½ percent per month (18 percent APR). If the consumer makes a $400 payment to the company, the interest charge that appears on the next statement will be $1.50. The company will have calculated this $1.50 charge by subtracting the $400 payment from the $500 owed and then applying the 1½ percent interest charge to the $100 outstanding balance.

According to a VISA Card official, about 37 percent of VISA's cardholders, whose charges account for half the dollar volume of total charges, take advantage of the adjusted balance method by paying off the entire balance before the billing period is over (*Changing Times,* December 1980). This means that the consumer does not *owe* any interest on charges made during the previous thirty days. As the cost of making thirty-day, interest-free loans increases, some bank card companies have begun adding a transaction fee each month to help defray the cost of their credit-card divisions. Others charge an annual fee that the consumer pays for the privilege of carrying the card regardless of the number of times it is used. Still other credit-card companies are changing their interest computation procedures to the previous balance method.

The **previous balance method** gives no credit to consumers for payments made during the billing period. This means that even if you pay off your balance in full, you still owe interest on the charges you made during the month. It is as if you have borrowed a sum of money for an entire month regardless of any payments you make. For example, if a consumer pays $400 on a $500 outstanding balance to a company charging an 18 percent APR and using the previous balance method for computing finance charges, the consumer will owe $7.50 in interest for the month. This is five times the amount that would be owed if the credit-card company used the adjusted balance method. The reason for the difference is that the previous balance method does not subtract any payments before computing the interest owed. Therefore, in our example, the 1½ percent monthly interest rate is applied to the entire $500 balance (1½ percent × $500 = $7.50).

A third plan for computing interest charges is called the **average daily balance method.** It requires creditors to compute the outstanding balance each day in the billing period by adding charges and subtracting payments on the day they are received. These daily balances are then totaled and divided by the number of days in the billing period to give an average daily balance. The APR is then applied to this balance. For example, if the previous balance is $500 and the monthly interest charge is 1½ percent, and if the consumer pays $400 on the fifteenth day of a thirty-day billing period during which nothing else is added to the charge card, the interest would be $4.50 based on an average daily balance of $300. The average daily balance is ($500 × 15 days) + ($100 × 15 days) ÷ 30 days = $300. And the interest charges are 1½ percent times the average daily balance.

Under this system, making your payment early in the cycle lowers your interest cost, whereas delaying payment increases it. If you do not pay until the last day of the cycle, this method amounts to the same cost as the previous balance method. But at least with the average daily balance method the interest cost is partly based on consumer decision making. A comparison of all three plans is made in Table 8-2.

Shopping for Open-End Credit. Table 8-2 presents data that show what these three plans mean to a consumer with an outstanding balance of $400, who then pays $300 by the fifteenth day of the billing period. As you can see, an annual percentage rate of 18 percent is assumed (1½ percent per month), but the method of computation of the finance charge results in charges that vary considerably.

The previous balance method is clearly the most expensive for the consumer and the most remunerative from the creditor's point of view. But the lower cost of the average daily balance method would be less obvious if the consumer chose to pay at the very

Table 8-2. Three Methods of Computing Finance Charges on Open-End Credit Accounts

	Adjusted balance	Previous balance	Average daily balance
Monthly interest rate	1½%	1½%	1½%
Previous balance	$400	$400	$400
Payments made on the 15th day	$300	$300	$300
Interest charge	$1.50	$6.00	$3.75
	($100 × 1.5%)	($400 × 1.5%)	(average balance of $250 × 1.5%)

SOURCE: Board of Governors of the Federal Reserve System, *Consumer Handbook to Credit Protection Laws* (December 1978).

---

end of the billing cycle. This would drive up the average balance on which the interest charge is made. The adjusted balance method is generally the least-expensive method.

If you are considering getting a credit card, you would do well to read their disclosure statements. Look at their APRs, their computational methods, their annual fees, and their service charges. No federal law limits the annual percentage rate that a creditor can charge or the way APRs can be used in computing a credit card's finance charge. However, many states do have **usury laws,** which limit the maximum interest rate that banks can charge on loans. These laws vary from state to state and sometimes depend on the amount financed. In Massachusetts and New Mexico, for example, the monthly APR for credit cards cannot exceed 1½ percent for the first $500 and 1 percent for all amounts above $500. And in nine states (Maine, Massachusetts, Michigan, Mississippi, Nebraska, North Dakota, New Mexico, Rhode Island, and Vermont), creditors are not permitted to include new purchases when computing the average daily balance (*Changing Times,* April 1980). These state regulations are certainly helpful to know, but the real question to consider when you are deciding whether or not to get a credit card is how the credit rules fit your particular needs.

Table 8-3 presents a summary of the major credit cards and compares their features and costs. As you can see, some credit cards are accepted at more places than at others. Some have annual fees, credit limits, and extended payment plans. As a rational decision maker, you should treat the decision to seek credit as you would any other consumer problem:

1. *Identify the problem.* Do you find that you need credit? For example, you may find it difficult to check into a hotel without a card or to carry enough cash for a long trip.

2. *Identify the options in light of your values, goals, and standards.* Do you have any reservations about owing money? Are you able to handle your debts in a responsible manner?

3. *Collect information about various credit cards.* How many and what kinds of retailers accept the card? Do you have enough income to qualify? What are the credit limits and fees associated with the card? What are the interest rates and how are the finance charges computed? The information in Table 8-3 should help with some of these questions.

4. *Weigh the costs and the benefits of the various cards and match them to your needs.* For example, if you will use the card primarily for identification, try to find one that charges by the transaction rather than one with an annual fee. Of course, if you use the card frequently, an annual fee may be cheaper than paying every time you use the card. If you plan to carry a balance from month to month, check the APRs carefully and make sure the card allows for this.

Table 8-3. The Major Credit Cards and How They Compare

	VISA	MasterCard
Issued through	About 12,500 banks, credit unions, and savings and loan associations affiliated with VISA USA, San Francisco	About 11,100 U.S. financial institutions affiliated with Interbank Card Association, New York City
Approximate number of cardholders	87,000,000 worldwide	79,700,000 worldwide
Approximate number of retail outlets	2,000,000 U.S. 1,000,000 foreign	2,000,000 U.S. 1,300,000 foreign
Minimum income to get card	Set by issuer; credit history considered	Set by issuer; credit history considered
Annual fee	Generally $10 to $20 where charged; sometimes free; sometimes charge made per transaction	Generally $10 to $20 where charged; sometimes free; sometimes charge made per transaction
Average credit limit	About $1,000	$918
Extended payments permitted	On all goods and services and cash advances	On all goods and services and cash advances
Interest rate on extended payments	Set by issuer; typically 12% to 18% and higher; some cards offer interest-free grace period	Set by issuer; typically 12% to 18% and higher; some cards offer interest-free grace period
Cash advance	Generally from $50 up to credit limit; interest rate set by card issuer, often less than rate on extended payments; usually no grace period; bank may assess flat charge at time of advance; available through participating banks in U.S. and abroad	Same as VISA

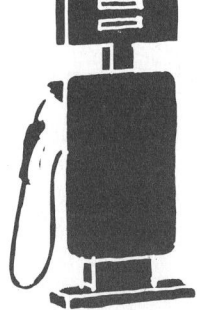

SOURCE: Reprinted with permission from "Beat the Rising Cost of Credit Cards," *Changing Times* (December 1980), p. 61. © 1980 Kiplinger Washington Editors, Inc.

5. *Make a decision and apply for your card.* If you get a card, move to steps six and seven. Monitor your behavior and that of the credit-card company to see that you made the right decision. If you do not get the card, you have a right to know why. We will discuss the right to know later in this chapter. But you will probably want to apply to a second or possibly a third credit-card company. Knowing why the first company turned you down could be important information.

6. *Review and evaluate your decision.* Save your monthly credit statements and periodically re-

American Express	**Diners Club**	**Carte Blanche**
American Express American Express Plaza New York, NY 10004	Diners Club Ten Columbus Circle New York, NY 10019	Carte Blanche Corp 3460 Wilshire Blvd. Los Angeles, CA 90010
11,000,000 worldwide	4,000,000 worldwide	850,000 worldwide
410,000 U.S. and foreign	450,000 U.S. and foreign	More than 250,000 U.S. and foreign
$12,500; credit history considered	$18,000; credit history considered	$16,000; credit history considered
$35 for basic card; $10 for each additional card; $35 for Gold Card, $10 for unlimited additional cards	$40 for two cards, $10 for each additional card	$35 for first card, $15 for additional cards
No preset limit	No preset limit	No preset limit
Only on airline tickets	None	Only on airline tickets
18%	None	12%
Only with Gold Card at Amexco offices and participating banks in U.S. and abroad; basic card has check-cashing privileges up to $1,000 per check every seven days in North America and every 21 days abroad at Amexco offices; Gold Card has check-cashing privileges up to $2,000 per check and $4,000 per month; both cards have check-cashing privileges for smaller amounts at participating hotels, motels, and airline counters	Up to $500 at more than 100 locations outside U.S.; service fee may be charged; check-cashing privileges up to $250 at participating hotels and motels in U.S. and Canada; additional credit line available to qualified cardholders through Chase Manhattan Bank	None; check-cashing privileges at some U.S. and foreign hotels

view them. Has your outstanding balance shown a tendency to get larger? What goods and services are you charging on your card? Are these the uses you envisioned when you first applied for the card? If you are having difficulty handling credit, these questions may make the reason more obvious. Perhaps you should consider putting the card away for a while. Try a "credit-less" month or two.

7. *Take responsibility for your actions.* Do not blame the credit-card company or advertising if you find it difficult to control your credit behavior. On the other hand, you have certain rights under the law and

you should not be afraid to use them if there is a billing error or if you have received poor service.

THE HIDDEN COSTS OF CREDIT

Although the Truth in Lending Law requires a full disclosure of the terms of a credit contract, it is still possible for consumers to be confused by the fine print of the contract. There are a number of clauses that seem to defy comprehension and yet can have serious effects. Box 8-3 presents some of these, with their English translations. You should be especially leery of **acceleration clauses,** which are found in many loan contracts. An acceleration clause requires that the entire debt become payable in one lump sum if the consumer fails to meet a single payment. Obviously, if you miss a payment because of financial difficulties, you are not likely to be able to pay off the entire loan when the next payment is due. This may mean that whatever you purchased on credit will be repossessed. And if it isn't worth as much as the value of the loan, you may be liable for the remainder.

Sources of Credit

Now that you understand the costs as well as the benefits of consumer credit, you may be interested in learning about the major sources of that credit. In the subsections that follow, we will list and evaluate where you can go in your search for credit. Table 8-4 lists the major holders of installment credit in the United States in the order of their importance. As you can see, there are a number of institutions that serve this consumer need. We deal with them in the order of their importance, and we add nonregulated sources as well. The object throughout is to provide more information and thus help you make better decisions about where to seek credit.

COMMERCIAL BANKS: FULL-SERVICE INSTITUTIONS

Until the passage of the Depository Institutions Deregulation and Monetary Control Act of 1980, commercial banks were the only financial institutions permitted to offer all financial services, from personal and real estate loans to savings and checking accounts. Today, other financial intermediaries such as savings and loan associations and credit unions also offer most of these services, including a type of

Table 8-4. Major Holders of Consumer Installment Credit, January 1982

Source	Dollars (billions)
1. Commercial banks	148.2
2. Finance companies	88.9
3. Credit unions	45.9
4. Retailers	28.2
5. Savings and loan associations	11.7
6. Other	7.2

SOURCE: *Federal Reserve Bulletin* (March 1982), p. A 42.

checking account. Nevertheless, commercial banks continue to dominate the consumer credit market. They supply almost half of all installment loans and open-end credit.

Loans from commercial banks generally take one of two forms: secured or unsecured loans. A **secured loan** is one for which the borrower must offer some guaranty beyond a promise to repay the loan. This generally takes the form of **collateral**—something of value pledged to assure loan repayment and subject to seizure upon default. Collateral can be property owned by the borrower or money that is on deposit in a savings account at the participating bank. Sometimes a loan can be secured by the purchase itself. For example, automobile or furniture loans are generally considered secured loans, because the bank's risk is lower. This means that the interest rate on the loans will also be lower, resulting in a lower cost to the consumer.

An **unsecured loan** requires only the consumer's promise to repay. These loans are generally offered for shorter periods and at higher interest rates than are secured loans. There are many forms of unsecured loans, including cash advances on bank credit cards and overdraft advances that are automatically extended whenever you write checks for more than you have in your checking account. Banks also offer small, unsecured loans repayable in monthly installments, but this form of unsecured loan is not very popular with bank loan officers. Given the administrative costs involved and the small size of these loans, banks prefer to offer overdraft protection or advances on credit cards.

BOX 8-3
Do You Speak Credit?

The following credit-language translations were done by the Federal Trade Commission's Bureau of Consumer Protection. These typical, standard-form contract provisions are used in states where they are permitted. One or more may be in a contract.

Acceleration Clause

Contract Language: Default in the payment of any installment of the principal balance or charges hereof or any part of either shall, at the option of the holder hereof, render the entire unpaid principal balance hereof and accrued charges thereon, at once due and payable.

Translation: If I miss a payment, you can make me repay the whole loan immediately.

Insecurity Clause

Contract Language: If the Debtor fails to pay any installment of any advance secured hereby or part thereof, or if there is a breach of any of the covenants, agreements, or warranties contained herein or in the credit agreement, or if the Secured Party shall feel insecure, all sums then owing under said credit agreement shall immediately become due and payable without demand or notice.

Translation: If you start to feel insecure about getting paid back, you can demand that I pay the entire amount at any time.

Late-Fee Clause

Contract Language: In the event Debtor defaults for fifteen days in making any of the aforementioned payments when the same become payable hereunder, creditor may charge the debtor a delinquency or collection charge of 5 percent of the amount of payments in default or the sum of $5, whichever is less.

Translation: You can charge me a late fee if I'm fifteen days late, and if I can't pay on time just once, my state law may let you charge me a late fee on all my other payments, too.

Waiver-of-State-Property-Exemption Clause

Contract Language: Each of us hereby, both individually and severally, waives any or all benefit or relief from homestead exemption and all other exemptions or moratoriums to which the signers or any of them may be entitled under the laws of this or any other State, now in force or hereafter to be passed, as against this debt or any renewal thereof.

Translation: If I do not pay, you can take even the personal belongings the state law allows me to keep.

Waiver-of-Right-to-Privacy Clause

Contract Language: The undersigned, jointly and severally, waive any right of privacy of any nature in connection with this instrument, regardless of whether or not the debt evidenced thereby may be contested, and agree that the Lender may at his or her option communicate with any persons whatsoever in relation to the obligation involved, or its delinquency, or in an effort to obtain cooperation or help relative to the collection of payment thereof.

Translation: If I don't pay, you can tell all my friends and relatives and my boss that I'm a deadbeat.

Right-to-Collect-Deficiency Clause

Contract Language: The Creditor may retain the goods as its property or may sell or otherwise dispose of the item pursuant to the (State) Uniform Commercial Code, whereupon Debtor shall be liable for and shall pay any deficiency on demand.

Translation: If you repossess what I bought from you and you do not get a good resale price for it, I'll still owe you the difference. (For example, if you take back a perfectly good $500 TV and can get only $150 for it, I lose the TV and still owe you $350.)

Attorney's-Fee Clause

Contract Language: In addition, if this agreement is referred to any attorney for collection because of any default or breach of any promise or provision hereunder by Debtor, Debtor agrees to pay an attorney's fee of 15 percent of the total of payments then due, plus the court costs.

Translation: It is a real hassle for you to sue me to collect, so I'll pay for your lawyer.

Confession-of-Judgment Clause

Contract Language: To secure payment hereof, the undersigned, jointly and severally, irrevocably authorize any attorney of any court of record to appear for any one or more of them in such court in term or vacation, after default in payment hereof, and confess a judgment without process in favor of the creditor hereof for such amount as may then appear unpaid hereon, to release all errors which may intervene in any such proceedings, and to consent to immediate execution upon such judgment, hereby ratifying every act of such attorney hereunder.

Translation: If you ever sue me because I have not paid, I agree in advance that you should win—even if I have a good reason for not paying. In fact, your lawyer can represent me.

CONSUMER FINANCE COMPANIES

Some financial institutions specialize in small consumer loans. These **consumer finance companies,** usually listed in the yellow pages of the phone directory, often do business across the country, unlike local commercial banks. They sometimes advertise on national television, and in general they try to make the business of borrowing money as appealing as possible. Because they specialize in small, unsecured loans, their rates are generally higher than those of commercial banks. On the other hand, their rules for qualifying are not as rigid as those of banks.

Many states have usury laws, which limit the amount of interest a loan company can charge. These laws can interfere with a lender's ability and willingness to loan money. Such laws are particularly important to finance companies, because finance companies generally charge the highest rates. But before you say "Good riddance" to such companies, remember that they do serve a consumer need. They are the financial institutions most willing to lend to high-risk, low-income consumers. If legislation forces finance companies and other lending institutions to lower their rates, finance companies will respond by tightening the qualifications consumers must meet to obtain loans. It is ironic that when usury laws are the most effective, they discriminate against low-income borrowers. So instead of getting a loan from a finance company at 24 percent interest, low-income borrowers must either forgo the loan entirely or borrow from a loan shark at exorbitant rates.

CREDIT UNIONS

Credit unions are the third most important holders of consumer installment debt. They are cooperative financial institutions that accept deposits from and offer loans to only their members. The most common way to join a credit union is to belong to a definable group such as teachers, government employees, union members, or the like. Because the members of a group are normally employed by a common organization and have similar jobs, the risk of loaning money is lessened. As a consequence, credit unions frequently have the lowest interest charges in the community. They also often have the advantage of being able to deduct loan payments directly from your paycheck. This can be very convenient for the consumer, and it also reduces the cost of administering the loan. The only drawback for the average consumer is in gaining admittance to the credit union. However, even this problem is lessened by the policy of most credit unions of allowing people to join if a close relative is already a member. It is probably worth your time to investigate this possibility if there is no credit union affiliated with your place of employment.

RETAIL OUTLETS

Retail outlets such as department stores, furniture stores, and jewelers were once almost as important in offering installment credit to consumers as banks and finance companies are today. As Figure 8-3 shows, they are still important, but over time they have fallen to a distant fourth in the race to provide consumer credit. Nationwide chain stores such as Sears and J.C. Penney offer consumers both forms of short-term credit: installment credit and open-end credit. As we mentioned earlier, installment credit is closed-end in the sense that the loan has a specific amount and a specific repayment period. An example of such a debt might be purchase of a $600 washer and dryer from Sears that includes an agreement to pay back the amount in equal monthly installments over the next year.

Open-end credit (revolving credit) allows the consumer to buy store merchandise and then repay the loan in any amount each month, subject to a minimum payment. The credit revolves in the sense that as the debt is repaid, the consumer can reuse the same credit line to purchase more goods.

SAVINGS AND LOAN ASSOCIATIONS

According to Table 8-4, savings and loan associations are the least important source for consumer credit, despite the fact that they had almost $12 billion in installment loans outstanding in 1982. The reason for their low profile can be found in the reason for their existence: They were established to finance home building. As a result, most of their loans are long-term mortgages for residences and apartment complexes. To attract money for this purpose, savings and loan associations were given the right to pay more

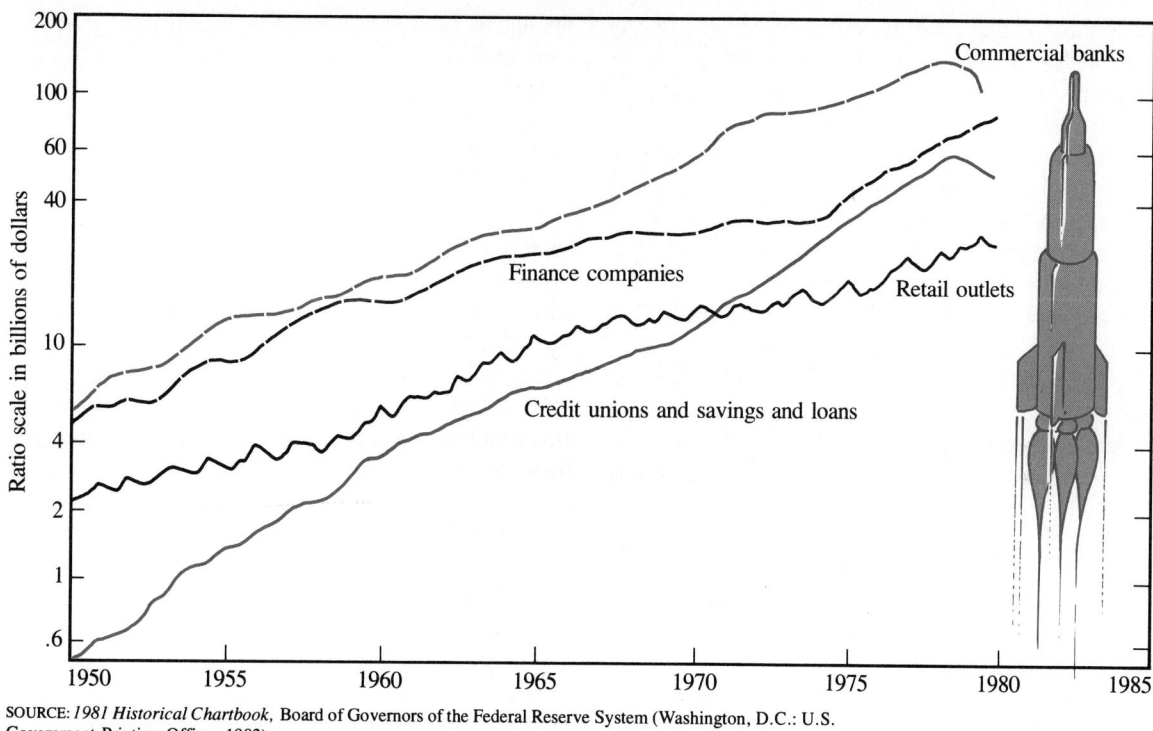

Figure 8-3. The growth of installment credit by source: 1950–1981.

SOURCE: *1981 Historical Chartbook,* Board of Governors of the Federal Reserve System (Washington, D.C.: U.S. Government Printing Office, 1982).

interest on savings accounts, but they were prohibited from issuing checking accounts to customers. With the passage of the Monetary Control Act of 1980, these regulations are being phased out, and the distinction between full-service commercial banks and the more recently established savings and loan associations is practically nonexistent. This means that savings and loans will function in about the same way as commercial banks do now. They will open personal loan departments, grant check overdraft protection, and issue bank-style credit cards. You can expect them to offer the same deal as their major competitors, commercial banks.

FAMILY AND FRIENDS

Important sources of consumer loans that are not regulated by federal or state agencies are your immediate family and friends. We have no objective way of determining how large a portion of consumer debt is held by this group, but any discussion of the sources of consumer credit would be seriously lacking if it did not consider this alternative. Most of us have been on both ends of the borrower-lender relationship, and we know the advantages as well as the disadvantages of such loans. On the plus side, there are neither applications to fill out nor references to supply, and the decision to lend is generally made fairly quickly. The disadvantages can be great, however. If repayment is delayed, friendships can dissolve and family relationships can be strained. Often it is more difficult to repay such loans, because they seldom fit easily into your budget. You do not get a monthly statement, and borrowers' memories seem to be especially flawed.

If you do decide to seek a loan from a friend or a relative, it is generally best to proceed in a businesslike manner. You should draw up a contract stating the amount of the loan, the interest rate, and the repayment schedule. Be sure to consult the section on finance charges and the annual percentage rate in this chapter, because they can make a difference in the interest rate. For example, if you borrow $100 at 8 percent interest and begin to repay in twelve equal monthly installments, you should not pay $9 per month. Although this may seem correct ($9 × 12 months = $108 × 8 percent) it is *not*. You do not have the use of the $100 for an entire year, because you begin to repay that money the very next month. The best approximation of an 8 percent APR in which you begin to repay by the following month and continue in equal installments for one year is to divide the loan in half ($100 ÷ 2 = $50) and compute the 8 percent interest charge on this average loan balance. This results in a finance charge of $4 (.08 × $50) and a monthly payment of $8.67, rather than $9. On the other hand, you may decide to avoid the hassle and pay whatever interest rate your friendly lender wants to charge.

LIFE INSURANCE

One of the less-obvious places to go for a loan is your life insurance company. If you have a life insurance policy that has some cash value in addition to its death benefits, you can probably borrow against the cash value and dividends that have accumulated from the time you began the policy. We will discuss these policies in more detail in Chapter 17, but some of the features of such policies are relevant to this chapter. For example, many life insurance policies charge comparatively low interest rates—most are under 10 percent and many are between 5 and 8 percent. Part of the reason for the low interest rate can be attributed to the fact that many of these policies were written years ago when other interest rates were also low. Once the rates are stated in the policy, they can't be changed. Another reason for the below-market interest rate is that you are actually borrowing your own money. Such life insurance policies are built-in savings accounts that pay off when the policyholder reaches a certain age. If you borrow from it, you are simply getting some of the long-term benefits early (and paying an interest fee for the privilege).

Another feature of life insurance loans is that the company can never refuse to lend you the money. Again, the reason is that all you are doing is borrowing against your paid-in benefits. And finally, you can repay the loan on any schedule you like. Or if you prefer, you can choose not to repay it. In this case, when the policy matures or when the policyholder dies, the insurance benefits will be reduced by the amount of the loan plus the interest owed.

PAWNBROKERS

Another source of consumer loans that can be used as a last resort is one of your local pawnbrokers. You will generally find these folks near the municipal jail and surrounded by bail bondsmen, unseemly bars, and boarded-up stores. The characters who frequent such neighborhoods are not typical college freshmen. On the other hand, if you need a loan badly enough, you may want to consider this source.

Pawnbrokers specialize in loans secured by personal property. You must bring in some article of value, such as a guitar, a stereo, or a class ring, and the pawnbroker will take it as collateral for a loan that is generally about half of the resale value. You generally have up to one year to reclaim your collateral by paying back the loan and the finance charge in one lump sum. The APR for such a transaction varies, but it is rarely less than 36 percent. If you do not reclaim your pawned article, the pawnbroker has the right to sell it. If the sale brings more revenue than the amount of the loan and the accumulated interest, you have a right to the excess. However, it is rare for such surpluses to exist, let alone to be repaid to the borrower.

Applying for Credit

It is sometimes said that the only two things that are certain are death and taxes, and not necessarily in that order. We might add a third item—consumer credit. The vast majority of Americans seek credit at some point in their lives. You may already have done so. You may have applied for a car loan, a credit card, or a department-store charge plate. Whether you got the credit or not, you probably do not know why you did or did not get it. This section will provide you with that information, so that the next time you decide to apply for credit you will know what creditors are looking for.

In order to obtain credit, an individual must demonstrate that he will be able and willing to repay the debt.

THE THREE C's:
WHAT CREDITORS ARE LOOKING FOR

Whenever a consumer applies for credit, whether it is for closed-end credit, such as an installment loan, or open-end credit, such as a credit card, the lender wants to know whether the prospective borrower has both the ability and the willingness to repay the debt. This overriding concern can be divided into the three C's: capacity, character, and collateral.

Capacity. There are many questions on a credit application that refer to the ability of a consumer to repay a debt. Creditors ask for employment information—how much you earn, what you do, and how long you have worked. They also want to know what your expenses are, so they ask questions about whether you have current loan payments, how many dependents you have, and whether you pay alimony or child support. These may seem to be personal questions—they are. But the rationale for asking them is not simply idle curiosity; the creditor wants to know whether you have the ability and the budget flexibility to repay the loan.

Character. The consumer's willingness to repay the loan is a quality that is quite distinct from his or her ability to shoulder the debt. Stories of prominent, affluent people who obtained large loans and then flew off to Tahiti never to be seen again are legion among bank loan officers. Of course, these are exceptional cases, but they do happen. Creditors want some assurance that consumers will repay the debt. This willingness, or character, is often demonstrated by your **credit history**—that is, your track record of past borrowing activity. Creditors want to know who has given you credit in the past, how much credit you were given, and whether you repaid your bills on time and in full. They also look for signs of stability by asking questions such as: How long have you lived at your present address? Do you own or rent? Are you insured, and for how much?

Collateral. We discussed collateral earlier, but in this context it serves as additional debt insurance for the creditor. Basically, the creditor wants to know whether you have any assets. An **asset** is anything of value that you own that could be used to pay off your

BOX 8-4

Qualifying for Credit

Banks, oil companies, and major retailers are always looking for ways to reduce their losses on bad credit risks without turning down good customers. This search has led them to outside consultants who often tailor a score card system to meet the needs of a particular creditor. The following score card was developed by the Fair, Issac Companies of San Rafael, California, a consulting firm that has created more than 900 scoring systems. This particular score card is a two-step process. Step 1 assigns points to various responses that applicants make when they fill out a credit application. For example, homeowners get 25 points, renters 15 points, and someone living at home with parents would score only 10 points. Stability and white collar jobs are highly rated as you can see from looking at the point totals for years at current address, occupation, and years on the job. In this score card, a major credit card such as VISA or MasterCard give more points than a department store card. And if one of your credit references is a finance company, you lose six points. The applicant's score is totaled at this point and the creditor's scoring guidelines are applied. On this particular example, you would have to score 100 points to obtain credit, although the cutoff can be adjusted up or down depending on how much risk the creditor was willing to take. If you were a borderline case, the creditor would move to Step 2 and seek additional information from a credit bureau. Take the test and see how you score.

Sample Score Card

STEP 1 - APPLICATION DATA

Own/Rent	OWN 25	RENT 15	OTHER 10				
Years at Address	BELOW .5 12	.5-2.49 10	2.5-6.49 15	6.5-10.49 19	over 10.49 23		
Occupation	PROF/EXEC 50	SEMI PROF. 44	MANAGER 31	OFFICE 28	BL. COLLAR 25	RETIRED 31	OTHER 22
Years on Job	BELOW .5 2	.5-1.49 8	1.5-2.49 19	2.5-5.49 25	5.5-12.49 30	over 12.5+ 39	RETIRED 43
Finance Co. Ref.	YES 5	NO 11					
Dept. Store/ Major C.C.	NONE GIVEN 0	DEPT. STR. 11	MAJ C.C. 16	BOTH 27			
Bank Reference	CHECKING 5	SAVINGS 10	CK & SV 20	OTHER REF 11			
Source	NEW CUST 5	PRES. CUST 5	FORM. CUST 18				

Application Score _____   Final Score _____

STEP 2 - CREDIT BUREAU INFORMATION

Number of Inquiries Where Credit was Denied	0 3	1 11	2 3	3 −7	4 −7	5-9 −20	NO RECORD 0
Worst Reference	NO RECORD 6	ANY DER. −29	ANY SLOW −14	1 SATIS. 17	2 SATIS. 24	3+ SATIS. 29	

SOURCE: The Fair, Issac Companies. Reproduced by permission.

loan in the event that you are unable or unwilling to do so. The "assets" part of the application asks you to list those physical assets—your house, your car, or other consumer items—that could be sold to repay the debt. Creditors may also want to know how much is in your savings account and where your savings accounts are and whether you have any investments in stocks, bonds, or real estate. All of this information may be used in processing your credit application.

THE CREDITOR'S DECISION TO ACCEPT OR DENY APPLICATIONS

In the final analysis, the creditor can accept or deny your credit. This decision hinges on the characteristics outlined in the preceding section, but the importance attached to each element of the three C's varies among creditors. Some creditors also employ scoring systems, such as the one in Box 8-4 to help them decide which loan applications to pursue further and which ones to deny almost immediately. For the consumer who wants credit, such variations in the lending policies of creditors could well mean that one would accept and another would deny the same credit application. A person deemed an acceptable risk by one creditor may be immediately turned down by another creditor. But there are certain legal guidelines that all creditors must follow, and there are certain rights that all credit applicants have. These are discussed in the next sections.

The Equal Credit Opportunity Act

Whatever criteria creditors use, the Equal Credit Opportunity Act, passed in 1974 and put into effect in October 1975, requires them to apply these criteria fairly, impartially, and without discrimination. This does not mean that everyone is guaranteed credit. It does mean that discrimination on the basis of age, sex, marital status, race, color, religion, national origin, or receipt of public assistance (welfare) is expressly forbidden. Discrimination can take several forms besides that of denying you a loan that you otherwise qualify for. You may also be discouraged from applying for a loan, or you may obtain a loan on terms different from those granted to others with similar incomes, expenses, collateral, and credit histories.

CREDIT WITHOUT DISCRIMINATION

We will elaborate on three of the most common types of discrimination prohibited by the Act: discrimination on the basis of age, sex, and receipt of public assistance.

Age Discrimination. Many consumers complain about being denied credit solely on the basis of their age. This is especially true of retired persons and young consumers. The law states that a creditor may ask your age, but if you are old enough to sign a binding contract (usually eighteen or twenty-one depending on your state law), a creditor may not:

1. Deny credit solely because of your age.
2. Decrease credit because of age or retirement.
3. Deny credit because credit-related insurance is unavailable to persons your age.
4. Ignore your retirement income in rating your application.

On the other hand, creditors are allowed to take age into account if it does have a bearing on your ability to repay the loan. For example, a creditor can ask when an applicant plans on retiring, because a person's ability to repay a loan may be adversely affected by retirement. Or an older person may not be considered a good credit risk on a large loan with a small down payment and a long repayment period. A seventy-year-old's right to a thirty-year mortgage with only a 5 percent down payment is not guaranteed by the Act because such loans would not make good economic sense.

Sex Discrimination. Both men and women are protected by law from discrimination based on sex and marital status, but the law was especially designed to prohibit practices that make it difficult for women to get credit. Before the act was passed, many creditors refused to acknowledge a woman's participation in the family's credit history, because they assumed that the family's credit was based solely on the *husband's* ability and willingness to pay. In the past, some creditors would automatically close a single woman's account when she married. Other creditors would cancel credit on learning of a divorce.

Under the Equal Credit Opportunity Act, denial of credit cannot be based on an applicant's racial or ethnic background.

The law now states that creditors may not require a person to reapply for credit just because he or she has married or has been widowed or divorced. Women may also continue to use their maiden name or a combined last name on their credit accounts. In addition, creditors cannot ask for information about a husband or an ex-husband when a woman applies for her own credit, unless she depends on spousal support to qualify for the account or unless she is still married and living in one of the community-property states— states in which husband and wife share all property and debts equally. These states are Arizona, California, Idaho, Louisiana, Nevada, New Mexico, Texas, and Washington.

Public Assistance. The Equal Credit Opportunity Act also prohibits denial of credit to persons on Social Security, welfare, or any form of public assistance. In the past, these forms of assistance usually led to a quick dismissal of the applicant. Now, these factors may affect a person's application only if they relate to his or her credit worthiness. For example, a mother who receives money from Aid to Families with Dependent Children (AFDC) may have to disclose the number and ages of her children, because these benefits will terminate as the children grow older.

WHAT TO DO IF YOU ARE DENIED CREDIT

Credit is not a right; it is a privilege. Nevertheless, if you are denied credit, you have the right to know why. Under the Equal Credit Opportunity Act your application must be acted on within thirty days. If you are turned down, the reasons must be stated or you must be told in writing how to obtain this information. The creditor must also tell you whether a credit report was used, and he or she must give you the information necessary to contact the relevant credit bureau. If the creditor violates this law, you may sue for actual damages plus punitive damages of up to $10,000. But before you go off to find a lawyer, you should first check your credit record at the local credit bureau.

A **credit bureau** is a firm that assembles credit information and other information about consumers and then sells this information to other businesses that are interested in a consumer's ability and willingness to repay loans. There are over 2,500 credit bureaus in the United States, and they process 150 million credit reports in an average year.

Contrary to popular belief, the credit bureau does not make a value judgment about how good or bad a credit risk you are. Instead, they simply collect and store information about you that banks, financial companies, retailers, and your employer are willing to give them. This information may include your repayment patterns on old loans, your occupation, records of any court proceedings against you, and even your marital history. This record is then furnished to prospective creditors for a fee, and the lender ultimately decides whether or not to extend you credit. If you are denied credit, a good place to begin your search for the cause of the denial is with your credit record at the local credit bureau.

If a prospective lender denies you credit because of an unfavorable credit report, you have the right to request the information directly from the credit-reporting agency. The 1970 Fair Credit Reporting Act went into effect on April 25, 1971. It is the scorekeeper that ensures fairness and objectivity in a consumer's credit report. You may request in writing or in person a summary of your file from the credit bureau. If such a request is made within thirty days of a credit denial, the credit bureau is not allowed to charge you for this information. The summary must tell you the sources of the bureau's information and it must list everyone who has received a copy of your report within the last six months.

If you find that the report contains false, incomplete, or obsolete data, you should challenge its accuracy and ask the credit bureau to recheck its information. If the bureau finds the information to be incorrect, it must change its report. The bureau must also notify (at no cost to you) those who have previously received the report. Any information in your report that is more than seven years old (except for bankruptcy, for which the time constraint is ten years) must be deleted as being obsolete.

If you disagree with the credit bureau's findings and it refuses to change them, you have the right to file a 100-word statement, which will be sent in all future reports. You may also request that this statement be mailed to anyone who has sought information about your credit rating during the last six months. If you believe the intent of the Fair Reporting Act has been violated, you have the right to sue.

Fair Credit Billing Act

Even if you have no difficulty obtaining credit, you may have some disagreement with your creditors (or their computers) over their billing procedures. Our modern credit network is so tied to computers and other electronic marvels that it is a wonder that humans can understand it. Most consumers have had or will have some problem in their credit statements. The 1974 Fair Credit Billing Act, which went into effect in October 1975, was passed to give consumers some clear and definable rights in their disagreements with their creditors.

CORRECTING BILLING ERRORS

A billing error may be as simple as an error in arithmetic, or it may be as complex as a charge made by someone not authorized to use your account. I once received two charges on my VISA card that were made in Calcutta, India. I have never even been to India, let alone charged something there on my account. If you notice an incorrect charge on a credit account, the procedure to follow is straightforward:

1. Notify your creditor in writing within sixty days at the address indicated on your bill. Remember, a phone call is *not* sufficient for this purpose, because it will not preserve your rights under the law.
2. In your letter, be sure to include your name, address, and account number as well as the reason the bill is wrong.
3. Do not withhold payment on the portion of the bill you agree with.

The creditor is required to acknowledge your letter within thirty days, and your account must be corrected within two billing periods but in no case longer than ninety days.

> **BOX 8-5**
>
> ## It Pays to Know Consumer Credit Laws
>
> Shirley McIntosh had a problem. Her 1978 Oldsmobile was running poorly and she took it into a local garage to be fixed. The mechanic told her the carburetor was giving her trouble and agreed to fix it for $95. The garage did the work and Shirley paid for it with her VISA card. However, this was only the beginning.
>
> A month later, Shirley took the car back to the garage citing the same problem. The mechanic agreed to look at it, and when she returned, he claimed to have fixed the problem. A few days later she was back in the garage with a more irate look on her face. Once again, the mechanic looked at the car, but this time he said she needed a *new* carburetor.
>
> Fortunately, Shirley knew the credit laws and realized that she did not have to pay for something that was never fixed right in the first place. Despite the fact that she had paid her VISA bill, she wrote to her credit-card company explaining the situation and asking for her money back. Because Shirley qualified for this credit clause, she received a $95 credit on her next bill.
>
> Where did the $95 come from? The local garage discovered very quickly that this money was charged against its bank account. When the garage owner discovered this, he called the bank immediately. The bank executive explained, "If a customer has a complaint about an item or a service and has run through the normal procedures, we simply credit his or her account and debit *yours*. These decisions are made automatically. It is the law. According to the Fair Credit Billing Act, the consumer has the right to redress when the bill is more than $50 and the charge is made within 100 miles of home or in the customer's home state, provided that the consumer has tried to settle the issue with the merchant."
>
> The garage owner was furious, but there was little he could do about it. The only alternative in this case was to go to court, and $95 was hardly worth the trouble.
>
> 1. Were you aware of this provision of the Fair Credit Billing Act before you read this chapter? Is it in the interest of bank-card issuers or merchants to tell consumers about this law?
>
> 2. What types of businesses are most likely to be affected by this law? Does it apply to merchandise purchased with a department-store charge card?
>
> 3. Are there any loopholes in the law? For example, what would have happened if the service had been performed while Shirley was on a vacation in another state?

STOPPING PAYMENT FOR DEFECTIVE GOODS OR SERVICES

If you receive damaged goods or poor-quality services purchased with a credit card, the Fair Credit Billing Act can be invoked to stop payment. But first, you must attempt to resolve the dispute with the merchant. If the merchant refuses to take back the merchandise or make the necessary repairs, you have the right to withhold payment. This right is limited to a credit charged on a bank card or any card *not* issued by the store in which you made your purchase. Thus, it does not apply to a Sears card or to other department store cards or to a gasoline credit card. In addition, the sale must amount to more than $50 and must have taken place in your home state or within 100 miles of your home.

If you refuse to pay because the goods or services are defective, the merchant may sue you for payment. However, a defect in goods or services is a legitimate defense, and in cases in which the amount involved is small, the likelihood of a suit is fairly small. The Federal Trade Commission has even put out a flyer on how to use this law to protect yourself against faulty or unnecessary automobile repairs. It is in the *Facts for Consumers* series and is called "Credit Cards: Auto Repair Protection" (1978). See Box 8-5 for a typical example of the use of this provision.

If it is determined that the creditor made a mistake in your bill, you will not have to pay the disputed amount or any finance charge on that amount. This was the pleasant resolution of my India story. The company simply deleted the charge from my bill.

However, if the credit-card company continues

to insist that you pay a disputed charge, you have little recourse outside the court system. Your final salvo is to write a letter to the creditor within ten days of receiving the unfavorable response. Once the company receives your letter, it can begin reporting you to credit bureaus and other creditors, but it must also tell these people that you are disputing the charge. The creditor must also send you a list of everyone to whom a report of your delinquency has been issued. After the matter is settled, the creditor must advise everyone about the final resolution.

REPORTING LOST OR STOLEN CREDIT CARDS

If you lose a credit card, you must act quickly if you hope to avoid a financial loss, although your liability is limited by the Truth in Lending Law to $50 of unauthorized charges per card. An easy way to protect yourself against these losses, which can mount up quickly when several cards are involved, is to keep a list of all your credit cards and their account numbers.

Whenever you are issued a credit card, the company is required by law to provide you with a self-addressed, stamped form to assist you in notifying it of the loss. If you are a typical consumer, however, you probably didn't keep this envelope, or you don't know where you put it. The best alternative is to make a note of the address *as soon as you get it*. The proper address is noted on the back of the card. Remember, if you lose the card, it will be much more difficult to obtain this information.

Losing a credit card is a problem, but losing your credit rating can be a disaster. In order to avoid this, you need to know the difference between using credit and abusing credit. In the next section, we review some rules that may help you to distinguish between these two options by establishing some limits to your credit behavior. We also present some alternatives for consumers who overextend their credit.

How Much Credit Equals Too Much Debt?

There is no magic formula to determine how much debt a consumer can safely afford. The decision to take on additional debt depends on your stage in the life cycle, your current and potential income, and your values. For example, a newly married couple in which both the husband and wife borrow money to complete their medical-school training could afford a significantly higher debt load than a newly retired couple trying to get along on Social Security and a company pension. The young couple can expect their income to grow dramatically over the next few decades, thus making the burden of their debt considerably lighter. The older couple can foresee no large increase in their incomes, and if health problems develop, their expenses could also rise. Thus, two couples with identical current incomes could come to quite different conclusions about how much debt they could afford.

Nevertheless, there are some general principles that you should consider before you enlarge your indebtedness. As a general rule, it is not a good idea to go into debt to pay for ordinary expenses such as food, clothing, or rent. If you have to take a loan to go to the grocery store or to buy clothes, you are heading for trouble. These expenditures should be paid for with your normal income. For more expensive and less frequently purchased items such as houses, automobiles, and major appliances, most consumers have good reason to seek loans.

But even here, one must be careful. Can you afford these loans? How many is it safe to have at one time? And where can you go and what rights do you have if you miscalculate your ability to repay these loans? The following sections answer these questions by offering you some guidelines for anticipating credit problems *before* they develop, as well as for handling these problems as they arise.

SOME GUIDELINES FOR ESTABLISHING CREDIT LIMITS

There are several ways to establish a personal debt limitation. Some are fairly complex, whereas others can be calculated in a few minutes. But the important point to remember is that *none* is foolproof. A seemingly rational consumer can be caught in a credit squeeze even with the best-laid plans. Having said this, we present three plans.

Debt Ceiling. Set a ceiling on your total amount of short-term debt and compare it to your current debt load. Your income can support only a limited amount of debt. Once you go beyond this point, you will either be unable to pay or your lifestyle will have to be downgraded considerably before you are able to reduce the debts.

Most credit counselors use a formula to determine the ceiling that a consumer's income can support. Worksheet 8-1 presents three of the more common methods that money managers recommend to estimate what an installment-loan ceiling should be, excluding home mortgage payments. Method A is the most generous formula in the sense that it allows the largest debt ceiling before sounding an alarm. It assumes that a consumer can handle a debt load equal to 20 percent of his or her annual take-home pay. For someone earning $1000 a month after taxes, this amounts to a credit ceiling of $2400.

Method B was derived from a rule that states that one should never owe more than he or she can pay off by devoting 10 percent of his or her monthly take-home pay to this repayment task for eighteen months. This amounts to a debt ceiling of 15 percent. (You can verify this by using the data from our previous example—10 percent of $1000 times 18 months equals $1800, or 15 percent of the consumer's income.)

Method C considers the importance of necessity expenditures in calculating a safe debt ceiling. If the consumer who earns $1000 a month spends $500 each month on food, clothing, and shelter, then the debt ceiling is $2000. ($12,000 minus a $6000 necessities expenditure = $6000 × ⅓).

Method C is a more accurate formula than method A or method B, because it can take abnormally large (or small) expenditures on necessities into account when calculating a sustainable debt ceiling.

After you have filled out the top of Worksheet 8-1, compare your debt ceiling to your current debt load by totaling your outstanding debts, excluding your home mortgage. The list of loans should include your current balance in all closed-end loans, such as auto or personal loans, that have a definite repayment schedule, and all open-end loans, such as credit-card balances, that require only a minimum payment. Don't be surprised if you have exceeded your debt ceiling. This is common, especially for young adults who borrow money to finance their education. But this should alert you to the dangers of overextending yourself.

Debt Liquidation Timetable. Establish a timetable for liquidating your consumer debt. This technique calls for you to pay off all your outstanding installment and credit-card debts on a regular basis. This might mean resolving your debts once a year, or it could mean waiting as long as three years to clean your consumer debt slate. A plan such as this one might suit a consumer whose income is steady but increases during certain seasons. A postal worker, for example, might be assured of getting overtime pay during the peak holiday season each year. This extra income might be used to pay off the consumer debts that accumulate during the year. A teacher whose paycheck is divided into twelve monthly installments might get extra pay for teaching summer school. This extra income could be used to clean up the debts that build up over a year or two.

This technique has two serious drawbacks. First, the job that you were counting on to give you the extra income may not materialize. Second, you may develop that "mañana syndrome"—you tell yourself that it is all right to get deeper into debt, because you are going to pay it all off in a couple of years anyway. Only a well-disciplined consumer should try to apply it.

Assessment of Net Worth. Set up a balance sheet with the value of what you own (assets) on one side, and the value of what you owe (liabilities) on the other. This is considerably more involved than the first technique we cited, but it is similar to the process that commercial lenders require before they approve or reject your loan application. The difference between your assets and liabilities is called your net worth, a concept discussed in Chapter 6. In general, loans are denied to people whose net worth is negative, that is, those whose liabilities are greater than their assets. If you find that your net worth is very low or negative, you have probably reached your debt limit, and you would be ill advised to take on additional debt even if someone is willing to loan you more money.

WORKSHEET 8-1
Three Methods for Estimating Installment Debt Ceiling

Method A

Step 1   Enter annual after-tax income.   _____

Step 2   Multiply by 20 percent.   _____

Method B

Step 1   Enter monthly after-tax income.   _____

Step 2   Multiply by 18 months.   _____

Step 3   Multiply by 10 percent.   _____

Method C

Step 1   Enter annual after-tax income.   _____

Step 2   Subtract yearly expenditures for the necessities (food, clothing, shelter, and so forth).   _____

Step 3   Multiply by 33⅓ percent.   _____

To compare debt ceiling to current debt:

1. Enter results:
   Method A   _____
   Method B   _____
   Method C   _____
2. Enter current short-term loans:
   a. Credit cards
   _____
   _____
   _____ $_____
   _____

   b. Installment loans
   _____
   _____   _____

   c. Education loans
   _____
   _____   _____

   d. Automobile loan
   _____   _____

   e. Other loans
   _____
   _____   _____

                              Total loans $_____

3. Subtract current debt load from the A, B, and C estimates of debt ceiling. A negative number indicates that you have overextended your debt ceiling.

CREDIT COUNSELING

It is not unusual for consumers to overextend themselves financially, and it is easy to tell when this has happened. Being unable to make payments on time, getting delinquency notices, receiving letters from collection agencies, and seeking new loans to pay off old debts are all trouble signals. These situations call for help. One of the best approaches is to seek some form of credit counseling. Five out of six families in credit trouble can be helped by credit counselors. Sylvia Porter (1979) estimated that without the counseling services that exist today, the number of consumers who declare personal bankruptcy would rise by 50 percent.

Credit counselors can be found in a number of institutions. Some universities provide these services in their home economics or business departments. Most credit unions and other creditors also provide help. But one of the best places to seek counseling is in a nonprofit community-based organization such as the Consumer Credit Counselors Service. There is probably one in your community, and a consumer who has overextended his or her credit would do well to contact it. Basically, credit counselors advise consumers on money management problems and assist in providing a common-sense plan for paying off debts. They do not loan money and they do not encourage consumer bankruptcy. They will contact the relevant creditors if this seems advisable, and they will prepare a repayment plan that is acceptable to all parties.

If you are unable to locate a local branch of the Consumer Credit Counselors Service, write to the National Foundation for Consumer Credit, 1819 H Street N.W., Washington, D.C. 20006 for the address of the nearest one. Another group that may help with credit counseling is your local Family Service Agency. You can find the nearest one by writing to the Family Service Association of America, 44 East 23rd Street, New York, N.Y. 10010.

DEALING WITH BILL COLLECTORS

You do not have to be in serious financial trouble to cross paths with a bill collection agency—a firm that regularly collects debts owed to other businesses. Even a merchant error can lead a bill collector to get in touch with you. Often your first notice will come in the form of a letter—frequently a friendly reminder. But if you ignore it, you could be in for a real war of words. In the past, correspondence from a bill collector to a consumer could verge on harassment. The collector could phone you at all hours of the night and even threaten you with lawsuits or the loss of your reputation.

In order to eliminate these abuses, the Fair Debt Collection Practices Act was passed in 1977. Under this Act, abusive, deceptive, and unfair debt-collection practices are expressly forbidden. Debt collectors cannot phone you or visit you in person at inconvenient times—generally before 8:00 A.M. or after 9:00 P.M. Neither can they call you at work if your employer disapproves. In addition, they cannot:

1. Use threats of violence.
2. Use obscene language.
3. Use telephone calls to annoy you.
4. Make you accept a collect call.
5. Advertise your debt.

Also, debt collectors must stop their efforts to get in touch with you if you notify them by mail that you do not owe the debt. However, they can reinitiate their efforts if you receive proof of the debt, such as a copy of the original bill.

If a debt collector violates this Act, you have the right to sue for "actual damages," that is, personal and financial costs sustained in the course of the transaction in question. You also may sue for $1000 in "punitive damages"—money sought to punish the wrongdoer. In a case that involves many consumers, you may institute a class-action suit with punitive damages of up to $500,000. However, if you sue in bad faith or simply to harass a bill collector, you can be held liable for the court costs. Before you decide to sue, you might consult your state attorney general's office or write to the Federal Trade Commission, "Debt Collection," Washington, D.C. 20580.

WAGE GARNISHMENT

If you are working but refuse to pay a debt, a creditor can, under some circumstances, get a court order that instructs your employer to set aside a portion of your wages until the debt is repaid. This is called **wage**

Some creditors are able to obtain money they are owed by using the courts to gain access to the debtor's wages, but the Fair Debt Collection Practice Act prohibits abusive or deceptive collection practices.

garnishment, and it has been used by creditors for years. However, the Wage Garnishment Law (part of the Consumer Credit Protection Act) limits the amount that an employer can garnish from an employee's salary. In no case can the employer withhold more than 25 percent of take-home pay. A second provision of the law limits the employer even further in the case of low-wage employees. Before any garnishment can take place, an employee's weekly take-home pay must exceed thirty times the federal minimum hourly wage. If the minimum wage is $3.40 per hour, then $102 of take-home pay is exempt each week, or $408 monthly. But above this minimum, salaries can be garnished until 25 percent of take-home pay is withheld.

Another section of the law prohibits an employer from firing employees because of wage garnishment. This section is enforced by the U.S. Department of Labor's Wage and Hour Division. If an employer willfully violates the law, he or she is subject to a $1000 fine and/or a one-year prison sentence.

Bankruptcy: The Last Resort

In spite of all your efforts to avoid financial insolvency, you may find that you simply cannot pay off your debts. If you find yourself in such a predicament, bankruptcy may be your only alternative. In a typical year, over 200,000 Americans file for bankruptcy, and many more give it serious consideration. What is bankruptcy and what are its advantages and limitations?

Bankruptcy is a court action that declares a person free of most debts because he or she is declared incapable of paying them. It is a serious matter, because it stays on one's credit record for ten years and seriously impairs one's ability to obtain credit well into the future. Once a person becomes bankrupt, he or she cannot file again for six more years. Nevertheless, all consumers have a legal right to declare bankruptcy, and the courts are likely to grant it unless fraud or dishonesty are involved.

Because bankruptcy proceedings can be very involved, it is generally a good idea to retain a lawyer to

The laws of each state enumerate the items a family is allowed to keep in Chapter 7 bankruptcy.

help, especially if one owns property. The procedure for starting a bankruptcy action consists of filing a petition with the bankruptcy court requesting that you be declared bankrupt. You will also be required to file a Statement of Affairs that describes your personal background and financial history. You must also file a list of your creditors (Schedule A) and your assets (Schedule B). After you have filed your papers, the court clerk will inform your creditors, and a court appearance called "The First Meeting of Creditors" will be scheduled. When you attend this meeting, you may be questioned about your case, and a trustee who represents the creditors will be appointed to sell your assets and distribute the proceeds to the creditors.

Not all of your debts will be canceled by a successful bankruptcy proceeding. Some debts, such as taxes, alimony, child support, and loans that have nonbankrupt cosigners, will remain in force. For example, banks often get both the husband and wife to sign for a loan. If the husband goes bankrupt, he need not repay the loan. However, his wife, who cosigned the loan, remains legally obligated to repay it. Thus, it is especially important for married couples to decide whether they should jointly file for bankruptcy. Joint filing has the added benefit of doubling the value of the assets one is allowed to keep after the bankruptcy is completed.

Bankruptcy law was not intended to encourage consumers to use it to get out of their debts, but neither was it intended to wipe them out financially. All states have laws governing what a bankrupt individual is allowed to keep. In California, for example, bankruptcy law exempts certain personal belongings such as household furnishings, appliances, one piano, one radio, one television, a three-month supply of food, one shotgun, one rifle, and certain works of art. A Californian may also keep tools necessary for a trade, a cemetery lot, and an inexpensive automobile. He or she may even keep a maximum of $1000 in a savings and loan account. Other states have different rules.

In an effort to minimize the variability among state laws, the Federal Bankruptcy Code, Public Law 95-598, established federal exemptions effective October 1, 1979. This code is not mandatory for either the debtor or the state. Virginia, Ohio, and Florida have chosen to deny these exemptions, but in all other states the debtor may choose to use these federal exemptions or the ones issued by the relevant state.

According to the Federal Bankruptcy Code, a debtor is given the following exemptions:

1. $7500 worth of equity in a home (commonly referred to as the homestead exemption).

2. A motor vehicle worth up to $1200.
3. Items of household furnishings, goods, clothing, appliances, books, animals, crops, or musical instruments worth up to $200 each.
4. Jewelry worth up to $500.
5. Other property worth up to $400 (plus any unused portion of the homestead exemption).
6. Implements, professional books, or tools of the trade worth up to $750.
7. Dividends, interest, or loan value accrued on any unmatured life insurance contract worth up to $4000.
8. Any unmatured life insurance contracts.
9. Professionally prescribed health aids.
10. Income from Social Security, unemployment, disability, public assistance benefits, alimony, and child support payments.

The type of bankruptcy we have just described is technically known as a **Chapter 7 Bankruptcy,** or a **straight bankruptcy.** The Bankruptcy Act also contains a section that allows for the restructuring of a consumer's debt. This section is called **Chapter 13,** ''Adjustments of Debts for Individuals with Regular Income.'' This chapter of the Act is often called the **wage-earner plan,** because it is aimed at the consumer who has a steady job but simply cannot repay debts on time. Under this plan, the debtor files a statement with the local bankruptcy court agreeing to give a portion of his future earnings to a court-appointed trustee whose job is to repay the creditors in no more than five years. The filing of this plan halts all creditor action against the debtor, and a hearing is held during which the creditors may object to the plan. However, as long as the creditors can expect to receive as much under this plan as they would if the debtor filed a straight bankruptcy, the plan will generally be approved.

Once the court accepts the plan, it orders the debtor's employer to garnish his wages and send the money to the court-appointed trustee. This plan binds the creditors as well as the debtor to the repayment schedule. On successful completion of the agreement, the court discharges the debtor of all debts. On the other hand, if the plan proves unworkable, the debtor can file for a straight bankruptcy.

A Chapter 13 wage-earner plan has a number of advantages over a Chapter 7 bankruptcy. The Chapter 13 plan allows the debtor to retain possession and control of his property and relinquish only future income. This means that the Chapter 13 debtor does not have to liquidate all his assets as he would in a regular bankruptcy. In effect, the debtor can hold the creditors in check until his check comes in. Unlike straight bankruptcy, a successful Chapter 13 proceeding also protects anyone who cosigned a note with the debtor.

Another benefit is that a person demonstrates his or her willingness to repay debts, albeit over a longer time period. This is sometimes viewed as a good sign by future creditors. At least the person did not declare personal bankruptcy or simply refuse to pay the debt. Instead he or she chose the wage-earner plan, which allowed lenders to get back most of what was owed them.

Summary

Consider these facts. In a given year:

- Short-term consumer debt exceeds $300 billion, or between 16 and 19 percent, of the disposable income of all American consumers.
- Over 50 percent of American households are repaying one or more installment debts.
- More than 75 percent of American families have at least one nongasoline credit card, and 25 percent have three or more.
- In a typical year, Americans file over 200,000 bankruptcy petitions under Chapter 7 of the Federal Bankruptcy Code.

In short, the use and sometimes the abuse of credit has become a way of life in Consumer America.

In this chapter we have tried to outline the costs of consumer credit, as well as its benefits. There are few of us who can get along without any credit at all, and even fewer for whom a creditless existence would be better than one in which credit is used to wisely augment buying power.

If you are going to use credit, however, you must understand the rules of the game. This includes knowing the principal sources of credit, how to apply for credit, your legal rights in the process, and what to do if an error is made on your credit record. Once you have established your credit, you need to continue to evaluate your credit and your credit behavior, and you need to guard against overextending yourself. If you do run into trouble that credit counseling cannot solve, you have two options: straight bankruptcy or the wage-earner plan. Neither plan is ideal, but it may be the only way to achieve a new start.

As you know, we have covered a lot of material in this chapter, but because credit has become such an important part of our lives, we have to understand its role and how it works. A great deal of legislation has been passed in this area from the Consumer Credit Protection Act in 1968 to the Federal Bankruptcy Code revision in 1979. Consumer rights have never been as well established as they are today, and you would do well to learn about them. But responsibilities are equally important. Our vast credit network runs on trust. All parties must make an honest effort to use and offer credit in a responsible manner. But if you get into financial difficulties, you do not give up your rights. And if you believe that you have been dealt with unfairly, there are a number of government agencies, including the court system, that are designed to help you.

REVISITED

After her unpleasant encounter with the credit department at Stern's, Barbara decided that it was going to be a long time before she put herself through that trauma again. "Besides, who needs credit anyway," she thought to herself. "If you can't afford to pay cash for something, you shouldn't buy it." But somewhere in the back of her mind was a feeling of rejection and the nagging question: Why wouldn't they give her credit?

1. If Barbara had been aware of her rights, what questions could she have asked that might have helped her find out why she was denied credit?

2. Why do you believe she was denied credit? Did her job and her lack of credit at other stores have any bearing on her case?

3. How might Barbara establish a good credit history? How could her parents help?

KEY TERMS

acceleration clauses
adjusted balance method
annual percentage rate (APR)
asset
average daily balance method
bankruptcy
bill consolidation loan
Chapter 7 (straight) bankruptcy
Chapter 13 bankruptcy (wage-earner plan)
collateral
consumer finance companies
credit
credit bureau
credit history
credit unions
finance charge
installment (closed-end) credit
open-end (revolving) credit
previous balance method
rule of 78
secured loan
unsecured loan
usury laws
wage garnishment

QUESTIONS

1. How important is credit in the United States today? Give some examples that illustrate your point.

2. Make a list of the advantages and disadvantages of consumer credit. Given your current situation, should you seek credit? Explain.

3. If you borrowed $1000 for one year on the installment plan at 12 percent APR, would you pay a finance charge of $120? Explain.

4. If you are considering opening a credit account, which method of calculating finance charges would you

least prefer—adjusted balance, previous balance, or average daily balance?

5. What is the difference between a secured and an unsecured loan? Which one is likely to have a lower APR? Why?

6. What are usury laws and how do they affect consumers?

7. Using the system in Box 8-4, estimate your ability to obtain a loan. Do you qualify?

8. If you believe that there has been an error in your billing statement, what should you do? What must the creditor do in response? What law guarantees these rights?

9. What does garnishing your wages mean? What rights does a debtor have with respect to wage garnishment?

10. What are the differences between personal bankruptcy and a Chapter 13 bankruptcy? List some situations in which one might be preferable to the other.

PROJECTS

1. Using Table 8-3, make a list of three or four prominent credit cards and compare them with respect to: finance charges, annual fee, ease of use, average credit limit, and cash-advance privileges. Which card would be the best buy for the typical college student? The typical business executive? A retired teacher?

2. Let us assume that you need $500 for some unexpected expenses. Do some comparison shopping among the sources of loans cited in this chapter and compare their relative costs. Which source offers the lowest finance charges? Where could you get the longest repayment schedule?

3. Go to a local credit bureau and ask whether you can obtain information on your file. What information do they have? Is it accurate?

4. What forms of credit counseling are available in your community? Do a telephone survey of the services they offer. Is there a charge for these services?

REFERENCES AND READINGS

American Bar Association. *Your Guide to Consumer Credit and Bankruptcy.* Chicago, Ill.: American Bar Association, 1980.

"Bankruptcy Reform." *Family Economics Review,* Summer/Fall 1980.

"Beat the Rising Cost of Credit Cards." *Changing Times,* December 1980.

Board of Governors of the Federal Reserve System. *Consumer Handbook to Credit Protection Laws.* Washington, D.C.: Board of Governors of the Federal Reserve System, 1978.

"Credit Cards: Auto Repair Protection." *Facts for Consumers from the Federal Trade Commission.* Washington, D.C.: Federal Trade Commission, 1978.

"Do You Qualify for a Loan from a Commercial Bank?" *Bottom Line,* October 1980.

Federal Reserve Bank of New York. *Consumer Credit Terminology Handbook.* New York: Federal Reserve Bank, 1979.

"How to Shop for Credit." *Consumer Reports,* March 1975.

Kwitney, Jonathan. "Little-Noticed Change in Credit Law Gives Unhappy Consumers a Chance to Get Even." *Wall Street Journal,* September 28, 1980.

"Managing Your Credit to Make It Work For You." *Changing Times,* April 1980.

Milberg, Aaron S., and Shain, Henry. *How to Do Your Own Bankruptcy.* New York: McGraw-Hill, 1978.

"The New Rules About Bankruptcy." *Changing Times,* May 1979.

Noble, Alice. "Bill of Equal Rights—Cha-a-a-a-arge." *Fresno Bee,* January 14, 1981, p. C1.

Porter, Sylvia. *Sylvia Porter's New Money Book for the 80's.* New York: Avon Books, 1979.

"A Screwy Rule That Shortchanges Borrowers: The Rule of 78." *Changing Times,* September 1980.

"What Are Your Rights When You Bank By Machine?" *Better Homes and Gardens,* February 1981.

Did You Know That...

- current fashion influences our choices of all sorts of consumer goods, from tennis shoes to televisions?

- our choice of certain fashions tells other people about our values, standards, and goals?

- the process used to evaluate the purchase of a shirt and a stereo is the same?

- the word "textiles" refers to products such as carpeting, draperies, sheets, shirts, pants, and jackets made of fibers and fabrics?

- you should analyze your needs and your budget before going shopping?

- using the buying process described in this chapter will increase your satisfaction with your purchasing decisions?

Comparison Buying in Fashionable America: Textiles and Household Durables

Fashion, Style, and Fads
The Buying Process
The Buying Process: Textiles
The Buying Process: Household Durables

Neighborhood CAPSULE

Can We Afford It?

Jim poured two cups of coffee while Heather read the paper. Their daughter had spent the night with a friend and planned to be gone the whole day, so Heather and Jim had slept in and were having a leisurely breakfast.

"There's a sale on washers and dryers at White's Appliance this weekend," Heather said. "Prices have been reduced 30 percent on all brands. This may be just what we've been looking for."

"It really would be terrific not to have to go to the laundromat. I'm really getting tired of one of us spending a couple of hours there each weekend," Jim replied.

Jim's work schedule as a librarian was quite predictable, but Heather's job as assistant manager at a grocery store required some unusual hours. They had previously discussed how convenient it would be to do the washing at home and how it would allow more free time for family activities. There was plenty of space for the equipment in the garage of the house they had been renting for a year.

"Do you think we can really afford it now?" Heather asked.

"I'm not sure, let's figure it out," Jim answered. "How much will it be?"

"The ad says around $425 on sale," Healther replied.

They decided that the equipment should last at least ten years. On an initial cost of $425, they determined that the annual depreciation would average $42.50 per year. Their savings account contained enough money to pay cash, because they had been planning for this purchase for several months. They calculated that the interest they would lose on the money in their savings account would be around $20 for the first year.

"I've discovered that doing the washing at home would add about $60 a year to our utility bills," Heather commented. "How much money should we plan to spend for repairs?"

"I think around $25 should cover it," Jim replied. "When we add it all up, the cost comes to $147.50 a year. Do you think this is really better than going to the laundromat?"

"Sure," Heather answered. "We spend around $3.50 a week there, and that comes to over $180 a year!"

"It really would be a lot more convenient to do the washing in between other jobs here at home. And remember how that broken dryer ruined my sweater last month when it got too hot?" Jim added.

"OK, so we've agreed that we want and can afford the washer and dryer, especially now that it's on sale. The ad lists several brands. I wonder which one is best for us," said Heather.

"I think we should investigate a little bit before we go shopping," Jim replied. "I'd like to know more about the advantages and disadvantages of an electric versus a gas dryer." "All right," Heather said, "let's finish breakfast and go to the library. We can find the most current information in consumer magazines. I'd like to know a little more about those new energy labels I saw when I was shopping last week."

"Good," Jim agreed. "Then we'll go to White's Appliance and be able to ask good questions. We might even find out that we can get a better price at another store, despite the sale."

A strong force affects every aspect of our lives. It influences our choice of carpeting and cabinetry, refrigerators and recreation, automobiles and art. It encourages manufacturers to produce, merchandisers to sell, and consumers to purchase. This force is **fashion,** which has been defined by fashion authority Paul Nystrom as "the prevailing style at a given time." Few consumers understand the impact that fashion has on buying decisions of all kinds. Fashion explains the popularity of sleek, fastback, Z-like automobiles, the color of towels we favor at a given time, the style of furniture we prefer, the type of window coverings we select for our homes, and the choice of a wok rather than a fondue pot for a wedding gift. Fashion, however, is constantly changing. And that change can become uneconomical if consumers do not understand its impact on their decision making. This chapter explores fashion's impact and provides guidelines for comparison shopping and decision making in the areas most affected by fashion: clothing, household textiles, and consumer durables such as furniture and appliances.

We define fashion, see how it enhances our lives, and explore how styles become fashionable and influence choices available to consumers. We introduce the **buying-process model,** which shows you how to analyze your needs, your budget, and your options; how to narrow your choices; and how to make purchasing decisions. We apply the buying process throughout the rest of the text, usually focusing on one category or area of the family budget. In this chapter we first apply the buying-process model to clothing and household textiles. We combine clothing and household textiles such as bedding, towels, carpet, draperies, and upholstered furniture because they are made of the same materials—fibers and fabrics—and so can be investigated and evaluated in much the same way. Then we apply the buying process to the purchase of other household goods such as wood furniture, kitchen appliances, and television sets. Rather than supplying buying information for every household product, we provide a basic buying process that can be applied to all household goods, and we illustrate the buying process with specific examples. Our intent is to teach you how to analyze your individual needs and your budget, how to find necessary information, and how to weigh the costs and benefits of the alternatives so that you will be able to make wise buying decisions.

Fashion, Style, and Fads

Fashion plays a major role in our selection of food, housing, transportation, and recreation. It describes both the prevailing or preferred way of dressing, writing, behaving, or buying at a particular point in time *and* the effect that such behavior has on others as a signal of social standing or status. For example, a Mercedes-Benz or a Porsche might be considered the most elite car in the United States. If we drive one of these cars, we are "in fashion," and we are demonstrating that we have the money and the status to go with it. Not everyone who drives a Mercedes is wealthy, of course, just as not everyone who drives a battered Volkswagen is needy. Similarly, not everyone who wears designer clothing is as rich as the price tags might imply. But the point is that we use fashion to enhance ourselves and to make ourselves and our homes more attractive.

Fashion has several specific characteristics in addition to signaling status:

1. *Fashion is constantly changing*. It reflects a need for novelty and a desire for change. Fashion changes in apparel are the most recognized, but fashion changes cut across a wide spectrum of consumer goods (Kefgen and Touchie-Specht, 1981). The tail fins on cars in the 1950s, the disco dancing influence on music and clothing in the 1970s, the patriotic color schemes of 1976, and the growth in the number and specialization of small kitchen appliances that began in the 1970s and continues today—all are examples of changing fashion.

2. *Fashion cannot exist in isolation*. Fashion "is the code language of status" (Konig, 1973), and as such allows us to rapidly and nonverbally share information about ourselves with others. It requires an audience that is aware of what a fashion signals. A Mercedes-Benz has much more status now than it did in 1960, when more people preferred the bigger, more extravagant American cars. We create beauty in our environment through fashion. We adorn our bodies to please ourselves and to attract others. We plan and produce goods with a specific purpose, but also with an eye to attractiveness. The reaction of other people to our appearance and possessions helps us form our self-esteem. We like to be admired. To have other people imitate us builds our ego and increases our status.

3. *Fashion is followed*. Fashion deals in trends and cycles, as we will see here. People adopt a fashion for a while, then abandon it and adopt a newer fashion in order to be more up to date, more special and unique. For example, the dominant colors in the

Figure 9-1. Whether a style becomes a fad, a fashion, or a classic depends on sales volume over a period of time.

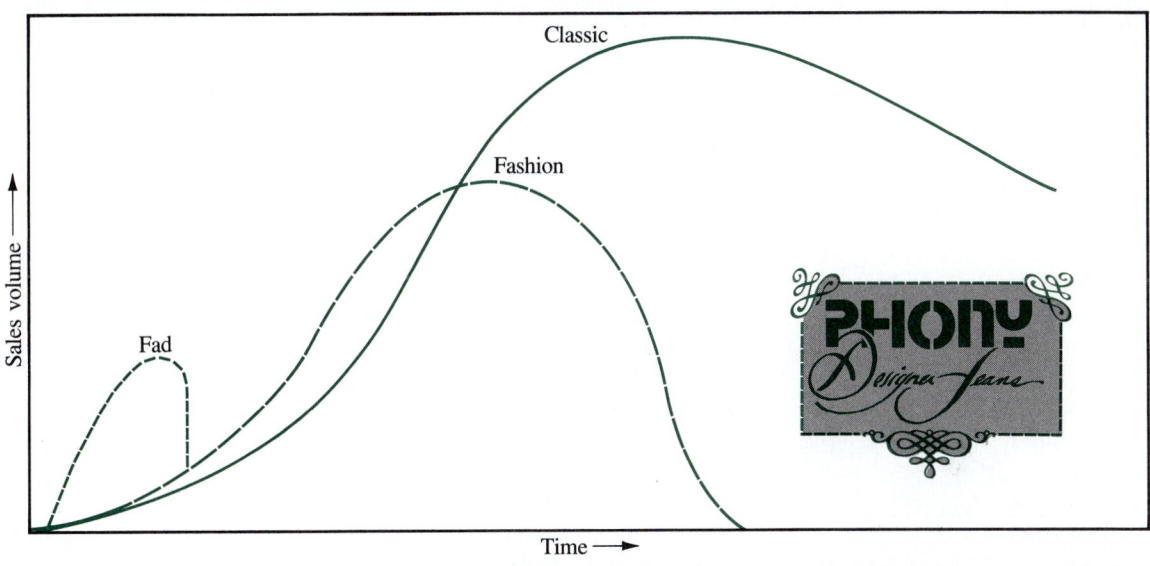

late 1960s for household goods from refrigerators to carpeting to bath towels were avocado and gold. These colors gave way to earth tones in the 1970s and they are in turn yielding to newer choices. Clearly, nothing forces a consumer to purchase fashionable goods. There is, however, subtle peer pressure to look and act in ways that reflect the group as a whole. What parent has not heard a child complain, "If I wear that, the other kids will laugh at me"? Although the sanctions that fashion imposes are vague, their power should not be underestimated.

4. *Fashion is not style*. A **style** is a particular design or line, such as a turtleneck sweater, a pressback chair, or a French Provincial settee. Its design characteristics never change. To become a fashion, a specific style must be accepted (purchased and used) by the majority of a group. For example, English and American eighteenth-century oak furniture has become increasingly fashionable in the last decade. This popularity has given rise to reproductions and to the manufacture of household accessories that complement them. Styles that endure—that change little and are continuously accepted over a long period of time—are called **classics**. They include tuxedos, Rolls Royces, and bentwood rockers. A short-lived fashion is called a **fad**. Fads are usually adopted by small groups of people and can quickly come and go (see Figure 9-1). For example, the clothing fad of the "punk look," complete with short ragged hair dyed in vivid colors, was adopted by some young people for a short time. Because home furnishings are more expensive than clothing, most people do not buy faddish furniture; it would be out of fashion before it wore out.

5. *Fashion is a luxury*. Following style trends requires that consumers have enough money to replace or add to their possessions. In other words, fashionable merchandise is often a "want" rather than a "need." For those who wish to be fashionable on a limited budget, classics are the most economical choices, because they do not become dated and can be used until they wear out. This helps to explain the popularity of classic looks in furniture, cars, and clothing.

Figure 9-2 Merchandise acceptance curve, or fashion cycle.

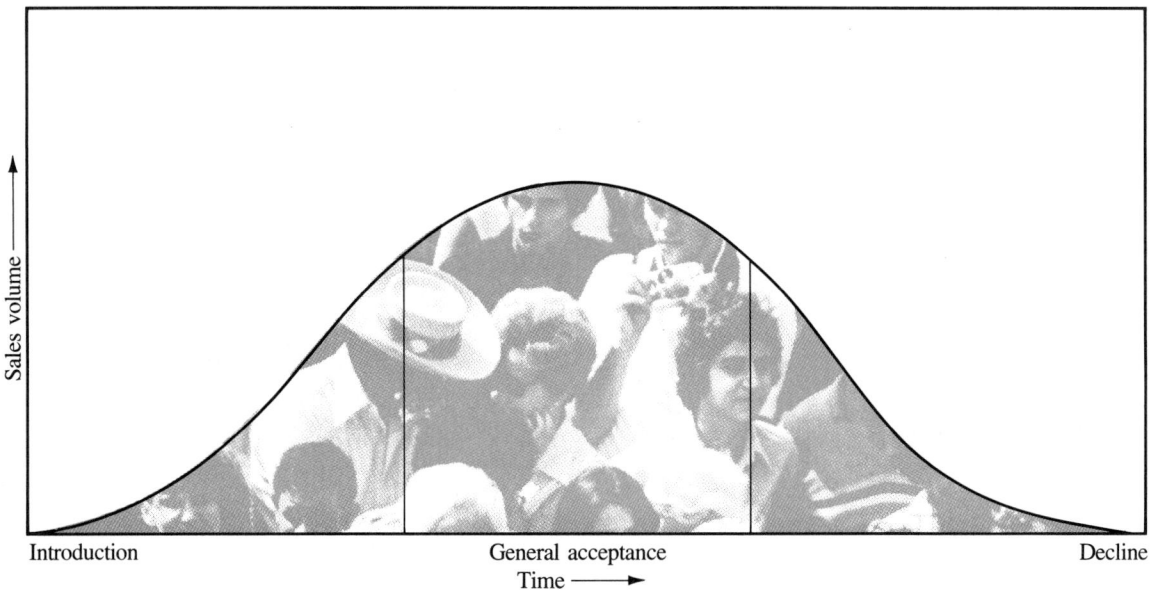

Introduction — General acceptance — Decline
Time →
Sales volume ↑

6. *Fashion follows a cycle.* The **fashion cycle** (see Figure 9-2) begins when a small group—*fashion leaders*—start to use an innovative product that, in the beginning, is experimental and expensive. If the product proves satisfactory, more people purchase it. Soon it is copied and imitated, often by using less-expensive materials or production methods. As it is sold to an increasing number of people, it achieves peak acceptance. Then fashion leaders begin to search for something new. The original fashion tends to be offered at reduced prices in specialty stores at the same time that lower-priced discount stores introduce it. As the first fashion declines, a new one emerges. In the final phase, consumers cannot be enticed to purchase the first fashion, and it becomes obsolete, that is, no longer current. Obviously, sales measure a product's acceptance—and decline.

An example of this **merchandise acceptance curve** can be found in evolving furniture styles. Mediterranean-style furniture, popular in the 1960s and 1970s, is massive and has ornate carving. As its popularity increased, less-expensive materials were used for construction, and the carved wood was replaced with molded plastic. After a time, Mediterranean-style furniture proliferated at discount stores and even at swapmeets. It has now been replaced by other styles.

INFLUENCES ON FASHION

Now that you understand that fashion is an integral, constantly changing part of your life, it is time to explore the causes of fashion changes to understand the role they play in consumer decision making. A number of elements influence fashion: politics, technological developments, social attitudes, religious beliefs, and government decrees. Fashions mirror the times by reflecting values, goals, and standards, and so are influenced by many of the same factors that influence values (see Chapter 2). For example, career-oriented women in the late 1970s, influenced by social attitudes, chose the classic blazer for their working wardrobe. They were trying to meet the wardrobe standards, set in a predominately male business world, that would indicate the seriousness of their career goals. The effects of politics and current events can be seen in the Chinese influence in some furniture and fabric design that has emerged since travel to and trade with China has been renewed. Finally, the economic impact of decreasing energy resources has diminished the interest in backyard swimming pools and has increased the use of wood-burning stoves for home heating.

For the economic, political, technological, social, and religious developments of an era to influence our fashions, there must be a leader to introduce a style. Three theories have been advanced to explain who this leader is and how fashions are adopted.

The oldest theory is commonly called the **trickle-down theory.** It suggests that a style is gradually accepted at progressively lower socioeconomic levels. Centuries ago, royalty served as leaders, and fashion spread as a result of this leadership. In the late nineteenth and early twentieth centuries, wealthy industrialists became the fashion leaders.

Today the trickle-down theory has limited application in developed countries, because increased speed of communication and transportation make it possible to introduce new styles to fashion leaders at all social and economic levels simultaneously. This has led to the **trickle-across** or **mass-market theory** of why fashion is adopted. Today's fashion leaders may be movie or recording stars, television personalities, sports figures, politicians, or campus or community leaders. They can be influential locally, nationally, or internationally. This theory recognizes that society is composed of many diverse groups of people, each with its own needs, wants, and fashion leaders. The trickle-across method of adopting fashion gave us disco dancing from *Saturday Night Fever*, jogging and jogging clothing for all occasions inspired by the Olympics and marathon running, the Cuisinart food processor and its imitators promoted by the media, the popularity of Jelly-Belly candy, and "Reagan red" for everything from napkins to wall coverings.

The **bottom-up theory** suggests that fashion filters up from the young, particularly from the young of lower-income groups because they feel freer to experiment with newer fashions. One recent example of this theory is the 1960s denim revolution, in which workers' bluejeans were adopted by the young. Because of the sheer numbers of the "baby-boom" generation, their clothing choices could not be ignored. Soon denim was shown in the couture collections in Paris, and it has since become acceptable for all ages and most occasions.

FASHION DICTATORS?
A common misconception is that designers dictate fashion and offer only what they like. A closer examination of the dynamics of fashion shows that this is not the case. Designers of consumer goods such as furniture, appliances, automobiles, and houses have thousands of ideas each year. From these, manufacturers choose to produce only those products that they think will sell. Then retailers select some of the manufacturers' offerings, based on market research and on previous sales records. Consumers make the ultimate decisions about what to buy or whether to buy. When many consumers make the same choices, a product is either declared fashionable or is rejected. Fashion is not a function of opinion, but of sales. Even strong sales promotions cannot change the direction in which a fashion is moving. Perhaps the best-known example is the Edsel, marketed by the Ford Motor Company in the mid-1950s. Despite heavy advertising, consumers did not buy the car, and it was quickly withdrawn from the marketplace. In 1970, women rejected midi (calf-length) dresses, also introduced with great fanfare. More recently, consumers rejected a small appliance that only cooked hot dogs. In the final analysis, consumers decide what is fashionable and whether fashion is worth the price.

The Buying Process

In Chapter 2, we introduced the concept of a decision-making model—a way of sorting out purchasing and other consumer decisions to achieve maximum satisfaction from investments of both time and money. This model is particularly important when it comes to buying **consumer durable goods**—items such as radios, television sets, carpeting, washing

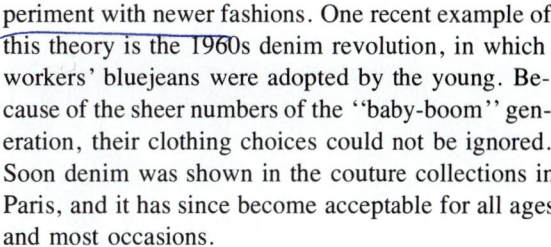

The first step in buying a durable good is determining what you need.

machines, and refrigerators. Consumer durables have several characteristics: (1) they are expected to last for several years, (2) they are often bought with credit, (3) they wear out and depreciate, or lose value, (4) they must be repaired or maintained, and (5) they may be insured.

When applying the decision-making model to the purchase of these and other major items, it is particularly important to account for fashion as well as for personal values and goals. All three make a difference in the decisions you make—and perhaps in the amount of rational thought you put into the buying process.

In this section of the chapter, we apply a variation of the decision-making model, called the buying-process model, to two kinds of purchasing decisions: decisions about textiles/clothing and household consumer durables. Some of these items are purchased often, whereas others are seldom purchased. You buy socks more often than you buy a new refrigerator, but in your lifetime you may spend almost as much to keep your feet warm as you do to keep your food cold. Nevertheless, in both cases the concept of comparison buying is essential. Acquiring the habit of comparing and shopping around as part of the decision-making process not only makes you a wiser consumer but also saves you money, helps you invest your time more wisely, and makes you more satisfied with what you buy. But before going on to look at some buying decisions, let us first compare the decision-making model (see Chapter 2) to the buying process model used here. The seven steps of the buying process model are:

1. Determine what you need.
2. Review your budget.
3. Investigate options.
4. Narrow your choices.
5. Make a choice.
6. Evaluate your choice.
7. Accept responsibility of ownership.

DETERMINE WHAT YOU NEED

This first step is like the first step of the decision-making model—*identify the problem*. Determine your physical and psychological needs and wants in relation to the purchase. Clarify your values and standards, and establish goals. Be sure to gather input from every family member affected by the decision, so everyone's needs will be identified as precisely as possible by asking:

1. Who will use the product?
2. What do I want the product to do?
3. What physical needs am I trying to meet?
4. What role does fashion play in my choice? How important is fashion in this purchase?
5. Will the product be used daily, weekly, or only occasionally?
6. Is the appearance of the product as important as its performance?
7. What size or quantity will give me the most satisfaction for my money?
8. How long do I expect the product to last?

> **BOX 9–1**
>
> **Merchandise Acceptance Curve: An Application**
>
> Consumers who wish to have fashionable clothing, household goods, or other durable goods can chart the progress of a particular look or trend. They can then purchase as early in the merchandise acceptance curve (see Figure 9–2) as they can afford to. For the fashion conscious, purchases made at the decline stage may actually prove to be relatively expensive. For example, let's say that Bob and Bill, equally interested in wearing fashionable clothing, see a new-style sportswear jacket. Bob decides to buy it in the introductory stage for $70, but Bill decides to wait until it is less expensive. One year later, Bill buys a jacket similar to Bob's for $50. Both men quit wearing their jackets at approximately the same time, because the style is declining in fashion. In this example, Bill wears his jacket for two years at an annual cost of $25, whereas Bob wears his for three years at an annual cost of $23.33. In addition, he had the satisfaction of having the new style for a longer time. Understanding and applying the merchandise acceptance curve can increase consumer satisfaction with buying decisions, particularly for those who want to be fashionable.

9. How does the cost of product care affect my selection?
10. Will owning the product require me to buy other products or accessories?
11. Will the purchase save me or my family time?

REVIEW YOUR BUDGET

Decide approximately how much money you can afford to spend in light of your values, goals, and standards. Decide who will do the buying and look at the overall budget to make sure it can accommodate the purchase. (See Chapter 6 for help in setting budgetary priorities and in making tradeoffs.) Ask yourself:

1. If I purchase the item, what am I giving up?
2. How does the purchase fit my goals, values, and standards?
3. How important is fashion in the purchase? How can I most economically apply the merchandise acceptance curve? (See Box 9-1.)
4. Can I pay cash for the product without using money from my emergency fund?
5. If I cannot pay cash, how will I pay?
6. If I must get a loan, how will the payment plan fit into my budget? (See Chapter 8 for help in selecting a loan.)
7. Will I be paying back the loan for longer than the usable life of the product?

INVESTIGATE OPTIONS

As in Step 3 of the decision-making model, you should seek advice and collect information about variations in product features, appearance, and durability. Sometimes, personal experience or a friend's experience can be a good source of information. Because it is relatively inexpensive to test a new brand of canned peaches, personal experience is a good source of information. Even if you do not like the peaches, you lose little money. But it can be costly to use the same technique with a durable good such as a video cassette recorder. Professional purchasing agents and retail buyers would not think of making a decision without first gathering technical preshopping data. You, as a consumer, should do the same. (See Chapter 5 for sources of technical information available to consumers.) The number of sources you consult and the amount of time you spend on research should be proportional to the amount of the expenditure involved. It would be irrational to spend weeks to investigate a new brand of peaches, for example.

Products marked "seconds" or "irregulars" sell at lower prices. They may have minor flaws, primarily in appearance, that do not affect their performance. Clothing, household linens, furniture, and appliances are often available in this condition. The flaw might be crooked stitching in clothing or a scratched finish in durable goods. Evaluate your needs and standards and consider these products, because purchasing irregulars can save money.

Do not overlook the savings possible by purchasing used rather than new products. Retailers often have used appliances for sale at substantially lower prices. In addition to standard retail outlets (see Box

> **BOX 9-2**
>
> ## Where to Buy?
>
> There are many types of stores that serve consumers. The type you choose depends on your budget, the time you have available for shopping, and your preference regarding personal service.
>
> *Chain store:* A chain store is an organization of stores managed from regional or national headquarters. It may specialize in one product, such as food or shoes, or it may carry everything from hats to hardware. Chain-store prices tend to be lower than those of independently owned stores, because the chain can buy and sell in larger quantities. Larger chains may have their own brands of merchandise. Customer service and sales personnel are available, but limited.
>
> *Independent store:* An independent store is a family business with one location. It may offer telephone ordering, delivery, credit, and special ordering at the customer's request. These services and the smaller volume of sales may cause prices to be higher than those of chain stores.
>
> *Department store:* A department store usually carries clothing and household goods. If it is part of a chain, it may offer slightly lower prices than an independently owned store. Some department stores that cater to middle-income or upper-income families may offer customer services such as ordering special merchandise, free gift wrapping, attractive decor, and special consultants to help in product selection. The cost of these services is included in the prices of all the store merchandise.
>
> *Discount store:* A discount store is a retail store that attracts customers by offering lower prices than those charged by competitors. This is done by eliminating customer services, such as gift wrapping and store restaurants, by minimizing sales staff, and by streamlining store decor and using all floor space for selling purposes.
>
> *Mail order service:* Mail order services originally developed because people lived far from retail stores. This method of selling has boomed in the last decade. Catalogs feature accurate descriptions of products, and they usually include photos. Customers who shop at home save time and gasoline, and they can shop at their own convenience.
>
> *Manufacturer's outlet:* A manufacturer's outlet is often located near the place of manufacturing. Merchandise usually costs half of its retail price or less, and it is available because there is a surplus that was not purchased by retail stores. Some merchandise may be irregulars or seconds, so look for flaws. To locate outlets in your community, look in the telephone directory, check with the Chamber of Commerce, read local newspapers, or ask friends.

9-2), newspaper classifieds, swapmeets, garage sales, auctions, and second-hand stores may yield the bargain you are looking for.

Sometimes you can get what you want without spending any money. For example, you may be able to use barter (see Chapter 7). As you focus on alternatives, ask yourself:

1. What do technical magazines or books say about the features, the appearance, the durability, and the care of the brands and models available?
2. What do I know about the features and the durability of the product from previously using it?
3. What are the opinions of friends who have used the product?
4. At what stage of the merchandise acceptance curve should I purchase?
5. What are the complaint or repair histories of the various brands or models?
6. What are the time and energy costs of using various brands or models?
7. Is the product a fad or will it have lasting appeal for me?
8. Should I purchase the product new or used?

Finally, you might consider the do-it-yourself option. Granted, it is difficult to do it yourself for many goods and services (not many of us can build our own cars or airplanes), but you may be able to make clothes and furniture or attempt minor plumbing repairs. Even preparing a meal at home may be considered part of the do-it-yourself trend when you consider that the alternative is to buy a restaurant meal.

Obviously, it takes time to do the labor yourself. Many of us buy goods and services that we could have provided for ourselves, because we cannot or do not wish to invest time in the task. After all, no one places a zero value on the opportunity cost of his or her time. But if it is possible to do tasks yourself, you can often substantially raise your level of living.

NARROW YOUR CHOICE

As a result of the research you did in Step 3 of the buying process, you should have selected one or two specific models or styles. As in Step 4 of the decision-making model, you should weigh the costs and benefits of the styles you chose. You can begin to shop around at various types of stores (see Box 9-2) and ask questions to verify and expand your knowledge of the product. Read all printed, point-of-sale product information such as labels, hangtags, and warranties. Do not rely on the claims of salespeople. Ask yourself:

When making a major purchase, a consumer must consider not only quality and cost but practical considerations as well.

1. Which brand or model will best meet the needs I determined in Step 1 of the buying process?
2. What are the monetary and time costs of selecting various brands or models?
3. How does the warranty for one brand or model compare to the warranty for other brands or models? (See Chapter 5 for a discussion of warranties.)
4. Are repair facilities available if I need them? What is the reputation of the facility?
5. If durability is important, which product is the best buy?

MAKE A CHOICE

As in Step 5 of the decision-making model, select the product that will give you the greatest satisfaction in light of your comparison shopping. If one product is not clearly superior, consider choosing the one with the fewest negative characteristics, or postpone the purchase until an acceptable alternative becomes available.

EVALUATE YOUR CHOICE

As in Step 6 of the decision-making model, you need to periodically evaluate your purchase to see how it is withstanding consumer use and maintenance. This increases your product knowledge and leads to a higher level of personal satisfaction with buying decisions. Ask yourself:

1. Does the product perform as I expected it to? If not, why not?
2. Did I buy the right size? (Whether you are buying a refrigerator for a small kitchen or a pair of shoes, size is always important.)
3. Will the product last as long as I expected it to? If not, why not?
4. Does the product require more costs (money and time) for care and maintenance than I expected it to?
5. What characteristics does the product have that I want to avoid in a future purchase?
6. What characteristics does the product lack that I want in a future purchase?
7. Did I purchase at a stage in the merchandise acceptance curve that was right for me?

ACCEPT RESPONSIBILITY OF OWNERSHIP

Product ownership entails not only rights, but responsibilities. As we discussed in Chapter 5, a buyer can assure satisfaction and good performance by doing certain things both before and after a purchase. Moreover, because the costs of processing returned merchandise are passed on to the consumer, it is in everyone's interest to be a responsible buyer. When you have purchased a good or a service, don't forget to ask yourself:

1. Did I file the sales slips, the warranty information, the instruction booklets, and the other information in a place where I can find them if I need them?
2. Do I know how to use the product properly so that I can prolong its working life? If not, do I have the information I need to learn to use it properly?
3. Do I know the procedures for lodging a complaint?
4. Did I ask all necessary questions about the product? Did I compare what the salespeople told me to information from other sources?
5. Did I follow all the steps in the decision-making process to ensure my satisfaction with the purchase?

You have just reviewed the buying-process model based on the decision-making model. As we apply the buying process throughout the remainder of this text, you will see that the information you seek and the questions you ask will vary from product to product. As you study the use of the buying-process model, you will become adept at inventing your own questions about a purchase. The rest of this chapter applies the buying process to the purchase of clothing and household textiles, and household consumer durables such as wood furniture, kitchen appliances, and stereos. We explore the purchase of clothing and household textiles in depth because a large share of the average family's budget is spent on textile products. Our second example reinforces the process and offers suggestions for sources of product information.

The Buying Process: Textiles

Textiles are fabrics that are woven or knitted. Textiles, in the form of clothing, account for 8–9 percent of a typical family's expenditures. Textiles are also used for floor coverings such as wall-to-wall carpeting and indoor-outdoor carpeting; for window coverings such as draperies and blinds; for upholstery on sofas and chairs; and for household linens such as blankets, sheets, bedspreads, and towels. All these uses account for 11–12 percent of a family's budget expenditures, certainly a substantial part.

DETERMINE WHAT YOU NEED

When choosing clothing and household textiles, you should consider your physical needs as well as your psychological needs for fashion and performance. For example, sheets with colorful designs may give pleasure, yet white or pastel sheets are available at one-third the cost, and they perform just as well. Only you can decide which will fulfill your needs best, but the questions outlined in Step 1 of the buying process and the information in the following sections should put you on the right track.

Household Textiles. Household textiles fulfill physical needs, such as keeping the floor warm or a room dark. They also fulfill psychological needs, such as providing attractive surroundings or indicating status. Some household textiles last a relatively short time, whereas others are durable goods. Because of the diversity of household textiles, you should identify personal needs for each purchase. In addition to asking the questions in Step 1 of the buying-process model, ask yourself:

1. Which is most important to me—appearance or durability?
2. How much wear and tear must this product withstand?
3. Is deterioration or fading from sunlight a consideration?
4. Is anyone in the household allergic to a specific fiber?
5. Do I want this product to be washable?

Clothing. Most of us buy clothing more frequently than we buy other types of textiles. Americans have more clothing than they need for physical protection, indicating that the psychological needs for status and self-esteem are being met with fashionable clothing purchases.

The best way to determine clothing needs is to take an inventory of what you already own. Worksheet 9-1 provides a simple inventory format that can

WORKSHEET 9-1
Wardrobe Inventory

	Coordinates
	suits
	women—dresses
		Separates
		pants
		sweaters
		jackets
		women—
		  skirts,
		  blouses
		men—
		  shirts
			Coats
			jackets
			topcoats
			raincoats
			poncho
				Accessories
				shoes
				ties
				belts
				hats
				jewelry
				gloves
					Miscellaneous or special activity items

Leisure or work active sports, work at home					
Casual school, relaxing, spectator sports					
Business/tailored school, work, dates, travel					
Semidress or formal entertaining, parties, formal occasions					

be adapted to anyone's needs. Taking stock of your present wardrobe alerts you to your clothing needs based on your job, your leisure time activities, your current wardrobe, your values, and your standards. Analyze the inventory results by asking yourself:

1. Do you have appropriate clothing to keep you physically comfortable? If not, what additional items are needed?
2. Do you have appropriate clothing for your job and leisure activities? If not, what is lacking?
3. Have you met your fashion standards to your satisfaction?
4. Do your separates (pants, sweaters, and so forth) work well together? Which ones can be worn with several other items? Are there any that you cannot coordinate with anything else in your wardrobe?
5. Are there some items that you are not currently wearing that could be altered, restyled, or worn in combination with other items?
6. Do you have one or two predominant colors in your wardrobe? If so, your clothing will be more interchangeable, and you will require fewer shoes, coats, and so forth.
7. Do your accessories (shoes, belts, and so forth) coordinate with the rest of your wardrobe? Do you need any key accessories in order to wear certain items in your wardrobe?
8. Is it more important that you have many lesser-quality clothes or fewer better-quality clothes?

When you have answered these questions, you have begun to identify your clothing and household textile needs. You may even have discovered that you have fewer needs than you thought. The next step is to see how much you can afford to spend to meet these needs.

REVIEW YOUR BUDGET
Review your budget, and clarify values, goals, and standards in reference to clothing and household textiles. Consumers have found that despite high inflation in the costs of other goods, retail apparel and textiles have remained among the most stable categories in the Consumer Price Index over the past fifteen years. Two basic factors are responsible for this stability: First, the textile and apparel industry consists primarily of small, highly competitive firms. Second, consumers have put up more resistance to price hikes in clothing than to similar increases in the costs of other goods. Many consumers value a tank of gas or a week's worth of groceries more highly than they do a new bedspread, and they therefore "make do" with the textile products they already own when there is a squeeze on their pocketbook. To help you make a decision about purchasing a textile product, ask yourself the questions outlined in Step 2 of the buying process. Then consider:

1. How does the initial cost of the item fit into the family budget?
2. Will the item have to be drycleaned? If so, how often can I afford to have that done?
3. How much will I use the item? (A shirt purchased for $25 and worn only twice is much more expensive than one purchased for $40 and worn thirty-five times.)

INVESTIGATE OPTIONS
Investigating options and information about features, appearance, durability, and care of textiles and clothing means learning about fiber content, fabric construction, coloring methods, finishes, and product construction.

Fiber Content. The **fiber content** of a textile is its basic ingredient. It may consist of natural fibers such as cotton and wool or of man-made fibers such as nylon and polyester. The 1958 Textile Labeling Act, which regulates the labeling of apparel, floor coverings, draperies, bedding, and other household goods, is enforced by the Federal Trade Commission (FTC). Labels must include the percentages of all fibers used in the product in order of their predominance. The "generic" or family name (cotton or nylon, for example) of the fiber must be stated, although including trade names (Supima or Qiana, for example) is optional. The fiber content is not a complete indication of performance, but it can help consumers who understand the characteristics of various materials to choose between products made of different fibers. Table 9-1 includes the generic names, some common

Table 9-1. A Guide to Fibers Used in Clothing

Generic name	Trademarks	Characteristics	Suggestions for care
Acetate	Acele, Estron, Chromspun	Moth and mildew resistant; high luster; colors sensitive to fading from atmospheric gases if not solution dyed; dissolves in acetone and nail polish remover.	Drycleaning may be preferred; remove oily stains before washing; heat in washing, drying, or pressing may set stains permanently; use low temperature in laundering and ironing.
Acrylic	Acrilan, Creslan, Orlon, Zefran	Soft, warm, lightweight, nonallergenic; quick drying; resistant to sun rotting.	Can be drycleaned; is machine washable and is dryable at moderate temperature (check label).
Cotton	Supima	Cool, comfortable to wear, strong, durable. Wrinkles easily unless treated with wrinkle-resistant finish; subject to damage by mildew.	Bleach only if label indicates it is safe; remove oily stains before washing; heat in washing, drying, and pressing may set stains permanently.
Flax (linen)	None		Can be drycleaned (check care label).
Glass	Betaglas, Fiberglas, Fiber Glass	Does not shrink or burn; limited resistance to abrasion; resists moths and mildew; most resistant of all fibers to sun rotting; resistant to soil and stains.	Wash by hand unless label lists other methods; do not iron; do not mix with other items in washing; drycleaning is recommended; remove soil by soaking; do not rub, twist, or wring.
Modacrylic	Dynel, SEP, Verel	Used in children's sleepwear because it is flame retardant; resistant to sunlight; soft, quick drying.	For washable items, use warm water and low heat in dryer; dryclean or fur cleaning suggested for fur-like items.
Nylon	Antron, Cantrece, Qiana, Vivana	Strong fiber; low in moisture absorbency; develops static electricity unless treated.	Machine washable; dries at low temperatures; scavenges color (wash whites separately).
Olefin	Durel, Herculon	Does not absorb water; soil and stain resistant; strong, except on long exposure to sunlight.	If washable, use low wash and dry temperatures; do not iron 100% olefin fabrics; may be drycleaned.

Continued next page

Table 9-1. *Continued*

Generic name	Trademarks	Characteristics	Suggestions for care
Polyester	Dacron, Encron, Fortrel, Kodel, Quintess, Trevira	Strong, quick-drying, wrinkle resistant; retains heat-set creases and pleats; resistant to sunlight; has a tendency to pill; develops static electricity unless treated.	Launder in warm water; dry in low heat; fabric softener will prevent static; may be drycleaned, with the exception of pigment prints.
Rayon	Bemberg	Absorbent; comfortable to wear; weak when wet.	May be drycleaned; pretreat oil spots before washing; iron on wrong side to prevent shine.
	Avril	Stronger than regular rayon when wet.	May be washed and ironed without special care.
Silk	None	Strong, luxurious fiber; may tend to water spot; subject to static electricity; white silk may yellow with age; low resistance to sun rotting.	Drycleaning is usually preferred; if washable, use moderate temperatures in washing, drying, and pressing; use a mild soap or detergent.
Spandex	Elura, Lycra, Monvelle (Spandex + nylon)	Good elasticity and recovery; resistant to perspiration, body oils, and detergents; lightweight.	Avoid constant overstretching (give garments a rest); do not use chlorine bleach; machine wash in warm water; dry at lowest heat, shortest cycle.
Triacetate	Arnel	Holds permanent pleats; mildew resistant; white may be chlorine bleached; burns and melts.	Can take higher pressing temperatures than acetate; can be laundered or drycleaned
Wool *Virgin wool:* fiber never used before. *Reprocessed:* reworked from fabric never used by consumer. *Reused:* reclaimed from products that have been used.		Resilient, springs back into shape; has excellent insulating properties; subject to damage by clothes moths and carpet beetles; burns slowly.	Drycleaning is usually preferred. If washable, use moderate temperatures in washing, drying, and pressing; use mild soap or detergent and use as little agitation as possible. To press, use a press cloth and moist heat (steam iron or damp press cloth).

SOURCE: Adapted from Madelyn C. Williams, "A Consumer's Guide to Fibers, Fabrics and Finishes" (California Department of Consumer Affairs).

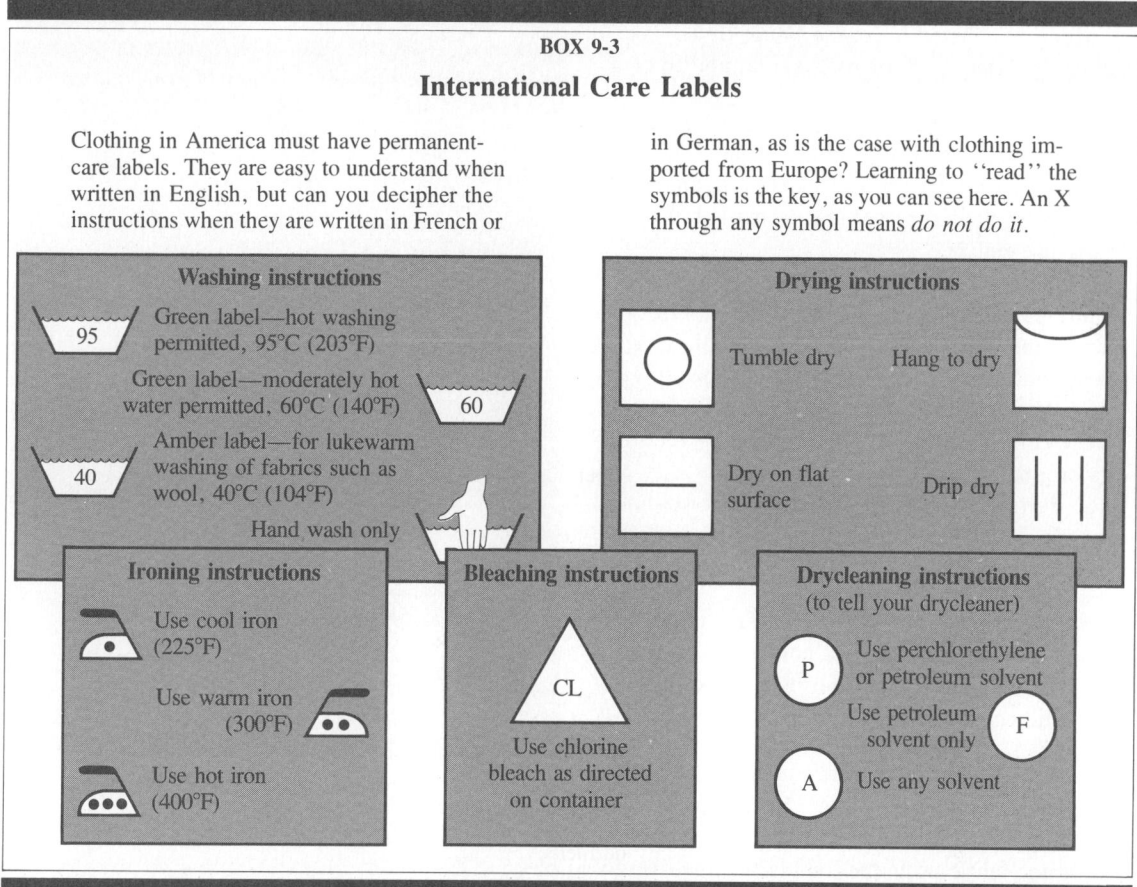

brand (trade) names, performance characteristics, and suggestions for care. The table applies to household textiles used for carpeting, upholstery, draperies, bedding, and clothing.

Fiber content is the major determinant of the method of product care. As a result of the Permanent Care Labeling Act of 1972 (expanded in 1981), most clothing and household textiles must have a permanent, legible, easily understood care label that has appropriate instructions for washing, bleaching, drying, ironing, and/or drycleaning. Such labels provide preshopping information, and they reduce confusion regarding garment care (see Box 9-3). When choosing fiber content:

1. Check labels and hangtags for product care.
2. Determine the resiliency of the fiber by crushing the fabric in your hand and observing its appearance when it is released.
3. Rub two pieces of the fabric together to check for static cling. If they stick together, they may stick to you as you wear them, or they may attract dirt when they are used in the home.
4. Fabrics that are susceptible to static cling absorb less body moisture, so they are less comfortable to wear.
5. Check Table 9-1 for specific problems with mildew, moths, sun rotting, and so forth.

Fabric Construction. **Fabric construction** is of three basic types: *woven,* yarn interlaced to form a fabric (basketweave, twill); *knit,* yarn looped to form a fabric (jersey knit, doubleknit); and *nonwoven,* loose fibers bonded or adhered to form a fabric (felt). To evaluate the future performance and durability of a fabric:

1. Pull the fabric in all directions. A stable fabric should not pull off-grain. This is particularly important for draperies, because unstable fabrics hang unevenly.
2. Do the thumb test: Grip two edges of the fabric with one hand and press down on the fabric with the thumb of your other hand. A durable fabric does not "give" or show slipping or separating of yarns. A single knit, or jersey knit, will show some stretching, but it should gradually return to its original shape.
3. Rub the fabric surfaces together. The fabric should not look rubbed and there should not be any pills (tiny balls of fiber).

Coloring Methods. **Coloring methods** are numerous, and they often depend on fiber content. As a consumer, your main goal is to determine the permanence of the solid color or printed design:

1. Check labels for descriptions such as "solution dyed" or "color fast"; they indicate good color stability.
2. Hold the fabric up to the light. Does the dye go through the fabric or just sit on the surface?
3. Slightly dampen the fabric and rub the surfaces together, or better yet, against a white fabric. Does the color come off?
4. Scratch printed fabrics with your fingernail to see whether the color comes off.
5. If possible, examine the color in natural, fluorescent, and incandescent lighting. The color may appear different under different lights.

Finishes. **Finishes** are chemicals applied to fabrics to improve their durability, the ease of care, their appearance, or their feeling. You may have noticed that washable clothing often is wrinkle resistant, that carpets are frequently soil resistant, and that tents are usually water repellent. Finishing processes may be listed on labels or hangtags, allowing consumers to choose products with or without these features. Your

In shopping for clothing, one must take into account the characteristics of fabrics in addition to style and fit. A stylish outfit will get little useful wear if it wrinkles or soils easily.

decision should be based on your need and your budget, because the use of finishes slightly increases product cost.

Product Construction. **Product construction** is the final factor that affects performance. There are four aspects of construction to consider: style (the design or line of the upholstered furniture, carpet, suit, or whatever); supportive materials (chair stuffing, carpet backing, or suit collar interfacing); construction details (stitch length, placement of textile design); and finishing details (such as lining and trims).

A style, as we have seen, can be faddish, fashionable, classic, or totally out of fashion. The most important consideration is whether you like it—whether it suits your personal taste.

Supportive materials add shape or stability. They

are found in collars, cuffs, front button plackets, and waistbands of clothing. They help stiffen and pleat the top few inches of draperies, they give stability to rugs and carpets, and they provide cushioning in chairs, sofas, mattresses, and pillows. To evaluate supportive materials, ask:

1. Do the supportive materials wrinkle or distort the outer fabric?
2. Are they securely sewn or bonded (specially treated with heat or chemicals) to the product?
3. Can the supportive materials be cared for as easily as the outer fabric? Will they last as long as the rest of the product?
4. Is the cushioning of sofas, mattresses, and so forth free of lumps? Does it provide adequate padding for the furniture frame or springs? Is its quality equal to that of the outer fabric?

Construction details include stitch length, seam finishes, hem appearance, comfort or fullness, and matching of the design. The following checklist offers an effective way to determine the quality of product construction.

1. Is the machine stitch short enough to be durable (tug on the seams to check for pulling) without causing a pucker seam?
2. Are the seams stitched, turned, or enclosed to prevent raveling?
3. Are the seams pressed flat, particularly where one seam crosses another?
4. Are hems invisible from the right side? They should be, unless a visible hem is a design feature (for example, a top-stitched hem).
5. Is there adequate fullness in the material to allow for pleats and gathers if they are part of the design? This is a consideration in buying items such as pants, dresses, jackets, draperies, and upholstered furniture.
6. Is the design matched? Do the stripes, plaids, floral, geometric, or pictorial prints come together to create a balanced appearance?

Inspect clothing to see whether:

1. The sleeves are set into garments without tucks or puckers (unless these are design features).
2. The collar is set onto the garment so both sides are symmetrical.
3. The cuffs button properly, with the buttonhole on the upper portion of the cuff.

For household textiles:

1. Does upholstered furniture "creak" when you sit on it? (It shouldn't.) Do cushions fit snugly? (Zippers are put in to give a neat fit, not to ensure ease of removal when cleaning.)
2. Do cushioning materials in sofas and chairs provide adequate back support?
3. Does upholstered furniture pass the "tipability" test? Place your knee on a cushion and put your full weight against the chair or sofa back. The chair or sofa should not tip over.
4. Check upholstered furniture to see that tacks, staples, or nails used to secure fabrics to wood frames are firmly attached and will not catch clothing or scratch people.
5. Are chair or sofa cushions reversible? Are sofa cushions the same size, so that they are interchangeable?
6. Are pleats in draperies securely stitched?
7. For carpets, the deeper and denser, the better. Compare identical styles (one plush to another plush, for example) by bending the carpet back on your hand to reveal the length and density of the yarn.

Finishing details include items such as linings, buttons, buttonholes, zippers, and trims. Let's use a checklist to help evaluate quality:

1. Are buttons securely fastened? In furniture, they should be hand-sewn through the filling. This is especially important for sofas, chairs, and pillows in households with children.

2. Are buttonholes properly spaced and sized correctly to accommodate buttons?
3. Do zippers zip smoothly? The zipper should be well covered by the outer fabric, unless otherwise indicated by design.
4. Trims such as welt cording, braid, and so forth should be straight. Stand back and look at the product from several angles to spot "wavy" or irregular trim application.
5. Linings should hang smoothly and evenly without causing distortion. Coats and jackets should have their linings firmly attached at the shoulders and sleeve caps to prevent pulling or showing at the sleeve hem. Drapery linings should be 1 inch shorter than the draperies themselves.

So far, we have provided basic preshopping information. Your decision to seek more technical information at the library should depend on your experience with the product and its cost. You may decide that you have enough information to buy a tailored suit, for example, but that you want more information on carpet construction techniques before making a carpet purchase.

With a more critical eye and with increased knowledge of textiles, you are now ready to plan your shopping trip.

When to Purchase. You can get more for your money by knowing when and where to buy clothing and household textiles. Taking advantage of sales is an ideal way to save money, particularly on clothing. If apparel has not sold within three or four weeks, most stores will reduce the price (that is, mark it down) by 20 percent. Additional reductions of 50–60 percent are often made in subsequent weeks to speed sales and to make space for newer merchandise. Because apparel usually appears in stores several weeks in advance of its season, markdown prices may occur during the season of use. For example, bathing suits are first marked down at the end of May. This coincides with the beginning of summer, the peak of swimwear use. Table 9-2 provides a more complete calendar for obtaining price savings.

Recently, sales have become a way of creating a demand for a fashion. Fashion apparel, sheets, towels, and bedspreads are on sale *before* the season, particularly in stores that are fashion leaders. Sales are usually promoted in newspapers, and the advertisements indicate that a product is selling at preseason reduced prices.

A word of caution—do not buy an item only because it is on sale. If it doesn't fit into your current household or wardrobe and suit your lifestyle and your budget, it is not a bargain, regardless of the price.

Most consumers purchase clothing and household textiles at department or specialty stores. With some research, greater savings on clothing, bedding, table linens, and curtains can be found at manufacturer's outlets, Salvation Army or Goodwill stores, second-hand stores, swapmeets, or garage sales. Consumers who shop for bargains must be armed with information on textiles, and they must be able to judge quality construction. Those who are prepared stand a good chance of finding a real bargain.

NARROW YOUR CHOICE AND CHOOSE

As a result of your investigation, you should have a clear picture of the product features, appearance, durability, and care that you and your family want in clothing and household textiles. You should also have a clear picture of the price you can afford. Applying your knowledge of the fashion cycle and the merchandise acceptance curve will be helpful, too. For most consumers, the general acceptance stage of an item is probably the best time to buy, because individuality of style and quality of materials and construction will be available for a reasonable price. Purchases made earlier will be more expensive, whereas purchases made later may be made of lower-quality materials and have a shorter time "in fashion." Fads, of course, have the shortest life of all. Applying this information can be particularly important for textile products you purchase with several years of use in mind (carpeting, draperies, or upholstered furniture, for example), so you will be happy with the decision as long as you use the product.

Clothing and household goods are often purchased primarily for their appearance. People make choices based on personal *taste*—our judgment of

Table 9-2. Shopping Calendar for Textile Savings

January
Bedspreads
Carpeting
Dresses
Furs
Handbags
Infant wear
Lingerie
Men's clothing, especially shirts and coats
Sheets
Shoes
Sportswear
Suits
Towels

February
Curtains and draperies
Dresses
Men's shirts
Rugs
Sportswear
Women's hats

March
Children's shoes
Hosiery
Infant wear
Spring clothes for all groups
Winter coats

April
Dresses
Infant wear
Lingerie
Men's and boys' suits
Women's and children's coats

May
Bathing suits
Handbags
Lingerie
Sheets
Sportswear
Towels

June
Boys' clothing
Dresses
Summer clothing

July
Bathing suits
Children's clothing
Dresses
Handbags
Infant wear
Lingerie
Men's shirts
Shoes
Sportswear
Summer fabrics

August
Back-to-school clothes
Bathing suits
Coats
Curtains and draperies
Fall fashions
Furs
Men's clothing, especially coats
Rugs
Sheets
Towels
Bedspreads

September
Back-to-school clothing
Children's clothing

October
Back-to-school clothing
Hosiery
Lingerie

November
Automobile seat covers
Children's clothing
Children's and women's coats
Dresses
Fabrics
Men's and boys' shoes
Men's and boys' suits

December
Carpeting
Children's clothing
Men's and women's shoes
Men's and boys' suits
Winter clothing
Women's and children's coats

what is attractive or beautiful. Taste is an individual matter, because the standards for evaluating beauty are a result of family, cultural, social, and educational experiences.

When comparison shopping for apparel and household textiles:

1. Take a list of correct sizes and measurements. Try clothing on, because standard sizing really does not exist.
2. Take color swatches and compare them in natural, fluorescent, and incandescent light.
3. Read labels and hangtags for fiber content, textile

238 Economic Decisions for Consumers

information, product guarantees, and so forth.
4. Compare the quality of materials and workmanship as described in Step 3 of the textile-buying process.
5. Look for permanent-care labels on clothing and household textiles.
6. Consider current fashion trends and personal tastes.

Make a choice, or postpone the decision until you have found a product that meets your needs.

EVALUATE YOUR CHOICE
To increase your knowledge and skill as a textile or clothing buyer, pay attention to product performance:
1. Do you use the product a little or a lot? Can you figure out why?
2. Did you choose the correct color and size?
3. Would a lesser-quality or a higher-quality product suit your purpose better?
4. What do you like most about the fiber content? Least?
5. Does the fabric construction keep its shape? Is it heavy enough or dense enough for your purpose?
6. Is the product fading, pilling, or hard to keep clean?

ACCEPT RESPONSIBILITY OF OWNERSHIP
Once you have made your clothing and textile purchases, your responsibilities as a consumer revolve around proper use and care of the items. This includes following use and care directions as precisely as possible. Do not assume, for example, that an item labeled "hand wash" can be safely machine washed or drycleaned. Make sure that your washer and dryer function properly, that you use appropriate wash additives (detergent, bleach, and so forth), that you use correct washing and drying temperatures, and that you launder or dryclean textiles before you store them away for a season or longer. Some problems with clothing or household textiles are not apparent until after the articles have been used or cleaned. Occasionally, the fabric shrinks excessively, buttons disintegrate, bonded fabrics separate, or artificial suedes lose their nap or texture. If problems do become apparent, immediately return the product to the place

Sometimes problems with fabrics do not become apparent until after they have been cleaned.

of purchase. Most retailers will gladly exchange faulty merchandise. However, you should be aware that a merchant has *no* obligation to give an exchange or a refund just because you change your mind.

It is important to choose a good drycleaner. Look for someone who has been certified by a state licensing board. Ask friends and neighbors for recommendations.

If problems occur after drycleaning, go to the cleaning establishment first. If textile damage is the drycleaner's fault, attempt to resolve the problem with him or her. Sometimes, the fault lies with the manufacturer, who may have mistakenly mislabeled the garment or made a poor choice when combining fabrics and notions (buttons, trims, and the like). For example, let us say that you take in slip covers for drycleaning, according to label instructions. When you pick them up, you find that the welt cording has shrunk and looks puckered. This is the manufacturer's fault, not the drycleaner's, so return the slip covers to the place of purchase.

If the retailer, the consumer, and the drycleaner cannot agree on who is at fault, the textile product can be sent to the International Fabricare Institute in Joliet, Illinois. Its laboratory can perform tests to determine the cause of the problem. Another way to obtain redress is to report the problem to the Better Business Bureau (BBB) in your area. Many metropolitan BBBs have an arbitration panel that will listen to all the facts, study the evidence, and recommend a solution.

The Buying Process: Household Durables

Every year, Americans spend over $200 billion on consumer durable goods (television sets, radios, stereos, furniture, washing machines, refrigerators, and so forth). Consumers are surrounded by such items, from electric toothbrushes and hair dryers to microwave ovens and vacuum cleaners. Because durable goods are purchased less often than nondurable goods (food and clothing, for example), consumers may have difficulty in recognizing quality. And because durable goods are expensive, it is important for consumers to make rational and careful buying decisions. Let us apply the buying-process model to household durable goods.

DETERMINE WHAT YOU NEED

Because consumer durable goods last a long time, it is crucial to spend time to define needs. Choices made on the basis of only a few factors may lead to future problems and dissatisfaction. For example, a single person living alone may feel that a small refrigerator is more than adequate for his or her needs. But if he or she were to marry, his or her lifestyle would change dramatically. If children arrive, the small refrigerator would be woefully inadequate. Of course, the "almost new" refrigerator could be sold, but consumer durable goods do not hold their value. In other words, they depreciate quickly. A three-year-old refrigerator that cost $500 new might sell for as little as $150. This is bad news for the consumer who does not forecast his or her lifestyle well, but it is good news for the consumer who buys the used item. If you are not sure of your future plans, consider buying used consumer durables that have over half of their expected lifetimes ahead of them. The lifespan of an appliance depends on its complexity, its workmanship, and the care it receives.

Determine what tasks you want the appliance to perform in addition to its one or two major tasks. For example, some refrigerator/freezers are equipped with an optional cold water dispenser. List both the features that you and your family expect the product to have (needs) and those that you would like it to have (wants). Then prioritize these features by considering their costs and benefits. You will be able to refine and adjust this list during product investigation (Step 3). Besides the questions from Step 1 of the buying process, ask yourself:

1. How much floor or wall space is available for the product?
2. What work capacity does my family need from the product?
3. What special features do we need? Want?
4. What are the current fashion trends for the product, and how do they fit my values, standards, and goals?
5. Is my house adequately equipped with energy (gas, electricity, and water) to operate the product?

REVIEW YOUR BUDGET

Examine your budget to see how much you can afford to spend for an item, once you have determined that you need it. In calculating the total cost of an appliance or a new piece of furniture, consider the purchase price as well as the costs of interest, operation, maintenance, repair, and depreciation.

Purchase Price. Let us say that you are considering buying a new stereo (speakers, turntable, and so forth.) The purchase price you can afford is $1000, and you expect to use the stereo for fifteen years. Do you have the cash? Have you considered the opportunity cost of being unable to buy other goods? If you decide to finance the stereo, can you afford the payment? ($1000 at 18 percent interest for three years equals a monthly payment of approximately $36.)

Interest. A further cost of owning a durable good is the interest on the purchase price. Consumers may be charged 14 percent to 18 percent or more if they borrow part or all of the cost of the item (see Chapter 8). If $1000 were financed for three years at 18 percent interest, the explicit interest charges would be $300. When you pay cash, the implicit interest must be calculated, that is, the interest you could have had if you had left your money in savings. If $1000 were left in savings at 10 percent interest and compounded annually, it would earn $330 in interest in three years. So consumers have an interest cost whether they finance the purchase (explicit interest) or pay cash (implicit interest). In our example, the annual interest costs average $20 ($300 ÷ 15 years).

Operation. Most consumer durables require energy (electricity, gas, batteries, or water) for operation. Chapter 11 discusses energy costs and the efficiency of various durable goods in detail. Generally, operation costs are based on product brand, quantity of usage, and local utility costs. In our example, we estimate that the annual cost of electricity for the stereo will be $45.

Maintenance and Repair. This expense is usually smaller the first few years of ownership for products covered by warranties (see Chapter 5). The stereo

Buying a durable good involves more than just the purchase price. The consumer must also keep in mind the costs of operation and maintenance, not to mention . . .

maintenance and repair might only involve buying a new needle occasionally. However, consumers should anticipate some repairs over the lifetime of a product, and they should set money aside for this purpose (see "Emergency Fund," Chapter 6). The stereo is not a high repair item, so we estimate maintenance and repair to average $20 a year for the fifteen-year life expectancy.

Actual Costs for Three Years. The out-of-pocket costs of consumer durables is highest in the first years of ownership whether cash or credit is used to pay for the product. Actual costs for the stereo are $41.42 monthly or $497 annually for three years.

	Monthly	Annually
Purchase price plus interest	$36.00	$432.00
Operation	3.75	45.00
Maintenance/repairs	1.67	20.00
	$41.42	$497.00

But because consumer durables are expected to last many years and because we "consume" only a portion of the good each year, we need to analyze the dollar cost of the depreciation and service flow of the purchase or investment.

Depreciation. **Depreciation,** or lessening of value, occurs most in the first year of product ownership, because most consumers prefer to buy new things. To see how this works, consider that the average annual depreciation of the stereo is $66 (purchase price of $1000 divided by life expectancy of fifteen years). But it would be impossible to sell the stereo for $934 ($1000 minus $66) after one year. Despite this disparity, if a consumer intends to use a durable good for several years, the average depreciation figure should be used to determine the annual cost of the investment. This method of cost analysis recognizes the **service flow**—the amount of usage during the entire lifespan of the item, rather than only in the first few years of ownership. For the stereo, then, the total average annual cost above the purchase price is $151:

Depreciation	$ 66 ($1000 ÷ 15 years)
Interest	20 ($300 ÷ 15 years)
Operation	45
Maintenance and repairs	20
Annual average cost	$151

By determining annual average costs, consumers can better evaluate whether they should purchase, rent, or lease the product, in light of family needs and anticipated amount of product use. For example, you may decide that owning a stereo is worth the investment, but when you analyze the annual average cost of snow skis, you might decide to rent the equipment. Determining monetary costs, however, is only half the process of reviewing your budget or making a cost-benefit analysis.

Benefits. The benefits of investing in durables can be both monetary and nonmonetary. There are few if any monetary benefits of owning a stereo. On the other hand, the monetary benefits of purchasing a food freezer might include reduced food bills, less food spoilage, and less time (opportunity cost) and gas spent for grocery shopping. Monetary benefits should be estimated and compared to the annual average cost

depreciation. If the buyer needs to sell the item for some reason, he will find its value has plummeted.

of product ownership to see whether benefits equal or exceed costs. The nonmonetary benefits of a purchase might include convenience, better service, improved decor, and pleasure or comfort. A stereo provides many such benefits. A freezer provides convenience and better service by providing adequate space to store a large quantity of food. The food is available for use at any time, and it can be purchased in fewer shopping trips, both of which save time.

When you do a cost-benefit analysis, remember that you have to live with your choice for a long time, so it is a good idea to buy the best quality you can afford. If you choose to buy a poorly made product that is used often, you may find that the flaws produce disappointment and irritation that can build over time.

After you have determined that you can afford to buy a product, consider the timing of the purchase. The prices of many consumer durables are reduced during August and September, when newer models are being introduced. January and February are also clearance months, because retailers are trying to reduce their inventory tax obligation (see Table 9-3). Purchasing a sale item can save you 20 percent to 25 percent of the product price.

Table 9-3. Shopping Calendar for Household Goods

January
Small electrical appliances
Sporting goods
Water heaters

February
Air conditioners
Clothes dryers
Furniture
Pianos
Typewriters

March
Luggage
Winter sporting goods

April
Kitchen ranges
Microwave ovens
Outdoor furntiure
Paint, wallpaper
Vacuum cleaners

May
Furniture
Housewares
Televisions
Outdoor furniture

June
Cameras and accessories
Furniture
Typewriters

July
Air conditioners
Camping equipment
Refrigerators, freezers
Woodburning stoves

August
Camping equipment
Freezers
Patio furniture

September
China
Dishwashers
Furniture
Glassware
Hunting equipment

October
Bicycles
Clothes dryers
Fishing equipment
Furniture
Kitchen ranges
Microwave ovens
Washers

November
China
Furniture
Glassware
Radios
Silverware
Televisions

December
Winter sporting
   goods equipment
Post-Christmas clearance
   on everything

INVESTIGATE OPTIONS

After identifying your needs and analyzing your budget, gather information about the product in general, as well as data about appearance, features, durability, operating costs, and repair records for specific brands and models.

It is not our intention to tell you how to select every durable good that you might purchase in your lifetime. The potential selection of durable goods is infinite, and technological developments change the standards that are used to judge quality. The main point here is that product information is available to help you evaluate quality and make a choice. For example, let us say that you want to buy bedroom furniture: a low chest of drawers, a high chest of drawers, and a headboard. You should go to the library and investigate the general features of *case goods*—furniture made entirely or almost entirely out of wood. Box 9-4 provides a sample checklist for evaluating case goods, but applying it requires knowledge of wood and wood finishes (1, 13, and 14) and furniture construction (5, 6, and 9). Checklists of this type as well as information about wood, wood finishes, and furniture construction techniques can be found in reference books on furniture selection and in periodicals such as *Better Homes & Gardens*.

You can find general information and brand and model comparisons in two periodicals—*Consumer Reports* and *Consumers' Research*. If you want to buy a washer, for example, you can get information to answer questions such as: Will a front-loading or a top-loading washer be best for my family? What

BOX 9-4
Shopping for Case Goods

The major difference between high-quality and low-quality furniture is in the type of wood used. The belief that solid wood furniture is superior to veneered wood furniture (made of two or more layers) is quite common, but often invalid. Furniture of low, medium, and high quality may be made of solid wood, veneered wood, or a combination of the two.

Solid wood furniture is easily repaired or refinished, its edges show no layers, and there is no chance that the surface may become loosened. Veneer is strong and light weight, and its surface resists warping, checking, and swelling.

Checklist for Shopping for Case Goods
1. Is the article made from soft wood or hard wood? Is it kiln dried?
2. Do doors shut tightly without sticking?
3. Are doors held shut with magnetic catches?
4. Are doors and drawers flush with openings?
5. Have corner blocks been used for reinforcement?
6. Has dovetail construction been used on drawers?
7. Are dust panels provided between drawers?
8. Do drawers slide easily on guide strips or ball bearings?
9. Are legs attached with mortise and tenon or dowel joints?
10. Do legs stand squarely on the floor?
11. Have insides of drawers, backs of chests, and undersides of tables and chairs been sanded and finished?
12. Are surfaces free from defects when viewed in good light and touched with fingertips?
13. Are exterior surfaces solid, veneered, or wood-finish stain?
14. Has a protective plastic coating been used on surfaces that will receive hard wear?
15. Is the hardware attractive and securely attached?
16. Will the furniture piece fulfill your requirements for use, style, color, and size?
17. Is the piece of furniture within your planned budget?

SOURCE: Courtesy of JoAnn Crist, Creative Interior Design Lecture Series.

washer capacity do I need (12, 16, or 20 pounds)? Do I want bleach and fabric softener dispensers? How many washing cycles do I want? How many temperature combinations do I want? How does one brand compare to another in removing sand or clay from fabrics? Once you have this information, you can compare it to your needs. Consumer guides can't tell you what to do, nor should they be followed blindly. But they can help you find out what factors to consider in a decision.

The information-gathering process should include determining the importance of financial factors such as service, design, operating costs, and, of course, price. Table 9-4 shows the degree of importance of these factors for ten major appliances. As you can see, service and operating costs are important for air conditioners, whereas for a freezer, service is not important, but operating costs are. Price and design features for both of these items are of moderate importance.

By recognizing and investigating various factors in shopping for appliances, consumers can minimize their true annual cost of ownership. The federal government has begun to help consumers to compare operating costs by testing major household appliances in laboratories that simulate home use. In 1980, the Energy Policy and Conservation Act mandated that all new air conditioners, dishwashers, water heaters, humidifiers, ovens and ranges, and heating equipment other than furnaces be accompanied by estimates of their annual energy cost. As we will see in Chapter 11, these energy-cost ratings are important.

Table 9-4. Factors in Shopping for Appliances

Appliance	Importance of:			
	Service	Price	Design features	Operating costs
Air conditioner	Yes	Moderate	Moderate	Yes
Television	Yes	Yes	Yes	No
Range	No	Yes	Yes	No
Refrigerator	No	Moderate	Yes	Yes
Freezer	No	Moderate	Moderate	Yes
Dishwasher	Moderate	Moderate	Yes	Moderate
Clothes washer	Yes	Moderate	Moderate	No
Dryer	Moderate	Moderate	Moderate	Moderate
Vacuum cleaner	No	Yes	Moderate	No
Microwave oven	No	Yes	Yes	No

SOURCE: From *Personal Money Management* by Thomas E. Bailard, David L. Biehl, and Ronald W. Kaiser. © 1980, 1977, 1973, 1969 Science Research Associates, Inc. Reprinted by permission of the publisher.

NARROW YOUR CHOICE

Now that you have focused on your needs, reviewed your budget, and gathered the necessary information, you are ready to choose a particular piece of furniture or an appliance. By this stage, you should have been able to compare and evaluate products from several manufacturers and you should have chosen two or three brands that might be suitable. Now you are ready to go to the stores. Find out the brands a merchant carries and the services he or she offers; get acquainted with the dealers to see who can offer you the best deal. Browse through the store; ask questions. If you are considering a stereo, listen to it, try the dials, test it to see whether it is easy to set the records on the turntable. If you are shopping for furniture, try it on for size. Sit on chairs for 10 to 15 minutes to check for comfort. Lie on beds or sofa beds. Check drawers, doors, or other movable parts of cabinets and chests to check for convenience and performance. Look carefully at the insides of refrigerators to check the number of shelves, the location of the drawers, and the keepers for meat, eggs, and dairy products. Examine the setup and the features of range/ovens. Read labels carefully. It is illegal to deceive a buyer about the composition of a product, so plastic must be labeled as such, and wood must be identified as solid, veneer, wood product, or simulated wood grain.

This is also the time to apply your knowledge of the fashion cycle. If one criterion for this purchase is fashion, select a product that is moving toward general acceptance rather than away from it.

Be sure to compare warranties (see Chapter 5). Occasionally, stores offer more extensive warranties than manufacturers' warranties, at no additional cost. This competitive device encourages consumers to buy from them rather than from other dealers. Store warranties are valuable only from well-established businesses that are likely to be around to honor the extended warranty. Be sure to get it in writing. Box 9-5 offers other suggestions for negotiating the best deal in the store.

MAKE A CHOICE

Now that you are armed with comparison-shopping information, you are ready to choose. You should anticipate that you may not be able to buy the best brand or model available because of budget constraints. You will, however, have the satisfaction of knowing that you have selected the product that best meets your needs without exceeding your budget.

BOX 9-5

In the Store: Getting the Best Deal—and What You Want

People who sell durable goods often earn commissions, that is, they earn a percentage of each sale that they make. They are, therefore, highly motivated to sell the highest-priced model and to close the sale as soon as possible. Be sure that in dealings with salespeople that you take adequate time to consider all the alternatives. Leave the store, if necessary, to think it over.

In some stores, and with some products, consumers can negotiate a price reduction. The way to do so is to ask for a reduction in the list or sticker price. This is particularly common during the purchase of a stereo or an automobile. Consumers who gather information on brands and models from consumer periodicals are familiar with typical markups and selling prices and know what price reduction is reasonable.

Another way to save is to bargain for a larger trade-in allowance. A considerable leeway is available when trading in automobiles, typewriters, vacuum cleaners, refrigerators, or sewing machines. If you are naive, you may receive only part of the anticipated allowance, but if you are informed and patient, you can bargain for the full amount.

You can get an indirect price reduction by negotiating for extra features or services (no extra cost for an appliance in a decorator color, free delivery or installation, or no billing for 30, 60, or 90 days). When shopping around, consider the total cost of the deal: product price, trade-in allowance, delivery and installation costs, billing procedure, availability of free extended warranties, and convenience of servicing if repairs are needed.

EVALUATE YOUR CHOICE

As a result of using the buying process, you should get many years of consumer satisfaction from your purchases. Using a product will give you knowledge of materials and features that can be used during the buying process of other consumer goods.

ACCEPT RESPONSIBILITY OF OWNERSHIP

Once you have purchased a consumer durable, your responsibilities revolve around the proper installation, use, and care of the product. This means carefully following the instruction book, the hangtags, and the labels. Store this information with the purchase receipt in a handy place. Take advantage of the free lessons that often come with items such as a microwave oven or sewing machine. This will help you get maximum use and satisfaction from the purchase.

More than likely, at the time of purchase or as the end of the warranty approaches, you will be asked to purchase a **service contract.** This is appliance repair insurance. You pay a predetermined amount of money each year in order to get specific repairs or servicing without charge. Service contracts are available for all major household appliances and sometimes for stereo equipment. Because these contracts entail sales costs, commission costs, and a profit for the seller, they are rarely a bargain for consumers. Base your decision about whether to buy a service contract on the first year's performance of the appliance. If the appliance does not seem like a "lemon," put half of the monthly cost of the service contract into a special repair fund. (See Chapter 6 on budgeting for emergencies.) If repairs are needed, you will be prepared. In the meantime, your money is earning interest.

If you do have problems with an appliance, be responsible for checking the instruction book before you schedule a repair appointment. Approximately 25 percent of repair calls could be avoided if people checked to be sure that the item was plugged in, turned on, and properly connected. Keep receipts of all repair work done, whether covered by warranty or not. These receipts may be needed to prove that the product should be replaced because of excessive repairs. A growing number of Americans are trying to save time and money by doing their own repairs. One major appliance manufacturer, General Electric, is making that easier. It now sells repair manuals and 94 common replacement parts, and it provides detailed advice on how to fix problems with five major appliances. The GE program, dubbed the "Quick-Fix System," covers washers, dryers, refrigerators, dishwashers, and ranges. Because of safety considerations, it does not apply to televisions, air conditioners, or microwave ovens. Manuals and replacement parts are sold by GE dealers. See Chapter 5 for a more complete discussion of the complaint process.

Summary

A fashion is a style accepted by a large group of people at a given time. There are fashions in clothing, household goods, food, automobiles, housing, and entertainment—fashion affects all areas of our lives. Fashion is the result of economic, social, political, and technological factors, and it is transmitted through fashion leaders. Politicians, entertainers, community or campus trend setters all may be fashion leaders. Consumers who understand fashion and the merchandise acceptance curve can make rational, economical buying decisions. By applying the decision-making model to the buying process, a consumer will be able to determine needs, analyze his or her budget, investigate options, and narrow choices. After choosing a product, a consumer needs to evaluate the purchase decision and accept responsibility for ownership. The buying process can be applied to any consumer purchase. The amount of time spent on the process should be in proportion to the product cost; a poor choice in buying an expensive product will be a psychological and financial disappointment.

This chapter applied the buying process first to clothing and household textiles, then to household goods such as kitchen appliances, televisions, stereos, and case goods. Physical needs for comfort and protection as well as psychological needs for status, beautiful surroundings, and self-esteem of all family members should be considered in the buying process for all such items.

In this chapter we also discussed budget review, which includes determining *costs* (purchase price, interest, operation, maintenance and repair, and depreciation), as well as benefits of purchase (convenience, better service, improved decor, and pleasure or comfort). We stressed the need to thoroughly investigate options, take adequate time to narrow choices, and choose the product that best suits needs and budgets. Taking responsibility of ownership of consumer durables includes ensuring proper installation, use, and care of the product.

Neighborhood REVISITED

1. Using the consumer buying-process model presented in this chapter, outline the steps that Heather and Jim should go through before buying a new washer and dryer. Did they skip any steps?

2. If Heather and Jim did not have cash for the washer and dryer, what steps would they follow to determine whether they can afford the purchase?

3. Based on the buying process for household durables, what questions should Heather and Jim ask when they go to White's Appliance Store? What sales tactics should they watch out for?

4. Would it make sense for Heather and Jim to purchase a service contract after the warranty runs out? Explain your reasoning.

KEY TERMS

bottom-up theory
buying-process model
classics
coloring methods
consumer durable goods
depreciation
fabric construction
fad
fashion
fashion cycle
fiber content
finishes
merchandise acceptance curve
product construction
service contract
service flow
style
textiles
trickle-across (mass-market) theory
trickle-down theory

QUESTIONS

1. What are the seven steps of the buying process?

2. What are the differences between a style, a fashion, a fad, and a classic? Give an example of each.

3. Identify fashion trends that have occurred in the last two decades for refrigerators, carpeting, ovens and ranges, automobiles, and beds.

4. Fashion is truly a luxury from a personal economic viewpoint. Discuss the contributions and costs to society of fashion changes.

5. What do you own that is a result of the trickle-across fashion influence? The bottom-up influence?

6. What factors affect the performance of textile products in general? What special factors should you look for when purchasing household textiles?

7. What factors should be considered when reviewing a budget during the buying process for consumer durables?

8. Name four magazines that often have articles on product information useful during the buying process. How can you locate additional information?

PROJECTS

1. Research a particular fashion to determine its place on the merchandise acceptance curve. How long is the entire lifespan from introduction to decline?

2. Select a product that interests you and that costs at least $500. Follow each step of the buying process: identify your needs, consider your budget, gather information, and narrow your choices. Determine the exact make and model that you would purchase and where you would buy it.

3. Call a local store and inquire about the cost of a service contract for the life expectancy of a clothes washer and dryer or a color television. Investigate the frequency of repair of the item and the typical repair costs. Would it be economically wise to buy the service contract? If so, under what conditions?

4. Take an inventory of your wardrobe and decide what additions you need for the coming season. Develop a budget for these items by checking newspaper advertisements and mail-order catalogs. Create a schedule for purchase.

5. Interview consumers to see how important flame-retardant finishes are to them. Have them consider the finish on children's sleepwear, the need for it on children's sportswear, and the need for it on all children's clothing. Include questions about the need for this finish on upholstered furniture, carpeting, draperies, and sleepwear for adults. Try to determine how much consumers are willing to pay for this protection. Report your findings to the rest of the class.

REFERENCES AND READINGS

Bailard, Thomas E.; Biehl, David L., and Kaiser, Ronald W. *Personal Money Management,* 3rd ed. Chicago: Science Research Associates, 1980.

Brown, Jan. *Buy It Right: A Shoppers Guide to Home Furnishings,* 3rd ed. Mundelien, Ill.: Career Institute, 1974.

Consumer Information Center. "Consumer Information Catalog." Pueblo, Colo.: Consumer Information Center, issued quarterly.

"Do it Yourself Sources for Appliance Parts." *Workbench,* January/February 1980.

Evans, M. Stanton. "Publishers Page." *Consumers' Research,* July 1980.

Gerner, Jennifer L., and Bryant, W. Keith. "Appliance Warranties as a Market Signal?" *The Journal of Consumer Affairs,* Summer 1981.

Gordon, Leland J., and Lee, Stewart M. *Economics for Consumers,* 7th ed. New York: D. Van Nostrand, 1977.

Greenwood, Kathryn Moore, and Murphy, Mary Fox. *Fashion Innovation and Marketing.* New York: Macmillan, 1978.

"Handbook of Buying." *Consumers' Research,* October 1981.

Jarnow, Jeannette A., and Judelle, Beatrice. *Inside the Fashion Business,* 3rd ed. New York: Wiley, 1981.

Kefgen, Mary, and Touchie-Specht, Phyllis. *Individuality in Clothing Selection and Personal Appearance,* 3rd ed. New York: Macmillan, 1981.

Konig, Rene. *A La Mode.* New York: The Seabury Press, 1973.

Paul H. Douglas Consumer Research Center. "The Product Liability Controversy: A Handbook for Consumers." Washington, D.C.: Consumer Federation of America, 1979.

"Quick Fixes for Small Appliance Problems." *Popular Mechanics,* August 1979.

Ruffin, M. D., and Tippett, K. S. "Service-life Expectancy of Household Appliances: New Estimates from USDA." *Home Economics Resource Journal,* 1975.

Rush, A. F. "Appliance Repairs: How to Make Sure You Get What You Pay For." *McCalls,* February 1980, pp. 131–134.

Tortora, Phyllis G. *Understanding Textiles,* 2nd ed. New York: Macmillan, 1982.

Williams, Madelyn C. "A Consumer's Guide to Fibers, Fabrics, and Finishes." Sacramento, Calif.: California Department of Consumer Affairs.

Did You Know That ...

- *many Americans suffer from malnutrition, and malnutrition is almost as common among the rich as among the poor?*

- *food expenditures account for 15 to 30 percent of American family budgets?*

- *bread and other grain products are not more fattening than foods such as milk or fruit?*

- *good health depends on the consumption of a wide variety of foods from the Basic Four food groups?*

- *food labels can reveal the major ingredients in packaged foods and therefore aid in comparison shopping?*

- *the two most frequently used food additives are sugar and salt?*

- *substances that are poisonous in food may occur naturally?*

10 Food: More Than a Matter of Taste

Food for Thought, Fuel, and Fat
Guides to Good Nutrition
Government Labeling
Safety and Quality
Codes: Prices and Dates
Hazards to Food Safety
Back to Nature: Health Foods and Vitamins
Getting Good Nutrition at Reasonable Prices

Neighborhood CAPSULE
Winning the Grocery Game

Joyce Mattson dreaded the trip. She hated to shop for groceries! It was a constant reminder that inflation was destroying her attempts to get ahead. Each time she or her husband Rod got a raise, it seemed that prices went up, too.

As she stood in front of the meat counter, she glanced up and saw a friend, Alicia Morales. After a greeting and an exchange of news about family happenings, Joyce complained to Alicia about the high cost of food.

"Yes, I know what you mean," Alicia replied. "But we did something about it."

"You're kidding! What can be done?" asked Joyce.

"We made a game out of our food budget. We chose a set amount of money, $80 a week, and we never spend more than that. And sometimes we spend less," replied Alicia.

"That's impossible!" Joyce exclaimed. "There are five of you. I usually spend close to $100 a week for the three of us. How do you do it?"

Alicia explained that the whole Morales family got involved. First, they found a self-service store that carried only staple items such as canned goods, flour, sugar, paper goods, and cleaning supplies. Although it is a bag-it-yourself operation, they felt it was well worth the separate trip. They stocked up on staple items, buying enough for a couple of months all at once. This made them more alert to the advantages of buying other items in quantity, especially meat, and especially when it is on sale.

"Today I came here to buy two beef roasts, because they're on sale. I like to start with a large cut of meat, and then have 'planned-overs.' After all, if you begin with stroganoff, you only have left-over stroganoff."

Joyce nodded her head in agreement. She began to see that she could do these things, too. Alicia continued, "We stopped wasting bits of meat and vegetables, and with left-over beef or chicken bones, we have the beginnings of terrific soups."

"You sound like my neighbor—she does the same thing with chicken and with fresh vegetables from her garden," Joyce said.

"Right! We all work in our garden. And sometimes we take family outings to pick seasonal fruits or visit a local manufacturer. Last weekend we went to a cheese factory. It was fascinating, plus the bulk cheese was really inexpensive."

"Gee," Joyce exclaimed, "that sounds terrific! We love lasagna and fettucine."

"We do too. We've found that the Mexican dishes with rice, beans, and tortillas are still our favorites, but pasta is a close second. Last summer our garden was so full of carrots, zucchini, peas, and beans that I began to experiment with wok cooking, too."

"You know," Joyce said to Alicia, "you have really inspired me. I've used coupons, bought fruits and vegetables in season, tried store brands, and even made a shopping list most of the time. But I see now that by planning ahead, I can save more money—and have some fun while I'm doing it."

Although we may not think of it when we look at people around us, the biggest health problem in America is malnutrition. Most of us think of starving children with big dark eyes when we hear this word. But if we think of nutrition as the process by which we take in and use the **nutrients** (food substances) essential for good health, **malnutrition** can also mean eating too much, eating too little, or eating too little of the foods we need to maintain good health.

Americans, it seems, are preoccupied with nutrition and food—eating it, buying it, and getting rid of its aftereffects. Although we are exercising more and eating less, the U.S. Department of Agriculture (USDA) reported in 1977 that the average American male was 20 to 30 pounds overweight, and his female counterpart was 15 to 30 pounds overweight. In addition to the $400 billion we spend each year on food, we spend $100 million on reducing pills or special diets to lose weight.

Besides being a national preoccupation, food is expensive. Food expenditures account for 15 to 30 percent of family budgets. Chapter 6 explored the need to budget for food, and Chapter 7 dealt with the effects of inflation on food prices. In this chapter we look at food as nutrition, as a matter for government regulation, as the source of some consumer misunderstanding, as a consumer good that might be misrepresented, and as an especially important topic for applying decision-making skills. When we're finished, you should have a better idea of some of the issues and forces that affect your food choices, as well as of the way the government protects and regulates the quality of food. Most important, however, you will have some specific skills to use in enhancing your nutrition and stretching your food dollars.

Food for Thought, Fuel, and Fat

Everyone knows that we need food to provide ourselves with energy to keep our hearts pumping blood, our lungs breathing, and our bodies functioning in a normal, healthy way. The energy that food supplies is measured in **calories,** the amount of heat produced as a by-product of the utilization of food. Normally, if we take in fewer calories than we need to meet our energy requirements, we lose weight. The reverse, as so many people have found out, is also true.

FACTORS THAT AFFECT CALORIE NEEDS

The major factors that affect how many calories we need to function normally at a healthy weight include:

1. *Activity level*. Running obviously requires more energy, and thus more calories, than watching television. As you can see from Table 10-1, the more active you are, the more calories you need. The less active a person, the more likely he or she may be to take in more calories than he or she can burn off.

2. *Age*. Younger people burn more calories than older people, primarily because growth and a higher activity level add to their energy needs.

3. *Size*. A bigger person (in basic bone and muscle structure) needs more calories to function and maintain body size.

4. *Sex*. Because men are usually larger, they need more calories. But women, when pregnant or nursing an infant, for example, may need extra calories, too.

Table 10-2 shows how many calories it takes to maintain the desirable weights of women or men of various heights (sizes) and ages. Height, weight, age, and calorie intake are important, but you can change only one of them—calorie intake. If you are overweight and would like to change, you have two choices. You can increase your activity level or decrease your calorie intake. Each decrease of 3,500 calories causes a weight loss of one pound. In other words, by making no other changes, you could lose one pound a week by consuming 500 calories a day less than you usually consume, or by dancing your socks off for two hours every night of the week.

FACTORS THAT AFFECT FOOD CHOICES

Making decisions about food we eat requires more than counting calories. Food choices are often emotional rather than logical. Habits we learned in our families ("Clean your plate—or else . . ."), as well as the additional benefits that food can provide (comfort, security, relief from boredom, reward, or status), can affect our choices throughout our lives. It is not unusual to eat for reasons other than hunger. In America, for instance, food—and hearty eating—plays a major role in traditional family and social events and holidays. The Thanksgiving turkey and pumpkin pie, the Fourth of July barbecue or picnic, the Halloween trick-or-treat candy, and the wedding feasts and cakes are all part of the values and ceremonies that we associate with food—and that we may seldom question.

Our lifestyles may also affect food choices. If we are busy and in a hurry, we may skip breakfast, grab something quick and available for lunch, and eat snacks for dinner, rather than plan a full meal. We are

Table 10-1. Calories Expended in Various Types of Activities

Type of activity	Examples	Calories used per hour
Sedentary activities	Reading, writing, eating, watching television or movies, listening to the radio, sewing, playing cards, typing, office work, and other activities done while sitting that require little or no arm movement.	80–100
Light activities	Preparing and cooking food, doing dishes, dusting, hand washing small articles of clothing, ironing, walking slowly, performing personal care, doing office work and other activities while standing that require some arm movement, and rapidly typing, and doing other activities while sitting that are more strenuous.	110–160
Moderate activities	Making beds, mopping and scrubbing, sweeping, light polishing and waxing, laundering by machine, light gardening and carpentry work, walking moderately fast, doing activities while standing that require moderate arm movement, and doing activities while sitting that require more vigorous arm movement.	170–240
Vigorous activities	Heavy scrubbing and waxing, hand washing large articles of clothing, hanging out clothes, stripping beds, walking fast, bowling, golfing, and gardening.	250–350
Strenuous activities	Swimming, playing tennis, running, bicycling, dancing, skiing, and playing football.	350 or more

SOURCE: *Food and Your Weight,* U.S. Department of Agriculture, Agricultural Research Service, Home and Garden Bulletin No. 74, Washington, D.C. (1977), p. 4.

Table 10-2. Daily Calorie Allowance Based on Desirable Weight for Height*

	Women					Men			
Height (in.)	Weight (lbs.)	Age 22	Age 45	Age 65	Height (in.)	Weight (lbs.)	Age 22	Age 45	Age 65
60	109 ± 9	1,700	1,550	1,450	64	133 ± 11	2,500	2,300	2,100
62	115 ± 9	1,800	1,650	1,500	66	142 ± 12	2,650	2,400	2,200
64	122 ± 10	1,950	1,800	1,650	68	151 ± 14	2,800	2,600	2,400
66	129 ± 10	2,000	1,850	1,700	70	159 ± 14	2,875	2,650	2,450
68	136 ± 10	2,050	1,900	1,700	72	167 ± 15	2,950	2,700	2,500
70	144 ± 11	2,200	2,000	1,850	74	175 ± 15	3,050	2,800	2,600
72	152 ± 12	2,300	2,100	1,950	76	182 ± 16	3,125	2,875	2,650

SOURCE: Adapted from National Academy of Sciences, National Research Council, Food and Nutrition Board, *Recommended Dietary Allowances,* 8th ed. (Washington, D.C., 1974), p. 29.

*Weights and heights without shoes or outer clothing

not really making decisions, we are haphazardly taking in food without much thought as to whether it is providing us with the nutrients we need. Perhaps saving time is not worth the results in this case.

The results of poor food choices can be increased susceptibility to illness, high blood pressure, and depression, as well as greater risk of death from coronary artery disease, stroke, kidney disease, and diabetes. Poor choices do not provide the body with adequate vitamins and minerals to maintain body functions. Obese people (those who are 20 percent or more above ideal body weight) have an increased hazard during surgery, pregnancy, and childbirth, because excess body weight places a strain on internal organs, particularly the heart and the circulatory system. Research continues on both the causes of overweight and obesity and the effects of these conditions on health.

Guides to Good Nutrition

How can you tell whether you are making good food choices? In order to help consumers make wise selections, the U.S. Department of Agriculture has divided food into categories, creating the concept of the **Basic Four food groups.** You probably learned about them in school. They are still the simplest and most effective way of remembering how to select good food.

Figure 10-1 shows that the Basic Four consist of meat (or other protein sources), dairy products (milk and cheese), fruits and vegetables, and cereal and grain products. By eating at least the recommended quantities, staying within appropriate calorie levels, and choosing a variety of foods, you will get adequate amounts of all the necessary nutrients.

The Basic Four is a simple and effective guide for consumers. Nutritionists and dietitians, however, most often evaluate the quality of a diet in a more detailed way. They compute the nutrient content of foods by the **U.S. Recommended Dietary Allowances (RDAs)**—standards established by the National Academy of Sciences. As with the need for calories, the amount of each nutrient needed varies according to age, sex, and size.

RDAs are recommendations, *not* average requirements, for groups of average, healthy people. To allow for individual needs and for a margin of safety,

Figure 10-1 A guide to good eating using the Basic Four food groups.

Eat daily:

1. Milk group
Cheese, yogurt, ice cream and other milk-made foods can supply part of the milk

3 or more glasses milk—children
Smaller glasses for some children under 8
4 or more glasses—teenagers
2 or more glasses—adults

2. Meat group
Meats, fish, poultry, eggs, or cheese—with dry beans, peas, nuts as alternates

2 or more servings

3. Vegetables and fruits
Include dark green or yellow vegetables; citrus fruit or tomatoes

4 or more servings

4. Breads and cereals
Whole grain or enriched breads, cereals; pasta, rice

4 or more servings

This is the foundation for a good diet. Use more of these and other foods as needed for growth, for activity, and for desirable weight.

SOURCE: U.S. Department of Agriculture.

Table 10-3. Calories, Protein, Vitamins, and Minerals Needed to Meet RDAs for Children, Men, and Women of Various Ages

Age	Calories*	Protein† (% of U.S. RDA)	Vitamins (% of U.S. RDA)					Minerals (% of U.S. RDA)	
			A	C	Thiamin	Ribo-flavin	Niacin‡	Calcium	Iron
Children									
1–3	1,300	35	40	70	50	50	30	80	85
7–10	2,400	55	70	70	80	75	50	80	60
Men									
15–18	3,000	85	100	75	100	110	55	120	100
23–50	2,700	90	100	75	95	95	45	80	60
51+	2,400	90	100	75	80	90	35	80	60
Women									
15–18	2,100	75	80	75	75	85	30	120	100
23–50	2,000	75	80	75	70	75	30	80	100
51+	1,800	75	80	75	70	65	25	80	60
Pregnant	+300§	+50§	100	100	+20§	+20§	35	120	100§
Nursing	+500§	+35§	120	135	+20§	+30§	35	120	100

SOURCE: B. Peterkin, J. Nicholas, and C. Cromwell, "Nutrition Labeling: Tools for Its Use." Agricultural Information Bulletin No. 382, U.S. Department of Agriculture (Washington, D.C.: U.S. Government Printing Office, April 1975), p. 47.

*Calorie needs differ depending on body composition and size, age, and activity level.

†U.S. RDA of 65 grams is used for this table. In labeling, a U.S. RDA of 45 grams is used for foods providing high-quality protein, such as milk, meat, and eggs.

‡Will provide RDA for niacin if RDA for protein is met. Some niacin is derived from tryptophan, an amino acid present in protein.

§Add to allowance for appropriate age.

---

the RDA exceeds the requirement of most individuals, so that the needs of at least 95 percent of the people in each age-sex group are met. For example, the RDA for adults is based on the needs of the age group that has the highest need for a specific nutrient (usually teenage boys). The RDA is expressed in a percent of the amount necessary rather than in the quantity by weight (see Table 10-3). As you can see, most adults do not need 100 percent of the RDA for each nutrient.

Nutrition experts in the USDA Agricultural Research Service have analyzed over 700 common foods for their nutritional values. Examples are shown in Box 10-1. A free publication called *Nutritive Values of Foods* (1977) is available from the U.S. Government Printing Office. It contains the results of their research, which may be helpful in analyzing your specific diet. Classes in nutrition do this in detail, often with the help of computers.

The body of information about what constitutes a healthy diet is growing, yet there is an ongoing controversy regarding appropriate levels of fat and cholesterol consumption. Consumers would be wise to keep up to date regarding nutrition and to use this information when making food selections. To help consumers make decisions, the federal government requires manufacturers to print the RDA content on many food packages. We will discuss this regulation

> **BOX 10-1**
>
> ## Compare Nutrient Levels
>
> Some foods that we eat supply very few nutrients compared to the number of calories they supply. We sometimes say that these foods have "empty calories." Candy, soft drinks, some snack foods, and alcoholic beverages fall into this group. Foods high in calories and low in other nutrients are described by nutritionists as having a **low nutrient density.** Foods low in calories and rich in other nutrients (many vegetables and fish) have a **high nutrient density.** Listed below are some examples of each. Which are the low-nutrient-density foods? Place a check next to each one that is low in nutrients compared to its calorie content.
>
> | Food | Food energy (cal.) | Protein (gm) | Fat (gm) | Vitamins | | | | | Minerals | |
> |---|---|---|---|---|---|---|---|---|---|---|
> | | | | | Vitamin A (I.U.) | Vitamin C (mg) | Thiamin (mg) | Riboflavin (mg) | Niacin (mg) | Calcium (mg) | Iron (mg) |
> | 1 cake doughnut | 125 | 1 | 6 | 30 | trace | .05 | .05 | .4 | 13 | .4 |
> | 2 slices whole-wheat bread | 120 | 6 | 2 | trace | trace | .12 | .06 | 1.4 | 50 | 1.6 |
> | 8 oz. orange juice | 120 | 2 | trace | 550 | 120 | .22 | .02 | 1.0 | 25 | .2 |
> | 8 oz. cola | 96 | 0 | 0 | 0 | 0 | 0 | 0 | 0 | 0 | 0 |
> | 10 potato chips | 115 | 1 | 8 | trace | 3 | .04 | .01 | .01 | 8 | .4 |
> | 2 cups popcorn with oil and salt | 80 | 2 | 4 | 0 | 0 | 0 | .02 | 0 | 2 | .4 |
> | 1 oz. gumdrops | 100 | trace | trace | 0 | 0 | 0 | trace | trace | 2 | .1 |
> | 1 medium banana | 100 | 1 | trace | 230 | 12 | .06 | .07 | .8 | 10 | .8 |
> | 1 cup broccoli | 40 | 5 | 1 | 3,880 | 140 | .14 | .31 | 1.2 | 136 | 1.2 |
>
> Were you surprised at the lack of nutrients in the cola drink? Probably not, but how about the doughnut and the potato chips? Foods such as cola drinks and gumdrops are excellent examples of foods that have "empty calories."
>
> SOURCE: Adapted from Agricultural Research Service, *Nutritive Values of Food* (Washington, D.C.: U.S. Government Printing Office).

as well as those that require disclosure of product content information in the next section.

Government Labeling

On a typical trip to the supermarket, we choose from 11,000 items—from fresh foods to canned goods to packaged snacks to frozen goods of all kinds. Six thousand new and improved products each year come from an increasingly sophisticated food processing and producing industry. At the same time, hundreds of products that were new and improved last year are discontinued. Some of the new products and some of

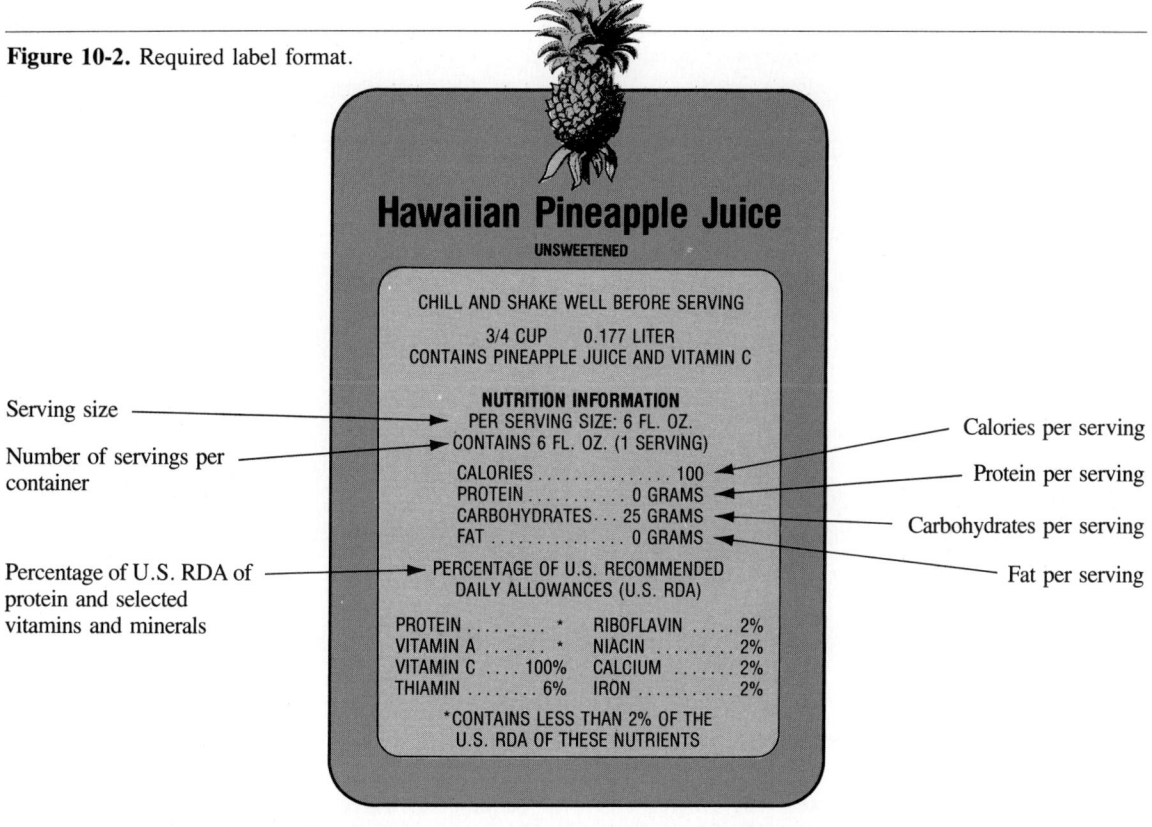

Figure 10-2. Required label format.

those already on the shelves are complex mixtures of food and chemicals. The chemicals do everything from enhancing flavor to replacing flavor to preventing spoilage. In addition, when we fill up our grocery carts, we choose foods that are packaged or canned, so we can't actually see the product. Product changes and the use of advanced food technology and packaging create the need for new, and often unexpected, decisions in the market, as well as for up-to-date product information. All we have are labels to tell us what food is inside, what has been added to it, and what nutritional value we can expect from it. Let us look at some of the federal and state laws that require and regulate product information on labels.

NUTRITIONAL LABELING

As of January 1975, any food that is **enriched,** or **fortified,** with nutrients (such as vitamin C) or any food that makes a nutritional or dietetic claim ("high protein," "low calorie," and so forth) must have a nutritional label. This allows consumers to compare and evaluate the cost of the enrichment. Nutritional labeling on other products is voluntary. All labels must use a standard format (see Figure 10-2). The information includes:

1. Serving size.
2. Number of servings per container.
3. Calories per serving.
4. Protein per serving (in grams).
5. Carbohydrates per serving (in grams).
6. Fat per serving (in grams).
7. Percent of U.S. RDA of protein and selected vitamins and minerals.

Because this labeling is based on the RDA for the group with the highest need (usually teenage

Figure 10-3. Required product information.

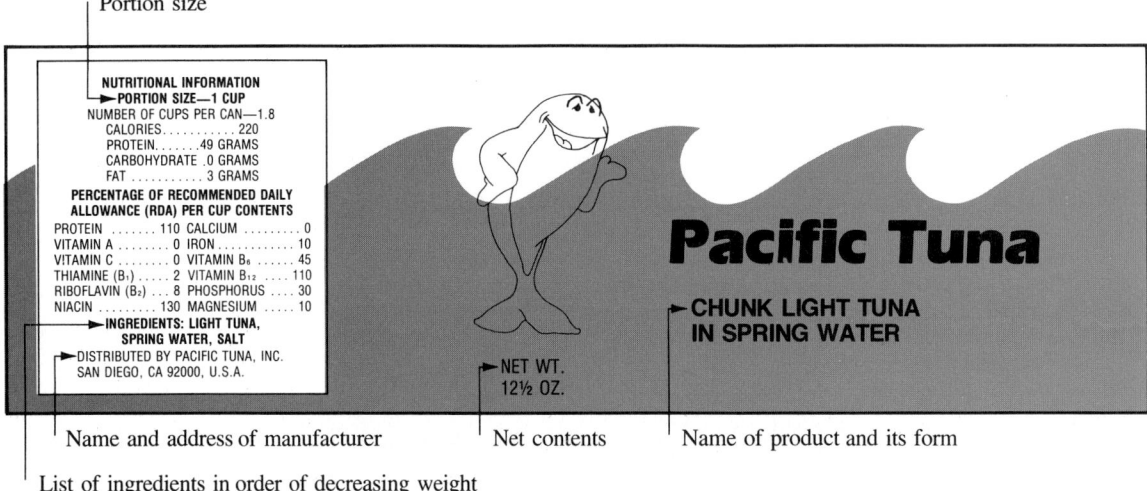

boys), the percentages do not reflect what all people need. Most people do not need 100 percent of each nutrient, so meals may be planned for the needs of various ages. According to Table 10-3, a 7-year-old child needs only two-thirds as much protein (55 percent of the RDA) as a woman needs (75 percent of the RDA). But if a woman is nursing an infant, she needs twice as much protein (75 percent plus 35 percent) as a 7-year-old.

It is important to remember that one food need not supply a whole day's worth of nutrients. Breakfast cereal, for example, is just one part of a meal, one nutrient source. The accumulation of nutrients consumed during meals and snacks is what is significant.

FAIR PACKAGING AND LABELING ACT

In addition to nutritional information, consumers need to know about the quantity and quality of the food they buy. During the 1950s and 1960s there was a tremendous growth in the number of canned, packaged, and frozen goods, from entrees to vegetables to desserts. Consumers found product comparison difficult, because standard product descriptions or information about container size were not required. As a result of the Fair Packaging and Labeling Act (FPLA) of 1966, we find such information on most food products sold nationally. Specifically:

1. Name of the product and its form ("fruit cocktail in heavy syrup").
2. Net contents (weight or fluid volume).
3. Portion size, if number of servings is stated.
4. Name and address of processor, distributor, or packer.
5. List of ingredients in order of decreasing weight.

Figure 10-3 illustrates how Star-Kist has met these requirements.

The FPLA, as it was passed by Congress, improved what was a bad situation. But as a result of food-industry lobbying, the law is considerably weaker than the version originally introduced in Congress. The FPLA required the food industry to establish guidelines for standardizing the way net contents are listed. Before 1966, one juice manufacturer might have measured only in ounces, whereas another measured in quarts and ounces. As a result comparison was more difficult. Now, all manufacturers of similar products use the same unit of measurement. Canned or bottled juices, for example, are measured and labeled in fluid ounces (48 fl. oz.), then in quarts (1½ qt.), and then in liters (1.42 L.). The FPLA also required individual industries to set standards to clarify adjectives such as "small" or "giant" and to standardize package sizes. Now there are only five toothpaste sizes rather than fifty-seven. Finally, the FPLA required industry to set standards to prevent excessive **slack fill.** This refers to the practice of not filling a box completely full and letting customers assume that the contents had settled. Consumers who judged the quantity by the box size were often fooled. Although some settling of cereals or crackers, for example, is understandable, the industry now controls how much slack fill is allowed after settling—generally 10 percent.

Despite the help FPLA has given, consumers still lack some information necessary for decision making. For example, on 265 specific food products ranging from ice cream to mayonnaise, there may be no list of ingredients. The federal government has decided that these foods fall under an **identity standard;** that is, their ingredients are so standard and well known that they require no labeling. Considering that over 125 separate ingredients, in any combination, have been approved for ice cream, this seems a bit ridiculous. Yet as long as labels do not make nutritional claims, an ingredient list is not required. Within the last decade, however, several states have passed laws requiring ingredient labels on *all* food products sold in those states, and many manufacturers voluntarily include such labels.

NEED FOR OTHER KINDS OF LABELING

Besides more complete labeling of ingredients, consumers need more specific information regarding weight and contents. Currently, "net contents" includes both the food and the liquid in a can or a package. So a 10-ounce can of green beans may contain 7 ounces of beans and 3 ounces of liquid, whereas a competitor may offer 8 ounces of beans and 2 ounces of liquid. Listing the drained weight, or the dry weight, would make price comparison more accurate.

It becomes even more difficult to determine the contents of a food package when the product is complex, as is the case with many convenience foods. If

The Fair Packaging and Labeling Act requires that products come in just a few standardized sizes rather than the myriad, sometimes confusing sizes available in the past.

you have ever wondered how much beef is in a pot pie or how many apples are in an apple pie, you were wondering about the **characterizing ingredient,** that is, the main ingredient that gives a product its identity. Because the amount of an ingredient can vary from one brand to another, it would be useful to know the percentages of the ingredients in each brand of food when comparison shopping.

The origins of ingredients would be useful information for people with allergies, chronic heart disease, or other ailments. For example, a product may contain vegetable oil, but consumers don't know whether the oil is saturated or unsaturated or corn or cottonseed. Identifying specific spices, flavorings, and colorings and the food source of fats and oils in food products would help consumers by eliminating some of the worry and guesswork that lack of information brings.

The heart of the consumer decision-making process depends on complete and accurate product information. Such information can be obtained from package labels or as a result of product use. The costs of more-detailed labeling will be passed on to consumers, who in turn will need to be more informed in order to use the information. Consumers who want this information, recognizing that minuscule price increases may result, should tell manufacturers their wishes.

Safety and Quality

In addition to providing nutritional and content labeling, the government provides consumers with other kinds of information about food appearance and flavor. Through inspection of meats and poultry, milk and milk products, eggs, and fresh produce, the government gives us a sense of the relative quality of these foods. Within each category, some grades (categories that indicate degrees of physical quality) are better than others—and usually cost more. If there were no inspection and grading, consumers could be deceived about the quality of what they buy. Inspection also provides a measure of the safety of the food, that is, its freedom from disease and contaminants. In this section we look at the specific kinds of information we receive through inspection and grading. Keep in mind, however, that no food is graded for nutritional quality (high nutrient density). You will have to make that judgment yourself.

MEAT INSPECTION AND GRADING

Because meat quickly spoils and is the most expensive part of the family food budget, it was the first food to be inspected and regulated to ensure safety and quality. Federal standards for both the cleanliness of the product and the plant were first set in 1906, and were strengthened as a result of the Wholesome Meat Act of 1967 and the Wholesome Poultry Act of 1968. All states must meet minimum sanitation requirements for meat and meat products (sandwich meats, sausage, and so forth). The U.S. Department of Agriculture (USDA) inspects fresh and processed meat products sold locally or nationally. Although inspection is required, USDA grading is done only at the manufacturer's request.

Beef is graded "U.S. Prime" (available primarily to restaurants), "U.S. Choice" (most commonly found in grocery stores), "U.S. Good," "U.S. Standard," "U.S. Commercial," or "U.S. Utility." Veal, mutton, and lamb are graded "U.S. Choice" (available to restaurants and consumers alike), "U.S. Good," "U.S. Standard," "U.S. Utility," or "U.S. Cull." Pork is not usually graded, because all cuts are considered tender. Consumers generally find only USDA Grade A poultry in the market. Lesser grades of meat and poultry are usually used in processed foods such as canned soups and sandwich meats.

Meat grades are determined partly by the quantity of fat found in muscle tissue. More fat is found in certain muscles, because the animal moves these muscles less. More exercise means less-tender meat. So fat content, muscle location, and the age of the animal are criteria for determining grading and price.

THE REST OF YOUR DIET

After meat, milk and milk products take the largest chunk out of the average food dollar. The U.S. Public Health Service grades milk for freshness and indicates how long milk has been stored and under what conditions. There are three grades of fluid milk—A, B, and C. Generally, consumers find only grade A in their dairy cases.

Varieties and prices of fluid milk are based on the butterfat content of the milk itself. Whole milk usually has 5 percent butterfat. Lowfat or nonfat fluid milk may be 5 to 8 cents less per quart because some of the fat has been removed to make butter. The fat content of cream can vary from 20 percent for light table cream to 37 percent for heavy whipping cream. Evaporated milk has only about one-half the water content of whole milk, and it is less expensive to use because shipping costs decrease when the water is extracted. The same is true for powdered milk. By

Table 10-4. USDA Grades for Some Fruits and Vegetables

Product	Top grade	Second grade	Third grade	Fourth grade
Apples (all states but Washington)	U.S. Extra Fancy	U.S. Fancy	U.S. No. 1	U.S. Utility
Apples (Washington)	Washington Extra Fancy	Washington Fancy		
Broccoli (Italian sprouting)	U.S. Fancy	U.S. No. 1	U.S. No. 2	
Celery	U.S. Extra No. 1	U.S. No. 1	U.S. No. 2	
Corn (husked, on the cob)	U.S. Fancy	U.S. No. 1	U.S. No. 2	
Grapefruit (all states but Arizona, California, and Florida)	U.S. Fancy	U.S. No. 1	U.S. No. 1 Bright	U.S. No. 1 Bronze
Grapefruit (Arizona and California)	U.S. Fancy	U.S. No. 1	U.S. No. 1	U.S. Combination
Grapefruit (Florida)	U.S. Fancy	U.S. No. 1	U.S. No. 1 Bright	U.S. No. 1 Golden
Lima beans	U.S. Extra No. 1	U.S. No. 1	U.S. No. 2	
Oranges (all states but Arizona, California, and Florida)	U.S. Fancy	U.S. No. 1	U.S. No. 1 Bright	U.S. No. 1 Bronze
Oranges (Arizona and California)	U.S. Fancy	U.S. No. 1	U.S. Combination	U.S. No. 2
Oranges (Florida)	U.S. Fancy	U.S. No. 1 Bright	U.S. No. 1 Bright	U.S. No. 1 Golden
Turnips	U.S. No. 1	U.S. No. 2		

using evaporated or powdered milk in a reconstituted form (with water added) for cooking or drinking, families can decrease food expenditures.

Eggs are available in six sizes, ranging from "jumbo" (30 ounce minimum per dozen) to "peewee" (15 ounce minimum per dozen). Standards for sizes and grades are regulated by the U.S. Department of Agriculture. Eggs are graded "U.S. Grade AA" ("Fancy Fresh"), "U.S. Grade A," or "U.S. Grade B." Grade AA and Grade A are the best quality for frying, because the yolks are large and round and the whites are firm and stiff. Grade B eggs have the same nutritional value, but they have a thinner consistency. The color of the eggshell (white or brown) reflects the breed of hen and not the quality or nutritional value of the egg.

The United States does not require inspection or grading of fish or shellfish. Even though inspection by the Department of Commerce is available on a voluntary basis for a fee, only about 25 percent of fresh or processed fish is protected by inspection. Because many fishing boats lack refrigerated storage facilities and because some processing plants undoubtedly cannot meet minimum standards, it is important to purchase from reputable firms and to learn to judge the freshness of fish.

As with seafoods, the grading of fruits and vegetables is voluntary. Grades are based on shape, color, maturity, size, and absence of blemishes. As Table 10-4 shows, the symbols and terms used do not allow consumers to easily distinguish the top quality from the second or third quality.

After this discussion of grading, you may want to throw in the towel. You are not alone. Because of consumer complaints across the nation, the USDA began public hearings on the grading issue in 1980. The proposals under consideration are:

1. Adopt a completely uniform grade-name policy using U.S. Grades A, B, and C or U.S. Grades AA, A, and B for all graded foods.
2. Keep the present system of grade names for meat and fresh fruits and vegetables, and use U.S. Grades AA, A, and B or A, B, and C for all other graded foods.
3. Retain present grade names but adopt a separate color-coding system in which one color represents one quality level for all graded foods.
4. Require grade labeling at the retail level even when a product is graded and labeled at the wholesale or packer level (now, grade labeling at the retail level is voluntary).

Codes: Prices and Dates

As we have seen, information on food packages is essential in decision making. Most packages today have two additional pieces of data—a product code and a date. Both practices are controversial and have received extensive consumer attention. The product code has also been the topic of an angry interchange between consumers and the food packaging and distributing industries.

UNIVERSAL PRODUCT CODE

You may have noticed a recent addition to food packages in the form of a grid of lines, bars, and numbers. This is the **Universal Product Code (UPC).** When read by a light scanner, the UPC indicates the brand or manufacturer of the product (Hunt-Wesson), the specific product (tomato catsup), and the product size (15 ounces). It appears on 92 percent of the products typically sold in grocery stores (*Los Angeles Times*, September 21, 1980). The UPC is designed for use by electronic cash registers and scanners at the checkout stand. When a checker moves the item over the scanner, the UPC triggers the machine to charge a customer the amount of money the machine has been programed by the store to charge. The code has no price information in it per se, only product identification. The transactions are flashed on an electronic readout panel visible to the consumer and the checker and are, at the same time, printed out in detail on the register receipt (see Figure 10-4).

The use of the UPC and electronic scanners has been controversial. The UPC and scanners provide retailers with accurate, up-to-date inventory counts, allowing them to order and stock more efficiently to meet customer demand. And the system may speed up the checkout procedure and reduce checker error. All of these seem to benefit consumers. But the new system does not require that prices be marked on individual items. If a can of green peas didn't have a price marked on it, would you remember its price when you looked at frozen or fresh green peas? A price comparison would be difficult, especially with a shopping cart full of groceries!

In 1980, over 1,500 supermarkets (out of 35,600) in America were using electronic scanners. Conversion to the system is occurring rapidly in supermarkets, sales from which account for 77 percent of all grocery sales (*Los Angeles Times*, September 21, 1980). Many cities and states have passed laws that require **item pricing,** that is, each product must be individually priced. But many of these laws are temporary measures, because consumers, industry, and legislators are still studying the effects of the new system.

UNIT PRICING

Unit pricing is the cost calculation for a small unit of measure—an ounce, a gram, or a pound. Figure 10-5 shows how to calculate the unit price. This information is provided on the shelf tag along with the price for the entire item. Those who favor the elimination of price marking on individual food packages claim that consumers do not use price information for comparison. A recent study of unit pricing indicates otherwise. Over 1,000 shoppers at a supermarket chain that had used unit pricing for over six years were surveyed. Of these shoppers, 73 percent were aware of unit pricing, and 85 percent of those who were aware of it used it to make choices among product brands and product sizes (Aaker and McElroy, 1979).

Figure 10-4. Universal Product Code (UPC) and Unit Pricing for two products.

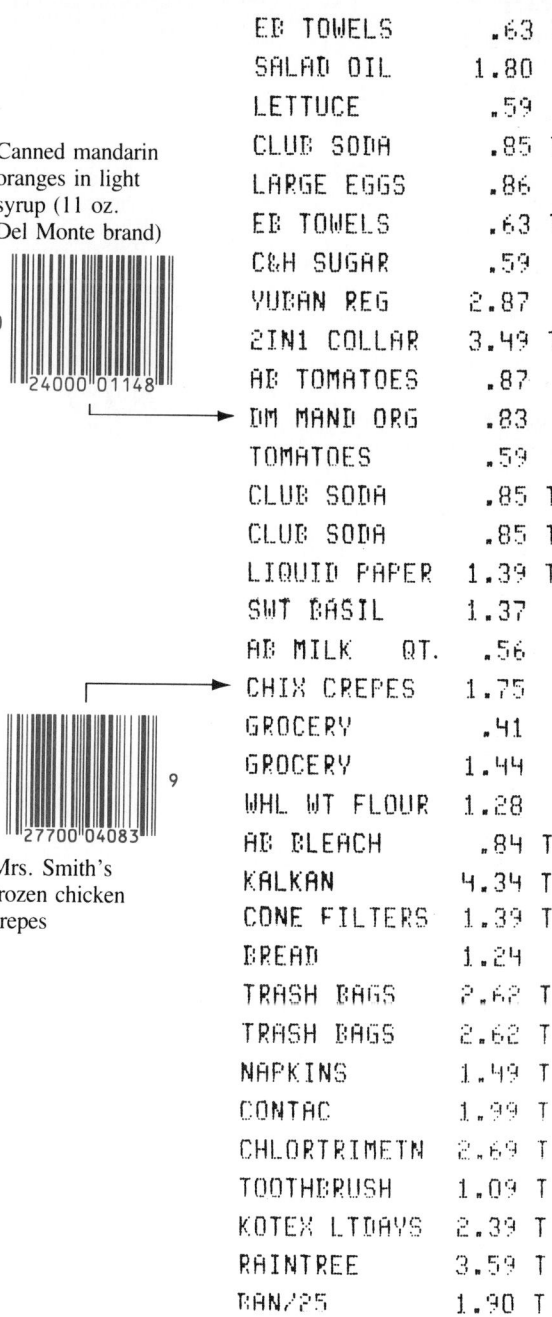

Canned mandarin oranges in light syrup (11 oz. Del Monte brand)

Mrs. Smith's frozen chicken crepes

Figure 10-5. Unit pricing.

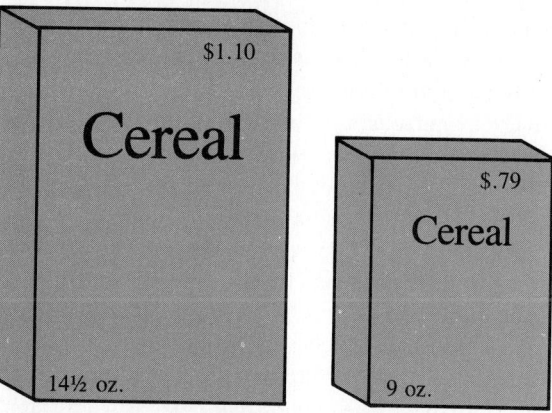

To determine which is the best buy, you could divide:
$.79 by 9 oz. (8.8 cents per lb.)
and $1.10 by 14½ oz. (7.6 cents per lb.)
or
You could look for the unit price on the shelf tag.

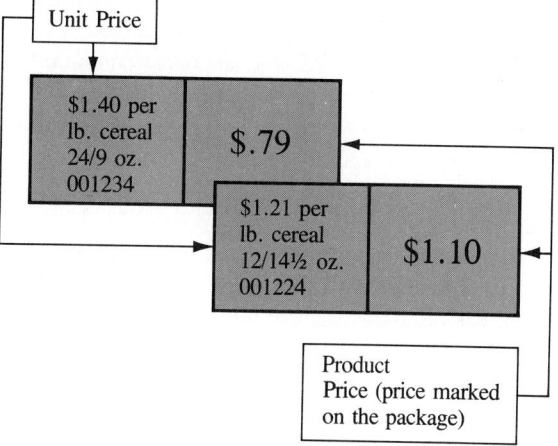

For most canned or packaged goods, the unit price is the price per pound.

Small items and personal care products will often show the price per ounce.

Most liquids are priced per pint.

Other items may be priced per 100 square feet or per 100 count.

FRESH, AGED, OR STALE?

The last time you purchased milk, yogurt, or cottage cheese, did you notice the date stamped on the bottom of the container? The practice of putting a **sell-by date (pull date)** on perishable foods is common for major manufacturers. This date indicates when a product should be sold or removed from the shelf. It does *not* mean that the product will spoil by a certain date, because it allows the consumer time for home storage and eventual use. Because pull dates are actual dates (August 28) rather than codes, they are sometimes called *open dates*.

If you look at other packaged goods such as canned vegetables or boxed cake mixes, you will probably find a date on these packages as well. But it may not look like a date, because it is most often in code. The dates hidden within the codes tell one of three things—expiration dates, packaging dates, or dates of manufacture. Some codes indicate an **expiration (use-by) date,** that is, the last day that the product can be used with proper performance or safety. Expiration, or use-by, dates are commonly found on sandwich meats and spreads or on bread-dough products in the refrigerated section of the store. Some manufacturers also record the pull date in code on items such as peanut butter, mayonnaise, and snack foods.

For products with somewhat longer shelf lives, two more methods of dating are often used. The **pack** or **packaging date** indicates when products as diverse as pasta, nuts, breakfast cereals, and tea have been placed in the containers that we see on grocery shelves. The **date of manufacture** indicates when the ingredients were all mixed together and processed to form the product. This date is often used by canners of fruits, vegetables, and soups. The shelf lives of such products vary from six months to several years from the date of manufacture or packaging. So even if these dates were decoded (open), they would be less helpful to consumers.

Many consumer specialists advocate a uniform system of open dating for packaged foods. Some major cities, such as New York, and a few states now require this. When shoppers in New York were polled, 75 percent of them used open dates to judge freshness, indicating the usefulness of this informa-

Figure 10-6. Sample packing codes.

General Mills, Inc.

Dating policy:
This company did not respond to our request. Its products are coded.

Sample code (first 4 digits):
Although the company failed to provide information about its code, we identified it as the date of packing.

```
         Year
         (1976)
          |
         F629 A
          |    \    \
        Month  Day  Plant
        (Nov)  (29th)
```

H = Jan   M = May   D = Sep
J = Feb   A = Jun   E = Oct
K = Mar   B = Jul   F = Nov
L = Apr   C = Aug   G = Dec

General Foods Corp.

Dating policy:
Most products are coded with the date of packing.

Shelf life:
The company says its coded products are good for at least 12 months after the coded date.

Sample code (first 4 digits):

```
        2005
        |    \
      Year   Day of year
      (1982) (Jan. 5)

      001 = Jan 1 through
      365 = Dec 31
```

SOURCE: Adapted from *Blind Dates: How to Break the Codes on the Foods You Buy* (New York State Consumer Protection Board, 1982).

tion. Open dating has also made it possible for store personnel to rotate stock properly and thereby substantially cut losses caused by waste. See Figure 10-6 for an example of packing codes.

Consumers can use open dating when selecting food at the store, as well as when keeping track of its freshness at home. Because most of us do not have sufficient information about dating policies, we would like to recommend an inexpensive pamphlet "Crack the Codes." This booklet (available for 25 cents from Montgomery County Office of Consumer Affairs, 611 Rockville Pike, Rockville, Md. 20852) lists major food manufacturers, identifies their dating policies, explains how to decode the dates, and includes suggested shelf-life limits whenever possible.

The Food and Drug Administration sets standards for the levels of contaminants allowed in processed and packaged foods.

Hazards to Food Safety

Besides regulating food labels and grading standards, the federal government inspects food for safety. Food inspectors look for substances not intentionally added to food. Such contaminants may enter food during growth, harvest, transport, processing, packaging, or storage. Food technologists rank hazards to food safety in order of their importance as:

1. Microbiological (food poisoning caused by bacteria).
2. Nutritional (inadequate or excessive nutrients).
3. Environmental (heavy metals such as lead; plastics).
4. Natural toxicants (such as oxalates in rhubarb and spinach).
5. Pesticide residues (such as malathion on fruit).
6. Food additives (those that cause disease, particularly cancer).

Consumers seem to worry most about the more visible or controversial contaminants, such as food additives, pesticide residues, and "filth"—small stones, rodent hairs, and insect parts. It may surprise you to learn that the FDA has set allowable levels of filth; if the levels are above what is permitted, the food cannot be sold. Although these levels are low, critics have argued that they are too lenient. Yet a standard of zero contaminants would be unrealistic. Completely uncontaminated food would be very expensive, and enforcing the law would be virtually impossible.

In the home, insects are frequent and troublesome contaminants. With the exception of cockroaches, however, they are seldom health hazards. If you find weevils or pantry beetles in foods such as cereals, pasta, crackers, dried fruit, nuts, or spices, you can save the food. First, check all packages. If food is contaminated, either throw it away or kill the bugs by freezing the product for at least two days or by placing it in a warm (130°) oven for two hours (stirring to ensure heat penetration.) The food will then be safe to eat.

To illustrate the seriousness of microbiological hazards in the homes, we have included Box 10-2, "Sally and Salmonella." But most consumer con-

> **BOX 10-2**
>
> ## Sally and Salmonella
>
> Early in the morning on a warm summer day, Sally cut up a chicken on her cutting board. She wiped the board with a damp sponge and cooked the chicken. After the chicken had cooled, she deboned it and cut it up on the cutting board. She also chopped celery and onion on the board. She mixed these ingredients with mayonnaise and put the salad in a covered bowl. A while later she put the salad in an ice chest and took it to a picnic. The ice chest sat in partial sun on the picnic table until afternoon, and when opened the ice had all melted. The chicken salad was served and remained on the picnic table for a couple hours before all of it was eaten.
>
> The next day, people who ate the chicken salad got sick with varying degrees of vomiting, diarrhea, abdominal cramps, fever, and headache. An elderly woman became critically ill and diagnostic tests showed she had salmonellosis—a gastrointestinal infection caused by salmonella bacteria. The chicken salad was identified as the source.
>
> What did Sally do wrong?
>
> 1. *The cutting board.* Raw chicken (and other poultry, meat, fish) may carry salmonella bacteria. The bacteria contaminated the cutting board; the board was not thoroughly washed. Salmonella bacteria grew on it, then contaminated the cooked chicken when it was cut on the board. (Cooking destroyed the salmonella that were present in the raw chicken.)
>
> 2. *The chicken salad.* Moist protein foods are especially good places for bacteria to grow. The mayonnaise made the chicken more moist and vulnerable. The mayonnaise was not the source of the bacteria, however—it was the chicken.
>
> 3. *The temperature.* The contaminated chicken salad might not have made anyone sick if it had been eaten fresh or kept very cold. But it was not chilled in the refrigerator before it went in the ice chest. The ice melted in the chest so the temperature was not cold enough to keep bacteria from growing. Later the salad was left on the warm picnic table where the temperature was ideal for rapid multiplication of the bacteria.
>
> 4. *The time.* Enough total time elapsed (4 or more hours) when the chicken salad wasn't cold to give the salmonella bacteria time to multiply to unsafe levels. Everyone who ate the chicken salad was infected by the bacteria, which multiplied in their intestinal tracts. Older people are especially vulnerable to attacks by salmonella.
>
> Sally should have:
>
> 1. Thoroughly washed and rinsed her cutting board immediately after using it for raw chicken, using hot water, detergent, a brush, and even diluted chlorine bleach.
>
> 2. Thoroughly chilled the salad in the refrigerator—overnight, for example, before taking it to the picnic.
>
> 3. Used enough ice in the chest, or replenished it, to keep the foods good and cold (below 40° F). Putting the ice chest in the shade—even covered with a blanket—would have helped.
>
> SOURCE: Wenck, Dorothy, "True Life Stories of Salmonella and Staph," *Today's Homemaker* (Cooperative Extension Service, University of California, July/August 1981).

troversy and regulation has centered around the last two hazards—pesticide residue and food additives. We will focus on these two matters for economic and consumer decision makers.

PESTICIDE RESIDUE

Pesticides are used to prevent damage and destruction of crops. Even with pesticide use, however, U.S. farmers sometimes lose as much as one-third of their crops to pest destruction. Part of the reason for the high loss is the high standards we have for how food should look. We allow for little visible evidence of insect damage, even if the food remains wholesome. Who wants to share his or her apple with a worm? Probably no one, but does it really matter if a snail ate part of a lettuce leaf?

Of course, pesticides in high enough doses could be harmful to humans. So the Environmental Protec-

4. Served the chicken salad immediately and returned it to the ice chest rather than letting it stand on the warm picnic table.

5. Better yet, not taken a vulnerable food like chicken salad on an all-day picnic. As an alternative, she could have taken cans of chicken, a jar of mayonnaise, and the chopped vegetables, and mixed a chicken salad just before serving time.

Remember These Facts

- Most incidents of food poisoning occur because food handlers do not follow good sanitation and health practices.
- Food poisoning bacteria need food, water, a temperature between 60–120° F, and time to grow. At cold temperatures—below 40° F—bacterial growth is very slow. At temperatures above 165° F, bacteria are destroyed.
- The most vulnerable foods are low-acid, moist protein foods—eggs, meat, poultry, fish, beans and peas, dairy products, puddings, custards, salads of potato, macaroni. Least vulnerable are fresh fruits and vegetables; acid foods—canned fruit, pickles, fruit salad; dry foods—breads, cereals, cakes, cookies.

To prevent food poisoning, vulnerable foods should be protected from contamination, and kept very cold or very hot until eaten. Leftovers should be chilled quickly in the refrigerator (spread out large quantities in shallow pans to speed the process). Vulnerable foods should not stand at room temperature for longer than a *total of 4 hours,* including preparation time.

tion Agency (EPA) establishes tolerance levels, based on the toxicity of each pesticide, for those who work with the pesticide, and it establishes residue levels for crops that receive the pesticide. The USDA and FDA assist in monitoring inspections of the harvest. Most health experts believe that the standards are safe.

There has, however, been criticism of the effectiveness of the monitoring programs, as well as concern for the safety of individuals who work in the manufacture or application of pesticides. Crop lands are spread throughout our country, from border to border and from ocean to ocean, making inspection prohibitively expensive. There have been violations of regulations, but there has never been a documented case of consumer poisoning from pesticide residue on foods. Research continues on the potential hazards of pesticides and on alternative ways to control pests. For example, biological control has been used in which a nondestructive insect such as a ladybug is introduced into the environment to feed on destructive pests such as aphids. At the same time, perhaps Americans should reconsider the standards of appearance that they require for fresh produce. Must fruit be picture pretty to be delicious?

FOOD ADDITIVES

The safety and merits of cyclamates, saccharin, red dyes, and sodium nitrate all became conversation topics among health-conscious consumers in the 1970s. Each of these is a **food additive,** a substance or combination of substances found in food as a result of processing, production, or packaging to (1) make foods more appealing by improving flavor, color, and texture; (2) increase the nutritional value; (3) prevent spoilage and increase the shelf life; or (4) improve performance or ease of preparation. In short, the almost 1,900 additives put in our food are designed to increase our satisfaction with the products. So why all the concern? In a word—safety.

Additives such as sugar, salt, and vinegar have been used for centuries to improve flavor and prevent spoilage. Sugar in its various forms (including corn syrup and dextrose) and salt are still the primary additives today. They account, in fact, for 93 percent of the 139.6 pounds of additives that each of us consumes each year (see Figure 10-7). The other 7 percent, which includes over 1,800 different additives, has been the focus of negative comments by consumers. Figure 10-8 shows the purpose of the most common food additives. You might be most familiar with the largest category of additives—*flavorings*—which includes all herbs and spices. *Thickeners* and *stabilizers* improve and maintain the texture of foods. *Leavening* causes foods to increase in volume. *Acidity controllers* neutralize or alter sourness; *emulsifiers*

Figure 10-7. Average annual consumption of food additives.

SOURCE: Adapted from *Nutrition Today* magazine, P.O. Box 1829, Annapolis, Maryland 21404, © July/August 1973, with permission.

enable oil to stay dispersed in water; *preservatives* prevent the growth of microorganisms such as mold; *firming agents* prevent foods from becoming mushy; *coloring agents* improve appearance (make cherry pop red, for example); and *curing agents* prevent discoloring and rancidity or spoiling.

Many people question the use of additives, because additives seem mysterious. Additives, as a rule, do not have simple, common names. Neither are they usually used in home cooking, which is consumed shortly after it is prepared.

Since the passage of the Food, Drug, and Cosmetic Act of 1938, the FDA has been regulating the use of food additives. Initially, their responsibility was only for labeling, but in 1958 the Food Additives Amendment was made to the 1938 regulation. One section of that law is the **Delaney Clause,** which initiated a rigid screening process to evaluate the safety of new food additives before marketing.

The Delaney Clause specifically prohibits the use of any additive that has been linked to cancer in people or animals under any circumstances. For example, in the late 1960s, cyclamate, an artificial sweetener, was proven to cause cancer in rats, so it was banned from food. In order to reach the level of cyclamate intake found to cause cancer in rats, a person would have to drink at least 138 12-ounce bottles of cyclamate-sweetened soft drinks daily (Clydesdale, 1979). Although consuming 138 bottles seems impossible, the law does not allow cyclamate to be used now, because large doses have been shown to be carcinogenic, or cancer-causing.

At least 700 additives were already in use in 1958, so they were not tested. These additives were placed on a **Generally Recognized As Safe (GRAS)** list, because they had been in use with no previous problems. Because a few GRAS additives were later found to be potentially hazardous, in 1969 the FDA was directed by Congress to test all GRAS substances. As a result, some additives, such as red dye number 2, were removed from food. For increased safety, since 1976 *all* food additives undergo periodic review.

The Delaney Clause eliminates only the carcinogens that are purposefully added to food. But carcinogens may occur naturally in our food. Coffee has

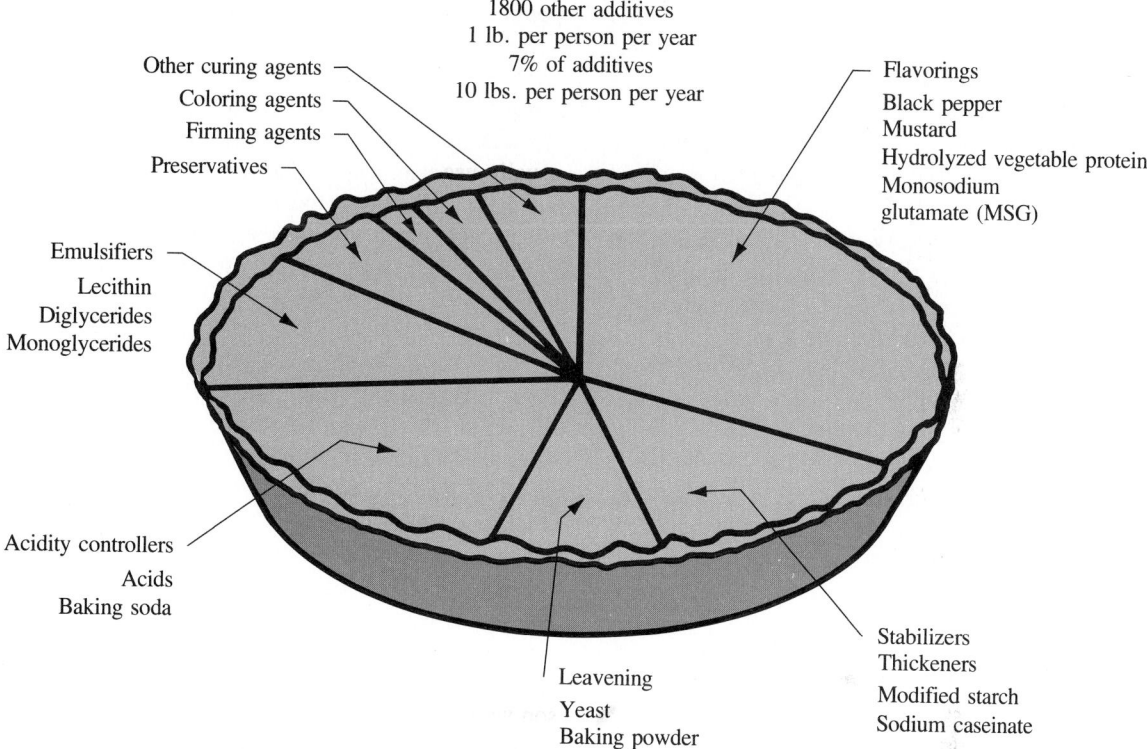

Figure 10-8. Common food additives other than sugar and salt (see Figure 10-7). The ones shown here constitute 6.4 percent of all additives, or 10 pounds per person per year. The remaining .6 percent, or 1 pound per person per year, includes 1,800 other additives.

SOURCE: Adapted from *Nutrition Today* magazine, P.O. Box 1829, Annapolis, Maryland 21404, © July/August 1973, with permission.

caffeine, cabbage contains thiourea, and flour and orange juice contain patulin. All of these substances can cause cancer when consumed in large enough doses, and they therefore cannot meet the standard required for food additives. Consequently, some scientists suggest that the Delaney Clause is too rigid. They recommend that the benefits gained from using a specific additive be weighed against the risks, rather than automatically outlawing its use for all people. This has been tried with saccharin, a sugar substitute. In high doses—the equivalent of consuming 875 12-ounce bottles of saccharin-sweetened soft drinks daily—saccharin is carcinogenic (Clydesdale, 1979). But it remains on the market to provide a choice for diabetics and others whose health may be endangered by sugar consumption. Products that contain saccharin bear a warning such as: "Use of this product may be hazardous to your health. This product contains saccharin, which has been determined to cause cancer in laboratory animals."

COSTS AND BENEFITS OF SAFETY

The food safety controversy centers on the costs and benefits of creating a risk-free food supply compared to those of accepting a minimal risk as determined by specialists of toxic, or poisonous, substances. Some consumers have called for the elimination of all food additives, but as we saw in the decision-making model in Chapter 2, decisions involve opportunity costs, or tradeoffs. Let us do a cost-benefit analysis of the effect on consumers of eliminating additives from our food. Because consumers usually accept sugar, salt, herbs, spices, and leavening agents, we will exclude these additives from our analysis.

The elimination of some additives may result in *higher ingredient costs*. Saccharin and aspartame, for example, are less expensive and lower in calories than sugar—desirable features to many consumers. If only sugar or honey could be used as sweeteners, the prices of foods now using saccharin would rise. Because the overall demand for sugar and honey would also increase, foods that now contain these ingredients would increase in price.

Distribution costs as well as ingredient costs determine product cost. Anyone who has shopped for bread knows that whole-wheat breads without additives can be as much as 25 percent more costly than white bread with additives. The additive-free bread requires daily distribution because it becomes stale quickly, which increases its cost. In a normal year, U.S. grocery stores return 100 million pounds of spoiled bread to the producers (*Consumer Reports*, July 1980, p. 411). In a world nagged by hunger and malnutrition, "natural" means more waste—and that drives costs up.

Vernal S. Packard, professor of nutrition at the University of Minnesota, has another objection to the concern about additives. He argues that calcium propionate, a mildew retardant used to prolong bread shelf life, might sound terrible, but it does occur naturally in raisins and Swiss cheese. "Without preservatives, the bread gets stale faster; it may go moldy with the production of hazardous aflatoxin" (*Consumer Reports*, July 1980, p. 411). *Spoiled food at home* increases family food costs and may endanger family safety when people consume food that is not visibly spoiled, but spoiled nonetheless.

Without additives, we would need to accept that *some foods would change appearance*. Colorings are responsible for the appearance of soft drinks and the reddish color of sandwich meats and frankfurters, for example. Certainly we could become accustomed to these changes. *Food selection* would also change. Staples such as margarine or other convenience foods, for example, would change drastically or leave the market entirely. The decreased selection of frozen, canned, and packaged foods could be a blow to families for which time for food preparation is scarce.

If we choose, then, to eliminate additives from our food supply, we might incur higher food costs, shortened time for safe food storage, health risks, and changed appearance and selection of food. In exchange, we would receive the benefit of zero risk of illness from food additives. In light of this, the federal government has chosen to ban only carcinogenic food additives. The decision to consume food additives and in what quantity is up to the individual consumer, who must do his or her own cost-benefit analysis.

Back to Nature: Health Foods and Vitamins

During the 1960s, as a result of concern about the safety and usefulness of food additives, some individuals began to purchase more fresh fruits, vegetables, and whole-grain food products grown without chemicals and processed without preservatives. This trend gave rise to specialty stores, restaurants, and food processors catering to the "health-food" consumer.

Health foods have been heavily promoted as cure-alls for everything from lack of energy to the common cold. They are supposed to taste better or be healthier. But health food is such a vague term that it has no nationally accepted legal definition. The Federal Trade Commission, whose job, in part, is to monitor deceptive advertising, has said that the term " 'health food' is undefined, indefinable, and inherently deceptive." But it continues to be widely used because of a persistent belief by many consumers that the term indicates better quality.

Specialty food producers generally agree that health foods can include foods for special diets, such as those for vegetarians, or foods used as nutrient supplements, such as brewer's yeast. These foods are not necessarily free of chemical additives; neither are they grown without pesticides. In a 1978 study, researchers from Wayne State and Michigan State uni-

Products marketed as "health foods," "natural," and "organic" are not necessarily free of additives or pesticides, but they do cost more.

versities bought ten brands of bread, half from supermarkets and the other half from health-food stores. All ten had traces of pesticide residue. In a similar study conducted at the University of Florida, twice as many of the health foods had pesticide and bacterial contamination. And the health foods cost about 70 percent more than their supermarket rivals (*Consumer Reports,* July 1980, p.414).

NATURAL AND ORGANIC FOOD

Natural food is another vague category of foods that has no nationally accepted legal description. Generally, a **natural food** is one that does not contain artificial preservatives to increase shelf life, emulsifiers to prevent separation of the ingredients, or artificial flavorings or colors to enhance taste or appearance. This label may also mean that the food has been minimally processed, as is whole-wheat flour as opposed to white refined flour. However, only one state, Maine, has incorporated this definition into law. And even if all states followed suit, there is nothing to prohibit a product such as Quaker's 100% Natural Cereal from containing 24 percent sugar—three times as much as an "unnatural" rival, Kellogg's Corn Flakes. Many other granola cereals have natural oils added that increase fat content of the diet. As you can see, "natural" does not necessarily mean that the food is free of all additives or that it is the best nutritionally.

Another confusing term is **organic food,** which refers to foods grown with organic fertilizers, such as compost and manure, and untreated with chemical pesticides. Technically, "organically grown" is a more accurate label, because all food is organic (that is, derived from living organisms). It is difficult for consumers to be sure that organic growing techniques have been used, because adjoining farms may not be using them. For example, what if one farmer grows tomatoes organically and the surrounding farmers spray their tomato fields with pesticides? The spray is likely to drift across the organically grown tomatoes. In addition, it is impossible to prove whether food is grown organically once it goes to market. The buyer has only the seller's word on the matter. Many consumers, then, may be trying to improve the quality of their diets (for example, by eliminating pesticide residues), but they end up paying more for food without any guarantee that they have gotten what they wanted. Another reason that many consumers sometimes prefer organically grown foods is that they believe that such foods are more nutritious and have a higher vitamin content. But research shows otherwise.

The issue of buying organically grown food is, however, separate from using organic growing techniques in your own garden. Tomatoes grown commercially and then shipped and stored for several days cannot compare to tomatoes picked fresh off the vine at their peak of ripeness. And you can, of course, eliminate the need for pesticides by picking the hornworms off your tomato plants, a process that would not be economical for commercial growers with hundreds of acres.

There are many abuses in the use of the terms *health food, organic food,* and *natural food.* The Federal Trade Commission, because of its concern about their use on labels and in advertising, has suggested that more specific definitions be established. At this time, no policy has been proposed.

DIETARY SUPPLEMENTS

Because many people feel that they aren't eating properly or getting good nutrition through their diets, they often use various kinds of supplements to try to make up for the deficiencies. Others feel that if a little supplementing is good, a lot will be even better and will help them achieve "supernutrition." **Vitamins** and **minerals** (that is, substances that are necessary in small amounts for normal growth and health) are probably the most common supplements. Others, such as seaweed and brewer's yeast, are taken to supply other nutrients as well as vitamins and minerals. In fact, Americans spend over $1.2 billion per year for vitamin pills.

The problem is that a good diet should supply most of the vitamins and minerals a person needs. There has been some controversy over the need for high doses of some vitamins. Linus Pauling, for example, supports the use of vitamin C as a preventative of the common cold. Generally, however, it is wise to take large doses of a vitamin only on your physician's advice. Some vitamins, such as vitamins A and D, can make you ill if you take too much.

When you do have to shop for vitamin supplements, how should you choose among the many brands? Should you take natural vitamins? Are they worth the extra cost? By law, all vitamins must have the same chemical composition, so that those that are made synthetically (made out of chemical compounds) are the same as natural vitamins that are extracted from foods. In addition, research shows that our bodies cannot tell the difference between "natural" and synthetic vitamins (Labuza, 1975).

Because one company manufactures 60 to 70 percent of all the vitamins sold in the United States and packages them in different labels, the only real differences among brands are in dose size (500 milligrams, 250 milligrams) and in price. When shopping for vitamins, then, buy the least-expensive brand available in moderate doses, using the RDA as a guide. Or better yet, avoid the expense by eating a balanced and nutritious diet.

Getting Good Nutrition at Reasonable Prices

Now that you know about the Basic Four food groups, RDAs for essential nutrients, and food labeling and grading policies, you are ready to make specific purchases. Because food prices have been rising faster than the prices of most other budget items, there is a feeling among some consumers that nutritious foods such as eggs, milk, meat, fruits, whole grains, and vegetables are just too expensive for their budgets.

Is it possible to eat well on a low or moderate income? The answer is yes, if the principles of decision making and good buying habits are applied. In 1965 to 1966 and in 1977 to 1978, the U.S. Department of Agriculture (1980) conducted national food-consumption surveys to determine the relationship between income level and the quality of diets. As might be expected, both surveys showed that as income levels rose, so did the amount of money spent on food.* Both surveys also showed that the proportion of people who had diets rated "good" or "fair" increased as income increased. But 37 percent of the families with incomes of $5000 or less also had diets

---

*We must add that the proportion of income spent on food declines as income rises. According to the Bureau of Labor Statistics, in 1980 families that earned less than $14,000 yearly spent at least 30 percent of their income on food, whereas those with incomes of more than $34,000 spent only 20 percent.

Food: More Than a Matter of Taste   273

Lower-income families get more for their food dollar than higher-income families.

Table 10-5. Nutrient Return Per Dollar

		Household income	
Nutrient	Unit	Under $5000	$20,000 and over
Protein	g	45	41
Calcium	mg	470	440
Iron	mg	9.1	7.7
Vitamin A	IU	3,720	2,930
Thiamin	mg	.89	.72
Riboflavin	mg	1.2	1.0
Vitamin C	mg	61	56

SOURCE: U.S. Department of Agriculture, *Family Economics Review* (Fall 1979), p. 18.

rated "good," proving that it is possible to eat well on a small budget.

The same surveys compared the consumption of key nutrients of low-income and high-income families (Table 10-5). In each case, the low-income families got more nutrients for their money. They did this by avoiding low-nutrient-density foods such as soft drinks, snack foods, and "gourmet" convenience foods. Instead, they ate poultry, eggs, liver, potatoes, dry beans, and enriched cereals and flour.

PLANNING, SPENDING, EATING—AND DECISION MAKING

Good nutrition on a budget does not happen automatically. It takes careful planning and decision making. Using the decision-making model (see Chapter 2) should give you a rational approach to the problem and a way of solving it to your satisfaction:

Step 1: Define the Problem. You want to have a good diet on your current income, getting the best and most for your food dollars.

Step 2: Clarify Values, Goals, and Standards. Consider how your values, goals, and standards limit your food choices. For example, you may be willing to pay a higher price for convenience (a value); you may have decided to avoid food additives as much as possible (goal); and you may think that taste is the main criterion for food selection (standard).

Step 3: Seek Advice and Information. Keep track of the money you spend on each food category for a month (Worksheet 10-1). Use electronic cash-register receipts as an aid, if they are available. Determine which category you are spending too much on. The USDA found that families who get the best diets for their money divide their budgets according to the

WORKSHEET 10-1
Record of Spending for Groceries

Dairy products: milk, cheese, yogurt, ice cream, and so forth.	Meat: meat, poultry, fish, eggs, dried beans, peanut butter, and so forth.	Fruits and vegetables: fresh, frozen, and canned (all varieties).	Breads and cereals: bread, cereal, pasta, rice, tortillas, and so forth.	Other items: fats, sugars, beverages (colas, alcohol), seasonings, dressings, and so forth.	Paper goods: towels, napkins, toilet paper, foil, and so forth.	Personal care items: toothpaste, shampoo, deodorant, and so forth.	Miscellaneous items: toys, magazines, cooking utensils, and so forth.

Nonfood items can account for 20 to 30 percent of spending in grocery stores.

1.
2.
3.
4.
5.
6.
7.
8.
9.
10.
11.
12.
13.
14.
15.
16.
17.
18.
19.
20.
21.
22.
23.
24.
25.
26.
27.
28.
29.
30.
31.

Figure 10-9. Optimal division of the consumer's food dollar. Note these costs are for food *only*. Nonfood items such as paper goods, cleaning supplies, magazines, and household accessories average 20 to 30 percent of a typical grocery bill.

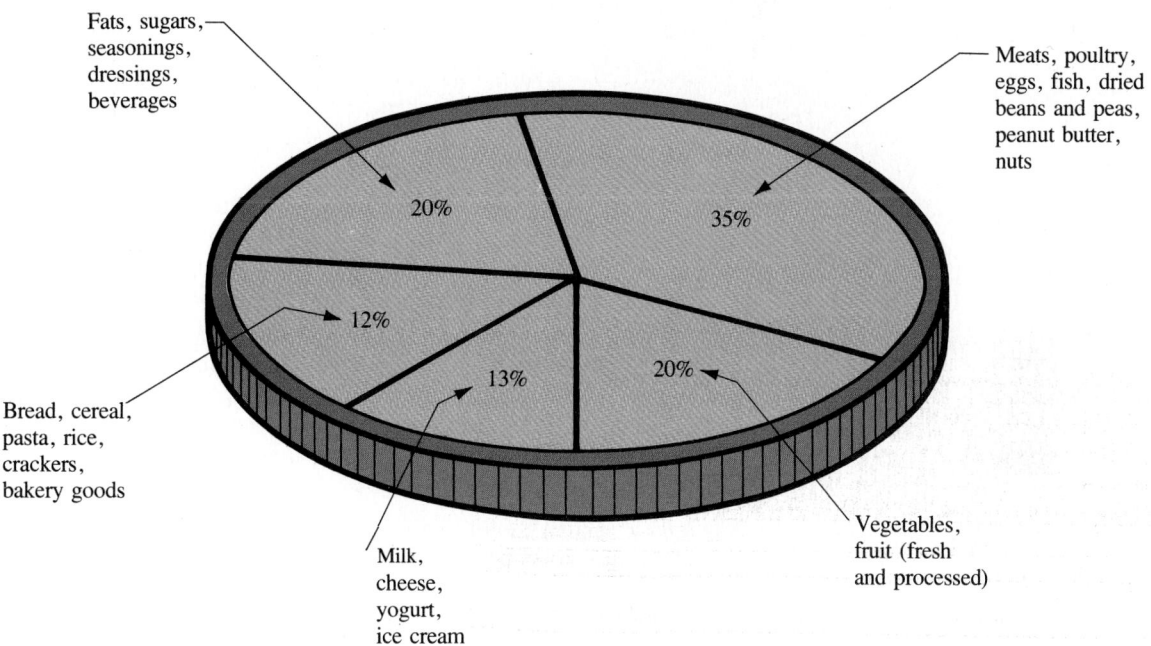

pattern shown in Figure 10-9. Look for ways to sharpen your planning and buying skills:

1. To eliminate waste, make sure that family members like and eat the foods you buy.
2. Keep track of what you throw away. Adjust your buying habits so that you purchase and prepare less of some foods or dishes that always seem to be tossed out.
3. Plan a weekly menu of all meals and snacks and compare it with recipes. When you shop, buy only the items you need to prepare the meals on the menu.
4. Plan meals around weekly advertised specials, which are usually cheaper.
5. Take a shopping list with you to the store. Resist buying anything that is not on the list. In particular, avoid high-priced impulse items such as gourmet foods or out-of-season fruits and vegetables.
6. Make only one trip to the store each week. Extra trips can mean extra purchases that you probably don't need.
7. Shop only when you have a full stomach. Studies indicate that shopping on a full stomach can cut your food bill.
8. Buy in quantity, if your budget and your storage space permit you to do so. Lower bulk prices and the effects of inflation make this an especially useful technique for families.
9. Shop around. Applying the principles of comparison shopping can really pay off in lower food bills. For example, a grocery store that operates on a

Those who spend a great deal of time clipping coupons and hunting for food bargains must weigh time costs against money saved.

self-service, no-frills, no-games-or-contests basis and that is open a limited number of hours daily usually has lower prices than a 24 hour, full-service store or a corner grocery or convenience store.

10. Buy store or house brands; they can save you 20 to 40 percent of the cost of each item and they are just as nutritious and wholesome as brand-name products. They often are made by brand-name manufacturers.

11. Use your calculator. Even though it may be complicated at times, try to determine which sizes are the least expensive. Divide the price by the number of ounces or grams to find the unit price. It probably isn't worth it to do this for a whole basket of groceries, but it might be worth it for higher-priced items. Or shop in stores that post the unit price on the shelf tag (see Figure 10-5).

Reexamine your spending patterns:

1. Are you getting most of your protein from beef and pork? If so, you might consider replacing them to some extent with poultry, liver, and heart, which are high in protein but cost much less. And you might use more plant protein in the form of dried beans and peas, soy protein, peanut butter, and cereals. Plant proteins can also extend small quantities of meat in soups, casseroles, and salads, while providing necessary levels of protein. Oriental, Mexican, and Italian dishes, for example, often use little or no meat.

2. Lower the amount of meat per serving. Two-ounce or three-ounce servings provide sufficient protein and cost less.

3. Choose simpler, cheaper foods for snacks. Processed snacks such as potato chips, candy, or soft drinks are expensive and low in nutrients. Other foods, such as home-popped popcorn, fresh fruit, raw vegetables spread with peanut butter or cheese, and homemade juice bars are more nutritious and less expensive. Remember, water is an inexpensive alternative to soft drinks.

Keep your eyes open for articles in popular magazines on food buying. Check the local newspaper for articles on food and nutrition. They can give you recipes, food-buying tips, and more information about areas of consumer concern. Use the federal government's pamphlets as sources of information about food (write to Consumer Product Information, Pueblo, Colorado). You might also want to enroll in a nutrition or meal-planning class at your college or adult-education facility.

Step 4: Weigh the Costs and Benefits of Information and Planning. Costs of information gathering might include: (1) time spent reading food labels, unit-pricing shelf tags, and food-buying and nutrition articles, and (2) increased food prices, if manufacturers are required to provide more information on packages and if stores are required to individually mark items. Benefits might include: (1) increased knowledge of food buying and nutrition, (2) lower family food costs, and (3) better diet and better health.

Costs of planning might include time necessary to (1) analyze diet, (2) choose menus in advance and make shopping lists, and (3) change food-preparation habits and try new recipes. Benefits might include: (1) saving fuel and time by making fewer trips to the

---

BOX 10-3

Men in the Kitchen

A growing percentage (approximately 30 percent) of men are actively involved in food shopping. Many men live alone or help their spouses. Consider George Portlock:

It was a beautiful Saturday. George Portlock was visiting his daughter, and they were just finishing breakfast. She needed some minor repairs done around her house, and she asked her dad, who was retired, to help. "The least I can do is make breakfast for you in return," she told him.

George was proudly telling his daughter how much he was learning about housekeeping, especially about buying and cooking food. His wife, Jo, had died a few months before. Before Jo died, he had occasionally cooked breakfast or dinner, but he had never had to plan, buy, and prepare meals on a daily basis.

"You know," he said, "my favorite thing to do is to buy a large piece of meat and put it in the slow cooker. Then I toss in a few vegetables—potatoes, carrots, some beans, maybe—and let it cook for several hours. That way I have a well-balanced meal, and it will last a couple of days. I'm even learning to put one or two individual servings in the freezer for another time.

"I looked through the cookbooks that we have, and I found the times and temperatures for roasting meats. So far, I've made four roasts, and I had meat for sandwiches as well as for one or two main meals from each roast.

"Not everything I've done has been perfect of course. You would have laughed if you had seen the macaroni I made. I had one friend over for dinner, and I decided a cup and a half of macaroni was about right as a side dish for the roast beef. I poured it into the boiling water, and ten minutes later I had enough macaroni for a dozen people.

"But I'm learning. This week I used the pressure cooker for the first time. Jo used it a lot to make spaghetti, stew, and chicken soup. She really planned things well—so I'm trying to do the same thing."

1. What other food-buying or preparation suggestions do you have for George? Keep in mind that he is interested only in simple recipes and would rather not follow a recipe at all.
2. Individuals who live alone often eat poorly. Why does this tend to be so? Does this affect both men and women? Does age make a difference?
3. Where can people obtain basic food-buying and preparation information?

---

store, (2) less food waste, (3) better diet and better health, and (4) lower family food costs.

Step 5: Make a Decision. By applying the techniques you have learned, you should get a higher level of satisfaction from your food-buying decisions.

Step 6: Evaluate Choices and Review Decisions. As your income increases or decreases or as your family changes, use the decision-making process we have outlined to sharpen and review your food and nutrition decisions. Recognize money and time as the scarce resources they are.

CONVENIENCE FOODS

Our ability to get good nutrition at reasonable prices has been affected by the growing array of convenience foods—those foods that require less work or the addition of fewer ingredients than their home-prepared counterparts. These foods range from frozen orange juice and green beans to Hamburger Helper and TV dinners to foods made mostly of artificial ingredients, such as Tang and Cool Whip. Because there are so many kinds of convenience foods and because they are so widely used, they deserve discussion here. Why do Americans choose these foods, and how can they be sure they are getting the most for their convenience-food dollar?

Americans select convenience foods because they save time. As families get smaller, as more people live alone, and as growing numbers of women seek employment outside the home, time becomes

Table 10-6. Fast Food Meals and RDAs

Food	Serving size (oz.)	Calories	Fat (gm)	Carbohydrates (gm)	Total sugars (gm)	Sodium (mg)	Percentage RDA*									
							Protein	Vitamin A	Thiamine	Riboflavin	Vitamin B₆	Vitamin B₁₂	Niacin	Calcium	Phosphorus	Iron
Burger King Whopper	9	660	41	49	9	1083	57	12	51	30	19	67	55	9	29	26
Jack-in-the-Box Jumbo Jack	8¼	538	28	44	7	1007	61	9	56	41	13	70	57	13	29	24
McDonald's Big Mac	7½	591	33	46	6	963	59	5	52	33	13	63	55	23	44	23
Wendy's Old-Fashioned Hamburger	6½	413	22	29	5	708	62	8	36	26	13	83	45	8	24	27
Roy Roger's Roast Beef Sandwich	5½	356	12	34	0	610	63	5	38	29	16	37	60	2	28	23
Burger King Chopped-Beef Steak Sandwich	6¼	445	13	50	0.7	966	67	5	48	34	25	40	66	15	37	30
Hardee's Roast Beef Sandwich	4½	351	17	32	3	765	41	4	36	22	10	47	42	8	29	17
Arby's Roast Beef Sandwich	5¼	370	15	36	1	869	52	4	36	21	10	53	56	5	35	20
Long John Silver's Fish	7½	483	27	27	0.1	1333	72	5	17	12	16	133	24	3	46	3
Arthur Treacher's Original Fish	5¼	439	27	27	0.3	421	46	3	11	6	10	27	18	2	32	3
McDonald's Filet-O-Fish	4½	383	18	38	3	613	35	3	39	19	6	23	25	14	27	9
Burger King Whaler	7	584	34	50	5	968	48	3	38	20	7	60	31	8	50	12
Kentucky Fried Chicken Snack Box	6¾	405	21	16	0	728	78	4	21	25	19	40	72	6	35	14
Arthur Treacher's Original Chicken	5½	409	23	25	0	580	57	3	12	10	24	10	87	2	33	4
Wendy's Chili	10	266	9	29	9	1190	50	51	20	169	18	47	8	9	27	27
Pizza Hut Pizza Supreme (½ 10 in. pizza)	7¾	506	15	64	6	1281	61	36	59	40	17	43	49	41	46	24
Jack-in-the-Box Tacos (2)	5½	429	26	34	3	926	35	25	16	13	15	27	18	20	33	12

*Recommended Daily Allowance for an adult woman as set by the National Academy of Sciences National Research Council.

SOURCE: Copyright 1979 by Consumers Union of the United States, Inc., Mount Vernon, NY 10550. Excerpted by permission from *Consumer Reports*, September 1979.

more precious. We are willing to pay other people to make the pizza dough, bake the meat pie, or shell the peas. Convenience foods eliminate the need for special pans and utensils or exotic spices; all that's needed is an oven for heating. And when we're finished, cleanup is a snap.

The tradeoff to save time costs consumers money and, in some cases, nutritional value. Approximately two-thirds of commonly purchased convenience foods cost more money than their home-prepared or fresh counterparts. (Notable exceptions include frozen orange juice and frozen French fries.) Sometimes you pay double or triple the cost of preparing the food at home. Is it worth it? That depends on what your time is worth to you and how you would use the time you save by using convenience foods.

Despite their higher costs, convenience foods often give lower nutritional value when compared to homemade foods. The main dishes or extras usually contain less meat, perhaps as little as one-fourth the meat of homemade dishes (Lerza and Jacobson, 1975). The sugar, salt, and fat content are often higher than in prepared or fresh foods, and convenience foods often contain preservatives and other additives.

Besides the time-saving benefits they offer, convenience foods expand our food choices by making seasonal fruits and vegetables available year round. Freezing preserves the appearance, the texture, and the nutritional value of most foods. So we can have corn on the cob at Christmas dinner.

A different type of convenience food is available at fast-food restaurants. If we want a hamburger, a taco, pizza, or chicken, it is quickly ready for us. Many people purchase a third of their meals in fast-food restaurants. Table 10-6 shows the nutritional values of some of the best-known fast-food items. Notice that fat and sodium levels are often quite high, as are calories. Of all the meals listed, which are the most nutritious?

As you can see, convenience foods are neither good nor bad. You will need to judge them individually on the basis of their costs, their time and money benefits, and their nutritional values.

Summary

Because food expenditures account for 15 percent to 30 percent of a family budget, it is a subject that interests consumers and merits their study. Wise food selection should be based on the Basic Four food groups, individual calorie needs, and Recommended Daily Allowances. Food package information can be extremely useful to consumers when they search for nutritional value. Labels usually include nutritional data, product content information, and, sometimes, inspection and grading designations. Consumers can find additional information and codes on food packages. These include the Universal Product Code (UPC) and dates that indicate freshness.

Consumers are interested in food safety, particularly as it relates to pesticide residue and food additives. Some experts think that the federal regulations such as the Delaney Clause are too rigid. Some consumers are concerned about the safety of food additives and pesticide residue, so they have tried to avoid them by choosing natural or organic foods. Both *natural* and *organic* are vague terms that are of dubious value to consumers.

The challenge for consumers, then, is to apply the decision-making process and comparison-shopping techniques to obtain a nutritious diet and keep their food budgets balanced.

Neighborhood REVISITED

1. Joyce and Alicia discussed many ways to stretch food dollars. In what ways does your family make its food dollars go farther?

2. Are there places in your community, such as fruit orchards or food factories, where you can buy from the source? Investigate how much money can be saved by buying from the source. Be sure to consider the cost of transportation.

3. Does your community have limited-service stores that offer lower prices on staple or nonperishable items? In what quantities must you buy such items?

KEY TERMS

Basic Four food groups
calories
characterizing ingredient
date of manufacture
Delaney Clause
enriched (fortified)
expiration (use-by) date
food additive
Generally Recognized As Safe (GRAS) list
health foods
high nutrient density
identity standard
item pricing
low nutrient density
malnutrition
minerals
natural food
nutrients
organic foods
pack (packaging) date
pesticides
sell-by (pull) date
slack fill
unit pricing
U.S. Recommended Dietary Allowances (RDAs)
Universal Product Code (UPC)
vitamins

QUESTIONS

1. What basic functions does the food we eat fulfill? What factors affect our specific food choices? Do people in other countries eat foods that we would not eat? Do you think the reverse is true?

2. What are the four general groups of foods that serve as the basis of an adequate diet? What factors sometimes stand in the way of changing poor eating habits?

3. What information is required on food packages and labels? Have you ever used the information to make food choices? Do you need other information that is not currently required?

4. What is the Delaney Clause and what does it require? Name one additive that has been used differently as a result of this regulation. Identify the change. What impact has this change had on your food choices?

5. What percentage of the RDA do you need for: calories, protein, vitamin A, vitamin C, thiamin, riboflavin, niacin, calcium, and iron?

6. What do the words *natural* and *health food* imply to consumers? Do you think consumers are getting their money's worth when they buy these foods? Explain your answer.

7. What are the costs and benefits of using convenience foods?

PROJECTS

1. Consider all of the buying suggestions recommended in this chapter. Which would have the most effect in reducing food budgets? Which would take the least amount of time and offer the best results?

2. Make a record of all the foods and beverages you eat for three to five days. Count the number of servings of the Basic Four foods that you eat each day. Compare the results to the number of servings recommended in Figure 10-1. How can you improve your dietary habits? What specific foods can be added to or substituted for low-nutrient-density foods?

3. Interview ten consumers concerning the use of the UPC in conjunction with the elimination of individual prices on packages. Include the issues of decreased costs and ease of price comparisons. Report your findings to the class.

4. List ten or fifteen products that you commonly eat at home. Visit three or four grocery stores, including a neighborhood convenience store, a supermarket, and a discount store. Record the prices of the items and total the bill for each store. What conclusions can you draw from the results?

5. Visit a grocery store that features unit pricing and locate the least-expensive brand among five similar products. Record the brand name, the size, the price, and the amount of time it took to gather the information. Now go to a store that doesn't have unit pricing and find the least-expensive brand among five similar products. Record the amount of time necessary to do this with and without a calculator. What did you discover?

REFERENCES AND READINGS

Aaker, David A., and McElroy, Bruce F. "Unit Pricing Six Years After Introduction." *Journal of Marketing,* (Fall 1979).

Agricultural Research Service. *Nutritive Value of Foods.* Home and Garden Bulletin no. 72. Washington, D.C.: U.S. Government Printing Office, 1977.

Briggs, George, and Calloway, Doris Howes. *Bogart's Nutrition and Physical Fitness,* 10th edition. Philadelphia: W. B. Saunders, 1979.

Clydesdale, Fergus. *Food Science and Nutrition: Current Issues and Answers.* Englewood Cliffs, N.J.: Prentice-Hall, 1979.

Deutsch, Ronald. *The New Nuts Among the Berries.* Palo Alto, Calif.: Bull Publishing, 1977.

"Fast Food Meals and RDAs." *Consumer Reports,* September 1979.

Ford, Barbara. *Future Food: Alternate Protein for the Year 2000.* New York: William Morrow, 1978.

"It's Natural! It's Organic! Or Is It?" *Consumer Reports,* July 1980.

Jones, Judith Lea, and Weimer, Jon P. *Food Safety: Homemakers' Attitudes and Practices.* Agricultural Economic Report no. 360. Washington, D.C.: U.S. Department of Agriculture, 1977.

Labuza, Theodore P. *The Nutrition Crisis: A Reader.* St. Paul, Minn.: West Publishing, 1975.

Lappé, Frances Moore. *Diet for a Small Planet.* New York: Ballantine Books, 1971.

Lehman, Phyllis. "More Than You Ever Thought You Would Know About Food Additives." Parts I, II, and III. *FDA Consumer,* April, May, and June 1979.

Lerza, Catherine, and Jacobson, Michael. *Food for People, Not for Profit.* New York: Ballantine Books, 1975.

Los Angeles Times, Advertising Supplement, Part VIII, September 21, 1980.

Montgomery County Office of Consumer Affairs. "Crack the Codes." Rockville, Md.: Office of Consumer Affairs, 1979.

Morella, Joseph J., and Turchetti, Richard J. *Nutrition and the Athlete.* New York: Mason/Charter, 1976.

Sherwin, Sally. *Seven Steps to Rockbottom Food Costs.* New York: William Morrow, 1976.

Traub, Larry G., and Odland, Dianne D. *Convenience Foods and Home-Prepared Foods,* Agricultural Economics Report no. 429. Washington, D.C.: U.S. Department of Agriculture, 1979.

U.S. Department of Agriculture. "Cost of Food at Home—U.S. and Regions," *Family Economics Review,* (Summer/Fall 1980), pp. 42–46.

U.S. Department of Agriculture. "Food." Home and Garden Bulletin no. 228. Washington, D.C.: U.S. Government Printing Office, 1980.

Wenck, Dorothy A.; Baren, Martin; and Dewan, Sat Paul. *Nutrition.* Reston, Va.: Reston Publishing, 1980.

"What's Your Nutrition I.Q.?" *Consumer Reports,* February 1977.

Whelan, Elizabeth, and Stare, Fredrick J. *Panic in the Pantry: Food Facts, Fads and Fallacies.* New York: Atheneum, 1975.

Did You Know That...

- *the United States has 5 percent of the world's population and consumes 30 percent of the world's energy?*

- *a well-fed person uses about as much energy each day as a 100 watt light bulb left on for 24 hours?*

- *half of all cars in the world are in the United States, and they consume about 7 million barrels of oil daily?*

- *you can increase your car's mileage by 20 percent without incurring any major expenses?*

- *an electric water heater is the most energy-expensive electric appliance an average family can own?*

- *a 40 watt fluorescent lamp gives off more light than a 100 watt incandescent bulb, even though it uses less energy?*

- *thousands of solar water heaters were being used in Florida and California in the 1920s?*

- *the largest solar-heated building in the world is in Saudi Arabia?*

- *all large electric appliances must be tested for their energy efficiency, and the results, called the Energy Efficiency Rating (EER), must be prominently displayed wherever the appliance is sold?*

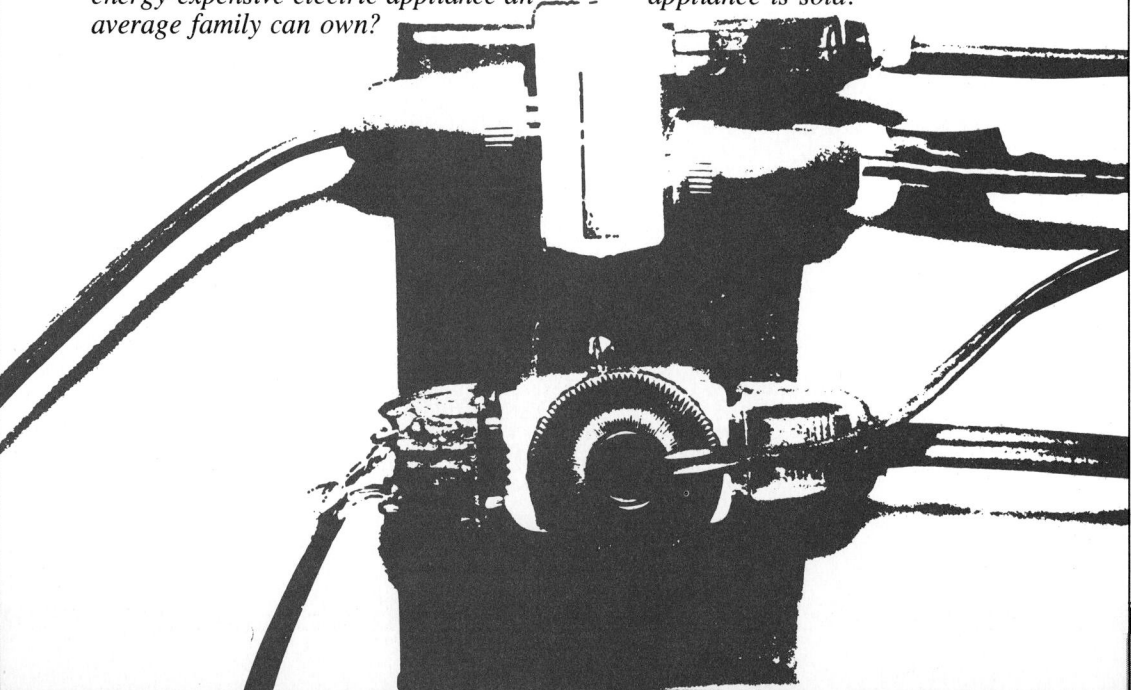

Energy: Conservation Pays

Energy: How Much, What, Who?
Energy and Transportation
Energy Use in the Home
Energy and Your Future

Neighborhood CAPSULE
The High Cost of Commuting

Frank and Melody had just finished their last class of the day and were driving home together, when Melody said, "Let's take the bus to school tomorrow, Frank. It's more energy efficient and cheaper, too."

"Well, I don't know much about energy efficiency," Frank said, "but I know it's not cheaper. Anyone who's had Economics 1 knows that."

It had been a long day, and Melody couldn't resist the temptation to say, "You don't know much about anything, and besides, didn't you drop that course?"

"Yes, but I took it over again and got a C."

"So that makes you an economist?"

"Look," Frank continued, "it costs us 35 cents each way on the bus. That's $1.40 for both of us round trip. It's only about five miles each way, and I get twenty miles per gallon in my Chevette on a bad day. The way I figure it, that's only a half gallon, which is cheaper, even at today's prices."

"But you're not figuring the *total* cost of our trip. By the time you include depreciation, wear and tear on the car, the semester parking sticker, auto insurance, and general maintenance, the real cost is actually higher," Melody concluded smugly. "Why, I'll bet your car's average cost per mile is closer to 20 cents. Just look at the mileage charges on a rental car to see whether or not I'm correct."

"Those extra costs are irrelevant!" Frank continued. "I have most of those expenses whether I drive to school or not. Once I have a car, I have to insure it and maintain it, just as I have to accept the fact that next year it will be worth less than it is this year. And besides, I never have to wait ten minutes to take my car somewhere. My time and privacy have some value too, you know."

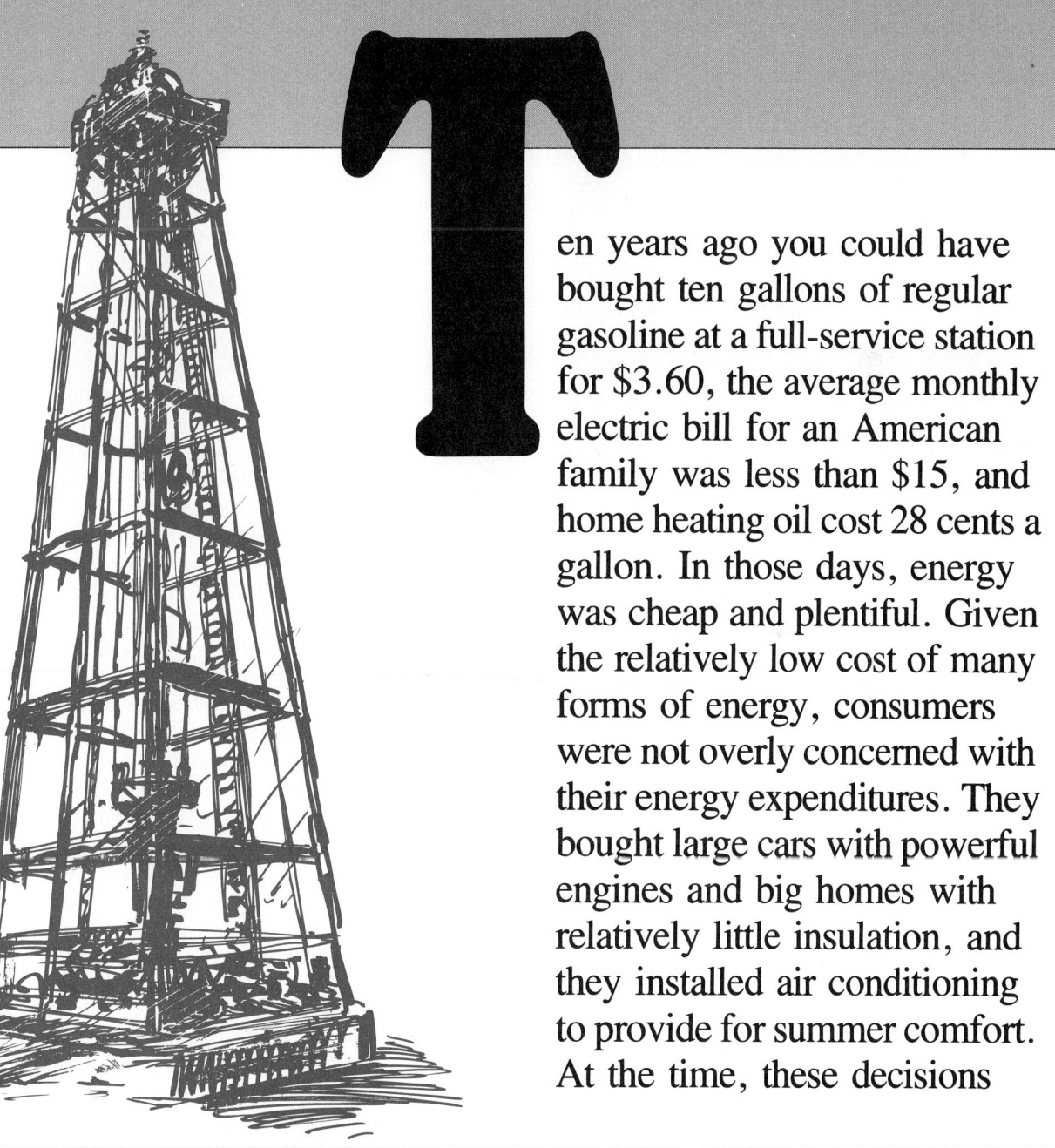

Ten years ago you could have bought ten gallons of regular gasoline at a full-service station for $3.60, the average monthly electric bill for an American family was less than $15, and home heating oil cost 28 cents a gallon. In those days, energy was cheap and plentiful. Given the relatively low cost of many forms of energy, consumers were not overly concerned with their energy expenditures. They bought large cars with powerful engines and big homes with relatively little insulation, and they installed air conditioning to provide for summer comfort. At the time, these decisions

Fossil fuels are currently our most valuable energy source. However, once they are used, they cannot be replenished.

seemed to make good sense. There was even some talk about eliminating electricity meters, because the use of cheap, nuclear-based electricity would have made it uneconomical for someone to read a meter. It was thought that electricity bills would become like the charges for water in most communities—you would pay a flat monthly fee and then you could use as much as you wanted.

The realities of the 1980s are vastly different from those of the 1970s. The prices of conventional forms of energy—such as oil, natural gas, and even coal—have risen dramatically since 1973, and nuclear power has not demonstrated its ability to provide the safe, cheap, trouble-free electric power that many people predicted. Today, consumers are much more concerned about their energy expenditures and about the energy costs of houses, automobiles, refrigerators, and even waterbeds. Higher energy prices make it more worth-while for the consumer to allocate more time to energy decision making.

Another concern of many consumers is the impact of their consumption on world-wide energy demand. Post-industrial-age consumers (see Chapter 2) are interested in minimizing their energy demands for the good of the environment. They are more "eco-conscious" than other consumers, and they see **energy conservation** as having social as well as economic value. These consumers point to the voracious energy appetite of the American economy, and they say that we cannot continue to use up a disproportionate share of the world's resources. Of course, one expects an economy with an annual GNP of $3 trillion to consume a great deal of energy, and it does. Currently, the United States has 5 percent of the world's population, and it consumes over 30 percent of the world's energy, including 49 percent of the natural gas, 30 percent of the oil, and 20 percent of the coal. In a typical year, 230 million Americans use more energy to air condition their homes and businesses than 800 million Chinese use for all purposes (Miller, 1980).

From a global perspective, it may be difficult to maintain our current share of the energy pie, because other nations will begin demanding a larger share as their economies begin producing more. We have an added problem here, because many of our most useful energy sources—oil, coal, and natural gas—are nonreusable. Once they are gone, they cannot be replenished. Whether or not you agree with postindustrial-age values, you should realize that worldwide energy demand will increase throughout the remainder of the twentieth century. Because technological breakthroughs take time and are unpredictable, Americans are going to have to learn to cope with high energy prices. This means becoming better decision makers regarding energy expenditures and energy conservation. The first section in this chapter outlines energy usage in the United States: How much we are using, what our major energy sources are, and who the energy consumers are. The next sections single out the two most cost-effective areas for personal energy saving: transportation and housing. Chapters 12 and 13 cover transportation and housing in detail, but here we emphasize the benefits that intelligent decision making can bring in conserving energy and saving money. In the final section, we take a look at our energy future and discuss potential solutions to our energy dilemma.

Figure 11-1. A comparison of energy consumption and population growth in the United States, 1850–1980.

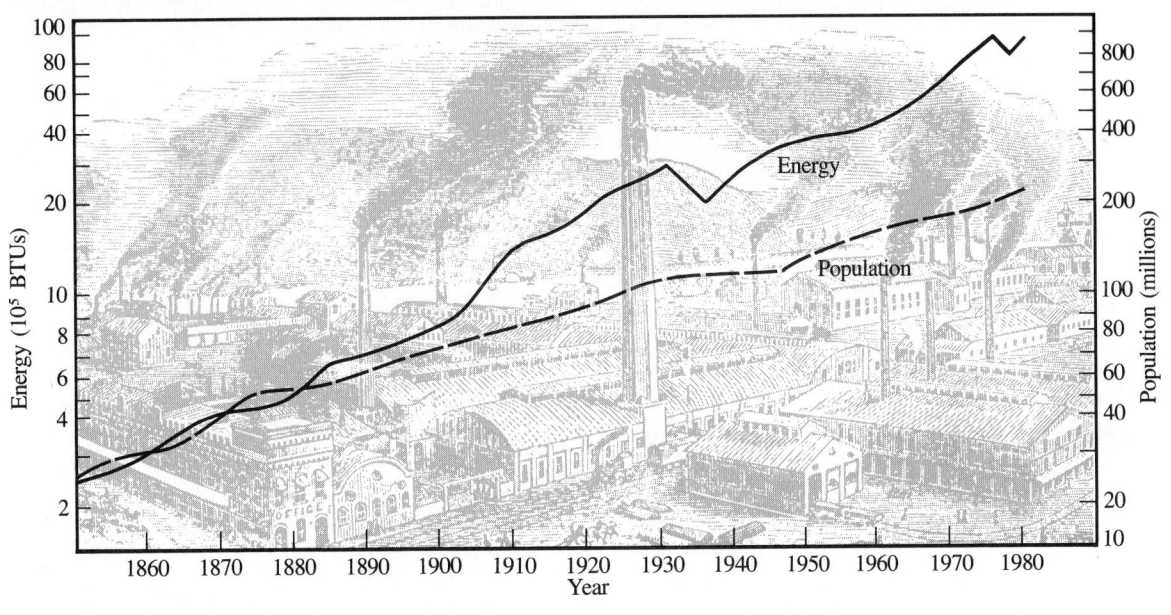

SOURCE: Reprinted with permission from John M. Fowler, "Energy and the Environment," *The Science Teacher* (December 1972), published by the National Science Teachers Association.

Energy: How Much, What, Who?

Whenever you turn on a light, start your car, eat dinner, or bicycle to school, you are using **energy**. Energy is defined as the ability to do work. At the most basic level, a person needs energy from food to survive. A typical well-fed American consumer uses about as much energy each day as a 100 watt light bulb uses in 24 hours (Hayes, 1977). But energy consumption goes far beyond food; it includes the energy used to provide us with our way of life—the energy to plow fields, transport people, provide shelter, and so forth.

If we measure energy as many scientists do, in **kilocalories**—the amount of heat energy needed to raise the temperature of one kilogram of water by one degree Celsius—we can estimate that an average person needs about 2,000 kilocalories per day to survive.

In order to provide for the most basic needs of their people, early agricultural societies used about 12,000 kilocalories per day per person. Early industrial societies that had power machinery (eighteenth-century England, for example) averaged 60,000 kilocalories in daily energy use for each inhabitant. In the United States today, the per capita energy consumption has reached 250,000 kilocalories per day, with only a few thousand of those derived from food.

Life in twentieth-century America has become energy dependent. For example, many of us live many miles from where we work. This means we must commute long distances—a significant energy expenditure in that a gallon of gasoline contains about 30,000 kilocalories. The electricity we use in our homes is also a significant part of our increased energy use, because during each kilowatt hour, 1,160 kilocalories are used. Even the polyester fabrics we wear use energy—it is made from petroleum. In addition, all record albums and plastic items are energy-rich, petroleum-based products. If all the energy that the average American uses daily were derived from coal, each of us would need about 78 pounds of coal to supply our needs.

Figure 11-1 illustrates the trend in American

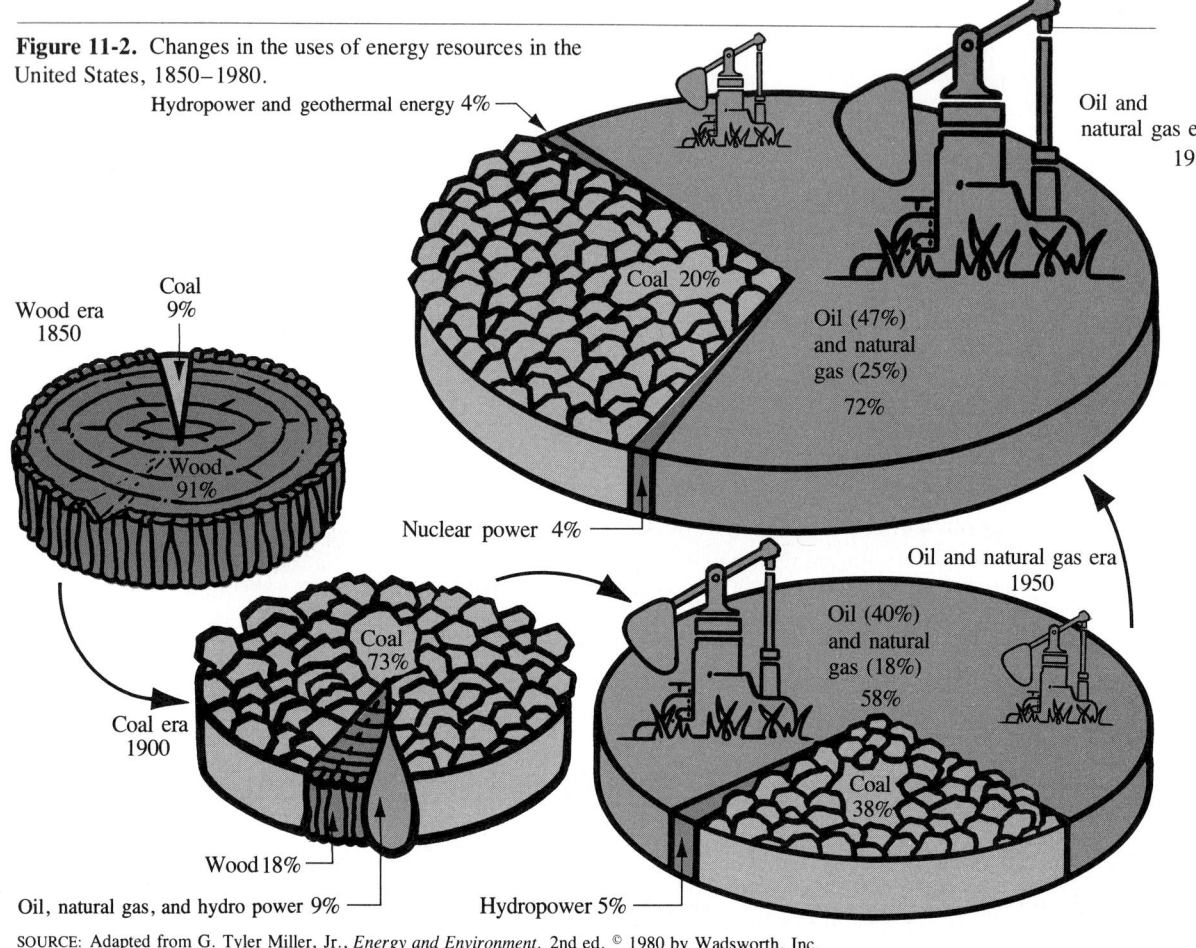

Figure 11-2. Changes in the uses of energy resources in the United States, 1850–1980.

SOURCE: Adapted from G. Tyler Miller, Jr., *Energy and Environment,* 2nd ed. © 1980 by Wadsworth, Inc. Reprinted by permission of the publisher.

energy use from 1850 to 1980. The population growth gives some perspective on the causes of increased energy use. After all, a larger population consumes more energy. Notice that energy consumption and population grew at parallel rates until the end of the nineteenth century, when the United States entered the age of high mass consumption. From this time forward, energy growth outstripped population growth, except during the 1930s, when energy consumption showed a decline. If energy costs continue to outpace the overall inflation rate, the last quarter of the twentieth century may repeat the 1930s pattern and halt our seemingly endless need for more energy.

What are our energy sources? Figure 11-2 illustrates the sources of energy in the United States over the last 130 years. In the mid-nineteenth century, Americans depended on wood, a form of stored solar energy. By 1900, however, the United States emerged as an industrial civilization largely dependent on coal, oil, and natural gas. These sources of energy are often called **fossil fuels,** because they are the remains (fossils) of plants and animals that died millions of years ago. Although the mix of these energy-giving fuels changed over time as the United States moved from the coal era to the oil and natural-gas era, we could still be said to be solar dependent, because all of these fossils

Figure 11-3. Uses of energy in the United States, by sector.

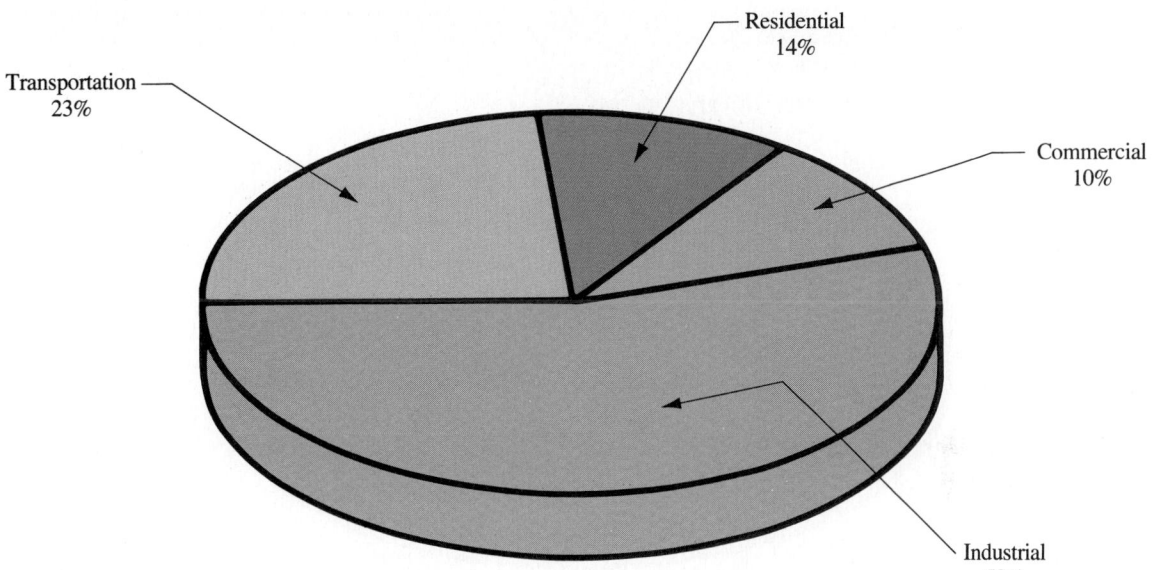

SOURCES: Adapted from G. Tyler Miller, Jr., *Energy and Environment,* 2nd ed. © 1980 by Wadsworth, Inc. Reprinted by permission of the publisher.

depended on the sun at one time. Certainly, no one would dispute our current quandary, which is: How can we continue to use up a finite energy source?

It is certainly not solely the responsibility of consumers to solve America's energy dilemma. The various levels of government and industry must also play important roles, but we as consumers can do much to help. And in the process of adjusting our individual energy budgets, we have the added satisfaction of knowing that we are contributing an important part of the overall solution. Imagine that our energy problem is a large jigsaw puzzle with millions of pieces. Many of these pieces belong to consumers, and if we neglect to put them in their proper places, no effort by industry or government will ever be able to reconstruct the whole picture.

How much of the energy puzzle do consumers control? Figure 11-3 shows the uses of energy in the United States. As you can see, American industry uses 53 percent, firms engaged in commercial activity (banks and retail stores, for example) use 10 percent, private residences consume 14 percent, and various forms of transportation use 23 percent. Consumers have a limited voice in how commercial and industrial sectors use energy, but we have a major impact on residential and transportation uses. By examining our consumer roles in these two areas, we can save ourselves money as well as contribute to conserving more of the world's energy for the future. Informed decision making about transportation use can pay handsome dividends for us and for those around us. We turn now to some specific opportunities for saving energy and money.

Energy and Transportation

According to the Department of Agriculture, in 1979 transportation cost the average household $965—13 percent of its after-tax income. This was the third straight year that a larger share of disposable income was used for transportation than for food prepared in

Figure 11-4. Transportation uses of energy in the United States.

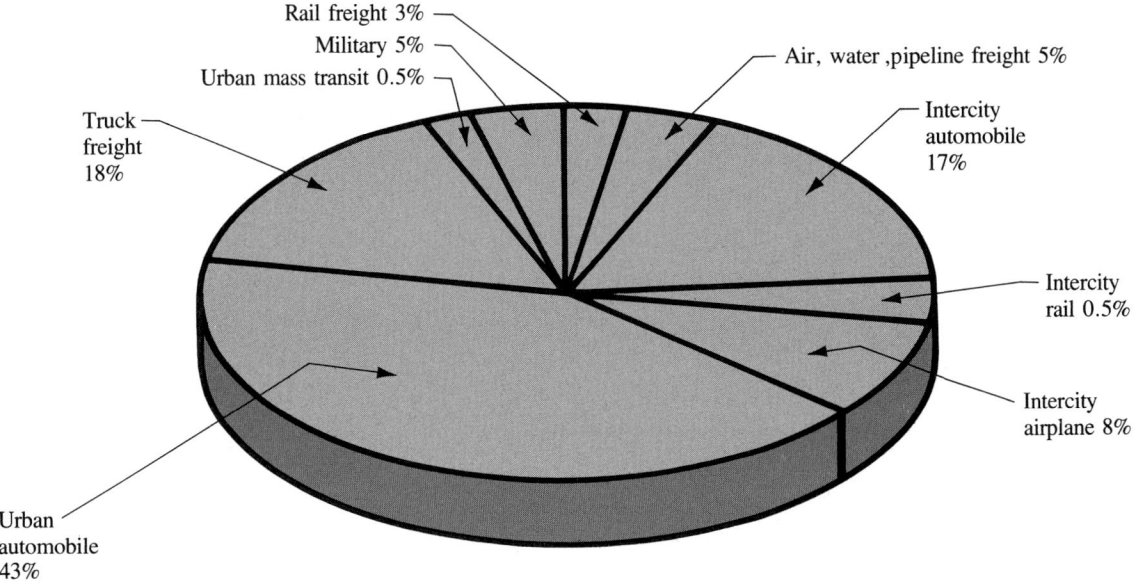

SOURCE: Adapted from G. Tyler Miller, Jr., *Energy and Environment*, 2nd ed. © 1980 by Wadsworth, Inc. Reprinted by permission of the publisher.

the home, which averaged 12.3 percent of disposable income that year (*Food News for Consumers,* June 1980). Clearly, when an expenditure looms this large in the consumer's budget, it merits separate consideration. We discuss transportation in detail in Chapter 12, but here we focus on one specific aspect of transportation: energy cost. We will look at alternative ways for consumers to satisfy their need for transportation, while minimizing their energy expenditures. In the process we will review different forms of personal transportation, from the automobile to the moped, as well as mass-transit alternatives such as trains and buses.

THE AUTOMOBILE

Almost one-fourth of the American energy budget is spent on transportation, and, as Figure 11-4 shows, a majority of that energy goes to fuel automobiles. At the present time Americans have over 130 million cars, about half of all the cars in the world. In an average year, twice as many households have new cars delivered as have babies. These cars use resources on a grand scale. It takes almost 7 million barrels of oil a day to feed and maintain these vehicles—more petroleum than is consumed for *all other uses* combined. In addition, each year 72 percent of the rubber, 30 percent of the zinc, and almost 20 percent of the aluminum produced in the United States are used to produce new automobiles, which are eventually discarded at the rate of about 6 million a year.

With rising resource costs and with the average price of a new car exceeding $10,000, we would expect consumers to reevaluate their past consumption habits in relation to automobiles. Perhaps you have thought about whether to purchase a new car or repair your old one. As you will see in Chapter 12, new cars today are more energy efficient than older ones, but the question here is whether the fuel savings justify the additional expense. This calculation may be more heavily weighted in favor of your old car if you choose

Table 11-1. Sources of Increased Energy Efficiency for Automobiles

Sources	Estimated percentage increase in fuel economy (miles per gallon)
No Costs	
Changing driving habits	5.0–10.0
Cruising at 50 mph rather than at 70 mph	12.0–35.0
Correcting tire pressure	5.0
Minor Costs	
Using synthetic oil	2.0
Getting regular tuneups	6.0–12.0
Installing radial tires	3.0–5.0
Major Costs	
Installing manual transmission	10.0
Eliminating air conditioning	5.0–12.0
Getting a lighter car (by 100 pounds)	2.8

to follow some of the suggestions presented here.

Table 11-1 presents some of the ways to make a car more energy efficient. The average American car gets about 15 miles per gallon (mpg), so a 10 percent increase in fuel economy would increase mpg to 16.5. If you drive 10,000 miles per year, a 10 percent fuel-economy increase will save 60 gallons annually. This should save about $90 at $1.50 per gallon. If you drive more, the savings would be even larger. If you follow all of the tips in the table, you can increase your fuel economy by as much as 50 percent. Then again, you might not, because drivers and driving conditions vary from place to place. Nevertheless, in the Shell Mileage Marathon for automobiles, the winner averaged 377 miles per gallon (Hayes, 1977).

The fuel savings suggestions in Table 11-1 are broken down into three categories: those involving no costs, those involving minor costs, and those involving major costs. As we have stressed before, any decision you make depends on more than the explicit dollar costs. The decision to conserve fuel is no exception. Once again, we have to introduce the element of implicit opportunity costs (time costs). Conservation often requires spending more time, if one is to save some money. Conservation may also entail a change in habits and customs as part of the decision-making process. For most consumers, driving becomes almost second nature. They often drive a certain way out of habit, seldom observing or analyzing their behavior. Conservation, at least initially, requires a mental override whereby consumers consciously change the way they drive and even their attitudes toward driving. Whether you choose to adopt any or all of these conservation tips depends on your values and customs, the opportunity costs, and the dollar costs outlined in the table. But before you can weigh the costs and benefits of fuel conservation, you need information.

Better Mileage with No Dollar Outlay. Driving habits include a variety of behaviors. The way you accelerate from a stop, the way you behave in traffic, the number of trips you take, the average distances you drive, and even the way you start your car all affect the mileage you get from a gallon of gasoline.

In order to understand why personal driving habits can have an important impact on your car's fuel efficiency, all you need to remember is that every time you accelerate, you spend energy to overcome friction, and every time you brake, you use friction to negate the energy you spent to help you accelerate. This continuum of spending energy to get your car rolling and then dissipating that energy by braking is one of the most energy-costly activities of driving. This stop-and-go driving accounts for most of the difference in the Environmental Protection Agency's estimates of fuel economy between city and highway driving. To get better fuel economy, you need to be alert to the traffic flow and to the speed that the traffic lights allow. In some cases, there seems to be no pattern, but more and more cities are using traffic engineering and are timing their signals to provide for a safe, orderly flow of traffic at a steady speed. Even if there is no definite pattern, you can still save gasoline by avoiding sharp accelerations or "jackrabbit starts" when the light turns green. You can also save gasoline by consolidating short trips. Going to the market, picking the children up at a dance class, making a bank deposit, and visiting a friend in the hospital could involve four separate trips. If you could consolidate them, you

Table 11-2. Comparison of Fuel and Time Costs at Different Automobile Speeds

Speed	MPG	Distance	Driving time	Fuel needed
50	18	350 miles	7 hours	19.4 gallons
70	15	350 miles	5 hours	23.3 gallons

> **BOX 11-1**
>
> **Average Tuneup Checklist**
>
> 1. Check the battery condition, as well as the electrical cables and terminals.
> 2. Test the ignition and check how efficiently each cylinder compresses the entering gas-air mixture.
> 3. Inspect spark plugs; clean or replace as necessary.
> 4. Inspect distributor (usually involves replacement of the electrical-system ignition points and the condenser).
> 5. Adjust engine timing so that spark plugs fire when the piston compressing the air-gas mixture is at the precise position to deliver maximum power.
> 6. Check fuel system, including cleaning and adjustment of the carburetor and automatic choke and cleaning or replacement of the positive crankcase ventilation (PCV) valve.

---

would use considerably less fuel. One final tip on driving concerns idling your car's engine. It is obvious that you get zero miles per gallon when the engine is idling, but many consumers still believe that they have to warm their engines before they can drive off. This is no longer true. As long as you begin at a moderate speed, there is no need to let the engine idle after starting the car. That only wastes fuel.

Decreasing speed also saves fuel. Cruising at 50 miles per hour rather than at 70 miles per hour can increase fuel economy from 12 to 35 percent, depending on auto design and wind resistance. Of course, it takes longer to get where you are going—time is the opportunity cost of the lower speed. The opportunity cost of your time is a factor to include in your cost-benefit analysis, just as you include money costs. In some cases, it may make sense to go faster, depending on the relationship between time costs and fuel costs.

Table 11-2 compares fuel and time costs. The information is based on the assumption that driving at 50 miles per hour gives about 20 percent better gas mileage and saves about four gallons of gasoline during a 350 mile trip. On the other hand, it takes two hours longer at the slower speed. It makes economic sense to travel slower if the value of the four gallons exceeds the value of the two extra travel hours it takes to get there. This calculation depends, of course, on the price of gasoline and on the value of the driver's time. At 1978 gasoline prices (63 cents per gallon), the savings totals $2.52, or $1.26 per hour. It is little wonder that speeding was a major problem then. Very few consumers consider their time worth so little. But if gasoline were $5 per gallon, the savings would be $20, or $10 per hour. Clearly, this is a much more powerful incentive for conservation.

Routine inspection of tire pressure offers another opportunity to save energy. Keeping the tires as hard as the owner's manual allows minimizes friction and thus raises gas mileage. The five minutes it takes to check the tires can save between $1 and $2 per fillup. If you save $1 dollar per five-minute check, you will have an after-tax saving of $12 per hour.

Fuel Savings Involving Small Dollar Costs. A motor tuneup is probably the best way to increase a car's mileage (see Box 11-1). Generally, tuneups should be done about once a year. According to the U.S. Environmental Protection Agency, "keeping an automobile tuned up can on the average improve fuel economy 6 percent, compared to an untuned automobile." Other estimates double this figure (Porter, 1979).

The cost of a tuneup varies, but a tuneup can generally be done for less than $100. Of course, fuel conservation is only one reason to have a tuneup. Other reasons include prolonging the life of the engine and ensuring the safety and dependability of your major form of transportation. But in some instances, conservation alone may justify a tuneup. One way to tell whether conserving gas justifies a tuneup is to estimate the change in your car's gas mileage after you get a tuneup. If you are a typical driver, you will get between 6 and 12 percent more miles per gallon after the tuneup. Let us assume that you average 8 percent better mileage as a result of the tuneup. If you use 500 gallons per year at your pretuneup mileage, your 8 percent mileage increase saves you 40 gallons (.08 × 500 = 40). Multiply the average cost of a gallon of gasoline by the number of gallons saved to find the value of the fuel savings:

Price of gasoline × gallons saved = Fuel conservation
   per gallon   savings

   $1.60   ×   40 gallons   = $64

Compare this cost to the price of a tuneup to see whether conservation alone makes a tuneup worthwhile.

You can also **retrofit** your car to increase fuel efficiency. This means replacing less-energy-efficient parts with more-energy-efficient ones. Most retrofit techniques work because they reduce friction. Recently developed synthetic oils, for example, are more slippery and thus lubricate better than older, more traditionally formulated motor oils. Less friction within the engine allows the motor to expend less energy on moving its internal parts and more on propelling the car. Radial tires also lower a car's fuel consumption by lessening the friction, although in this case the friction occurs between the tire and the road. Radial tires can increase miles per gallon by 3 to 5 percent. Does such a saving justify the additional cost of a set of radial tires? The answer depends on fuel saving and the size of the cost differential. By now you should be able to compute them and arrive at your own conclusion. But most calculations favor a radial retrofit only if you are already in the market for a new set of tires. In this case, the only cost of retrofitting your car with radials is the *difference* between the price of a set of conventional tires and the cost of radials. Chapter 12 gives more details on purchasing tires, including a discussion of federal tire-grading regulations.

Major Expenditures and Fuel Efficiency. The conservation suggestions listed above can all be tried with your current automobile. On a new car, you can also apply all of these techniques, and you can choose other optional equipment that will further improve its effi-

The lighter a car is, the more miles it will get to the gallon.

ciency. For example, if you choose a manual transmission (preferably one with five forward gears), you can expect to get 10 percent better mileage than a similar car with an automatic transmission. If your new car weighs less than your old car, you can add another 2.8 percent to your fuel economy for every hundred pounds. This can result in a 25 percent improvement in fuel economy if your new car weighs 900 pounds less than your old one. If you can do without air conditioning, you may save another 5 to 12 percent, although recent studies show that such a saving is almost nil at highway speeds if you have to leave your windows open to cool off. The additional wind resistance (friction) negates the fuel economy gained by eliminating air conditioning. It is highly unlikely that fuel savings alone will pay for the expenses involved in purchasing a new car. Of course, circumstances differ among individuals. For example, a consumer who uses his or her car sparingly and drives only 4,000 miles a year will be less likely to consider fuel efficiency an important criterion for getting another car. On the other hand, a salesperson who drives 35,000 miles a year will have an entirely different cost-benefit calculation.

During a major transit strike, many New Yorkers discovered the advantages of the bicycle.

OTHER FORMS OF PERSONAL TRANSPORTATION

The automobile is not the only form of personal transportation. People use everything from private planes to roller skates to get them from one place to another. The range of choices is quite large, but we will focus on the bicycle, the motorcycle, and the moped, all of which offer attractive energy-saving alternatives to cars. Of the three alternatives, the bicycle is the most energy efficient.

The Bicycle. Bicycling is not only more efficient than using mopeds or motorcycles, it is even more efficient than walking, because of the mechanical advantage of gears and wheels. A bicyclist traveling at 10 miles per hour uses only 25 kilocalories per mile, whereas a pedestrian walking at 2.5 miles per hour uses five times that amount per mile, even though he or she is traveling one-quarter as fast. Because a gallon of gasoline contains 30,000 kilocalories, the bicyclist obtains the energy equivalent of more than 1,000 miles per gallon—considerably more miles per gallon than a Volkswagen or a Chevette. And the bicyclist uses food rather than petroleum for energy (Hayes, 1977). The bicycle's value becomes even greater when you realize that 43 percent of all urban driving involves trips of less than five miles and that in traffic, both cars and bicycles travel at the same average speed—13 mph (Miller, 1980).

If the bicycle is such a great invention, why doesn't everyone ride one? In Holland almost everyone does. Holland has 11 million bicycles and 13 million people. In the United States, over 10 million bicycles are sold every year, and the United States is estimated to have more than 100 million bikes nationwide. But there are several factors that limit their use:

1. *Comfort.* Bicycles, like their two-wheel cousins the motorcycle and the moped, have no roofs. As anyone who has ever been caught bicycling during a rainstorm can tell you, it can be miserable. And in cold weather or in snow storms, bicycling is extremely difficult.

2. *Safety.* A bicycle takes only one-thirtieth of the space of an automobile, which is good if you want to reduce congestion but bad if you want to be seen. Small vehicles and bikes are frequently overlooked by motorists, with tragic results for the cyclist. In the United States alone, more than 1,000 people are killed in bicycle accidents each year, and another 500,000 are injured, mostly from collisions with cars. Add to this the fact that modern bicycle brakes are unreliable in wet weather, and you have some important reasons for not using the bicycle to commute to work.

3. *Poor facilities.* Despite the fact that there are about 30,000 miles of bikepaths and bicycle lanes in the United States, a major complaint of bike riders is the inadequacy of safe bikeways. A Philadelphia survey showed that 38 percent of all bicycle owners would use their bikes to commute to work if this problem could be corrected (Environmental Protection Agency, 1974). This survey also points out the problem of finding secure parking facilities. Where can you put your bike once you are at work? Another problem is that of perspiration. If showers were readily available at the workplace, more commuters would probably be willing to ride their bikes during the warm summer months.

4. *Health*. Although there is evidence that moderate exercise of the kind that bicycling provides can help stimulate the heart and the circulation, it does not take into account the problems a bicyclist has when he or she is caught in heavy traffic, where the air is rich in lead, hydrocarbons, and carbon monoxide from the exhausts of idling autos and may have unhealthful effects on the bicyclist.

5. *Time*. The opportunity costs of the potential bicyclist's time must also be considered. Although autos and bikes average identical speeds in heavy urban traffic, their speeds differ radically as traffic lightens. At 10 miles per hour, a bicycle can commute 20 miles in 2 hours, but the same distance can be covered in only 30 minutes in a car, which can easily average 40 mph.

The Moped. Some consumers neglect the bicycle because of the basic muscle power it requires. For these folks, and for the fainthearted who prefer motored transportation, the **moped** may be a viable option. The moped can be operated like a standard bicycle, because it has pedals and gears, but it also has a small one- or two-horsepower engine capable of powering the vehicle up to 30 miles per hour. This hybrid is very popular in Europe, and it has world-wide distribution of almost 40 million. Moped prices range from $400 to over $1000, and the moped gets over 100 miles per gallon and has a better safety record than its better-known cousin, the motorcycle.

With all of these advantages, it is little wonder that ownership of mopeds in the United States has risen dramatically in recent years. The National Highway Traffic Safety Administration (NHTSA) estimates that only 25,000 Americans owned mopeds in 1974, but by 1980 there were almost 1 million on American roads. The NHTSA expects that by 1984 there will be over 2.5 million of these vehicles putting along our streets (*Consumers Digest*, 1981). Because the vehicle is a cross between a bicycle and a motorcycle, some states have chosen to view it as similar to a bicycle and impose few regulations. Other states have opted to treat it more like a motorcycle and require the operator to be licensed and to register the moped.

Motorcycles. Motorcycles are more energy efficient than cars, but they are less efficient than mopeds or bicycles. Some smaller motorcycles may weigh less than 300 pounds. They have modest engine sizes (generally less than 200 cubic centimeters), can get up to 70 miles per gallon, and cost between $600 and $1500. Larger varieties can have engines that rival those of small cars, as does the 1340 cc engine in the huge Harley-Davidson that many police officers ride. As with most cars, the larger the engine, the lower the gas mileage. Besides having higher energy costs, larger cycles are priced two to three times higher. Insurance is another cost that must be considered before deciding to buy a motorcycle. We will discuss automobile insurance in detail in Chapter 12, but consumers should be aware that a motorcycle that weighs under 300 pounds costs about 50 percent more for a basic insurance package than a car does. For big cycles (those over 300 pounds), insurance rates are three times the basic automobile insurance rate (Porter, 1979). A final problem to consider is one's physical ability to handle a 300 or 500 pound machine. Most consumers have little problem with a 50 pound bike or a moped that weighs less than 100 pounds. But could they pick up a motorcycle if it toppled to the ground?

MASS TRANSIT

Transportation is a necessity; personal transportation is a luxury. In our society most people insist on mobility, but going it alone is not best for energy conservation. In your own everyday experience, you see dozens of automobiles traveling here and there with only one person in them. Kenneth Boulding, an economist at the University of Colorado, once remarked that if the United States were to be visited by intelligent beings from outer space, their initial impression would probably be that the dominant form of life here consists of hard-shelled creatures with soft pulpy insides, who are propelled by wheels, although the creatures are capa-

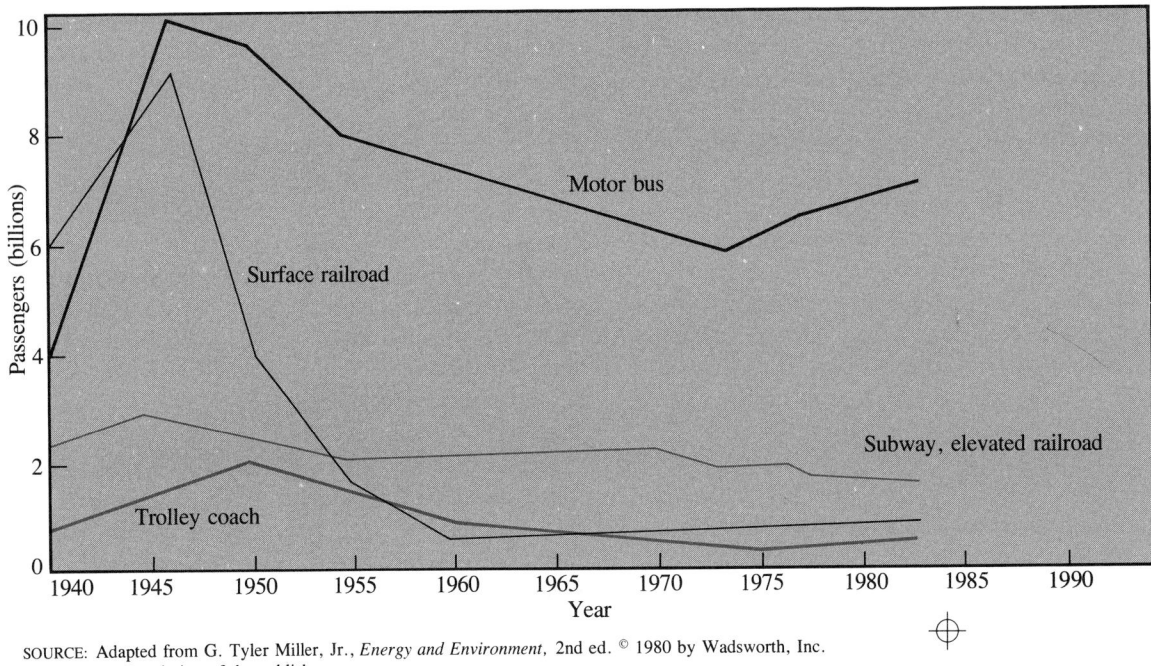

Figure 11-5. Mass transit use in the United States.

SOURCE: Adapted from G. Tyler Miller, Jr., *Energy and Environment*, 2nd ed. © 1980 by Wadsworth, Inc. Reprinted by permission of the publisher.

ble of sluggish motion on their own when not encased in their natural external skeletons (Heilbroner, 1975). Because urban cars carry an average of 1.4 persons at a time, Boulding's characterization does not seem so farfetched.

Figure 11-5 illustrates the number of passengers using mass transit from 1940 to the present. Notice that the peak was achieved in 1945, at the end of World War II. From then until 1974, a steady decline took place. The decline resulted from logical decision making by individual consumers, and it eventually led to some massive transportation problems and congestion. After World War II, consumer incomes began to rise steadily. Good, low-cost housing became available on the outskirts of most major cities, and the real price of gasoline began to decline. Higher incomes, lower-density housing, cheaper gasoline, and the construction of new freeways (see Box 11-2) all weighted the consumer's cost-benefit calculations away from mass transit and toward personal transit. Of course, the private car has always had several advantages over the bus or the trolley. The car is convenient both in terms of scheduling—it is available on a moment's notice—and in terms of convenience—it offers door-to-door service. The automobile also offers something that Americans find lacking in mass transit—privacy. These benefits were significant in motivating people to buy cars. And once people bought cars, once it became normal to have a car, the cost calculations became loaded against mass transit.

The average cost of owning an automobile is quite high (see Chapter 12), but once you have a car, the marginal cost of a particular trip is considerably lower than the average cost of owning an automobile. The **marginal cost** of a trip is the cost of getting in the car and going somewhere. In essence, this is the price of gasoline, and it could vary between 3 and 10 cents per mile. A four-mile commute might result in an out-of-pocket expense of 40 cents. Private bus companies, on the other hand, must charge enough to lower service, which results in fewer riders, lower revenues, and increased fares once again.

Over the 1974 to 1979 period, the downward trend in mass transit ridership began to reverse. The rising price of oil coupled with increased governmental subsidies led many consumers to reevaluate their cost-benefit calculations for transportation. With the help of the Federal Department of Transportation, cities such as Atlanta, Denver, Los Angeles, Portland, and St. Louis reduced bus fares, increased service, and witnessed a resurgence in consumer interest. Free fares in downtown Seattle tripled the number of daily bus rides and reduced automobile traffic by 7 percent. These developments, when combined with the rising cost of gasoline, offer some hope for the future of mass transit.

RIDESHARING: A PERSONAL ALTERNATIVE TO MASS TRANSIT

It's nice to leave the driving to someone else, especially when commuting to work. But buses can be late, crowded, and generally uncomfortable, and the weather (and sometimes fellow passengers) can be unpleasant at times. If you would like to reduce your transportation-energy consumption and save money, but you do not like mass transit, you should consider **ridesharing.** Under this arrangement, commuters who live and work near one another share driving, and usually the expenses of commuting, by taking only one vehicle. When they take turns driving, they belong to what is called a *shared-driving car pool*. Although car-pool drivers should carry additional automobile insurance, most insurance companies offer a 10 percent discount for reduced commuter work mileage. A *shared-riding car pool* uses only one car and one driver, and it results in even greater savings because of further reduced insurance costs.

Table 11-3 shows the annual per-person costs of commuting to work with and without ridesharing. As you can see, even in a short 10 mile commute, a two-person car pool can cut driving costs by $300 for a subcompact Chevette, and by $500 for a larger car such as a Chevrolet Caprice or a Ford LTD. A long commute, say 40 miles one way, would cost almost $2200 if driven alone in a subcompact, but it would cost only $1250 if car pooled with another person,

---

BOX 11-2
The Highway Trust Fund: Biased Against Mass Transit?

The Public Highway Act of 1956 established the Highway Trust Fund, which by 1976 was receiving about $6.7 billion a year from taxes on gasoline, trucks, buses, tires, and vehicle parts. Since 1956, these funds have been used to finance 90 percent of the costs of interstate highways and freeways, the construction of which has encouraged urban sprawl. After a long battle by environmentalists, the Federal Aid Highway Acts of 1973 and 1976 allowed more money from this fund to be used for other purposes. States can use funds approved for interstate highways for mass transit, paratransit (moving small groups of people), and other transportation programs. But this alternate use is discouraged, because the federal government puts up 90 percent of the cost of highway projects and only 80 percent of the cost of substitute projects. Thus, states and cities must put up twice as much money for mass transit as for highways.

There has been pressure to set up a separate trust fund for mass transit, but such an approach could be disastrous. It would separate planning for highways from planning for mass transit, and it would emphasize expensive, highly technological mass transit projects that do not solve many urban transportation problems. The United States needs to eliminate the Highway Trust Fund and create a transportation fund. Revenues from such a fund might be used to plan and finance balanced, integrated transportation programs rather than programs that overemphasize highway or mass-transit schemes that waste money, energy, and material resources (Miller, 1980).

---

cover their **average cost,** which includes maintenance, wear and tear on the equipment, and insurance, in addition to the cost of gasoline and wages. This marginal-versus-average-cost dilemma is at the heart of the decline in bus ridership. Because the automobile is almost always more convenient, bus fares have to be equal to, and preferably lower than, the marginal cost of driving. Private bus companies in most urban areas simply cannot meet the competition. As mass transit costs rise, companies raise fares or

Table 11-3. Annual Costs (Per Person) of Commuting to Work (in 1979 dollars)

Cost Category:
Operating = costs for gasoline, oil, tires, repairs and maintenance.[1]
Owning = costs for insurance, depreciation, finance charges, taxes and license fees.

One-way commute (miles)	Vehicle type	Cost category	Drive alone	Ridesharing Options				Vanpool	
				Shared-driving carpool[2]		Shared-riding carpool[3]			
				2-person	4-person	2-person	4-person	8-person	12-person
10	Subcompact (Pinto, Chevette, etc.)	Operating	$412	$206	$103	$206	$103		
		Owning	314	192	114	157	79		
		Total	726	398	217	363	182	$ 82	$ 54
	Standard (LTD, Caprice, etc.)	Operating	620	310	155	310	155	372	248
		Owning	442	272	161	221	111	454	302
		Total	1062	582	316	531	266		
20	Subcompact	Operating	823	412	206	412	206		
		Owning	439	306	192	220	110		
		Total	1262	718	398	632	316	163	109
	Standard	Operating	1240	620	310	620	310	372	248
		Owning	617	433	272	309	155	525	357
		Total	1857	1053	582	929	465		
40	Subcompact	Operating	1646	823	412	823	412		
		Owning	548	427	306	274	137		
		Total	2194	1250	718	1097	549	327	218
	Standard	Operating	2480	1240	620	1240	620	372	248
		Owning	771	604	433	386	183	699	466
		Total	3251	1844	1053	1626	813		

1. Gasoline costs based on $1 per gallon.
2. Shared-driving: Poolers take turns using their cars and must carry car insurance that covers driving to and from work. Each pooler gets a 10 percent insurance discount because of reduced work mileage.
3. Shared-riding: One person's car is used. Insurance is based on distance being driven to and from work and must be provided for only the pool car. Car costs are shared equally by poolers.
SOURCE: "Rideshare and Save—A Cost Comparison," Federal Highway Administration, U.S. Department of Transportation, 1979.

---

sharing expenses—almost a $1000 saving. These data are based on 1979 gasoline prices, about $1 per gallon. Today, the savings are even greater.

Ridesharing combines the convenience and assurance of personal transit with the lower cost and energy-saving qualities of mass transit. The difficulty comes in locating ridesharing companions. Many cities and counties promote ridesharing by setting aside special lanes for car poolers and by providing free telephone service for matching drivers and riders. Louisville, Kentucky has been particularly successful in its ridesharing program. The California Department of Transportation is using the Commuter Computer, developed by ARCO, to help match ridesharers. This

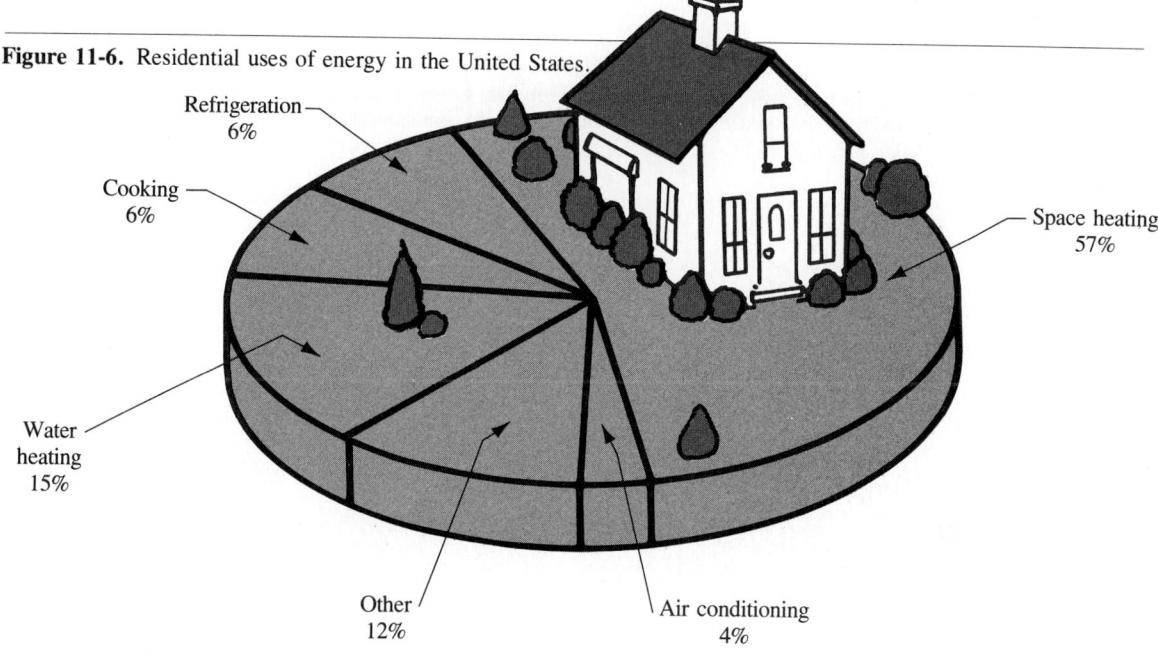

Figure 11-6. Residential uses of energy in the United States.

SOURCE: Adapted from G. Tyler Miller, Jr., *Energy and Environment*, 2nd ed. © 1980 by Wadsworth, Inc. Reprinted by permission of the publisher.

saves California commuters an estimated 2 million gallons of gasoline a year (*People Power*, 1980, p. 244).

For more information on ridesharing programs write or call:

Commuter Computer
3325 Wilshire Boulevard, Ninth Floor
Los Angeles, California 90010
(213) 380-7433

Commuter Connection
3020 Bridgeway Boulevard, Suite 106
Sausalito, California 94965
(415) 332-8333

Energy Use in the Home

The second most important area in which consumers can personally affect their energy demand is in home energy use, which accounts for 14 percent of America's total energy use. Government agencies, public utilities, and universities have all sponsored studies to test various home energy-saving strategies. In the sections that follow we present the results of these studies and offer some ideas on how to conserve residential energy use. Of course, which strategy you choose to adopt depends on your evaluation of the costs and the benefits. But as we mentioned earlier, energy use has both a personal and a society-wide dimension. On a personal level, one's strategy should be to adopt the energy conservation techniques that promise the greatest benefit for the lowest cost. On a society-wide level, American consumers will see a decrease in the demand followed by a decline, or at least a more modest rise, in the real price of energy, if they begin to conserve energy. Both of these developments would give consumers more money to spend (or save) than they would have if they did not conserve energy.

MEASURING HOME ENERGY USE

Home energy costs differ among households for a variety of reasons. Geographic location, size of the family, the type of residence, and the sources of available energy are among the most important. Figure 11-6

Figure 11-7. How to read your gas meter. Read the large dials only. (The small dials at the top are for test purposes.) On each dial, a hand points between two numbers. Write down the smaller of these numbers. Read the larger dials from left to right. For example, the reading in the illustration below is 6084.

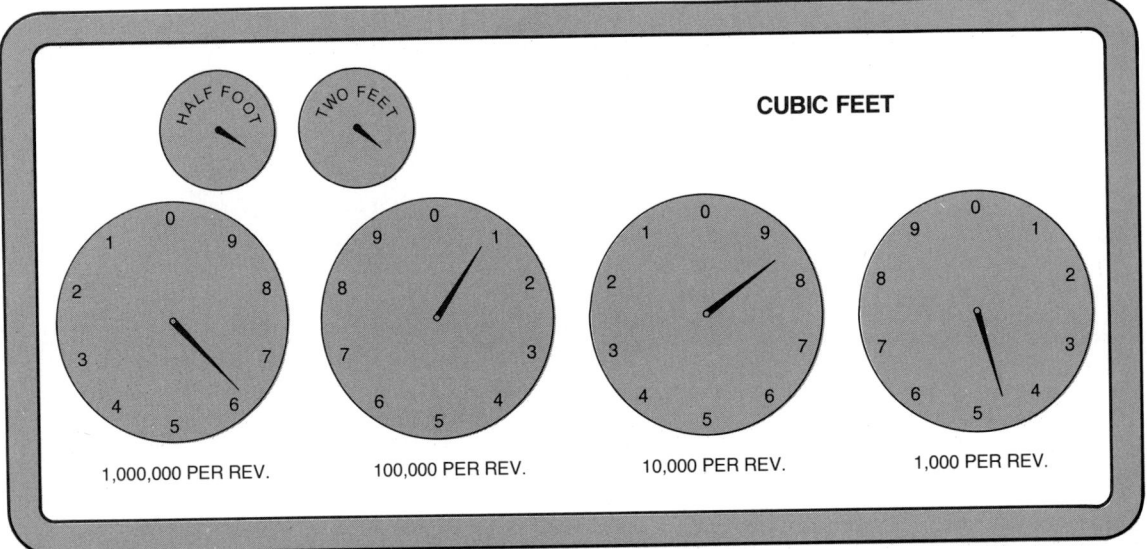

SOURCE: Adapted from "Answer Book" (Anaheim, Calif.: Southern California Gas Company, 1981).

cuts across all of these factors and develops a profile of total residential energy use in the United States. Most home energy use (57 percent) is devoted to heating or cooling. In fact, the vast majority of the energy we use in our homes is aimed at either heating or cooling something. For example, water heating uses 15 percent of our domestic energy, and refrigerator/freezers and cooking appliances each use 6 percent. When household air conditioning needs are added (4 percent) only 12 percent of household energy remains for tasks such as lighting, and running appliances such as televisions, stereos, and clock radios. Figure 11-6 is based on national data, so in order to estimate your personal potential payoff from home energy conservation, you need some information about how much energy you are currently using, what kind of energy it is, and where it is being used.

For most consumers, monitoring energy use in the home should be no more difficult than calculating a car's miles per gallon. All homes and most apartments have meters conveniently located so the gas and electric company can determine the energy usage over a period of time, usually a month. Company meter readers perform this task, but you can be your own meter reader once you understand the basics of the system.

Reading the Gas Meter. Natural gas is measured by volume, generally in cubic feet. A standard gas meter looks like the one in Figure 11-7. The important dials are labeled A, B, and C. Read the dials from left to right, and record the lowest number next to the pointer. The only exception to the "lower-number rule" occurs when the pointer is between the 0 and the 9. If you are not certain whether the pointer has reached a particular number, look at the dial immediately to the right to see whether the needle has passed 0. If it has not passed 0, record the lower number for the first dial. After your next reading, subtract the smaller number from the

Figure 11-8. How to read your electric meter. The dials are like watch faces lined in a row (every other dial moves counterclockwise). The reading for a five-dial meter is 16,064. The reading for a four-dial meter is 6,064. When the pointer is between two numbers, record the lower of the two numbers. When the pointer seems to be directly on a number, look at the dial to the right; if the pointer on the right-side dial has passed 0, write down the number the pointer seems to be on; if the pointer on the right-side dial has not passed 0, write down the lower number of the first dial.

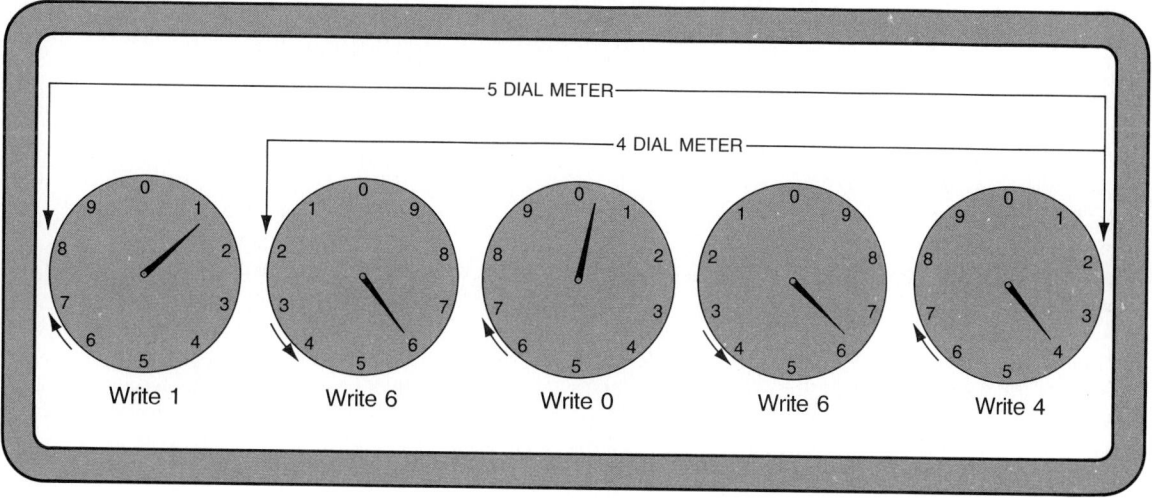

SOURCE: Used by permission of Southern California Edison Company.

larger one to determine how much gas you have used over the period of time. To gauge the dollar effectiveness of your energy conservation, multiply the amount of gas you have used by the cost per hundred cubic feet of gas. Many utility companies charge by an energy measure called a **therm**—the amount of heat energy required to raise the temperature of 100,000 pounds of water by one degree Fahrenheit. Because a hundred cubic feet of gas contains approximately one therm of energy, you can multiply the change on your meter by the price of therms (usually between 30 and 80 cents) to estimate your natural gas costs.

Reading the Electric Meter. Your electric consumption is measured in kilowatt-hours, abbreviated kwh. One kilowatt-hour is 1,000 watts of electricity used for one hour, or 100 watts (a 100 watt bulb for example) used for 10 hours. All electrical appliances sold in the United States have a wattage rating label on them. To determine the number of kilowatt-hours used by an appliance, simply multiply the wattage rating by the number of hours the appliance is used. A color television, for example, may use 200 watts per hour. If the set is used an average of six hours per day, the monthly electricity usage will rise by six hours × 30 days × 200 watts (36,000 watt-hours or 36 kilowatts). At 6 cents per kwh, the power to run your TV set will cost about $2.16 per month.

Electricity meters are read in much the same way as gas meters. The only difference in the meters is the number and the location of the dials. There are generally four or five dials on the meter, and they are read using the same "lower-number rule" suggested above. Look at Figure 11-8 and read the meter yourself before looking at the answer provided. Once you know the number of kilowatt-hours used, multiply it by the price of those hours (usually 6 to 8 cents per hour) to determine the cost of electricity over that period.

Table 11-4. Estimated Average Monthly Kilowatt-hour Consumption of Electric Household Appliances*

Electric Appliance	Kilowatt-hours used per month	Average wattage†	Frequency of use in home
Blanket	24	177	6 mo. (nighttime)
Blender	1	386	15 min. per week
Clock	1	2	continuous
Clothes washer	9	512	26 loads per month
Clothes dryer	87	4856	26 loads per month
Coffee maker	9	894	Two 8 cup pots per day
Dishwasher	35	1201	1 rinse-hold and 1 complete wash per day
Freezer (frost-free)			
16 cu. ft.	150		continuous
20 cu. ft.	158		continuous
24 cu. ft.	167		continuous
Frypan	16	1196	1 hour per day
Garbage disposal	3	445	1 minute per day
Hair dryer	1	381	15 min. per week
Iron	6	1008	2 hours per week
Knife	<1	92	15 min. per week
Mixer	1	127	2 hrs. per week
Microwave oven	16	1450	18 min. per day
Radio	7	71	3 hours per day
Radio/phonograph	9	109	3 hours per day
Range	98	12200	3 meals per day
Range with self-cleaning oven	100	12200	1 cleaning per month
Refrigerator (frost-free)			
12 cu. ft.	101		continuous
16 cu. ft.	150		continuous
20 cu. ft.	209		continuous
24 cu. ft.	262		continuous
Room air conditioner	92–250		3–7½ hr. per day (summer) 10,000 BTU
Television (black and white)			
tube	30	160	6 hours per day
solid state	10	55	6 hours per day
Television (color)			
tube	55	300	6 hours per day
solid state	37	200	6 hours per day
Toaster	3	1146	5 minutes per day
Toothbrush	<1	7	3 minutes per day
Trash compactor	4	400	20 minutes per day
Water heater	500	4474	continuous

*Kilowatt-hours are for a typical family of four and based on national averages. More or less may be used, depending on family habits.
†Average wattage is taken from the nameplate of the appliance.
SOURCE: Southern California Edison Company, *Residential Conservation Handbook* (1980).

Using a clothesline rather than an electric dryer not only saves electricity but also makes clothes feel and smell fresh.

Additional Meter Monitoring. Utility companies list on the bill the amount of energy consumed for a month, in kilowatt-hours for electricity or in therms for gas. Recently, many companies have begun to include comparative figures for present and past years, both by month and by daily average. If your daily average in August was 15.8 kwh this year and 20.2 kwh last year, it could mean that it was cooler this year and so you used less air conditioning, that you have been conserving by setting the thermostat higher, or both. It is for you to determine. But with information such as this on the bill, you get an indication of what your habits save you or cost you.

SAVING ENERGY IN THE HOME

With the help of your local public utility company and with a few lessons on meter reading, you can begin to get a better idea of how much energy you consume at home. The next step is to put yourself and your home on an energy diet. Instead of counting calories, you will count kilowatts. Table 11-4 presents the average monthly energy consumption of most electric appliances. As you can see, unplugging your electric toothbrush or even permanently abandoning your television set will do little to reduce your energy bill. The major users of electrical energy are appliances that heat or cool. Water heaters, air conditioners, refrigerators, freezers, ranges, and clothes dryers head the list of energy users. Together, they account for most home electricity costs. Have you ever returned home after an extended vacation expecting your electric bill to reflect your absence, only to discover that your utility bill was just about the same? The reason is simple. The water heater, the refrigerator, and the freezer continue to operate in your absence. If you vacationed during the hot summer months, the refrigerator and freezer may have worked even longer to overcome the additional house heat.

Reducing your personal energy budget throughout the year calls for several strategies. There is no simple cure-all. We divide these strategies into three parts, as we did for transportation: (1) cheap techniques, (2) minor expense-saving strategies, and (3) major expense-saving plans. Consumers will not be able to employ all of these techniques (some of which you may already know), but energy decisions will certainly improve if they get better information about the alternatives.

Cheap Techniques. The single most effective quick-fix conservation technique is regulating your home thermostat. At one time 72 degrees was considered to be the optimal temperature for a home, and most thermostats were set at that temperature. If you are willing to deviate from that norm by 6 degrees (78 degrees in the summer and 66 degrees in winter), you will save an estimated 15 percent on your energy bill. Larger savings can be achieved, of course, if you are willing to change the temperature even more. Other simple conservation practices are closing your drapes at night during the winter, washing and drying only full loads, turning your water-heater thermostat to a lower setting, cooking with a microwave oven, avoiding preheating your oven, matching the stove's burner to the size of your pots and pans, and lighting only work areas rather than entire rooms. Box 11-3 lists these and other simple energy-saving tips.

Minor Cash Outlays: Retrofitting Techniques. Turning down the thermostat during the winter to save energy is similar to changing driving habits to get more miles per gallon. There is no direct cost, but you will have to change your habits and adjust to a different lifestyle. Other changes in energy consumption involve more than a simple change in behavior; they require investments in energy-saving equipment. Buying and installing new equipment (retrofitting), for example, upgrades the energy efficiency of an energy-using system by changing some of its components.

Because retrofitting a building or a home costs money, you should estimate the benefits *before* you spend your money. One commonly used way to estimate the usefulness of a particular retrofit is to calculate the **payback period**—the time it takes to get back your investment as a result of lower energy expenditures. The shorter the payback period, the more profitable the retrofit.

Home Heating
Keep room temperature at 65 degrees or lower. Turn control down at night or when you are away from home. Consider installing a thermostat with a setback feature that does this automatically.

Draw draperies at night to limit heat loss. Open them on sunny days to let heat in.

Close damper when fireplace is not in use.

Check the furnace filter monthly. Replace when dirty.

Check heater filter. Hold it to the light; if light does not pass through readily, replace filter. Cleaning is not recommended (unless heater has a permanent filter).

Turn off furnace pilot at end of heating season, but *only* if you are capable of relighting it.

Laundry
Wash and dry full loads of clothes. Adjust water level for the size of the load.

Wash clothes in warm or cold water.

Don't overdry clothes. Follow manufacturer's instructions for drying time.

Remove lint from dryer filter before each load.

Remove accumulated material from dryer moisture exhaust.

Consider drying laundry outdoors. Let solar energy do the job.

Lighting
Keep bulbs and fixtures clean. Accumulations of dust can lower lighting levels.

Turn off unnecessary lights.

Use reflective, light-colored interior decor whenever possible.

Natural lighting should be used whenever it does not interfere with air conditioning.

Water Heating
Take fast showers.

Repair leaky faucets.

Install water-savings showerheads that restrict water flow.

Operate dishwashers only for full loads.

BOX 11-3

Energy Conservation Tips

Set water heater thermostat below normal. Turn to "pilot" position when you are away for extended periods of time (one week or longer).

Use cold water for operating garbage disposal and for prerinsing dishes.

When handwashing dishes, avoid rinsing under continuous hot running water.

Cooking

Do not preheat gas oven. Preheat electric oven only for baked goods requiring precise temperatures at the start of the cooking cycle.

Keep pots and pans covered.

Adjust top burner flame to fit pans.

Reduce burner flame to "simmer" after cooking starts.

Cook by time and temperature. Avoid opening oven door while food is cooking.

Do one-place cooking. Prepare an entire meal using only the oven, the broiler, or the top burner.

Turn all burners off when not in use.

Use a steamer or a pressure cooker to cook several foods at the same time.

Use a microwave oven.

Air Conditioning

Hang a thermometer on the wall and check it to see that room temperature stays above 78 degrees.

Investigate an energy-saving unit. Before buying a room air conditioner, compare the Energy Efficiency Ratios (EERs). The higher the number, the more cooling you get from the electricity.

Cut down the use of heat-producing equipment by restricting the use of major appliances (dishwashers and dryers) to early morning or evening. Turn off unused lights.

Clean or replace filters. Clogged filters make your air conditioner work harder and less efficiently.

Shield outdoor air conditioners from sunlight. Be sure that you don't shield the air flow. Plants or lattices are excellent sunscreens.

Keep units clean. Dust or dirt particles can block air flow and waste energy.

Set thermostat higher if you are away from home for most of the day.

Locate thermostats away from heat sources.

Turn thermostat off when you are away from home for 24 hours or more, unless you live in a climate in which air conditioning is needed to prevent damage to furniture or paintings.

Do not overcool. Maintain as warm a temperature as comfort permits to minimize cooling costs and equipment use.

The size of your air-conditioning system is vitally important. An oversized system turns on and off too often, decreasing the efficiency of the unit. An undersized unit operates almost continuously on hot days. Either way, you'll waste energy.

Shade window areas from direct sunlight with window awnings or plants.

Refrigerators and Freezers

Allow food to cool before refrigerating. Your refrigerator has to work harder to cool hot food.

Check your refrigerator door seals occasionally. A misaligned door or a buildup of soil around the gaskets lets cold air out. To test the seal, close the refrigerator door with a dollar bill between the gaskets. If there's resistance as you pull the bill out, the seal is tight.

If refrigerator frost becomes more than ½ inch thick, it acts as an insulator and makes your refrigerator work harder. Defrost frequently, but never use an ice pick or a knife. You could puncture cooling tubes or seriously damage freezer walls.

Keep condenser coils clean (bottom or rear of the refrigerator). If they accumulate dust and dirt, operation will be impaired and cold temperatures cannot be maintained.

Open refrigerator doors only when necessary. Loss of cold air results in unnecessary cycling of the compressor, increasing the amount of electricity used.

Set refrigerators at warmer temperatures during vacations, and leave them fairly empty. When unused for longer periods, refrigerators and freezers should be unplugged, cleaned, and left open.

Figure 11-9. Recommended insulation standards for climate zones of the United States.

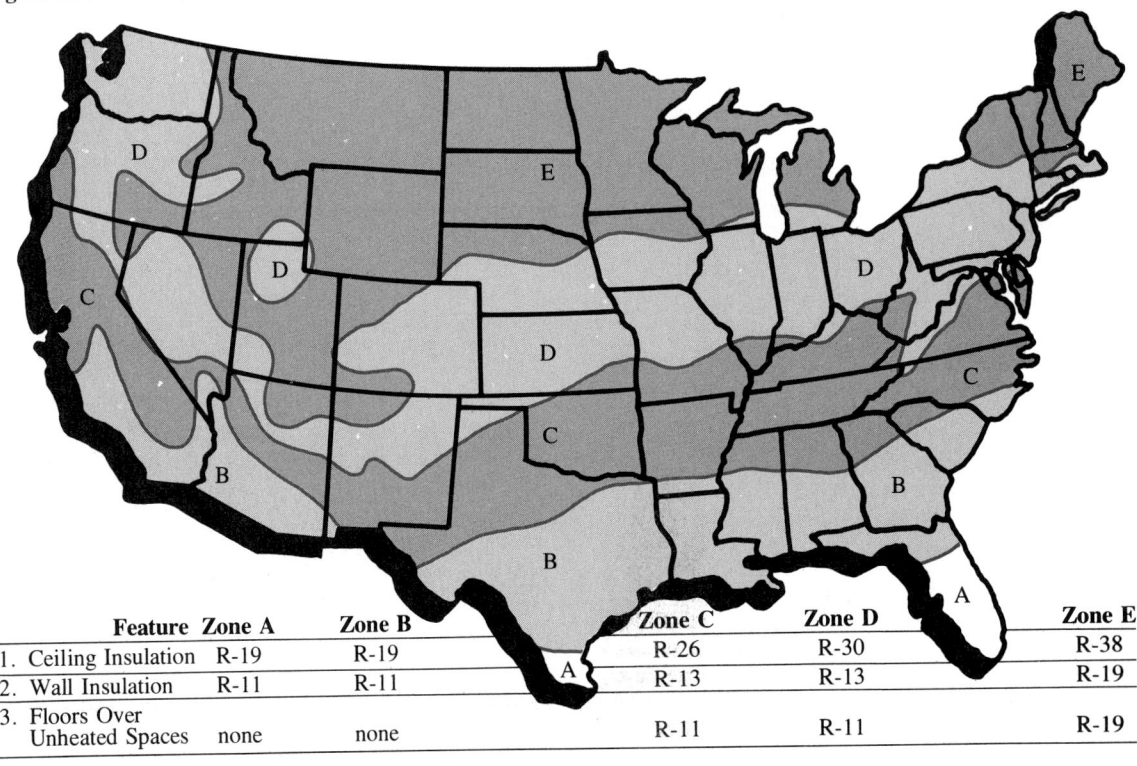

Feature	Zone A	Zone B	Zone C	Zone D	Zone E
1. Ceiling Insulation	R-19	R-19	R-26	R-30	R-38
2. Wall Insulation	R-11	R-11	R-13	R-13	R-19
3. Floors Over Unheated Spaces	none	none	R-11	R-11	R-19

SOURCE: U.S. Department of Housing and Urban Development, *The Energy-Wise Home Buyer* (Washington, D.C.: U.S. Government Printing Office, 1979).

To calculate the payback period, divide the cost of the retrofit by the annual energy saving. For example, if a new furnace costs $3000 and is 20 percent more efficient than your old one, the payback period can be calculated once you are able to estimate how much money you are saving as a result of the 20 percent decrease in fuel consumption. If the 20 percent decrease in your annual heating bill is $200, then the payback period is 15 years ($3000 ÷ $200 = 15 years). This is a long payback period, but if fuel costs were to double, so would fuel savings, with the result that the payback period would be cut in half. Here are some suggestions for energy-conservation techniques that offer short payback periods:

1. *Insulation* is high on everyone's list of conservation techniques. More than one-third of all American homes were built before 1940, when there were few or no standard requirements for insulation. By some estimates, about 30 percent of the residences in the United States are completely uninsulated, and another one-third are underinsulated (Stobaugh and Yergin, 1979). When standard insulation was installed in a test house in Washington, D.C., the annual energy consumption decreased by 25 percent. In a three-year study conducted in Portland, Seattle, and Spokane, a $981 investment reduced fuel consumption by 50 percent, with a payback period of less than four years (Tsongas, 1977).

The amount of insulation that is most energy efficient and economically justifiable is determined by the climate in a particular area. Figure 11-9 shows the recommended insulation standards for ceilings,

---

BOX 11-4

Choosing the Most Cost-Effective Home Insulation

Two homes stand side by side in Mt. Airy, Maryland, forty miles northwest of Baltimore. The homes are identical in almost every respect—in size, in age, in floor plan, and in method of heating (all electric). Even the families that occupy the two homes are similar—married couples with two young children. However, one of the houses has utility bills that are 50 percent lower than the other's. Both homes are part of a government study on the economic effects of conservation techniques in the home. The study has found that one of the most cost-effective forms of household energy conservation is insulation.

A few years ago, it was common to recommend a certain number of inches of insulating material to achieve a given level of energy conservation. But today, there are so many different types of insulation material, from mineral to wool to foam, and so many different ways of applying the insulation, from rolling it on to blowing it in, that an inch of one material may not have the same energy-conserving effect as an inch of another. This is the basic reason for the creation of the R-value, which measures the ability of a given insulating material to resist heat transfer.

All stores that sell insulation are required to have the manufacturer's R-value fact sheet for each type of insulation sold. These sheets identify the type of insulation, the manufacturer, the R-value, and the coverage capability. Given these facts and the price of different insulation materials, here is how to decide which one to buy.

1. Find out what R-value you need. This varies with the part of the house you are insulating and the climate (see Figure 11-9).

2. Decide what kind of insulation to install. Do you want to use a loose fill and blow the insulation in, or do you prefer a blanket type of insulation? You should consult with a building-supply house (or two) to see which method suits your need.

3. Measure the area you are going to insulate. Multiplying the length by the width gives you the area in square feet. Check the R-value fact sheet to see how much insulation you need to get the desired R-value. If you install more insulation than you need, you will waste money.

4. Shop for the best deal. To find the lowest cost, compare the dollar cost per unit of R-value. Here is an FTC-recommended way of calculating cost:

price of the package	÷	square feet of insulation needed for a given R-value	÷	the R-value number	=	cost per unit of R-value

The smaller the number, the more economical the package of insulation.

---

walls, and floors in different regions. Generally speaking, the milder the weather, the lower the recommendations. Notice, too, that the standards are listed as **R-values.** The R stands for resistance to heat transfer from the outside of the house to the inside of the house. R-values are more accurate than inches as a means of measuring the performance of insulation. The higher the R-value, the greater the resistance to heat flow. For more details on selecting the most cost-effective insulation, see Box 11-4.

2. *Caulking and weather stripping* are two additional energy-saving devices that are simple, cheap, and efficient. Caulking is a putty-like substance that can be squeezed into cracks and crevices where outside air might seep into the house. Weather-stripping performs the same function, but it comes in strips made of felt, foam rubber, vinyl, or interlocking metal. Plugging air leaks can lower home heating and cooling costs by as much as 10 percent, and given the low price of the materials, the payback period may be less than one year.

3. *Storm doors and windows* are forms of insulation that can be helpful in cold climates. In some cases, energy savings of up to 15 percent in lowered fuel costs have been documented. If you are renting a home or an apartment, an investment in storm windows would not be cost effective, because the payback period is not short enough. But you might consider taping a sheet of clear

The efficiency of your lighting system is related to the amount of lumens produced per watt of electricity used.

plastic film to the inside of the windows. This has been shown to be nearly as effective as exterior storm windows (although not as pleasing to look at), and the price is exceptionally low (Porter, 1979).

4. *Lighting* your home is another area in which some minor changes could lead to long-term savings. First, you should remove light bulbs or lower their wattage in areas where bright light is not needed. Second, wherever possible, replace incandescent light-bulb fixtures with fluorescent ones. Fluorescent lights last twenty times longer and produce more light per watt. A 40 watt fluorescent lamp, for example, will produce more light than a 100 watt incandescent bulb. The wattage rating measures electricity used, not light given off. Engineers measure light in units called **lumens.** A bulb that gives off 900 lumens is twice as bright as one that emits 450 lumens. Higher-wattage bulbs tend to give off more lumens and thus are more efficient than a combination of lower-wattage bulbs. A 100 watt bulb might be rated at 1750 lumens, whereas two 60 watt bulbs together might have only 1740 lumens. The new long-life bulbs last longer partly because they deliver less light (lumens). This, coupled with their higher price, makes them a poor buy, unless you are lighting an area where the bulb is difficult to replace. If you follow these tips, you can save up to 4 percent of your electricity costs (Porter, 1979).

5. *Other indoor energy savings* can be achieved with a variety of retrofits. Insulating your water heater with a wraparound blanket and installing reduced-flow shower heads that conserve hot water can reduce your energy bill up to 5 percent. Replacing oven and furnace pilot lights with electric ignition devices may seem like a small change, but oven pilot lights account for more than 40 percent of the fuel that ovens consume.

6. *Exterior energy conservation* can also be an important part of a retrofit program. Trees planted on the southern side of a house give pleasant cooling shade during the summer months and do not interfere with the winter sun's rays, because they conveniently shed their leaves in fall. This type of energy conservation is known as a **passive solar technique,** because it uses the sun's energy and doesn't require a mechanism with moving parts. Large, south-facing windows under an overhanging roof are also examples of passive solar design; they allow the sun's rays to penetrate and warm the home's exterior when the sun is low in winter, and they block rays in the summer when the sun is high overhead.

Major Expenditures on Energy Conservation. Consumers have many opportunities to try low-cost and no-cost energy-conservation strategies but few chances to make major expenditures for energy conservation. But major conservation strategies are just as important. A family may buy only three refrigerators over its entire life cycle, but it will have to live with each decision for an average of 15 years. A poor energy choice will cost hundreds of dollars over the life of the purchase, whereas an energy-efficient choice will pay dividends over the life of the purchase. A similar argument can be made for buying, building, or renovating a home. The size of the total expenditure coupled with the infrequency of the expense requires that consumers spend more time gathering information and investigating energy options.

One of the most interesting energy options available today is **solar energy.** We discussed passive solar techniques earlier, but in this section we focus on **active solar systems,** which use the sun's energy but also require mechanical parts.

A primary example of active solar technology is the solar water heater. Such heaters consist of panels, each about three by seven feet, which are bolted on the roof facing south. The panels, generally made of aluminum, glass, plastic, and copper, catch and concentrate the sun's rays, which in turn heat the water or air that flows through pipes in the panel. Fans or pumps then circulate the heated air or water through a heat exchanger, which transfers the solar heat to a storage tank. Cool water is returned to the solar panel, and the water in the storage tank is generally hot enough to be used in the house. Three panels are enough to satisfy the hot-water needs of an average house, and it is estimated that one-third of all American houses are suitable for this type of conversion (Maidique, 1979).

Contrary to popular belief, solar water heating is not a new idea. It has been available to American consumers since the early part of the twentieth century. Twenty-five percent of the homes in Pasadena, California had solar water heaters in 1920. Miami, Florida had over 50,000 solar water heaters still in place in 1950; most were over twenty years old. Americans abandoned their solar water heaters for a very good reason—cost. Natural gas was so much cheaper to use, when it was readily available, that people turned their backs on active solar technology. Now, with rising energy costs, many people are reconsidering solar power. Many new housing developments, such as those in Davis, California, are having solar water heating and space heating built in before the homes are sold. One estimate indicates that California alone will have 1.5 million solar installations by 1985 (Stobaugh and Yergin, 1979). The world's largest solar-heated building, a 325,000-square-foot athletic field, is in the heart of oil country—Tabuk, Saudi Arabia.

If there are solar facilities in Saudi Arabia, it is probably worth your while to consider solar heating. But, in order for the choice to make economic sense, you must consider the costs and the benefits. Suppose, for example, that for $2400 you could buy a solar water-heating system that would satisfy 75 percent of your hot-water needs each year. If you owned an aver-

To be efficient and economical, solar water heating methods must be well thought out.

age electric water heater, you might be using 500 kilowatt-hours per month (see Table 11-4), and at 8 cents per kwh, this amounts to $40 per month, or $480 per year. With a solar water heater, you would save $360 per year (.75 × $480), and your payback period would be 6.7 years ($2400 ÷ $360). This would justify going solar, and you would have two added benefits: (1) you would be protected against a further rise in the cost of electricity, and (2) the solar system would increase the value of your house. Of course, if you had a natural-gas water heater, the energy costs of which are generally a third of electricity costs, the payback period would be tripled (almost 20 years) and the system would not be justifiable on purely economic grounds.

Consumers also make large investments in refrigerators and air conditioners. The Federal Trade Commission now requires that all large electrical appliances be rated for energy efficiency. The standard measure is called the **energy efficiency ratio (EER).** The EER typically ranges from 4.0 to 12.0. The higher the EER, the greater the energy efficiency

Saving money and energy for summer cooling can be a real challenge.

of the unit. An air conditioner with an EER of 4.0 costs three times as much to operate as one with an EER of 12.0. The EER is computed by dividing the cooling power of the appliance (rated in **British thermal units [Btu]**) by the watts consumed. For example, a unit that produces 8,500 Btu per hour and uses 1,000 watts per hour has an EER of 8.5. You may find another model that produces the same output (8,500 Btu) but uses only 900 watts per hour. The second unit has an EER of 9.4 (8,500 ÷ 900). Because it uses less, it has a higher EER, which can be translated into an energy saving of 100 watts per hour or 0.1 kilowatt (1 kilowatt equals 1,000 watts).

To determine your annual energy saving, multiply the hourly energy saving by the number of summer cooling hours in your area. In Bangor, Maine, which averages 360 summer cooling hours annually, the air conditioner with a 9.4 EER would save 36 kwh each year (.1 × 360). To determine dollars saved, multiply the annual kilowatt saving by the cost of a kilowatt. At 5 cents per kilowatt-hour, the more-efficient unit would save a Maine family $1.80. But in New Orleans, for which the FTC estimates that there are 2,090 cooling hours, the saving would be $9.95. So a $10 difference in the cost of the two units would be paid back in the first year in New Orleans but would take almost six years to pay back in Maine.

Your local electric company can tell you the average number of cooling days in your area, if you wish to make the comparison yourself. The FTC now requires that all literature that accompanies air conditioners list the **seasonal energy efficiency rating (SEER),** and the expected average cost of the energy the air conditioner will use. Although this allows consumers to make some rough comparisons between models, it does not give them a precise indication of the cost, because seasonal cooling hours vary from place to place (from 40 hours in Anchorage to 3,950 in Honolulu) and because the price of a kilowatt hour of electricity varies from 2 to 14 cents. To make an informal comparison between two units with the same cooling power (Btu rating), obtain the information needed to use the following formula:

$$\frac{\text{difference in watts}}{1{,}000} \times \text{summer cooling hours} \times \text{cost per kilowatt-hour}$$

Suppose the comparison is between two 9,000 Btu air conditioners—unit A, which uses 860 watts per hour and has an EER of 10.5, and unit B, which uses 1,100 watts per hour and has an EER of 8.2. The difference in watts is 240. Let us also assume that the local utility company says that there is an average summer cooling load of 2,000 hours and that the price of electricity is 8 cents per kilowatt-hour. How much would the more-energy-efficient unit save each year?

$$\frac{240}{1{,}000} \times 2{,}000 \text{ hours} \times \$.08 = \$38.40$$

The difference in wattage per kilowatt times the number of summer cooling hours times the price per kilowatt-hour gives the answer—$38.40. Of course, if the cost of electricity rises, the saving from the more-efficient unit also rises. In the 1970s, electricity could generally be purchased for 4 cents a kilowatt-hour. In the 1980s, 8 cents per kilowatt-hour is closer to the average price. The increase doubles energy savings and cuts payback time in half.

Energy and Your Future

The energy story of today is clearly one of conserva-

Proposed space solar power satellites would beam microwave energy to earth for conversion into electrical power. Such a satellite would be 30-40 square miles of solar cells and would weigh 100-150 million pounds.

tion. By conserving energy, consumers prolong the useful life of nonrenewable resources and, at the same time, spend less money. But what new developments can you, as a consumer, look forward to in the near future? What will your energy budget be like in the year 2000? This final section addresses these questions.

One source of energy that we can count on indefinitely is the sun. Broadly defined, solar energy includes not only direct radiation from the sun, but energy resulting from the interaction of the sun's rays and the earth. Such interaction can take the form of wind power, water power, ocean power, and **biomass** (the sun's energy stored in plants such as wood). Most interactive processes require a large investment in the resources that make windmills or dams that produce electricity. Biomass in the form of wood has been the most available form of solar energy for consumers who burn it to heat their homes. Partly because of the rise in the cost of fuel oil, the use of wood as a residential fuel grew sixfold in New England from 1970 to 1978. Today, 18 percent of the households in Maine, New Hampshire, and Vermont rely on wood as their primary source of heat (Holzman, 1978).

The President's Council on Environmental Quality recently estimated that 23 percent of America's energy use in the year 2000 will come from some form of solar power. The two most promising ways of delivering that energy to the consumer are by using solar heating with solar panels and by using electricity produced through **photovoltaic cells.** There are already more than 2 million solar water heaters in Japan, and because the average cost of a solar water heater is $2500 in the United States, solar water heating is already cheaper than electric systems in most parts of the nation. Photovoltaic electricity is not yet common, but it holds great promise.

The photovoltaic cell is made from silicon, which is made mostly of sand—the most abundant solid element on earth. The silicon is "contaminated" with gaseous impurities, and then a thin layer of aluminum is deposited on it. The result is a photovoltaic cell, which converts the sun's rays into electrical current.

Today, electricity generated from photovoltaic cells is more expensive per kilowatt than electricity from local public utility companies. However, as sales increase and newer, more efficient techniques are discovered to produce these cells, their costs should fall

Use of photovoltaics for household electrical needs is in experimental stages but could be the wave of the future if costs of installation continue to drop.

dramatically. The prices of transistors and computers, for example, fell as production increased and technological advances were made. A transistor that costs 20 cents today cost $200 when it was first introduced. The Department of Energy's (DOE's) Photovoltaics Division has projected a set of price goals that they hope the solar industry will meet.

In 1977, photovoltaics cost about $15,000 per kilowatt. By 1980 that price had fallen to $5,000. When the price falls to $500 per kilowatt, homeowners can begin carefully considering photovoltaics. If the average household could purchase enough solar cells to get 3 kilowatts of power ten hours per day, it would produce 900 kilowatt-hours per month. At 5 cents per hour, this power is worth $45. In three years, the $1500 investment could be covered, and from then until the panels needed replacing (approximately 20 years), the power would be virtually free. Of course, power is also consumed at night, so either a storage facility would have to be purchased or a utility company would have to supply the evening power. But the utility company could also purchase the excess power generated during the day. Imagine having your own "mini" power station that sold electricity to the utility company. This could be achieved by allowing your meter to run backward as well as forward. This "excess power" would be generated at the "peak-load period" in the summer, when utility companies strain to produce enough electricity to meet urban needs.

If you have questions about solar energy, write to the National Solar Heating and Cooling Information Center, P.O. Box 1607, Rockville, Maryland 20850.

Summary

Until the last decade, American energy costs were relatively low and were getting even lower. New discoveries of oil, coal, and natural gas expanded energy supplies, and consumers were not terribly concerned about prices. From about 1900 to 1974, energy use generally grew more rapidly than population. Over this period, the American economy became heavily dependent on fossil fuels such as coal, oil, and natural gas, which supplied 92 percent of America's energy needs in the 1970s. When the price of oil was abruptly raised in 1974, consumers and producers alike began to look for ways to cut back on their energy demands. American consumers can most affect energy use in transportation (23 percent of U.S. energy consumption) and in homes (14 percent of U.S. energy consumption).

The American automobile uses a vast amount of energy, but it also offers great potential for conserving energy and saving money. All changes, however, involve opportunity costs, and some changes are quite expensive. Nevertheless, by changing driving habits, by correcting tire pressures, and by getting regular tuneups, a driver can get from 25 to 40 percent better mileage. If you are willing to trade your automobile for another form of personal transportation (a moped or a bicycle, for example), you can save even more. Mass transit offers the greatest savings, but the personal costs may be greater than the benefits.

The greatest opportunities for cutting home energy costs are in heating or cooling systems, because expenditures for refrigeration and heating account for 88 percent of the average home's energy bill. Reading utility meters is as essential for measuring energy expenditures and savings as counting calories is for someone on a weight-loss diet. Once you have estimated your energy budget, it is time to look into ways to save by making minor changes, such as adding insulation and weather stripping and changing lighting. Both minor and major expenditures (buying solar water heating units or new refrigerators, for example) should be analyzed by the payback method—estimating the number of years it will take to pay off the investment in energy conservation. The energy efficiency ratings on new appliances help consumers quantify the value of the energy savings, so that they can compare the long-run costs of various models.

Your energy future will probably contain some nontraditional energy sources. In the short run, solar energy in the form of hot-water heat and biomass offer the most promise for energy saving. In the long run, it may be possible to convert the sun's energy into electricity by means of photovoltaic cells. The cost of electricity produced by these cells has fallen sharply since they were introduced, and if the Department of Energy's projections are met, photovoltaic cells will be a viable energy option for homeowners before 1990.

REVISITED

Now that you have read the chapter, answer the following questions about Frank and Melody's argument over the cheapest form of transportation.

1. Is it more expensive for them to take the bus or to continue to use the car? If they traveled separately, which form of transportation would cost more? If the price of gasoline were $5 per gallon, would the answer change?

2. How would society in general benefit from Melody's suggestion to use the bus?

3. If both Frank and Melody had bicycles, would the car still be a cheaper alternative? More convenient? Under what circumstances might your answer change? Consider weather, bike paths, traffic congestion, and parking space.

KEY TERMS

active solar
average cost
biomass
British thermal units (Btu's)
energy
energy conservation
energy efficiency ratio (EER)
fossil fuels
kilocalories
lumens
marginal cost
moped
passive solar
payback period
photovoltaic cells
R-values
retrofit
ridesharing
seasonal energy efficiency rating (SEER)
solar energy
therm

QUESTIONS

1. Describe the general changes in the uses of energy in the United States from 1850 to the present. Rank American energy sources in order of importance in 1850, in 1900, and today.

2. How much of the American energy transportation budget is used for automobiles? Buses? Planes?

3. List four ways to improve a car's energy efficiency.

4. What does the term "retrofit" mean, and how does it apply to energy conservation in transportation?

5. Give an illustration of the relationship between fuel costs and time costs. How does this explain the speeding behavior of certain drivers?

6. If you were choosing between a bike, a moped, and a motorcycle, what criteria would you use to help you decide? List the benefits and drawbacks of each form of transportation. Which would you choose? Which would you have chosen if you were five years younger or twenty-five years older?

7. Describe the pattern of mass-transit ridership since World War II. Why did people abandon mass transit in the 1950s and 1960s? What could make mass transit a better competitor to personal transportation?

8. Here are two meter readings:

	June 20	July 20
Electricity (kwh)	97640	98481
Natural gas (cu. ft.)	1310	1340

a. How many kilowatt hours were used by this household?
b. If the cost of electricity is 6 cents per kwh, how much would the electric bill be?
c. Many gas companies charge by the therm, not by the cubic foot. If a therm costs 70 cents and there are 1.1 therms in a cubic foot of gas, how much is the gas bill?

9. What is the difference between passive solar strategies and active solar strategies? How would you classify the following solar strategies?
a. Planting a tree.
b. Building a greenhouse.
c. Installing a solar water-heating system with an electric backup unit.

10. The yearly energy consumption of an electrical appliance depends on the climate, the EER, and factors such as the time of day and the thermostat setting. Here is an example of the consumption of two room air conditioners:

	Unit I	Unit II
Size (Btu/hr)	10,000	10,000
Watts	860	1,800
Operating hours	600	600

Calculate the following:
a. The EER of both.
b. The annual amount of electricity used for each in kilowatt-hours (kwh).
c. The annual energy savings of the more-efficient model, assuming a 5 cent per kwh cost.
d. The approximate payback period if a more efficient air conditioner costs $100 more.
e. The change in the length of the payback period if electricity costs 2 cents per kwh, or 10 cents per kwh.

PROJECTS

1. Evaluate your car in terms of its energy efficiency. What can you do for no cost or for minor cost to save money? What will the total cost be? Would it be worth it to you? Why?

2. Call your local utility company and get the current charge per kilowatt-hour of electricity and per therm of natural gas. Read your own meter at the beginning and end of a normal week. Then try to conserve. Keep a log of your conservation tactics for the next week. Once again, read your own meter and compare the energy and dollar savings. Compare your experience with others in the class. Given your time and expenditures, how much did you earn per hour of your labor? Was it worth it?

3. Locate a local company that installs solar water heaters. Get a cost estimate, and then calculate whether solar would be a good investment.

4. Compare the prices of three comparably sized refrigerator/freezers. Do their costs bear any relationship to their EERs? Is the one with the lowest EER the best buy? Explain.

5. Make a list of all your electrical appliances. Rank them in order of importance. Could you do without any of them for one week? Try it, and estimate your energy savings by reading your meter.

6. Calculate the out-of-pocket cost of commuting to class by car, by bus, and by bicycle. Which is the least expensive? Do you use the least expensive alternative more often, or do you consider other nonmonetary costs? Explain.

REFERENCES AND READINGS

Christener, Anne M. "The Energy Conservation Crisis." *Journal of Home Economics,* Winter, 1979, pp. 32–35.

Commoner, Barry. "The Case for Solar Energy." *Challenge,* September/October 1979, pp. 35–40.

"Energy Conservation." *Consumer Reports 1982 Buying Guide Issue,* December 1981.

Environmental Protection Agency. *The Bicycle vs. the Energy Crisis.* Washington, D.C.: U.S. Government Printing Office, 1974.

Hayes, Denis. *Rays of Hope.* New York: W. W. Norton, 1977.

Heilbroner, Robert. *The Making of Economic Society.* Englewood Cliffs, N.J.: Prentice-Hall, 1975.

Hogan, M. Janice. "Does Less Energy Equal Less Happiness?" *Forum,* Spring/Summer 1981, pp. 9–11.

Holzman, David C. "Wood Fuel Makes Strong Comeback." *People and Energy,* May 1978, pp. 5–6.

Maidique, Modesto A. "Solar America" in Stobaugh and Yergin (1979). pp 183–215.

Miller, G. Tyler, Jr. *Energy and Environment.* Belmont, Calif.: Wadsworth, 1980.

"Motorcycles for Beginners." *Consumer Reports,* June 1981, pp. 353–362.

"Motorcycles: Half the Wheels, Twice the Mileage." *Changing Times,* March 1981, pp. 78–80.

Porter, Sylvia. *Sylvia Porter's New Money Book for the '80s.* New York: Avon Books, 1979.

"Saving Energy Dollars." *Consumer Reports,* October 1981, pp. 563–594.

Schultz, Neil. "How to Get 100 Miles Per Gallon." *Consumers Digest,* January/February 1981, pp. 46–50.

Stein, Richard G. *Architecture and Energy.* Garden City, N.Y.: Anchor Books, 1977.

Stobaugh, Robert, and Yergin, Daniel, eds. *Energy Future: Report of the Energy Project at the Harvard Business School.* New York: Random House, 1979.

Tsongas, George A. *Home Energy Conservation Demonstration Project: Final Report for Chevron USA.* August, 1977.

U.S. Department of Agriculture. *Food News for Consumers.* Washington, D.C.: U.S. Government Printing Office, June 1980.

U.S. Department of Agriculture. "Heating With Wood." *Fact Sheet.* Washington, D.C.: U.S. Government Printing Office, March 1981.

U.S. Department of Housing and Urban Development. *The Energy Wise Home Buyer.* Washington, D.C.: U.S. Government Printing Office, 1979.

Wells, Malcolm. "Confessions of a Gentle Architect." *Environmental Quality,* July 1973, pp. 51–57.

Wells, Malcolm, and Spetgang, Irwin. *How to Buy Solar Heating and Cooling Without Getting Burnt.* Emmaus, Pa.: Rodale Press, 1978.

Did You Know That...

- *there are two major costs of owning an automobile—fixed costs of ownership and variable costs of operation?*

- *octane rating measures a gasoline's ability to stop engine knock, but it has nothing to do with how much energy the gasoline has or the quality of the gasoline?*

- *there is a federally mandated tire-grading system that helps consumers compare the quality of tires?*

- *half of all new-car buyers get auto service contracts to supplement their warranties, but the quality of these contracts varies greatly?*

- *three out of every four cars sold for personal use in the United States are used cars?*

- *it is a federal offense to tamper with an automobile's odometer?*

- *on an average day, Americans spend $55 million for automobile repairs that are unnecessary, faulty, or fraudulent?*

- *in addition to the written warranty consumers receive when buying a car, there are also implied warranties? There can also be secret warranties that consumers should know about.*

- *with one phone call consumers can find out whether their car has a safety defect that has required a recall?*

- *the ratio of automobiles to mechanics in the United States is 450 to 1, about the same ratio as the number of people to physicians?*

- *if you are a typical driver, you will be involved in two traffic accidents in the next eight years, one of which will be your fault?*

12

The Automobile: Wheels and Deals

Basic Automobile Decisions
The Costs of Automobile Ownership and Operation
Shopping for a Car
Automobile Repairs
Automobile Insurance

Neighborhood CAPSULE
Her Dasher Was a Dog

Margaret McNamera was a price-conscious consumer. When she decided to get a new car, she shopped around, read the latest consumer information, and finally purchased a brand new Volkswagen Dasher stationwagon.

On her way home, Ms. McNamera began to have doubts about the car. When she tried to blow the horn, the windshield wipers went on. So of course she wasn't surprised when the horn beeped when she turned on the windshield wipers. By the time she arrived home, the car had barely enough power to make it into her garage.

During the next eleven months, Ms. McNamera made twenty trips to the dealer. The service-department manager was always friendly and courteous—they were soon on a first name basis. But Volkswagen offered only a limited warranty, and Margaret was never compensated for her time or her inconvenience. Here is a brief log of her troubles:

- 1,200 miles: The brakes squealed, the passenger window would not close, and the car vibrated when in first gear.
- 2,100 miles: The car rattled in reverse.
- 3,800 miles: The engine lost power and the cylinders misfired.
- 5,100 miles: The accelerator pedal stuck in traffic. Fortunately there was no accident.
- 5,400 miles: The battery failed and had to be replaced.
- 6,200 miles: The horn began blaring, and Ms. McNamera had to have it disconnected at a service station.
- 7,000 miles: The engine began spouting oil.
- 7,500 miles: The car would not start and had to be towed to the dealer.
- 8,400 miles: Ms. McNamera turned on the windshield wipers and the horn honked uncontrollably until the fuses blew.
- 9,200 miles: The window on the driver's side stuck halfway and the door jammed. The dealer propped the window closed and advised Ms. McNamera not to use the door. To get out of the car she had to climb over the gear shift.
- 12,000 miles: The warranty ran out and so did Ms. McNamera's patience.

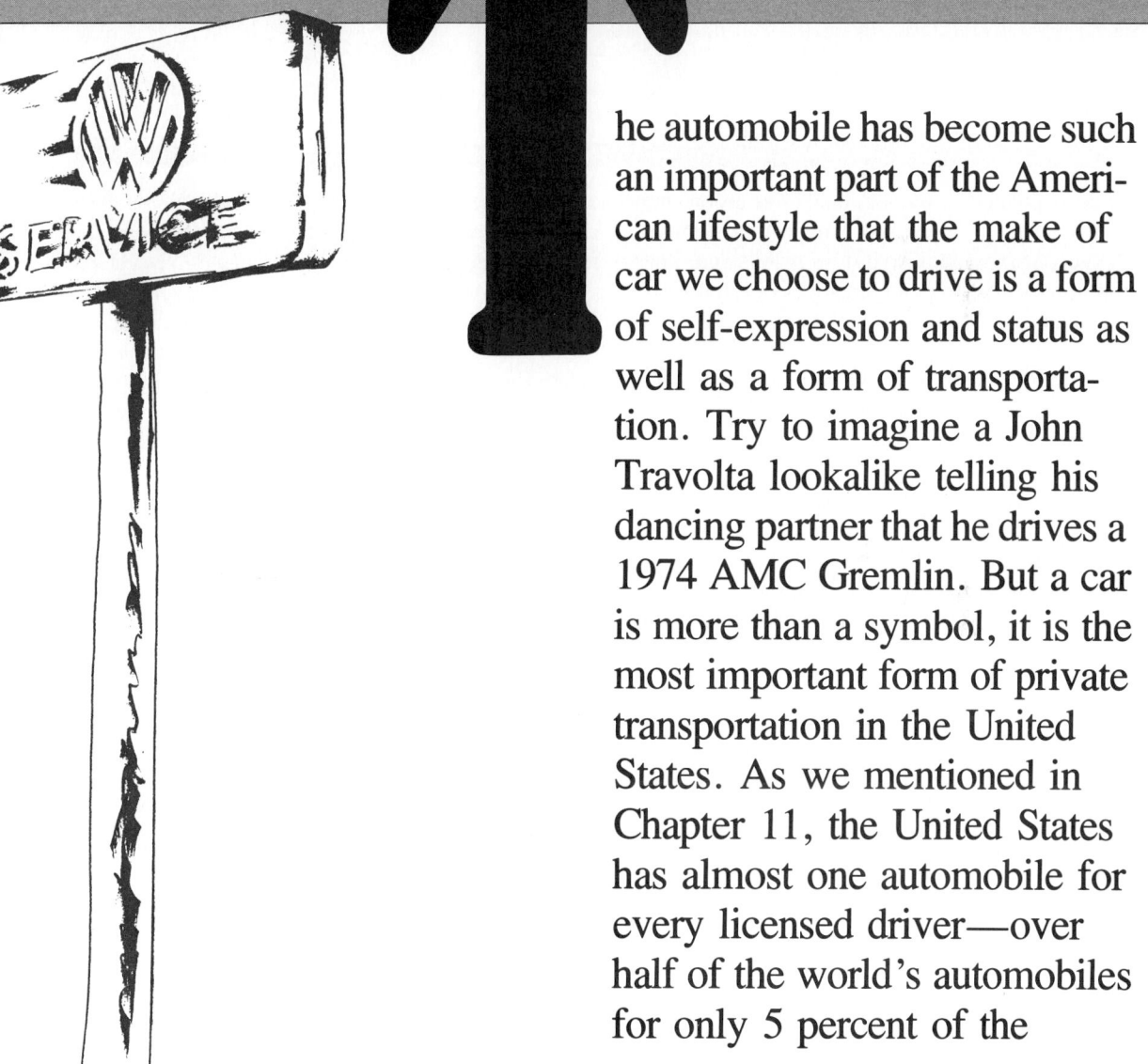

The automobile has become such an important part of the American lifestyle that the make of car we choose to drive is a form of self-expression and status as well as a form of transportation. Try to imagine a John Travolta lookalike telling his dancing partner that he drives a 1974 AMC Gremlin. But a car is more than a symbol, it is the most important form of private transportation in the United States. As we mentioned in Chapter 11, the United States has almost one automobile for every licensed driver—over half of the world's automobiles for only 5 percent of the

Table 12-1. Decision Matrix for Evaluating Auto Desirability

	Alternatives						
Criteria	New car	Used car	Lease	Buy	Subcompact car	Midsize car	Van
Low initial cost	−	+	+	−	+	0	−
Low maintenance cost	+	−	+	−	+	0	−
High gas mileage	+	−	0	0	+	0	−
Comfort	+	−	0	0	−	+	0
Safety	+	0	0	0	−	0	+
Size	0	+	0	0	−	0	+
Multi-use	0	0	0	0	−	−	+
Reliability	+	−	0	0	0	0	0

world's population. An automobile is the second most expensive item an individual American household will ever purchase, ranking just below housing. Thus, being a good consumer requires some basic knowledge about purchasing and maintaining an automobile.

Before you look for a car, you must decide why you want it and what kind of car suits you best. We address these questions in the first part of the chapter. But the decision to get a car is only the first decision you must make. The costs of ownership include the more obvious costs of gasoline and oil, as well as insurance and depreciation costs. Our objective throughout the chapter is to alert you to various options that may save you money and time when you own an automobile.

We begin the chapter with a discussion of the types of cars available, their characteristics, and how they might fit your needs. We then go on to explore the costs of ownership and operation. These costs far exceed monthly finance or leasing payments. Then we explore various shopping strategies and options, such as buying a used car or leasing a car rather than buying a new one. Regardless of the strategy you choose, you will need to know some of the information about auto repairs and warranties presented in the following sections. Finally, we look at the world of automobile insurance and its role in consumer affairs, and we offer some tips for getting better automobile insurance rates.

Basic Automobile Decisions

An automobile is a major consumer expenditure, and as such it merits a greater degree of deliberation than choosing a tube of toothpaste. Using a decision-making model such as the one in Chapter 2 can help you avoid costly errors. This means taking some time to identify the reason you are considering getting a car. By doing so, you will define the problem by identifying the causes of your search. Maybe your old car needs some major repair work, or maybe your present car is not energy efficient and your gasoline bills are high. Or maybe you are moving into a different stage in the life cycle and your present car is too big, too small, or too dumpy for your changing needs. Whatever the reasons, it is important to take some time to outline them.

There are many reasons for looking for another car, but their relative importance varies from one consumer to another, because no two consumers have identical values, goals, and standards. Table 12-1 lists some auto characteristics that could be important in a consumer's automobile decision-making process. Cost criteria such as purchase price, maintenance costs, and gasoline mileage are listed along with comfort, safety, and reliability. The list is not exhaustive, but it should give you some idea of the considerations that affect a car-buying decision. The top row of the table lists various transportation alternatives. You could buy a used car, a new car, a large car, or a small car, or you could lease rather than buy. After establishing the relevant characteristics and alternatives, your next step is to collect information.

The information-gathering process involves reading, visiting car showrooms, and consulting knowledgeable people about their experiences with

---

BOX 12-1

A Comparison of New Car Models: Some General Characteristics

The Environmental Protection Agency (EPA) issues an *Annual Gas Mileage Guide* for all new cars and light trucks. The guide gives information on relative fuel economy, engines, transmissions, fuel systems, and body types. We used information from a recent issue of this guide to list the basic classifications and their characteristics.

Minicompact cars are those that have less than 85 cubic feet of passenger and luggage space. They seat four, although the rear seats generally have little leg room. Their fuel-economy estimates vary from 15 miles per gallon for the Porsche 928 to 38 mpg for Renault's Le Car. The Honda Civic and Prelude mileage estimates are in between.

Subcompact cars have more than 85 cubic feet but less than 100 cubic feet of space. The interior space is larger than that of the minicompact, but the maximum seating capacity is still only four. Most Toyotas and Datsuns fall into this category, as do the domestically produced Chevrolet Chevettes, Dodge Omnis, Plymouth Horizons, and Volkswagen Rabbits. Gas mileage can be as high as 42 mpg for the VW Rabbit or as low as 9 mpg for an Aston-Martin, but averages between 20 and 30 mpg are more common for this group.

Compact cars have between 100 and 110 cubic feet of passenger and luggage space. Generally, these cars have room for four or five passengers, and they strike a compromise between the fuel economy of their smaller cousins and the roominess and smooth ride of their larger rivals. Examples are the AMC Concord, the Buick Skylark, the Oldsmobile Omega, and the Volvo. Even the prestigious Rolls Royce is in this category and has the dubious distinction of getting the lowest fuel-economy rating in this group—10 mpg. The typical mpg for compacts ranges from 15 to 25.

Intermediate or mid-size cars are either large compacts or small full-size sedans. They are generally a foot shorter than full-size cars, can carry five passengers in reasonable comfort, and have more than 110 but less than 120 cubic feet of room. Only a few foreign cars, such as the Mercedes-Benz 450 SEL and the Saab 900, belong under this heading. Many American models (the Cadillac Seville, the Chrysler LeBaron, the Cougar XR7, and the Chevrolet Citation) belong to this category. Short-distance mileage estimates for these cars range from 15 to 20 mpg. The Citation is a real exception at 24 mpg.

Large cars are the biggest sedans sold in the United States. They have more than 120 cubic feet of interior space, and not one imported car qualifies. Six passengers can be accommodated, and the top-of-the-line models include Cadillac DeVille and Brougham, Chevrolet Impala and Caprice, Lincoln Mark VI, and Oldsmobile Ninety-Eight. Mileage estimates are much closer among members of this group; no car gets less than 12 or more than 19 miles per gallon.

If you are interested in getting a free guide to the latest information on the newest models, they should be available at your dealer's showroom or write to Fuel Economy Distribution, Technical Information Center, P.O. Box 62, Oak Ridge, Tennessee 37830.

---

particular cars or styles. (See Box 12-1 for some additional information that may be helpful in your decision.) These data can then be transformed into positive or negative reinforcements for choosing a particular alternative. In Table 12-1, a plus sign indicates that a given alternative has the positive characteristic listed at the left. A negative sign indicates that a given alternative does not have the characteristic, and a zero indicates that no definite judgment can be made. For example, the minus sign at the intersection of the "Low initial cost" and "New car" columns indicates that a new car does *not* have a low initial cost. The used car has a plus sign, which indicates that it is lower in cost than the other alternatives. The "Leasing" and "Subcompact cars" columns also have plus signs, because these alternatives are likely to involve low initial costs.

When you have filled in the table, you are ready for Step 4—comparing the costs and benefits of the alternatives. Keep in mind that your evaluation is subjective and may not reflect another consumer's circumstances. For example, good gas mileage is not as important to someone who drives infrequently as it is to someone who commutes 40 miles to work every day. Safety may be a more important issue to a carpool driver who takes young children to school than to a college student who skydives on weekends. The interior size of an automobile may be less important for someone living alone than for a big family or even for someone with a large pet.

When you have compared the costs and the benefits of various models and have seen how they stack up against your criteria, you are ready to make your decision. Recall from Chapter 2 that this is not the end of the decision-making process. You still must periodically review and evaluate your choice, and you must, of course, accept the responsibility for your action. But before you take the plunge, you ought to understand more about the basic costs of automobile ownership.

The Costs of Automobile Ownership and Operation

As we mentioned earlier in this chapter, the decision to buy a car can be quite complex, and one consumer's rationale for buying a car might be quite different from another's. One person may be looking for basic transportation, whereas another wants considerably more than a good work car (perhaps he or she wants the car to reflect his or her personality or to project an image of prosperity). But regardless of whether one is looking for bare-bones economy or a car with "personality," a rational decision maker does not want to spend more than he or she has to. We have divided the myriad expenses associated with automobile ownership into two basic kinds: fixed and variable. Both are important and should be estimated *before* you decide to purchase a car.

FIXED COSTS
As you may recall from Chapter 6 on budgeting, **fixed costs** are expenses that do not change. They are costs that will be with you as long as you own your car, and they are not directly related to the number of miles you drive. They are the costs of ownership as opposed to the costs of driving. Fixed costs include depreciation, insurance, interest, taxes, and parking fees.

Depreciation. **Depreciation** is the loss in value of the vehicle during the time you own it. It can be measured by subtracting the current market value of your car from the purchase price. For example, if you paid $7000 for your car three years ago and today you can sell it for $3000, your car has depreciated $4000. As soon as you drive a car out of a dealer's showroom, depreciation is at work, and it will, with few exceptions, continue to whittle away at the value of your car as long as you own it. Depreciation is generally most severe in the first year of ownership. In a 1982 study, the Department of Transportation (DOT) estimated that an "annual trader" who buys a large car every year loses about $2457 in depreciation whenever he or she sells or trades the car in. In ten years, this amounts to a depreciation cost of $24,570 (10 × $2457). Car owners who buy a new car every two years see their new car depreciate $2457 in the first year and $1421 in the second year for a total of $3878 every two years. "Two-year traders" lose only $19,390 in depreciation, because they purchase only five cars over this period and depreciation costs decline as the vehicle ages (5 × $3878). Savings in depreciation would be even larger for a three-year trade-in cycle, but some of the savings in depreciation are lost in additional expenses such as tire replacements and automotive repairs, not to mention the possibility that newer models may get better fuel economy than older ones and thus may be less expensive to operate.

Insurance Costs. These costs are more closely related to the type of coverage you choose rather than the number of miles traveled. We will explain this in more detail later in this chapter. Because cars are damaged in minor as well as in major accidents and because other kinds of damages can occur, drivers take out insurance to protect themselves from having to pay for repairing the harm to the car and themselves.

Interest. Interest is another fixed cost that does not vary with the number of miles driven. If you choose to get a loan for your car, you will pay a finance charge each month for the privilege of using someone else's money. As we mentioned in Chapter 8, the size of this charge depends on the size of the loan, the

Table 12-2. The Cost of Financing a Car

Annual percentage rate	Number of months	Amount of the loan					
		$8000		$9000		$10,000	
		Monthly payment	Total finance cost	Monthly payment	Total finance cost	Monthly payment	Total finance cost
18%	36	$289.21	$2411.56	$325.37	$2713.32	$361.52	$3014.72
	48	235.00	3280.00	264.37	3689.76	293.75	4100.00
	60	203.14	4188.40	228.54	4712.40	253.93	5235.80
22%	36	305.52	2998.72	343.71	3373.56	381.90	3748.40
	48	252.04	4097.92	283.55	4610.40	315.06	5122.88
	60	220.95	5257.00	248.57	5914.20	276.18	6570.80

length of the repayment period, and the interest rate. Table 12-2 illustrates some of the financing costs of car loans. If, for example, you borrow $8000 and agree to repay it in forty-eight equal monthly installments at an annual percentage rate (APR) of 18 percent, your monthly payment will be $235. This means that at the end of your payment period, you will have repaid the $8000 plus $3280 in finance charges. A 22 percent interest rate would raise finance costs on this loan to $4100. If a difference of 4 percent in the APR can cost you over $800, it pays to shop around for the lowest interest rate. So in addition to looking for the best car price, you should also look for the lowest-priced money. You might want to review the sources for a loan discussed in Chapter 8 before you decide to buy a car.

If you choose to pay cash for your car, there is still a cost: the interest you will lose by not leaving your money in a bank. This is the opportunity cost of paying for your car immediately. To calculate this cost, use the following formula:

$$V_f = V_p (1 + i)^n$$

where
V_f = value of future savings
V_p = value of present savings
i = interest rate on savings
n = number of years

For example, $8000 would grow to $11,680 if left in an account that paid 10 percent interest for four years:

$$V_f = \$8000 (1 + .10)^4$$
$$V_f = \$8000 (1.46)$$
$$V_f = \$11,680$$

The interest on $8000 would have amounted to $3680 at the end of the four-year period ($11,680 − $8000 = $3680). If you compare the opportunity cost of using your money ($3680) with the finance cost in Table 12-2, you will get a better idea of which is cheaper. The finance charge on an $8000 loan for four years at 18 percent interest is $3280. This is less than your interest earned on $8000, because as we mentioned in Chapter 8, you don't have the use of the entire $8000 over the four-year period. You begin paying the loan back as soon as you get the car, so you are really only paying interest on an average balance of $4000.

The editors of *Changing Times* magazine received some serious criticism when they performed similar calculations and suggested that "a car buyer might come out ahead by borrowing to pay for a car rather than taking money out of savings to pay cash" (*Changing Times*, December 1980). In many instances, borrowing comes out ahead, or virtually as cheap as, paying cash—when you include the opportunity cost of the lost interest on your savings. Box

BOX 12-2
Finance Charges Per $1000 Borrowed

Number of months	Interest rate (annual percentage rate)					
	12%	14%	16%	18%	20%	22%
36	$195.80	$230.39	$265.65	$301.47	$337.89	$374.84
48	264.02	311.67	360.33	410.00	460.66	512.28
60	334.80	396.10	459.08	523.58	589.63	657.08

To find the finance charge:

1. Divide the loan amount by 1000.
2. Find the amount for the number of months and the annual percentage rate.
3. Multiply the answers from 1 and 2.

For example, the finance charge on $6500 loan at 18 percent (APR) for 4 years would be:

1. $6500 ÷ 1000 = 6.5
2. Finance charge per $1000 = $410
3. 6.5 × $410 = $2665 in finance charges

12-2 lists the finance cost per $1000 borrowed at various interest rates for three, four, or five years. If you are not sure whether it is cheaper to borrow or to use your savings, use the savings formula to calculate the opportunity cost of your savings interest lost, and then compare this to the financing costs in Box 12-2. For example, would it still be cheaper to leave your money in an account paying 9 percent interest if the loan rate for 48 months was 22 percent APR?

There are other reasons that borrowing may be preferable to paying cash for your car. Some consumers have great difficulty saving, and if they were to drain their savings by paying cash, it would take a long time to rebuild them. Given the importance of having an emergency fund (see Chapter 6), you may be giving up more than just the interest on your savings if you use savings to buy a car. You may be threatening your economic security.

A second consideration that the calculation doesn't include is the impact on your after-tax income. Because interest paid on loans is tax deductible, the true cost of borrowing money is actually less than the finance charge shown in Box 12-2. However, if your interest income is taxed, your principal will grow more slowly, and the opportunity cost of using your own money will also be less than our simple calculation shows it to be (that is, less than $3680). How much less depends on the severity of the tax rate. Of course, it may be possible to earn the 10 percent interest assumed in the calculation and avoid, or at least defer, the tax bite by putting your savings in a tax-deferred Individual Retirement Account (IRA) or a tax-free All Savers Certificate. We will discuss these options in Chapters 16 and 17. As the after-tax return on your savings rises, the opportunity cost of using your own money also rises. And given the tax advantages of borrowing, financing your car becomes more cost effective.

Taxes and Licensing Fees. These fees vary considerably among states, and they may include sales tax on the purchase, inspection and licensing fees, and property taxes. The ALA Auto and Travel Club recently found that for a subcompact, such costs averaged

Table 12-3. Cost of Owning and Operating Automobiles and Vans, 1982

Size	Suburban-based operation (cents per mile)						
	Original vehicle cost depreciated	Maintenance, accessories, parts, and tires	Gas & oil (excluding taxes)	Garage, parking, and tolls	Insurance	State and federal taxes	Total cost
Standard (with standard equipment, weighs more than 3,500 lbs. empty)	7.7	6.0	7.3	0.8	3.3	1.5	26.6
Midsize (weighs less than 3,500 lbs. empty)	6.2	5.6	6.6	0.8	3.3	1.3	23.8
Compact (weighs less than 3,000 lbs. empty)	5.9	5.0	5.3	0.8	3.3	1.1	21.4
Subcompact (weighs less than 2,500 lbs. empty)	4.7	4.8	4.5	0.8	3.1	1.0	18.9
Passenger van (weighs less than 5,000 lbs. empty)	10.7	7.2	8.9	0.8	4.4	1.9	33.2

SOURCE: U.S. Department of Transportation, *Cost of Owning Automobiles and Vans, 1982* (Washington, D.C.: U.S. Government Printing Office, 1982).

$72.93 annually in New Hampshire, $164.08 in Los Angeles, and $274.90 in Hartford, Connecticut (*Changing Times,* September 1980).

Garage Costs. These are simply the costs of parking. In a major urban area, garage fees can be a significant component of automobile ownership. In Manhattan, for example, there are "car hops" who charge a monthly fee for finding safe street parking for cars. Urban mass transit is generally the most convenient way to commute to work; thus, a person's car may sit idle during most of the week. Because street sweeping occurs with some regularity, idle cars must be moved to other areas during sweeping hours. Owners often find it cheaper to pay car hops to move their cars and thus avoid parking tickets and towing charges. These additional costs must be considered as part of the cost of ownership, and they help to explain why car ownership for people living in Manhattan is only one-quarter of the per-capita level in the nation as a whole.

VARIABLE COSTS

Costs directly associated with the amount of driving are called **variable costs** (costs of operation). The two most significant costs in this category are for fuel and maintenance.

Fuel. Gasoline or diesel fuel is a major expense for vehicles of all sizes, although the size and weight of the vehicle directly affects the cost of the fuel (see Table 12-3). The Department of Transportation has estimated that the difference in gasoline costs alone between a standard-size car and a subcompact amounts to $3380 over the life of the two autos. This calculation was made when the price of unleaded gasoline was $1.35 per gallon. Higher gasoline prices

BOX 12-3
Octane Ratings and Automobile Performance: Does It Pay to Buy Premium Gasoline?

Gasoline is a major expense, even for someone who owns a fuel-efficient automobile. But gasolines are not all the same. Some offer higher octane—the so-called premium gasolines—whereas others have less octane and are called "regular." There are no federal standards for the terms "premium" or "regular." How do you know whether you are getting your money's worth? Should you buy higher-octane gas? Will you get better mileage?

First, you must understand that the octane rating of a gasoline is simply a measure of its resistance to engine knock. It is not a measure of power or quality. However, if your engine is designed for a higher-octane gasoline than you are now using, your car will burn the gasoline unevenly and will thus be less efficient and less powerful. If a knock is loud and persistent, it can severely damage your car's engine and require costly repairs. On the other hand, if you are using gasoline with too much octane, you are paying more than you need to.

Second, you should be aware that federal law requires all gasoline pumps to bear a bright yellow sticker showing the octane rating of the gas in each pump. With the help of this information, you can save money, conserve energy, and protect your car's engine.

To determine whether your current gasoline has too much or too little octane, follow these steps suggested by the Office of Public and Consumer Affairs in the Department of Transportation.

1. Have your car tuned by a competent mechanic to exact factory specifications. Make sure that it is in good mechanical condition.
2. Wait until the gas is low, then fill up with the brand you usually buy, specifying the grade (premium, regular, or other) as recommended by your owner's manual. Drive a few miles until the engine is warmed up, come to a complete stop, then accelerate hard. If the engine knocks or pings on the gasoline with the recommended rating, use up the tank and refill with the next higher grade. Repeat the acceleration test. If the engine does not knock, this is the octane you need. If it does knock on this higher octane, see your mechanic. You have mechanical problems.

If the engine does not knock or ping on the gasoline with the recommended octane rating, use up the tank and refill with the next lower grade, or octane. Repeat the acceleration test. If the engine knocks, the lower grade is inadequate for your car's needs, and you should go back to the higher octane. If the engine does not knock, you probably can use the lower grade safely.

 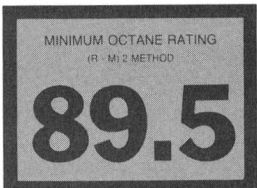

lead to even greater differences. But one way to avoid some of the high cost of gasoline is to make sure that you do not buy a more expensive grade of gasoline than you need to (see Box 12-3 for details on octane rating).

The fuel-economy estimates that you see on all advertisements for new cars (and that must be prominently displayed on all new cars) are not predictions of the mileage you will get in that car. They measure only the relative fuel economy of various new models driven under identical test conditions. According to the Environmental Protection Agency, estimated fuel economy reflects trips for local errands, driving to work, and general stop-and-go driving in urban and suburban areas, but not in heavily congested traffic. As we mentioned in Chapter 11, driving habits alone can affect miles per gallon by over 25 percent. But there are other factors beyond a person's control that can lower (or raise) a car's fuel economy, according to the EPA. Winter temperatures, for example, are a hindrance to fuel economy. Cars get better mileage when the air temperature is over 70 degrees Fahrenheit (20 degrees Celsius). At 20 degrees Fahrenheit there can be an 8 percent loss in fuel economy. Wind can also play a role in fuel economy. Driving into a 10 mph headwind lowers fuel economy by 6 percent. Snow and rain also reduce a car's mileage. Rain and wet roads will cause a 5 percent decrease in fuel economy, and snow and ice can account for a 20 percent reduction. From these examples you can see why cars in Maine or Minnesota get significantly lower gas mileage than identical models in Florida or Texas.

Maintenance Costs. These costs include everything from tuneups and oil changes to replacing tires and paying for unexpected repairs. Paying attention to the owner's manual will pay dividends by giving better fuel economy and by helping to avoid major repair expenditures. Although most drivers know this, they seldom act on it. One study showed that fewer than one-third of all new-car buyers even bothered to read the manual, let alone to follow the prescribed maintenance procedures. If you accept your responsibilities, you may well find that you will be like the car owners interviewed in *Money* magazine who all went well over 100,000 miles in their cars. The one factor that was common to all of these car owners was not the type of car they owned or the kind of driving they did, but the fact that they all met or exceeded the automobile manufacturers' maintenance requirements as stated in their owner's manual.

EVALUATING COSTS

Now you have a general idea about the kinds of costs involved in owning and driving a car. But before you can make a decision about buying or selling your car, you ought to have a more specific idea about costs. If you had to pay for each mile driven in your car, just as motorists pay for the right to drive on toll roads and

The cost of owning a car is more than the sticker price; it also includes fuel, maintenance, and sometimes inconvenience.

turnpikes, how much would your car cost? Would 5 cents per mile be a reasonable estimate, or would the cost be 25 cents or more per mile?

Table 12-3 shows the U.S. Department of Transportation's estimates of the costs per mile of owning and operating five different types of vehicles over their lifetimes. These data were estimated on the assumptions that the car is purchased new, is owned for twelve years, and is driven 120,000 miles before junking. They further assume that the car is driven under suburban conditions and that it is driven more during its early years than its later years. All of the variable and fixed costs that we mentioned in the last sections are included, except the cost of financing. Thus, the table slightly underestimates the actual cost of driving.

As you can see, the least-expensive car to own is a subcompact, which costs an average of 18.9 cents per mile. If you had to pay by the mile for a standard (full-size) car over its ten-year life, you would pay over 26 cents for every mile you drove. A passenger van is the most expensive vehicle, with a per-mile average of 33.2 cents. To get the Department of Transportation's estimate of the total cost of any of these vehicles, multiply the total per-mile cost by 120,000. Thus, the passenger van costs almost $40,000, whereas the subcompact costs about half that much. You could buy and operate two subcompacts for about the same amount as you could operate one van.

Even though a van costs twice as much to operate as a subcompact, is it irrational for consumers to buy vans? Of course it isn't. The benefits as well as the costs must enter into the decision. Some of the benefits of a van are obvious, such as the passenger roominess and the large cargo area. Others, such as safety, are less obvious but could be very important. In a head-on collision between a van and a subcompact, the occupants of the van have a smaller risk of injury. And if you have ever carpooled or gone camping, you know that a van is far more comfortable than a subcompact. For a van to be preferred over a subcompact, its benefits would have to be twice as great—a subjective judgment that consumers must make based on their individual values and goals.

As you can see in Table 12-3, depreciation is clearly the largest single expense for new-car owners. And because the Department of Transportation estimates are based on a twelve-year car ownership pattern, they probably underestimate the per-mile depreciation charges. The average new-car owner trades in when the car reaches 50,000 to 55,000 miles and is approximately 5.2 years old (Porter, 1979). Although this is less than half of the life of the car, the car's value has fallen (depreciated) by two-thirds. As a general rule, depreciation becomes a smaller component of total cost as a car ages. The figures in the depreciation column would all double if only first-year costs were included. The second most important cost is that of gas and oil. Because the subcompact gets the most miles per gallon, its average cost per mile is lower than that of any other model. But here again, these estimates understate the real cost of driving, because they are based on gasoline prices ($1.35 per gallon). The costs of maintenance, accessories, parts, and tires are the third most significant expenses for car owners. Unlike depreciation

Table 12-4. Costs in Cents Per Mile According to Usage and Type of Car

Years of use	Miles driven per year for subcompacts		
	10,000	*15,000*	*25,000*
1	27.2¢	20.4¢	14.9¢
2	26.5	19.9	14.8
3	25.8	19.5	14.7
4	23.7¢	18.2¢	14.2¢
	Miles driven per year for compacts		
	10,000	*15,000*	*25,000*
1	33.7¢	25.3¢	18.8¢
2	33.0	25.1	18.8
3	31.9	24.4	18.5
4	29.8¢	23.0¢	17.9¢
	Miles driven per year for standard cars		
	10,000	*15,000*	*25,000*
1	38.6¢	28.9¢	21.3¢
2	37.9	28.6	21.2
3	36.9	27.9	21.1
4	34.1¢	26.2¢	20.4¢

SOURCES: "The Real Cost of Driving Your Car," reprinted with permission from *Changing Times* magazine, © 1980 Kiplinger Washington Editors, Inc. (September 1980), p. 22, and *Sylvia Porter's New Money Book for the 80's*, by Sylvia Porter. Copyright © 1975, 1979 by Sylvia Porter. Reprinted by permission of Doubleday & Co., Inc. Both are based on Hertz Rent-A-Car data.

expenses, which decline as a car ages, maintenance costs rise over time. Tires wear out, batteries go dead, and engines need major overhauls as a car's mileage mounts. Again, these figures are only estimates, and a good consumer can save hundreds of dollars by comparison shopping, as Box 12-4 shows.

Of course, all of these per-mile costs are averages. We cannot stress this point often enough. If, in the first year, you drive your new car more than the 14,500 mile Department of Transportation estimate, the per-mile costs will decline because the fixed costs of depreciation, insurance, and so forth will be averaged over more miles. For example, depreciation costs for a new standard-size car are estimated to be $2457 in the first year. This averages less than 10 cents per mile for a car driven 25,000 miles. Of course, your variable costs (maintenance and gasoline) will rise as you drive more, but for new cars driven 100,000 miles or less in the first five years of ownership, fixed costs are generally more important than variable costs. Table 12-4 makes this point using

BOX 12-4
Tire Buying Made Simpler

In the days when gasoline was sold by the gallon and a dollar could buy more than three gallons, a car was sometimes referred to as "a set of wheels." But even then, wheels were of little use without tires, which came in a myriad of sizes. Tire brands, styles, and treads were very difficult for the consumer to evaluate in a straightforward manner. Today, however, there is uniform tire-quality grading that can be of significant help to a person who is considering purchasing new tires.

The first question to ask, of course, is whether you *need* new tires. The answer to this question is a definite yes if the grooves on the tread are 1/16 of an inch deep or less. All modern tires are equipped with tread wear bars that cut across the tread when the tire reaches a certain level. If you are unsure of the amount of tread wear, push a penny between the tread. If Lincoln's head is not at least partially covered, it is time to consider replacing the tire. Under no circumstances should you wait until the tire is "bald," that is, without tread. Bald tires can lose traction and increase the possibility of a blowout at high speed.

Once you have decided to purchase new tires, you will want to do some comparison shopping. This is when a knowledge of the Uniform Tire Quality Grading System can pay significant dividends. The system rates three significant tire characteristics: tread wear, traction, and temperature resistance. As of October 1, 1980, all passenger-car tires sold in America must have tread-wear, traction, and temperature ratings molded on the tire sidewall. This allows the consumer to make an informed choice among competing brands of tires.

The tread-wear grading system uses a numerical range of 50 to 200. The Department of Transportation has already established the tread-wearing capability of an "average" tire. Such a tire receives a rating of 100. If a particular tire gets 20 percent more miles on the government's test course, then it will be given a tread-wear rating of 120. The higher the rating, the more miles per tire under similar road conditions. Of course, because driving terrains and habits vary, the precise number of miles per tire also vary. But for comparisons between tires, the exact number of miles is irrelevant; the proportions remain constant. A tire with a rating of 120 can be counted on to give 20 percent more service than a tire with a rating of 100.

Traction and temperature resistance are graded alphabetically. The ratings assigned by the Department of Transportation are A, B, and C. A tire rated A has better traction than one rated B. A grade C tire is considered adequate under normal conditions, but has poor traction on wet roads. The temperature grades represent the tire's resistance to the heat that develops naturally as a result of friction. At highway speeds, tires can develop high temperatures that can reduce tire life and, in some cases, lead to sudden tire failure. The grade C tire meets the minimum federal safety standard. Grades A and B exceed the standard.

The tire you choose should be related to the type of driving you do, to the general condition of the roads, and to the climate in your area. If you live in an area with frequent rainfall, traction is obviously an important criterion. If you frequently travel long distances at high speed, the temperature-resistance rating is important. The tread-wear rating may be important if you plan on keeping the car a long time. The grading standards can not tell you which tire is best for you, but they can give you the information you need to make a rational choice.

When shopping for an expensive durable item such as a car, consumers should be well-prepared. Not only should they have a good idea of what they're looking for and how much they want to spend, but they should also be aware of sales tactics.

data from the Hertz Rent-A-Car fleet. For every year of ownership, a car driven 25,000 miles has average per-mile costs that are 40 to 44 percent lower than those of one driven only 10,000 miles.

There are many other ways of lowering your real driving costs. These may include getting a better deal on your new car, buying a used rather than a new car, leasing rather than buying, finding a good mechanic, and getting a better automobile-insurance package. In sections that follow we explore these topics with an emphasis on decision making. But before you can begin to save money on your car, you have to own or lease one. In the next section we deal with the problems of looking for a car.

Shopping for a Car

The decision to buy a new car is rarely made solely because it would be cheaper to buy a new car than to buy a used one or to fix the one you already have. Depreciation on a new car in the first year alone will probably exceed the cost of repairs to any car with fewer than 100,000 miles on it. Nevertheless, 6–10 million new cars are sold each year. Even subtracting the number of cars purchased for business use, somewhere between 3 and 5 million new cars are purchased for personal use every year. Add to this the 13–15 million used cars that consumers purchase each year and the 1 million cars leased for personal use by consumers, and it is obvious that all consumers need to be better informed about the automobile selection process. In the following sections we review the three major choices—buying a new car, leasing a car, and buying a used car.

NEW CAR BUYING STRATEGIES

Few experiences can be as traumatic as buying a new car. In most cases, there are only a few dealerships for any particular make, and their profit is directly related to the kind of bargain they can make with the consumer. There are various strategies that you should be aware of *before* you venture into the showroom full of sparkling clean, aromatic automobiles. Unfortunately, many consumers are unaware of these techniques and often wind up paying hundreds and perhaps thousands of dollars more than they have to for a car.

The first step in the buying process must involve a realistic assessment of what you are looking for in automotive transportation. Roominess, comfort, style, high performance, fuel economy, and reliability are only a few of the features to be considered. Obviously, there are tradeoffs involved in getting a car that meets these standards. You may be forced to give up some acceleration performance in order to get better fuel economy. You may have to sacrifice style for roominess. These are decisions you should make well before you begin to talk seriously with an automobile salesman. If you don't, you may wind up with a car you never really wanted. If you are making a family decision, it is especially important that everyone involved have some input about these tradeoffs.

Second, decide how much car you can afford. Place an upper limit on the monthly allocation for automotive needs that includes the monthly payment for a car loan and the costs of auto insurance, maintenance, parking, taxes, and gasoline. A general rule is that not more than 15 percent of your monthly income should be devoted to transportation.

Third, get information about the types of cars you are considering. Much of this information can be obtained in consumer-oriented periodicals such as *Consumer Reports,* which publishes an annual *Buying Guide* issue and generally reports on all new cars in its April issue. Such periodicals describe and evaluate the newest models and report on the repair records of previous models. Another important piece of information is the wholesale price of the car, that is, the dealer cost. Newsstands generally carry several periodicals that list dealer costs for most models.* If these are unavailable, you can generally estimate the dealer's cost by cutting the sticker price by 20 percent. The average markup is a bit higher than this for larger cars and slightly lower for compacts, but this is a good general rule.

---

*Some examples are *Edmund's Car Prices, Auto Dealer Costs, Car Fax, Better Homes & Gardens Car Prices,* and *Consumers Digest Buying Guide.*

If you know the exact make, model, and body type of the car you want, you can write to Car/Puter International Corporation, 1603 Bushwick Ave., Brooklyn, New York 11207. Car/Puter will send you a computer printout of the wholesale price of the car plus prices for various options. The service costs $15, and it can be reached by telephone. Call 800-221-4001. Given all of these information sources, it is little wonder that fewer than 10 percent of all new-car buyers actually pay the manufacturer's suggested price. So when the salesperson offers to lower the price, don't be surprised or feel any obligation. It is just good business.

Your homework assignment also includes finding out how much your present car is worth as a trade-in. Current used-car prices are published monthly in the National Automobile Dealers Association (NADA) *Official Used Car Guide* or in the *Kelley Blue Book Market Report.* Banks and other lending institutions, such as credit unions, always have the most recent issue. Ask to see it, or purchase it yourself at a local newsstand, bookstore, drug store, or supermarket.

Two common practices that you should be wary of when buying a new car are called low balling and high balling. When using the **low-ball technique,** a salesperson will quote a very low price on the car, perhaps 25 to 30 percent below the sticker price. But when you try to buy the car, you discover that the salesperson "made a mistake" and forgot to include some important costs. Or no mistake may be mentioned, but your trade-in car is appraised at half of its wholesale value. The **high-ball technique** is a deliberate overestimate of the value of your trade-in. You may get $500 to $1000 over the wholesale value of your older car, but the dealer refuses to come down on the retail sticker price of the car or adds some extra charges into the final price. By obtaining good information and by knowing the wholesale value of your car and the dealer's cost of the model in question, you should be able to quickly spot either of these techniques.

Finally, as you saw in Table 12-2 and Box 12-2, interest rates can have a significant impact on the cost of financing an automobile. It is generally a good idea to shop for credit *before* you shop for a car. This allows you to determine the price of the car separately from the price of the financing. Auto dealers sometimes earn a significant return by getting their customers to use a particular finance company or bank. In essence, the dealer earns a fee for bringing in business. Having your financing arranged in advance also saves you the trouble of filling out the forms in the dealer showroom. These forms can provide the dealer with information that makes it more difficult for you to get the dealer to give you a discount from the sticker price. For example, if you live near a dealership, you might prefer to buy the car there rather than across town. If you fill out a credit application, the dealer will know where you live, and he or she may not offer you as low a price as someone who lives farther away.

Now you are ready to enter the battleground—the dealer's showroom. Steel yourself against the urge to buy a car on the first visit. Take a test drive. Ask about the warranty. Get a feel for the car, and then leave. Look at the competitive models and visit other dealerships before you decide to bargain. If you like a particular model but seem unable to strike a good price, consider purchasing its corporate twin. The Lynx, sold by Mercury dealers, is essentially the same car as the Ford Escort. The same is true for the Dodge Omni and the Plymouth Horizon, as well as for the corporate quadruplets from General Motors: the Buick Century, the Chevrolet Celebrity, the Oldsmobile Ciera, and the Pontiac 6000. For other models, see *Consumer Reports*.

You may be unable or unwilling to bargain with your local new-car dealer. This should not deter you from looking over the cars and taking a test drive. All you need to do is to indicate to the salesperson that you are considering a purchase, but you are not going to decide today. Then you can go to a car-buying service to complete the purchase. Some credit unions or local savings and loan associations can help you to get in touch with one of these services. Such services normally have agreements with one or two dealers of every automobile make sold in your area. For a fee, which varies from $150 to $500, the buying service will see that you get the car of your choice at factory cost. The factory warranties and even the rebates will be the same as if you had purchased the car directly from the dealer. A few of the better-known services are:

American-wide Auto Buying Service, Inc.
2507 David Broderick Tower
Detroit, Michigan 48226

Motor Club Auto Buying Service
14411 West Eight Mile Road
Detroit, Michigan 48235

United Auto Brokers
1603 Bushwick Avenue
Brooklyn, New York 11207
(This is Car/Puter's purchasing division and has a toll-free number: 800-221-4001.)

LEASING A NEW CAR

Some consumers do not buy new cars, they rent them. This may not seem unusual, because most of us know of two or three major car rental companies. But instead of renting cars for a day or a week, many consumers are now renting cars for two or three years. This rental arrangement, called a **lease**, has a number of advantages. First, a lease car is easier to obtain, partly because the buyer puts down a smaller amount of cash and partly because the rules for computing a customer's financial eligibility are less strict. For example, a family could lease three cars, whereas they could only qualify to borrow enough money to buy one. Secondly, the leasing company may provide repairs and insurance all in one neat package. Under such a "full-maintenance agreement" the driver need not make any outlay for the car other than the lease price and the cost of gasoline and oil. This means that he or she can budget exactly for the cost of driving. Finally, if the car is used for business purposes, leasing a car greatly simplifies recordkeeping for tax purposes. One simply adds up monthly leasing bills. Of course, the costs of using a personal car for business are also deductible, but figuring some of these ex-

> **BOX 12-5**
>
> ## Only $98.35 a Month!
>
> Debbie and Kevin had been married for twelve years. Their little girl, Robin, was in grade school, and Debbie was looking for a job to supplement the household income.
>
> "You're going to need your own car to go to work," Kevin remarked, as he looked over the automobile ads in the newspaper. "Let's get a small, gas-saving model so you won't just be working for the car payment."
>
> "I'm not sure that I'll need a car," Debbie replied. "We're not far from the bus stop, and I'll probably get a job downtown."
>
> "Nonsense," Kevin replied. "I don't want you to wait in the snow and the rain for some overcrowded bus with all kinds of weirdos on it. We are going to get you a car."
>
> "But where are we going to get the money for a down payment?" Debbie asked.
>
> "I've got it! Here it is!" Kevin went on. "A brand new Mazda GLC for only $300 down and $98.35 per month on our personal lease plan for thirty-six months. There's our answer. For less than $100 a month. Let's go look at it."
>
> "It sounds too good to be true," Debbie remarked skeptically. "Let me look at the ad."
>
> Sure enough, the ad did state in bold type that the cost was $98.35 per month for thirty-six months on a personal lease plan. In smaller letters there was something about "residual value, $2485." But the meaning wasn't really clear to either of them. They decided to go to the showroom and have a look the next day.
>
> The following evening, a shiny red Mazda GLC was parked outside their house, and they had a personal lease plan.
>
> 1. Did they follow a logical consumer decision-making process?
> 2. What kind of decision making did they go through about mass transit? How could you have done it differently?
> 3. Will this couple's transportation expenses rise by only $98.35 per month? What additional costs will they have to bear?
> 4. What does "residual value" mean in the context of a personal lease plan? Are Debbie and Kevin in for a surprise at the end of the thirty-six-month lease period?

penses (especially depreciation) can be complex. If the car is used for business one-third of the time, it is easy to justify one-third of the leasing cost as a business expense, but it is more difficult to argue that one-third of the depreciation was related to business driving.

Of course there are also disadvantages to leasing. Generally, there is a penalty for ending the lease early. And even if the contract is fulfilled, one still does not own anything of value. In one type of lease, called a **closed-end lease,** one pays a flat fee every month and then turns the car back in at the end of the lease period. In another, more common contract, the **open-end-lease,** one is obligated to buy the car at the end of the lease period for a depreciated amount, the **residual value.** An advertisement might offer a brand new Volkswagen Jetta Diesel, "A Family Sports Car," for only $202.15 per month. The fine print must mention the length of the lease period, say forty-eight months, and the residual value ($5,621 in a recent ad). Generally, the leasing company agrees to sell the car for the lessee if he or she decides not to pay this residual amount. However, if it cannot get someone to pay this amount, then the consumer must come up with the difference. So, in addition to monthly payments, he or she may have a large balloon payment at the end of the contract. Of course, it is also conceivable that the car will be worth more than the anticipated residual value. In this case, a consumer with an open-end lease will actually get to keep the difference.

The decision to lease rather than buy should not be made before the costs and benefits of each are weighed. If you prefer not to argue with dealers over the price of a new car and if you prefer to *know* how much car maintenance will cost rather than hoping you didn't get a lemon, a closed-end, full-maintenance lease could be the best option. And with a closed-end lease, you don't have to worry about the residual-value problem of open-end leases. Of course, a closed-end, full-maintenance lease is also the most expensive monthly lease. Eliminating the full-maintenance lease will lower your cost, and opting for an open-end lease will lower your lease price, because you share some of the repair and depreciation risk. Of course, no matter what kind of lease you choose, you will still never "own" the car. If you buy a car and then hold onto it, you will be free of payments at about the same time that some long-term personal leases are up. If you hold a typical new car for ten years, you might save enough in the nonpayment years to pay cash for your next car.

BUYING A USED CAR

Three out of every four cars sold for personal driving are used cars. In a good year, 15 million used cars will be sold in the $30 billion used-car industry. To understand why business is booming in the used-car industry, all you have to do is to walk into a new-car showroom and look at the sticker prices. In 1981, the average price of a new car broke the $10,000 mark for the first time, and prices have not fallen since then. Used cars have one major advantage over new cars—they are cheaper. Depreciation has taken its toll, and the changes in style may have further eroded the market value of older vehicles. In other words, you may be able to get more transportation value for your money from an older car. But there is always some risk.

There are four major outlets for used cars: new car dealers, used car dealers, rental car companies, and private owners.

Franchised New-Car Dealers. New-car dealers generally sell only the most marketable, late-model cars that they take in on trades. They have a service facility for repairing and maintaining cars, and they often provide a written guaranty that the used car will be free from defects for a specific time period or for a certain number of miles. This guaranty, called a **limited warranty,** is similar to those discussed in Chapter 5. New-car dealers will take your old car in trade (which is convenient for you), but you will probably net less money than if you sold it yourself. Given the kinds of cars and services offered at new-car dealerships, it is understandable that they sell almost 50 percent of all used cars, but they usually charge the highest price listed in the National Automobile Dealers Association (NADA) blue book of used car prices, too.

Used-Car Dealerships. Used-car dealers often have lower-priced cars on their lots, but they usually do not have their own service facilities, and they seldom sell cars that they take in trade. They buy their cars in wholesale auctions, sometimes in different states, or they purchase them from other dealers or fleet owners. They have been known to buy cars that will not pass inspection in one state and sell them in another state that does not have such inspection laws. Taxis, police cars, and other late-model, high-mileage fleet vehicles often appear on these lots. In the past, some dealers rolled back the odometers on high-mileage cars to make them appear less used. This happens less today, because it is a federal offense (see Box 12-6). As a group, used-car dealers are the riskiest people to buy cars from because of their disreputable records. Of course, there are always exceptions to this rule, but a University of Wisconsin study funded by the Federal Trade Commission concluded that "those who trade with a used car dealer get a worse deal than those who buy from a private seller" (*Focus,* 1978).

Rental Cars as Used Cars. A small but growing segment of the used-car market involves purchases from large fleet owners such as rental car companies. In major cities, Hertz, Avis, National, and others are beginning to sell their cars directly to the public. They often provide some type of warranty, and you can usually see the maintenance record of any car you are considering—two advantages that few used-car dealers offer. But you will also get a car that has had 80 to 100 different drivers who have had no vested interest in treating the car with care. These cars also have more miles on them than comparable cars owned by individuals, but many of these miles may have been relatively less-demanding highway miles rather than the strenuous stop-and-go traffic miles that wear out

> **BOX 12-6**
>
> ## The Odometer Law
>
> A federal law passed in 1972 makes it illegal for anyone to do anything that would cause a vehicle's odometer to show the wrong mileage. No one, not even the vehicle's owner, is permitted to turn back or disconnect the odometer (except to perform necessary repairs). The federal law also requires that anyone who sells a vehicle or transfers ownership in some other way must provide the buyer with a signed statement indicating the mileage registered on the odometer at the time of the transfer. If the seller knows that the registered mileage is incorrect because the odometer has been broken or previously tampered with, he must include a statement to that effect on the mileage-disclosure form. When you purchase a vehicle, be certain that you receive a mileage-disclosure statement before the transfer of title.
>
> Anyone who illegally tampers with an odometer or fails to provide the required mileage-disclosure statement may be sued in a private civil action by the person wronged by the violation. If the suit is successful, the person will recover $1500 or three times the amount of actual damages, whichever is greater.
>
> If you suspect that an odometer has been tampered with, call the National Highway Traffic Safety Administration, 202-426-0670, or the Department of Justice, 202-724-6786.

an engine faster. Selection is also more limited in the fleet-owner outlet, and fleet owners will not accept your old car in trade. Despite these drawbacks, the good reputation of the companies plus the availability of a warranty and a maintenance record make this option worth consideration.

The Private Seller. This is the smallest used-car outlet, accounting for about 20 percent of all vehicles sold. Nevertheless, it is an important outlet for consumers, because they may be on either side of the transaction. If you buy from a private party, you should get a lower price than a dealer would charge for the same vehicle. The average markup from the wholesale blue-book price on a used car is 22 percent, but it can be as high as 50 percent if the car is transported long distances or sold by one dealer to another. Use the same procedure we suggested earlier to find the value of a given used car—look at the *NADA Official Used Car Guide* or the *Kelly Auto Market Report* available at credit unions, at banks, or for sale at newsstands and bookstores. You should also scan the classified ads in your local newspaper to see what the average price for a given car model and year is. Used-car prices rise in the spring and early summer as people begin to think about taking vacations and as the weather makes used-car buying less difficult. You should also time your buying to avoid inflation; November is a good month to buy used cars, and spring and early summer are good times to sell (see Box 7-5).

Information and Decision Making in the Used-Car Market. No matter which outlet you choose to buy from, there is always some risk involved in buying a used car. You could make the wrong decision and wind up with a lemon instead of the peach you thought you were getting. One way to lessen your risk is by obtaining information about the car you are considering. The Federal Trade Commission has made an effort to provide such information with a 1981 ruling that required all commercial used-car dealers to disclose any known defects in the car and to describe any warranty on a **buyer's guide window sticker.** However, in 1982 Congress overruled this and effectively repealed the regulation. Thus, the burden of information is clearly on the consumer. For example, you should ask to see evidence of the reliability of the car, proof of servicing, mechanics' records, and the like. Rental-car companies and private sellers will probably have such servicing records, and you should certainly ask for them. This kind of information will support assertions such as, ''I just had the brakes relined'' or ''I just had the engine rebuilt'' or ''I

One of the rules of thumb in looking for a used car is never to shop at night or when it is raining.

always take the car in for servicing." In addition, records give you an idea of the costs of maintaining the car. These costs can be expected to rise as the car ages. Finally, general information about the frequency of repair records for most used cars can be found in the *Consumer Reports* annual *Buying Guide*. In an average year, *Consumer Reports* receives over 250,000 replies from its readers on the repair records of the autos they own. These responses are then summarized by model and year in the *Buying Guide*. By looking up the record of a given used-car model, you can discover trouble spots to investigate before you buy, and you will have some indication of the reliability of the model you are considering.

In addition to seeking information, there are a number of general rules to follow when you are in the used-car market.

1. Never buy a car at night or when it is raining. Both conditions can obscure defects in the car and make it appear to be better maintained.

2. Avoid buying an "orphan," that is, a car that is no longer in production. Cars such as Dodge Diplomats, AMC Ambassadors and Matadors, and General Motors Opels are examples. Parts for such cars may be expensive and hard to get.

3. Be wary of used cars that are loaded with options such as power windows, power seats, power antennas, and the like. Cars seldom age gracefully, and they are less likely to do so if they are filled with technological contraptions that are waiting to cause trouble.

4. Never buy a car without taking it for a test drive. This should include some hard acceleration, emergency stops, and parking.

5. If you think you have found the car you want, have your mechanic look it over. It is well worth a $30 investment to avoid a mistake that may cost hundreds of dollars.

6. Check for recalls. Many vehicles have defects that are discovered after the cars are sold to the public. The owners of these cars are notified by the

automobile company that their cars are being recalled and that the defect will be fixed at no charge. Since 1966, there have been 3,000 recalls involving 80 million vehicles, but not all of those recalled have been repaired. For example, 1 million owners of 1971 to 1976 Ford Pintos and 1975 to 1976 Mercury Bobcats were told of a defective fuel system that could lead to explosion and fire. This defect had reportedly killed twenty-five people, and yet two years after the recall, 350,000 unfixed Pintos and Bobcats remained on the road (*Changing Times,* October 1980). In 1979, safety defects led to the recall of 9 million cars, trucks, and motorcycles. Before you buy a used car, call the National Highway Traffic Safety hotline at 800-424-9393. Give the year and the model of the car, and a computer will check for recalls. If such a recall exists, you will be sent a card to put the car's vehicle identification number on and send to the auto manufacturer, who will then check to see if the car was repaired. If it wasn't, the manufacturer will pay for the necessary repairs.

Automobile Repairs

Whether you decide to buy a new or a used car or you decide to keep your old one, you can be sure that in the not-too-distant future you will have to get your car serviced and repaired. According to NHTSA, Americans spend over $50 billion a year in repairs and service. Even more disheartening is the NHTSA estimate that 40 percent of these consumer expenditures are caused by improper diagnosis and unnecessary or poor repairs. In this section, we cover some of the major factors involved in getting your car repaired—warranty coverage, service contracts, and selecting a mechanic.

AUTOMOBILE WARRANTIES

According to Murphy's law, "If anything can go wrong, it will, and generally at the worst possible moment." Automobile breakdowns certainly follow this general principle. However, a knowledgeable consumer can be prepared, and he or she can thus lessen the impact of these annoying incidents. This means knowing one's rights and responsibilities concerning the automobile. Research indicates that consumers are largely ignorant about warranties. And if your car breaks down, it may be important to understand just what your warranty covers. We discussed warranties in Chapter 5, but automobile warranties are so important that we will repeat some information here.

A **warranty** is an assurance that a product is in working order and will give good service for a reasonable period of time. If properly understood, a warranty can save thousands of dollars in repairs. Our purpose here is to guide you through the jungle of automobile warranties so that you will be able to survive in the real world.

Types of Warranties. Automobile manufacturers' warranties may be full warranties or limited warranties. The difference between the two is in consumers' rights, not in the length of the warranty period or in the number of parts covered by the warranty. Currently, only American Motors offers full warranties; all other manufacturers offer limited warranties. Under a full warranty, the manufacturer is required to give the consumer a refund or replace the automobile if the defects are not repaired in a reasonable time period. In addition, under the Magnuson-Moss Warranty Act of 1975, the manufacturer must compensate the consumer for incidental expenses such as those for food, lodging, and rental cars, if there are unreasonable delays or other problems in honoring the warranty. American Motors thus agrees to lend its customers a car if their automobile has to be left overnight, and it further agrees to reimburse the owner up to $150 for extra expenses if the car breaks down while the owner is more than 100 miles away from home.

Under a limited warranty, the manufacturer is not required to compensate the consumer for time or expenses incurred or to provide alternate transportation. The warranty is limited to fixing the car. You may be inconvenienced by taking your car back to a dealer dozens of times, but you will still not be protected under the Magnuson-Moss Act, as long as the dealer is legitimately trying to repair the car.

A limited warranty is only one form of what is known as an **express warranty,** that is, a statement about what the prospective consumer can expect from the product. However, the manufacturer's written warranty is only one form of express warranty. Claims made by the salesperson, especially if they are in writing, are another form of express warranty. Television commercials and advertising brochures can also be considered express warranties. If you see a pickup truck bouncing around on rough roads, the implication is that, if the truck were handled the same way by a consumer, it would be able to withstand the treatment. Recently, a Ford pickup truck advertisement was used as evidence in just such a case, and the consumer won. This court ruling may make such dramatic commercials a thing of the past (*Consumer Reports,* October 1979).

All products sold also carry *implied warranties*—implicit statements that the product is usable and will not fall apart or break down under normal use (see Chapter 5). Twenty-five states have explicit provisions for implied warranty protection. And every state except Louisiana has adopted Section 2-719 of the Uniform Commercial Code, which governs the sale of all items purchased in the United States. This section states that "where circumstances cause an exclusive or limited remedy (warranty) to fail of its essential purpose, remedy may be had as provided in this Act." If, for example, your automatic transmission breaks down 500 miles after the 12,000 mile warranty expires, you could argue that the limited warranty did not provide an effective way to ensure that you received a serviceable automobile.

Another type of warranty that has only recently come to light is the so-called **secret warranty.** This is a form of extended protection that is sometimes provided by the manufacturer when a particular problem habitually develops beyond the limited warranty period. It should not be confused with a recall, in which all owners are notified of a particular defect and are invited to have it repaired at an authorized dealer's expense. A secret warranty is never announced publicly; only the local dealers are notified, and then, at their discretion, repairs are made.

BOX 12-7

The Center for Automotive Safety

Since 1900, more than 2 million Americans have died from traffic accidents—many more than the 1.2 million deaths Americans suffered in *all* our wars. Recognizing the many problems connected with automobiles and highway safety, Ralph Nader and the Consumers Union (publishers of *Consumer Reports*) joined forces in 1970 to create a public-interest, non-profit consumer organization called the Center for Auto Safety.

The Center now operates independently of its founders, but its goals are still the same: to eliminate the causes of auto accidents and to speak for consumers on automotive issues. To do this, the Center operates as a clearing house for consumer complaints. It receives over 15,000 letters annually from frustrated car buyers complaining about vehicle defects. The Center also conducts research on increasing safety through automobile and highway design. With over 50,000 traffic deaths per year, this is very important work. And according to the Center's literature, "More than 50 percent of these deaths and injuries are caused by hazards such as exploding gas tanks, inadequate occupant protection, steering wheels that lock, brakes that fail, tires that blow out, hazardous guard rails, weak bridge railings and other mistakes in building cars and highways."

The Center depends on the public for its support. If you are interested in learning more about it, or if you have an auto complaint, write to: The Center for Auto Safety, 1223 Dupont Circle Building, Washington, D.C. 20036.

The Center for Automotive Safety, for example, uncovered a secret warranty program covering rust damage to 1969 to 1973 Fords. Under this plan, favored customers (or those who complained about the problem) had their rust problems repaired at no cost. But not all Ford owners were notified (see Box 12-7 for more on the Center's work). It has been reported that Chevrolet replaced millions of rusted front fenders on Vegas under a similar secret warranty plan. *Consumer Reports* (October 1979) also claimed to have uncovered evidence of a similar plan covering

General Motors' new lightweight automatic transmission, which often failed shortly after the limited warranty expired.

Enforcing Warranty Rights. According to Clarence Ditlow, head of the Center for Automotive Safety, "There are two types of consumers who have a better than average chance in pressing warranty claims. The first is the long-time customer of one dealership; the second is the obnoxious customer, who goes in and raises hell. As it's currently set up, the system is designed to wear the customers down" (*Consumer Reports,* October 1979). If you are a price-conscious consumer who shops for the best deal, you probably won't fall into the first category, so you may have to be a bit obnoxious. But you also need to know and follow the rules of the game.

In order to get the best results, you should keep good records and discuss your complaint with your local dealer first. In many cases, this will result in a satisfactory solution. If it doesn't, then call the manufacturer's representative in your area; generally, the phone number is in your owner's manual. If you are still not satisfied, call corporate headquarters and ask for the consumer service representative. This exhausts your in-house complaint possibilities, but there are other remedies available. There are over twenty national Consumer Action Panels (Auto CAPs*) for automobile problems. These panels are special offices established to help resolve disputes between consumers and the automobile industry. After receiving your complaint, they will ask the manufacturer to reinvestigate the problem and report back to them on the action taken. If the dispute still exists, they will sponsor a hearing and make a recommendation that is not binding on the manufacturers but that manufacturers generally accept. If you still have a problem, Box 12-8 may give you ideas for other sources of help.

AUTO SERVICE CONTRACTS

A common practice among new-car and used-car dealers today is to offer the buyer a service contract

---

*To find out if there is an Auto CAP in your area, write to your Better Business Bureau, the Chamber of Commerce, or the National Automobile Dealers Association (NADA), 8400 West Park Drive, McLean, Virginia 22101.

BOX 12-8

Lemon Aid

"I bought a lemon." This statement seldom refers to fruit; generally it refers to a poorly made automobile that is continually breaking down. If you buy a lemon and cannot get satisfaction from the dealer or the auto maker, you can still do quite a bit before you have to hire a lawyer and go to court. The Maine Bureau of Consumer Protection has published the *Down-Easters Lemon Guide,* from which this list was adapted:

1. By law, all new cars have an implied warranty to provide safe, efficient, trouble-free transportation.
2. If something is wrong with your new car, you must give the dealer a reasonable number of chances to repair it.
3. If the dealer will not or can not fix the defect within a reasonable time, and further, if the defect substantially impairs the car's value, you have a right to get a replacement or a refund. (Note: The problem must be major, not just a rattle or a clock that keeps poor time.)
4. To get a replacement or a refund, you must give the "lemon" back to the dealer. This procedure is called "revocation of acceptance." This should include giving the dealer some reasons in writing and indicating that you are canceling your insurance and registration.
5. Do not forget to contact your lender and inform him or her of the situation and where the car may be found. You may wish to "play it safe" and continue to make payments to avoid the possibility of being sued for the outstanding debt balance.
6. This bold maneuver will generally result in a successful settlement. But if it does not, let the dealer know that you plan to hire an attorney. In most cases of this sort, the dealer or manufacturer will have to pay your attorney fees as part of the settlement.

If you do need an attorney, the *Lemon Guide* has a special section on law citations and the legal background of successful suits in which lemon victims got their money and expenses back. For $1.50, you can get the publication from the Maine Bureau of Consumer Protection, Augusta, Maine 04333. There is no charge for Maine residents.

that is sometimes called an **extended warranty plan.** As they often say, "For only a few pennies a day, you can have peace of mind." The Federal Trade Commission estimates that 50 percent of all new-car buyers purchase this additional protection against having to make automobile repairs. Are these consumers making a wise decision?

First, you should understand that there is a major difference between a warranty and a service contract. A warranty is provided by the manufacturer or seller at no extra cost. A **service contract** is an agreement in which the buyer agrees to pay a certain fee to a service contractor (who may be the auto manufacturer, the dealer, or some independent firm), who in turn agrees to maintain or repair the car for a given period of time. The service contract is purchased separately from the car, and you don't have to buy it from the dealer. But are these contracts good deals? Each case is a bit different, and only you can decide. But before you decide to pay the extra money, answer the following questions developed by the Federal Trade Commission's Bureau of Consumer Protection:

1. *How much does the service contract cost?* Although manufacturers' service contracts generally offer the same coverage for all their new cars, the price depends on the car model. Independent company and dealer service contracts base the contract price on the car make, the model, the condition (new or used), what is covered, and the length of the contract. Most contracts cost between $100 and $345 and can last from a few months to five years or 50,000 miles. A dealer may offer more than one type of contract. You may be able to choose your coverage and cost.

2. *What other costs are there?* After you have paid the selling price, you may have other expenses. Service contracts, like insurance policies, often ask you to pay part of the cost of any problem that develops. Some contracts ask you to pay a fee for each unrelated repair, and some contracts ask for one fee each visit for all repairs. Frequently, contracts limit the amount paid for towing or rental-car expenses. You may also have to pay cancellation or transfer fees if you sell your car or wish to end the contract.

3. *What does the contract cover?* A service contract may cover repairs on all parts of your car or only major mechanical repairs. (For example, the car engine may be covered for major repairs, but you may have to pay for gaskets and seals.) Some contracts also pay for maintenance, towing, and rental-car expenses. Contracts may offer different coverage for different parts. Do not assume that something is covered if it is not written into the contract.

4. *What will my service contract give me that my warranty will not?* On a new car, your warranty coverage and your service-contract coverage may overlap for a year or so. If they do, you should compare the coverages and decide whether you can justify the additional expenses for the added coverage you get from having a service contract.

5. *How will my repair bills be paid?* Your service-contract company may pay the selling dealer or mechanic directly, or you may have to pay for the work and ask the service-contract company for reimbursement.

6. *Where can my car be serviced locally? What happens when I am traveling or when I move?* Under most service contracts, your car can be serviced only by the selling dealership. In some contracts, you may use any mechanic you choose. Manufacturers have dealerships nationwide, and service is available if you travel or move. Some service-contract companies and dealers offer nationwide service, so you will get service if you travel or move. Other companies give you service only in a specific geographical area.

7. *What special requirements do I have to meet?* Some service contracts require you to use a certain brand of motor oil when you have your car serviced, or they may require you to get your car serviced at specific intervals.

SELECTING A MECHANIC

Even if you have the world's best automobile, you will eventually have to bring it in for repairs and servicing. When you do, you will face the problem of finding a good mechanic. Given the ratio of automobiles to mechanics in the United States (about 450 to 1), it is little wonder that it is hard to find a good mechanic who can deal with your problems on a moment's notice. Just as you wouldn't want a poorly trained doctor caring for your family, so, too, you

You should be just as careful in choosing a garage or mechanic as you are in choosing a hospital or doctor.

wouldn't want an inept or unprincipled mechanic taking care of your car. The tight supply of mechanics compared to the demand for them makes it easier to understand why Americans spend so much on automobile repairs and servicing. The mystique that surrounds the servicing of a car (the strange-sounding names such as "universal joint" and the odd procedures such as "repacking the wheel bearings") leaves consumers easy prey to unscrupulous or incompetent mechanics. The $20 billion estimate cited earlier for unnecessary, faulty, or fraudulent auto repairs amounts to $55 million per day. To help avoid these unnecessary expenditures, you ought to spend some time selecting your repair shop.

Automobile repair shops come in all shapes and sizes, from the one-mechanic garage to the service station to the mass-marketing franchise shop such as Tuneup Masters or Aamco to department-store auto-service departments such as Sears and J.C. Penney. With such an array of sellers, it seems difficult to choose one. But there are some guidelines to follow:

1. Avoid garages that are located near highways and that are oriented toward transient business. These shops have the worst record for fraud, for a good reason—they never expect their customers to come back.

2. Find a local garage, especially one in which you can actually talk to the mechanic who is working on your car. Look for a mechanic who is familiar with your kind of car. This can be especially important if you have a foreign car. Ask friends or acquaintances who own similar cars to recommend someone.

3. Always get a written estimate for the repair work *before* anyone begins working on your car. After the work is completed, the mechanic should give you a detailed invoice of all work done and parts supplied. If the mechanic is unwilling or unable to do so, go somewhere else.

4. Ask if the mechanics have passed any of the voluntary testing programs. The most common are the tests administered by the National Institute of Automotive Service Excellence (NIASE).

5. Consider learning to do simple repairs and

servicing yourself, possibly by taking a course at a local community college. By being your own minor mechanic, you will save some money and learn more about how your car operates.

You can also provide yourself with a bit of "consumer insurance" by paying for the work with a bank credit card such as a VISA card or a Master-Card. It will take about 30 days for this charge to show up on your statement, and in the meantime you will have an opportunity to see whether the repair was successful. If you are not satisfied, you can return to the mechanic for an explanation. If you are still not satisfied, you can inform the bank of the disagreement, and it will have to disallow the charge. As we saw in Chapter 8, this is the law. Of course, the mechanic could take you to court, but chances are that if you are honestly dissatisfied with the work, you will never be troubled by a lawsuit.

Automobile Insurance

On the average, there is almost one motor vehicle accident every second of every year in the United States. The odds are good (or bad) that you will be involved in an accident that ranges in severity from a fender-bender to a multiple-car collision in the next four years. A recent government publication noted that the average motorist will be involved in an accident twice during an eight-year period and will be at fault for one of them. With these kinds of odds, all drivers need some type of automobile insurance. In the sections that follow, we outline the basic insurance package and how to shop for insurance; then we offer some ideas about no-fault insurance.

THE BASIC INSURANCE PACKAGE

Automobile insurance is just another form of **insurance,** which can be defined as an agreement between a consumer and an insurance firm in which the consumer gives up a small fixed amount of money today in order to be protected from a potentially greater loss in the future.

Not all states require automobile insurance, but they all require that operators of motor vehicles be financially responsible for any damage that may be done by their vehicles. If you are involved in an accident in which someone is injured or in which there is significant property damage, you will be required to demonstrate that you are able to pay for a minimum level of damages. If you cannot, your driver's license will be suspended. For most people, financial responsibility is assured by having an automobile insurance policy. The six forms of insurance in all insurance packages are:

1. Bodily injury.
2. Property damage.
3. Collision.
4. Comprehensive physical damage.
5. Medical.
6. Uninsured motorist.

Liability Insurance. The first two categories are sometimes referred to as **liability insurance** because they are invoked only if the insured person is judged to be responsible (that is, liable) for the accident. The amount of the driver's liability is potentially unlimited, because he or she can be sued for any amount of money. But the amount that the insurance company is willing to pay is limited by the size of the protection stated on the insurance policy. You will frequently hear about or see such figures as $100,000/$300,000 (or simply 100/300). These are the limits of the insurance company's guaranties in the event that you have an accident for which you are to blame. In the case of a 15/30 policy, the insurance company agrees to pay a maximum of $15,000 for a bodily-injury claim to any person you may have hurt, provided the injury claims for all people who have been hurt do not exceed the $30,000 limit established under that policy. A 100/300 policy increases those limits to $100,000 for each person and $300,000 for the entire claim. If you have a 15/30 policy, have an accident that is your fault, and get claims of $50,000 against you, you are stuck with a $20,000 bill, even after the insurance company pays its share. Given the size of today's lawsuits, a 15/30 policy is hardly adequate, and yet it is the amount that most states accept as proof of financial responsibility.

Property-damage liability insurance is always sold in the same package as bodily-injury insurance, and it is only paid if the policyholder is judged to be at

The Automobile: Wheels and Deals   343

All automobile insurance policies include basic coverage against property damage.

fault. It is invoked when the policyholder's car damages someone else's property—generally another car—although it covers all property, including houses, telephone poles, shrubbery, and bicycles. The limit of this portion of an auto insurance policy varies depending on the desired level of protection, but $10,000 to $50,000 limits are most common. If you add a $10,000 property damage policy to your 15/30 bodily-injury coverage, you will get a 15/30/10 policy. But if you are at all aware of the cost of repairs these days, you can easily see how a $10,000 property-damage policy is hardly enough to protect you against someone else's claims. It is quite conceivable that a multiple-car collision could result in three or four times that amount of physical damage. And, if you happen to hit just one Ferrari, your $10,000 property damage insurance will not help much.

Collision Insurance. While liability insurance covers injuries and damages to other people, you may also need insurance to cover your personal losses and damages to your car. **Collision insurance** protects you when your car is damaged in an accident with another car or with an object such as a tree or a telephone pole. The amount of this coverage is limited by the value of your car at the time of the accident. Because liability is not the most important question in such cases, your insurance company will generally appraise the damages and send you a check for the necessary repairs without regard to who was at fault. If another driver was involved and was judged to be at fault, your insurance company will collect from him or her.

Another important provision of most collision insurance is the amount of damage that the policyholder is willing to pay for *before* the insurance company begins paying the claim. This is called the *deductible* amount, and it commonly varies from zero to $500. If you have collision coverage with a $100 deductible clause and you do $500 worth of damage to your car by backing it into a tree, the insurance company will only pay $400 to repair the damage, because the first $100 is deductible. Having the insured person agree to assume some of the insurance risk is called **co-insurance,** and it is common to many types of insurance policies, such as health insurance and homeowner's insurance. The more the risk (the larger the deductible), the lower the premium. A higher deductible amount reduces the number of small claims that must be processed by insurance companies, and part of the resulting reduction in administration is passed along to the consumer in the form of lower payments. Many insurance companies refuse to write zero-deductible policies, and even if they do, most insurance experts do not view zero deductible as a good deal (see Box 12-9). If your collision damage was someone else's fault, your insurance company will reimburse you for the deductible amount once it collects from the guilty party.

Collision insurance is optional. There are no state laws that require you to replace or repair your own car, but if you borrow money to buy a car, the lender generally requires collision insurance as a condition of the loan. In your decision-making process about whether or not to buy collision coverages, you have to weigh the costs of the coverage against the

---

BOX 12-9

How Large a Deductible?

You can reduce your automobile insurance premiums significantly by increasing the deductible, that is, the set amount of loss that you will pay before the insurance company has to honor its obligations. On a standard auto insurance policy, you can expect to reduce the cost of your collision insurance by the following percentages, if you agree to raise your deductible:

- 15 percent for raising the deductible from $100 to $200
- 10 percent for raising the deductible from $200 to $250
- 35 percent for raising the deductible from $250 to $500

Some insurance experts recommend that the deductible amount equal about 5 percent of the value of the car. Thus, if a car is worth $10,000, a $500 deductible is about right under the 5 percent rule. These experts argue that the $100 deductible policies are a vestige of the past, when new cars cost about $2000. Other experts recommend that the deductible equal one week's pay. This rule is probably better, because it more clearly reflects the size of the loss that could be absorbed. Thus, if you earned $10,000 a year, a $200 deductible would be appropriate. A third possibility uses a payback method such as the one used in Chapter 11. The payback method focuses more clearly on the costs and benefits of increasing the deductible. Ask your insurance agent how much the cost of an insurance premium would fall if you raised the deductible limit. This is a benefit. Divide this benefit into the proposed change in the deductible amount to see how many years it would take for you to accumulate the difference and in effect, insure yourself. For example, if you currently pay $100 for collision coverage with a $100 deductible amount and your premium would be reduced by $15 annually if you raised the deductible to $200, you would get a payback in 6.66 years:

$$\frac{\text{change in deductible}}{\text{reduction in premium}} = \frac{\$100}{\$15} = 6.66 \text{ years}$$

If you figure that you will not have a claim for the next seven years, raising the deductible will save you money.

A second point to consider if you itemize your tax deductions is that all uninsured losses in excess of $100 are deductible from federal income tax if they exceed 10 percent of your adjusted gross income. State tax laws may be more lenient where casualty losses are concerned, but in any case, you cannot claim this deduction if you are subsequently reimbursed by your insurance company or another party. Thus a high deductible amount may have certain tax advantages that make it even cheaper than the payback principle indicates.

---

benefits. Many consumers misunderstand the benefits of collision coverage and the obligations of the insurance company. If you are involved in an accident and you have collision coverage, the insurance company is required only to restore your automobile to its previous condition; it is not required to buy a new car if your five-year-old Chevrolet is totaled in an accident. The collision insurance simply covers the average value of a five-year-old Chevrolet. As a general rule, it costs four times as much to repair a car as it does to build it from scratch. Thus, if 30 percent of your car is damaged, it is probably cheaper for the insurance company to pay you the estimated value of the car rather than to pay more to have it fixed. Given the rapid rate at which an automobile depreciates, the cost of collision insurance quickly exceeds the benefits. Once your car is worth less than (could be replaced for) $1000, most experts agree that you should stop paying for collision coverage.

Comprehensive Physical-Damage Insurance. **Comprehensive insurance** is also optional, but insurance companies frequently require you to purchase collision insurance *before* you are allowed to buy comprehensive insurance. This coverage provides protection against most hazards other than those from collision, including theft, fire, natural disasters, and vandalism. The insurance company may require a deductible of $50 or $100. If a deductible clause is not required, you may want to take it anyway to get lower rates.

Medical Insurance. Medical insurance covers any medical expenses incurred as a result of a automobile accident, and it covers all members of the policyholder's immediate family, whether they are in the family car, in someone else's car, or are pedestrians. This policy also covers all other passengers in the insured vehicle. Coverage varies from $2000 to $10,000, and payments are made regardless of who is at fault. If you already have good medical insurance, such coverage may be redundant for your family, but of course your passengers are another question. Because the cost of such coverage is generally small, most drivers purchase medical insurance.

Uninsured-Motorist Bodily-Injury Insurance. What happens if you are injured by a hit-and-run driver or by someone who has no insurance? To protect yourself, you can get **uninsured-motorist insurance** for yourself (the policyholder) and all family members whether you are in someone else's car, are in the insured automobile, or are simply an unlucky pedestrian. Such coverage is generally sold in amounts equal to the minimum financial responsibility laws of the state. In essence, uninsured-motorist insurance sets up bodily-injury liability insurance for the other guy in case you are involved in an accident in which he is at fault but cannot pay because he has no insurance. Suppose, for example, that you are driving through an intersection, and Frank, an uninsured motorist, runs the red light and hits your car, injuring you and your daughter. Because Frank has no insurance, your uninsured-motorist coverage will pay for all your medical bills and for any additional claims that result from injury to you or your daughter. If you are unable to work for two weeks, for example, you would be reimbursed by this coverage. Uninsured-motorist insurance does not cover damage to your car, however. Collision insurance covers that. And uninsured motorist insurance is limited to some amount usually equal to the minimum financial responsibility laws of the state.

LOOKING FOR AUTO INSURANCE

Now that you understand the fundamentals of automobile insurance, you know what to look for in a policy. It may surprise you to learn that according to most surveys, only about one out of every four consumers shops around for auto insurance. Many people probably believe that the rates of various companies are all about the same, because companies are all regulated by the state. But in this case, state regulation does *not* mean uniform pricing. In a sample of eleven insurance companies in the Los Angeles area, the California Department of Insurance found that the average car owner can save between $100 and $400 per year by simply "shopping around." As Insurance Commissioner Wesley J. Kidder said, "Dramatic differences exist and the time spent shopping can indeed be worthwhile" (*Los Angeles Times,* October 16, 1978).

Before you go shopping, however, you would do well to consider your individual needs and to set some limits on the amount of coverage you want. The most important step is to determine how much liability insurance (bodily and property damage) you need. In most cases, insurance experts recommend that consumers opt for higher-coverage rather than the lower-coverage policies. Increasing liability coverage from 15/30/5 to 100/30/50 will cost only a few dollars more, and the extra security is generally deemed worth the extra cost.

Once you decide how much liability protection to buy, you must next decide whether to purchase collision and comprehensive insurance. If you get a large loan to finance a car, you will not have the option to refuse these coverages, but for an older car, you must decide. Consumers Union recommends that consumers seriously consider discontinuing collision insurance when a car's value drops below $1000. This is especially good advice in that the cost of uninsured damage in excess of

$100 can be subtracted from taxable income (see Box 12-8). So the costs of repair of collision damage reduce taxes—in effect, Uncle Sam shares some of the risk.

As far as medical insurance and uninsured motorist protection are concerned, it is generally best to settle on a minimal but adequate amount of coverage and to get quotations from various insurers with this amount in mind. If you already have good medical coverage, you might consider omitting medical insurance from the agreement to sign on with a particular insurance company. But if you car pool or frequently take nonfamily members as passengers, you should get medical coverage.

Most insurance agents are like other salespeople—they want to get your business. And if they have to, they will offer you the best deal possible. But you can help yourself by knowing what questions to ask and by demonstrating that you are a price-conscious consumer. In order to save yourself valuable time, first contact the insurance agent by telephone. Tell him or her the type of coverage you are looking for; the make, the model, and the year of the car you wish to insure; and when you need the coverage to begin. Keep the following tips in mind:

1. *Co-insurance means less-costly insurance premiums.* If you are willing to accept a higher deductible amount on collision and comprehensive insurance, you will get a lower price. Ask about the rates for different levels of co-insurance.

2. *If you cannot afford the coverage you want, consider trading your collision and comprehensive coverage for better liability protection.* Remember, even if your car is stolen and never recovered, the cost to you will be only a few thousand dollars. On the other hand, if you get stuck with a large lawsuit, the cost could be hundreds of thousands of dollars. For example, if you were to do without collision coverage and were in an automobile accident that totally destroyed your 1980 Ford Mustang, the most you would lose would be a few thousand dollars. And if the other motorist were at fault, his or her company would have to pay that sum. If you were to do without liability protection or were to buy a minimum, $30,000 policy and you permanently disabled someone in an accident that was your fault, you could face a $200,000 lawsuit. Which is potentially more damaging to your future, the loss of a car or the loss of $200,000 of your earnings?

3. *Look for discounts.* Some insurers provide discounts to nondrinkers, to nonsmokers, to people who have had driver training or have good driving records, and to car poolers. Sometimes, good students and small-car owners can also get discounts. The idea behind discounts, besides the fact that they are sales gimmicks, is that people with these characteristics tend to have fewer accidents and are better insurance risks. Nondrinkers never have their abilities impaired by alcohol, and nonsmokers do not take their eyes off the road to look for cigarettes or to light up on their way home.

4. *Consider insuring your car on your parent's insurance policy.* It is often cheaper to add another car to an established policy than to buy a new policy. This is especially true for young drivers who do not have established driving records. One study showed that male drivers under age twenty-five pay almost 80 percent more for insurance than the average adult over age twenty-five *(Journal of American Insurance,* 1980).

5. *Don't get speeding tickets.* In other words, obey the law. Traffic citations make it more difficult to change insurance companies and more expensive to stay with a given company, because citations are an indication that a person is a high-risk driver. If you cannot switch companies, your ability to comparison shop will be extremely limited.

6. *Never allow your current auto insurance coverage to lapse until you have an agreement with another company.* Insurers are skeptical of accepting a new driver who does not currently have an auto insurance policy. This means that your shopping should begin two or three months before your policy expires.

7. *Avoid duplication of coverage.* For example, if you already belong to an auto club, don't buy towing insurance. If your existing health insurance is adequate and you don't car pool or take nonfamily members as passengers, you don't need medical coverage.

WORKSHEET 12-1
Comparison of Auto Insurance

Type of Insurance	Desired Amount of Coverage	Company Name or Agent	
		Insurer 1	Insurer 2
Bodily injury liability (per person or per accident)	$100,000/$300,000	$89	$150
Property damage liability (per accident)	50,000	49	(included above)
Collision	6,000 *		
$100 deductible		123	142
$500 deductible		60	83
Comprehensive	6,000 *		
$100 deductible		42	44
$500 deductible		19	21
Medical (per accident)	10,000	23	24
Uninsured motorist (per person or per accident)	$15,000/$30,000	16	23
Cost per year with $100 deductible		342	383
Cost per year with $500 deductible		256	301

*Wholesale value of auto

8. *Pay annually*. Many insurance companies have a variety of payment plans, but if you can pay once a year, you will avoid extra finance and handling charges. In addition, you will avoid the six-month rate hikes that can occur with shorter policies.

9. *Do not drive to work*. If your car is used only for pleasure and not to commute to work, you can save substantially. In Chapter 11 we outlined some of the alternatives to commuting by car. Bicycling, using mass transit, and ridesharing offer great promise in reducing insurance costs.

Use a form similar to Worksheet 12-1 when you do your comparison shopping.

Even though you have obtained price quotations from various insurance agents, your task is still not complete. You must consider three other factors: ease of claim settlement, company cancellation policies, and the financial reliability of the company. No company enjoys paying claims, but some are more difficult to deal with than others. Check the most recent issue of the *Consumer Reports Buying Guide* for its recommendations about companies that settle claims easily, and talk to the agent about the process. You should also inquire about a company's cancellation policy. If a company makes no pledge about renewing a policy, you could wind up paying higher premiums in the future while you cast about looking for another insurer. Finally, you should consult *Best's Insurance Reports* (available in your library) for information about the financial conditions of various insurance companies. Nothing would be more upsetting than to find yourself insured by a company that could not meet its obligation to you in the event of a major accident. In short, you must weigh the *quality* of the insurer in addition to the quality of the insurance offered.

NO-FAULT INSURANCE

When consumers buy insurance policies, most of them realize that a portion of their premium pays for expenses other than claims. Obviously, your friendly insurance agent smiles so broadly partly because of the commission that will soon find its way to his or her pocket. But most consumers do not know the extent to which expenses other than claims payments eat into their insurance dollar. Less than half, and in some cases less than a third, of every premium dollar finds its way back to a claimant. This low payout ratio is partly caused by the expenses of elaborate trial procedures and other legal expenses associated with arguing in court over who was at fault and how much the injured party should receive. In an effort to limit this cost, some states have instituted a plan called no-fault insurance.

No-fault insurance applies only to the bodily-injury liability section of automobile insurance policies. The rest of the policy is treated just as it is in other states. Under the no-fault system, the injured parties collect from their own insurance companies regardless of who is to blame for the accident. Instead of spending weeks and sometimes years trying to determine who bumped whom, the injured parties are reimbursed by their own companies within a few days for medical care and lost wages. It is still possible to go to court if large judgments against the offending party seem warranted, but claims below a stipulated amount or "threshold level" are normally settled quickly, without an elaborate courtroom battle. By avoiding protracted litigation, insurance companies should be able to provide better claims service at lower cost. At least that is the theory behind the movement toward no-fault auto insurance.

Currently, almost half of the states have enacted some form of no-fault insurance, and the results seem to depend on whom you ask. The American Trial Lawyers Association sees no-fault as an unmitigated disaster, in part because it tends to decrease the number of lawsuits and thus the demand for lawyers' services. In states where no-fault has not been successful, the problems seem to revolve around the size of the threshold level that triggers court cases. No-fault procedures are no longer followed once the threshold level is reached, and a low threshold level leads to most injury cases being treated in the traditional "fault system." In Nevada, for example, where the threshold level was set low ($750), the no-fault system never got a fair chance to operate. Things got so chaotic that the state legislature actually repealed the no-fault law and went back to the fault system. In states in which the threshold level was set higher, most impartial observers argue that no-fault insurance has resulted in lower premiums and better service. In Massachusetts, for example, during the first four years of operation the cost of liability insurance dropped by more than one-third, and in Michigan, no-fault insurance was credited with reducing the claim settlement time from sixteen months to less than thirty days. These are impressive results that could be duplicated in other areas.

The drive to create a nationwide no-fault insurance law seems to have withered. It was once thought that such a law would soon be forthcoming and that it would dramatically lower insurance premiums. Given that drivers do have accidents in other states, a national insurance law would simplify motorists' legal situation. As it stands now, the laws of the state in which the accident occurs govern rights and responsibilities. Drivers from a no-fault state are still fully liable for injuries to other motorists when driving in states without no-fault.

Summary

In the United States, automobiles are almost a way of life. Consumers are more likely to drive a car than they are to exercise their right to vote. Getting from place to place has become so important to most of us that we might add transportation costs to the traditional list of necessities such as food, clothing, and shelter. In the early 1980s, we spent considerably more on our automobiles than on our clothing. We have become so used to the automobile that we almost take these expenditures for granted, as a fact of life.

In this chapter we have emphasized that automobile expenditures should be subject to the same decision-making process as other important expenses, and that there are many areas in which wise decision making can lead to greater satisfaction and save money as well. The major areas of decision making are: identifying the kind of car desired, evaluating the costs of ownership and operation, shopping for a car, getting auto repairs, and shopping for automobile insurance.

Consumers should outline the major qualities they want in a car and then compare various options so that they can select the car that suits them best. The costs of an automobile can be divided into the costs of ownership (fixed costs) and the costs of operation (variable costs). Depreciation is one of the most important of the fixed costs, and it falls most heavily on consumers who buy new cars and trade them in frequently. The cost of financing a car is another fixed cost, and it is probably just as economical to borrow money to buy the car as it is to pay cash, as long as the opportunity cost of using one's own money is included. Gasoline and oil are the most expensive variable costs, but they vary by 50 percent depending on the size and the gas mileage of the vehicle. The Department of Transportation estimates that a new car driven for twelve years and 120,000 miles costs its owner an average of 26.6 cents per mile; a subcompact costs an average of 18.9 cents per mile driven.

Used cars are more frequently purchased than new cars. Almost three-quarters of all cars purchased in the United States in a given year are used. Leasing is another alternative to buying a car that has grown in importance as the price of new cars rises. But leases come in many varieties, and consumers should understand all the terms *before* they choose this option.

Whether consumers buy new or used cars or even undertake lease plans, they should understand warranty rights and learn how to find a good mechanic, since 20 percent of all auto repair work is estimated to be unnecessary, poorly done, or outright fraudulent.

Automobile insurance is the final area for which consumers should know their rights and compare prices. By raising deductible limits and by increasing liability insurance coverage consumers can generally improve their protection without paying more.

Neighborhood REVISITED

The transmission was making strange sounds when Ms. McNamera brought her Dasher back to the dealer. He pleasantly but firmly reminded her that her warranty was up. He was certain that they could fix the problem, but she would have to pay an estimated $400 for the repairs.

As Ms. McNamera pondered the question of whether a jury would convict her for murdering the service manager, her eyes wandered to the Ford dealership across the street, where banners read, "Top Dollar for Your Trade-in—Discount Days Are Here."

She managed to drive her Dasher across the street, and within two hours she was driving her new Ford. She was even chuckling to herself over the $2000 trade-in she had gotten on her clunker, but she didn't consider that the dealer charged the full sticker price for the new car. Ms. McNamera was simply happy to be rid of her lemon.

1. What should Ms. McNamera have done to get the problem with her Dasher resolved? Would she have qualified for a refund or replacement under the "lemon aid" legislation?

2. Would Ms. McNamera's rights have differed if her Volkswagen had come with a full rather than a limited warranty? Explain.

3. Did she get a good deal on her new Ford?

4. Do you know of any similar cases of new-car defects? Did the consumers involved press their claims? Why or why not?

KEY TERMS

buyer's guide window sticker
closed-end lease
co-insurance
collision insurance
comprehensive insurance
depreciation
express warranty
extended warranty plan
fixed costs
high-ball technique
insurance
lease
lemon aid
liability insurance
limited warranty
low-ball technique
no-fault insurance
open-end lease
residual value
secret warranty
service contract
variable costs
uninsured-motorist insurance
warranty

QUESTIONS

1. Explain why the automobile has become such an important component of the American lifestyle.

2. State your personal rationale for purchasing a car.

3. List the five classifications of sedans sold in America as determined by the Department of Energy.

4. What are the two major kinds of costs of owning an automobile? Give two examples of each.

5. Discuss how consumers can lower the per-mile costs of driving.

6. How can tread wear be measured to see whether new tires are needed? How would you use the Department of Transportation's tread-wear grading system to compare tire costs?

7. How can you estimate the dealer cost for most new car models? How can you estimate the value of the car you own? How does this information help in buying a new car?

8. What are the advantages and disadvantages of leasing a new automobile? Do these depend on the kind of lease you get? Explain.

9. What are the four major outlets for used cars? Which is generally the most expensive? The riskiest?

10. Describe the major kinds of warranties that a new car may have. Explain the difference between full and limited warranties.

11. Summarize the guidelines that consumers should follow when they find that they have purchased a "lemon."

12. What are the six essential elements in all auto insurance packages?

13. Explain the difference between liability insurance and collision insurance.

14. What part of your insurance package is most affected by no-fault as opposed to fault insurance? What are the advantages and disadvantages of the no-fault system?

15. A Federal Trade Commission study found that new cars have four times as many defects as any other warranted products. The same study also found that twice as many new-car complaints were unresolved after a month compared to the number of unresolved complaints about other products. Why do new cars have so many more defects, and why does it take longer to settle the claims?

PROJECTS

1. Using the Uniform Tire-Quality Grading System as a basis for comparison, price three different brands of tires of the same size and quality. Try to include at least one national brand as well as one regional trade name. Are there significant differences in price? Can the salespeople explain the differences? Can you?

2. Go to three new-car dealerships and get a copy of their new-car warranties. Compare them. In what ways do they differ? Do they make a significant difference in your choice of a car? Explain.

3. Contact three auto insurance agents and get an estimate for the cost of insuring your automobile at your current coverage. (If you do not have a car, use the coverage amounts in Worksheet 12-1.) Fill in the following worksheet. Could you save money by changing agents? How much can you save by going to a higher (or lower) deductible? By buying liability coverage?

Comparison of Auto Insurance

Type of Insurance	Desired Amount of Coverage	Company Name or Agent		
		Insurer 1	Insurer 2	Insurer 3
Bodily injury liability (per person or per accident)	_____	_____	_____	_____
Property damage liability (per accident)	_____	_____	_____	_____
Collision	_____*			
$100 deductible		_____	_____	_____
$500 deductible		_____	_____	_____
Comprehensive	_____*			
$100 deductible		_____	_____	_____
$500 deductible		_____	_____	_____
Medical (per accident)	_____	_____	_____	_____
Uninsured motorist (per person or per accident)	_____	_____	_____	_____
Cost per year with $100 deductible		_____	_____	_____
Cost per year with $500 deductible		_____	_____	_____

*Wholesale value of auto

4. Imagine that you are going to purchase a new car. Choose a certain body style and model classification, and then estimate the first-year cost of driving using the following worksheet, which was developed by the U.S. Department of Transportation. Compare your costs to those of your classmates who chose other makes or models.

Worksheet for Calculating Costs in Any Locality

1. Amount paid for car $ _____
2. Cost of accessory items $ _____
3. Cost per tire $ _____
4. Price of gasoline per gallon (including tax) $ _____
5. Price of oil per quart (including tax) $ _____
6. Annual cost of insurance $ _____

7. Estimated cost of daily parking $_____
8. State registration fee $_____
9. Sales, titling, and/or personal property tax $_____
10. Labor charge per hour for repairs $_____
11. Monthly interest cost (monthly payment ×number of months of loan − amount of loan ÷ number of months of loan) $_____
12. Term of auto loan (months) $_____
13. Mileage for 1 year $_____

Fixed (ownership) cost (first year)	Total	Cost per mile (total ÷ line 13)
14. Depreciation (25 percent of line 1)	$_____	_____ cents
15. Accessories (line 2 ÷ 12)	$_____	_____ cents
16. Insurance (line 6)	$_____	_____ cents
17. Registration fee (line 8)	$_____	_____ cents
18. Finance (12 × monthly interest cost)	$_____	_____ cents
19. Sales, titling, and/or property tax (line 9)	$_____	_____ cents

Variable (operating) costs (first year)

	Total	Cost per mile
20. Gasoline (annual gallons used × line 4)	$_____	_____ cents
21. Oil (line 13 ÷ owners manual oil-change requirement × line 5)	$_____	_____ cents
22. Snow tires (2 × line 3 × .25)	$_____	_____ cents
23. Maintenance and repair (line 10 ÷ 23.42 × first-year repairs and maintenance from lines 2, 3, 4, and 5)	$_____	_____ cents
24. Parking (250 × line 7) or actual days parked × daily cost + tolls	$_____	_____ cents
25. Total estimated first-year cost (add lines 14–24)	$_____	_____ cents

READINGS AND REFERENCES

"Beat the Dealer." *Consumers Digest,* November/December 1980.

"Buying A New Car: How to Drive Home a Bargain." *Changing Times,* October 1981.

"Good Reasons for Buying an Old Car." *Changing Times,* September 1981.

Maine Bureau of Consumer Protection. *Down-Easter's Lemon Guide.* Augusta, Me.: Maine Bureau of Consumer Protection, 1980.

Nader, Ralph, et al. *The Lemon Book.* Ottawa, Ill.: Caroline House Publications, 1980.

"No-Fault Car Insurance Works in Michigan." *Changing Times,* August 1979.

"Pay Cash or Borrow." *Changing Times,* December 1980.

Porter, Sylvia. *Sylvia Porter's New Money Book for the 80's.* New York: Avon Books, 1979.

"The Real Cost of Driving Your Car." *Changing Times,* September 1980.

"Recalls: Why So Many Are Flops." *Changing Times,* October 1980.

Skidmore, Felicity. "The Used Car Rip-Off." *Focus,* Spring 1978.

"State Discloses Local Auto Insurance Rates." *Los Angeles Times,* October 16, 1978.

"The Trouble With Auto Warranties." *Consumer Reports,* October 1979.

U.S. Department of Energy. *Gas Mileage Guide: California.* Washington, D.C.: U.S. Government Printing Office, annual issues.

U.S. Department of Transportation. *The Car Book: A Consumer's Guide to Car Buying.* Washington, D.C.: U.S. Government Printing Office, 1981.

U.S. Department of Transportation. *Common Sense in Buying a Safe Used Car.* Washington, D.C.: U.S. Government Printing Office, 1976.

U.S. Department of Transportation. *Common Sense in Buying a New Car.* Washington, D.C.: U.S. Government Printing Office, 1978.

U.S. Department of Transportation. *Cost of Owning and Operating Automobiles and Vans, 1982.* Washington, D.C.: U.S. Government Printing Office, 1982.

"Want to Hold Down Your Auto Insurance Costs?" *Journal of American Insurance,* Fall 1980.

"Your Car Can Last 100,000 Miles and More." *Changing Times,* April 1980.

Did You Know That...

- the choice of whether to buy or rent depends on more than personal preferences?

- the cost of housing accounts for 25 to 40 percent of a family's budget?

- in most American cities landlords can raise rents as often and as much as the market allows?

- approximately one-third of all new homes being built today are mobile homes?

- renters should carefully read month-to-month rental agreements or leases to see whether such agreements or leases prohibit subleasing, changing the color of interior paint, or having overnight guests?

- landlords are required to provide access to hot and cold water and to provide a working sewer or septic tank connection? They must also promptly make repairs such as fixing leaky roofs or plumbing and replacing broken windows.

- newer styles of home loans are available for which the loan payment can fluctuate from one year to the next?

- the federal government regulates movers of household goods and has given consumers protection when they buy this service?

- the supply of rental units is at a thirty-five-year low and the costs of home ownership are escalating?

13

Housing: Home Sweet Home

To Rent or to Buy?
The First Step: Identifying Your Needs
The Second Step: Estimating How Much You Can Afford
The Third Step: Exploring Housing Options
The Fourth Step: Choosing Your Housing
The Fifth Step: Moving
The Sixth Step: Evaluating Your Choice
The Seventh Step: Accepting Responsibility

Neighborhood CAPSULE
New Ways to Fulfill a Dream

Sharon had invited her sister, Pat, and her five-year-old nephew Ryan over for dinner. Now that they'd eaten, Pat and Sharon were doing the dishes, while Ryan played outside.

"You know, Sharon, I really envy you for being single and having your own apartment. Since Ernie and I separated and Ryan and I moved back home with Mom and Dad, I've really felt cramped. Don't get me wrong, they've been terrific, but . . ."

"I know what you mean, Pat. I've often thought about you and Ryan. Sometimes he seems confused by the two sets of rules—yours and Mom's."

"If only I could buy a place of my own—it wouldn't have to be much. But the few thousand dollars from the divorce settlement doesn't come close to a down payment, so I guess I'll start looking for an apartment."

"I really wish I could buy a place, too," Sharon responded. I've been saving my money, and every time I think I'm getting close, the interest rates go up, or something."

Both women were silent for a moment. Then Sharon said, "I stopped by those new condominiums over on Grand Avenue. They look terrific, with a swimming pool and a recreation hall. Some of the plans, the three-bedroom ones, were two-story, although I wouldn't need that much space."

"How much were they?" Pat inquired.

"Between $65,000 and $80,000."

"Wow, that means around a $12,000 or $15,000 down payment, doesn't it?" Pat asked. "My $5,000 doesn't even come close!"

"Mine either," Sharon moaned. "Wait a minute," she continued. "If you have $5,000 and I have, well, actually almost $4,000, together we could almost do it."

Pat laughed, "Yeah, too bad we're not married!"

"No, I'm serious, Pat. Banks are beginning to loan money to unmarried people who want to buy a house together—even to two women together. You and I have always gotten along, and I love Ryan. What do you say?"

"You are serious, aren't you? Well—it would be terrific. But do you really think it's possible? I've only been working for the phone company for three months. Do you really think we could get a loan?"

"I don't know, but we could ask. After all, I've had my job for almost five years."

356 Economic Decisions for Consumers

Whether to buy or rent a home, an apartment, a condominium, a cooperative, or a mobile home is an important decision—one that is not made very often in most cases and that is becoming more and more of a problem for many of us. In recent times the middle-class American dream has been to own a single-family suburban home, and the booming economy of the 1950s and 1960s led a growing population to believe that this was their right. But as you are probably aware, not everyone prefers that lifestyle. Many people choose to rent apartments, particularly in big cities, either for financial reasons or because they want to avoid the work and responsibilities that go with home ownership.

Today, however, the choice of whether to buy or rent depends on many factors besides preference or even personal economics. Our national economy in the last few years has been characterized by rising housing costs (caused by a steadily increasing demand for and an equally steady decline in the building and availability of new housing), double-digit inflation, increasing interest rates on home loans, and other factors that have forced some people to rent who, in years past, would have bought. At the same time, however, changes in the density and construction of housing and in our attitudes and lifestyles have made it possible for more people to buy homes, albeit not the detached, single-family suburban dwellings of the past. In addition, renters have begun to assert their rights and to realize that they are not completely at a disadvantage with their landlords. And other renters have realized that renting is the best situation for them—that they would rather have the flexibility that renting affords.

Because housing accounts for 25 to 40 percent of a family's budget, it is important to carefully consider housing decisions. The consumer has many factors, both personal and economic, to keep in mind, from determining whether to rent or buy to choosing a living space to establishing good relations with a landlord to obtaining the best financing for a home. This chapter will help you focus on those decisions and, we hope, give you some tools for making satisfactory housing decisions.

To Rent or to Buy?

At first glance, the decision whether to buy or rent seems easy. If consumers do not have the money for a down payment and the income to support the monthly payments, they have to rent. This reasoning is based on old assumptions, though; it doesn't consider other factors such as one's values, goals, family size, lifestyle, stage in the life cycle, or career. Examining the roles of these factors and the advantages and dis- advantages of both buying and renting gives us a starting point for later discussions of the types of housing and for other aspects of the two sides of the housing coin.

ADVANTAGES OF RENTING

Most people rent shelter at some point in their lives. The first time is usually when a young adult moves out of his or her parents' home and becomes self-supporting. Renting has also become common for single adults, students, couples without children, people with little interest in or time for homeowner chores, retired people, those who want small living quarters (such as a one-bedroom or studio apartment), and those who have to move often because of their jobs.

Perhaps the major advantage of renting is that it doesn't require major cash outlays. A renter may have to pay the equivalent of two or three months' rent for deposits, but that is a relatively small amount compared to a down payment required of a buyer.

Renting also allows flexibility. Even when a renter has a **lease**—a written agreement with the owner about the amount of rent to be charged for a specific length of time, as well as about other aspects of their relationship—he or she can usually move more easily and cheaply than a homeowner. A tenant can relocate because of job transfers or changes, an increase in family size or income, the desire for a better or more convenient location, and so on.

Rentals may also have attractive facilities. Recreational facilities such as game rooms, swimming pools, and health clubs provide places for relaxation and meeting others. Laundry facilities also make it possible for renters to avoid having to buy their own appliances or visit the laundromat.

Finally, for many people, renting means freedom from home repairs, gardening, maintenance, worry, and drudgery—and from responsibility for them. Even if they pay a monthly fee for this freedom, most renters find it a small price to pay. Many retired people, for instance, are ecstatic to be rid of a lifetime of homeowner chores, expenses, and responsibilities.

One of the main advantages of renting is freedom from home repairs, maintenance, and gardening.

DISADVANTAGES OF RENTING

Although renters are free from responsibilities, they cannot claim any rights to the property. They may be restricted or prohibited from making inside or outside changes to suit their own preferences, and they are governed by the needs and desires of the owner. Without a lease and without rent control, owners can raise rents at their own discretion and as high as the market will allow. They can ask tenants to leave, refuse to make repairs, let the property deteriorate, or make tenants unhappy in many other ways. Renters do have recourse, but uncertainty and lack of control are always there.

Another major disadvantage of renting is that there are no financial breaks for tenants. Renters help cover the owner's payments on the property, taxes, insurance, maintenance, and repairs, even though they receive no benefits for their contributions. Although the owner is accumulating **equity**—the increasing money value of the property over and above what he or she owes on it—the tenant gets nothing. Whereas the owner gets several kinds of tax credits and deductions, most tenants get no tax benefits.

ADVANTAGES OF BUYING

In addition to the financial benefits we have just listed, many of the advantages of owning one's own living space involve the feelings one has about one's property. The feelings of pride and independence are satisfying. People can live as they want, decorate according to their personal needs and tastes, and have more privacy than in a rental unit. They don't have to answer to anyone else or worry about being asked to leave. For many people, the feelings of security and responsibility in home ownership are very important.

Owning a home is usually a good financial investment, too. Because of inflation and rising demand, most homes increase in value, especially when compared to the prices of other goods and services. Between 1975 and 1981, the median price of existing homes rose over 100 percent, compared to a 68 percent increase in the Consumer Price Index. That means that a house worth $40,000 in 1975 was worth $80,300 in 1981. Although the increase in housing values will probably not continue at that spectacular rate in the 1980s, some geographic areas may continue to experience rapid rises. Because of the tendency for homes to keep pace with consumer prices, they have been a traditional hedge against inflation for middle-class families.

Another financial advantage of home ownership, and a disadvantage of renting, is that property taxes and interest on home loans are deductible from federal income tax returns. Homeowners can also deduct the costs of certain home improvements and repairs, such as energy-saving improvements (insulation, solar heating, and so forth). They can also save on income tax if they do their own home repairs, as we will see later in this chapter.

DISADVANTAGES OF BUYING

With the advantages, of course, come the disadvantages. Homeowners have to pay taxes, loan payments, and insurance, and all three expenses may increase faster than income. In recent years, state property taxes have been increasing at such a fast rate that many states passed measures to roll them back. California's Proposition 13, for example, and others like it in other states, are said to represent a "homeowner's revolt." If a loan has an interest rate that

> **BOX 13-1**
>
> ## Buying Doesn't Always Pay
>
> Monthly outlay for rent is not directly comparable to the costs of home ownership, because with ownership, there are annual tax deductions of loan interest and possible profit when the house sells. Professor Michael S. Johnson of Cornell University uses a computer to estimate the break-even point of the rent versus buy decision. In the following example, a married couple with three tax exemptions is considering the purchase of an $80,000 house. The break-even point depends on their income and on how long they expect to live in the house. The table shows how much rent per month they can pay before they would be better off buying.
>
> The figures are based on the assumptions that both rents and house prices will rise by 8 percent a year; that there is a fixed-rate mortgage at 15 percent for 25 years; that annual maintenance costs 1.5 percent of the home's value; that insurance costs 0.5 percent; that utilities cost $125 a month; that annual property taxes are 2 percent of the initial market value; and that the money used for a down payment could earn 14 percent a year if invested elsewhere.
>
> Generally, the higher the couple's income, the more advantageous it is for them to buy, because higher tax brackets allow greater benefits for ownership. Note that the break-even figure declines the longer the couple owns the home, because there is more time for price appreciation and equity build-up.
>
> If you would like an individualized computer analysis, send for a questionnaire to Housing Computer Analysis, c/o Michael S. Johnson, Department of Consumer Economics and Housing, MVR Hall, Cornell University, Ithaca, New York 14853. There will be a nominal charge for the analysis, but the questionnaire is free.
>
> **Initial Monthly Break-even Rents for a Couple with Three Tax Exemptions Contemplating Buying an $80,000 Home and Owning It for the Periods Indicated**
>
> | Income | 1 year | 2 years | 3 years | 4 years | 5 years | 10 years |
> |---|---|---|---|---|---|---|
> | $20,000 | $1,454 | $1,066 | $936 | $870 | $830 | $748 |
> | 30,000 | 1,382 | 997 | 869 | 805 | 767 | 694 |
> | 40,000 | 1,279 | 897 | 772 | 712 | 676 | 615 |
> | 50,000 | 1,210 | 830 | 707 | 647 | 614 | 559 |
> | 60,000 | 1,189 | 809 | 685 | 627 | 593 | 539 |
>
> SOURCE: Buy Now or Wait?" *Changing Times* (November 1981), p. 31. Copyright © 1981 Kiplinger Washington Editors, Inc. Used with permission.

changes with interest rates in the economy, budgeting may be difficult, particularly if the payment goes up.

Upkeep on a house can take a lot of money—and time. Repairs are often expensive and unexpected, and postponing them can damage or decrease the value of the property (not to mention one's enjoyment in living). And all the time spent gardening, repairing, and working on a house is time that can't be spent doing anything else—it is leisure foregone. For many new homeowners, the feeling of not having time for other activities is sometimes overwhelming. In addition, money spent on the house cannot be spent on anything else; homeowners sometimes have to forego vacations, new cars, furniture, or many other purchases, both big and small. Thus, the opportunity costs of home ownership are considerable.

Home ownership also restricts mobility. If consumers have to or want to move, they have to sell their property—which involves getting a reasonable price, a good buyer, and possibly a real estate agent. Then they must put up with the one- to three-month wait that it takes to process the sale.

Listing the advantages and disadvantages of buying and renting obviously doesn't get one very far in decision making. It gives only the basic information needed to begin thinking about a choice. If you want to do a rent versus buy analysis for financial considerations only, Box 13-1 will interest you. In the rest of the chapter, we follow both options through the decision-making model presented in Chapter 2.

The First Step: Identifying Your Needs

Whether you rent or buy, your first step in choosing housing is to determine what you need and expect from your living space. Here are some of the questions that have to be answered before you can choose among the available housing options:

1. How many bedrooms do you need?
2. How many bathrooms?
3. How large a kitchen is needed? Will you eat in the kitchen or do you prefer a separate dining area?
4. Do you need a separate room for recreational activities (such as watching TV), or will the living room do?
5. What other special-purpose rooms are needed (for example, laundry room/area, sewing/crafts room, and so forth)?
6. How much storage space is needed?
7. How much outside private space do you need for pets, play, patio, garden, and other activities?
8. What kind of garage or parking facilities do you need?

Be sure to consult everyone in the family when making these decisions, because everyone has to live in the housing that's chosen—maybe for a relatively long period of time. It is important to ensure that housing supplies living space, protection from the elements, utilities, and convenience. Many forms of shelter might meet these needs, including single-family houses, multifamily dwellings, and mobile homes. We will look at each of these in detail, but first let us consider budget.

The Second Step: Estimating How Much You Can Afford

Once you have identified the needs and goals of your household, the next step is to study your budget to estimate how much you can afford to pay for loans or rent. This will help you decide which form of shelter you should choose. It will also save you time and frustration, because you will not be tempted to look at places you cannot afford.

The amount of money you can spend for housing depends on your present monthly income, your expenses for needs other than housing, and the amount of cash you have available. Use Worksheet 13-1 to estimate these figures. Calculate your current regular monthly net pay, and be realistic. Do not include overtime pay or future raises that are not a certainty. Add any other reliable income to that amount, such as Social Security payments, stock dividends, and so forth, to find the total of your present monthly income.

Next, determine monthly expenses for all spending, excluding housing expenses (rent or mortgage and utilities). Be sure to calculate annual and semiannual payments (for insurance, taxes, and so forth) in the monthly averages. By subtracting the nonhousing monthly expenses from your income you have an estimate of how much you can afford for rent or housing payments. In the example in Worksheet 13-1, the family's total net income is estimated as $2000 and the nonhousing expenses are $1300, leaving $700 for housing. In many regions of the United States, this would be a generous amount to cover rent and utilities, but it might not be enough for mortgage payments.

A second guideline often used by financial counselors to determine a ''safe'' housing budget is to not spend more than 25 percent of one's budget for annual **recurring costs,** such as rent or loan payment, taxes, insurance, utilities, and maintenance. In our example, the family would find that it should spend $500 rather than $700 on housing if they followed this guideline.

The largest portion of money spent for ownership goes for the loan payment. This portion will of course vary according to geographic location, initial cost of the house, and the size of the down payment. As a rough guide, you can estimate that two-thirds of your monthly housing costs will go for the loan payments only. The remainder will be spent on real estate taxes, insurance, utilities, repairs, maintenance, and association fees (for maintenance of facilities used by all tenants or owners within a housing complex). In

WORKSHEET 13-1
Estimating What You Can Afford to Pay for a House

STEP 1
Figure out regular monthly net pay after deductions for taxes, Social Security, pension, union dues, and so forth. (Include only what you can definitely count on.)

	Your estimate	Example
Sources of income		
Wages (after deductions)	$ _____	$ 1275
Social Security, disability or pension benefits, etc.	$ _____	$ 0
Alimony, child support	$ _____	$ 0
Interest on savings accounts	$ _____	$ 15
Stock dividends, bond income, etc.	$ _____	$ 0
Other income (such as from a second job)	$ _____	$ 710
Total net income	$ _____	$ 2000

STEP 2
Figure out regular monthly expenses (excluding rent and utilities).

Expenses		
Education	$ _____	$ 20
Food (groceries, eating out, etc.)	$ _____	$ 350
Clothes (new clothes, laundry, etc.)	$ _____	$ 100
Personal care (cosmetics, hair care, personal hygiene)	$ _____	$ 50
Medical or dental bills (plus prescriptions)	$ _____	$ 40
Home furnishings and expenses	$ _____	$ 60
Recreation (movies, vacations)	$ _____	$ 60
Gifts (for birthdays, holidays)	$ _____	$ 55
Car expenses (auto loan, insurance, gas, oil, maintenance, etc.)	$ _____	$ 255
Life and health insurance	$ _____	$ 50
Childcare expenses	$ _____	$ 100

Continued next page

Installment loans (charge accounts, credit cards)	$_____	$ 50
Regular savings	$_____	$ 75
All other miscellaneous expenses	$_____	$ 30
Total (nonhousing) expenses	$_____	$ 1300

STEP 3
Subtract the total in Step 1 from the total in Step 2 to get the amount available for housing expenses.

Total available for housing	$_____	$ 700

SOURCE: Adapted from *Home Buyers Information Package: A Guide for Buying and Owning a Home,* U.S. Department of Housing and Urban Development (1979).

our example, only two-thirds of the $500, or $333, should be spent on a mortgage payment according to this guide.

Many people want to buy a house so much that they believe no sacrifice is too great. But it helps to have guidelines to avoid being "house poor" (that is, having a house and nothing else). One rule of thumb in real estate is that families can afford a house that costs two to two and a half times their annual net income. If we apply this to our example, the family would be able to afford a house costing $48,000 to $60,000.

High prices and interest rates have caused many families to ignore these guides. It is estimated that two-fifths of today's home buyers are spending more than 25 percent of their incomes for recurring costs. This is more likely for families at or below the median income level—approximately $24,000 in 1981. In high-cost areas such as San Francisco and Los Angeles, over half of the buyers spend more than 25 percent (*Changing Times,* March 1979).

Lenders (banks and savings and loan associations) also began to ignore these guidelines in the last half of the 1970s because of rising home prices and rising family incomes, the latter caused in part by an increase in the number of two-income households. It was felt that, because the amount of home loan payments was fixed, homeowners would eventually spend a smaller percentage of income on housing. Today, new financing methods have created loans for which the payments can fluctuate 10 to 20 percent, so consumers are advised to be more cautious about exceeding these guidelines.

For decisions about your personal housing budget, you should apply all of these guides realistically. It may be wise to purchase a home worth *two times* your annual net family income if (1) you can make only a small down payment, necessitating higher monthly payments; (2) you have heavy debts, car payments, or college tuition; or (3) your income is irregular each month because you are in sales, construction, or another occupation for which income varies. Also, allow for the likelihood that property taxes, interest rates, and costs of repair for an older home will increase. If these are not possibilities, then the rule of *two and a half times* income applies, because your budget is more stable.

Besides determining income and expenses, you will need to determine how much cash you have available for housing. When you buy housing, you have to pay a **down payment,** which may be as low as 1 percent or as high as 20 percent, although 10 to 20 percent is typical. In addition, there will be **closing costs** (discussed later in this chapter), which vary according to geographic location and are 3 percent or more of the selling price.

It is common to require renters to pay the first month's rent in advance plus a **deposit,** which could include the last month's rent plus additional fees for cleaning, security, and the like. Some states set maximum limits on such deposits, but even these limits might allow the deposit to total three month's rent. If a space rents for $300, one could pay $1200 in advance of moving day.

By this time, you should have a rough estimate of how much of a deposit or down payment you could make. A perusal of local classified newspaper advertisements will help you draw some conclusions about your financial ability to rent or purchase shelter in your area.

The Third Step: Exploring Housing Options

Whether you choose to rent or buy, you will find three basic types of shelter: single-family homes; one-unit living spaces in multiunit dwellings such as apartments, cooperatives, or condominiums; and mobile homes. Each type has distinct characteristics.

SINGLE-FAMILY HOMES

By far the most popular choice of housing for Americans is a single-family detached home on a large, preferably half-acre, lot. What Americans are seeking is more privacy and freedom. There is more physical space between households as well as more interior space than is found in apartments. The overall population density in neighborhoods is less, which can mean less noise and pollution. Of the 100 million homes that will exist in 1990, 80 percent have already been built (*Real Estate Today,* August 1980). This means that we have a realistic picture of the appearance that single-family homes will have in this decade.

The trend in single-family homes in the 1960s and early 1970s was toward increasing interior size (in the 1970s, the size rose from an average of 1500 square feet to 1750 square feet). Increasing interest rates, housing prices, and associated costs have reversed this trend (Breckenfeld, 1980). Luxury and comfort have also been important features of newer homes. In 1963, for example, 19 percent of all new homes had central air conditioning, 13 percent had two and a half (or more) baths, and not enough had fireplaces to be included in the data. By 1978, 58 percent of all new houses had central air conditioning, 25 percent had at least two and a half baths, and a whopping 64 percent had at least one fireplace. These features were included, despite drastically increased building costs (*Real Estate Today,* August 1980).

Lot size, in contrast to house size, has been decreasing. Today, in heavily populated areas an acre might contain eight houses rather than four. As the price of land and the demand for single-family housing have risen, builders have had to put more houses on the land they acquire. Perhaps the increased luxury inside is an attempt to compensate for the decreased space outside.

MULTIUNIT HOUSING COMPLEXES

Some multiunit housing is designed specifically for rentals, whereas other multiunit housing may be purchased or rented, as are cooperatives or condominiums. **Apartments,** which are always rentals, offer a broad selection of living arrangements. They may consist of one unit (an efficiency apartment) above a garage or in a remodeled basement or of a small number of units clustered around a common garden or yard as in a duplex (two units) or a fourplex (four units). Two or three-story apartment buildings with private patios or balconies are common in the Southwest and West. High-rise apartment buildings in cities may provide closeness to jobs, to shopping, and to cultural events. Luxury high-rises may include spectacular views and recreational facilities such as handball courts, swimming pools, and health spas.

A **cooperative** is an apartment building or a group of dwellings owned by a nonprofit corporation that holds legal right to the building or dwellings. The residents of the building are the stockholders and they own a share of the corporation proportionate to the living space that they occupy. For example, if an apartment contains 2 percent of the living space of a dwelling, then the occupant has a 2 percent ownership share. He or she has the right to occupy that space for as long as he or she owns the stock, as well as the right to sell the stock at will. Apartments are sometimes converted to cooperatives, providing an opportunity for ownership. Because cooperatives are nonprofit, unlike apartments, and because cooperative members have a personal interest in the maintenance of the property, cooperative apartments cost about 20 percent less than comparable landlord-owned apartments.

The residents elect a board of directors to operate the cooperative. The board makes decisions regarding maintenance, upkeep, insurance, subletting, and rules of conduct for owners and their guests (parking, noise, and so forth). This board also determines the amount of monthly fee or lease payment that will be charged for the right to live there (for loan payments, maintenance, insurance, and so forth). One may need to apply to this board if he or she plans extensive remodeling or for approval to lease or rent the space to someone else.

A **condominium** is a group of housing units that may be built to be sold as separate units or may be converted from apartment buildings. They may be stacked side by side or may be stacked one on top of another. A condominium owner holds title to the living quarters plus a proportionate interest in common areas such as lobbies, corridors, grounds, and recreational facilities. The homeowners either elect a board of directors for the association or hire a management firm to make decisions and take care of landscaping, upkeep, and repair of common areas. Buyers arrange their own loans, pay their own tax bills, and pay a fee to the association for exterior maintenance. Owners may refinance or sell their units or rent the property as they see fit.

In 1979, for the first time, the number of condominium starts (starting to be built) exceeded the number of private rental starts (not subsidized by any government agency) (Breckenfeld, 1980). Condominiums are growing in popularity because they offer all the financial advantages of buying a single-family home, they often cost less money (because they are smaller, have common walls between units, and have higher population density), and they provide some of the benefits of renting, such as freedom from direct responsibility for maintenance and upkeep.

MOBILE HOMES

Mobile homes of the 1980s have more in common with apartments than with travel trailers. "Single wides," usually about 700 to 800 total square feet, are most prevalent. "Double wides," with as much as 1,200 to 1,400 square feet, are built and towed to the site in separate sections and then joined together. In either case, the cost per square foot is less than half the cost of a conventional house and usually includes kitchen appliances and some furniture. For example, purchase of a single-wide costs between $12,000 and $20,000, whereas double-wides range in price from $18,000 to $50,000. Mobile homes, sometimes called manufactured homes, offer a low-cost, minimum-upkeep alternative, which helps explain why approximately one-third of all new homes are mobile homes.

The quality of construction is an important consideration in selecting a mobile home. Buyers should avoid mobile homes with (1) floors that sag, buckle, or squeak, (2) roofs that show evidence of leaking and that are not insulated, (3) roofs and walls that are too flimsy for the weather, and, (4) doors and windows that do not allow exit in case of fire.

Prospective buyers of mobile homes must find a suitable place to park their home. Once installed, mobile homes are difficult and expensive to relocate, which explains why 98 percent of all mobile homes are mobile only once—when they are transported from the factory to a lot, space, or pad. In most cases, one must rent a pad in a mobile-home park. Rental fees include property taxes, grounds maintenance, recreational and laundry facilities, and perhaps some utilities.

Most mobile homes are purchased with personal property loans, as with automobiles. Loans typically last for ten to fifteen years and require a down payment of 10 percent to 25 percent of the purchase price. Shopping around for the loan could save hundreds of dollars, with the best deal probably available from a credit union if one has access to one. A few lenders now make loans for mobile homes like they do on permanently located homes. This trend is ex-

pected to increase, since the cost of mobile homes is becoming closer to the cost of a permanent home than of a car. Also, newer mobile homes are larger and more difficult to move. Because they are more difficult to steal, some of the lender's risk is diminished. One risk factor is that many mobile homes depreciate, or diminish in value, over time. However, good-quality, well-maintained mobile homes in prime locations can and do appreciate, or increase, in value.

NEW OR OLD?

Decision making about a type of housing must include a consideration of the age of the dwelling. New houses, condominiums, and apartments may be more energy efficient, may make better use of space, and may have more up-to-date style features (appliances, counter tile, skylights, and so forth). But they also may have less space for the money and higher prices or rents, they may lack the charm or interest of older homes or apartments, and they may require, if one is buying, an investment of several thousand dollars for landscaping, fencing, window coverings, and other decorator features.

Perhaps because of these factors, 70 percent of buyers choose older resale homes. First-time buyers like the lower prices of resale homes, despite the fact that, depending on age, such homes require more repair and maintenance and may be in less-desirable neighborhoods. In addition, personal tastes may influence renters and buyers; many people prefer the look and feel of older homes and apartments, and they may even enjoy renovating them.

WHETHER RENTING OR BUYING: INVESTIGATE

Besides deciding to rent or buy and choosing a particular type of shelter, consumers need to consider the geographic location and the construction features of the structure.

Geographic Location. Between 1950 and 1975, record numbers of families moved away from the cities and into the suburbs—regions of clean air, fewer people, and little crime. Gradually, small businesses, major department stores, office complexes, and even industry followed, diminishing many of the qualities consumers sought in suburbia. As a result of these changes and as a result of higher housing costs in the suburbs, many consumers are moving back into the cities, often to newly constructed apartments or condominiums. The choice of city, suburban, or country living is often dictated by one's job. But when deciding on geographic location, consider:

1. The cost of transportation to work, school, place of worship, shopping, and entertainment.
2. Whether property taxes are likely to increase drastically.
3. The quality of the schools (which sometimes has a direct relationship to property taxes)—are schools suitable or will you feel the need to pay for a private school?
4. Air or noise pollution (this may affect your health) from factories, airports, freeways.
5. Crime (statistics are available from the police department).
6. Zoning and development—what are the long-range plans for the area in terms of industry, airports, freeways, and other housing?

To obtain this type of information, talk to friends, relatives, and neighborhood residents, read local newspapers, and visit real estate offices, the planning department of the city, the school board, and the local police department.

Physical Construction. Once you have chosen a location, you need to investigate specific neighborhoods and houses. Worksheet 13-2 provides a checklist that will help you to evaluate the quality and convenience of each neighborhood. By acquainting yourself with neighborhood characteristics and features, you can determine which neighborhoods do not meet your needs and standards and save time by excluding them from your search.

After selecting several neighborhoods, you should be prepared to evaluate a particular house or apartment. Use Worksheet 13-3 as a checklist during inspection and for comparing one choice to another. Information about warranties, cost of utilities, insulation, and the like is available from the landlord, owner, or real estate agent. To use the worksheet

WORKSHEET 13-2

Neighborhood Inspection Checklist

Neighborhood Quality	Yes	No	Not important
1. Are the homes well cared for?	☐	☐	☐
2. Are there good public services (police and fire departments)?	☐	☐	☐
3. Are roads paved?	☐	☐	☐
4. Are there sidewalks?	☐	☐	☐
5. Is street lighting adequate?	☐	☐	☐
6. Is there a city sewer system?	☐	☐	☐
7. Is there a safe public water supply?	☐	☐	☐
8. Are the public schools good?	☐	☐	☐

Neighborhood Convenience

	Yes	No	Not important
1. Will you be near your work?	☐	☐	☐
2. Are schools nearby?	☐	☐	☐
3. Are shopping centers nearby?	☐	☐	☐
4. Is public transportation available?	☐	☐	☐
5. Will you be near childcare services?	☐	☐	☐
6. Are hospitals, clinics, or doctors close by?	☐	☐	☐
7. Is a park or playground nearby?	☐	☐	☐

Neighbors

	Yes	No	Not important
1. Will you be near friends or relatives?	☐	☐	☐
2. Will you be near other children of the same ages as your children?	☐	☐	☐
3. Will you feel comfortable with the neighbors?	☐	☐	☐
4. Is there an active community group?	☐	☐	☐

Continued next page

Does the Neighborhood Have:	Yes	No	Not important
1. Increasing real estate taxes?	☐	☐	☐
2. Decreasing sales prices of homes?	☐	☐	☐
3. Lots of families moving away?	☐	☐	☐
4. Heavy traffic or noise?	☐	☐	☐
5. Litter or pollution?	☐	☐	☐
6. Factories or heavy industry?	☐	☐	☐
7. Businesses closing down?	☐	☐	☐
8. Vacant houses or buildings?	☐	☐	☐
9. Increasing crime or vandalism?	☐	☐	☐

	Good	Fair	Poor
What is your overall rating of the neighborhood?	☐	☐	☐

SOURCE: Adapted from *Home Buyers Information Package: A Guide for Buying and Owning a Home*, U.S. Department of Housing and Urban Development (1979).

most effectively, adapt it to your personal needs with sketches or notes. For example, because first impressions are important, consider the front or entrance of each dwelling. Is it pleasant and clean, with easy access? Are there more stairs than you can handle on a daily basis? Is there enough space inside? Is the floor plan logical and convenient for your needs? Room size is often deceiving, so imagine your furniture in each room.

Layouts of kitchens and bathrooms can be critical in time management. Consider lighting, storage, continuous counter space, and ventilation in terms of your needs and your family size. Make sure all appliances and fixtures work. Is there enough space in the bathroom for two people to use the mirror? Does the kitchen have room for a table and chairs? Awareness of these factors and those shown in Worksheet 13-3 will prepare you to make a specific renting or buying choice.

Prospective buyers should be aware that **new-home warranties** are now available from the National Association of Home Builders. The coverage is transferable, so subsequent homeowners are also protected. During the first year of ownership, the builder guarantees the materials, the structure, and the quality of workmanship. During the second year, heating, air conditioning, wiring, plumbing, and structural flaws continue to be covered. And for eight more years, the owner is insured against major structural defects. This coverage is offered as a "feature" with some new homes and, of course, is included in the purchase price. At approximately $2 per $1,000 of selling price (for example, $160 on an $80,000 home), it is a bargain for homeowners.

Those who have decided to buy should also be aware of the real estate adage that it is better to buy an attractive, well-maintained home similar in value to others in the neighborhood than to buy the most expensive home in a lesser neighborhood. Remember, home ownership provides an investment as well as shelter, and the value of a home is tied to the quality and value of neighboring homes.

The Fourth Step: Choosing Your Housing

Although you have done all the groundwork for a housing decision, you need one more important piece

WORKSHEET 13-3

House Inspection
Inside the House—Structure and Systems

Inspection item	Condition		Item under warranty?	Additional comments
	Adequate—not a problem	Inadequate—needs repair or replacement		

1. Structure of house
   support posts
     (basement)
   floor beams
     (basement)				

2. Floors				
3. Stairs (treads, handrails)				

4. Plumbing system
   water pipes OK?
   sewer pipes OK?
   water pressure OK?
   toilets work?
   sinks and faucets?
   drains work?
				Cost of water bills last year $

5. Heating system
   what type?
   how old?
   kind of fuel?
   when serviced last?
				Cost of heat last year $

6. Hot water heater
   how old?
   capacity or
     recovery rate?				

7. Electrical system
   how old?
   fuses or circuit
     breaker?
   no. of volts or amps?
				Cost of electricity last year $

8. Cooling/air conditioning
   evaporative
     or cooling?
				Cost to use last year $

9. General room layout (traffic patterns)				

10. Kitchen
   size of kitchen
   stove/oven
   refrigerator
   dishwasher
   disposal/sink
   counter space
   cabinets/shelves
   electrical outlets
   floor condition
   windows/ventilation				

Continued next page

11. Bathrooms 　　no. of bathrooms 　　toilets, showers, 　　　tubs OK? 　　tiles and floors? 　　lighting and ventilation?				
12. Living room/dining room 　　size OK? 　　fireplace?				
13. Bedrooms 　　no. and size 　　closets adequate? 　　windows?				
14. Storage space				
15. Windows in house				
16. Doors in house				
17. Walls and ceilings				
18. Basement 　　leaks or dampness? 　　lighting OK?				
19. Attic 　　signs of leaks? 　　insulation? 　　signs of rodents?				How much insulation?

SOURCE: *Home Buyer's Information Package: A Guide for Buying and Owning a Home,* U.S. Department of Housing and Urban Development (1979).

of information before you place your signature on a rental or purchase agreement: your rights and responsibilities. The Federal Fair Housing Law, Title VIII of the Civil Rights Act of 1968, makes it illegal for anyone to discriminate on the basis of race, religion, sex, color, or national origin. In many states, other forms of discrimination (such as those based on marital status) may also be illegal. Discrimination in housing may be subtle, but as a result of it you may be denied the chance to look at housing in a particular neighborhood, you may be denied the chance to look at a specific dwelling, or you may be pressured into paying more for rent or a house than others would. Box 13-2 describes illegal discriminatory practices and tells how to contact your local office of the U.S. Department of Housing and Urban Development (HUD) if you feel you have been a victim of discrimination.

RENTING

Besides the features on the housing checklist, there are a few unique considerations for renters concerning security, convenience, and personal preferences. Are children allowed? If so, are there age restrictions? Are pets allowed, and if so, are there special rules regarding their care? If you are renting in a multiunit dwelling, will there be a manager or a superintendent on the premises at all times? If not, will someone be easy to contact to solve problems? What specific security measures are available in the parking facility,

> **BOX 13-2**
>
> ## Dealing with Discrimination in Housing
>
> How discrimination may affect you:
>
> 1. You may be denied a chance to look at or buy a particular house in a particular neighborhood.
> 2. You may be "steered" by real estate brokers into looking at houses only in certain neighborhoods.
> 3. You may be pressured into paying more for a house than others would.
> 4. You may become so discouraged that you decide not to buy at all.
>
> Discrimination is sometimes hard to detect. Some of the ways it is practiced include:
>
> 1. You are told the house is sold when it is not.
> 2. You are told that there are other offers or that there is no one to show you the house.
> 3. You are asked to leave your phone number, and if the exchange is for a minority area, no one calls you back.
> 4. You are told the seller has decided not to sell or has raised the price.
> 5. The broker says he or she has nothing available in your price range and refuses to show you the listing of houses for sale.
> 6. You can't get an appointment or the broker cancels an appointment.
> 7. You are told that the house is not what you want, is too expensive, or is not desirable.
> 8. The owner is out, sick, sleeping, or whatever.
>
> SOURCE: *Home Buyer's Information Package: A Guide for Buying and Owning a Home,* U.S. Department of Housing and Urban Development (1979).
>
> If you think you have been discriminated against, write down a few notes about how you think discrimination was practiced:
>
> 1. The names of the real estate agency, the seller, or other persons you think discriminated against you.
> 2. The date, time, and place it occurred.
> 3. How you think you were discriminated against.
> 4. The names of any witnesses who were with you when the discrimination occurred.
>
> Call the people who can help. Get in touch with your local civil rights organization or the local office of the U.S. Department of Housing and Urban Development (HUD). The steps they take on your behalf usually include:
>
> 1. Taking down the facts of your case.
> 2. Sending out an investigator ("tester") to check whether your rights were denied in any way.
> 3. If they agree that you were discriminated against, contacting the seller, the real estate broker, or other persons involved to work out an agreement.
> 4. If they cannot work out an agreement or if the person denies having discriminated, beginning the legal process for filing a formal complaint before the state civil rights commission or the state or federal courts.
>
> Remember, if you think you have been discriminated against, you can and should do something about it.

in the corridors, and so forth? Are there safe and clearly marked fire exits? Some of these factors may be included in rental agreements or in contracts that identify the rules of conduct and the payment required of the tenant. Contracts and rental agreements may also list the services that the landlord agrees to provide, and such contracts are signed by both tenant and landlord.

Rental Agreement. Basically, there are two kinds of rental agreements: month-to-month agreements and leases. With a **month-to-month rental agreement** the rent can be raised monthly, although this is not likely. Payment of each month's rent is usually assumed to indicate that the renter continues to accept the terms of the agreement. In addition, the landlord can evict the tenant and change the terms of the agreement (rental fees, responsibility for expenses, and restrictions). A lease, however, as we have already seen, fixes the rent payment and conditions of the rental for a period of time, usually a year. In times of high inflation, this provides renters with more budgetary security.

The majority of rental agreements and leases are written to protect the landlord. Often, standard forms such as those purchased in stationery stores have clauses that may be illegal in the state where one lives. The forms may misstate current laws or fail to inform tenants of their rights. Such agreements or leases, although legally unsound, may frighten tenants into complying with the terms or discourage tenants from demanding the protections provided by state law. Uninformed landlords may also believe these forms to be legal and may operate accordingly.

In deciding whether to sign an agreement or a lease, you should examine its provisions carefully and weigh what you are getting against what you are giving away. To check on local and state laws affecting housing rights, get in touch with your state consumer affairs agency (listed in Appendix III), a local consumer affairs agency, the local city hall, or a tenant's rights organization. A month-to-month agreement or a lease should indicate:

1. The amount of the monthly fee and the day of the month it is due. If a prepayment of the last month's rent is required, it should be so stated.
2. The amount of any required deposit and the conditions under which part or all of it will be returned.
3. Who pays for utilities, repairs, replacements, insurance, and the like.

In addition, a lease should state how it will be renewed when it expires, whether on a month-to-month basis, at a renegotiated rental rate and time period, or automatically extended with the same terms.

You should personalize the rental agreement or lease to include everything you have been promised. For example, if you have been told that the dwelling comes with appliances or furniture, make sure each item is specified. If the landlord has promised to paint the interior, to make repairs, and so forth before you move in, have this written into the contract. If you have been promised use of common recreational or laundry facilities, be sure that this use is included, as well as the cost, if any, for such use.

Most rental agreements or leases list the landlord's policies regarding overnight guests, children, pets, noise, and so forth. Failure to comply may result in eviction or a cancelled lease. This probably sounds reasonable, but consider that some leases include clauses that prohibit immoral behavior—judged by the landlord, naturally. Another common restriction may prohibit having overnight guests by requiring that the dwelling be occupied only by the tenant and the tenant's immediate family. Leases may prohibit subleasing, changing the color of interior paint, or hanging pictures on the wall. Be cautious of other clauses that make you liable for all repairs, that allow the landlord to enter the premises even when you are not there (except for an emergency, of course), or that require you to follow regulations that have not yet been written. If you disagree with any of the stipulations and convince the landlord that they should be changed, write these changes into the contract. If the landlord does not agree to changes that you feel are essential, you have two choices. You can sign the contract and hope that a problem doesn't arise, or you can look for another place to rent. Naturally, if you choose the first, you need to be prepared to accept the consequences, which may include the possibility of eviction.

Most landlords require a deposit to cover the cost of cleaning, breakage, or loss when a tenant moves out. This "refundable" deposit can equal from one to three months' rent, and it is supposed to be returned if the dwelling is left clean and in good condition. A cleaning charge is commonly assessed against this deposit, however, regardless of how clean you leave the house or apartment, and the final judgment usually rests with the landlord.

1. Make a list of all damage that already exists. It is best to do so on a "walk through" with the manager or owner. Make a carbon copy of this list. Sign the list immediately, and have the manager do the same.
2. Take photographs that show the condition and contents of the dwelling and the yard on the day

you move in, and repeat the process on the day you move out. Have them developed by a company that puts a date on their pictures.

3. Save copies of all bills for maintenance, cleaning, repairs, or improvements you make.

4. Investigate state and local laws that regulate security deposits and refunds, so that you know your rights and responsibilities. When you move out, discuss the refund with the owner or manager, keeping these regulations in mind. If you encounter resistance, showing the owner the pictures and other documents will usually prove your point. If not, you can go to small claims court. (See Chapter 5.)

Landlord-Tenant Relations. Considering the number of tenants in the United States, it is logical to assume that some landlord-tenant disagreements may arise. Many such disputes focus on a landlord's failure to provide necessary repairs or livable dwellings. Even though there is no federal landlord-tenant law covering privately owned housing, in recent years most state courts have extended rights to tenants, by the application of an **implied warranty of habitability**, to ensure that landlords provide decent conditions. This warranty requires that rentals conform to building, safety, and sanitation codes. At the very least, this means that there are no roof leaks, broken windows, or broken doors; that plumbing works, including access to hot and cold water and a working sewer or septic tank connection; that the heater, lights, and wiring work safely; that the floors, stairways, and railings are in good condition; that the property is clean and free of pests when it is rented; and that there are enough covered garbage cans. Box 13-3 presents a case study involving the landlord's responsibility to provide habitable housing and problems that can arise.

In some states, tenants have the legal right to withhold part or all of the rent to force landlords to make repairs. Approximately half of the states allow tenants to deduct repairs from the rent, and each of these states has specific procedures and restrictions for this process. Some states limit the portion of a month's rent that can be used or specify how often this can be done. Many states also have specific legal procedures for rent strikes. Unfortunately, if tenants

---

BOX 13-3

Landlord-Tenant Relations: A Case Study

"Hey, Tony," Nanette called out. "We've received a registered letter."

Tony came into the room as Nanette tore open the envelope. The look on her face indicated shock. "We're being sued!" she exclaimed.

"You're kidding! Who would do that?" Tony asked.

"Well, it says here that it's Robert Jensen, our past landlord from the house on Columbia Avenue. He claims that we caused damage to the draperies, carpet, plumbing, and backyard. He's suing us for $5,000 to cover damages, lawyer's fees, and two months' rent for the time the house was empty during repairs."

"I can't believe this. We moved from there because he wouldn't fix the plumbing. Remember how the shower leaked and kept the bedroom carpet soggy? We waited three months for him to fix that before we gave up and moved out. Those damages aren't our fault."

Nanette nodded in agreement. "Well, what do you think he means about the draperies?" she asked. "They weren't in very good condition when we first moved in—they were faded and had snags. It's true that our cat did climb on them once in a while, but they weren't really much worse than when we moved in."

"And I fixed the backyard before we moved out, remember?" Tony asked. "Snoopy dug those holes, but I filled them back up. There never was a lawn back there anyway."

"We just can't afford this," Nanette moaned. "What should we do?"

1. What can this couple do to protect themselves? Where can they go to get accurate advice?
2. What are the laws in your state that might provide legal protection for this couple?
3. What could this couple do to avoid being in this situation in the future?

---

exercise any of these options, the landlord may ask them to move. Such "retaliatory eviction" is prohibited in certain circumstances, but it is often difficult to establish in court.

BOX 13-4

Rent Control: A Problem or a Solution?

In the late 1970s, many apartment owners raised their rents in an effort to keep up with taxes and energy and maintenance costs. When the increases seemed excessive, angry tenants responded with picket lines and rent strikes. When rents continued to escalate, apartment dwellers in many regions developed enough clout to successfully convince local governments to initiate **rent control,** regulations that state under what conditions rent can be increased and what percent increase is allowable.

Confusion and inequities have been the hallmarks of rent-control legislation ever since it was imposed nationally during World War II. Critics of rent control usually cite New York City as an example of the negative effect of such measures. This city, which has had rent control since 1943, lost between 25,000 and 30,000 rental units each year between 1974 and 1979. Mortgage money for new rent-controlled apartments virtually vanished during the same time. Both situations are blamed on the fact that rent-controlled apartments are not as profitable as other forms of real estate or investment (*Los Angeles Times,* October 21, 1979).

Those who favor rent control point out that most measures exempt new construction. In addition, most measures usually allow increases to ensure that landlords get a "just and reasonable" return on their investment, usually tying new allowable increases to the Consumer Price Index.

When local regulations are being formulated, consumers have a responsibility to evaluate both long-term as well as short-term costs and benefits for tenants and landlords. The tradeoff of lower rents in the short term may not be worthwhile if it results in inadequate rental housing for consumers in the long term.

The Future of Renting. At least 26 million households in America are renters—over one-third of the total. Renters make up over half the households in cities such as San Francisco, Los Angeles, and New York—the three most expensive cities in terms of home ownership. As costs of owning increase and with houses and condominiums as well as apartments available for rent, more people are choosing this option. Yet some real estate experts predict a rental-housing shortage in the 1980s because of increased demand and limited supply. These reasons coupled with consumers' needs for housing at affordable prices will make the issues of landlord-tenant relations and rent control controversial throughout the decade (see Box 13-4).

BUYING A HOME

You may have come to the conclusion that your family's financial and personal circumstances warrant purchasing a home. Besides your budget and your personal situation, two factors in the housing market will affect your chances of making a purchase. The first is supply and demand. If there are only a few buyers and many sellers in your community, you will be able to negotiate a reasonable price for your home. This "buyer's market" might occur in places where winters have been excessively cold several years in a row, where population has declined, or where building or housing units have exceeded the demands of a region, such as is the case in St. Louis. On the other hand, if you have to compete with other home buyers for a limited number of homes, you are in a "seller's market" and may have to pay more, as in Los Angeles or Washington, D.C. As a result of decreased housing starts nationally in 1974–1975 and in 1980–1981, more and more Americans may be facing seller's markets.

A second factor is the availability of financing, or money for a loan. As interest rates rise, the cost of financing increases dramatically. For example, at interest rates of 10 percent, a family that could afford a house payment of $878 a month and a 20 percent down payment could buy a $100,000 house. But at a 17 percent rate, they could only afford a $60,000 house. Table 13-1 shows the impact of rising interest rates more completely. Because the national median price of existing homes is more than $78,000, it is not surprising that fewer families purchase homes when interest rates soar.

Finding Your Dream Home. All of the factors we considered when searching for a rental apply to looking for a home to purchase. Do not be pressured into buying the first house you see. Refer to Worksheet

Table 13-1. Impact of Rising Interest Rates on Monthly Mortgage Payments*

Loan amount	18%	17%	16%	15%	14%	12%	10%
$ 60,000	$ 904	$ 855	$ 807	$ 758	$ 711	$ 617	$ 527
80,000	1,205	1,140	1,076	1,011	948	823	702
100,000	1,507	1,426	1,345	1,264	1,185	1,029	878
125,000	1,884	1,782	1,681	1,581	1,481	1,286	1,098
150,000	2,261	2,139	2,017	1,897	1,778	1,543	1,317
175,000	2,637	2,495	2,353	2,213	2,074	1,801	1,537
200,000	3,014	2,852	2,690	2,529	2,370	2,058	1,756

*Estimated monthly payments for principal and interest only on a 30-year loan, allowances for taxes, insurance, and other impounds not included.

SOURCE: California Federal Savings and Loan Association (1980). Used with permission.

13-3 and ask questions. Take a flashlight with you so you can see into those dark corners. Worksheet 13-4 provides a more detailed checklist for evaluating the structural condition of the building and grounds. Be sure to bring and consult other members of the household. Because you may be living in the house for a long time, it is important that the rest of the family be happy with the choice.

The two most common sources of homes for sale are owners and real estate brokers. You can learn about homes, condominiums, and mobile homes for sale by owners by checking the classified ads in the newspaper, reading bulletin boards in stores and other locations, asking friends, and looking for signs on lawns and streets. But not every seller wants to put up with the trouble of advertising, showing the property, or dealing with the paperwork of selling. This is where **real estate brokers** come in handy. A broker, usually through his or her agents, handles all the ins and outs of selling the home for the seller, and he or she may take care of the buyer's side of the deal, too. Real estate agents and brokers are licensed by the state to perform these services (the legal responsibilities and extent of their work vary from state to state) for a **commission,** that is, a percentage of the sales price of the property.

Real estate brokers and agents have several main functions:

1. They acquire listings of properties for which they act as agents. In some states, such as California, brokers cooperate and compile all listings into a computerized book (the *Multiple Listing* book) that shows all the houses available in a given area. Thus, a buyer can go to a broker and find out about many more properties than the ones that the broker has in his or her office. There is no restriction on the buyer to purchase a property from another broker, but the two brokers (and their agents, if any are involved) split the commission.

2. They negotiate the highest price that the buyer will pay and the lowest price that the owner will accept.

3. They show prospective buyers property, usually without charge, because they expect to be paid when they sell a house. If you are new to an area, a real estate agent or broker can be particularly helpful in showing you areas and houses you may be interested in, which can save you time. You may also feel obligated to that person, although you are not legally bound to buy anything.

Before you choose a broker or a real estate agent, try to research his or her reputation. Ask your friends or workmates for recommendations, talk to the person to see whether you like her or him, and check with the Better Business Bureau to see whether there have been any complaints.

Most brokerage societies or real estate boards (that is, groups of brokers) have rules against price competition and have instituted a standard fee for services of 6 to 7 percent of the selling price. As you

WORKSHEET 13-4
Home Inspection
Outside the House—Structure and Grounds

Inspection Item	Condition		Item under warranty?	Additional comments
	Adequate—not a Problem	Inadequate—needs Repair or Replacement		
1. Foundation				
2. Brickwork				
3. Siding				
4. Exterior paint				
5. Porch(es)				
6. Windows and screens				
7. Storm windows				
8. Roof				
9. Gutters and downspouts				
10. Chimney(s)				
11. Walls and fences				
12. Garage				
13. Driveway and walks				
14. Grounds and landscaping				
15. Drainage and septic systems				
16. Other items outside the house				

SOURCE: *Home Buyer's Information Package: A Guide for Buying and Owning a Home*, U.S. Department of Housing and Urban Development (1979).

well know, the price of housing has increased over the last few years faster than the prices of many other commodities, which has meant an automatic and substantial raise for brokers. As a result, many homeowners sell their homes themselves or go to cut-rate or alternative brokers. These brokers provide advertising, signs, and flags, and they line up prospective buyers and provide advice to owners. Basically, they do everything except show the house to prospective buyers, a job left to the seller. Most alternative brokers will not be able to list houses in the computerized *Multiple Listing* book used by conventional brokers, but they may offer a similar service on a smaller scale. For these services, they charge 1 to 4 percent. Consumers should feel free to ask brokers about whether the commission fee is negotiable, because competition by alternative brokers has created more fee flexibility. If there is no commission or a reduced commission, there will be a lower selling price, making the property more attractive to a buyer.

When You Decide to Buy. From looking at comparable homes in similar neighborhoods, you should be able to decide what a fair sales price is for a specific dwelling. Do not be deceived by quick cosmetic fixes (such as a cheap paint job on the front door or carpeting or fancy wallpaper that hides defects) or by the owner's furniture and appliances. Look for the real value in the house: quality construction inside and outside, lot size and landscaping, the size of the house and the number of rooms, structural improvements, and the convenience and quality of the neighborhood.

If you are seriously considering a dwelling, it may be wise to pay an expert to explore the home for problems with structure, wiring, termites, plumbing, and the like, before you sign a contract. Inspection is particularly useful for a home 10 years old or older. It may cost as little as $50 or as much as $250 for larger homes. For newer homes, for which the risks are fewer, you might want to postpone inspection until after you have made an offer for the home, but make the offer contingent on the satisfactory results of the inspection. This information can save you hundreds of dollars and may serve as a bargaining point. Also ask about **easements** for the property—the rights of an individual, business, or government to have access through or over the property. You will want to know all of these conditions and restrictions.

After you are familiar with the house and its problems, as well as its charms, investigate the seller's situation. Sellers almost always ask for more money than they are willing to accept. But look, too, for other factors. If the house has been on the market for a long time, the owner may be eager to sell and may accept a lower price. Your first offer should be below your safe limit. You can expect the seller to accept or reject it quickly—within a day or two. If the seller rejects your offer, he or she may make a counter offer with another price or different terms. You, of course, could do the same.

If and when you and the seller agree on price, you will need to put up a deposit, often called **earnest money**—usually $100 to $1,000. This deposit is evidence of the seriousness of your intention, and it is usually applied to the down payment later. At the same time, you will draw up an **earnest agreement** or **binder**—a written offer to buy the home at a given price. The binder should contain a clause such as "contingent upon the buyer's obtaining financing," and both you and the seller need to sign and date it. The advantages to the buyer of a binder is that the price of the house is fixed and it provides proof that the offer has been accepted; thus, it is important to get the seller to sign the binder as soon as possible. This leaves you and the seller free to work out the details of the agreement. In most cases, if the seller accepts your offer and you change your mind, you forfeit your deposit.

The next step is to draw up a **contract of sale,** also called a purchase and sales agreement, or a contract of purchase. This contract protects both buyer and seller, because it clarifies the terms and the conditions that must be met. If one or more of the terms are not met, the contract can be cancelled. And if the fault is not yours, the deposit or earnest money will be returned. Often, the binder and the contract of sale are combined, which speeds up the buying process, but that procedure leaves everything open for negotiation until the last minute. Here is a partial list of conditions that should be included in a purchase contract:

1. The name(s) and address(es) of the seller(s) and buyer(s).

2. A description of the property.
3. The price of the house.
4. The amount of the deposit (earnest money), and who holds it until the closing.
5. The date and time of the closing.
6. Where the closing will take place.
7. A provision to extend the closing date.
8. A provision for disposition of the deposit if something goes wrong.
9. The amount of the broker's fee (if any).
10. The adjustments to be made at the closing (taxes already paid by the seller, fuel adjustments, points or extra service charges for a home loan paid by the seller or the buyer).
11. The details of what is included in the sale (carpeting, appliances, curtains, light fixtures, and so forth).
12. Special conditions of the sale (for example, the seller will repair broken windows, pay for a termite inspection and treatment, and so forth).
13. Inspections you can make before closing.
14. Property easements.

Blank purchase agreements can be obtained at stationery stores, sometimes from banks or savings and loan associations, or from attorneys, or they can be personally devised (a sample is provided in Figure 13-1). Brokers provide these forms and complete them as part of their services. Changes can be made in the standard purchase agreement as long as the buyer and the seller agree. Before you sign an agreement: (1) make sure that all of the terms of the agreement are filled out properly, (2) add any special conditions you want included, and (3) delete any terms or conditions in the standard agreement that do not apply to you or that you do not want included.

Loans and Mortgages. A **mortgage** is a claim against **real property,** that is, land and everything permanently fixed to it, such as buildings, fences, and so forth. A mortgage is given by the buyer (mortgagor) to the lender (mortgagee) as security for the money borrowed. That is, if you want to borrow money to buy a house, you give the lender a claim to the property so that if you do not or cannot pay for it, the lender can take the property in place of the money you owe. The **mortgage note** is the written agreement the buyer signs with the lender to repay the loan. It states the loan **principal,** which is the specific amount borrowed, the interest rate, and the specific details of the payment plan, which allows the mortgagor to reduce the debt gradually through monthly payments on the principal. This form of repayment is called **amortization.** The mortgage note also states whether there is a **prepayment penalty**—a charge for paying off the loan before it is due. Prepayment is often done when the house is sold to another person who has negotiated his or her own mortgage with a different lender. Some buyers assume the loan of the seller, that is, they accept all conditions and terms of the mortgage note and become responsible for its payment. Such **assumable loans** are often available at lower interest rates than prevail at a given time and so are an asset for both buyers and sellers. Now that we know the basic vocabulary of mortgages, we can look at the terms and conditions of each type.

Fixed-Payment Mortgages. A **fixed-payment mortgage** has a payment and interest rate that stay at one level for the lifetime of the loan. Three types of fixed-payment mortgage loans are available. Although you may not be eligible for two of them, all three are available from commercial banks, savings banks, savings and loan associations, and insurance companies.

Conventional loans can be arranged in any way that satisfies both parties. They may require down payments that range from 5 to 25 percent, with a larger "down" sometimes receiving a lower interest rate. Interest rates are established by the lender, within the limitations of state statutes, and they are affected by the forces of supply and demand in the national money market. For example, if the demand for money rises, the interest rate on conventional loans might rise to 17 or 18 percent. If the demand drops, lenders offer conventional loans at a lower interest rate, perhaps 12 percent.

With a conventional loan, the money that the mortgagor borrows is secured by the value of the mortgaged property. If the borrower fails to make the monthly payments as agreed (that is, he or she **defaults** on the loan), the lender has the right to

Figure 13-1. Sample purchase agreement.

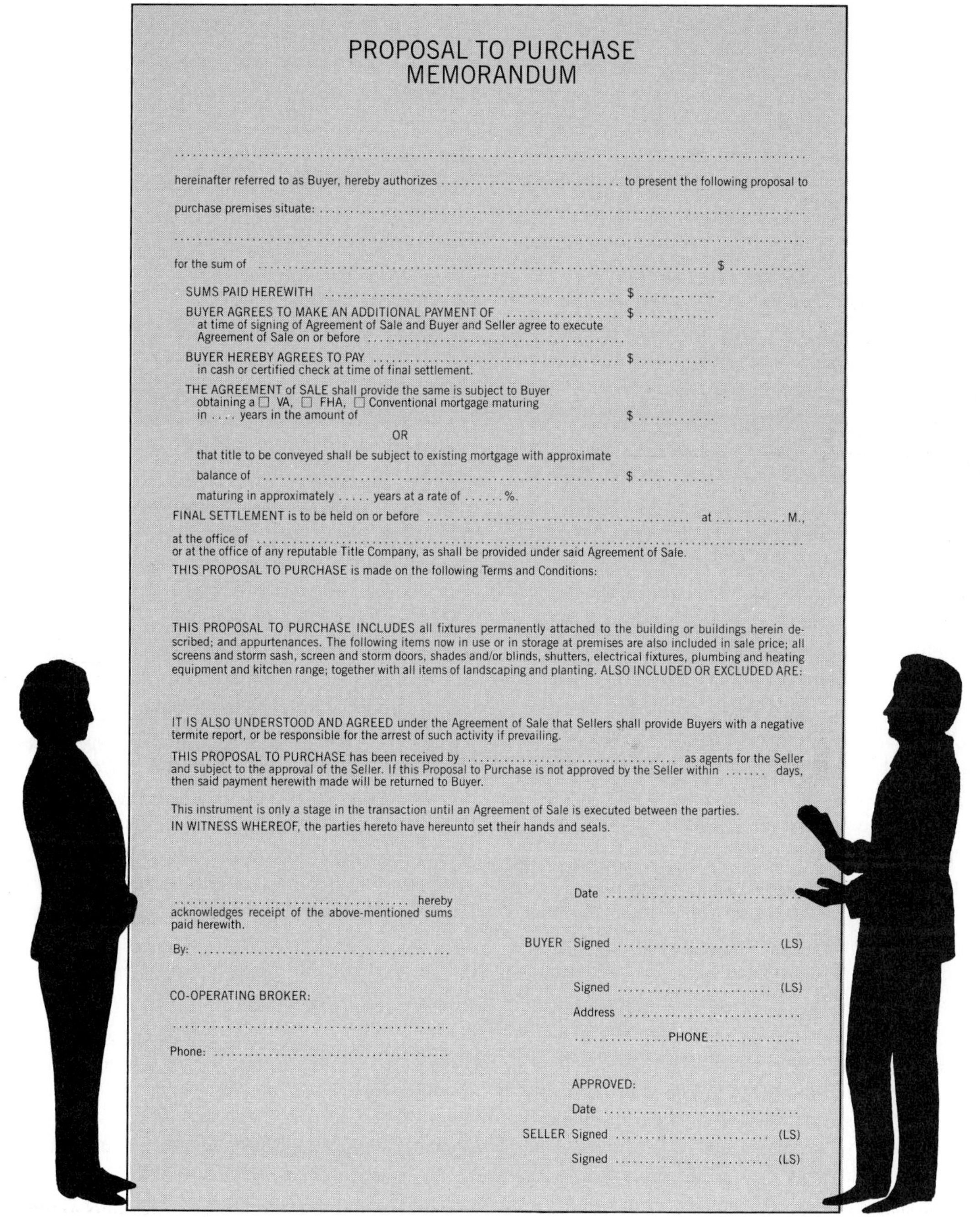

PROPOSAL TO PURCHASE MEMORANDUM

....
hereinafter referred to as Buyer, hereby authorizes .... to present the following proposal to
purchase premises situate: ....

....

for the sum of .... $ ....

   SUMS PAID HEREWITH .... $ ....
   BUYER AGREES TO MAKE AN ADDITIONAL PAYMENT OF .... $ ....
     at time of signing of Agreement of Sale and Buyer and Seller agree to execute
     Agreement of Sale on or before ....
   BUYER HEREBY AGREES TO PAY .... $ ....
     in cash or certified check at time of final settlement.
   THE AGREEMENT of SALE shall provide the same is subject to Buyer
     obtaining a ☐ VA, ☐ FHA, ☐ Conventional mortgage maturing
     in .... years in the amount of .... $ ....
                                         OR
   that title to be conveyed shall be subject to existing mortgage with approximate
   balance of .... $ ....
   maturing in approximately ..... years at a rate of ...... %.
FINAL SETTLEMENT is to be held on or before .... at .... M.,
at the office of ....
or at the office of any reputable Title Company, as shall be provided under said Agreement of Sale.
THIS PROPOSAL TO PURCHASE is made on the following Terms and Conditions:

THIS PROPOSAL TO PURCHASE INCLUDES all fixtures permanently attached to the building or buildings herein described; and appurtenances. The following items now in use or in storage at premises are also included in sale price; all screens and storm sash, screen and storm doors, shades and/or blinds, shutters, electrical fixtures, plumbing and heating equipment and kitchen range; together with all items of landscaping and planting. ALSO INCLUDED OR EXCLUDED ARE:

IT IS ALSO UNDERSTOOD AND AGREED under the Agreement of Sale that Sellers shall provide Buyers with a negative termite report, or be responsible for the arrest of such activity if prevailing.

THIS PROPOSAL TO PURCHASE has been received by .... as agents for the Seller and subject to the approval of the Seller. If this Proposal to Purchase is not approved by the Seller within .... days, then said payment herewith made will be returned to Buyer.

This instrument is only a stage in the transaction until an Agreement of Sale is executed between the parties.
IN WITNESS WHEREOF, the parties hereto have hereunto set their hands and seals.

.... hereby   Date ....
acknowledges receipt of the above-mentioned sums
paid herewith.
                                                BUYER Signed .... (LS)
By: ....

                                                      Signed .... (LS)
CO-OPERATING BROKER: Address ....
.... PHONE ....
Phone: ....

                                                    APPROVED:
                                                    Date ....
                                             SELLER Signed .... (LS)
                                                     Signed .... (LS)

foreclose—to seize the property and sell it to pay off the debt. For example, let us say that your neighbor is in a car accident and is unable to work for several months. As a result she cannot make her house payment. The lender would have the right to evict your neighbor, auction off the house, and take the proceeds to pay off the loan. If any money is left after the loan is paid, it would go to your neighbor.

With a conventional loan, **mortgage insurance** is available, which protects lenders against loss by default on at least part of the loan. Because of the diminished risk, private mortgage insurance may make it possible for the borrower to pay as little as 5 to 10 percent of the sale price for a down payment.

A second type of loan is the **Veterans Administration (VA) loan guarantee.** The purpose of this loan is to ensure that an eligible veteran or a veteran's widow can obtain financing for home ownership. The interest rate is fixed by the federal government rather than by money availability, and it is usually slightly lower than the interest rate on a conventional loan. The Veterans Administration generally does not make loans, but it offers a guaranty against loss to private lending institutions. The government promises to repay a certain percentage of the loan (usually 60 percent), so the borrower needs no other mortgage insurance.

To be eligible for a VA loan, the amount of the loan cannot exceed the VA's appraised value of the property. When you apply for a VA loan, a VA representative comes to the property to do an **appraisal**—an evaluation of what the property is worth—and to see whether, if you should default, the house can be resold for at least as much money as you paid for it. This guaranty of value makes VA loans safer for both borrowers and lenders. Because of this guaranty, VA loans are made for up to $100,000 for 30 years, with no prepayment penalty and with little or no down payment. During the 1970s, VA loans became available for mobile homes and mortgages on second homes, although under slightly different guaranty terms. All of these loan guaranties are available to veterans more than once if the previously guaranteed loan has been paid off and if the property has been transferred to another owner. Veterans are liable to the VA for loan losses if they default, until the VA releases them from this responsibility, usually at the time that the home is resold.

The Federal Housing Administration (FHA), established by Congress in 1934, insures home loans up to certain amounts for up to thirty-five years. **Federal Housing Administration loans** can have down payments as small as 3 to 5 percent of the appraised value of the house. This mortgage insurance was created to encourage and facilitate home ownership. As with VA loans, the maximum interest rate for FHA loans is usually below the prevailing market rate. It is set by the Secretary of Housing and Urban Development (HUD).

Application forms for FHA mortgage insurance are normally available through lenders. If the lender approves the loan after reviewing the application, the lender notifies the FHA, which in turn assigns a private appraiser to investigate the value of the property. As with VA loans, this is done to affirm that, in case of default, resale of the house would pay off the loan. When this appraisal is completed, the report and the application are forwarded to the FHA for review and approval. As a result of this procedure, FHA loans take a bit longer to process.

Because VA/FHA mortgages are at interest rates below the prevailing market rate, they are less profitable to lenders. As a result, lenders usually charge a lump-sum service fee **(discount points)** because they are agreeing to lend money at the lower, less-profitable rate. This practice increases their profit and still allows them to meet the interest rate allowed with VA/FHA loans. The amount of the lump-sum fee depends on the amount of the loan and the prevailing interest rates. One discount point equals 1 percent of the loan. Typically, two points are charged for each quarter percent difference between the interest rate available on conventional mortgages and the maximum rate of VA/FHA mortgages. For example, if the conventional rate is 13 percent and the ceiling rate on VA/FHA is 12 percent, you would pay eight (two points times four quarters of a percent) discount points. On a loan of $60,000, one point is equal to $600, so eight points equals $4800. This $4800 fee can be charged to the seller or the buyer, although both the FHA and VA have restrictions on buyers' paying points. As a result, if the seller agrees to a

The mortgage situation in today's housing market can be very confusing to the consumer.

VA/FHA mortgage package, the fees are usually passed on to the buyer in the form of a higher price.

Floating Payment Mortgage Types. One of the advantages of fixed-payment mortgages is that they represent a constant level expense in the family budget. Many families count on the fact that as inflation and income increase, the mortgage payment will be easier to bear. Now, new types of mortgages are available in which the mortgage payments can fluctuate. Experts in the financial community predict that these will become the prevalent forms of mortgages by the end of this decade.

Floating-payment mortgages were created by savings and loan associations and adopted by other lenders in an effort to protect themselves during periods of rapidly escalating interest rates. Historically, savings and loan institutions have been locked into long-term, fixed-rate mortgages, while trying to attract savings in a competitive market. As the overall demand for money has risen, they have had to offer higher interest rates to attract new money, or savings, to their business. This is done by raising rates on new mortgages, creating a situation in which new borrowers are bearing the total burden of—in effect subsidizing—older loans. Floating-rate mortgages are an effort to make the lending side of the banking industry more responsive to changes in the supply and demand of money as they shift some of the risk of rising interest rates to consumers. These floating mortgages can improve the capacity of the nation's mortgage lenders, 80 percent of which are savings and loan associations, to provide money for loans. The Federal Home Loan Bank Board believes that this will make more mortgage money available and will decrease interest rates. One industry expert agrees, and suggests that the cost of floating-rate mortgages will actually fall below the cost of fixed-rate mortgages (Salkin, 1981).

Floating-rate mortgages typically require lower-than-usual payments in the first few years of the contract in exchange for higher-than-usual payments in later years or at the time a house is sold. This payment pattern may more closely fit the income pattern of many borrowers and so make home ownership possible for more people. Let us look at these newer mortgage alternatives so that you can better understand what they could mean to you and your budget.

A **graduated-payment mortgage (GPM)** is a loan with a fixed interest rate. Monthly payments are arranged to be low at first, increasing each year for a stated time period—usually five to ten years. Because of low payments in the early years, all the interest actually due on the loan during that time is not paid. So the principal *increases* during this period, causing negative amortization. These loans are suitable for families whose income is low but will rise steadily. Currently, 25 percent of all FHA mortgage loans are

Table 13-2. Graduated-Payment Mortgages: The FHA Payment Schedules*

Year	1	2	3	4	5
1	$400.29	$365.30	$333.52	$390.02	$367.29
2	410.29	383.56	358.53	397.82	378.31
3	420.55	402.74	385.42	405.78	389.66
4	431.07	422.88	414.33	413.29	401.35
5	441.84	444.02	445.41	422.17	413.39
6	452.89	466.22	478.81	430.61	425.79
7	452.89	466.22	478.81	439.23	438.56
8	452.89	466.22	478.81	448.01	451.72
9	452.89	466.22	478.81	456.97	465.27
10	452.89	466.22	478.81	466.11	479.23
remaining payments	$452.89	$466.22	$478.81	$475.43	$493.60

*Payment schedules for five of the graduated-payment plans now available with HUD/FHA mortgages. In each case, the loan is for $50,000 for 30 years at 10% interest. In the first three plans, payments level off after the fifth year. In the other two, they increase for ten years before leveling off. The shaded area indicates level payments.

SOURCE: Department of Housing and Urban Development, 1979. Reprinted with permission from *Changing Times* magazine, © 1979 Kiplinger Washington Editors, Inc.

GPMs (*Consumer Reports,* 1979). FHA loans offer five payment schedules from which to choose (see Table 13-2).

One disadvantage of GPMs is that a buyer pays more interest, because reducing the principal takes longer with smaller payments. At first glance, this may not matter to you if you do not plan to live in a home until the mortgage is paid off. But because the principal has been reduced so little in the first few years, your equity does not grow as quickly as it does with a standard, fixed-payment loan. This means you will get less cash when you sell, so you may not have enough for a down payment on your next house. It will, of course, depend on how quickly homes are appreciating in your area, as well as on the price of the next home you choose.

The **flexible loan insurance program (FLIP)** is similar to the GPM, except that all or part of the down payment is kept in an interest-earning account from which some of the money is withdrawn each month to supplement the borrower's payment. With a FLIP loan, the amount of the down payment kept in the account and the level of payments can be tailored to individual circumstances. For example, if someone were to buy a $60,000 house and had $12,000 for a down payment, $7200 (60 percent) could be used as the actual down payment; the remaining $4800 (40 percent) would be placed in a special savings account. On a thirty-year loan at 10 percent interest, the monthly payment would be $425. During the first year of a FLIP loan, the borrower would pay $285, or two-thirds of the payment, and $140, or one-third, would be withdrawn from savings. Each year, the borrower's percentage would increase and a smaller percent would come from savings. In the sixth year, the borrower would pay the entire $425. FLIP loans can be individually designed according to the borrower's budgetary needs, but most of them are flexible only in the first five years.

FLIP mortgages may require a slightly higher interest rate than standard mortgages, and closing costs may be higher because lenders' service costs are greater as a result of monthly transfers out of savings to pay on the loan. As with GPM, this plan can present a risk for consumers whose income does not increase as anticipated.

Table 13-3. Summary of Adjustable-Rate Mortgage Plans Available

Plan	Interest rate index*	Interest rate adjustment period	Payment adjustment period	Maximum interest rate adjustment per year (percent)	Maximum periodic payment adjustment (percent)	Negative amortization restriction provision
1	6 mo.	6 mo.	6 mo.	none	7.5	yes
2	6 mo.	6 mo.	3 yr.	none	none	—
3	1 yr.	1 yr.	1 yr.	none	7.5	yes
4	3 yr.	2½ yr.	2½ yr.	none	18.75	yes
5	3 yr.	2½ yr.	2½ yr.	5	none	—
6	5 yr.	5 yr.	5 yr.	none	none	—
7	FHLBB	1 yr.	1 yr.	none	none	—
8	FHLBB	1 yr.	1 yr.	2	none	—

*Indexes 1 through 6 refer to treasury securities.
SOURCE: Mortgage Bankers Association of America, *Mortgage Points* (August 1981).

Another type of loan is an **adjustable rate mortgage (ARM),** sometimes called **adjustable mortgage loan (AML).** With an ARM the interest rate charged for the loan can rise or fall according to the supply of and demand for money at a national level, resulting in an increase or decrease in the amount of a loan payment. There is great flexibility of terms in this type of loan, making comparison by consumers both a complex and an essential task.

Regulations of terms of ARM loans differ at national banks and federally chartered savings and loan companies. They also vary from one state-chartered lender to another, depending on state legislation. Because of the heterogeneity of these regulations, we will confine our discussion to a comparison of federally chartered lenders only.

Consumers can compare seven basic features of ARM loans, all of which determine to what extent a monthly payment can change and how frequently the change can occur. Table 13-3 charts six of the seven features for eight common ARM plans in use today. Included are (1) the index used to determine rate changes, (2) the frequency of the interest-rate adjustment, (3) the payment adjustment period, (4) the amount of periodic rate change, (5) the maximum interest-rate change permitted over the life of the loan, and (6) restrictions regarding negative amortization. The seventh feature, provisions for extending the term of the mortgage, is not charted, because it simply depends on whether a national bank or savings and loan association is the lender.

The first feature to compare is the *index used to determine rate changes.* As we have mentioned, ARM's interest-rate fluctuation is caused by a change in the national supply of and demand for money. The index used to measure this change varies from one lender to another. National banks are allowed to use the Federal Home Loan Bank Board's (FHLBB) average of mortgage rates, the three-year Treasury securities rate, or the six-month Treasury Bill rate. Savings and loan associations may choose any verifiable index, as long as the index is beyond the lender's control. If the index rises, the lender can raise the interest rate on the loan. If the index drops the lender *must* decrease the interest rate. A change in the interest rate affects the amount of money the borrower owes; therefore, the choice of index is critical to the borrower. For example, one lender might use a short-term index such as the interest rate on six-month Treasury Bills, whereas another might use the Federal Home Loan Bank Board's average of mortgage rates as an index. Short-term indexes tend to be more volatile, causing dramatic changes in a payment, whereas indexes based on long-term rates have historically been higher. It is difficult to accurately predict future movement of interest-rate indexes, but experts seem certain that the cost-of-funds index, which is based on rates that savings and loan associations pay to depositors, will rise as savers transfer money into higher-paying certificates (*Changing Times,* December 1981). Therefore, consumers should avoid a mortgage tied to this index.

A second feature is the *frequency of interest-rate adjustment.* National banks cannot change the interest rate on loans more often than every six months. Savings and loan companies are not restricted and so theoretically could change the interest rate monthly, if the supply of and demand for money warrant it.

The *amount of periodic rate change* is also unrestricted for savings and loan associations. On the other hand, national banks can adjust their interest rates only a maximum of one percentage point at the end of each six-month period. Rate changes in excess of 1 percent can be carried over to the next adjustment period. The *payment adjustment period* determines when the monthly payment is affected by all the changes. For most plans this occurs at the same time that the interest rate is adjusted.

Another point of comparison is the *rate cap,* the maximum interest-rate change permitted over the life of the loan. No rate caps are required on loans from either savings and loan companies or national banks. However, the latter can adjust interest rates only a maximum of two percentage points annually, which does provide some restriction. Although they are not required to do so, some lenders do offer plans that include caps. Whenever rate changes exceed a specific amount, these loans provide the borrower with the option of increasing payments above the cap or of having the excess added to the principal balance. The latter choice increases the size of the loan. For example, let us say that the borrower has been making monthly principal and interest payments of $750 and the cap is a 7½ percent increase. If the rate change causes an increase to $825, the borrower has two options. One is to pay the full $825. The second option is to pay $806.25 ($750 plus the 7½ percent increase of $56.25) and have the remaining $18.75 added each month to the unpaid principal of the loan.

With all of these potential adjustments, consumers should look for the protection afforded by *restrictions regarding negative amortization.* Federal restrictions require savings and loan associations to adjust payments at least once every five years. National banks may not allow negative amortization to exceed 10 percent of the outstanding principal. These restrictions protect the equity that the borrower may anticipate using for a down payment in a future house.

The final comparison feature is the *term of the mortgage.* National banks are restricted to a maximum of thirty years, whereas savings and loan associations may offer a thirty-year loan that is extendable to forty years. As with other loans, the longer the term, the smaller the monthly payment, but the greater the total cost.

Creative Financing. The term **creative financing** refers to the combination of mortgage or loan instruments used in order to obtain adequate money for real estate purchases. It covers many different concepts, some of them new and relatively untested. Two arrangements that fit that description are **shared-appreciation mortgages (SAMs)** and **shared equity arrangements.** With a SAM, the lender or investor provides a lower interest rate in return for sharing in the increase in value of the home when it is eventually sold or refinanced. In a typical shared equity arrangement, the buyer is paired with an investor, who provides the down payment. The buyer occupies the property and pays the mortgage, taxes, insurance, maintenance, and repairs. At some future point, the property is sold or refinanced, and the investor gets back the down payment money plus a share of any appreciation that has accrued. According to *Changing Times* (December 1981), this concept is too new to evaluate, because few homes had been sold by this method at this point. As a result, both SAMs and shared-equity arrangements raise questions about deductions and capital gains that had not yet been resolved by the IRS.

When houses are slow to sell, sometimes a seller with a conventional, assumable loan is encouraged to offer a **wraparound mortgage.** Under this arrangement, the seller retains the original mortgage. The

Owners who choose to sell their homes without going through a broker are often amiable to creative financing plans, such as wraparound mortgages or taking back a second mortgage.

buyer obtains a new mortgage, often from the seller, at a lower-than-market rate, typically an average of the prevailing rate and the original mortgage. For example, let us say that the seller's assumable mortgage is at 9 percent and is five years old, and that the original loan of $43,000 is paid down to $41,000. The buyer agrees to pay $85,000 for the house, and he or she makes a down payment of $16,000. A lender gives a wraparound mortgage of $69,000 at 12 percent for 25 years permitting amortization over the same amount of time as the original loan. The buyer would make monthly payments of $700 on the $69,000 loan. The lender in turn would make the $325 payment on the original loan, pocketing the difference of $375. Because he lent only $28,000 ($69,000 minus $41,000), the lender's return is about 16 percent ($375 × 12 months ÷ $28,000), not the 12 percent for the wraparound. Note that both seller and buyer are obligated to both loans, and if the buyer defaults, the seller owns the property again.

The use of wraparounds is likely to increase because many mortgage bankers, in addition to individual sellers, are beginning to see that using wraparounds leads to more rapid sales (Garrigan and Higgins, 1981). For example, in 1982 Bank of America introduced "blended-rate custom home loans." These loans were initially available only to the borrowers that the bank had invited to participate or to their qualified buyers. Unlike a wraparound, the plan eliminates the need for financing by the seller and allows the seller to receive his or her equity. The buyer in turn is given an adjustable-rate mortgage at a lower-than-prevailing interest rate.

Further assistance to consumers who are interested in creative financing comes from an unlikely source, and perhaps one unfamiliar to most consumers. The Federal National Mortgage Association (FNMA), commonly called Fannie Mae, is one of the two largest purchasers of mortgages from banks and savings and loan associations. Mortgagors normally have no reason to care whether their home loans are sold to FNMA on the secondary market. But in 1981 FNMA announced its Resale Finance plan, which allows purchasers of a home on which FNMA holds the existing mortgage to obtain a loan at lower-than-prevailing rates. There are four eligibility requirements: (1) Fannie Mae must hold the existing mortgage, (2) the balance on the existing loan must be $10,000 or more, (3) the interest rate on the new loan must be higher than the existing rate, and (4) the home must be sold.

The Resale Finance plan relieves sellers of the risks and liabilities of creative financing, as well as provides them with their equity. Buyers benefit from a lower interest rate and a lower down payment, usually 5 percent. The new loan is conventional; the existing one can be conventional, FHA, or VA.

Another way to achieve the same goal that wraparound mortgages achieve is for the seller to *take back a second mortgage*. In this situation, the buyer makes a down payment, assumes the first loan, and accepts all of its terms and obligations. Then the seller lends the buyer the balance, with an interest rate equal to the return he would have gotten by using a wraparound. Let us use the previous example of a 9 percent assumable mortgage with a balance of

$41,000, a selling price of $85,000, and a down payment of $16,000. The seller taking back a "second" would loan the buyer $28,000 at 16 percent interest, making the seller's return and the buyer's total payments the same as for those of a wraparound. The advantage to taking back a second is that it is a slightly simpler process. However, if the seller takes back a second he or she is responsible for properly conducting the transaction and, as with a wraparound, does not come out with a large sum of cash.

In 1981, FNMA initiated the Home Seller's program for sellers who choose to take back a mortgage. The mortgage is originated with FNMA documents and follows the corporation's credit and appraisal guidelines. An FNMA-approved lender provides and processes the documents and collects monthly payments for the seller. The lender can charge a fee for these services. The advantage of the Home Seller program to both buyer and seller is that the loan transaction is conducted by trained specialists. Later, if the seller wants to convert the mortgage to cash, the lender can arrange to sell the loan to FNMA.

Choosing a Financing Method. Choosing the mortgage or financing method you prefer is complex, because of the many options. Your choice of financing should be based on the willingness of a lender to offer the option, the monthly costs of the option, the total cost of the option, the prevailing rate and expected future interest rate, and your own goals. Compare the offerings of all types of lenders, such as savings and loan associations, banks, mortgage corporations, and credit unions, considering these crucial points:
1. The initial monthly payment.
2. The initial interest rate.
3. How often the interest rate can change and what index is used to trigger these changes.
4. The limits, if any, on interest-rate changes.
5. How often your monthly payment can change, and how much notification you will be given.
6. The limits, if any, on negative amortization.

Closing Costs. **Closing** or **settlement** is the formal process by which ownership of real property transfers from seller to buyer. **Closing costs** for all services during this process are usually 3 to 4 percent of the total purchase price, and they are added to the down payment. In other words, you will need the amount of the closing costs in cash, besides the down payment. The 1976 revisions of the Real Estate Settlement Procedures Act (RESPA) require lenders to send you, within three business days after you apply for a loan, a booklet prepared by HUD that explains closing costs. Within the same period, the lender must provide you with a "good faith" written estimate of closing costs. Figure 13-2 shows a form that might be used for this estimate.

RESPA also requires the lender to identify any businesses or individuals from whom a buyer will be required to purchase services, such as appraisals or legal services. The law prohibits kickbacks, or "under-the-table" payments, from buyers or lenders to those involved in the real estate transaction (lenders, title insurers, or lawyers, for example). If the lender approves the loan, you must then be given a truth-in-lending statement that specifies the annual interest rate.

There are many fees that lenders charge to process or approve mortgage loans. A **title search** is usually required to review legal documents and public records to be sure that no one else has a prior claim to the property. When a title search reveals that there are no prior claims to the property, usually title insurance is written to guarantee that if a flaw in the title is found later, the title company will defend the insured and pay all legal fees involved. Bear in mind that title insurance issued only to the lender does not protect the buyer. If you buy an owner's policy, it is usually much less expensive if it is purchased simultaneously with a lender's policy, so ask the lender to include this. Other fees lenders charge include:
1. Loan origination fees—to cover administrative costs of processing the loan.
2. Credit report fees—to show how the prospective borrower has handled other credit transactions (for instance, with credit cards or other loans).
3. Assumption fees—to pay for the costs of processing papers on a loan assumed by a new buyer.
4. Appraisal fees—to pay for the costs of estimating the value of the house (paid by the buyer or the seller as specified in the sales contract).

Figure 13-2. Sample good-faith written estimate of closing costs.

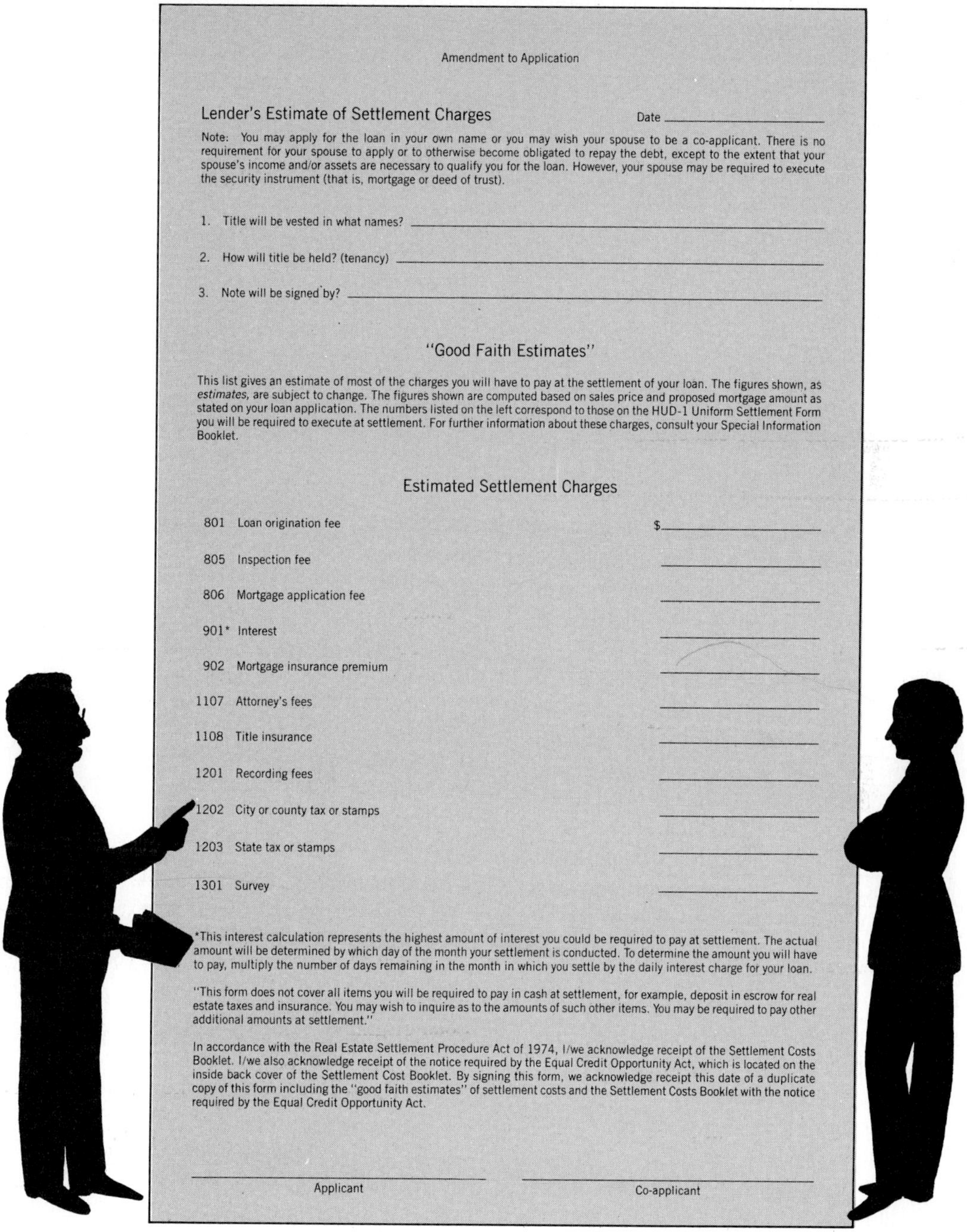

Amendment to Application

Lender's Estimate of Settlement Charges   Date _____

Note: You may apply for the loan in your own name or you may wish your spouse to be a co-applicant. There is no requirement for your spouse to apply or to otherwise become obligated to repay the debt, except to the extent that your spouse's income and/or assets are necessary to qualify you for the loan. However, your spouse may be required to execute the security instrument (that is, mortgage or deed of trust).

1. Title will be vested in what names? _____

2. How will title be held? (tenancy) _____

3. Note will be signed by? _____

"Good Faith Estimates"

This list gives an estimate of most of the charges you will have to pay at the settlement of your loan. The figures shown, as *estimates*, are subject to change. The figures shown are computed based on sales price and proposed mortgage amount as stated on your loan application. The numbers listed on the left correspond to those on the HUD-1 Uniform Settlement Form you will be required to execute at settlement. For further information about these charges, consult your Special Information Booklet.

Estimated Settlement Charges

801	Loan origination fee	$_____
805	Inspection fee	_____
806	Mortgage application fee	_____
901*	Interest	_____
902	Mortgage insurance premium	_____
1107	Attorney's fees	_____
1108	Title insurance	_____
1201	Recording fees	_____
1202	City or county tax or stamps	_____
1203	State tax or stamps	_____
1301	Survey	_____

*This interest calculation represents the highest amount of interest you could be required to pay at settlement. The actual amount will be determined by which day of the month your settlement is conducted. To determine the amount you will have to pay, multiply the number of days remaining in the month in which you settle by the daily interest charge for your loan.

"This form does not cover all items you will be required to pay in cash at settlement, for example, deposit in escrow for real estate taxes and insurance. You may wish to inquire as to the amounts of such other items. You may be required to pay other additional amounts at settlement."

In accordance with the Real Estate Settlement Procedure Act of 1974, I/we acknowledge receipt of the Settlement Costs Booklet. I/we also acknowledge receipt of the notice required by the Equal Credit Opportunity Act, which is located on the inside back cover of the Settlement Cost Booklet. By signing this form, we acknowledge receipt this date of a duplicate copy of this form including the "good faith estimates" of settlement costs and the Settlement Costs Booklet with the notice required by the Equal Credit Opportunity Act.

_____   _____
           Applicant   Co-applicant

A buyer may be required (on non-VA or non-FHA loans) to have mortgage or hazard insurance prepaid (for six months or one year) by the time of closing. Mortgage insurance protects the lender from loss caused by the borrower's default on payment of the loan. With conventional loans, this protection often allows the lender to require a small down payment. It is not the same thing as mortgage life, or disability insurance, which is designed to pay off a mortgage in the event of the physical disability or death of the borrower.

Hazard insurance protects the borrower and the lender against loss caused by fire, windstorm, and other natural hazards. It may be included in a homeowner's policy, which insures against additional risks, such as personal liability and theft. However, hazard insurance or homeowner's policies may not protect the buyer against loss caused by flooding. In special flood-prone areas identified by HUD, a homeowner may be required by federal law to carry *flood insurance* on his or her home. Such insurance may be purchased at low, federally subsidized rates in participating communities under the National Flood Insurance Act.

In **escrow,** or **impound accounts,** lenders hold funds in reserve to assure future payment for recurring items such as real estate taxes, mortgage or hazard insurance premiums, or annual assessments for municipal improvements such as sidewalks and sewers. Homeowners' association fees might also be included. If an impound account is used, the total annual costs of the recurring expenses are prorated monthly by the lender, and they are added to the monthly loan cost. The requirement for such an account may be negotiable, so feel free to discuss it with your lender. A few states now require that this special account earn interest for the borrower, rather than the lender. When closing, one may need to make an initial deposit into this reserve account.

Box 13-5 provides a checklist of all the things that should be done before closing.

The closing process is the final step, and it is a simple one. Its purpose is to transfer the title, or ownership, from the seller to the buyer. A typical closing is a meeting between the buyer, the seller, a repre-

---

BOX 13-5

What to Do Before Closing: A Checklist

1. Inspect the house one more time to make sure that everything is the way you expect it to be. If there has been any damage to the property, the seller must fix it before the closing. (Your purchase agreement should clearly state this.)
2. Make sure that the seller (and all his furnishings and trash) will be out of the house before your closing date. But remember, it is better not to let a house remain empty for too long.
3. Call your mover to confirm the moving date. Find out whether he needs a deposit, and make sure that you will have enough money to pay him.
4. Give your present landlord plenty of notice (at least 30 days). Check your lease.
5. Notify the gas, electric, phone, and fuel companies of your move so that they can shut off service in your present home and turn it on in your new one.
6. Check with the lender (or closing agent) to find out how much money you will need for closing costs. Federal law entitles you to know at least twenty-four hours before the closing what charges you will have to pay, including those that were not disclosed on your RESPA statement from the lender.

Be sure you have:
1. The right time, date, and place of the closing.
2. A paid insurance policy (or binder) for the house.
3. Receipts for other items you may have already paid for, such as the deposit on the house, mortgage application fees, or inspection fees.
4. Enough money for all closing costs in a certified check.

---

sentative or agent for the lender, and a real estate broker. Here is the usual agenda:

1. The lender's agent will ask for the paid insurance policy (or binder) on the house.
2. The agent will list the adjustments (what is owed to the seller, including the remainder of the down

payment, prepaid taxes, and so forth, and what the seller owes the buyer, including unpaid taxes, prepaid rents, and so forth).
3. The buyer will sign the mortgage, or deed of trust (the legal document giving the lender the right to take back the property if the buyer fails to make his or her mortgage payments).
4. The buyer will also sign the mortgage note (the promise to repay the loan in regular monthly payments of a certain amount).
5. The buyer will then be "loaned" the money to pay the seller for the house.
6. The title passes from the seller to the buyer, usually in the form of a deed (the document that transfers the title) signed by the seller.
7. The lender's agent will collect the closing costs from the buyer, usually in the form of a cashier's check, and he or she will give the buyer a loan disclosure statement (a list of all the items the buyer has paid for).
8. The deed and mortgage will then be recorded (put on file) in the town or county registry of deeds.

The Fifth Step: Moving

Once you have selected a home, you must prepare to move into it. Box 13-6 is a checklist of tasks that need to be done before you move. Some, such as numbers 7 and 8, should be done as early as six weeks before the move.

If you have only a small number of possessions or if you are not moving too great a distance, you may find it more economical to rent a truck and move your things yourself. This is especially true if you have friends or family members to help you.

If you decide to hire a moving company, be aware that the federal government has specific requirements for movers:

1. The movers must come on the promised day. The company can be fined up to $500 if it fails to do so.
2. Price estimates must be based on the moving company's actual physical inspection of whatever you ask it to move.
3. Before moving day, a mover must give you an order for service that states the estimated price of the move and the mutually agreed on pickup and delivery dates.

BOX 13-6

Moving Checklist

Have you:
1. Checked the condition of your new house to make sure that all the seller's things are moved out and that it is swept and free of all trash (in the basement, the attic, and the yard)?
2. Given your landlord plenty of notice?
3. Cleaned your apartment and had the landlord inspect it?
4. Returned your key to the landlord?
5. Arranged to get your security deposit back?
6. Notified all utility companies to shut off your present service and turn on service at the new address?
7. Notified your employer, the department of motor vehicles, credit-card companies, magazine companies, and so forth of your move?
8. Filled out change-of-address forms at the post office?
9. Notified your children's school or day-care center?
10. Made arrangements for your children during the move?
11. Checked with the moving company about the date of the move, the times of pickup and delivery, and the cost of the move (in a written estimate)?
12. Checked with the mover to make sure that all your belongings will be insured?
13. Checked with the rental company (if you plan to rent a truck or a van) about the date and the cost of the rental?
14. Arranged with family or friends to help you with the move?
15. Stocked up on plenty of boxes, cartons, rope, tape, and newspapers?
16. Made a list of items to be moved and marked the contents on the boxes?
17. Made a list of what items should be moved first (food, dishes, clothing, rugs) and where they should go in your new house?
18. Made sure you have all the keys to your new house and that they work properly?

4. Your property must be delivered and all services performed, with charges due and payable on moving day no higher than the estimate plus 10 percent (because of an inaccurate estimate). You have fifteen days to pay any amount over 110 percent of the written estimate.
5. The Interstate Commerce Commission (ICC) has established uniform charges for specific weights and mileage.

Do not postpone your move to the last minute. If you are rushed, things get broken and people sometimes get hurt working too quickly. If you have decided to use a moving company, schedule it to come a few days before you must actually vacate. This allows for mistakes and emergencies. After all, you can get by without your furniture for a day or two.

To protect yourself when using a mover, be around during the loading and unloading of your goods. You should:

1. Compare your inventory list with the mover's list of things loaded into the van.
2. Look at how the movers evaluate the condition of your furniture. Most movers use a code to indicate whether goods are scratched, marred, gouged, cracked, soiled, or whatever.
3. If you disagree with the evaluation of the condition, make sure it is changed. Because 25 percent of all moves end in a dispute over damages, this is important.
4. Observe the weighing of the empty truck and the loading, reweighing, and unloading of the truck to ensure that nothing is lost, stolen, or added to increase the loaded weight.
5. During the unloading check off the items on your inventory sheet.
6. Do not sign the mover's inventory release sheet until you have had time to discover all possible damage or loss.

If damage or loss does occur, you will want to make a claim. If, after contacting the mover, you are not satisfied, call the nearest Interstate Commerce Commission office, listed in the telephone directory. If you are still not satisfied, you may want to go to small claims court (see Chapter 5).

The Sixth Step: Evaluating Your Choice

Your choice of whether to rent or buy depends on your values, goals, standards, budget, stage in the family life cycle, and economic conditions. Because these factors can change, you need to occasionally reevaluate your housing decision. Let us briefly look at how economic conditions can affect your future decisions.

Despite rapid inflation, high interest rates, and energy shortages, all of which cause the cost of shelter to rise, the demand for additional housing units is stronger than ever. Young adults now reaching the prime home-buying age of twenty-five to thirty-four compose an ever-increasing proportion of the population. A second group that affects the need for housing is composed of those age sixty-five and over. Of the 19.5 million new households that are formed during the 1980s, more than 80 percent will be single-person or two-person households (*Real Estate Today,* August 1980). The shift toward smaller households increases the need for smaller housing units, particularly rentals. Providing suitable shelter for the unique needs and budgets of these households is a major challenge in the 1980s. So what is your housing future?

RENTING

Builders have shied away from construction of multifamily rental units in the last ten years because of increases in the costs of constructing and operating them. In 1976, Congress dealt a blow to the rental-housing industry when it reduced the tax deductions on new rental buildings. Simultaneously, the costs of building were rising as much as 15 to 20 percent a year. As a result, the supply of rental units is at a thirty-five-year low.

Renters will need to be clear about their rights and responsibilities as they face a national apartment-vacancy rate (the amount of rental units empty at any one time) of 4.5 percent—a figure that drops to 2 percent in major cities. As rents take an increasing portion of family budgets, renters may need to reevaluate their needs in relation to costs. Options to reduce costs include renting smaller spaces, sharing rentals with friends or family members, or returning to one's parents' home.

BUYING

Homeowners of the 1980s will face rising interest rates and prices. They may have to wait longer than their parents did to purchase so that they can accumulate a down payment. They may need to choose smaller, less-luxurious housing that is more affordable. To reduce housing costs, for example, buyers might give up extra bedrooms, extra bathrooms, finished basements, and landscaping. Prospective buyers may need to be more flexible about their expectations and consider mobile homes and condominiums as well as traditional single-family homes. They may need to compromise on location, because the most affordable housing is often available in less-desirable neighborhoods or suburbs.

Consumers should be alert to newer construction methods that can cut down expenses. One common cost-cutter is building **modular homes,** which are made of factory-manufactured sections arranged in various ways on a permanent foundation on the building site. "Wet" modular units include plumbing, baths, heating, and kitchen equipment, and "dry" modular units include living, dining, and sleeping rooms. Using modular units saves one-third of the costs of traditional construction methods.

Buyers as well as renters should consider sharing their space with other individuals or family members. Part of the home could be rented, or two single individuals or two families could buy the home jointly. Cooperation and flexibility of this sort allows needs and wants to be met despite economic constraints.

The Seventh Step: Accepting Responsibility

As with all decisions, a renter or a buyer has certain responsibilities. They include (1) making the rent or loan payment on time, (2) keeping the property clean, (3) maintaining the property by making necessary repairs or by asking the landlord to do so, and (4) refraining from causing damage to the property. By meeting these responsibilities, both renters and buyers can help keep down housing costs.

Doing maintenance and repair work oneself, rather than hiring someone to do it, can be a money saver for homeowners. Renters can offer to do such work in exchange for reduced rent. Before deciding to do it yourself, however, you should evaluate your skills, your abilities, and how much time the task will take in light of the cost of hiring a specialist. Owners who do repairs themselves save the labor cost of hiring someone else, and they also save income taxes on that money. For example, let us say that your home needs a new roof. You investigate and find that the average bid for the labor is $2000. How much do you have to earn to have $2000, after taxes? That, of course, depends on what tax bracket you are in. If you are in the 25 percent tax bracket, you would have to earn about $2667 (25 percent of $2667 is about $667) to pay for that labor. So you could spend your time working to earn $2667, give $2000 to the roofer for his or her labor, and give $667 in taxes to the Internal Revenue Service, or you could spend your time reroofing the house yourself and avoid paying $667 in taxes. Your decision should be based on how long it would take you to reroof the house compared to the time it would take you to earn $2667, to develop your skill at that particular task, and on which job (nonmarket production or labor-market production) you prefer.

Summary

Whether one rents or buys a home, the decision is an important one, because it is not made very often, so its consequences will be with one for quite a while. Renting requires a relatively small initial cash outlay, it allows for mobility, and it requires fewer responsibilities, but it does not provide tax deductions or equity. Buying can be a profitable financial investment that can provide feelings of pride and security, but it can also strain family budgets and restrict mobility and leisure. To decide which is best for you, you should clarify the needs and goals of all family members and evaluate them in terms of the family budget.

Renters and buyers will find housing options ranging from single-family homes to condominiums and mobile homes. Whether renting or buying, it pays to investigate various locations and to inspect physical construction. Consumers should be aware that it is illegal to discriminate in renting or buying because of race, religion, sex, color, or national origin.

Renters need to know the rights and responsibilities that relate to rental agreements, deposits, and the implied warranty of habitability. Buyers have a more complex task: to understand how to shop for a home, negotiate a deal, select a mortgage, and close the sale. Moving involves choosing between doing the moving yourself or hiring a specialist.

The housing decisions that one makes represent a substantial portion, perhaps as much as 35 percent, of a family budget. They should be made carefully, following the decision-making model, in order to reflect one's values and standards and satisfy one's goals within the constraints of one's budget.

Neighborhood REVISITED

1. How should Sharon and Pat decide whether buying is a better choice than renting? What advantages and disadvantages does renting have for each of these women? What advantages and disadvantages would each find in buying?

2. Do you think lenders in your community would give Sharon and Pat a mortgage loan? Why or why not?

KEY TERMS

adjustable mortgage loan (AML)
adjustable rate mortgage (ARM)
amortization
appraisal
assumable loans
closing (settlement)
closing costs
commission
condominium
contract of sale
conventional loans (fixed-payment mortgages)
cooperative
creative financing
default
deposit
discount points

down payment
earnest money
earnest agreement (binder)
easements
equity
escrow (impound) accounts
Federal Housing Administration (FHA) loan
flexible loan insurance program (FLIP)
foreclose
graduated-payment mortgage (GPM)
hazard insurance
implied warranty of habitability
lease
mobile homes
modular homes
month-to-month rental agreement

mortgage
mortgage insurance
mortgage note
new-home warranties
prepayment penalty
principal
real estate brokers
real property
recurring costs
rental agreement
rent control
shared-appreciation mortgages (SAMs)
shared equity arrangements
title search
Veterans Administration (VA)
wraparound mortgage

QUESTIONS

1. What purposes does housing serve for all families? What personal or individual needs might housing meet for you?

2. What alternatives to single-family houses exist in your community? What is your community doing in the areas of construction methods and building codes to reduce the cost of housing?

3. Imagine that you are employed by a national firm that requires you to move every two years. Discuss the pros and cons of renting and buying shelter under these circumstances. Consider also the pros and cons of purchasing mobile homes under the same circumstances.

4. What specific characteristics of a particular location should be investigated when searching for a place to live?

5. What is an implied warranty of habitability? Of what use is it to consumers? How can it be enforced?

6. What specific information should be included in a purchase contract?

7. Define mortgage note, principal, interest rate, amortization, prepayment penalty, loan assumption, closing, and impound account.

8. Describe why discount points are used and how they work.

9. What is the major difference between fixed-payment mortgages and floating-payment mortgages? Why are the latter now available to consumers?

10. How would individual families be affected if homeowners could no longer deduct property taxes and mortgage interest from income taxes?

PROJECTS

1. Investigate restrictions that are commonly encountered by potential tenants in your community. Consider restrictions such as "adults only," "no pets," and "no college students." If there is a tenant organization in your community, what is it doing about such restrictions? Report your findings to the class.

2. Investigate the current interest rates and terms available for FHA and conventional loans in your community. What floating-rate options are also available at this time? If you were buying a home now, which loan and terms would you prefer and why?

3. Organize a debate on the issue of rent control for your community.

READINGS AND REFERENCES

"Are Those New Low-Payment Mortgages Worthwhile?" *Consumer Reports,* January 1979.

Blumberg, Richard E., and Grow, James R. *The Rights of Tenants.* New York: Avon Books, 1979.

Breckenfeld, Gurney. "A Decade of Catch-up for Housing." *Fortune,* April 7, 1980.

"Buy Now or Wait?" *Changing Times,* November 1981.

"Can You Afford to Buy a House These Days?" *Changing Times,* March 1979.

Ehrbar, A. F. "It May Be Time to Rent." *Fortune,* August 24, 1981.

English, John Wesley, and Cardiff, Gray Emerson. *The Coming Real Estate Crash.* New Rochelle, N.Y.: Arlington House, 1979.

"Find a Mortgage You Can Live With." *Changing Times,* December 1981.

"Finding the Best Deal in a Mortgage." *Changing Times,* September 1979.

"The 5 and 10 Year Outlook for Housing." *Real Estate Today,* August 1980.

Garrigan, Richard T., and Higgins, Hugh K., Jr. "Originating Single-Family Wrap-Around Loans." *Mortgage Banker,* February 1981.

"Is There a Floating-Rate Mortgage in Your Future?" *Changing Times,* October 1980.

Meeks, Carol B., and Oudekerk, Eleanor H. "Home Warranties: An Analysis of an Emerging Development in Consumer Protection." *The Journal of Consumer Affairs,* Winter 1981.

Miller, Linda. "FNMA Resale Finance." *Seller/Servicer,* January/March 1981.

Mortgage Bankers Association of America. "FNMA Announces Ajustable-Rate Mortgage Program." *Mortgage Points.* Mortgage Bankers Association of America, August 1981.

Rothenberg, Henry H. *What You Should Know About Condominiums.* Radnor, Pa.: Chilton Book Company, 1974.

Salkin, Michael S. "Adjustable Rate Mortgages: The National Scene." *Mortgage Banking,* November 1981.

Stloukal, Robert A. *The Greatest Real Estate Book in the World.* New York: New York Times Book Company, 1980.

Turner, John F. *Housing by People.* New York: Pantheon Books, 1976.

U.S. Department of Housing and Urban Development. *Home Buyers' Information Package: A Guide for Buying and Owning a Home.* Washington, D.C.: U.S. Government Printing Office, 1979.

"When Renters Get Together." *Changing Times,* March 1981.

Did You Know That...

- *the United States is not among the top five countries with the highest life expectancies or the lowest infant mortality rates?*

- *if present trends continue, by 1987 Americans will be spending an average of $2000 per person for health care?*

- *about two-thirds of all personal health-care expenditures today are financed indirectly through third parties such as private insurance companies or the government?*

- *a presidential commission recently estimated that the United States will have a surplus of 70,000 doctors by 1990 and 145,000 by the year 2000?*

- *most prescription drugs are produced by more than one company, and many are much cheaper when purchased under generic names?*

- *taking ampicillin, a commonly prescribed antibiotic, increases the chance of pregnancy for a woman using birth-control pills?*

- *there are over 1,200 health insurance companies in the United States, but Blue Cross and Blue Shield account for almost 50 percent of all policies?*

- *dental insurance is the fastest growing form of health insurance in the United States?*

- *your habits and your personal lifestyle have a much larger impact on your health than the amount of medical care you buy?*

14

Health Care: What Happens When You Get Sick in Consumer America

Health Care in the United States
The Cost of Health Care
The Demand for Health Care
The Supply of Health Care
Prescription Drugs
Health Insurance: Private Plans
The Health Maintenance Organization
Alternative Health-Care Systems: Is There a Better Way?
Staying Healthy: The Best Way to Avoid the High Cost of Health Care

Neighborhood CAPSULE
Medical Care Costs and the Neighborhood HMO

Jimmy and Patty have been married for two years. They are living in San Francisco while Jimmy finishes his MBA. Patty is working as a speech therapist for a local school district. Patty's school district has several health-insurance options, and she chose the Kaiser Plan health maintenance organization (HMO) because it seemed to offer the best cost-benefit ratio. Jimmy is also covered, because he is Patty's spouse.

Helen, a neighbor, who is also in their HMO, was relating her latest experience with the plan to Jimmy and Patty.

"I really have been fortunate, despite my problems," Helen said. "You know, I'm sixty-four years old, and over the last six months I've fallen twice, broken my wrist and my ankle, had a stroke, and was hospitalized for over 100 days."

"How do you figure that you're *fortunate*?" Jimmy wanted to know.

"Well," Helen went on, "I came away with no bills. Now that really means something to me!"

"I'm sure it does," Patty confirmed. "But we are having a little problem with the HMO."

"A *little* problem," Jimmy chimed in. "Yes, she means that in two ways," and he winked knowingly at Helen.

"You mean you two are going to have a baby?" Helen blurted. "That's marvelous!"

"You wouldn't think it was so great if you knew the problem we are having," Jimmy continued. "I've been offered a terrific job in New York, but our wonderful HMO doesn't have a facility there. And because it's not an emergency situation, we're faced with a choice between asking for an extension on the job offer or paying all of the medical bills in New York."

"I could stay here and have the baby by myself," Patty said, "but we simply don't want to do that."

"Oh, I didn't know that our HMO placed restrictions on our plan," Helen said, somewhat downcast.

"There are always some restrictions," Jimmy said. "One of the first things I learned in economics was that there is no such thing as a free lunch."

"Or free medical care," Patty added.

The first sound you hear in the morning is the shrill pitch from your alarm clock. Your eyes open somewhat unwillingly. As you try to silence your mechanical tormentor, you become aware of a soreness in your throat. Once you arise, you become increasingly aware that you simply don't feel well. Your throat hurts, your head throbs, and suddenly you know that this is not going to be a routine day. This is one of those sick days. What should you do?

Most of us do not immediately reach for the phone to call a physician. Neither do we rush to the hospital. Most of us try to stick it out; we can beat or treat the illness by ourselves or with a little help from our friends. Why don't we seek medical aid immediately? One reason is very simple—the cost of such care can be rather high, both in money and time.

Despite our natural inclination to avoid buying medical care, it is one of the most important components of a consumer's budget. As such, it merits considerable study, both from society's view and from an individual standpoint. As a society, we must once again realize that there is no free lunch. If we choose to provide more medical resources, we must subtract resources from housing, transportation, national defense, or another sector. As consumers, we must also know that the high cost of health care will cause our insurance premiums and taxes to rise to pay these costs. As a result, we will have less income to spend on other consumer goods or less to save and invest. There is no cure-all for these tandem problems, but after studying this chapter, you should have a greater appreciation for the complexity of the problem and should be better able to minimize your individual health-care costs while maximizing your benefits.

We begin with an overview of the state of health care in the United States. How does our system compare with those of other nations? How much do we spend on health care? Where does the health-care dollar go? Then we look at the demand for and the supply of health care. Government-sponsored programs such as Medicare and Medicaid, coupled with the growth of the health-insurance industry, have lowered the price of medical care for some consumers and thus increased the amount they demand. Meanwhile, the supply of health-care facilities and personnel has not always kept pace with the increases in demand, which means higher prices.

Of course, there are ways that wise decision making can limit your health-care expenditures. Selecting your doctor, getting a second opinion on surgery, asking for generic drugs, and understanding your health-insurance program are a few of the ways that information can lead you to make more cost-effective decisions concerning your health-care dollar. Today, there are more alternatives than the traditional fee-for-service plan. Health maintenance organizations that stress preventive medicine are available in many areas. And many studies indicate that by following some common-sense guides on eating and exercising, you can improve your chances of staying healthy.

Health Care in the United States

Anyway you look at it, health care is a big business in the United States. In 1980, one out of every twenty employed persons was working in some area of health care, which means that more people work to keep us healthy than work to grow the food we eat. Health care is the third largest industry in the country. But how good is it? Is big always best? And more to the point, is health care efficient?

From the consumer's standpoint, one of the best ways to judge the effectiveness of America's health-care industry is by the output—health—rather than by inputs such as money, the number of workers, or other resources. Of course, this means that we must define and then measure health. Like singing while swimming under water, these can be difficult to do at the same time. The preamble of the charter of the World Health Organization (WHO) defines **health** as "a state of complete physical, mental and social well-being, not merely the absence of distress or infirmity." Such an ambitious definition makes it nearly impossible for any society to reach the goal of perfect health for its members. Nevertheless, it is possible to compare the state of health in the United States by looking at how we are doing compared to other nations.

Life expectancy at birth (that is, the number of years that a newborn child can expect to live) is an important measure of health care (see Figure 14-1). Comparing international life expectancies can be a tricky business, because differences between nations may reflect factors other than the quality of health care. Lifestyles, socioeconomic conditions, and the distribution of income can also play important roles. For example, the Japanese diet emphasizes fish and rice but not meat or dairy products. As a result, studies have shown a much lower level of saturated fats, serum cholesterol, and heart disease in Japanese than in similar populations in the United States, where heart disease is the leading cause of death (*Consumer Reports,* May 1981). Even at that, you might have

Figure 14-1. Life expectancy at birth for selected countries by sex.

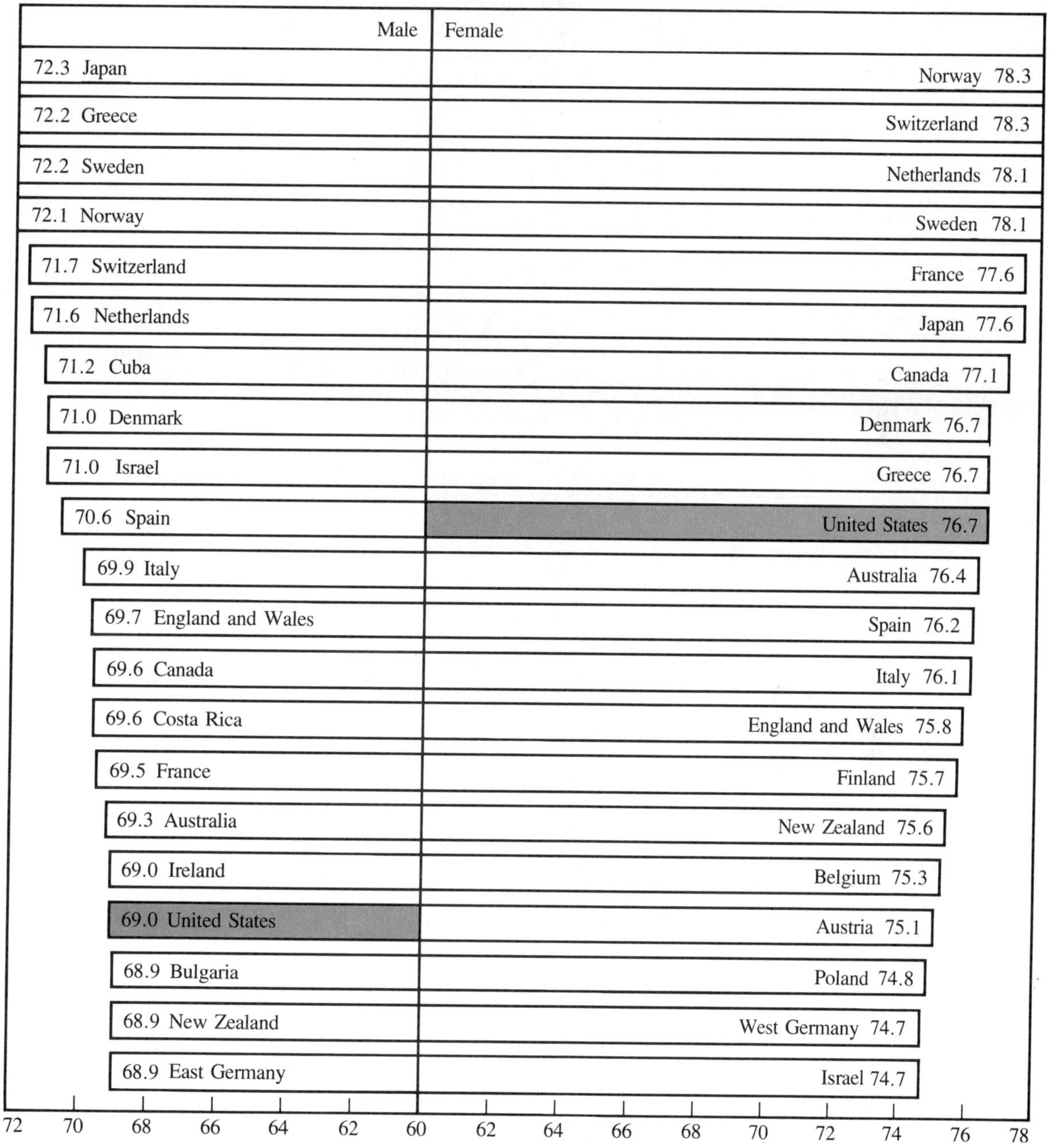
Male
Female
72.3 Japan
Norway 78.3
72.2 Greece
Switzerland 78.3
72.2 Sweden
Netherlands 78.1
72.1 Norway
Sweden 78.1
71.7 Switzerland
France 77.6
71.6 Netherlands
Japan 77.6
71.2 Cuba
Canada 77.1
71.0 Denmark
Denmark 76.7
71.0 Israel
Greece 76.7
70.6 Spain
United States 76.7
69.9 Italy
Australia 76.4
69.7 England and Wales
Spain 76.2
69.6 Canada
Italy 76.1
69.6 Costa Rica
England and Wales 75.8
69.5 France
Finland 75.7
69.3 Australia
New Zealand 75.6
69.0 Ireland
Belgium 75.3
69.0 United States
Austria 75.1
68.9 Bulgaria
Poland 74.8
68.9 New Zealand
West Germany 74.7
68.9 East Germany
Israel 74.7
72 70 68 66 64 62 60 62 64 66 68 70 72 74 76 78

SOURCE: World Health Organization and National Center for Health Statistics, *Health in the United States Chartbook* (Washington, D.C.: U.S. Government Printing Office, 1980).

Figure 14-2. Infant mortality rates for selected countries.

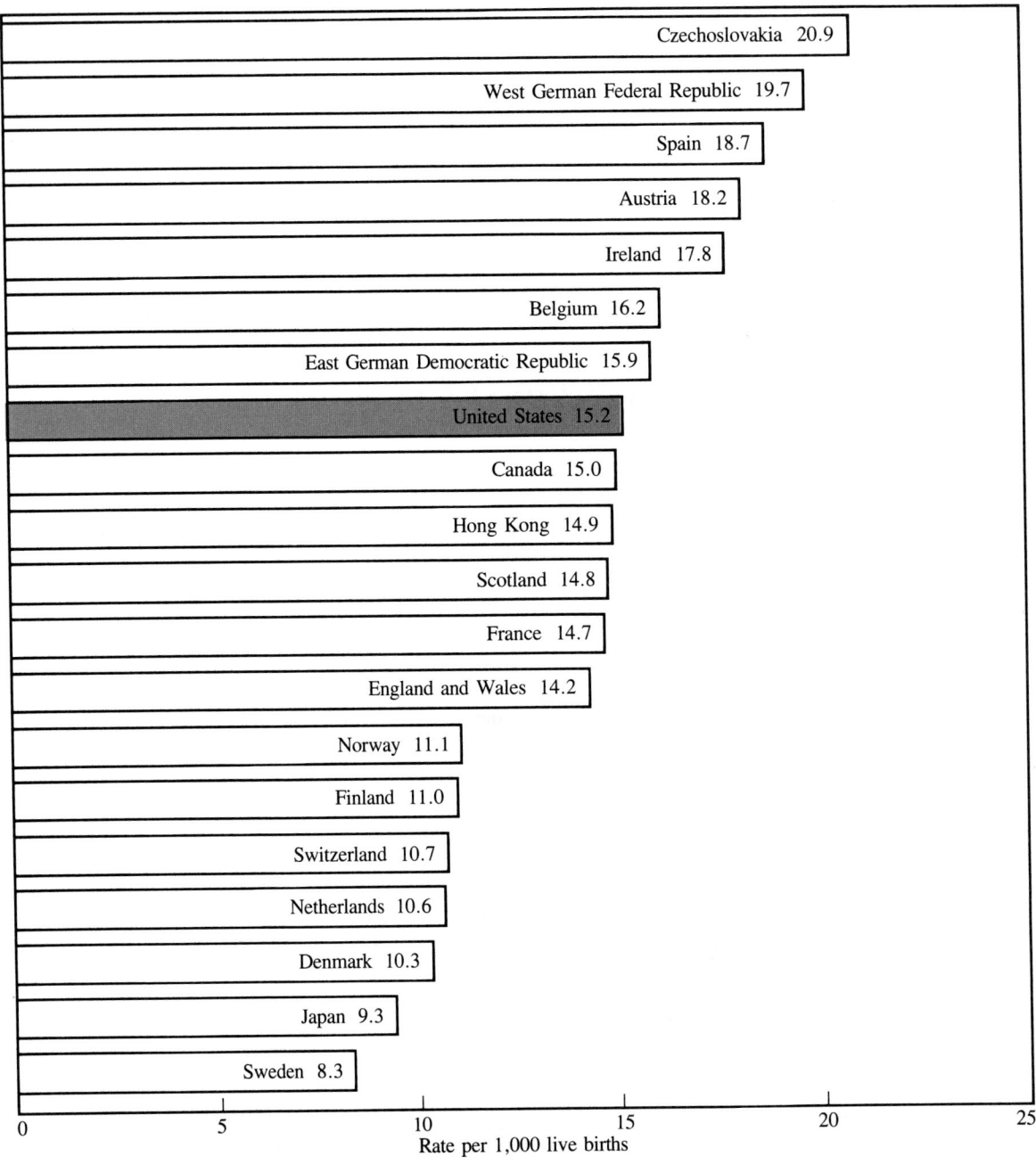

SOURCE: World Health Organization and National Center for Health Statistics, *Health in the United States Chartbook* (Washington, D.C.: U.S. Government Printing Office, 1980).

Table 14-1. Gains in Life Expectancies for Americans of Various Ages

Age	Sex	Life expectancy remaining		Life expectancy gain (percent)
		1939–1941	1978	
0	Male	62.8	70.2	11.8
	Female	67.3	77.8	15.6
20	Male	47.8	52.0	8.8
	Female	51.4	59.1	14.9
40	Male	30.0	33.6	12.0
	Female	33.3	39.9	19.8
50	Male	22.0	24.8	12.7
	Female	24.7	30.7	24.3

SOURCE: *Statistical Abstract of the United States* (Washington, D.C.: U.S. Government Printing Office, 1980).

expected the United States to rank among the top five nations in male or female life expectancy, but it does not. Of the twenty-one nations with the highest life expectancies for males, the United States is tied with Ireland for the seventeenth best record, with an average of sixty-nine years. According to the World Health Organization, American females do slightly better, with an average life expectancy of almost seventy-seven years. That is the same average as Greece and Denmark, but worse than seven other nations.

Another important indicator of health care is the **infant mortality rate,** that is, the number of children who die before their first birthday (see Figure 14-2). As you can see, the United States is not among the ten best nations in the category; our rate is almost twice as high as the world's leader, Sweden. Part of the reason for our relatively poor showing in infant mortality statistics reflects the startlingly high infant mortality rate for black children born in the United States. Their rate is twice as high as that of white babies, but of course this does not take into account other factors such as prenatal care, access to physicians and hospitals, and income levels, all of which serve to increase the difference in infant death rates.

Another reason for our higher rates is the accessibility and availability of health care in the United States. Many people living in rural areas or small towns do not have access to physicians or health-care facilities. The distribution of the population of the United States over a much larger geographical area than that of Sweden, Japan, or Denmark makes the logistics of supplying health care much more difficult. This geographic disadvantage weighs especially heavily on newborn infants who are delivered far from the nearest hospital.

We have clearly established that the American health-care system is not the unparalleled leader in delivering quality care to its citizens. However, we should not leave you with the impression that our system is an unmitigated disaster. Despite the fact that we are not first in health care, we are among the leaders, and the differences are not huge when one realizes that the life expectancy at birth in many nations is still less than fifty years and that every year infant mortality rates in many countries reach and exceed 100 per 1000 births.

If you are curious about how well the American health system has done in recent years, look at Table 14-1, which compares life expectancies for average Americans at various ages based on data from 1939–1941 and 1978. Notice that over this period, all age groups experienced significant gains in the number of years they could expect to live. In 1939, a twenty-year-old man could expect to live nearly forty-eight more years, whereas by 1978 he could expect to live fifty-two more years—a gain of over four years. A woman of the same age gained eight years. A woman

Figure 14-3. National health-care expenditures and percent of gross national product; selected years, 1950–1980.

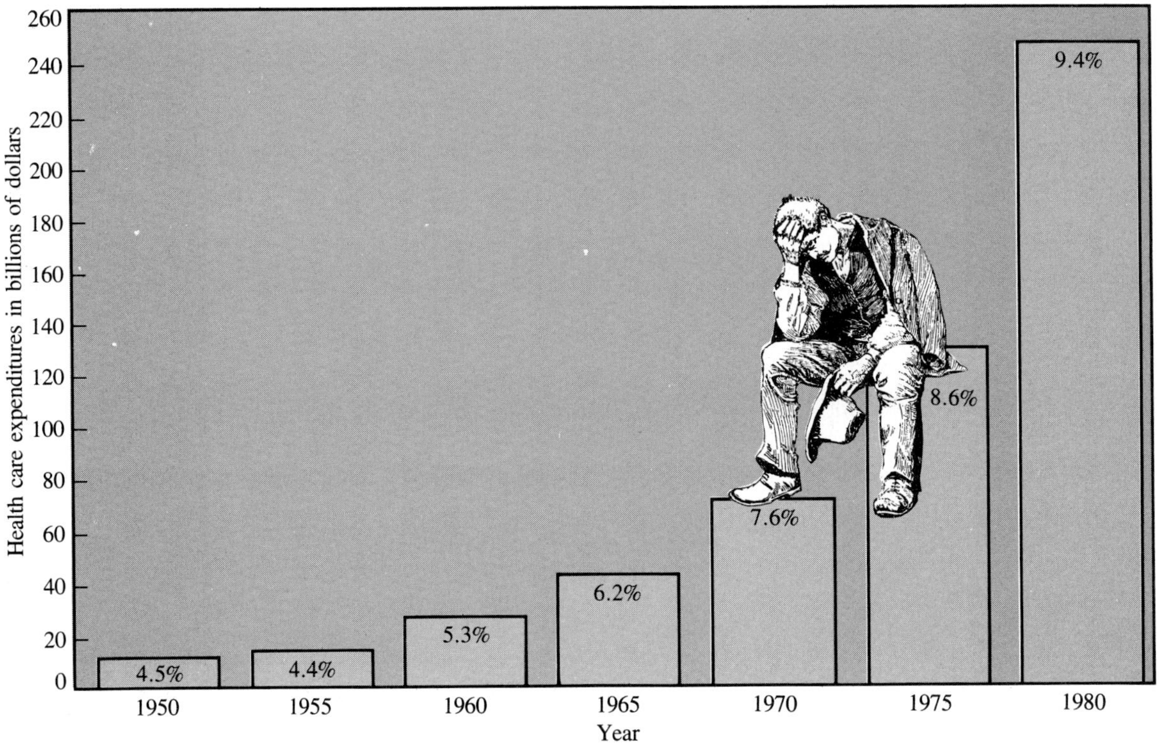

Year	% of GNP
1950	4.5%
1955	4.4%
1960	5.3%
1965	6.2%
1970	7.6%
1975	8.6%
1980	9.4%

SOURCE: Health Care Financing Administration, *Health in the United States Chartbook* (Washington, D.C.: U.S. Government Printing Office, 1980).

who was twenty in 1978 could expect to live to see her seventy-ninth birthday.

The Cost of Health Care

How have we managed to increase our life expectancies over this century? One of the ways is by devoting a larger proportion of our national income to the health industry. Figure 14-3 shows the overall rise in national health expenditures since 1950. As you can see, Americans have spent substantially more, and a bigger proportion of, the national income on health care. In 1950, expenditures were about $16 billion —only 4.5 percent of our Gross National Product (the value of all final goods and services produced in the United States during that year). By 1980, Americans were spending $247 billion, or 9.4 percent, of the GNP. Individually, Americans now spend $1067 per person every year, as opposed to $107 in 1950. Can this growth continue? Can we all keep paying more? Are we getting our money's worth? These and other questions need to be answered if we are to make ourselves better health-care decision makers.

The growth in health-care costs over the last thirty years has been linked to a number of factors: population growth, changes in the quality and quantity of health-related goods and services (sometimes called the "intensity factor"), and inflation. A study of the impact of these three factors on health-care expenditures between 1972 and 1979 concluded that

Figure 14-4. Sources of growth in personal health-care expenditures, 1972–1979.

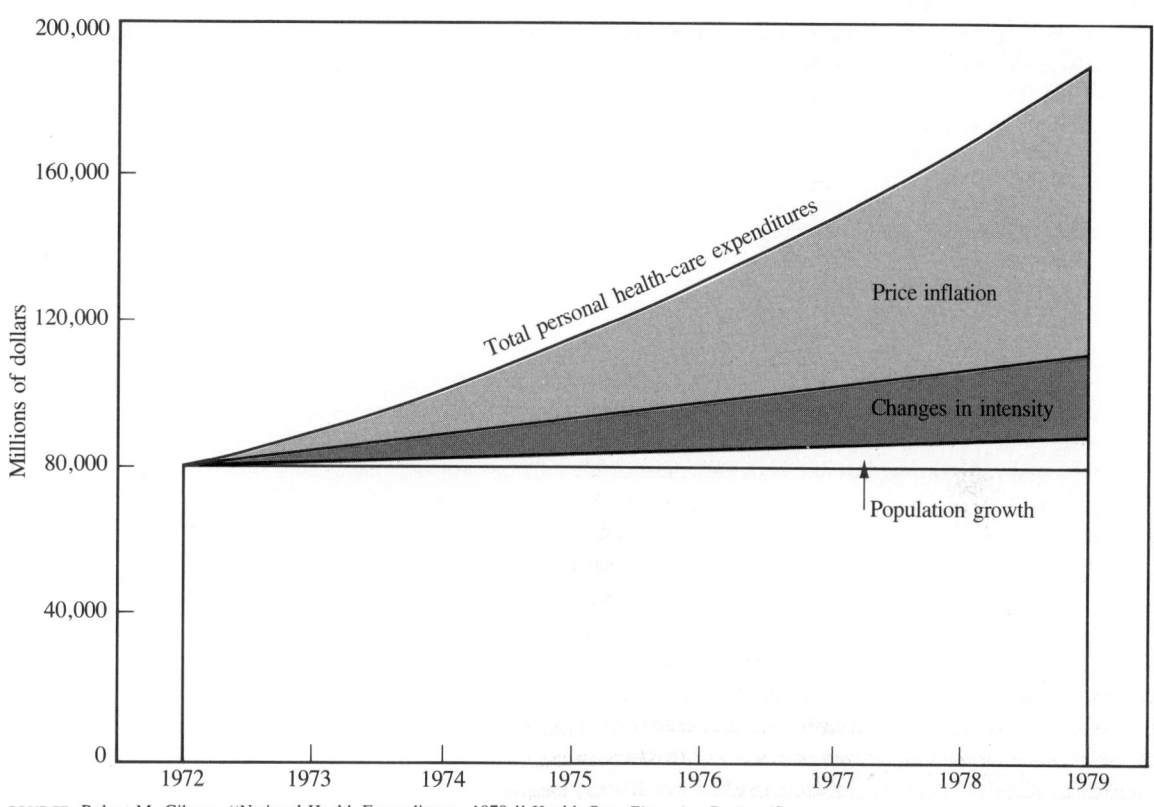

SOURCE: Robert M. Gibson, "National Health Expenditures, 1979," *Health Care Financing Review* (Summer 1980).

population growth was responsible for 7 percent of the increase over this period and that changes in the intensity factor accounted for over 27 percent of the expenditure increase. But the biggest factor (66 percent) was inflation. As the report stated, "Had there been no inflation between 1972 and 1979, personal health care expenditures in 1979 would have been $71 billion lower" (Gibson, 1980).

As Figure 14-4 indicates, inflation has been the major reason that health-care expenditures have been rising in the United States. In essence, the value of our health-care dollar has been shrinking over time. Of course, as we pointed out in Chapter 7, this is true for dollars in general, but it is especially true in the health-care industry, because prices in this sector have risen *faster* than prices elsewhere. Since 1950, the average annual rate of increase in the cost of medical care has been 5.2 percent—well above the inflation rate for that period. Even more alarming is the acceleration in this rate—from a little over 2 percent in the 1950s and early 1960s to over 9 percent by 1980. A 9 percent increase in costs will cause health expenditures to double in about seven years. This means that by 1987 we will be spending an average of $2000 per year on health care for every person in the United States.

How did health care become so expensive? And, more important, how can consumers avoid the high price of medical care? We cannot answer the second question until we give you a better understanding of

BOX 14-1
Where Does Your Health-Care Dollar Go?

In the text, we discuss the impact that inflation, population growth, and intensity of care have had on our health-care expenditure pattern. But you may be curious about who gets what proportion of those health-care dollars. In this pie chart, we have a breakdown of an average dollar spent on health care in the United States. The largest piece of the pie, 40 cents of every dollar, goes to pay for hospital care.

The second most important slice pays for physicians' services. Together, these two components account for almost two-thirds of every health-care dollar, with the rest going to pay for nursing homes, drugs, dental services, and administration costs. The biggest change in the shares of this pie has occurred in the hospital-care portion, which grew from 33 percent to 40 percent in less than fifteen years.

- 6.4% Dentists' services
- 6.7% Other personal health care
- 8%   Drugs and medical sundries
- 8.4% Nursing home care
- 11.2% Administration, prepayment, public health activity, research, and construction
- 19.1% Physicians' services
- 40.2% Hospital care

---

the first. To do that, we need to look more closely at the most important components of demand and supply.

The Demand for Health Care

The demand for medical care is not quite the same as the demand for automobiles or housing, although there are some similarities. The law of demand states that as the price of a commodity rises, consumers will buy less of it. This fits consumer behavior fairly well when it comes to cars, and even when it comes to housing. If some automobile producers raise their prices, one can shop around for a better deal, or one can postpone the purchase. But it is much more difficult to shop around for a lower-priced surgeon to take out one's appendix. And if the operation is postponed, the results can be fatal. Even if one could comparison shop, how could one judge quality? Most consumers are not equipped to make informed judgments about the quality of their treatment. If one is buying a car or looking for a house, he or she can take a test drive or preview the house to see whether it is suitable and in good condition. The medical-care market simply doesn't operate this way. Consumer information is very expensive, and it is generally unavailable.

There are a few avenues for consumers to pursue, however, if they want to know about a particular physician. The American Medical Association (AMA) provides a free computer printout profile of doctors' backgrounds, including age, education, and specialty. Write to: American Medical Association, Department of Data Release Services, 535 N. Dearborn St., Chicago, Illinois 60610.

Another problem with applying traditional demand analysis to the health-care market is that there are low economic incentives for spending time locating lower-priced health care. For medical care and hospitalization, the recipient of that care rarely pays the full price.

To use our automobile analogy, if you shop around and bargain hard in the car market (as we suggested in Chapter 12), you will pay a lower price and get a better deal. Thus, there is an economic incentive for practicing comparison-buying strategies. But for medical care and hospitalization, the recipient of the health-care service would not benefit as much from a lower price, because a large portion of the bill is generally paid by someone else—an insurance company or a government agency. These outside sources of payment are called third-party payers. Because third parties share any (and sometimes all) of the decrease in the cost of health care, many consumers have less incentive to look for lower-cost alternatives or even to ask about price. And because most (and sometimes all) of the immediate cost of a particular operation or hospital stay can be passed on to these third parties, there is less incentive for consumers to be price conscious. Why should they be if they know that their insurance or a government program will pay most or all of the cost?

Today, about 67 percent of all personal health-care expenditures are financed by third parties. The rest is paid directly by patients. Of the 67 cents of every health-care dollar that third parties pay, private insurance companies account for 27 cents, and gov-

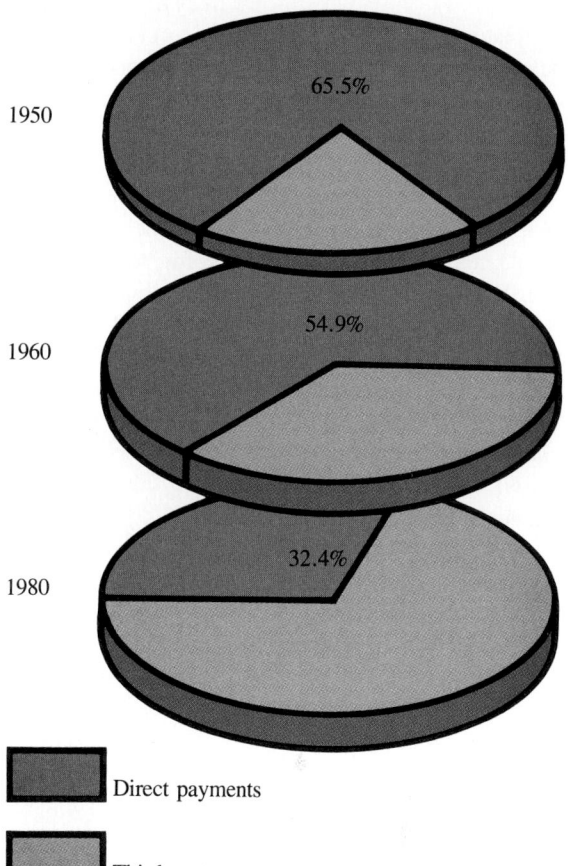

Figure 14-5. The proportion of medical-care costs paid directly by patients for 1950, 1960, and 1979.

■ Direct payments

▨ Third-party payments

SOURCE: Adapted from Robert M. Gibson and Daniel R. Waldo, "National Health Expenditures, 1980," *Health Care Financing Review* (September 1981).

ernment programs at the local, state, or federal level pay 40 cents. This distribution of the health-care cost burden has not remained constant over the last thirty years. As Figure 14-5 shows, the importance of third-party payments has increased dramatically since 1950. In that year, the proportions of direct payment versus third-party payment were reversed from what they are today. Because patients in 1950 paid two-thirds of their bill directly, they had a greater incentive to economize. This incentive still exists in areas such as dental services and prescription drugs, in which patients continue to pay over two-thirds of their bills directly. In the health-care industry, inflation correlates directly with the proportion of third-party payments. Hospital room charges, for instance, are most often paid for by third parties, and they have risen the most rapidly, followed by physicians' fees. Dentist fees and drug costs, however, have risen more slowly, because patients bear a larger share of the costs directly.

Another factor in the demand for health care is age. Whereas personal health-care spending averaged less than $300 per year for people under the age of nineteen, the average for those sixty-five and older was over $2000. The oldest one-tenth of the population uses one-third of the health care. And we can expect increased demand for health care as our nation's population ages. By the year 2000, some demographers estimate that the over-sixty-five age group will constitute 14 percent of America's population. This will put additional demands on our health-care delivery system.

Income change has also increased the demand for medical care. As incomes rise, people tend to buy more of some things and less of others. We touched on this phenomenon in Chapter 1 when we discussed the concepts of normal and inferior goods. Medical care is a normal good; as our incomes rise, we tend to purchase more of it. And one of the hallmarks of American economic history has been the slow but steady rise in real incomes and consumer purchasing power. A good example of the interaction of income and health-care expenditures is in the increased demand for orthodontics, the dental specialty that deals with straightening teeth and improving the bite. In 1950, crooked teeth may have been considered an unfortunate malady, but they were rarely corrected. Today, the proportion of the population that has had braces is much higher. It is rare to find a class of college students in which fewer than 10 percent have had braces. A large part of the reason is simply that families have more real income and can thus afford to have their children's teeth straightened. The child who grows to adulthood with "buck teeth" is a real exception. And more than likely, he or she will choose to have the orthodontia done as an adult.

A discussion of the demand for health care would not be complete without exploring the most important reason for an increase in the demand—namely, government programs. In 1980, the federal government spent $71 billion on health programs, an increase of 17 percent over the previous year's expenditures and the third largest part of the federal budget, after national defense and social security. When these federal moneys are combined with state and local health expenditures, government programs account for over 40 percent of all personal health-care spending. Moreover, their impact on demand has been even greater because they aim at those groups that have historically had unfilled health needs: the poor, the elderly, and the disadvantaged. Once the government began to subsidize their health care, these groups began to use more health services. This increased demand, to some extent, resulted in higher prices. Two-thirds of all government health-care expenditures are spent in two programs: Medicare and Medicaid.

MEDICARE: AID FOR THE ELDERLY

The **Medicare** program was established under Title XVIII of the Social Security Act, and it went into effect on July 1, 1966. It was originally designed as a federal insurance program to protect those age sixty-five and over from the high cost of hospital and physicians' services. On July 1, 1973, permanently disabled workers and their dependents and persons in need of kidney dialysis machines were added to the program. Nevertheless, 90 percent of those on Medicare are age sixty-five or over. In 1980, Medicare expenditures were over $36 billion, with about 17.3 million persons receiving benefits.

Once the Medicare program began, hospital admission rates for persons covered by the program rose markedly. In 1967, short-stay hospital admission rates were 260 per 1000 patients. By 1978, this rate had risen to 350 per 1000—an increase of about 33 percent. So Medicare was successful in making hospital care more affordable for the elderly, but it had the undesirable side-effect of increasing the cost of such care. Another quirk in the program was the schedule of fees for doctors, which provided for larger payments to physicians if their patients were in hospitals. This may be part of the reason that more elderly patients were put in the hospital, with the result that payments to doctors increased.

MEDICAID: HEALTH CARE FOR THE POOR

Another program that created an increase in the demand for medical services was **Medicaid**—a joint federal-state program that provides health-care funding to low-income persons. This program provides medical assistance to people who are eligible to receive cash assistance under one of the existing welfare programs such as Aid to Families with Dependent Children (AFDC), Supplemental Security Income (SSI) for the aged, blind, and disabled, or unemployment compensation. In 1980, Medicaid paid over $25 billion in benefits for 22 million people. By reducing the cost of medical care to segments of the American population that need it but often are unable to obtain it, this program increased demand and thus pushed prices higher. Together with Medicare, Medicaid accounted for one-third of the growth in personal health-care expenditures during the 1970s. Taxes pay for the costs of these programs, but other users of medical service must also bear the burden of higher prices brought on by increased demand. Some critics of the program also charge Medicaid and Medicare with the disappearance of the older tradition of charitable medical care provided by well-meaning doctors and hospitals. Nevertheless, no one can deny that medical care is more available to the poor and the elderly today than ever before.

The Supply of Medical Care

Trying to understand changes in the demand for medical care is like hearing only half of a good story. You can never be sure that you know what will happen until you hear the second half. In this section, the supply of medical care represents the second half of the story. As we said earlier, the two most important components of supply in the health-care industry are

Physicians are plentiful in large metropolitan areas with lots of potential patients, but they are often hard to come by in small towns and rural communities.

physicians and hospitals, which account for two-thirds of all health-care costs in the United States. In the next few sections, we explore how changes in these basic health-care deliveries can affect the prices you pay for health care.

PHYSICIANS

According to the American Medical Association, there were over 400,000 active physicians in the United States in 1979, or about 180 doctors per 100,000 people. There were also 123 accredited medical schools that graduated over 14,000 new doctors. Was this an adequate supply to fill our needs? The answer depends on who is asking the question.

A presidential commission, the Graduate Medical National Advisory Committee, predicted in its 1980 report that by 1990 there would be a *surplus* of doctors. It argued that if current trends continue, the United States will have a surplus of 70,000 doctors by 1990, and a surplus of 145,000 by the year 2000. According to the report, such an oversupply will increase rather than decrease the cost of health care because of the third-party payment system in our nation. The commission believes that physicians have a certain target level of income, and if each doctor has fewer patients, he or she will simply raise his or her fees in order to meet the level of expected income. This increase in fees will then be passed along to insurance companies or the government and will thus be reflected in higher health-care costs for the general public. The Committee's solution is to cut back on the number of new medical graduates and restrict the number of foreign medical graduates who are allowed to practice in the United States. In short, the report says that cutting back on the supply will cause doctors to have more patients and thus be able to make their projected incomes, even though they are charging less. This contorted sort of reasoning has prevailed in the past, beginning with the acceptance of the Flexner Report.

Abraham Flexner operated a prep school in Louisville, Kentucky in the early twentieth century. In 1910, the Carnegie Foundation asked him to evaluate the state of medical education in the United States, and his report became the basis for a radical restructuring of American medical schools. Flexner visited all of the medical schools and compared them to the one school that he felt gave adequate training—Johns Hopkins University. Largely as a result of his report, most of the medical schools were put out of business, so from 1910 until 1944, the number of degree-granting medical schools fell from 192 to 69, with a similar decline in the number of new physicians. It is interesting to note that anyone who received an M.D. from such a school before the certification procedures went into effect could continue to practice. The point was to restrict *new* entrants into the field, which of course would raise the incomes of those already practicing.

From 1930 to 1970, the incomes of physicians rose more rapidly than those of any other professional group. But from 1970 to 1980, physicians' purchasing power fell by more than 9 percent, according to the American Medical Association's periodic survey. Nevertheless, in 1980, physicians had an average income of $80,800, and they were earning an estimated 22 percent return on their investment in their medical education (compared to an average return of 10 to 11 percent for college graduates). The fact that physicians' salaries have grown more rapidly than those of other comparably trained professionals indicates that a supply bottleneck has given them the power to set prices and avoid competition. But the AMA survey that reported a decline in physicians' real income from 1970 to 1980, as well as the 1980 study, raised fears about a doctor surplus and indicated that we may be getting more doctors, more competition, and better prices in the near future. As Frank Sloan, director of the Health Policy Center at Vanderbilt University said, "It's getting harder for doctors to maintain a big cartel" (*Changing Times,* March 1981, p. 38).

The "oversupply" of doctors is an issue that bears more analysis, because it was used before to increase the cost of health care. If one were to believe the AMA and other spokespersons for the industry, the major solution is to cut back on the training of new physicians and restrict the number of foreign-trained physicians allowed to practice in the United States. Contrary to that conclusion, however, there is evidence of a shortage of physicians, rather than a surplus, in many parts of the United States. Table 14-2 shows the distribution of medical doctors by state. In Alabama, there are 122 doctors per 100,000 people, whereas in the District of Columbia there are almost 500 doctors per 100,000 residents. South Dakota has the fewest doctors compared to its population. It has 99, compared to a national average of 175 per 100,000 people. If there were a cutback in the number of graduates, would South Dakotans be better off? And these figures do not begin to indicate the paucity of physicians in the rural areas of states such as California, which appear to have more than their share. Even in California, many small towns have no doctors at all. How would a cutback in the number of new physicians help these towns?

INCREASING THE SUPPLY OF HEALTH-CARE PERSONNEL

It seems clear that a partial solution to the problem of too few physicians is to expand the number of people who deliver health-care services. One way to do so is to encourage doctors to use **physician assistants** in their practice. Just as medics augment the supply of

Table 14-2. Number and Rate per 100,000 Population of Active Medical Doctors by State

State	Medical doctors Number	Rate*	State	Medical doctors Number	Rate*
Alabama	4,554	122	Montana	965	124
Alaska	445	117	Nebraska	2,198	142
Arizona	4,229	182	Nevada	860	132
Arkansas	2,423	111	New Hampshire	1,376	159
California	47,891	217	New Jersey	12,870	176
Colorado	5,248	200	New Mexico	1,696	142
Connecticut	7,222	234	New York	44,458	251
Delaware	911	159	North Carolina	7,934	145
District of Columbia	3,322	499	North Dakota	780	122
			Ohio	16,366	152
Florida	15,456	182	Oklahoma	3,453	121
Georgia	6,925	138	Oregon	4,192	172
Hawaii	1,670	199	Pennsylvania	20,831	177
Idaho	928	106	Rhode Island	1,850	199
Illinois	19,704	176	South Carolina	3,640	128
Indiana	6,549	122	South Dakota	677	99
Iowa	3,424	118	Tennessee	6,498	150
Kansas	3,385	146	Texas	19,101	148
Kentucky	4,455	129	Utah	2,107	162
Louisiana	5,675	144	Vermont	970	199
Maine	1,562	144	Virginia	8,114	162
Maryland	9,851	240	Washington	6,460	174
Massachusetts	14,149	246	West Virginia	2,419	130
Michigan	13,513	147	Wisconsin	6,841	146
Minnesota	7,212	180	Wyoming	440	105
Mississippi	2,436	102			
Missouri	7,448	154	Total	377,683	175

*Rates based on civilian population as of July 1, 1978.

SOURCE: American Medical Association, "Physician Distribution and Medical Licensure in the U.S.," *Sourcebook of Health Insurance Data* (1978).

health-care services in the armed forces, physician assistants could help with medical services to patients on the home front. One study has shown that using paramedics could increase a physician's productivity by 74 percent (Golladay, 1973). Whereas an efficient medical practice could deal with 147 patients per week, the use of paramedics could increase that figure to 265, with no loss of quality. After all, is a shot given by a paramedic any less effective than the same treatment administered by a physician?

Using nurse-midwives is another alternative that could increase health care while holding down costs. **Nurse-midwives** are certified nurses who specialize in the care of pregnant women. They supervise pre- and post-natal care and assist during the delivery of a baby. Today, there are 2,200 nurse-midwives, but the potential for expansion is enormous. A pilot project was recently conducted in California's primarily rural Madera County. During the first eighteen months of the project, the death rate for newborn infants fell

Table 14-3. The Cost of Hospital Stays

Year	Average daily cost	Average length of stay (days)	Average total cost
1950	$ 15.62	8.1	$ 126.52
1955	23.12	7.8	180.34
1960	32.23	7.6	244.95
1965	44.48	7.8	346.94
1970	81.01	8.2	664.28
1971	92.31	8.0	738.48
1972	105.30	7.9	831.70
1973	114.40	7.8	892.00
1974	127.70	7.8	996.20
1975	151.20	7.7	1164.20
1976	172.70	7.7	1330.10
1977	197.90	7.6	1504.10
1978	221.90	7.6	1686.40
1979	248.60	7.6	1889.40

SOURCE: American Hospital Association, *Hospital Statistics* (1980).

from 23.9 to 10.3 per 1000 live births. Considering our nation's record for infant mortality, such a program merits expansion. And yet, according to Sally Tom, a certified nurse-midwife who represents the American Colleges of Nurse-Midwives, doctors are fighting to keep them from practicing (1980). She testified at a congressional hearing in 1980 that the opposition argument is generally based on the issues of "quality of care and of patient safety," but "fear of economic competition underlies much of the resistance to nurse-midwifery practices."

HOSPITALS

The cost of all components of health care is rising, but none is rising as rapidly as the cost of hospital care. As Table 14-3 shows, the average daily cost of staying in the hospital rose from $15.62 in 1950 to $248.60 by 1979. And although the average length of stay has shortened, the rise in the cost per day has boosted costs from a few hundred dollars to over $1800. Such a dramatic rise in the price led some people to remark that it would be cheaper to move into a first-class hotel with room service than go to a hospital. This rise in price is in part explained by the third-party payment system we explained earlier: 90 percent of hospital bills are paid by private insurers, Medicare, or Medicaid. The result is that doctors, patients, and hospitals often lack the incentive to economize.

The average patient's hospital costs have also risen, because more complicated and expensive tests are being ordered by physicians practicing defensive medicine—protecting themselves in case of lawsuits. Doctors and hospitals have discovered that they can be judged liable for damages in cases in which they misdiagnose or mistreat patients. These lawsuits are called **malpractice suits,** because the patient argues that the defendant did not follow accepted procedures or did not perform all the tests to see whether a certain condition existed. As a result of the multimillion-dollar awards that some patients have received, many doctors and hospitals are ordering more tests to protect themselves against the possibility of malpractice suits. Companies that insure health practitioners have also raised their rates dramatically, given the size of the malpractice awards. Most of these increased insurance costs ultimately get passed along to the health consumer in the form of higher prices.

The third-party payment system, coupled with the malpractice penalties for omitting a test or failing to take every precaution, helps explain why thousands of people are hospitalized each year for treatment that they could obtain as outpatients at a hospital or a clinic and why others are given expensive tests or surgery that they do not need. According to some estimates, as many as one-half of all surgeries are unnecessary. For example, based on recent surgical records, someone living in Ohio is three times as likely to have surgery as a Pennsylvanian but only half as likely as a resident of New Jersey. Do people in New Jersey really need six times more surgery than their Pennsylvania neighbors? The possibility of unnecessary surgery seems very real. To counteract this, some insurance companies are now encouraging their policyholders to seek second and third opinions *before* they submit to surgery (see Box 14-2). Medicare and Medicaid *always* pay for a second opinion when nonemergency surgery is recommended.

Contrary to popular belief, the high cost of hospital care does not result primarily from increasing

---

BOX 14-2

Getting a Second Opinion *Before* Surgery

At one time, it was almost unheard of for patients to question their doctor's opinion, especially with regard to having an operation. But you should be aware that even doctors may disagree about the best way to handle a medical problem. Because all surgery costs both time and money and because there are certain risks no matter how minor the surgery, it is a good idea to have a second opinion. A second opinion should *not* be used to delay an emergency operation such as an appendectomy, but when there is time, a second opinion will often give one additional information so that one can make an informed choice about whether surgery is the best alternative. Operations that are usually not emergencies include: tonsillectomies, gall bladder operations, hysterectomies, and some cataract operations.

The Department of Health and Human Services suggests that one find the answers to the following questions before agreeing to nonemergency surgery:

1. What is the doctor's diagnosis?
2. What operation does the doctor plan to do?
3. What are the likely benefits of the operation?
4. What are the risks of the surgery and how likely are they to occur?
5. How long would the recovery period be and what is involved?
6. What are the costs of the operation? Will your insurance cover all of these costs?
7. What will happen if you do not have the operation?
8. Are there other ways to treat your condition?

There are several ways to get a second opinion. One is to ask your physician to recommend someone. A second way is to contact your local medical society or medical schools for names of local doctors who specialize in the relevant field. Or you can call the government's toll-free number, 800-638-6833 (in Maryland, 800-492-6603), to locate a specialist near you.

There are a number of advantages to telling your doctor that you want a second opinion, not the least of which is that you can have a copy of your records sent to the second physician. In any event, be sure that you know the names of the recommended surgical procedure and the tests you have had. If the second doctor agrees with the surgical plan, he or she will normally refer you to the original doctor for surgery. If there is disagreement, at least you will have some facts to discuss with your first doctor. Do not be afraid to assert yourself, because it is *you* who will be undergoing the surgery.

---

payroll costs. Despite the fact that the salaries for hospital personnel have risen and a few well-publicized strikes have occurred, the proportion of total hospital expenses attributable to payroll costs has been steadily decreasing since 1962, when they were over 60 percent of the total. By 1980, labor costs had fallen to only 50 percent of community hospital expenditures. The rising cost of hospital care is related to the structure of the hospital itself.

Community hospitals are nonfederal, short-term, general and special hospitals that provide care to the public. They account for 92 percent of all hospital admissions, with most other admissions going to federal veterans hospitals. These institutions are overwhelmingly nonprofit undertakings that were started from community fund raising, gifts from wealthy patrons, or Catholic or other religious groups. Their original purpose was primarily to provide charitable care for the poor and the terminally ill, but after their founding they quickly came to serve the nonpoor as well. In return for being able to bring their patients to the hospital for treatment, physicians normally donated their services for the poor, who occupied the majority of the hospital beds.

With the institution of federal and state programs for the poor, the number of charity cases in community hospitals has diminished, but the essential feature of the doctor-patient referral scheme has not. Because

Part of the high cost of hospital care can be attributed to the fact that hospitals often spare no expense in trying to attract doctors to their facilities.

the physician brings patients to the hospital, the hospital must cater to the physician, not the patient. This scheme is like the relationship between a travel agent and a resort hotel. The hotel does not, under any circumstances, want to alienate the person responsible for booking its customers. This point explains why patients often feel like second-class citizens. As Herman Somers (1969) put it, "The doctors make a special point that the hospital cannot practice medicine, that the patient is the doctor's, not the hospital's—a precious distinction which strikes at the unity and authority of the hospital."

This need to satisfy physicians leads to a number of problems. Because they want to assure doctors that their patients will always have a bed, hospitals may add new wings or renovate old ones. This expansion, however, adds to the fixed cost (overhead) of the hospital. Because hospital admission rates have been virtually constant since 1976 but the number of beds has kept growing, occupancy rates have been declining. In Los Angeles alone, an estimated 10,000 beds are empty every day. In the Los Angeles area, some private hospitals have been accused of offering kickbacks to physicians who send patients to their facilities.

In addition to guaranteeing enough bed space, hospitals are under pressure to provide the most modern technological equipment, even if this equipment is not used often enough to justify its cost. Hospitals fear that physicians will simply move their patients to hospitals that do have more-sophisticated facilities. According to the American Council of Life Insurance Institute, the rapid growth in use of the CAT scanner, a sophisticated x-ray and computer diagnostic tool, is a case in point. According to the Institute, these machines, which cost over $.5 million, are so popular that there are enough CAT scanners in southern California hospitals to fill the needs of *all* the hospitals west of the Mississippi River. As a result, they are underused, and a portion of their cost is simply added to the cost of hospital care in the form of higher room charges or other fees.

HEALTH SYSTEM AGENCIES: THE CONSUMER COUNTERATTACK

Consumers know that all these hospital costs are eventually recovered from the consumer either in higher insurance premiums or higher taxes. In 1974, the National Health Planning and Resources Development Act was passed to create a nationwide multilevel network to help contain these rising costs with the help of consumers. Under this Act, the nation is divided into more than 200 health-service areas, each headed by a local planning unit called a **Health System Agency (HSA).** Most HSAs are governed by ten to thirty volunteer board members chosen by local government officials or community groups. A majority of the board must be composed of consumers who represent the area's socioeconomic population.

The powers of Health System Agencies are substantial, so consumers who are active in them can have a direct impact on the health care provided. On the local level, HSAs have the authority to disapprove all proposals for federally funded health projects such as mental health centers or alcohol- and drug-abuse programs. On the state level, they have a major voice in the State Health Planning Development Agency, which is charged with approving all requests by individuals or organizations wishing to spend $150,000 or more for additional health facilities or medical equipment. These powers enable HSAs to help prevent the expansion of a hospital when others in the area already have vacant beds. Between August 1976 and August 1978, this program prevented $3.4 billion of unnecessary expenditures for health facilities, services, and equipment (*People Power,* 1980). Its success indicates that consumer involvement and proper planning can make a difference. But HSAs are only the beginning in the consumers' battle to slow the rise in the cost of medical care.

THE NEW JERSEY HOSPITAL COST CONTAINMENT PLAN

A New Jersey plan for containing costs allows hospitals to charge a flat fee for the patient's ailment, rather than charging for the actual services rendered. By 1983, all of New Jersey's hospitals are expected to adopt this system, and Georgia, New York, and Maryland ara also planning similar programs. The new program uses a Yale University system that puts thousands of possible disorders into 383 categories called **diagnosis related groups (DRGs).** The state then establishes a standard price and a set number of days that a patient may stay and still qualify for these fees. For a tonsillectomy, for example, the hospital can charge $532.51, and the allowable length of stay is two to five days. If a patient spends less than two days or more than five days in the hospital, the fees are adjusted; otherwise the flat fee holds. The advantages of the system are a more uniform set of charges and an added financial incentive to the hospital to get someone well as quickly as possible (and thus pocket the difference between costs and charges).

One disadvantage that could develop among hospital staff is a "get-em-up, get-em-out" attitude that could put patients through a revolving door of admission, surgery, and quick discharge. The DRG system itself needs some refinement, because any plan to narrow all ailments into 383 categories results in some miscellaneous categories. Julie Micheletti, the DRG coordinator for the Freehold Area Hospi-

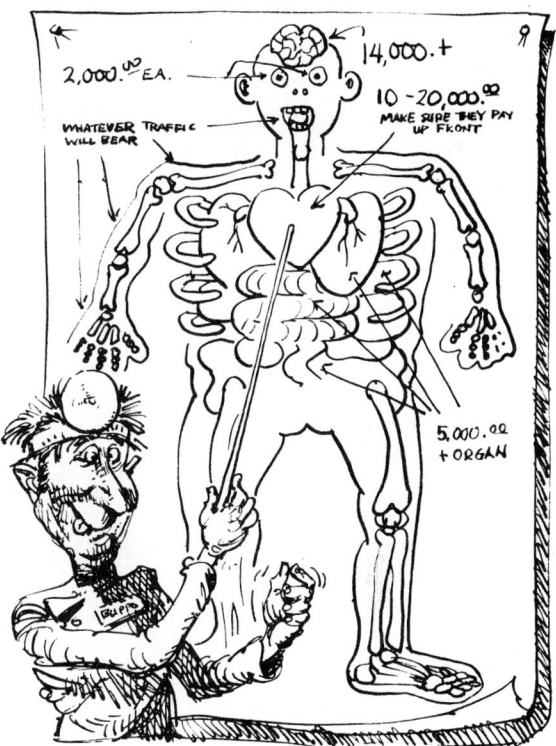

In the DRG system, disorders are classified into 383 different categories, for which the state then sets a standard price.

tal in Freehold, New Jersey, is not completely sold on the idea. According to her, some DRGs are just "dumpster categories." A headache, for example, is classified under DRG 333, and it could cost $1,982.16, because it is an "ill-defined indication of disease." The DRG system may be adopted nationwide, so consumers should be aware of it. For now, it is still viewed with a considerable degree of skepticism (Larson, 1980).

Although hospital cost containment has proved to be a difficult task, we have some reason to be optimistic, because health-care costs have been reduced in other areas. In the prescription-drug industry, a combination of increased competition and better consumer information has led to better prices for health-care buyers. In the section that follows, we trace this success story and cite some ways that consumers can lower their health-care costs by making more-informed decisions.

Table 14.4 The Fourteen Most Prescribed Drugs with Their Generic Equivalents

Generic name	Commonly prescribed brand names	Purpose of drug
Ampicillin	Amcill Omnipen Polycillin Principen	To fight infection (antibiotic)
Tetracycline	Achromycin V Panmycin Sumycin Tetracyn	To fight infection (antibiotic)
Acetaminophen/codeine	Tylenol with Codeine	To relieve pain, fever, and cough
Hydrochlorothiazide	Esidrix HydroDIURIL Oretic	For hypertension and edema (diuretic)
Penicillin V-K	Pen-Vee K V-Cillin K Veetids	To fight infection (antibiotic)
Chlordiazepoxide hydrochloride	Librium	To relieve anxiety and tension
Propoxyphene hydrochloride, aspirin phenacetin, and caffeine	Darvon Compound-65	To relieve pain (analgesic)
Erythromycin stearate	Erythrocin Stearate	To fight infection (antibiotic)
Amitriptyline hydrochloride	Elavil Endep	To relieve symptoms of depression
Diphenhydramine hydrochloride	Benadryl	Antihistamine (also for motion sickness and parkinsonism)
Diphenoxylate hydrochloride with atropine sulfate	Lomotil	To help control diarrhea
Meclizine hydrochloride	Antivert	To control nausea and vomiting, and dizziness from motion sickness
Chlorothiazide	Diuril	For hypertension and edema (diuretic)
Erythromycin ethyl succinate	E.E.S.	To fight infection (antibiotic)

SOURCE: *FDA Consumer*, "Generic Drugs: How Good Are They?" (Washington, D.C.: U.S. Government Printing Office, 1980).

Prescription Drugs

It may come as a surprise to you to learn that the prices of some of the components of health care have actually risen *more slowly* than the inflation rate. Prescription drugs is one such component. This means that the cost of the average drug prescription is *lower* in real dollars today than it was ten years ago. One of the chief reasons for this decline is the advent of **generic,** or non-brand-name, drugs. In 1966, generic prescriptions accounted for only 6 percent of all prescriptions; by 1978 they accounted for over 13 percent.

GENERIC DRUGS: A BARGAIN FOR THE CONSUMER

When a new drug is developed, it is usually patented and sold exclusively under a single brand name. Such patents last for seventeen years, after which any firm can manufacture the drug and sell it under the drug's generic or "official" name. The generic name usually describes the chemical composition of the drug—often some unpronounceable name such as chlordiazepoxide hydrochloride. The trade name of this chemical compound is Librium, a drug often prescribed to relieve anxiety or tension. Ampicillin is a generic name for a drug that fights infections. Some of the common trade names given by various producers of this drug are Amcill, Omnipen, Polycillin, and Principen. They are all ampicillin—they just have different trade names, because different companies produce them.

If you are familiar with wines, you know that the term generic is sometimes applied to a wine made from a specific grape, like Pinot Noir or Chardonnay. But unlike the production of generic wines, the production of generic drugs must proceed under strict supervision, so that no matter who manufactures them the end result is precisely the same. The Food and Drug Administration (FDA), which we discussed in Chapter 5, monitors all prescription drugs, both brand-name and generic, and tests them for purity and strength.

In 1979, the FDA drafted a list of the more than 5,000 prescription drugs approved for sale in the United States. About half of these drugs are available from more than one manufacturer, and the FDA has certified them as "therapeutically equivalent" to other brands of the same strength and dosage form (liquid, tablet, or capsule). They do not necessarily look or taste the same, but you can be sure that they are all equally safe and effective and that the body will absorb their active ingredients at the same rate.

Table 14-4 lists the fourteen most-prescribed drugs that are available generically. If you or someone you know is taking one of these drugs under a brand name, you can probably save money by asking

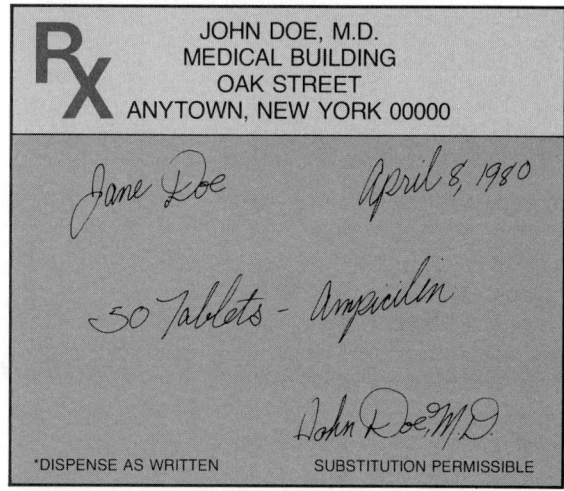

Figure 14-6. New York's Generic Drug Law requires that patients receive prescriptions on slips containing two lines for doctors' signatures. Substitutions are forbidden when doctors sign on the left-hand side over the statement "dispense as written."

your physician to write a generic prescription instead. Of course, this is only a partial list, but the six most popular generic antibiotics account for over 60 million prescriptions each year. Keep this list in a handy place; it could save you hundreds of dollars.

By 1980, over forty states had passed generic-substitution laws that either allow or require pharmacists to substitute generic for brand-name drugs, if the prescribing physician has no objection. In 1978, the New York legislature passed its Generic Drug Law, which provided for a standard format (see Figure 14-6) for all prescriptions written in that state. The placement of a doctor's signature on the right-hand side of the prescription slip signifies that the doctor has no objection to generic substitution. As a result, pharmacists are required to use the lower-cost generic drug.* This procedure has the added advantage of

---

*You might wonder why pharmacists must be *required* to use the lower-cost generic. The reason is that the profit margins are generally higher in the brand-name drugs, so it is more profitable for the druggist to use them. In addition, it is often easier (and cheaper) for the pharmacist to stock only one name brand.

Table 14-5. Brooklyn College Drug Price Survey of Flatbush–Midwood Area*

Pharmacy Address	Brand name Achromycin 250 mg/20 tabs	Generic equivalent Tetracycline hydrochloride 250 mg/20 tabs	Brand name Librium 10 mg/90 caps	Generic equivalent Chlordiazepoxide hydrochloride 10 mg/90 caps	Brand name V-Cillin K 250 mg/20 tabs	Generic equivalent Penicillin potassium 250 mg/20 tabs
1066 Flatbush Ave.	$3.95	$2.95	$12.45	$ 4.95	$4.45	$2.95
1148 Flatbush Ave.	$3.60	$3.10	$11.50	$ 4.75	$4.50	$3.75
1258 Flatbush Ave.	$4.50	$3.50	$17.95	$ 9.95	$4.50	$3.95
1490 Flatbush Ave.	$5.00	$4.00	$12.95	$ 8.95	$5.04	$4.00
1830 Flatbush Ave.	$4.50	$2.75	$13.95	(didn't carry)	$4.50	(didn't carry)
2064 Flatbush Ave.	$3.45	$2.85	$ 8.10	$ 4.45	$4.30	$3.10
2472 Flatbush Ave.	$2.95	$2.50	$11.50	$10.50	$5.95	$3.95

*Partial results of a NYPIRG survey as recorded by project director Carole Gould and student volunteers.

SOURCE: *People Power: What Communities Are Doing to Counter Inflation* (Washington, D.C.: U.S. Government Printing Office, 1980).

making it easy for physicians to prescribe generic drugs, even if they are not familiar with the generic name. Unfortunately, a 1979 study by the New York Public Interest Research Group (NYPIRG) found that 98 percent of the pharmacists surveyed were violating one or more provisions of the state law. According to NYPIRG (1980), "more than half of the pharmacists refused to dispense generic drugs even when the doctors had requested it." Largely because of this consumer survey, the New York Pharmacy Board fined fifty drugstores for noncompliance with the state law. Legislation is only half the battle. Consumers must also remain active to assure that such laws are enforced.

Requesting generics is not enough to get full value for your prescription dollar. Another important tool is comparison shopping. The price of a generic drug can vary enormously from one pharmacy to another. In April 1979, Brooklyn College Consumer Education Classes conducted a survey of local pharmacies. Some of their results are presented in Table 14-5. In every case, the generic drug was cheaper than its brand-name equivalent, but there were wide price variations among various drugstores. At some pharmacies, the brand name was actually *cheaper* than the generic sold at pharmacies only a few blocks away. Once again, it pays to comparison shop.

OVER-THE-COUNTER DRUGS

Not all drugs require a prescription. Many of our most common drugstore purchases are for standard problems such as headaches or sore throats. If one were to judge one's needs by viewing television commercials, the number-one health problem in the United States would seem to be the common headache or loose dentures. As far as headaches are concerned, there are really only two forms of over-the-counter medication, acetylsalicylic acid (aspirin) or acetaminophen (non-aspirin pain reliever). Bayer Aspirin is the largest-selling acetylsalicylic acid, and Tylenol is the best-known acetaminophen, although Datril is gaining recognition. Extensive tests have established that the only physical difference between various brands of aspirin is the size of the cotton plug in the bottle. The same analysis holds for acetaminophens. The smart consumer compares prices, chooses the least-expensive variety, and disregards those clever commercials that help drive the cost of the advertised brands up but do nothing to enhance their therapeutic value. A more-important concern, as Box 14-3 shows, should be the potential hazards of drug interactions.

Health Insurance: Private Plans

Now that you have some idea of the components of

> **BOX 14-3**
>
> ## Drug Interactions and Potential Health Threats
>
> Being a good decision maker in the area of health-care expenditures can be difficult because of the high cost of information. In the text we outlined some of the ways you can save money on prescription drugs by comparison shopping and by asking for generic drugs rather than their more expensive brand-name rivals. The effectiveness of the drug you take is a second area of concern that is just as important as saving money. Once again, information is important but often difficult to obtain. The Food and Drug Administration ruled that by 1981 pharmacists had to include **patient package inserts (PPIs)** whenever they sold one of the ten most commonly prescribed drugs. These inserts must be written in nontechnical language and they must describe the purpose of the drug; the side effects, risks, and benefits; and potential drug interactions. However when President Reagan took office in January 1981, these and other regulations that were to be put into effect were delayed indefinitely.
>
> A recent article by a pharmacologist presented some information about the interactions between drugs and commonly ingested foods (Romankiewicz, 1981). For example, citrus fruit juices such as orange juice or grapefruit juice can reduce the absorption of penicillin into the bloodstream. Thus, if you take ampicillin with orange juice, you will reduce the drug's ability to fight or control infection. Dairy products that are taken daily have a similar effect on tetracycline, another commonly prescribed antibiotic. One reaction that women who take contraceptives should be especially alert to is the effect that ampicillin (an antibiotic prescribed to fight infection) can have on the effectiveness of birth-control pills. In some cases, ampicillin has been shown to counteract the effects of birth-control pills, and the result may be an unwanted pregnancy. Alcohol is another potent reactor with certain drugs. Antihistamines can interact with alcohol to produce pronounced drowsiness. This may be a minor side effect if you are trying to rest, but it could be dangerous if you need to be alert to drive a car. Alcohol will also impair the effectiveness of most antibiotics. Bleeding from the stomach could result if alcohol is taken with aspirin.

supply and demand for health care, let us explore the most important ways to minimize health costs.

Health insurance—insurance designed to help cover expenses arising from sickness or injury and, in some cases, to provide income during disability, is probably the most common way to limit health expenditures. Based on past experience, about one out of every six Americans is hospitalized each year, so the need for health insurance is evident. For that one out of six, hospital bills alone will average close to $2000, with expenses for drugs and physician's services added to that. In addition to the actual expenses, the patient may not be able to work and may lose income. Such events can wipe out a family's savings, put tremendous debt on household members, and ruin the most carefully planned family budget. Because these kinds of risks are too great to accept, most people choose to pay for some form of insurance.

The rationale for obtaining insurance is fairly straightforward: A family wants to be assured that if illness or accident befalls them, they will remain financially secure. In 1981, more than 200 million Americans—nearly 90 percent of the population—had some form of private health insurance. This broad base of support makes it possible for health insurance companies to spread the risk over millions of families; thus, the healthy subsidize the sick. This is the same principle that automobile insurance companies use to spread the risk of loss caused by accidents (see Chapter 12). The premiums from insured drivers who do not have accidents help to pay for those insured drivers who do have a claim. This share-the-risk principle is basic to all types of insurance.

The private insurance industry is highly competitive, with more than 1200 companies writing policies for hundreds of millions of people. Some of these companies, such as Mutual of Omaha, Prudential, and Occidental, are set up like any other profit-oriented corporations. Their goal is to maximize their profits, because they are owned by stockholders, who expect a return on their investment. The average profit-making insurance firm pays about 80 percent of its premium income in claims. The other major kind of insurance company is a nonprofit membership corporation such as Blue Cross and Blue Shield, for which the goal is to charge a high enough premium to

Consumers are bombarded with insurance offers that claim to cover daily hospital expenses; often such payments are fixed in the policy, even though hospital costs are rising.

pay the health-care bills of its members and cover the costs of administering its plans. Blue Cross and Blue Shield plans cover almost half of all health insurance holders, and they pay out almost 95 percent of their premium income in claims.

Based on the payment ratio of nonprofit plans, one might think that nonprofit plans are the best choice. This may not be so. Before you are ready to make an intelligent decision about which health-insurance company to choose, you need to know something about the general provisions of health insurance policies. Almost every company offers a wide variety of plans. Some will be better suited to your needs than others. There is no way that we can cover a majority of these plans here, but we can lay out the basic categories of health insurance and what they do and do not cover. In many respects, the sections that follow parallel the sections on automobile insurance presented in Chapter 12. The concepts of co-insurance and deductible also apply to health insurance, but there is seldom any problem with who is at fault. If you become ill, the health insurance company pays for all covered expenses—it does not try to assess blame. But what does your policy cover?

The health insurance industry is undergoing dramatic change, because the costs of health care (and insurance premiums) are rising faster than the general inflation rate. This has led many companies to restructure their sales techniques, benefits, and programs. Nevertheless, you can still divide health-care insurance into these categories:

1. Basic coverage, which includes protection against the cost of ordinary, short-term hospital care, surgery, and doctors' services for nonsurgical care.
2. Major medical coverage, which provides broad protection against the costs of serious or prolonged illness.
3. Disability insurance, which provides income for people who are unable to work because of sickness or injury.
4. Dental insurance, which provides coverage for the costs of dental services.

BASIC COVERAGE

Basic coverage is insurance that covers the costs of ordinary hospital care, surgery, and doctor's services. Before the days of spiraling health-care costs, basic coverage and disability insurance were the only kinds of health insurance offered. Depending on the policy, basic-coverage benefits usually last a year or less, and they often have a stipulated maximum payment. These benefits are geared to the normal, everyday medical needs that many people experience, from hospital visits because of pregnancy or a broken leg to having one's tonsils removed or simply visiting a doctor because of illness. If your insurance plan has a basic-coverage provision, it probably includes hospital-expense insurance, surgical-expense insurance, and physician-expense insurance. But in many plans, it is possible to purchase these coverages separately.

Hospital-Expense Insurance. If a person has any health insurance coverage at all, it is most likely hospital-expense insurance, because it is the most widely held type. **Hospital-expense insurance** provides specific benefits for daily hospital room and board and for routine nursing care. It also provides for other hospital services such as laboratory tests, x-rays, anesthesia, the use of an operating room, drugs and medications, and even local ambulance service.

With hospital-expense insurance, as with all insurance policies, the benefits received, the number of days covered by the plan, and the value of the insurance depend on how much coverage a policy allows. These are always stated in terms of daily charges. For example, if the room-and-board benefit is $100 per day and the additional covered services are eight times that amount, one would be covered for $900 in charges for each day in the hospital.

Blue Cross uses a service-benefit approach when paying the room-and-board charges for the hospital confinement of one of its policyholders. With **service-benefit insurance,** the insurance carrier pays the full cost of a semiprivate room without regard to the specific dollar cost. The hospital bills Blue Cross and receives its payment directly from Blue Cross; the patient does not receive a check or pay the bill directly. A possible problem with this plan for Blue Cross policyholders is that they must make sure that the hospital qualifies for the plan and is considered a participating hospital. Otherwise, all charges may not be covered.

Another frequently purchased form of hospital-expense insurance is **hospital indemnity coverage;** it pays a fixed amount of money (indemnity) directly to the patient for every day that he or she spends in the hospital. The amount of money paid to the patient is unrelated to actual hospital expenses. Hospital-expense policies that use the indemnity approach are sometimes sold through the mail or with television ad campaigns. Insurance companies that sell hospital indemnity coverage often border on being disreputable. Remember, with rising hospital costs, $150 a day does not go very far in paying medical bills. These kinds of policies should be viewed only as supplements to other health insurance plans. A ten-day hospital stay for which charges average $250 per day leaves a patient with a hospital bill of $1,000, even after a daily indemnity of $150 is paid. One point to check *before* signing up for indemnity coverage is the manner in which insurance companies deal with preexisting ailments, that is, illnesses that a patient was treated for before subscribing to the insurance plan. If preexisting ailments are broadly defined, this clause can be used to deny payment. A final question to ask of these companies is what proportion of a policyholder's premiums are repaid to insured patients. This can be determined by looking the company up in the *Argus Chart of Health Insurance,* which should be available at your college or public library. If an insurance company is returning less than 65 percent of its premiums to its hospitalized policyholders, its policies are probably a poor buy.

Surgical-Expense Insurance. As the name implies, **surgical-expense insurance** provides benefits for the costs of surgical procedures performed as a result of accident or illness, but not for cosmetic procedures such as having a face lift. Benefits under this type of policy can follow either the indemnity or the service-benefit approach. Under the indemnity approach, an insurance company pays up to a certain amount, according to a price schedule of surgical procedures.

Consumers should be aware of what a health insurance package does or doesn't cover before taking out a policy.

But Blue Shield and an increasing number of other insurance companies are now moving to the service-benefit approach, in which they agree to pay for all surgical costs, as long as the charges are "usual, customary and reasonable" (UCR). The UCR reimbursement system is based on how much other physicians in the area charge for similar operations. For a participating Blue Shield physician, as long as his or her fee is below the ninetieth percentile (not in the top ten percent for the same operations), it is paid in full. For example, if 90 percent of all the physicians in a given area charge $300 or less for a tonsillectomy, then the insurance company would consider a bill of up to $300 reasonable, but it probably would not pay a doctor $350 for the operation, unless there were some unusual circumstances. Surgeons do not get bonuses for charging less. But because next year's UCR fees depend on this year's fees, some critics have argued that the system has a built-in upward bias (*Changing Times,* March 1981).

Physician-Expense Insurance. Physician-expense insurance provides benefits that help pay doctors' fees for nonsurgical care in the hospital, the home, or the office. This insurance does not cover routine check-ups, eye examinations, or immunizations, probably because preventive medical care is not a high priority for most insurance companies. Payments are usually made by the indemnity approach, with a limit on the number of doctor visits allowed per year. Some consumer advocates believe that this type of insurance is not very useful, because the risk of major expense is slight and the indemnity payments are low. Thus, the consumer can achieve the same level of protection by holding a financial reserve, a form of self-insurance. The nice part of holding a financial reserve is that it becomes a regular part of savings and can pay interest, rather than earning money for an insurance company.

MAJOR MEDICAL-EXPENSE INSURANCE

The three categories of insurance detailed above (hospital, surgical, and physician-expense) are basic coverage. **Major medical-expense insurance** is a backup plan that protects the policyholder from large, unpredictable medical expenses. It was introduced nationally in 1951, and its growth has been rapid. Today, over 140 million people are covered by major medical-expense insurance (*Sourcebook of Health Insurance Data,* 1981). It generally covers a much broader number of accidents and illnesses, including mental illness and sometimes alcoholism. In 1980, 93 percent of those covered by this kind of plan had maximum benefits of more than $100,000; a third of these had unlimited benefits.

A good major medical plan normally has a deductible amount, say $500, that limits minor claims and thus keeps administrative costs lower. It also has a co-insurance provision that requires a policyholder to pay a percentage, often 20 percent of the major medical expenses. Beyond this, however, the only limit is the maximum stated in the policy. In order to protect oneself against catastrophic illness, under no circumstances should this maximum be less than $100,000, and it should preferably be $1,000,000. Oddly enough, major medical insurance is usually the least-expensive form of private health insurance, and

Table 14-6. An Illustration of How Basic Coverage and Major Medical Coverage Work

Expense	Total charges	Basic coverage	Major medical coverage
Hospital room and board			
10 days of intensive care at $400 per day	$4,000	$3,000	$1,000
40 days of room and board at $200 per day	8,000	4,000	4,000
Other charges: laboratory, blood tests, drugs, medicines	2,250	1,500	750
Registered nurses fees			
10 days at $75 per day	750	—	750
Physicians' fees	2,050	1,350	700
Totals	$17,050	$9,850	$7,200
Less deductible of $500			−500
Balance subject to co-insurance			$6,700
Less co-insurance at 20 percent			−1,340
Amount paid by major medical insurance			$5,360

when the size of the risk is considered, it is a very good buy.

Table 14-6 shows how major medical coverage supplements basic coverage and considerably reduces an insured person's costs. For example, suppose Frank Jones develops a severe case of hepatitis, has to be hospitalized for a long time, and needs ten days of nursing care after he is discharged. Basic coverage pays $9850 of the total bill, but because it has certain maximum limits on how much it covers, it does not pay all of the bills for this illness. If Frank did not have major medical coverage, he would still owe $7200 to hospitals, doctors, and nurses. It is in cases such as this that the backup coverage of major medical insurance is so important. Of the $7200 in additional costs, major medical insurance pays $5360. The rest, $1840, Frank owes, because of the $500 deductible and 20 percent co-insurance provisions in his policy. Nevertheless, it would be a lot easier to pay $1840 than the $7200 left over after the basic coverage paid its share.

DISABILITY INCOME PROTECTION

In addition to the problem of rising medical bills, one has the problem of being unable to work and thus not receiving a paycheck to help pay other bills. **Disability income insurance** provides an income if one is unable to work because of sickness or injury. In 1980, about 90 million workers had some form of disability income coverage—9 out of every 10 members of the civilian labor force.

Not all disability policies are alike. Cash benefits usually range from one-half to two-thirds of one's regular gross income, depending on the policy selected. But because this money is nontaxable, the net change in one's earning power is less than one might imagine. The total amount of benefits paid also varies based on the extent of the disability and on whether the policy is short or long term. Short-term policies pay an insured person for two years or less. Long-term policies can last an indefinite period, but they rarely go beyond retirement age, generally assumed to be sixty-five. In addition to these conditions, most plans also have a **waiting period**—an amount of time between the onset of the disability and the beginning of the payments. This waiting period is like the deductible amount in other health-insurance policies; it lowers the claims and also the size of the

Belonging to a Health Maintenance Organization encourages the consumer to have regular "maintenance" on his or her body, but sometimes the care seems impersonal.

premiums. But be careful, do not accept a policy for which the waiting period may exceed your ability to financially maintain your household. A one-month waiting period is optimal for most families; it balances the advantages of lower premiums against the risk of a prolonged loss of income.

DENTAL-EXPENSE INSURANCE

Dental-expense insurance is the most rapidly expanding form of health insurance. In 1967, fewer than 5 million persons were covered, but by 1980 there were over 60 million people with some form of dental insurance. Unlike the other forms of private health insurance, dental insurance emphasizes preventive as well as remedial care. Most policies reimburse clients for routine oral examinations, including x-rays and cleaning, fillings, extractions, inlays, and dentures, as well as for oral surgery and orthodontics. The major problems with dental insurance are twofold. First, unless one belongs to a labor union or works for a large corporation or the government, dental insurance is difficult to get, because most insurance companies offer it only to large groups. Second, even if one is able to obtain dental insurance, the maximum payment to any policyholder in one year is generally low, rarely exceeding $1500.

The Health Maintenance Organization

A **health maintenance organization (HMO)** is a health-care plan that differs significantly from others we have discussed. An HMO offers its members comprehensive, coordinated medical services and hospitalization for a prepaid monthly or yearly fee. Once one is enrolled as a member and pays a fee, he or she is entitled to all the services without any further charge. HMOs normally have a staff of doctors who are paid a salary, and HMOs maintain hospitals that never bill members. In 1973, there were about fifty HMOs in the nation, but with the passage of the Health Maintenance Organization Act in the same year, the federal government began encouraging their expansion. By 1980, there were over 200 HMOs serving 8 million consumers in thirty-seven states. The most well-known and largest HMO is the Kaiser-Permanente Medical Care Program that has 3.5 million members in California, Colorado, Hawaii, Ohio, Oregon, and Washington.

HMOs are not the best solution for everyone. They can offer services only in a given geographical area, and they are limited by the specialties of their staff doctors. If a member becomes ill outside the HMO's area, he or she is covered only if the illness or accident is a genuine emergency. Otherwise, he or she is expected to return home for treatment. Another problem with many of these plans is that members are not allowed to choose a particular physician. They are treated by whoever is on call when they arrive.

On the other hand, there are many advantages to belonging to an HMO. Unlike private insurers, health maintenance organizations stress preventive care and encourage periodic checkups and routine immunizations. Partly because of the emphasis on prevention, persons covered by these prepaid plans tend to make more doctor visits per year than those covered by fee-for-service plans. However, a study conducted by the U.S. Department of Health and Human Services showed that the HMO group had fewer and shorter hospital stays, indicating that an ounce of prevention may well be worth the proverbial pound of cure. In addition, there may be a certain peace of mind in knowing that whatever the ailment, however long the treatment, and no matter what drugs are prescribed, the patient will never have any medical bills over and above the monthly HMO fee.

Alternative Health-Care Systems: Is There a Better Way?

In the 1960s and 1970s there was a tremendous debate over providing health care for everyone. It was fairly clear to all concerned that the major factor restricting access to American health-care institutions could be summed up in one word—money. Many people simply could not afford to be sick, and if they became ill, they did not have the financial resources to buy enough health care to become well again. Some nations, such as the United Kingdom and Sweden, decided to overhaul their health-care delivery systems and institute a program of **socialized medicine.**

Under this plan, many doctors, dentists, and other health-care specialists became government employees. Their salaries were paid by taxes in much the same way that American police, teachers, and civil servants are paid. Anyone in need of their services could obtain them without charge. This system does not provide "free" medical care, because someone has to pay for the resources used by patients. For Sweden and the U.K., this has meant massive governmental intervention in health care: paying bills from tax revenues; setting salaries for physicians, dentists, and other health-care personnel; and establishing regulations about the quality and quantity of care, in addition to deciding who qualifies. The record of socialized medicine has been neither all bad nor all good. As we mentioned previously, the Swedish infant mortality rate is the best in the world—a strong indication of a good medical system. On the other hand, Sweden has a tremendous shortage of dentists, partly because of government interference, and England has had doctor strikes over wages and working conditions. In the United States, there have already been so many complaints and even scandals involving our more-limited Medicare and Medicaid programs that the idea of having the federal government take over the wholesale provisioning of health care seems inconceivable in the next decade. However, there is a program that might be a middle ground between our current health-care system and socialized medicine. It is called national health insurance.

Most people in the United States have some form of health insurance, but a sizable minority do not. Estimates of the number of Americans without health-care coverage run from the Social Security Administration's high of 26 million to the Congressional Budget Office's low of 11 million. This means that the uninsured population represents between 5 and 12 percent of the United States population. Who are these people? Would they, as well as insured citizens, gain from a national health insurance program?

A breakdown of the uninsured population in the United States indicates that people who are young, nonwhite, poor, less educated, or living in rural areas, especially in the South and the West, are more likely to be uninsured. Young adults eighteen to twenty-four are almost twice as likely as any other age group to be

In the long run, habits and lifestyle have a greater impact on an individual's health than does quality of medical care.

without coverage. Although they account for only 11 percent of the total population, they represent 20 percent of those uninsured. Among employed persons, those earning less than $10,000 are most likely to be without coverage, accounting for 55 percent of the unprotected population. Is the institution of some form of government-sponsored national health insurance the best way to insure health-care services for the uninsured? Is it the best way to provide maximum coverage for those who are only partially insured? The answer at this time is not resolved, but it is clear that a national health insurance scheme would be very expensive.

The most comprehensive national health-insurance plan has been put forward by Senator Edward Kennedy. Under his revised plan, introduced in 1979, the entire population would be insured for a wide range of health services that would be provided at no cost to the patient. The cost of the plan for the elderly and the poor would be entirely underwritten by the federal government. Those who are employed would pay no more than 35 percent of their health insurance premiums, and their employers would pay the remainder. Under this revision, workers would be able to choose among insurance agents, Blue Cross–Blue Shield plans, HMOs, and so forth. The cost of this plan is estimated to be $40 billion per year, and given the results of recent political elections, there is little likelihood that it will pass in the near future.

Staying Healthy: The Best Way to Avoid the High Cost of Health Care

Research on the economics of health care has come to a startling conclusion. Habits and lifestyle have a much larger impact on health than the amount of medical care purchased. In other words, if people have good diets, exercise sensibly, and ingest few substances such as alcohol or tobacco, they will be considerably healthier.

There is already some evidence that shows the healthy impact of the movement away from smoking. Figure 14-7 shows the proportion of men and women who smoke tobacco. The precipitous decline in the

Figure 14-7. Percent of adults who smoke, by sex, for 1965, 1974, and 1798.

SOURCE: National Center for Health Statistics, *Health in the United States Chartbook* (Washington, D.C.: U.S. Government Printing Office, 1980).

proportion of men who smoke has already had an important impact on their mortality patterns and in their rate of hospitalization. Women do not show such a marked decrease in cigarette smoking, which has led to an annual age-adjusted increase in lung cancer of 7.7 percent for white women. As one observer noted, "The figures speak for themselves. Insofar as the rate of cancer deaths in this country is rising, the single largest factor is the vast increase in cigarette smoking by white women over the past generation" (Schwartz, 1980, p. 22). If men and women ever reach equality in their smoking, we will probably see a much more equal life expectancy as well.

Regular exercise is another important ingredient in maintaining health. Some of us are fortunate enough to have occupations that fulfill the need to exercise, but most of us are products of the post-industrial revolution—we buy machines or pay other people to do the tasks that require muscle power. We are left with sedentary mental tasks that may pay better but are not really as healthful. One of the most interesting studies done on the impact of occupational

There is no substitute for regular exercise in helping to keep one's body fit and healthy.

exercise on health was a time-series study on the bus drivers and ticket takers working on London's double-decker buses. These men (there were no women) were issued uniforms by the company, and over the years records were kept of their sizes. The ticket takers (called "squirrels") who went up and down the stairs hundreds of times each day stayed slim and healthy. The drivers, because they were sitting most of the time, got heavier with age, and their medical records showed a much higher incidence of heart attacks and other illnesses. Before you begin to quibble with the study on the grounds that the drivers were stressed by London traffic, remember that the "squirrels" had to answer questions, make change, deal with rowdy passengers, and recall who got on at the last stop. That was no easy job, either.

Summary

The health-care industry in the United States is big business. It employs 5 percent of the workforce and costs well over $200 billion every year. It can also be called a growth industry, because it accounts for a larger proportion of the GNP today (9.4 percent) than it did thirty years ago (4.5 percent). But with all this increased activity, there is still some question about its ability to produce adequate health care for all Americans. Certainly, death rates have fallen and life expectancies have risen, but the United States is still not at the forefront in many areas. Our infant mortality rates, for example, are still higher than those of many other developed nations, and our life expectancies are not the highest in the world, either. But there are other factors involved in death rates besides medical care.

Health-care expenditures have risen dramatically in recent years, largely because of inflation within the industry. These inflationary tendencies can be traced to changes in demand and supply. On the demand side, large segments of our population that had previously been excluded from the health-care market were brought in via the Medicare and Medicaid programs. Added to this factor was the increasing use of private insurers as third-party payers. The prevalence of third-party payments led to a decrease in the price consciousness of consumers, because they felt little of the direct cost at the time of treatment. It was only when their insurance premiums rose or their taxes went up that they related the rise in health-care costs to their personal budgets.

Changes in the supply of medical care have also played an important role in the pattern of health-care costs. Early in this century, government licensing restrictions cut the number of medical schools by over 60 percent, with a subsequent decline in the number of physicians and a rise in their average income. Recent government reports say that the United States will have a surplus of doctors by the end of this century, which will boost health-care costs even further. However, there is disagreement over the price effect of increasing the supply of doctors. Training additional health-care personnel, such as physician assistants and nurse-midwives, offers some hope for slowing the rise in costs.

Hospital cost containment is another area in which important strides can be taken to lessen inflation in health-care costs. The establishment of local Health System Agencies and the New Jersey experiment with fixed fees for certain treatments offer some hope in this area, although the basic doctor-hospital relationship makes it difficult for hospitals to avoid buying the latest equipment, even if it is expensive and underutilized.

Prescription drugs have not experienced rapid inflation, partly as a result of the advent of generic drugs. Consumers can save significantly by learning to ask for generic drugs that have been classified by the Food and Drug Administration as therapeutically equivalent to their brand-name competitors.

Most consumers protect themselves against the potentially devastating costs of medical care by buying insurance. Over 1,200 private insurance companies sell insurance, but almost all offer basic and major medical coverage. Basic coverage takes care of ordinary, short-term hospital care and doctors' services. But for broader, long-term coverage consumers need major medical coverage. Disability income insurance is a form of health insurance that provides a cash grant while one is unable to work. Dental-expense insurance is the fastest-growing form of health insurance, but it is difficult to obtain without belonging to a labor union or working for a firm.

Health maintenance organizations offer an alternative to private insurance plans. They often stress preventive care, and according to recent studies, their members spend less time in hospitals than privately insured consumers.

A number of alternative health-care plans have been tried in other nations and have been suggested for trial in the United States. Socialized medicine is practiced in the United Kingdom and Sweden, with mixed results. National health insurance seems to be a more likely plan for the United States, because it requires less government intervention than socialized medicine. But it is unlikely that such a plan could get through Congress in the near future.

The best way to improve your own health is to control what you eat and drink, to exercise frequently, and to avoid smoking. These personal habits are your responsibility, and they tend to affect your health more than your medical expenditures.

1. What would the optimal solution be for someone in Patty and Jimmy's situation? Would foresight be better than hindsight in this situation? How might they have avoided this predicament?

2. Are there other situations in which an HMO might be the best solution? Would a national health insurance plan have made Jimmy and Patty better off? Would it have made Helen better off?

KEY TERMS

basic coverage
community hospitals
deductible
diagnosis related groups (DRGs)
disability income insurance
generic drug
health
health insurance

Health Maintenance Organization (HMO)
Health System Agency (HSA)
hospital expense insurance
hospital indemnity coverage
infant mortality rate
life expectancy
major medical-expense insurance
malpractice suits
Medicaid

Medicare
nurse-midwives
patient package inserts (PPIs)
physician assistants
physician-expense insurance
service benefit insurance
socialized medicine
surgical-expense insurance
waiting period

QUESTIONS

1. How successful has the American health-care industry been in maintaining Americans' health? What evidence could you use to point to the health industry's success? Is there any evidence of failure?

2. List the major causes of the rise in health-care costs in the United States. Of all these factors, which was the most important during the 1970s?

3. How is the average health-care dollar spent? List the types of health expenditures in order of their importance. What proportion of the total do hospital care and physician services take?

4. What is a third-party payment system, and how is it related to the increase in health-care costs?

5. Compare the Medicare and Medicaid programs. How are they funded? Who benefits from them?

6. Have you or anyone in your family ever had nonemergency surgery? Was a second opinion sought? Why? How would you go about seeking a second opinion? Explain.

7. Explain how an increase in the supply of physicians could cause a rise in prices as predicted by the Graduate Medical Advisory Committee. Do you agree with its conclusion? Is there any evidence to contradict its hypothesis?

8. Why does the unique doctor-hospital relationship lead hospitals to buy expensive equipment that is already available and underused at nearby hospitals or to build new wings with additional rooms when other hospitals have high vacancy rates?

9. Is the high cost of hospital care primarily the result of increasing hospital payroll costs?

10. What is a generic drug and how does it benefit consumers?

11. What are the four basic types of health insurance? If you could afford only one, which would it be? Why?

12. What are the characteristics of the typical uninsured consumer? Would socialized medicine or national health insurance benefit uninsured consumers? Who would bear the cost of these programs?

13. Is it a consumer's responsibility to take care of his or her health? How can you improve your health without spending more money? Are there any costs associated with such health improvement?

PROJECTS

1. Write to the American Medical Association, Department of Data Release Services, 535 N. Dearborn Street, Chicago, Illinois 60610 and ask for a computer printout on your family doctor.

2. Is there a Health System Agency (HSA) in your area? If there is, attend one of its meetings and report to the class on the proceedings. Interview one of the board members and find out what he or she has done to help contain health-care costs in your locality.

3. Get two health-insurance policies and compare them. Do they use the service-benefit or the indemnity approach? Is there any form of co-insurance? What are their costs? Which would you recommend for a single person? Would your recommendation differ depending on a person's stage in the life cycle?

4. What are the advantages and limitations of a health maintenance organization? Find out whether there is an HMO in your area. Investigate its facilities and ask questions about benefits and monthly service fees. Can anyone in your area join the plan? Would you like to join? Why?

5. Survey local pharmacies to find the prices of one of the prescription drugs listed in Table 14-4. Are the generics always cheaper than the name brands? Do the results hold between pharmacies as well as among drug groups for a particular pharmacy? Is the price variation among drugstores related to the level of services provided? For example, do some pharmacies provide free delivery? Are some open longer hours? Are some more conveniently located? Compare your results with those found by the Brooklyn College students (see Table 14-5).

6. Alex McMahon, president of the American Hospital Association, was questioned about the use of increasingly expensive technological machines such as kidney dialysis machines that can prolong the life of terminally ill patients for a short period of time. McMahon said, "The patient's attitude is, 'I want the best, and the cost be damned.' People who raise questions about [the cost of] technology are usually healthy" (*Changing Times*, February 1981, p. 32). Do you agree with McMahon that any cost is reasonable if it prolongs human life, even for a short period of time? Take an informal survey of twenty-five people to see whether they agree or disagree with your view. Is there any unanimity on the basis of age group, occupation, or health status of those surveyed? Are the results related to their values?

REFERENCES AND READINGS

"Diet and Heart Disease." *Consumer Reports*, May 1981.

Fuchs, Victor. *Who Shall Live?* New York: Basic Books, 1974.

"Generic Drugs: How Good Are They?" *FDA Consumer*, 1980.

Gibson, Robert M. "National Health Expenditures, 1979." *Health Care Financing Review*, Summer 1980.

Gibson, Robert M., and Daniel R. Waldo. "National Health Expenditures, 1980." *Health Care Financing Review*, September 1981.

Golladay, Fredrick. "Allied Health Manpower Strategies." *Medical Care*, November/December 1973.

"Health Care Dollars and Sense." *Teaching Topics*, Spring 1978.

Health Insurance Institute. *Sourcebook of Health Insurance Data, 1980-81*. Washington, D.C.: Health Insurance Institute, 1981.

"How to Pay Less for Prescription Drugs." *Consumer Reports*, January 1975.

Klarman, Herbert E. *The Economics of Health*. New York: Columbia University Press, 1965.

Larson, Erik. "Hospital Program to Charge by the Ailment." *Wall Street Journal*, November 11, 1980.

Leamer, Laurence E.; Smith, Paul A.; and Bloch, Lawrence W. *Analyzing Health Care Policy: A Resource Guide*. New York: Joint Council on Economic Education, 1977.

"Long Life Can Strain Your Finances." *Changing Times*, August 1980.

"Midwives Hit Doctor's Tactics." *Fresno Bee*, December 21, 1980.

"Must Doctors' Fees Be So High?" *Changing Times*, March 1981.

Newhouse, J. P., and Friedlander, L. J. "The Relationship Between Medical Resources and Measures of Health." *Journal of Human Resources*, Spring 1980.

Romankiewicz, John A. "Don't Take Your Penicillin with Orange Juice." *Redbook*, May 1981.

"Runaway Hospital Bills: What We Can Do." *Changing Times*, February 1981.

Schwartz, Harry. "Looking At The Ways We Die." *Wall Street Journal*, December 9, 1980.

Somers, Herman M. "Economic Issues in Heath Services." In Chamberlain, Neil W. *Contemporary Economic Issues*. Homewood, Ill.: Irwin, 1969.

U.S. Bureau of the Census. *Statistical Abstract of the United States*. Washington, D.C.: U.S. Government Printing Office, 1980.

U.S. Department of Health and Human Services. *Health in the United States Chartbook*. Washington, D.C.: U.S. Government Printing Office, 1980.

U.S. Office of Consumer Affairs. *People Power: What Communities Are Doing to Counter Inflation*. Washington, D.C.: U.S. Government Printing Office, 1980.

van der Gaag, Jacques, and Perlman, Mark. *Health, Economics and Health Economics*. Amsterdam: North-Holland, 1981.

Wiener, Carolyn, et al. "Patient Power: Complex Issues Need Complex Answers." *Social Policy*, September/October 1980.

Did You Know That ...

- there are over 80,000 governments in the United States?

- transfer payments to individuals make up the largest portion of the federal budget?

- taxes are about 20 percent lower in the United States than they are in other developed nations?

- the federal income tax on individual income provides almost half of the federal budget revenues, yet before 1913 the income tax was unconstitutional, and as late as 1939 less than 4 percent of the population had to pay income tax?

- the Economic Recovery Tax Act of 1981 provided the biggest tax cut in American history?

- marginal tax rate is different from average tax rate and is crucial to tax planning?

- there is a simple formula to help one compare an investment that offers a tax-free income with an investment offering a taxable yield?

- there is a marriage tax built into the tax laws?

- you can get a tax credit when you pay someone to care for your child while you work, and the size of this tax credit varies inversely with your income?

- tax evasion is punishable by fine or imprisonment, but the art of tax avoidance is rewarded by lower taxes and more spendable income?

- you can significantly lower the likelihood that your tax return will be audited?

15 Government Services and Taxation: Paying Your Fair Share

The Government: An Overview
Taxation
The Federal Budget and Income Tax
Understanding the Federal Income Tax
The Dreaded Tax Audit
The Overall Tax Burden: Is It Fair?

Neighborhood CAPSULE
One Day in the Life of an American Taxpayer

"Can't you keep those kids quiet?" Dennis yelled as he threw down his pencil and rose from his desk. "How can I work on these tax forms with all this noise? I just can't concentrate."

"Why don't you take a break and have a cup of coffee," his wife remarked, trying to console him. "I'll take the children to the park for a few hours and let you have some peace and quiet."

"Oh, it's not their fault," Dennis mused as he accepted the cup of coffee. "I should have done this long ago. It just always seemed that I could put it off a little longer. But here it is April tenth and I still don't have our return done. You'd think that after doing this stuff every year I would have the procedures memorized."

"How could anyone memorize all those forms, Dennis? I'm just glad I don't have to do it. And I know it's especially hard this year because of our solar water heater. Don't forget to claim that as a deduction."

Dennis's face grew dark. "That's part of the problem. It isn't a deduction. It's a 'tax credit,' whatever that is. And I think we are entitled to get something off our taxes now that you're working and we are paying for childcare. But I'm just not sure how to do this. And I don't think I have all the right forms. Don't you think they should send me *all* the forms? Those IRS people have no mercy. I wish we could just get the government off our backs."

Most consumers are aware of the importance of government both in providing services and in demanding payment for those services. The 1970s and 1980s have seen an increase in this awareness, as consumers fight to get the most from their tax dollars. In this sense, consumers' desire to get the most for their tax dollars is no different from their attempt to get the best clothing or housing for their money. However, unlike purchasing a new coat or a residence, it is difficult to invoke the principles of comparison shopping when paying taxes. One cannot decide to pay more for public hospitals and less for national defense. Our elected officials make these decisions collectively. Nevertheless, consumers are not powerless. They can affect the expenditure process through political action—by voting for those candidates who are closest to consumers' individual positions on various issues and by making their views known to those elected. And just as important, consumers can learn the fundamentals of the tax system and make sure that they are not bearing an unusually large share of the tax burden. An understanding of the tax laws and a conscious effort at tax planning can really pay off for an individual consumer.

We begin this chapter with an overview of two of the major functions of government—providing goods and services and transferring income. Then we move on to the main topic of this chapter—taxation. First we look at the principles of taxation, and then we narrow our focus to the federal income tax. Our purpose here is to help you to understand the most important sections of your income-tax form and to give you some guidance on tax planning as well as in actually preparing the forms. For example, understanding the difference between marginal and average tax rates is essential to weighing the tax consequences of working overtime, taking a second job, or calculating your rate of return on an investment.

Tax laws change frequently, and even the most astute consumer may find it difficult to keep up. As a result, the sections on federal income tax are followed by some advice on how to find a professional tax preparer and what to do if you are called in for a tax audit. We conclude the chapter with a look at the fairness of the overall tax burden and the experience of one state that cut its property taxes by 50 percent in one year.

The Government: An Overview

How often have you heard someone talk about "the government"? In the United States, such a blanket term can have many meanings. There are over 80,000 governments in the United States, ranging from small townships and villages to the massive federal bureaucracy. With such a large collection of agencies exercising varying degrees of control over our lives and money, it is little wonder that many people have the idea that government has grown too big and has become unresponsive to taxpayers' needs. But the functions of government have not changed. It must still provide needed goods and services and transfer income from one group to another. Perhaps the difference is in our perception of the extent of services we are getting for our taxes and the number of people we as a society feel we can support. That perception may be correct, but it may also be the result of our lack of understanding of these government functions. However, an understanding of these functions is basic to an informed consumer's ability to live within the system. Let us start, then, with these functions and move to the more specific everyday realities of taxes and tax paying.

PROVIDING GOODS AND SERVICES

Regardless of how big government seems, almost everyone admits that a society needs a government to maintain order. Without a system of enforceable laws, society would rapidly deteriorate into anarchy, a situation in which "might makes right" and weaker members of society are terrorized by the strong. In order to avoid this, people have established laws to govern their behavior, and they have delegated the administration of these laws and their enforcement to the courts and the police. The resulting social and legal framework is like a giant rulebook. As long as people play by the rules, they can continue to function in society. If they violate these rules, they will be subject to a suitable punishment, which may vary from a small fine for a parking ticket to life imprisonment or even death for a serious crime.

All levels of government—local, state, and federal—participate in the basic law-and-order function. But in addition to ensuring the rule of law, government often provides other goods and services. On the local level, for example, government provides its citizens with fire protection and public schools. At the national level, the federal government maintains the armed forces. There is little debate over the necessity of spending tax dollars on fire protection, public education, and national defense, but there can be a heated debate over how *much* to spend and how to best achieve these ends. In the 1982 federal budget, for example, 25 percent of the expenditures are slated for

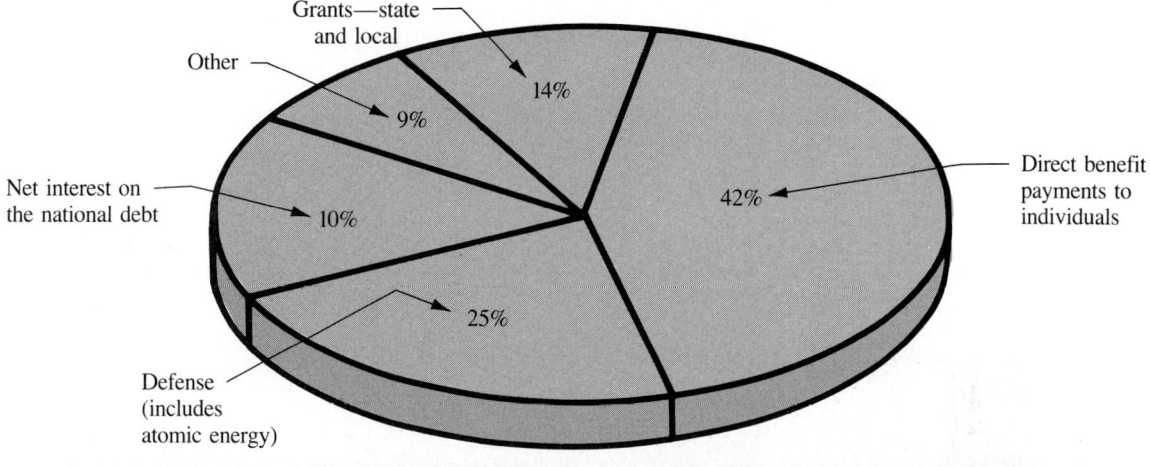

Figure 15-1. 1982 budget. Transfer payments to individuals absorb a greater proportion of the federal budget than any other function. Providing national defense takes a quarter of the budget, with grants to other governmental units, interest payments on the national debt, and the normal expenses of running a national government taking the rest.

national defense. Is this too much or too little?

Justice, fire protection, public education, and national defense are examples of what economists call **public goods.** A public good is a good or a service that the business sector would not produce in sufficient quantities, even though society as a whole would benefit. Why won't private firms produce an ample supply of public goods? The answer is simple: There is not enough profit in it. Imagine the difficulty a company would have in trying to provide national defense and selling it to its customers. Many people would refuse to pay, yet they would still be protected once the public good was produced. In other words, the company could not count on a payoff from all those who used the good. This problem of not being able to exclude the nonpaying public is sometimes called the **free-rider effect.** In essence, the nonpaying public gets a free ride, because it gets the service without paying for it. It is as if a company produced bread but only got paid for every tenth loaf, because they didn't control the distribution of bread. Whenever the free-rider effect is important, you can be sure that the private sector will either underproduce the good or not produce it at all.

In most cases, public goods must be provided by the government if they are to be produced at the required level. Private enterprise is simply not geared to providing such important services as national defense, lighthouses, and public parks, for which it is difficult to make all beneficiaries pay. Government can use its power to tax and thus can both provide goods and require the citizenry to pay for them. This is an important function of government and one that accounts for a significant share of total government expenditures.

TRANSFERRING INCOME

Aside from providing certain goods and services, another major task of government is to oversee **transfer payments**—unearned payments made to individuals for social reasons. Transfer payments can take the form of direct money payments, such as those for Social Security or veterans benefits, or they can be in-kind subsidies such as food stamps, public housing, or free medical care. Whatever their form, they contribute the largest proportion of the federal budget—42 percent in 1982 (see Figure 15-1). The programs that are composed exclusively of transfer

Figure 15-2. Federal government payments to individuals.

payments are called **entitlement programs.** This name is applied because Congress has said that certain groups are *entitled* to government transfer payments. As Figure 15-2 shows, government transfer payments have tripled since 1974. The reason for this growth has been Congressional legislation that has increased coverage of various social programs in addition to increasing the size of the individual payment and, in some cases (as we explained in Chapter 7), indexing the payments to the inflation rate.

The government controls transfer payments for a different reason than the one for which it oversees public goods. The free-rider problem does not apply here. The reason for transfer payments lies in our free-market economy. In a pure market economy, everyone is supposed to earn income by working. Some earn more than others by being more productive. But if for some reason, such as age, infirmity, or disability, a person cannot work, the system will not reward him or her with income. In the past, such unfortunate citizens had to depend on private charity, but in this century Americans decided that government should see that the truly needy have at least some income. Government, therefore, collects money from the income-earning members of society and transfers it to the needy. Taxes do not have to be used for transfer payments, but doing so is a political decision that most consumers accept in principle, even though they may disagree about how much should be spent or who should get it.

Taxation

Justice Oliver Wendell Holmes once said that taxation is the price we pay for civilization. There is more than a grain of truth in this observation, because we cannot maintain our society without a government, and we cannot maintain our government without the income it gets from taxation. But are we paying more than is

Figure 15-3. The tax burden in developed nations (taxes as a percent of GNP).

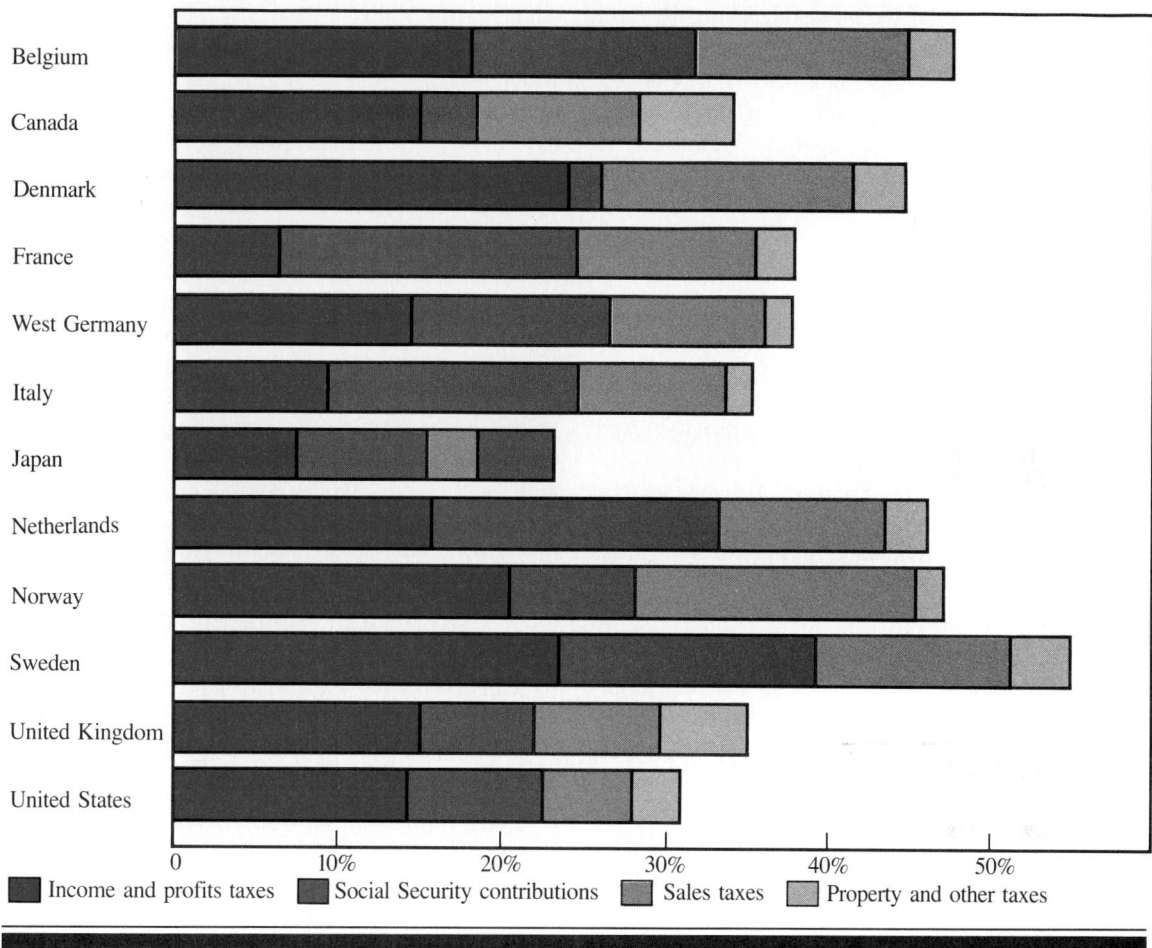

reasonable or just? According to the Tax Foundation, the average American works for two hours and thirty-nine minutes of each working day to pay for taxes. Of that, one hour and forty-one minutes goes to Uncle Sam; the rest pays state and local taxes. Is that too much?

Figure 15-3 gives some perspective on Americans' tax burden relative to that of other nations. The Organization for Economic Cooperation and Development (OECD), an association of some of the most highly developed nations in the world, collected the data. According to the OECD, the United States' tax burden is well below that of most other industrialized countries. Total taxes were a little over 30 percent of total output (Gross National Product) in the United States, whereas taxes averaged over 36 percent of output in the other nations. Japan is the only nation in the survey with a tax burden lower than that of the United States. In Sweden, the leader in this category, tax collections averaged over 50 percent of its Gross National Product; thus, in Sweden a typical taxpayer works for over half a day just to pay his or her taxes.

Compared to citizens of other developed nations, Americans do not appear to be overtaxed. However, we should point out that all taxes are not alike, and in nations with high tax rates, such as Sweden, government services are also more abundant. By focusing on the overall tax burden, we are also ignoring the types of taxes and the manner in which they are collected. In some nations, taxes are more heavily weighted toward personal income; in others, sales taxes and property taxes may be more important. To understand how taxation works, then, we need to know more about the basic principles behind it.

THE PRINCIPLES OF TAXATION

There are two basic views about deciding who should bear the burden of taxation. One school of thought argues that taxes should be levied on the **benefits-received principle.** This is a fairly straightforward approach that argues that because taxes provide goods and services, the households and firms that receive these benefits should pay for them. Because many government expenditures produce public goods such as national defense, highways, and parks, it is sometimes difficult to apply this theory. Nevertheless, we do have some taxes based on this principle. The gasoline tax, for example, is typically earmarked for financing road construction and maintenance. The assumption is that those who use the highways should pay for them when they buy gasoline and other petroleum products. Automobile- and truck-licensing fees may also be classified as benefits-received taxes, because the owners of these vehicles have the right to use them on public highways. Even a public good such as a lighthouse could be financed on a benefits-received principle if the cost of the lighthouse were paid out of a boat license fund. But for many public goods and for most transfer payments, the benefits-received principle cannot apply. How could welfare recipients pay for their benefits when they have little or no income?

Another approach to taxation is called the **ability-to-pay principle.** The idea here is that the burden of taxation should fall most heavily on the members of society who are most able to pay. In other words, citizens who have more income or greater wealth should be asked to pay a larger share of the cost of government.

There is a certain appeal to asking the better-off members of society to pay more for government. A $1000 tax payment would not burden a household earning $100,000 per year as much as it would burden a household earning $10,000. A share-the-wealth idea underlies the ability-to-pay principle.

The economic concept of **diminishing marginal utility** has also been used to support levying higher taxes on the rich. In this context, diminishing marginal utility refers to the fact that at low levels of income, households buy goods and services that are essential and are thus more useful (have the most utility). At higher levels of income, consumers spend their dollars first on essentials and then more and more on less-urgently needed goods or even on luxuries. The higher the income, then, the less usefulness or utility is achieved from the last dollar spent. If marginal utilities can be compared among households (and not all economists agree that they can be),* the last dollar spent by a household earning $100,000 will result in a smaller increase in utility than the last dollar spent by a household earning only $10,000. If this is true, then in order for all households to sacrifice equally, those with higher incomes must pay more money in taxes, because an equal dollar contribution would mean that the lower-income group would sacrifice more than its share.

Neither the ability-to-pay principle nor its corollary, the equal-sacrifice principle, gives us a guideline as to how much more higher-income groups should pay. If a tax rate were so high that no household was able to keep a portion of its increased income over some minimal amount, the tax system could destroy the incentive to work. In this case, tax rates would become **confiscatory tax rates**—all additional income would be confiscated, and as a result, the economic incentives to work more and thus earn more money would break down. Obviously, this can lead to chaos in the economy.

PROGRESSIVE, PROPORTIONAL, AND REGRESSIVE TAXES

Now that you understand something about the benefit and ability-to-pay principles of taxation, you are

---

*The argument against using the diminshing marginal utility concept in support of levying higher taxes on people with higher income hinges on one's inability to make objective interpersonal utility comparisons. So, although no one denies that the last $1000 spent brings less utility than the first $1000 spent, there is no way to prove conclusively that the last $1000 that a millionaire spends brings him or her less satisfaction than the first $1000 spent by a poor person, because one cannot objectively measure "utility" for purposes of comparison between two people.

Table 15-1. An Example of How a Progressive Income Tax Works

Taxable income bracket	Bracket tax rate (marginal tax rate)	Tax owed on bracket Income	Total tax owed on all income	Average tax rate
$2000 or less	0%	$ 0	$ 0	0%
$2001 to $3000	5%	$ 50	$ 50	1.67%
$3001 to $4000	10%	$100	$150	3.75%
$4001 to $5000	20%	$200	$350	7.00%
$5001 to $6000	30%	$300	$650	10.83%

ready to look at three basic types of taxes that are all classified by their relationship to household income: progressive taxes, proportional taxes, and regressive taxes.

Progressive Tax. Classifying the relationship between tax rates and household income is one of the most common ways to classify taxes. If a form of taxation takes a larger and larger fraction of a household's income as the family's income rises, it is called **progressive taxation.** Those who believe strongly in the ability-to-pay principle generally support the idea of a progressive tax. The federal income tax is the most well-known example of a progressive tax, although many states have progressive taxation, too. In this scheme, high-income people pay more, both in absolute dollar amounts *and* in percentage. For example, a tax that takes $2000 from a family that earns $20,000 and $10,000 from a family that earns $50,000 is a progressive tax, because it takes a larger proportion (20 percent) from the higher-income family than from the lower-income family.

Understanding the structure of a progressive tax is especially important in planning one's personal tax burden. Table 15-1 shows how a progressive income tax works. Taxpayers with different levels of income fall into different **income brackets.** According to the table, a person earning $4000 would be subject to a 10 percent **marginal tax rate,** sometimes loosely referred to as the "10 percent bracket." This does *not* mean that all of the $4000 is subject to a 10 percent tax. Only the income from $3001 to $4000 is subject to the 10 percent rate; income in the $2001 to $3000 bracket is taxed at 5 percent, and the first $2000 is not taxed at all. Thus, someone with a $4000 income would owe a total $150 in taxes ($0 on the first $2000 plus $50 on the next $1000 plus $100 on the last $1000). This is a progressive tax, because higher income brackets have higher taxes levied against them (see Figure 15-4).

The **average tax rate** is computed by dividing the total tax owed by total income earned. If someone earned $4000 and was subject to the marginal tax rates for each income bracket listed in Table 15-1, his or her average tax rate would be $150 divided by $4000, or 3.75 percent. Notice that in a progressive tax system, the average tax rate and the marginal tax rate both increase as incomes rise, but they are not equal to each other. The marginal tax rate applies only to a certain range of income, whereas the average rate is a general tax rate for total income. The relevant rate to consider in tax planning is the marginal, not the average, because if a taxpayer is able to lower his or her taxable income, it is always the reduction from the last dollar earned that is calculated. Thus, if someone earning $4000 is able to reduce his or her income subject to tax by $100, he or she lowers personal taxes owed by $10 (marginal tax rate × income reduction = .10 × $100). In this case, taxable income would equal only $3900 and total tax owed would be $140. We will return to these concepts in more detail when we discuss federal income tax.

Proportional Tax. **Proportional taxation** takes the same proportion of a household's income, regardless of the income level. When an income tax is propor-

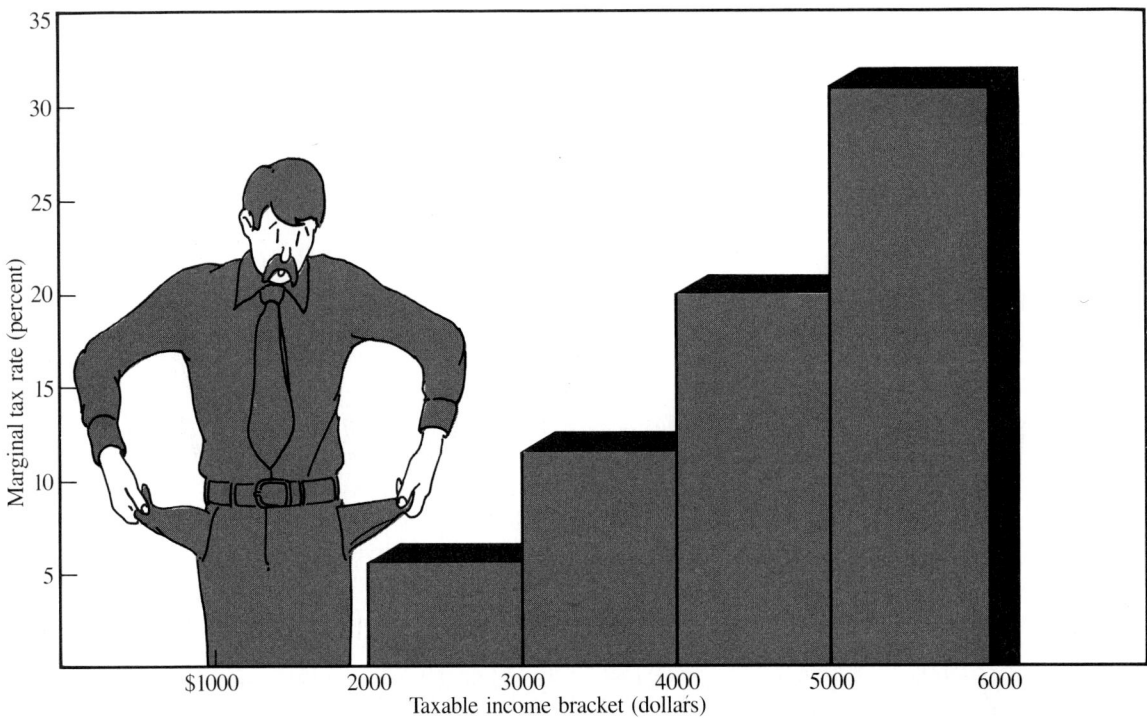

Figure 15-4. The structure of a progressive income tax.

tional, more money is taken away from higher-income groups, but the percentage of income taxed is equal for all households. Thus, if two families earn incomes of $20,000 and $50,000, respectively, per year, under a proportional income tax they would pay different amounts in taxes ($2000 and $5000, respectively), but the same proportion—10 percent. Milton Friedman, a Nobel Prize-winning economist, has suggested that the proportional tax is a more equitable and efficient way to tax income than our current progressive income tax. He argues that a proportional tax with virtually no deductions or loopholes could generate the same revenue as the progressive tax, and at lower rates, because the system would be so simple. If you can imagine a single-page tax form on which the only entries are questions about how much income you have earned, a box indicating the percent of taxation, and a line indicating how much tax is owed, you can understand the simplicity of the proposal. But because of the political and economic implications of a strictly proportional, no-deductions-allowed tax form, it faces an uphill battle in Congress. Nevertheless, a variation of the proportional tax, called the **flat tax,** has been gathering support. Recent research indicates that a flat tax of 19 percent on business and individual income could replace the current range of income rates and generate the same revenue if most tax deductions were abolished (Hall and Rabushka, 1981).

Regressive Tax. If a progressive tax takes a higher percentage of income as income rises, then a **regressive tax** is one that takes a lower percentage of income as income rises. Before you jump to the conclusion that a regressive tax is preferable because its impact declines as income rises, remember that the reverse is also true. A regressive tax takes a *larger* proportion of household income as income declines.

Figure 15-5. Federal budget revenues, 1982.

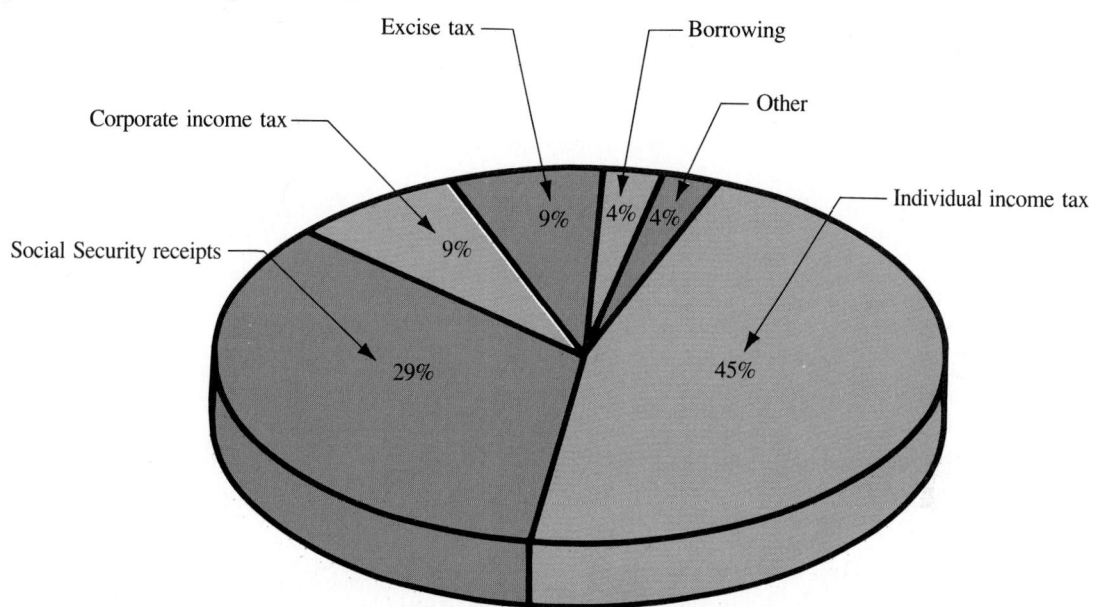

According to the ability-to-pay principle, the regressive tax is the least-preferred tax, because it places a disproportionate burden on the poorer segments of a community.

Examples of regressive taxes abound in most communities. Any tax that is not specifically indexed to a household's income level is a candidate for the regressive label. Take the almost universal state sales tax. In 1980, thirty states taxed consumer food purchases. A 3 percent tax on food sales might seem to be a proportional tax, because all consumers pay the same rate when buying food. However, the relevant rate is not the stated percentage of the sale item but the percentage of a household's income used to pay the tax. In the case of food, low-income families spend a much higher proportion of their budgets for this item. According to the Bureau of Labor Statistics, low-income families spend 22 percent of their incomes on food, whereas high-income families spend only 7 percent. Thus, a 3 percent food tax would be levied on 22 percent of a poor family's income but on only 7 percent of a well-to-do family's income. The Social Security tax is also a regressive tax, because there is a limit on the amount of income subject to this tax. A family earning less than $31,800 in 1982 paid 6.7 percent of its income in Social Security tax, but any amount over $31,800 was not subject to the tax. If a person earned $60,000, the average Social Security tax rate would have been only 3.55 percent, because about half of the income would not have been subject to any Social Security taxes.

The Federal Budget and Income Tax

In the last section we introduced the principles of taxation and the various classes of taxes. You now know the difference between regressive, proportional, and progressive taxes, and you have some idea of how a progressive tax structure works. In this section, we focus on federal taxes and apply some of the concepts learned in the previous sections. At the conclusion of this section you should know how the federal income tax works and should be ready to proceed to the next section, filling out income tax forms.

Figure 15-5 illustrates the federal government's revenues for fiscal year 1982. Individual income-tax receipts account for 45 cents of every federal tax dol-

> **BOX 15-1**
>
> ## Additional Federal Taxes
>
> Although the income tax is the most important federal tax, Americans are subject to a host of other federal taxes. Here is a partial list. Would you classify them as progressive, regressive, or proportional?*
>
> | Tax | Rate |
> |---|---|
> | Estate tax | 18% to 65% of taxable estate (after 1981) |
> | Social Security tax | 6.7% of wages up to $32,400 on both employer and employee |
> | Corporate income tax (1982) | 16% to 46% of taxable income |
> | Excise taxes (charged to manufacturers and passed on to consumers) | |
> | Tires (for use on highway) | 10 cents per pound (5 cents as of October 1, 1984) |
> | Fishing equipment | 10% of manufacturer's price |
> | Firearms, shells, etc. | 11% of manufacturer's price |
> | Airplane tickets | 5% of amount paid on domestic flights |
> | Diesel fuel and special motor fuels | 4¢ per gallon |
> | Lubrication oil (for use in highway vehicles) | 6 cents per gallon |
> | Alcohol | $10.50 per gallon |
> | Beer | $9 per barrel (31 gallons) |
> | Wine (still) | 17 cents to $10.50 per gallon, depending on alcohol content |
> | Wine (sparkling) | $3.40 per gallon |
> | Wine (carbonated) | $2.40 per gallon |
> | Cigarettes | $4 to $8.40 per thousand |
> | Cigars | 75 cents to $20 per thousand |
>
> *These taxes are as of 1982 and are subject to revision from year to year.
>
> SOURCE: Prentice-Hall. *Federal Tax Handbook 1982*, issued annually.

lar collected. An additional 29 cents is collected in the form of the Social Security payroll tax, with the remainder coming from corporate income taxes (9 cents), excise taxes, such as specific taxes on tires, firearms, and air travel (see Box 15-1), and public borrowing, which increases the national debt (4 cents). The federal income tax is obviously the most important source of revenue, although Social Security tax receipts are also important. The burden of these taxes falls on the consumer.

In 1982, the average taxpayer paid the government over $2200 in income taxes and another $1100 in Social Security contributions. Anytime you spend over $3000, you should take some time to evaluate your choices. Obviously, taxes are a necessity, because we could not have a civilized society without them. Nevertheless, it makes good sense to try to limit your tax liability by developing good decision-making habits. This means calculating the tax impact of just about every major decision you make before you make it. Given the fact that income tax is progressive as you work and earn more, your income is taxed at a higher rate. But the higher your tax bracket, the more the incentive (greater payoff) you have to finding ways to reduce taxable income by looking for legitimate loopholes. This is especially true for federal income tax.

FEDERAL INCOME TAX

In 1980, more than 133 million federal tax returns were filed by almost 60 percent of Americans. The rules on filing are fairly explicit, as Figure 15-6 dem-

Figure 15-6. Who must file an income tax return? Follow the arrows to find out whether you must file a federal income tax return. By answering "yes" or "no" to each question in turn and following the arrow to the next box, you will be led to one of two final boxes: "File a return by the due date" or "You do not have to file a return."

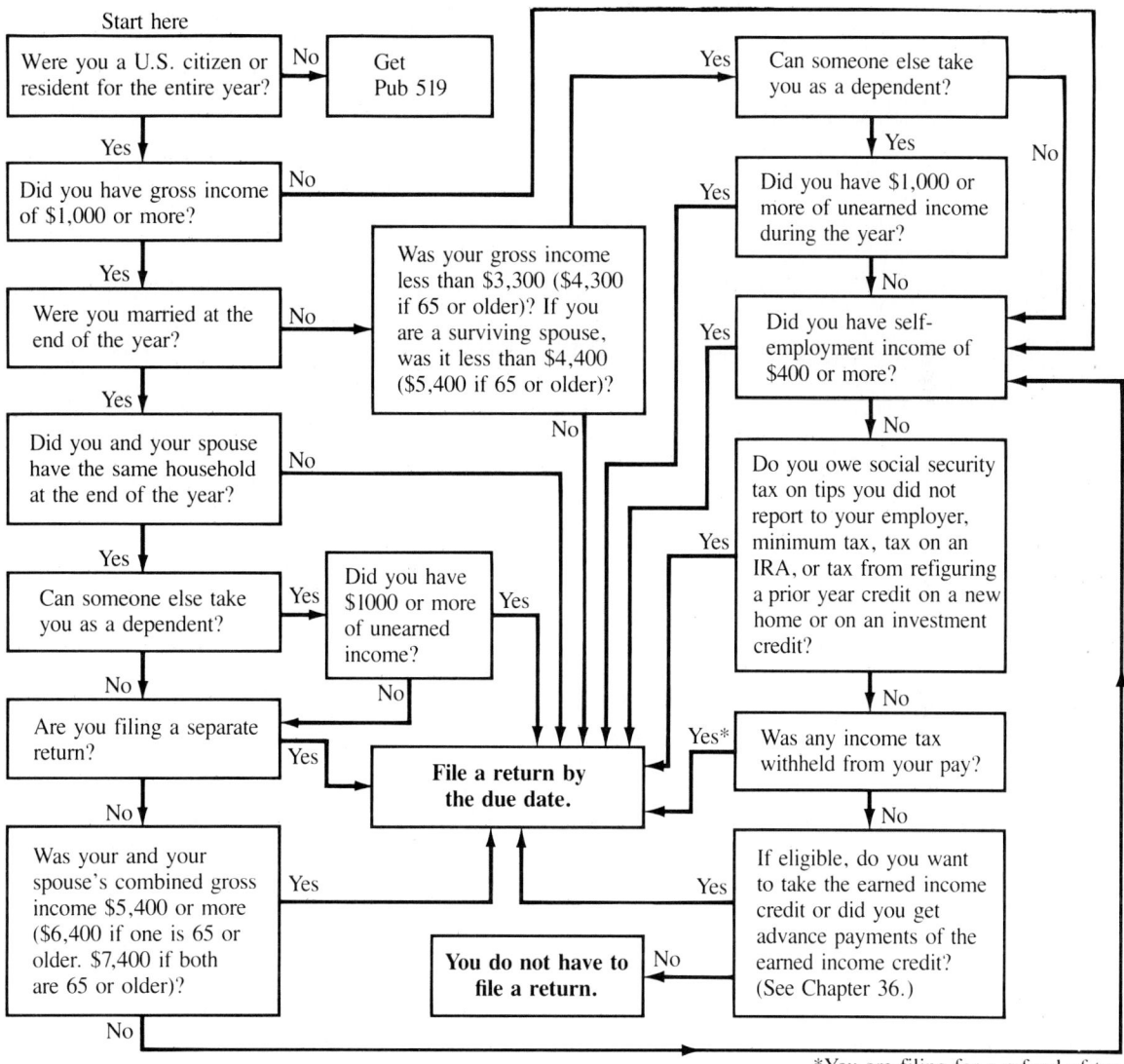

SOURCE: Internal Revenue Service, *Your Federal Income Tax*. (Washington, D.C.: U.S. Government Printing Office, 1982).

onstrates. The fact that almost every adult is required to make a report to the Internal Revenue Service has made the April 15 deadline for filing almost as well known as July 4. It may surprise you to learn that this was not always the case. As late as 1939, fewer than 5 million Americans (about 4 percent of the population)

BOX 15-2
The Economic Recovery Tax Act of 1981 and Supply-Side Economics

President Reagan's tax package, which became law in 1981, was one of the most sweeping pieces of tax legislation ever devised. It provides for a 25 percent cut in personal income taxes to be phased in over a three-year period ending July 1983. As of January 1, 1982, the highest tax rate on nonwage income was slashed from 70 percent to 50 percent. And after 1985, all tax brackets will be indexed for inflation, so that taxes will not rise just because incomes rise with inflation. Thus, in order to move into a higher bracket, a taxpayer's income will have to rise faster than the government's measure of inflation.

The 1981 Tax Act contains more provisions, but almost all of them are a product of an economic philosophy called **supply-side economics.** Supply-side economics stresses the importance of increasing production by using tax incentives to encourage savings, investment, and work effort. Supply-siders such as economist Arthur Laffer of the University of Southern California argue that high tax rates discourage work effort and investment by taking away too large a portion of workers', savers', and investors' incomes. Professor Laffer even argues that the disincentives from taxation can be so strong that they reduce government revenues. He drew the Laffer Curve to illustrate his point. The curve shows the relationship between tax rates and tax revenues. If tax rates are zero, obviously revenues will also be zero. And as tax rates rise, tax revenues also rise, up to point B. But if tax rates rise higher than B, the curve bends backward, indicating that smaller government tax revenues are associated with higher and higher taxes. Why would higher tax rates bring in less revenue? According to the supply-side economists, the reason is that at some point people decide that the income they get to keep after they pay their taxes is not enough reward for them to work or save or invest. For example, laborers refuse to work overtime, savers decide to spend their money rather than putting it in the bank and paying tax on the interest, and businesses decide not to expand their plants, because increased profits would mean higher taxes. In addition, higher taxes make it more tempting to hide income or cheat on tax forms. As tax evasion becomes more commonplace, it is more difficult to catch, and tax revenues fall. The solution, according to supply-side theory, is to lower tax rates. This can move the economy from point C to point B and can increase tax revenues by giving people a greater incentive to work, save, and invest. As laborers begin to work overtime again, as the number of two-income families begins to grow, as savers begin taking advantage of their tax breaks, and as businesses begin to earn tax credits with new investments, the gross national product will rise and government will automatically get more revenue, because incomes in general are rising. This is the principle behind the 1981 tax bill—the largest tax cut in the history of the United States.

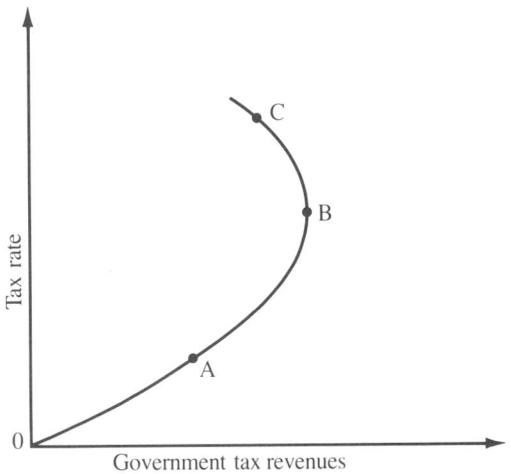

had to worry about filing tax returns. In fact, it took the passage of the Sixteenth Amendment to the Constitution (1913) to make the federal income tax legal. Before that, the Supreme Court had ruled that the federal government could not levy an income tax.

The early federal income tax forms were models of simplicity. There was a generous exemption for all families, so very few had to concern themselves with filling out the form. And the rates were low, varying from 1 percent to a top rate of 6 percent. Today, the

Table 15-2. 1983 Federal Personal Income Tax Rates For Single Taxpayers

Taxable income bracket	Marginal tax rate for each bracket (percent)	Tax owed on bracket income	Total tax owed	Average tax rate (percent)
$ 2,300 or less	0%	$ 0	$ 0	0%
2,301– 3,400	11	121	121	3.5
3,401– 4,400	13	130	251	5.7
4,401– 6,500	15	315	566	8.7
6,501– 8,500	15	300	866	10.19
8,501–10,800	17	391	1,257	11.6
10,801–12,900	19	399	1,656	12.8
12,901–15,000	21	441	2,097	14.0
15,001–18,200	24	768	2,865	15.7
18,201–23,500	28	1,484	4,349	18.5
23,501–28,800	32	1,696	6,045	21.0
28,801–34,100	36	1,908	7,953	23.0
34,101–41,500	40	2,960	10,913	26.3
41,501–55,300	45	6,210	17,123	31.0
Over 55,300	50	—	17,123 + 50% of additional income.	

tax schedule begins at 14 percent and reaches a maximum rate of 50 percent, although before the Economic Recovery Tax Act of 1981, income-tax rates on unearned income, such as on interest or savings accounts, stock dividends, and even on royalties from textbooks, reached as high as 70 percent (see Box 15-2). And tax forms are mailed to almost everyone. If you need additional forms, you usually have only to go to your local post office or bank to get them.

MARGINAL AND AVERAGE TAX RATES

As we mentioned earlier, the federal income tax is a progressive tax, because it takes a greater proportion of income as income rises. Different tax rates are applied to different levels of income. Table 15-2, based on 1983 tax rates for single taxpayers, shows that earned income between $2301 and $3400 is taxed at an 11 percent rate, whereas income between $3401 and $4400 is taxed at a 13 percent rate. The tax rate that applies to the last dollar one earns during the year is the marginal tax rate. As we noted earlier, the marginal tax rate should not be confused with the average tax rate, which is the proportion of total income that goes for taxes. The marginal rate applies only to the income in a specific bracket. According to Table 15-2, taxpayers who have taxable incomes of $15,000 are paying a 21 percent marginal tax rate only on income in the $12,901 to $15,000 bracket. On lower-bracketed income, they pay anywhere from 0 to 19 percent marginal rates. Thus, the average tax rate for a single person earning $15,000 is only 14.0 percent ($2097 ÷ 15,000)—considerably less than would be owed if the highest marginal rate applied to all brackets.

Why should one be concerned with the difference between average and marginal tax rates? At low levels of income, this knowledge is sometimes not very useful. But at higher levels of income, knowing the marginal rate can help one to decide how much of certain expenditures will be paid by the government. For example, if you have $20,000 in taxable income, a $1000 Christmas donation to your church will *not* cost you $1000. Why? Because you can deduct that contribution from your taxable income, thereby reducing the amount of money you owe taxes on. If Table 15-2 were the relevant tax table for you, a $1000 reduction in taxable income would result in a tax reduction of $280 (.28 × $1000). In effect, you would pay only $720 and the government would pick up the rest. This type of tax saving can be important if you are in a higher marginal tax bracket and can itemize your deductions.

At other times, knowing the marginal tax rate will be important in deciding where to put money. For example, suppose that you could earn a 12 percent taxable return by putting your money in a money-market fund or that you could earn a 9 percent return by putting your money in tax-free municipal bonds. Which gives you a better return? A $10,000 investment at 12 percent earns $1200 per year, whereas the same investment earns only $900 at 9 percent. But what proportion of that $1200 will be taken by taxes? To find out, you must know the marginal tax rate. If your taxable income is $20,000, your marginal tax rate is 28 percent, which means that you only get to keep 72 cents of each dollar in interest from your money-market fund. Your $1200 return is reduced to $864 after taxes. Thus, a 9 percent tax-free yield brings you $36 more ($900 − $864) than the taxable 12 percent return. For additional information on how to calculate this, see Box 15-3.

Another interesting facet of the progressive income tax is its relationship to inflation and government tax revenues. Inflation and the rise in consumers' incomes can push taxpayers into higher tax brackets and make them liable for increases in taxes, even though their real incomes (adjusted for the rise in prices) have not risen. Tax inflation has been a bone of contention between the government and taxpayers for some time. We discussed this two-way squeeze in Chapter 7; we discuss it again here to remind you of some of the drawbacks of progressive taxation. Some states, such as California, for example, have already indexed their tax brackets to limit the impact of inflation. The Economic Recovery Tax Act of 1981 provides for indexing the federal income tax after 1985. Once indexed, the tax brackets associated with a specific marginal tax rate are raised every year so that taxpayers are not taxed at a higher rate just because their incomes have kept pace with inflation. If Table 15-2 were indexed for inflation and if we experience an average annual inflation rate of 10 percent, all brackets would be raised by 10 percent, but the marginal tax rates would remain unchanged. This would mean that a single taxpayer could earn $2530 and still

---

BOX 15-3
What Is Tax-Free Income Worth to You?

As we have stressed, knowing and understanding your marginal tax rate can be crucial to good decision making. Often you will see or hear about tax-free investments. Generally, these investments offer smaller **yields**—rates of return on your money. But they may give you more after-tax dollars than investments that give you a higher return that you must share with the Internal Revenue Service. The following formula can be used to calculate whether a tax-free investment gives a better return than a taxable investment:

$$\frac{\text{tax-free yield}}{(1 - \text{marginal tax rate})} = \text{equivalent taxable yield}$$

For example, if a tax-free certificate offers 9 percent return and your marginal tax rate is 40 percent, you are getting the equivalent of a 15 percent taxable yield:

$$\frac{9 \text{ percent}}{(1 - .40)} = \frac{9 \text{ percent}}{.60} = 15 \text{ percent}$$

If you know the taxable yield and want to calculate the tax-free yield, simply subtract your marginal tax rate from one and multiply the answer by the taxable yield. The formula is:

$$(1 - \text{marginal tax rate}) \times \text{taxable yield} = \text{tax-free yield}$$

For example, someone with a 24 percent marginal tax rate who is considering an investment with a taxable yield of 10 percent would really only earn the equivalent of 7.6 percent after taxes:

$$(1 - .24) \times 10 \text{ percent} = .76 \times 10 \text{ percent} = 7.6 \text{ percent}$$

pay no taxes, because the current $2300 minimum bracket would be raised 10 percent to account for inflation. All other brackets would also be lifted by 10 percent, and the government would not get its windfall revenue increase.

Understanding the Federal Income Tax

Contrary to popular belief, the Internal Revenue Service is not trying to rob you blind. Its job is to enforce the tax laws so that the federal government receives enough money for its budget to provide the goods, services, and income transfers mandated by Congress. Congress, as the source of all federal tax law, is very aware that we do not like to pay taxes and can pay only so much. It does not want to strangle the taxpayers. It also knows that changes in the tax law can encourage certain behaviors and discourage others. Congress often tries to use taxes as policy tools as well as revenue makers. By being aware of tax laws, consumers can save money by taking advantage of Congressionally approved tax incentives.

Congress maintains some slack in the tax noose for many reasons. Some taxpayer expenditures, such as business or employment expenses, are given special treatment because they are seen as necessary costs of doing business and thus create income that will eventually be taxed. Other taxpayer expenditures, such as payments for medical care, alimony, and casualty losses, are tax deductible because they may involve financial hardship to the taxpayer (although alimony is taxable for the recipient). Still other tax provisions, such as tax incentives to encourage consumers to insulate their homes, may be included to encourage certain kinds of behavior. Finally, the tax laws have general provisions that allow all consumers to keep a certain amount of tax-free income, based on the size of the household or on special circumstances such as blindness.

It should be clear by now that not every dollar one earns during the year is subject to income tax. The income earned from wages, interest, rents, dividends, or other sources may not be part of **taxable income**—the income that is subject to federal income tax. In the following sections, we will outline in some detail the various forms of exclusions, deductions, exemptions, and tax credits that can and will reduce

Table 15-3. A Basic Outline for Calculating Income Tax

Your income
− Exclusions

Gross income
− Deductions (adjustments to income)

Adjusted gross income
− Zero bracket amount or excess itemized deductions

Income before exemptions
− Exemptions

Taxable income
× Tax rates from tax table

Tax from tax table
− Tax credits

Taxes due

your taxes. Understanding how the tax system works can lead to big savings if this understanding is coupled with good planning and decision making. Given the wide range of taxation, you need to anticipate the tax implications of every major decision you make, from buying a car to taking a vacation to insulating your home or getting your teeth fixed. And as your income rises, so does the value of tax planning. Knowledge and tax-planning strategies learned now will pay dividends now and even larger dividends in the future.

AN OVERVIEW OF TAX CALCULATIONS

Our objective in this section is to give a brief summary of what is involved in calculating the amount of federal income tax you owe, based on the amount of money you earn in a given year. Table 15-3 outlines all the steps we will be discussing. Some of the forbidding and unfamiliar words and phrases, such as "exclusions," "zero-bracket amount," and "adjusted gross income," may give many students an almost uncontrollable urge to shut their books at this

Psychiatric care is a legitimate tax deduction under the category of medical expenses.

point. For other students, the words on the page may begin to blur and run together. Do not be discouraged. No one expects you to look at Table 15-3 and instantly understand how the tax system works. Could someone from Mars know what a human being from Earth looks like if the only clue was a human skeleton? A skeleton is an important part of the body, but we must put some flesh on those bones for aliens to get some idea about what humans look like. The same is true for our tax system. Table 15-3 presents the skeleton; the following sections supply the definitions and the examples to fill it out. But you may find it handy to refer back to this table after you have read each section, in order to see how the pieces fit together.

At the conclusion of these sections you should review and understand the following terms:
exclusions
deductions
zero-bracket amount
exemption
taxable income
tax credit

We begin our analysis with exclusions.

EXCLUSIONS

As we mentioned earlier, not every dollar that a household receives is considered income. Certain forms of income are excluded from federal income taxation, and they are called **exclusions.** For example, all Social Security benefits are excluded from **gross income**—the income, minus exclusions, on which federal income tax is computed. The first $100 of stock dividends on an individual tax return or the first $200 on a joint return is another example of an exclusion. Interest on all-saver savings certificates is also excluded up to $1000 for an individual and up to $2000 for a joint return. Even a federal income tax refund (but not a state refund) is excluded from gross income. Exclusions come and go depending on the mood of Congress. To get a complete list of the exclusions and other tax rules applicable to the current tax year, get a free copy of Internal Revenue Service Publication 17, *Your Federal Income Tax—For Individuals*.

Look at Table 15-3 again. Once you have determined all of your exclusions, you are ready to report your gross income, which includes all income that is not specifically subject to exclusions. From here on, the only way to legally reduce your tax liability is through deductions, exemptions, or tax credits.

DEDUCTIONS

Deductions are specific taxpayer expenses that may be subtracted from gross income or adjusted gross income before going on to calculate taxable income. Those deductions that are subtracted directly from gross income are called adjustments to income, and they are often related to employment. Travel and moving expenses related to changing jobs, business entertainment, and depreciation on property used in one's business are three of the most important categories. However, there are other deductions that are unrelated to employment, such as alimony and interest penalties paid on early withdrawal from a savings account. If you qualify for any of these deductions, the only way to receive them is to file for them specifically.

Other deductions apply to all individual taxpayers, and they are subtracted from the adjusted gross income. The government realizes that all households spend a portion of their income for goods and services that are legally deductible under the tax laws. As a result, they automatically build some level of itemized deductions into the tax tables. In essence, they estimate your deductions for you. This built-in level of deductions is called the **zero-bracket amount,** or ZBA. In 1980, there were three zero-bracket amounts, each linked to filing status:

Filing status	Zero-bracket amount
Married, filing jointly	$3400
Single or head of household	$2300
Married, filing separately	$1700

It is interesting to note that a single person gives up a portion of the zero-bracket amount when he or she gets married. As single wage earners, people are entitled to take a $2300 ZBA, but once they marry, their combined ZBA cannot exceed $3400, regardless of whether they file jointly or separately. This is part of the so-called marriage tax discussed in Box 15-4.

Many taxpayers' itemized deductions exceed their ZBA. For them, the logical course of action is to file for the amount of itemized deductions they are entitled to. However, this means an increased burden in terms of recordkeeping and tax planning. It also means that taxpayers will have to use tax form 1040 (sometimes called the long form) rather than tax form 1040A (the short form).

The decision to use the long form rather than the short form is a voluntary one, but you should not make it until you have some idea about which expenditures are deductible. The Internal Revenue Service lists seven general categories of deductible expenditures:

1. Medical and dental expense.
2. Taxes.
3. Interest deductions.
4. Contributions.
5. Casualty and theft losses.
6. Employees' educational expenses.
7. Miscellaneous deductions.

We will not be able to go into great detail for any of these categories, but we will outline some of the most important ones. For more specific information, you should refer to the pamphlet we mentioned earlier, IRS Publication 17, *Your Federal Income Tax—For Individuals*.

Medical and Dental Expenses. As we mentioned in Chapter 14, health-care expenditures are some of our biggest and most important expenditures. Federal law allows people to deduct all of their medical, hospital, and dental expenses in excess of 5 percent of their taxable income. This can include transportation expenses for obtaining medical care. Some other legitimate medical-care deductions are payments for acupuncture, cosmetic surgery, eyeglasses, psychiatry, abortion, and vasectomies. Any prescribed

BOX 15-4

The Marriage Tax

When two wage earners get married, their zero-bracket amount (ZBA) of deductions is automatically reduced. In addition, given the progressive nature of the federal income tax, adding their incomes together puts them in a higher tax bracket, and so they pay a higher tax rate. For example, a single man and woman who each earn $15,000 a year would pay a marginal tax rate of about 25 percent. If they were married, their combined $30,000 income would be subject to marginal tax rates of 35 percent or more. The increase in married couples' taxes that results from a lower ZBA and a higher marginal tax rate has become known as the **marriage tax,** because it applies only when one is married.

The Economic Recovery Tax Act of 1981 included a special provision to ease this marriage tax. For the 1982 tax year, two-earner married couples are permitted to deduct 5 percent of the earned income of the lower-earning spouse, up to a maximum of $1500. For 1983 and beyond, the deduction doubles to 10 percent or a maximum of $3000. This lowers the marriage tax for all two-income families and erases it for some. In our example in which the husband and wife earn $30,000 and have no children, the marriage penalty in 1982 would have been $383. In 1982, the penalty is reduced to $153, and by 1983 the new reduction would wipe the penalty out completely.

How the marriage penalty will plummet

FOR A COUPLE WITH $30,000 IN EARNED INCOME AND NO CHILDREN				
Where Income Split Is:	1981 Penalty	1982 Penalty	1983 Penalty	1984 Penalty
80/20 ($24,000/$6,000)	$47 BONUS	$115 BONUS	$153 BONUS	$162 BONUS
60/40 ($18,000/$12,000)	$324	$153	$9	$20 BONUS
50/50 ($15,000/$15,000)	$383	$153	$6 BONUS	$31 BONUS
FOR A COUPLE WITH $50,000 IN EARNED INCOME AND NO CHILDREN				
80/20 ($40,000/$10,000)	$120	$94 BONUS	$265 BONUS	$247 BONUS
60/40 ($30,000/$20,000)	$1,350	$825	$427	$388
50/50 ($25,000/$25,000)	$1,455	$823	$348	$304
FOR A COUPLE WITH $70,000 IN EARNED INCOME AND NO CHILDREN				
80/20 ($56,000/$14,000)	$661	$134	$153 BONUS	$128 BONUS
60/40 ($42,000/$28,000)	$2,662	$1,754	$1,057	$1,018
50/50 ($35,000/$35,000)	$2,935	$1,977	$1,196	$1,162
FOR A COUPLE WITH $100,000 IN EARNED INCOME AND NO CHILDREN				
80/20 ($80,000/$20,000)	$29 BONUS	$674	$198 BONUS	$99 BONUS
60/40 ($60,000/$40,000)	$3,600	$2,906	$1,944	$1,970
50/50 ($50,000/$50,000)	$3,760	$3,346	$2,324	$2,290

The tables above assume that deductions equal 23% of income unless the taxpayer can't itemize; in that case the zero-bracket amount is used. All income is earned. The "1981 Penalty" column shows what the marriage penalty would have been this year if there had been no tax cut. BONUS indicates where married couples end up owing less in taxes than single people do.

SOURCE: Money, September 1981, p. 63.

medicines or drug expenses in excess of 1 percent of taxable income are also legitimate deductions. These include pharmaceuticals, birth-control pills, vitamins, and even whiskey, if a physician advises a person to take a certain dosage. You cannot, however, deduct a medical expense for which you were reimbursed by your insurance company.

Other Taxes. General sales taxes, personal property taxes, real estate taxes, and state or local income taxes are all legitimate deductions. Property and income taxes are generally the simplest taxes to keep a record of, because one generally pays them in lump sums. Because sales tax is a more difficult tax to estimate, the IRS provides tax tables to help people estimate the correct amount, depending on their income. Nevertheless, people will generally have greater deductions if they actually record their sales-tax expenditures. Ronald Reagan's 1979 tax return shows, for example, that he deducted $2148 for sales tax rather than accepting the IRS formula, which would have allowed him a paltry $727. Of course, most consumers would not have been in the same income class ($500,000) and thus could not have claimed as much (*Changing Times,* January 1981).

Interest Deductions. Every dollar one spends for the privilege of using someone else's money (interest) is tax deductible. All of the finance charges discussed in Chapter 8 may reappear as itemized deductions on a tax form. Home buyers take the most advantage of this deduction. Economists estimate that each year, four times as much tax revenue is lost through this deduction as is spent on federal subsidies to low-income housing. The interest deduction is probably the largest tax break the average middle-income person can take. This is especially important for recent purchases of homes or condominiums, because over 90 percent of such payments will be deductible as interest. For a family in the 35 percent bracket, the IRS forgives 35 cents of every dollar spent. Thus, tax law makes the federal government a silent partner in most home purchases.

Charitable Contributions. Donations of cash or property to recognized charitable, religious, or educational organizations are tax deductible. Your contribution can be made by check, in which case you automatically have a receipt, or it can be in the form of personal property, in which case you should have some proof of its fair market value and the date it was donated. For example, if you donate an old television set, you can only deduct the current market value of that set, not its original price. And it is a good idea to get the charitable organization to agree on the true value and to give you a receipt. You may even deduct transportation expenses and the cost of meals and lodging incurred as a result of charitable activity. Suppose, for example, that you volunteer your time to help at a nonprofit school for the blind. Perhaps you take some of the children on field trips in your car and you pay all your own expenses, including some overnight lodging. All of your expenses are deductible, but you cannot deduct anything for the value of your time.

Casualty and Theft Losses. The federal government recognizes your right to deduct the value of anything stolen from you or destroyed as a result of an accident. So if you are burglarized, if your car is in an accident, or if a tornado destroys your house, you may be eligible for this deduction, provided that your insurance company does not reimburse you. This deduction can be taken even if you never replace or repair the item in question.

Employees' Educational Expense. If you are employed and you are required by your employer or by law to continue your education, you can deduct the cost of the necessary training. If there is no legal requirement but the training will maintain or improve the skills required to do your present work, you are also allowed to deduct the cost of the education. This provision in the tax law was intended to aid workers in maintaining their productivity, but it has also spawned large numbers of "European vacations" that taxpayers claim are "educational." Abusers of this section have made IRS personnel skeptical of returns listing large educational expenses involving foreign travel. You would do well to check with the Internal Revenue Service *before* you plan to use this kind of deduction.

EXEMPTIONS

Once you have subtracted either your zero-bracket amount or your excess itemized deductions from your adjusted gross income, you are ready to calculate your exemptions. (For clarity, it might be a good idea to review Table 15-3 just to see where we are in the income tax calculation process.)

Exemptions are specific amounts of income that one is allowed to subtract from earned income *before* beginning to calculate taxes. The most important exemptions deal with the number of people in a household. In 1980, the federal government allowed a $1000 income exemption for every member of a taxpayer's household. The rationale behind this exemption is that there is a basic level of income needed to support a household and that the government should recognize this by not taxing this minimal amount. This means that a family of four filing one tax return could earn at least $7400 before paying any federal income tax ($4000 in exemptions plus $3400 zero-bracket amount).

One does not have to do any special calculations in moving from "income before exemptions" to "taxable income." The tax tables prepared by the Internal Revenue Service incorporate exemption bonuses and taxable income. Figure 15-7, which is a reproduction of part of a 1980 tax table for married people filing joint returns, illustrates how the IRS adjusts for exemptions. A family of four, for example, would owe no tax if it earned $7400 or less. Look at the income brackets in Figure 15-7 and find the one marked "Over $7350, but not over $7400." Then look at the column for four exemptions. The zero indicates that no tax is owed. If the family had a taxable income of more than $7400 but not more than $7450, it would owe $4 in federal income tax.

In our example, we are assuming that the family does not qualify for any other exemptions. This may not be the case. There are additional exemptions for taxpayers when they reach sixty-five or when they are legally blind. The rationale for these exemptions is less clear, because it probably does not relate to necessary living expenses. One might argue that these exemptions are based on need, but then why don't deaf persons or quadriplegics qualify for special exemptions? It is also interesting to note that full-time

Figure 15-7. An illustration of a tax table.

If Form 1040A, line 11, is—		And the total number of exemptions claimed on line 6 is—							
Over	But not over	2	3	4	5	6	7	8	9
		\multicolumn{8}{c}{Your tax is—}							
6,800	6,850	200	60	0	0	0	0	0	0
6,850	6,900	207	67	0	0	0	0	0	0
6,900	6,950	214	74	0	0	0	0	0	0
6,950	7,000	221	81	0	0	0	0	0	0
7,000	7,050	228	88	0	0	0	0	0	0
7,050	7,100	235	95	0	0	0	0	0	0
7,100	7,150	242	102	0	0	0	0	0	0
7,150	7,200	249	109	0	0	0	0	0	0
7,200	7,250	256	116	0	0	0	0	0	0
7,250	7,300	263	123	0	0	0	0	0	0
7,300	7,350	270	130	0	0	0	0	0	0
7,350	7,400	277	137	0	0	0	0	0	0
7,400	7,450	284	144	4	0	0	0	0	0
7,450	7,500	291	151	11	0	0	0	0	0
7,500	7,550	298	158	18	0	0	0	0	0
7,550	7,600	306	165	25	0	0	0	0	0
7,600	7,650	314	172	32	0	0	0	0	0
7,650	7,700	322	179	39	0	0	0	0	0
7,700	7,750	330	186	46	0	0	0	0	0
7,750	7,800	338	193	53	0	0	0	0	0
7,800	7,850	346	200	60	0	0	0	0	0
7,850	7,900	354	207	67	0	0	0	0	0
7,900	7,950	362	214	74	0	0	0	0	0
7,950	8,000	370	221	81	0	0	0	0	0
8,000	8,050	378	228	88	0	0	0	0	0

college students, regardless of age, can qualify for the $1000 exemption on both their parents' tax return *and* on their own, as long as their parents provide over 50 percent of their support. This exemption is clearly a boon to college students and their families.

TAX CREDITS

After you have taken care of all your exemptions, have taken your itemized deductions (or the zero-bracket amount), and have found your tax liability in the tax tables, you may further reduce your tax if you qualify for a **tax credit**. A tax credit is a dollar reduction in the tax bill that is determined after one has computed the tax owed on income. Like a tax deduction, it is intended to encourage a behavior by making it less expensive. Unlike a deduction, a tax credit returns the same number of dollars to taxpayers regardless of their marginal tax rate. For example, to a taxpayer in the 20 percent bracket, a $1000 tax-deductible church contribution saves $200 in tax liability. To a taxpayer in the 50 percent tax bracket, the same $1000 deduction saves $500 in tax liability. If, instead of giving taxpayers a deduction for church contributions, the IRS gave them a 20 percent tax credit, both taxpayers would save $200 in tax liability from a $1000 donation. The three most important tax credits are for childcare, residential energy conservation, and political contributions.

Childcare. If you must pay someone to care for your child so that you can work, you are allowed to deduct a portion of that cost directly as a tax credit. The maximum allowable expense is $2400 for one child and $4800 for two or more. If you earn more than $28,000 per year, you are allowed to take 20 percent of your childcare costs as a tax credit, which means that you can subtract a maximum of $480 for one child or $960 if two or more are cared for while you work. The 1981 Tax Act gives lower-income workers an even larger tax credit by allowing them to take a larger percentage of their childcare costs (up to 30 percent for families earning $10,000 or less) as tax credits. Thus, the maximum credit for a low-income family is $720 (.3 × $2400) for one child and $1440 (.3 × $4800) for two or more.*

Residential Energy Credit. Because the federal government (and many state governments) recognize the importance of encouraging consumers to conserve energy, they offer tax incentives in the form of tax credits to lower the cost of cutting residential energy use. In 1980, the federal government allowed taxpayers to take a credit of 15 percent of the first $2000 spent on energy-saving items for the home, such as insulation designed to reduce heat loss or gain, storm windows, caulking or weatherstripping, and automatic clock thermostats.

In addition to encouraging conservation, the federal government sought to speed the changeover to solar, wind, and other renewable sources of energy by offering individuals a credit of 40 percent of the first $10,000 spent on such items. Solar-energy equipment designed for heating the home or hot water, and solar- or wind-power projects for generating electricity qualify for this tax credit. If a credit exceeds the tax owed, it may be carried over to the next tax year.

Political Contributions. A third tax credit is for political contributions. Most of us realize that it costs money to run a successful political campaign. In the past, candidates often had to depend on large contributions from a few citizens to pay for campaign expenses. In order to encourage more taxpayers to get involved in the political process, the government offers a 50 percent credit on the first $100 ($200 on a joint return) paid to political candidates, to their campaign committees, or to national political parties. With this and all other credits claimed, one must have a receipt to document the contribution. But this tax credit, unlike childcare or energy credits, can be claimed on either the short form, 1040A, or the long form, 1040.

SEEKING TAX ADVICE: PROFESSIONAL TAX PREPARERS

If the federal tax laws seem a bit complex, there is a reason. Tax laws are used for more than obtaining tax revenue. The government uses the tax code to encourage some activities and to discourage others. Your goal should be to minimize your personal tax liability by following the guidelines established by law. This does not mean evading your taxes. **Tax evasion** is an attempt to pay less than one is legally obligated to pay, and it is punishable by fine and/or imprisonment. However, it is perfectly legal to engage in **tax avoidance**—techniques for decreasing taxes by engaging in those activities that are undertaxed or not taxed at all. By installing home insulation, for example, one can avoid paying taxes on part of the money spent on it. But how will you know whether such an activity is tax deductible, and how can you be sure that you will get the maximum tax refund? One of the easiest ways to handle this tax problem is to go to a professional tax preparer. This simple advice is not as easy as it may sound. In addition to the folks at the Internal Revenue Service, there are national tax preparation services such as H & R Block, local tax preparers, tax lawyers, and certified public accountants.

---

*The percentage for the tax credit rises at the rate of 1 percent for each $2000 decrease in family income. Thus, a family with a $20,000 income gets a 25 percent maximum tax credit ($600 for one child, $1200 for two or more).

454 Economic Decisions for Consumers

Taxpayers who are being audited should come prepared with documentation of all exemptions, deductions, and credits.

All may be able to help you with your tax return, but their skills and level of expertise will vary, and so will their prices.

If you have a simple return and plan to file the short form, the IRS will compute the tax for you. All you need to do is fill out the form, sign it, and enclose the wage form, called the W-2, sent by your employer. Most taxpayers are not keen on letting the IRS figure their taxes. The feeling is that there might be a conflict of interest, because the IRS is set up to collect money, not disburse it. Nevertheless, on a simple form there is little harm in letting the IRS do the work.

On a more complex form, especially when you plan to itemize your deductions rather than simply take the zero-bracket amount, some professional advice could be worth the expense, and it is tax deductible. As a general rule, tax lawyers and certified public accountants are best able to deal with the thorny problems of tax law, but they are also the most expensive sources of advice. If your tax statement is not unduly complicated, a better buy might be a local tax preparer who is allowed to represent taxpayers at an IRS hearing. In order to be certified to practice before the IRS, an accountant must pass a series of stringent examinations administered by the U.S. Treasury. This is your assurance of the tax preparer's competence, and it may be of real comfort to you if your return is chosen for further scrutiny by the IRS.

The Dreaded Tax Audit

The American tax system is built on voluntary compliance. There is no way that the IRS would be able to run the system if the majority of taxpayers refused to pay or cheated. Nevertheless, the Internal Revenue Service estimates that between $75 and $100 billion of income goes unreported every year. If this is true, how is the system policed? The Internal Revenue Service uses several techniques, including a spot check of randomly selected tax returns and guidelines

Table 15-4. Average Deductions Claimed by Taxpayers With Various Incomes

Adjusted gross income	Medical expenses	Taxes	Donations	Interest	Other
$10,000–$ 11,999	$1,071	$ 1,141	$ 522	$ 1,864	$ 406
$12,000–$ 13,999	1,004	1,255	557	1,868	447
$14,000–$ 15,999	1,000	1,380	513	1,993	460
$16,000–$ 17,999	657	1,531	508	2,164	468
$18,000–$ 19,999	657	1,646	568	2,149	441
$20,000–$ 24,999	561	1,876	570	2,280	455
$25,000–$ 29,999	498	2,245	644	2,456	480
$30,000–$ 49,999	503	3,007	869	2,880	613
$50,000–$ 99,999	668	5,309	1,825	4,585	1,136
$100,000–$199,999	963	10,001	4,676	7,933	2,123
$200,000 and over	1,510	26,699	25,913	19,633	7,269

about the average amount of deductions for a given income. Table 15-4 shows the average deductions for workers' income levels in a recent tax year. Given these guidelines, tax returns that claim an exceptionally large amount for a particular deduction are suspect. These tax returns are subject to greater scrutiny and are more likely to undergo a personal examination, sometimes called a **tax audit**. The IRS collects an additional $2 billion each year as a result of these audits.

Your chances of undergoing an audit are fairly small, because only about one in every fifty returns is selected each year. The odds range from one in two hundred for those using the short form to one in ten for those using the long form and reporting more than $50,000 of income. However, if you are one of the unlucky ones, you will be notified by mail that your return is being examined. Frequently, a face-to-face meeting is arranged during which the IRS agent will ask some questions about your return. You will know the purpose of the audit in advance, so come prepared with all of your documentation. If the IRS is questioning the size of your charitable donations, for example, bring the canceled checks plus any supporting material, such as receipts for in-kind donations of clothing, appliances, or other goods.

At the end of the meeting, the examiner will explain all proposed changes in your tax liability. If you accept this judgment, you sign an agreement. If you disagree, you may request an immediate meeting with the examiner's supervisor. After this, you must formally appeal the ruling if you disagree.

The IRS has only one appeal level, and cases are conducted as informally as possible. If you do not get a satisfactory settlement at this level, your only alternative is to take your case to court. There are three courts available to you: the United States Tax Court, the Federal District Court, and the Claims Court. If you choose not to pay the disputed amount first, you may argue your case only in the Tax Court. If your case involves a dispute of $5000 or less, the Tax Court provides the simplest form of redress. (You can write for a description of the procedures, free of charge, from the United States Tax Court, 400 Second Street N.W., Washington, D.C. 20217.) The Tax Court will travel to a convenient location near you to hear your case. There are only two catches here. First, you must file a petition with the Tax Court within 90 days of the formal IRS notice that you owe additional taxes. If you miss the deadline, you will have to pay the tax. Then your only recourse will be the Federal District Court or the Claims Court, for which you will need a tax lawyer. Second, if you have a small claim, the decision of the Tax Court cannot be appealed.

The Internal Revenue Service publishes its win-loss record of taxpayers' appeals each year. At all

Figure 15-8. Total revenue by major sources for state and local governments, 1980.

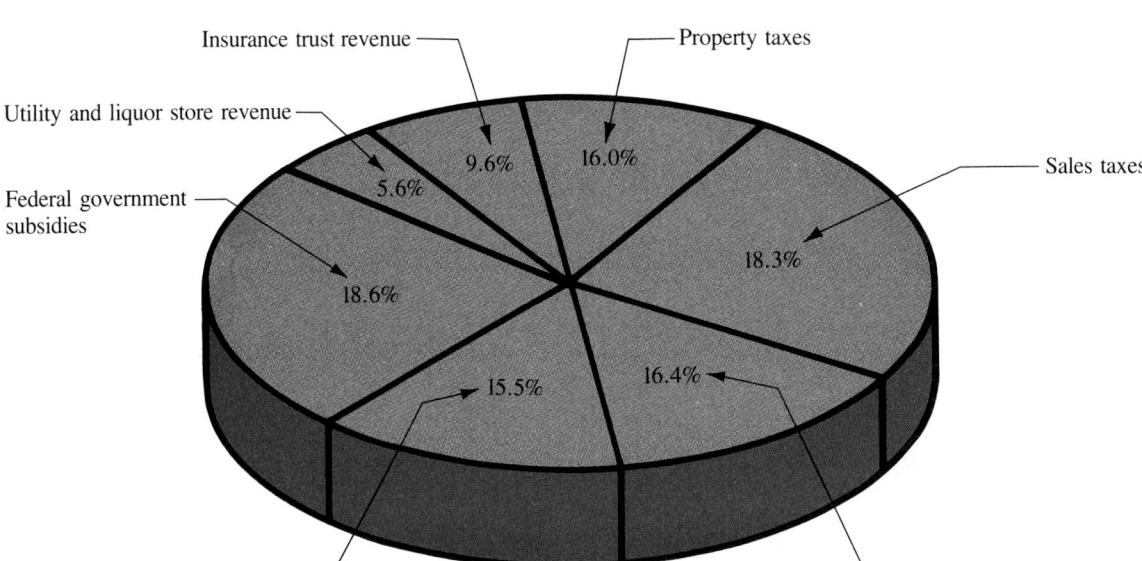

SOURCE: U.S. Bureau of the Census, Government Finances in 1979–80. (Washington, D.C.: U.S. Government Printing Office, 1981).

levels of appeal—the Tax Court, the Federal District Court, and the Claims Court—the IRS wins more than half of the cases. But their win-loss percentage has been lowest in the Claims Court, where they have won only 52 percent of the cases. Nevertheless, most tax experts agree that the Tax Court is the best place to appeal an IRS ruling if you have a strong case, because you do not need to retain counsel or pay the disputed tax, and the location of the hearing will be convenient. If your case is not strong legally but appeals to other taxpayers' sympathies, the experts recommend taking it to the U.S. District Court to be decided by a jury of your peers (*Money,* July 1981). As with all decisions, you must weigh the costs and benefits. The costs include your time and psychological stress, as well as the cost of lawyers' fees and other fees.

Appealing a particular tax ruling raises the broader question of the fairness of the tax system. This transcends the federal income tax and opens up the entire tax system to investigation. Who bears the tax burden and who gets the benefits?

The Overall Tax Burden: Is It Fair?

As we mentioned earlier, government covers a wide variety of agencies and levels. Thus far we have generally focused on the federal government, but state and local governments are an important part of the picture as well. In 1980, state governments collected almost 25 cents of every tax dollar, and local governments took about 15 cents. Figure 15-8 shows the combined tax revenues of state and local governments by source. If you compare this chart with Figure 15-5, you will see that state and local governments emphasize sales and property taxes, whereas the federal government depends on income taxes.

The amount of sales tax and property tax that a household pays is not directly linked to its income, as we saw earlier. Retired people, for example, often have only moderate incomes, and yet they may be

BOX 15-5
Cutting Local Property Taxes: Heads They Win, Tails You Lose

In 1978, Californians went to the polls in record numbers and voted to cut property taxes by over 50 percent. Their "yes" votes on Proposition 13 rolled back the tax on residential and commercial property to 1 percent of the 1975–1976 property value and limited increases in that value to an annual upward adjustment of 2 percent. As a result, property-tax revenues fell by over $7 billion. The voters said that they were tired of paying higher taxes and that they wanted some relief. We know from our previous discussion of taxes that a tax that is not directly related to income is probably regressive, and this is the case with local property taxes. But who benefited from this tax cut and what does this action mean for future tax policy in other states?

The Revenue and Taxation Committee of the California Assembly did a study of who received the benefits of the $7 billion property-tax cut. The figure here shows the distribution of benefits. Surprisingly, government and businesses obtained much larger gains than homeowners, who were largely responsible for the passage of the tax cut. The U.S. government and the State of California benefited, because their income-tax revenues rise every time taxpayers lose deductions. Because payments for local property taxes are deductible on income-tax forms, any reduction in property taxes leads to a reduction in deductions and a rise in taxable income. As far as Proposition 13 was concerned, a decrease in property-tax payments led to a $1.6 billion increase in federal income taxes and a $977 million rise in California income-tax revenues in the first year. Commercial, industrial, agricultural, and rental property taxes were also cut, so 40 percent of the $7 billion tax savings went to the owners of these properties. Some of this gain may have been passed on to consumers in the form of lower rents or lower prices for other goods, but much of it was retained by the owners. It is interesting to note that Howard Jarvis, the founding father of Proposition 13, headed an association of Los Angeles apartment-building owners—a group that had a great deal to gain from a reduction in property taxes. When apartment rents did not decline after the passage of the proposition, a strong movement for rent control developed in many California cities, because some renters believed that they did not get their fair share of the tax break.

Cutting the local government's principal form of revenue also had an impact on government services. The budgets of schools, libraries, public transportation, and recreation departments were all affected. The combined budgets of California's city and county consumer-protection agencies were cut by 45 percent. Almost 20,000 government employees were laid off, and many municipalities raised fees for such diverse services as garbage collection, libraries, and public parks.

People in other states witnessed this California experiment with mixed emotions. On the one hand, inflation has driven up the value of real estate and thus increased property taxes; on the other hand, tax revenues have been used to increase government services. It is difficult to cut taxes without trimming services. It is even more difficult to trim the local tax burden and still preserve the tax benefits for the local population. Obviously, there is no easy solution to this dilemma.

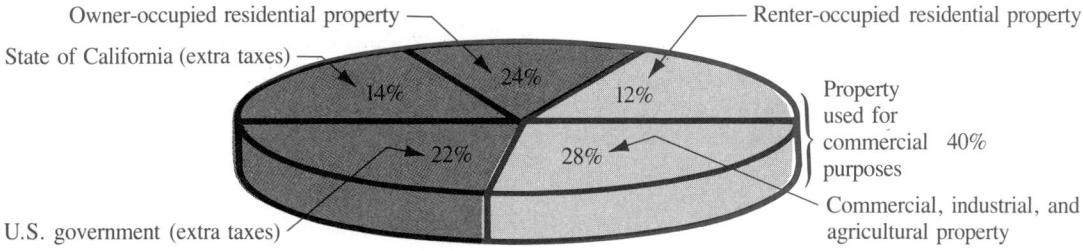

SOURCE: Copyright 1979 by Consumers Union of United States, Inc., Mount Vernon, NY 10550. Reprinted by permission from *Consumer Reports*, September 1979.

Table 15-5. Estimated Tax Rate by Income Levels (taxes as a percentage of income)

(1) Family income	(2) Federal taxes	(3) State and local taxes	(4) All taxes, or (2) + (30)	(5) Government transfer payments	(6) Net taxes, or (4) − (5)
Under $2000	22.7%	27.2%	50.0%	106.5%	−56.5%
$2000-$4000	18.7	15.7	34.6	48.5	−13.9
$4000-$6000	19.0	12.1	31.0	19.6	11.4
$6000-$8000	19.4	10.7	30.1	8.6	21.5
$8000-$10,000	19.1	10.1	29.2	5.5	23.7
$10,000-$15,000	19.9	9.9	29.8	3.9	25.9
$15,000-$25,000	20.7	9.4	30.0	3.0	27.0
$25,000-$50,000	25.0	7.8	32.8	2.1	30.7
$50,000 and over	38.4	6.7	45.0	0.4	44.7
Total tax on all income	21.7%	9.9%	31.6%	6.9%	24.6%

SOURCE: Roger A. Herriot and Herman P. Miller, "The Taxes We Pay," *Conference Record* (May 1971), p. 40.

liable for a high property tax on their homes. Low-income families tend to save very little, and many of their daily expenditures are subject to state sales taxes. As a consequence, people in higher income classes generally pay a smaller percentage of their incomes in sales taxes or property taxes. In general, state and local taxes can be labeled regressive, because they tax low-income households more heavily.

On the other hand, state and local governments provide goods and services that benefit low-income people as well as high-income people. Public education, welfare, and hospital care are only three of the many services provided at the state or local level that are open to all citizens. If the value of these subsidies is compared to the recipient's income level, the system tends to appear more progressive.

Table 15-5 presents the results of a study that estimated the overall burden of taxation in the United States on taxpayers by income level (Herriot and Miller, 1971). This study also included the effect of cash transfers such as Social Security and welfare benefits, but it excluded the impact of public goods such as education and medical care. As you can see, federal taxation was shown to be mildly progressive; families earning over $50,000 paid higher taxes than those earning less. But state and local taxes were strongly regressive—high-income families paid less than 7 percent of their income to the government, and low-income families paid much more. When all taxes were combined, the lowest income group still paid a higher percentage of their income than the highest income group, although the system was almost proportional for middle-income families. But when government transfers were included, the overall tax system emerged as a progressive one, because lower income groups get proportionately higher subsidies.

The data from Table 15-5 show that there is a mildly progressive tax system in the United States. This conclusion seems to fly in the face of the common folk wisdom that says that the rich don't pay any taxes or that they use special tax deductions called **loopholes** to avoid paying taxes. There is undoubtedly some truth to the statement that special tax provisions are sometimes written into the law to aid a particular taxpayer or group of taxpayers. However, part of the reason for these so-called loopholes is the multidimensional rationale behind the institution of taxes. Taxes do more than pay for the costs of government, although this is their primary reason for being. As we have said, taxes can be used to encourage certain forms of behavior and to discourage others. Energy tax credits, for example, are meant to lower the costs of conservation and thus increase consumer conservation activity. Presumably, this will lower the demand for energy and thus make people less reliant on undependable foreign energy sources. The energy tax credit is a tax loophole that not everyone will take advantage of, but does that make it unfair?

The tax on capital gains is another controversial tax loophole. **Capital gains** are increases in the value of assets such as stocks, bonds, or real estate during the time the assets are owned. Under the present tax law, if you hold an asset for more than one year and then sell it for a higher price, only 40 percent of your gain is taxable; 60 percent is tax free. Thus, if you bought 100 shares of stock two years ago for $1000 and sold them this year for $3000, your capital gain would be $2000. You would not have increased your taxable income by $2000, however, because only 40 percent of the gain is taxable. Thus, your taxable income would rise by only $800 (.40 × $2000). This tax loophole is especially helpful to consumers who are in higher tax brackets. However, the major purpose of the capital gains tax is not tax relief for the rich. Instead, it is aimed at encouraging savings and investment in productive assets. Of course, there is still disagreement on whether the capital gains tax achieves this goal in a fair and equitable manner.

Summary

Because the tax system must balance so many conflicting objectives, it is little wonder that the U.S. Tax Code comprises more than 6,000 pages of exceedingly fine print that often require attorneys to interpret. Given the complexity of the system, no one can expect you to emerge as an expert simply because you have read this chapter. Nevertheless, you should have a better understanding of the American tax system and your part in it.

The original purpose of taxation was to provide revenue for the government so that it could maintain order. The basic law-and-order function of government remains, but many other public goods and services have been added. On the federal level, over 40 percent of the budget is devoted to programs that transfer income to individuals for social reasons. Despite the size and the rapid growth of these income transfers, Americans are among the least taxed citizens of any highly developed nation.

Who bears the burden of taxation can be just as important as the size of the burden. Here, the benefits-received and the ability-to-pay principles can be used to justify different kinds of taxes. The ability-to-pay principle generally supports progressive taxes, which always take a higher proportion of income from those earning more. Two other classifications of taxes are those that take a higher percentage from lower-income consumers—regressive taxes—and those that take the same proportion from all income groups—proportional taxes. The federal budget depends heavily on the progressive income tax for its revenue. The progressiveness of the income tax is achieved by dividing a taxpayer's income into brackets and then applying a higher tax rate to each succeeding bracket. Knowing what tax bracket you are in can be very important for decision making and tax planning.

Understanding how federal income tax works is important if you want to minimize your tax liabilities without going to jail. Taking advantage of your legitimate exclusions, deductions, exemptions, and tax credits can lower your taxes significantly. If you choose to itemize your deductions, you will need to keep good records with regard to medical expenses, state and local taxes, interest paid, charitable contributions, casualty and theft losses, and employment-related expenses. Otherwise, you can accept the government's estimate of these deductions, called the zero-bracket amount (ZBA).

If you have a great deal of income from a wide range of sources, professional tax advice is practically a necessity. But even if your tax return is not complex, it is often helpful to have someone review your form, particularly a tax preparer who is certified to practice before the U.S. Tax Court.

Random and selective tax audits are important enforcement tools of the IRS. If you are audited, you should be prepared with records to substantiate your case. If the IRS still disagrees after seeing your evidence, you have the right to appeal your case.

Studies indicate that state and local taxes are largely regressive, whereas federal taxes are mildly progressive. When all taxes and income transfers are considered, the tax rate is actually negative for the lowest income groups, because their subsidies exceed their taxes. Overall, the system is progressive, because it takes more from higher income groups.

Some critics have challenged the conclusion that the U.S. tax system is progressive. They point to loopholes in the tax law, such as capital gains taxes, to illustrate the unfairness of the system. Many of these tax loopholes were designed to encourage specific taxpayer activities by rewarding them with lower taxes. What may appear to be unfair or unproductive loopholes to one taxpayer may seem to be necessary deductions to another. Nevertheless, it is true that under a progressive tax system, tax deductions are more valuable to higher-income consumers.

 REVISITED

Dennis continued to mutter as he went back to his desk in the study. "Why didn't I keep a file of medical expenses? Where are those canceled checks? I can't remember whether we gave that couch to the Salvation Army last year or the year before."

Dennis didn't hear his wife and children preparing to go to the park. He didn't answer their good-byes as they left the house, and the noise from their car didn't disturb him either. He was concentrating hard and blaming the Internal Revenue Service for his troubles.

1. If you were in Dennis' position, what would you do? Remember, it is April 10.

2. How could Dennis obtain additional information about his tax return? Where could he go to get additional forms?

3. Is Dennis' plight a result of Internal Revenue Service incompetence? Why didn't they send him *all* the forms? Why are there so many different forms in the first place?

4. How could Dennis avoid this situation next year?

KEY TERMS

ability-to-pay principle
average tax rate
benefits received principle
capital gains
confiscatory tax rates
deductions
diminishing marginal utility
entitlement programs
exclusions
exemptions

flat tax
free-rider effect
gross income
income brackets
loopholes
marginal tax rate
marriage tax
progressive taxation
proportional taxation
public good

regressive taxation
supply-side economics
taxable income
tax audit
tax avoidance
tax credit
tax evasion
transfer payment
yields
zero-bracket amount (ZBA)

QUESTIONS

1. List four examples of public goods. Do they all have the free-rider problem? Could they be produced by the private sector or must government always produce them? Explain.

2. The free-rider effect can apply to goods other than those produced by government. How does it apply to:
   a. Educational television stations?
   b. Coffee available in offices?
   c. Fourth of July fireworks displays?

3. Classify the following taxes according to whether they are based on benefits received or ability to pay:
   a. Income tax.
   b. Gasoline tax.
   c. Fishing license fee.

4. Many people argue that Americans are overtaxed. What comparative evidence do we have that seems to contradict this position? Is it still true?

5. What are the most important sources of revenue for the federal government? What are the most important expenditure categories? Did these categories dominate the federal budget twenty-five years ago? Fifty years ago?

6. What is the difference between the average tax rate and the marginal tax rate? Can the marginal tax rate have a significant impact on consumer expenditure patterns? How?

7. If the federal income-tax laws were rewritten overnight so that every citizen got a $2000 personal exemption but no other exemptions, credits, or deductions, and if the rate were made strictly proportional, say 15 percent, what would the impact be on the demand for lawyers, accountants, IRS examiners, and tax preparers? How would consumer expenditure patterns change? Would the government lose any weapons in its economic arsenal? What is the possibility of such a change?

8. What is the zero-bracket amount? What is its purpose? When does it make sense to keep tax records if you are not going to itemize your deductions?

9. What is the difference between a deduction and a tax credit? Which one favors high-income taxpayers?

10. What procedures can you follow to minimize the probability of having your tax return audited? If you are audited, what rights do you have? How can you appeal an IRS ruling?

PROJECTS

1. Get out your tax return from last year and calculate your average and marginal tax rates. Divide the amount of tax you owed by your taxable income to get your average rate. Then find the marginal tax rate from the tax table that applies to your filing status.

2. Call several local tax preparers and get a quote on how much they would charge to fill out your tax form. Are their prices different? Do they all offer the same services? For example, will they help you in case of an audit? Are they all licensed to practice in Tax Court?

3. Write for a free copy of IRS Publication No. 17, *Your Federal Income Tax–For Individuals*. How does it compare to commercially produced tax guides?

REFERENCES AND READINGS

"Don't Let the IRS Scare You." *Changing Times*, March 1980.

"The Growing Burden of State Taxes." *Consumer Research*, February 1981.

Hall, Robert E., and Rabushka, Alvin. "A Proposal to Simplify Our Tax System." *Wall Street Journal*, December 10, 1981.

Herriot, Roger A., and Miller, Herman P. "The Taxes We Pay." *Conference Board Record*, May 1971.

Holzman, Robert S. *Take It Off!* New York: Thomas Y. Crowell, 1981.

"How to Reduce Your Taxes: A Special Report." *Money*, February 1982.

Internal Revenue Service. *Your Federal Income Tax*. Washington, D.C.: U.S. Government Printing Office, 1982.

Lasser, J. K. *Your Income Tax*. New York: Simon & Schuster, annual editions.

Pechman, Joseph A., and Okner, Benjamin A. *Who Bears the Tax Burden?* Washington, D.C.: The Brookings Institution, 1974.

"Plan Now—Save Later on Taxes." *Consumers Digest*, January/February 1981.

Prentice-Hall. *Federal Tax Handbook*. Englewood Cliffs, N.J.: Prentice-Hall, 1982.

"Proposition 13: Who Really Won?" *Consumer Reports*, September 1979.

Smith, Stuart A., and Spragens, Janet. *How You Can Get the Most from the New Tax Law*. New York: Bantam, 1981.

"Solar Water Heaters: What They Cost, What They Can Save." *Consumer Reports*, May 1980.

Swartz, Thomas, et al. *Analyzing Tax Policy: A Resource Guide*. New York: Joint Council on Economic Education, 1979.

"Tax Angles on Divorce." *Changing Times*, June 1981.

"Tax Breaks for Saving Energy." *Changing Times*, September 1980.

"Ten Ways to Cut Your Taxes All Year Long." *Changing Times*, January 1981.

U.S. Bureau of the Census. *Governmental Finances*. Washington, D.C.: U.S. Government Printing Office, 1981.

"You Versus the IRS." *Money*, July 1981.

Did You Know That...

- you probably have an investment portfolio right now, even though you may not realize it?

- you can master a vocabulary of personal finance terms and then evaluate potential investments using these concepts?

- two banks can advertise the same interest rate, yet one pays less interest than the other because of different compounding or computing policies? The American Bankers Association estimates that there are fifty-four ways of computing interest on a savings account.

- in the near future (legally, by 1986), all interest-rate ceilings will be eliminated and the differences between commercial banks and other financial institutions will be small, because of the Depository Institutions Deregulation and Monetary Control Act?

- money-market funds offer the small investor high yields and liquidity for a small risk?

- there are significant differences between common stocks and preferred stocks?

- over the last decade there was almost no growth in the assets of stock-market mutual funds?

- the average annual rate of return on an investment in a college education varies from 8 to 12 percent?

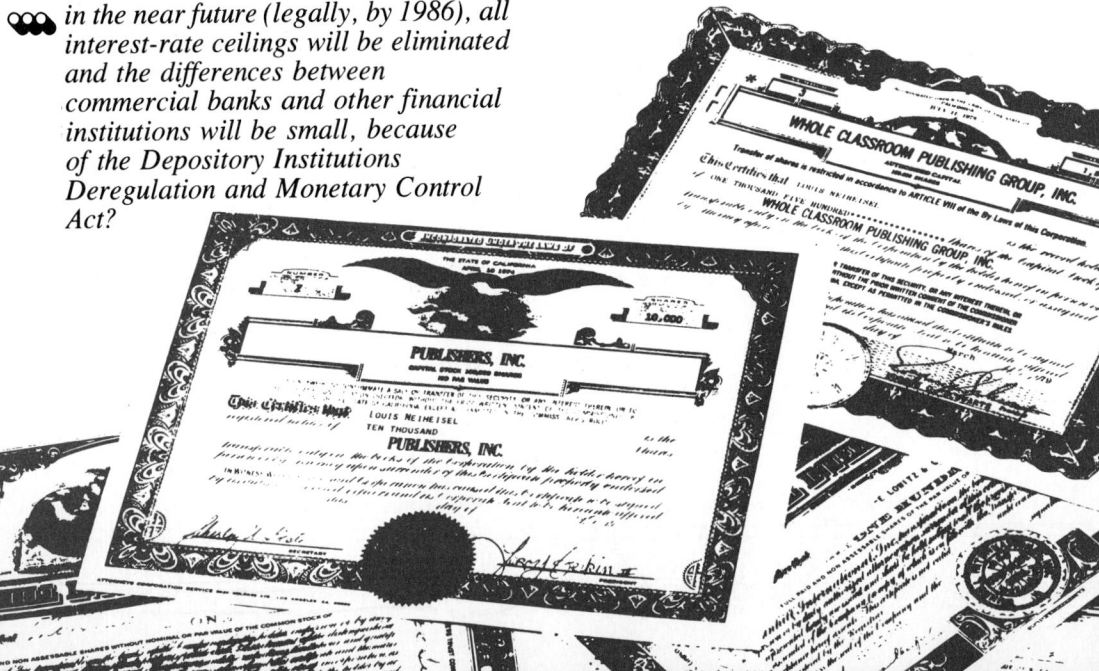

16

Saving and Investing: Is a Penny Saved a Penny Earned?

The Vocabulary of Investment an Personal Finance

Types of Investments: Creating an Investment Portfolio

Comparing Various Investments

Neighborhood CAPSULE

Family Decision Making: Where Should You Invest Your Savings?

The Dombrowski family had just finished an Easter Sunday feast. It had been a perfect combination of old-country traditions and American cuisine, from the Polish ham to the all-American apple pie. Now, as the final dishes were cleared and everyone began to move to the living room to relax and digest, Joe Dombrowski put his arm around his grandmother and guided her back to the dining room table.

"Grandma, let's sit down over here. I'd like to talk to you for a minute," Joe began. The other members of the family were vaguely aware of the essential elements of the conversation, but they decided to leave well enough alone. They didn't want to be involved in that conversation if Grandmother Dombrowski lost her temper. And they knew this was a distinct possibility.

"Grandma," Joe said after they were seated, "I know that Grandpa left you some money after he passed away. And I also know that you've been keeping it just where you and Grandpa always kept your money—in Polska Savings and Loan. But Grandma . . ."

Before Joe could finish his statement, his grandmother interrupted him with a sharp Polish statement that, roughly translated, means "Shut up."

"I don't want to talk about this, Joe. I want to relax and enjoy being with my family on Easter."

However, Joe was not about to take this answer as definitive. In fact, he had been chosen as the family representative because he was persuasive and he was his grandmother's favorite.

"Grandma," Joe began again. "You are just not earning enough interest on your savings. We could double your annual interest by putting your money into a money-market fund. Please, let me help you. Believe me, I know about this."

"Just a minute," his grandmother replied as she looked him straight in the eye. "You know about these things, do you? Well tell me this, Joe. Will your money-market fund lend my money to people who need it? Does it care about us? Can I walk down the street and talk to someone from this fund? And how do I know whether my money is safe? Is it insured?"

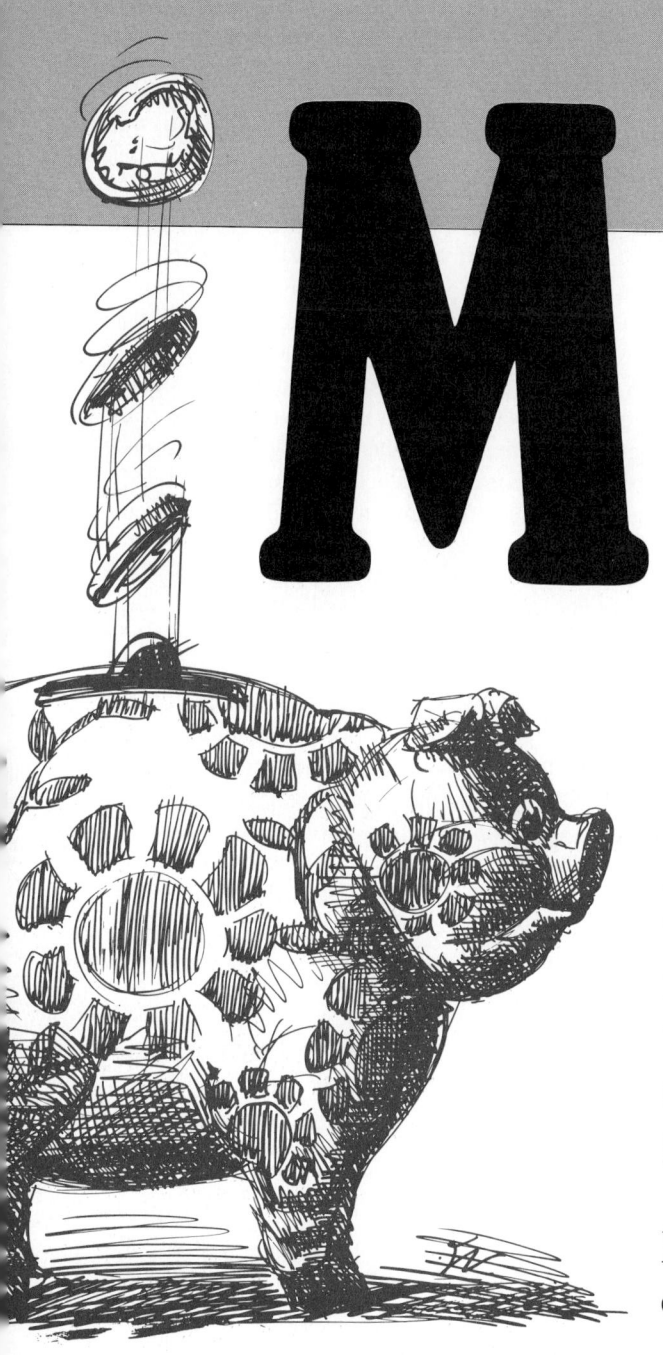

Most of us have fond memories of our first piggy bank and recall the implied parental message about the importance of saving. But as we grew up, we learned that stuffing money into a piggy bank is not the best way to save. For one thing, the money could be stolen, but more important, it is not doing anything for us. It is just sitting there. That's where the search for investments comes in. **Investments** are ways of using money in the present to create greater income in the future.

Interest—the income a lender earns for letting someone else borrow his or her money—is one kind of return on an investment. When you learned as a child that a bank would pay you interest for letting it keep your savings, it may have seemed like an unearned bonus for you—like getting something for nothing. The Internal Revenue Service perpetuates that myth by classifying interest and other nonwage income as "unearned income." As we saw in Chapter 15, until the Tax Act of 1981, this unearned income could be taxed at higher marginal rates.

Despite these misconceptions, interest income is not an unearned bonus. It is a legitimate reward for allowing someone else to borrow purchasing power. And there is a real opportunity cost involved, because one could be using that money for something else. The money could be used for a vacation, a quality stereo package, or some other investment.

Banks and other financial institutions are in the business of encouraging people to save a portion of their income so that other people and firms can borrow the money to increase their purchasing power. We discussed the demand for loans and credit from the borrower's perspective in Chapter 8. Borrowers want to minimize the finance charges (interest) they must pay to get this additional purchasing power. Savers, on the other hand, want to get as much interest as possible on their savings.

In the 1980s, traditional passbook savings accounts have been shown to be an increasingly inadequate form of investment for most consumers. Inflation, changes in the tax laws, and the appearance of many other forms of investment mean that today, more than ever, consumers need to understand the principles of investment and personal finance if they are to make wise decisions regarding their money. In this chapter, we begin with the fundamentals of investment, in order to give you a method for evaluating various types. We define and explain the concepts of yield, risk, and liquidity. We also emphasize the importance of planning for inflation and taxes when one makes investments. Then we move on to the sometimes confusing world of investments. Here, we apply our investment principles to a wide range of investments, from savings accounts to real estate and from the stock market to government bonds. Our objective is to give you information about each of these investment opportunities so that you can put them in perspective, understand the pros and cons of each, and see how they could potentially fit into your investment strategy.

The Vocabulary of Investment and Personal Finance

You would be hard pressed to find an area of business that is more confusing to the average consumer than the world of investment and personal finance. One of the most obvious reasons for this confusion is the jargon used by investors. It is so foreign to most of us that it could well be another language, "investese." Investment counselors, stockbrokers, bankers, and business professors seem quite at home when discussing "investment portfolios" and the problems of "liquidity," but many consumers are not. Many even avoid the concepts and the terminology. That, however, is not to their advantage. Without an understanding of the basic vocabulary and concepts of investment, consumers may cling to a few familiar kinds of investments or simply rely blindly on other people to make their decisions for them. Doing so limits both decision making and results. Taking the time to learn about investments now will give you information on some of the most important characteristics of investments that you will need to understand the principles of investment and to evaluate alternative investment opportunities.

YIELD

Have you ever played with the psychology of free association? This is the game in which one is presented with a word such as *white* and supposed to say the first thing that comes to mind. Perhaps you thought of the word *black*. What would you think of if you heard the word *yield*? If you are like most people, you probably thought of the yellow and black highway traffic sign. But if you were an investment broker, you would think of a percent sign or a dollar

Saving and Investing: Is a Penny Saved a Penny Earned?

People with money to invest are in great demand. They must be careful to investigate the risks of any investment scheme.

sign, not a traffic sign, because in investment terms **yield** refers to the *return on an investment*—the amount of money that an investment returns. It is often expressed as a percentage of the cost of the original investment. The annual amount of interest a savings account earns, for example, can be translated into an annual yield by dividing the interest earned by the original amount deposited in the savings account. For example, if you left $100 in your savings account for one year and the bank gave you $5 interest, the annual yield would be 5 percent ($5 ÷ $100). The annual yield on any investment is simply the additional income earned during the year, divided by the amount of the investment. The higher the yield, the better the return on the investment.

RISK
Risk is the possibility that a financial investment may lose rather than earn money. Financial risk can take two forms. Either the yield on the investment will be less than expected when one decides to invest, or one may actually lose a portion (or all) of the investment.

Investors want to limit their risk as much as possible for obvious reasons. No one wants to lose money. To some degree, one can lower the risk by gathering more information and by becoming more informed about a potential investment. But ultimately, risk is directly correlated with yield. Higher-yielding investments almost always have a higher risk factor than investments with lower yields. The reason is in the dynamics of the investment process and in the basic rationality of investors. For example, suppose we offered you two investment opportunities, A and B. Option A involves a risky venture such as drilling for oil. If you will invest $10,000 in the oil-drilling scheme and if we strike oil, we will give you your $10,000 back at the end of a year, plus $2,000 for your trouble—a potential yield of 20 percent. Under option B, we will accept your $10,000 investment and use it to help us build an addition to our steel mill—the largest and most productive of its kind in the world. At the end of the year, you can get your investment back with a 20 percent yield. Which option would you take? Both offer the same yields if everything goes right, but the oil scheme is much riskier, so if you are rational, you would invest in option B, the steel mill. Because almost anyone in his or her right mind would follow the same strategy, the yield on option A would have to be raised to attract investors. The dynamics of the market plus the rationality of investors make risk and yield move in the same direction. A higher risk necessarily must offer higher potential yield.

CAPITAL GAINS (AND LOSSES)
The value of some investments, such as shares of stock in a corporation or a piece of undeveloped land, may change yearly, monthly, or even daily. If the value of an investment rises so that the income derived from its sale is greater than the original cost, the investor is said to have earned a **capital gain.** Of course, an investment sometimes loses value over time. For example, if you sell some stock for less than you paid for it, you have sustained a **capital loss.** As we mentioned in Chapter 15, for income tax purposes 60 percent of the income received from a long-term*

---
*"Long term" is defined as holding an asset for more than one year.

capital gain is tax free. The remaining 40 percent is taxed at a person's marginal rate. Capital losses, subject to some constraints, are tax deductible.

Capital gains and losses are relevant only to those investments that can be sold to others. These investments are called **capital assets,** and they include any form of real or personal property other than those used in one's trade or business. Houses, stocks, bonds, paintings, and jewelry are some common forms of capital assets.

LIQUIDITY

Liquidity is an investment's potential for being converted into cash. If there is no difficulty in converting an asset into cash, it is said to be a highly liquid investment. On the other hand, if one has to wait for a buyer or if some prearranged agreement prohibits the sale for some time, then the investment is not liquid. Ideally, because investors would like to have their investment options open at all times, they prefer liquidity. No one wants to be locked into an investment when a better opportunity arises or when an emergency strikes. But once again, there is a tradeoff among goals. If you prize liquidity very highly, stuffing your mattress with cash gives you a great deal of liquidity. However, the yield on your investment is zero, and the possibility for a capital gain is also nil. On the other hand, although buying a house has the potential to offer a significant capital gain, a house is not highly liquid. We will discuss this tradeoff of goals and the evaluation of investments later in this chapter.

INFLATION HEDGES

Inflation can be a mortal enemy of investment. As we discussed in Chapter 7, an overall rise in the price level eats away at the purchasing power of money. A decade ago, inflation was running at about 4 percent annually. A savings account with a 6 percent yield would have been reduced to a real gain of only 2 percent (6% − 4%), but at least it would have been a positive 2 percent. The 9 percent inflation rate of 1980 resulted in a 3 percent *negative* yield (6% − 9%) in savings accounts that year. Given the realities of inflation, it is of critical importance to weigh an investment's ability to stay ahead of inflation. Investments for which the values tend to rise with inflation are called **inflation hedges.** From 1970 to 1980, the best inflation-hedge investments were precious metals such as gold and silver, for which values rose at a compound annual rate of 31.6 and 23.7 percent, respectively. Does this mean that they will always be good inflation hedges? It is difficult to predict the future, but between 1980 and 1982 the value of an ounce of gold fell from $800 to under $400, and the value of silver fell from $40 to less than $10. Both commodities have fluctuated since, but their rapid decline points out the risk factor that is generally associated with any highly touted inflation hedge. By its very nature, an inflation hedge depends on investors' confidence in its ability to outpace inflation. If that confidence is shaken, large declines in price are possible. What goes up can also come down. And sometimes it can come down very quickly.

INFORMATION, TRANSACTION, AND MANAGEMENT COSTS

By this time, you should begin to realize that cost involves more than the money paid to acquire an investment. Gathering information and making informed decisions involves time and monetary costs that may or may not result in deciding to undertake a specific investment. The greater the uncertainty about the quality of an investment, the more information one needs and the costlier it becomes. You may decide to subscribe to one of the investor newsletter services to get a better idea about the quality of various investments, or you may simply subscribe to a personal finance magazine such as *Money*. In either event, the time and the expense are part of the information costs, and they are tax deductible when used for investment purposes.

Some investments, such as stocks, bonds, and even real estate, require brokers or dealers to help in acquiring or selling. Payments for such services are **transaction costs,** and they can significantly cut into returns. Day-to-day managing of investments may also involve costs. If the value of an investment fluctuates frequently, as do the prices of gold, silver, and other precious metals, one may have to devote some time each day to evaluating its progress (or decline). Other types of investments, such as rental property, may require management or paying someone else to see that they are maintained. These costs may seem burdensome to some investors, whereas other investors may actually enjoy them. Your particular mix of investments should reflect your attitudes toward these necessary expenditures of money and effort.

TAX STATUS AND INVESTMENT STRATEGIES

As we discussed in Chapter 15, tax avoidance is desirable because it lessens one's tax burden. Thus, investing money with an eye toward tax laws can often increase disposable income. As we have already seen, capital gains, for example, are treated much more favorably by the IRS than income from interest or stock dividends in that the first 60 percent of a capital gain is tax free.

Tax-exempt **municipal bonds** can also help one avoid taxes. When cities and counties need to borrow money to improve their communities, they issue bonds to attract outside money to pay for these investments. A **bond** is a certificate of indebtedness for which the borrower agrees to pay a fixed amount of interest each year for the privilege of using the bondholder's money. At the end of some preset time period, generally from five to thirty years, the borrower agrees to "redeem the bond at face value"—buy the bond back for a certain sum of money, generally printed on the front (face) of the bond. This description of a bond applies to corporate bonds as well as municipal or federal bonds. However, interest paid on corporate and federal bonds is not exempt from federal income taxes.* This tax exemption allows municipalities and states to offer less interest and still sell their bonds, making it cheaper for them to finance their debt.

INVESTMENT TRADEOFFS

The ideal investment, like the ideal spouse, probably doesn't exist. But if it did, it would have a high yield with no risk, it would be highly liquid with tremendous potential for capital gain, it would be an inflation hedge, and it would shelter those gains from taxes. If you can find something that has all of these qualities

---

*On the other hand, cities and states are not allowed to tax the interest earned on federal bonds. But given the smaller income taxes of these levels of government, this tax exemption is much less important.

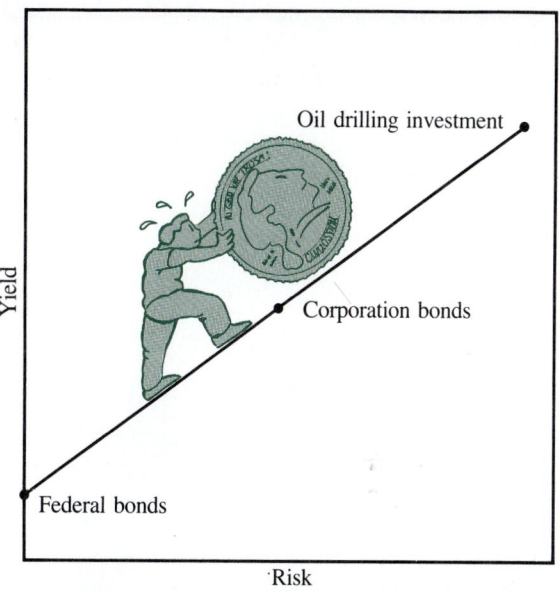

Figure 16-1. The relationship between yield and risk.

and no significant transaction or management costs, invest in it. Better yet, tell us how we can invest in it!

The impossibility of finding the "perfect investment" points up the conflict that is inherent among the terms in our investment vocabulary. Take the concepts of yield and risk, for example. All investors would like to maximize their return and minimize their risk, but some investors would be willing to accept a little more risk if the potential yield were higher. If the riskier investment did not offer a higher yield, no one would invest in it, as our earlier example about oil-drilling and steel-mill investments showed. Thus, there is a tradeoff between the variables, and there are different yields associated in systematic ways with their risks.

Figure 16-1 shows a hypothetical relationship between yield and risk, with some real-world examples to put it into perspective. For investors who dread financial risk, the least-risky investment consists of lending money to the United States government. In over 200 years, the federal government has never failed to pay its debts. And given the power to tax, there is no reason to assume that the government will

Figure 16-2. The relationship between yield and liquidity.

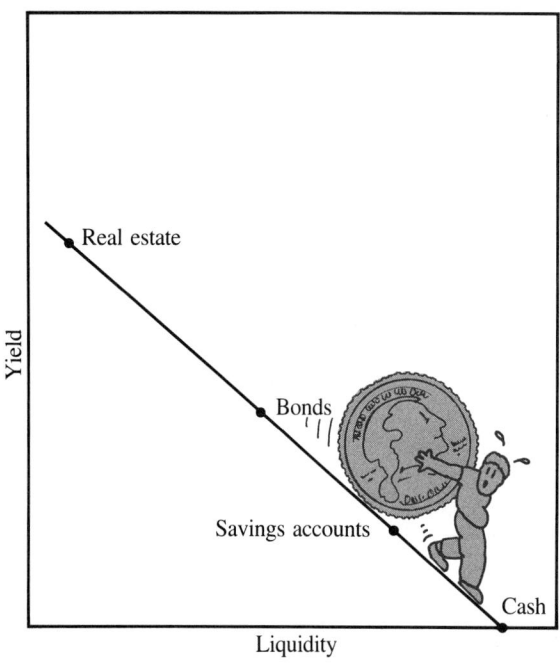

ever be in a situation in which it is unable to pay its creditors. The unhappy side of this enviable credit record is that as a result of this zero-risk situation, the federal government offers investors a very low yield. Corporate bonds cannot offer as much security as federal bonds, so corporations have to offer higher yields to attract investors. Extremely risky ventures such as drilling for oil are often called speculative investments, and they must offer even higher yields.

There are other tradeoffs, of course. For example, what is the relationship between liquidity and yield? All other conditions being equal, an investor would like to be able to earn a high yield and be able to convert the investment to cash instantly. Here again, you can see that because investments that provide greater liquidity are preferred over illiquid ones, they can offer a lower yield than those that are more difficult to convert to cash, as Figure 16-2 illustrates. In the last decade or so, real estate has offered a high return on investment. However, money invested in real estate is sometimes difficult to get back quickly. It is not very liquid. Corporate bonds offer greater liquidity because they are easier to sell than real estate, but their value can fluctuate, so investors may have to take a loss to get their money back immediately. Savings accounts offer low yields but very good liquidity, except on weekends and holidays, but even here, automatic teller machines are improving liquidity. But nothing is as liquid as cash.

A similar tradeoff often exists between investments offering a high annual yield and those offering long-term capital gains. It is often true that large capital gains can only be realized by reinvesting the profits of an enterprise and paying little or no return to current investors. Corporations often follow this strategy by paying their stockholders only a small percentage of their profits in dividends and reinvesting the bulk of their profits in new equipment, plants, or research. If this investment is successful, the price of the stock will rise, because other potential investors will try to buy the stock in anticipation of larger future dividends to stockholders. As these new investors bid up the price of the stock, the stockholders earn capital gains by selling to them.

The best investment for an individual consumer depends largely on the importance of the various investment tradeoffs. Some investors cannot sleep at night knowing that their investment involves some risk. Others are happy to accept a large degree of risk as long as the opportunity for a large capital gain or a high yield is in the offing. Some investors feel compelled to have as much information as possible before they make a decision. Others may simply be willing to accept the advice of a friend. The point is that one person's "ideal" investment may not be a good option for another person. You must evaluate your own standards for acceptable levels of risk, yield, and capital gains before venturing into the investment world. And you must realize that these factors are seldom present in all investments. You can generally obtain more of one factor only by sacrificing another. Table 16-3 (later in this chapter) compares the strengths of different investments using the terminology we previously explained. But before we can compare investments, we must first investigate options. We do this in the next section.

Types of Investments: Creating an Investment Portfolio

Now that you understand terminology and tradeoffs, it is possible for you to evaluate some of the typical investments available in the United States economy. Remember, no single investment is perfect for everyone, and investment goals determine the forms and varieties of investments. The mixture of investments that you choose to hold is called your **investment portfolio**. By acquiring new investments and getting rid of old ones, you can change your portfolio so that it more closely reflects your investment goals.

As you review the following investment possibilities, try to keep in mind the major concepts we have discussed:

- yield
- risk
- liquidity
- inflation protection
- information, transaction, and management costs
- tax status

SAVINGS ACCOUNTS

One of the best places to put your money to earn a safe yield is in a savings account at your local bank or savings and loan association. These institutions can offer more than 5 percent interest, and up to $100,000 of your savings is insured by a government-sponsored agency. (For details on insurance provisions for savings accounts, see Box 16-1.) Of course, a 5 percent yield may not seem very large when one considers the rate of inflation. Nevertheless, these accounts have certain advantages. They take almost no time to manage; information costs are virtually zero, because the maximum rates will be set by government decree until 1986; and transaction costs involved in putting money in or taking it out are also zero. Savings accounts are highly liquid and virtually risk free, but before you decide to plunk your money into the most convenient bank or savings and loan association, let us review the rationale for saving.

Why Consumers Save. On a society-wide level, an economy needs to have some members that hold their consumption below their income (that is, save) so that other members can borrow that purchasing power and spend. But on an individual level, why do consumers save? The three main reasons are: providing for an emergency, accumulating purchasing power for an expensive item, and providing for income in the long run. These reasons relate directly to budgeting and

---

BOX 16-1

How Safe Is Your Savings Account?

If you have ever seen a documentary about the 1929 stock market crash and the Great Depression of the 1930s, you must have witnessed a scene in which huge crowds gathered outside a bank hoping to get their deposits out. This frightening scene was all too real in the early years of the Depression, and more than a few people lost lifetime savings. You can get a feel for the scale of this catastrophe if you realize that the number of banks in the United States shrank from 25,000 in 1929 to 15,000 by 1934. The fear, the uncertainty, and the grief that this banking contraction forced the public to bear left an indelible mark on this country. As a result, Congress established the Federal Deposit Insurance Corporation (FDIC) to insure accounts in commercial banks. The FDIC was followed by the Federal Savings and Loan Insurance Corporation (FSLIC), which insures savings and loan deposits, and by the National Credit Union Association (NCUA), which insures deposits in affiliated credit unions. Each association is independent of the government and is financed by association members. Nevertheless, if a 1930s-like situation ever developed, there is little doubt that the U.S. Treasury would come to the rescue.

Currently, an account can be insured for up to $100,000. If you happen to be in the enviable position of needing more than $100,000 in insurance, you can do one of two things: you can go to another insured institution and open an account in your name, or you can open a second account at the same bank, but make it a joint account for you and a trustworthy partner (for example, your spouse). But before you begin to figure out how you are going to insure a million dollars at one bank, you might like to know that since 1934, the number of insurance payouts have been very few. In the FSLIC account, for example, only thirteen savings and loan associations have ever been forced to close and use the insurance fund.

Table 16-1. Year-End Value of a $1000 Savings Account Using Various Compounding Techniques for One Year

Compound technique	Nominal annual interest rate				
	6%	7%	8%	10%	12%
Annual	1060.00	1070.00	1080.00	1100.00	1120.00
Semiannual	1060.90	1071.22	1081.60	1102.50	1123.60
Quarterly	1061.36	1071.86	1082.43	1103.81	1125.51
Daily	1061.83	1072.50	1083.36	1105.22	1129.40

money management—the ways consumers define and achieve their financial goals.

1. *Saving for emergencies.* In Chapter 6 we discussed the basic principles of money management and budgeting. You may recall that one of the important components of budgeting is accumulating a fund that can be used in case of emergency. We suggested that an emergency fund should, at minimum, be equal to at least two months' income. It should be larger if one's monthly income is subject to large variations. For example, a full-time real estate agent or a construction worker would probably need a larger emergency fund than a nurse or a police officer, because he or she has less-regular income. An emergency fund should be readily available, but it should not be used unless there is no other alternative by which to meet one's budget. Once such a fund is depleted, every effort should be made to rebuild it as soon as possible.

2. *Saving for a specific purchase.* Buying a new car or taking a vacation might be another reason for saving. Any expense that is too large to be financed out of monthly income is a candidate for a special savings plan. Bank Christmas-club savings accounts are examples of this. Another common use for a special savings fund might be to provide a down payment on a house or a condominium. Saving for an expenditure of this type should be done on a regular basis, but the savings do not have to be available on a moment's notice. Therefore, the savings can be put into a longer-term savings or investment account and thus earn a higher interest rate.

3. *Saving for a long-term goal.* Putting aside money for the future with no specific purchase in mind may provide for income during retirement or simply enlarge financial holdings for heirs. This long-run savings is an investment for one's future and the future of one's family. The goal here is to obtain the highest possible yield, subject to other constraints such as the safety and tax status of the investment. We discuss this topic in more detail in Chapter 17.

No matter what the reason for saving, one should be aware of some minor differences in bank interest procedures that could result in one's earning a lower return.

The Importance of the Three C's: Compounding, Computing, Crediting. With a savings account, one not only earns interest on what one puts into it, but one earns interest on the interest itself, if it is left in the account. The concept of earning interest on previously paid interest is called **compounding.** Financial institutions have many different ways to compound interest. The simplest way is to do it once a year. A 6 percent interest rate that is paid annually will earn $60 interest on a savings account that has $1000 in it for one year. However, if another bank offers the same 6 percent interest rate but compounds the interest daily, the earnings will be $61.83. One can earn more with the second bank because the interest earned on January 1 and on each succeeding day earns interest on itself. Sometimes, banks will advertise that they compound interest daily. If they do, the effective yield will be higher. Table 16-1 shows the difference that compounding can make on a $1000 savings account at various interest rates.

Besides using various compounding techniques, banks and other financial institutions may also use various techniques in computing, or calculating, interest. The American Bankers Association estimates that there are at least fifty-four ways of computing interest on savings accounts. We will not try to outline all of them, but the most advantageous one to consumers is the "day of deposit to day of withdrawal" method. Under this plan, a depositor begins earning interest on the day the money is deposited and he or she continues to earn interest until the money is withdrawn. Some other less-favorable methods use the lowest monthly balance or offer interest only on money left on deposit for an entire quarter (three months). Still others penalize a depositor for making a withdrawal during the quarter or in the middle of an interest period.

A third factor to be consider is the procedure the bank has for crediting the interest to one's account. Some pay semiannually, quarterly, or even monthly. The system of crediting interest can be very important for a retired person who may be using that interest for living expenses. It may also be an important convenience for a consumer who needs the interest to make a specific purchase.

CERTIFICATES OF DEPOSIT

Financial institutions such as banks, credit unions, and savings and loan associations have developed a series of ingenious ways to pay more interest in the hope that this will entice more people to save with their firms. The **certificate of deposit (CD)** is an example of this innovative spirit. A CD is an agreement between a bank and a depositor that the bank will pay a guaranteed rate of interest over a specific time period, as long as the depositor agrees to leave a certain amount of money in the bank over that same period. With a CD, the depositor gives up some liquidity in order to gain a specific yield for a certain period of time.

Not all time certificates of deposit are alike. Some require larger deposits, whereas others require longer time commitments. The small-saver certificates offered by practically every bank and thrift institution require one to leave money on deposit for at least thirty months in order to earn the highest return,

Because interest rates on various types of savings and investment accounts fluctuate quite a bit, savings institutions post current rates prominently.

which is frequently twice as much as one could earn in a regular savings account. These small-scale certificates have no legal minimum size, and the interest rate on new issues is set by federal banking officials and is based on how much the federal government must pay to borrow money. Commercial banks are at a slight disadvantage in this market when compared to savings and loan associations, because they are required by a 1975 law to pay 1/4 percent less interest on these certificates than savings banks. The best rate available from commercial banks in 1981 on the certificates was 14.9 percent, whereas savings and loan associations and mutual savings banks could pay 15.15 percent interest. Once you deposit your money, the interest rate remains constant for thirty months, but if you choose to withdraw your money, you must pay an interest penalty.

Money-market certificates of deposit are another form of CD. Unlike small-saver certificates, money-market certificates tie up money for only twenty-six weeks (six months), and their interest rate is the same for all financial institutions. However, the minimum denomination is $10,000. No compounding

---

BOX 16-2

The Depository Institutions Deregulation and Monetary Control Act

In 1980, Congress passed the most far-reaching piece of financial legislation in over a generation—the Depository Institutions Deregulation and Monetary Control Act. There are many sections to this act, and we cannot outline all of them here, but consumers should know some of the most important ones and learn a little history besides.

The Banking Act of 1935 made it illegal to pay interest on checking accounts and it gave regulatory agencies the authority to impose ceilings on the interest that banks could pay on savings accounts and time deposits. In 1966, these regulations were extended to include almost all financial institutions and almost all forms of saving. These rates were quite low by recent standards (3 to 5 percent), and when consumers realized that they could get higher interest by taking their money out of these savings accounts, banks and saving and loan associations began to lose reserves. The system was further complicated by the appearance of **negotiable order of withdrawal (NOW)** accounts, which function like checking accounts but also pay interest. The combination of higher interest opportunities plus novel checking accounts led Congress to seek a complete reform of the system.

The Monetary Control Act (MCA) created a committee to oversee a gradual phaseout of all interest-rate ceilings by April 1986. Their first order of business allowed all banking institutions, from commercial banks and savings and loan associations to credit unions, to offer interest on checkable deposits, although they called for a 5¼ percent ceiling on these funds. However, given the potential differences in compounding, computing, and crediting, not all NOW accounts are alike. In addition, most banks require customers to maintain a minimum monthly balance in the account. Despite these requirements, most experts agree with Professors Richard Morse and Pat McDermott (1981) of Kansas State University, who wrote, "If a consumer is able to maintain a minimum or average balance of at least $200, the 'best' NOW account is more economical than any regular checking account. Moreover, many NOW accounts waive the minimum balance requirements for senior citizens (60 or 65 and older)."

In the near future consumers can expect a phaseout of all interest-rate ceilings because of the Act. This means that consumers will have to spend more time investigating the yields offered by competing financial institutions, but they will receive higher returns for this effort.

---

of interest is allowed, and a cash penalty is required if one chooses to withdraw the money early. Given these conditions, it is understandable that money-market certificates have offered higher yields than small-saver certificates in the past. Whether they will continue to offer higher yields depends in large part on the effect of the Monetary Control Act (MCA), explained in Box 16-2.

All-savers tax-exempt certificates are the most recent addition to the family of time certificates of deposit offered by banks and other savings institutions. Under the 1981 Tax Act (discussed in Chapter 15), from October 1, 1981 until December 31, 1982 all banks, savings and loan associations, credit unions, and mutual savings banks could offer a tax-exempt savings certificate that yielded 70 percent of the average interest rate paid by the U.S. Treasury. An individual investor could earn $1000 in interest from this certificate ($2000 for joint returns) and not pay any federal income tax on it. However, unless additional legislation is passed, the all-savers certificates cannot be purchased after 1982. Nevertheless, the tax-exempt nature of the investment reiterates the importance of being able to compare "after-tax yields." As we mentioned in Chapter 15, you can compare a tax-free yield with a taxable yield by using this formula:

$$\text{taxable yield} = \frac{\text{tax-free yield}}{1 - \text{marginal tax rate}}$$

Thus, consumers in the 40 percent bracket would

BOX 16-3

Choosing a Bank

Given the deregulation of banking interest rates and the increasing competition for deposits, selecting a bank is becoming a more important task for many consumers. Convenience has always been an important criterion in choosing a bank, and the Monetary Control Act has made this less of a problem by allowing most financial institutions to provide checking as well as saving accounts. One way to choose a bank, then, is to select the one that is close to home, is open at convenient hours, and has automatic tellers, statewide service, low charges, and high interest. Once again, no bank will come out the best in all departments, but you must set your personal range of acceptable tradeoffs. You can use the following worksheet to evaluate various interest-bearing checking accounts. The form is adapted from a survey done by Professor Pat McDermott at Kansas State University to evaluate local options.

	Banks		Savings and loan associations		Credit unions	
Yield Annual percentage rate Compounded Annual percentage yield Computed	Sample 5.25% Daily 5.39% Day of Deposit to Day of withdrawal					
Costs Check printing (per check) Overdraft fee Stop-payment fee	$0.02 $7.00 $3.00					
Schedule of Fees Balance Monthly account fee Check charge (per check) Balance for free checking How is balance calculated?	Under $1,000 $2.00 $0.20 $1,000 Lowest balance for the month					
Statements Frequency Checks included?	monthly yes					
Additional Services Safe-deposit box Traveler's checks Automatic teller Saturday banking	$12.00 free NO NO					

SOURCE: Adapted from Richard Morse and Pat McDermott, "Now Accounts: Costs and Benefits for Consumers," Kansas State University.

---

have to find an investment with a taxable yield of 20 percent to equal their return from a tax-exempt certificate paying 12 percent.

$$20 \text{ percent} = \frac{12 \text{ percent}}{1 - .40} = \frac{12 \text{ percent}}{.60}$$

GOVERNMENT SECURITIES

The federal government's debt is over $1 trillion, much of it owed to private citizens. Government debts are the least risky of all forms of investment, but they are also notoriously low in annual yield. However, not all government debts pay the same interest rate.

Two investors could lend the government identical sums of money and the more knowledgeable investor could earn twice the return of the other, because the types of and yields on certificates of government debt, called **government securities**, can vary enormously. Let us start with the best-known (and lowest-yielding) government security, the savings bond, and work our way up to the highest-yielding security.

The name U.S. savings bonds is as easily recognized as the names Coca-Cola and Chevrolet. But if consumers were asked to explain what a savings bond is and how it works, many of them would have a difficult, if not impossible, time doing it. All the posters, jingles, and television ads have conditioned Americans to accept U.S. savings bonds as a reasonable investment, but most of us do not know whether or not they are a good investment. In fact, one consumer group filed a protest with the Federal Trade Commission over the advertising of these bonds. They argued that the ads were false and misleading because the bonds are not a good investment.

U.S. savings bonds are similar to all other bonds—they are certificates of indebtedness whereby the borrower agrees to pay a certain amount of interest each year for the privilege of using the bondholder's money. But savings bonds are aimed at the small investor, and they are sold in only two forms: series EE and series HH bonds.

Series EE bonds are issued at a 50 percent discount of the value printed on the front of the bond—the **face value.** The smallest face value in the EE series is $50, so you could buy one of these bonds for $25. After you buy the bond, it begins to earn interest, which raises its value. So after seven years and ten months the cash value equals the face value. Once the government is willing to pay the face value of the bond, the bond is said to have matured. At this writing, the yield on EE series bonds is 9 percent, if they are held to maturity. No one may purchase more than $15,000 worth of these bonds in any year, but given their comparatively low yield, it is difficult to imagine that someone would buy that amount in a lifetime, let alone in one year.

Series HH bonds are purchased for their face value, and they pay 8.5 percent interest compounded semiannually if held for ten years. The smallest bond in the HH series is $500, compared to $50 in the EE series. One can buy more HH bonds than EE bonds—up to a maximum of $20,000.

Savings bonds do not offer extremely high yields. However, they do offer some tax advantages, because the interest earned cannot be taxed at the state or local levels. In addition, because the interest is not taxed until the bond is cashed in, one could purchase Series EE bonds at a discount during peak earning years, when he or she is in a high tax bracket, and then cash them in after retirement so that the interest earned would be taxed at a lower rate. But the time spent on this investment strategy may be better used in seeking another tax shelter that pays more than a 9 percent return. A final advantage of savings bonds is the "payroll savings plan," whereby an employer automatically deducts a portion of one's salary each month to buy bonds. This kind of forced saving yields a lower return than most other plans, but for consumers who find it almost impossible to save voluntarily, the plan does work.

Government securities do not always pay low interest rates. Besides buying U.S. savings bonds, an investor can purchase Treasury bills, Treasury notes, and Treasury bonds. The simplest way to buy these securities is through a bank or a broker, whose fees will be a tiny fraction of the cost. All of these securities must compete with bonds issued by private corporations and other government units, so the interest rate must be competitive. In recent years, these securities have offered twice the yield of ordinary savings bonds, along with most of the tax advantages. The major differences among **Treasury bills (T-bills),** Treasury notes, and Treasury bonds is the size of the minimum purchase and the length of time before they can be cashed in, or have matured. T-bills have the shortest maturities (anywhere from thirty days to one year) and the highest minimum denomination ($10,000). Treasury notes mature in one to ten years and come in minimum denominations of $5000 for notes running for four years or less and denominations of $1000 for longer terms. Treasury bonds run for more than ten years and are available in $1000 denominations.

Liquidity is not much of a problem for government securities, because there is a large market for them and brokers are constantly buying and selling old as well as new issues. However, everytime the services of a broker are used a fee will be charged. Thus, transaction costs are higher for T-bills, T-bonds, and T-notes than they are for savings bonds that can be purchased and redeemed at any bank. As far as risk is concerned, one can be certain that the federal government will not default (refuse to pay its debt). And once a T-bill or a T-bond is purchased, one knows with certainty what the yield will be. However, a problem may occur when one sells the bond before it matures. In this case, the value of the bond depends on the yield one gets versus the yield that another investor gets by buying a new bond. If a bond costs $1000 and pays $100 interest annually, it is yielding 10 percent. But if new bonds are yielding 20 percent, the value of the first bond is really only $500 to someone who has a choice between buying the old bond or a new one.

MONEY-MARKET MUTUAL FUNDS

If you like the idea of earning more than the savings-bond rate by buying larger government bonds, you may be even more pleased by the possibility of earning double that yield by investing in a **money-market mutual fund.** These funds, run by investment companies, pool investors' money to buy large bank certificates of deposit, high-paying government securities, and the high-yield bonds of major corporations. The funds require no day-to-day management on your part, and they are almost riskless (although not insured), because of the nature of the bonds and securities they hold. Liquidity is almost as good as that of a checking account, because most funds permit you to write checks on your account, subject only to a minimum amount, usually about $500.

If the combination of high yield, liquidity, and safety sounds good, you are not alone in your evaluation. When these funds began, few investors appreciated their advantages. Even by 1974 they had only $1.7 billion in assets. But as Figure 16-3 shows, these funds literally took off in the late 1970s and early 1980s, so by 1982 their assets exceeded $180 billion. The variety of funds currently available staggers the imagination. Some funds even specialize in tax-free bonds to provide nontaxable yields. The August 1980 issue of *Changing Times* listed sixty-eight funds and their major characteristics, along with addresses and phone numbers. You can obtain more recent data from *Donoghue's Money Fund Directory,* Box 540, Holliston, Massachusetts 01746.*

THE STOCK MARKET

When investments are mentioned, many people immediately associate the term with the stock market, and for good reason. Stocks have been a mainstay of investments for almost a century. Today it is impossible to watch a nightly news program or to read a local newspaper without seeing a reference to the stock market. But what are stocks and are they good investments for you?

To understand stocks it helps to look at them from a company's point of view. Whenever a company decides to expand its business or whenever a new company is being formed, it generally needs financial capital (money). There are many ways that a company could get this money, such as going to a bank and borrowing directly or selling bonds to the general public. However, both of these systems saddle the company with fixed periodic payments and interest on the debt. If the company is a corporation, it can raise money by selling stock, which entitles a buyer to an ownership interest in the corporation. To hold a **share of stock** is to own a piece, albeit a small piece, of the corporation itself. Once one becomes a stockholder, he or she has a right to a share in the profits of the corporation. However, unlike a bondholder, a stockholder is not a creditor of the corporation; he or she is an investor in the corporation. The return on an investment in stock is called a **dividend,** and it depends largely on the profitability of the corporation.

If one owns **preferred stock,** the size of the

---

*Most local newspapers list the current average yield of all major money market funds. If yours does not, look at a copy of *Barron's* in your library. This weekly financial newspaper is filled with investment data.

Figure 16-3. Assets of money-market mutual funds in (billions of dollars).

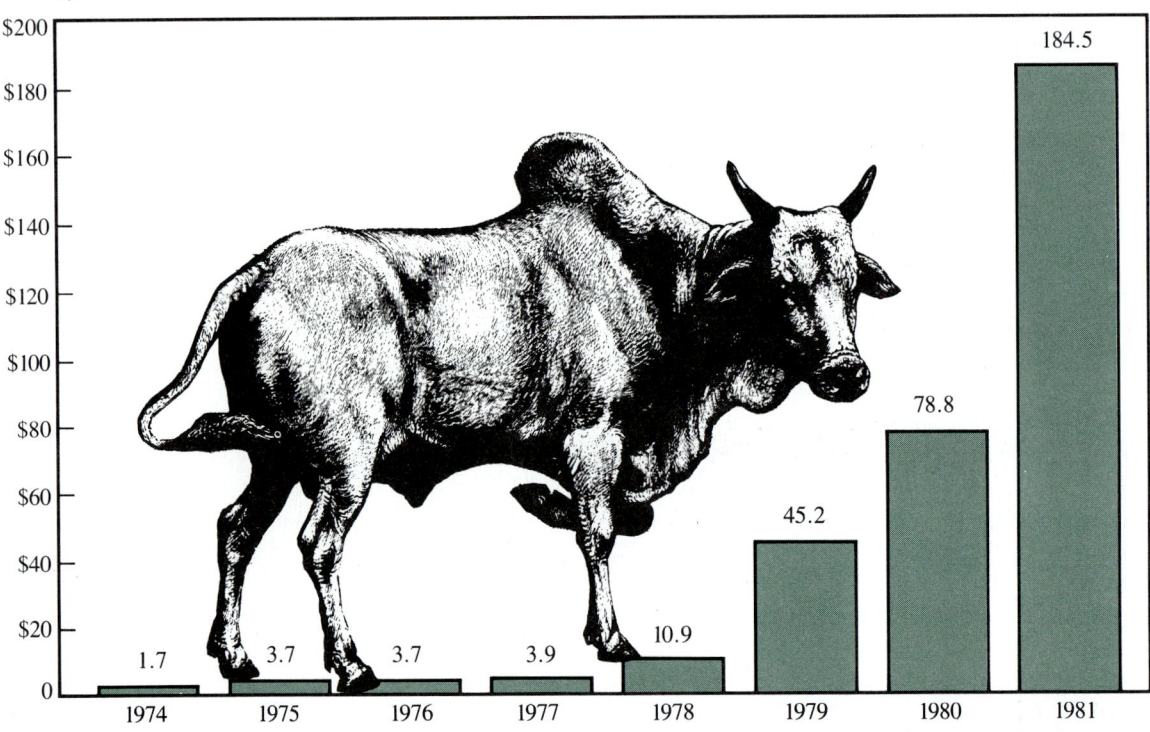

SOURCE: Investment Company Institute, *Mutual Fund Factbook* (Washington, D.C., 1982).

annual dividend is fixed by the corporation and never changes. In this regard it is similar to a bond, but unlike bondholders, preferred stockholders cannot sue the corporation if their dividends are not paid because of the lack of profitability. Preferred stockholders definitely have an inferior position to bondholders. However, they are "preferred" over other stockholders in the sense that their dividends must be paid before other stockholders receive their dividends. On the other hand, preferred stockholders do not have a voice (vote) in who should run the company, because preferred stock is always nonvoting stock.

Common stock is an investment in the ownership of a corporation that entitles the stockholder to share in the profits of the firm (if there are any) and also in the election of those who run the firm. Large corporations with publicly traded common stock have thousands of owners who seldom exercise their power to run the company. For example, if you owned 100 shares of IBM stock, you would own the equivalent of 0.00002 percent of the corporation. You would have 100 votes out of 583,900,000 potential share votes. If stockholders do not approve a corporate policy, it is generally easier for them to sell their shares and invest elsewhere than to go to corporate headquarters and attempt to change things. Because the everyday buying and selling of these shares determines the price of the stock, dissatisfaction among the shareholders will drive the price of a stock down and act as an indirect, but effective, way of controlling corporate management. As the price of a stock falls, the company becomes vulnerable to a takeover by another firm (or by a few disgruntled stockholders) who would replace the top management people.

The appeal of common stocks as an investment lies in their potential for increased dividends and capital gains. Unlike the interest return on a bond or on the dividends paid to a preferred stockholder, dividends on common stock can be raised at any time. Dividends are usually paid every three months (quarterly), and they may take the form of a cash payment, additional shares of stock, or a combination of both. If a corporation is doing exceptionally well, it may even declare an extra dividend. Capital gains accrue to stockholders who sell their shares of stock for a higher price than they paid for them. Because common stocks have the greatest potential for increased dividends, they are also more likely than preferred stocks to show capital gains. If the price of a stock doubles or triples, many corporations will declare a **stock split**—every common-stock shareholder will get additional shares based on the number of shares owned as of a certain date. For example, a 2 for 1 stock split for all shareholders of record on May 7 would credit someone who owned 100 shares of this corporation on May 7 with 200 shares.

Investing in the stock market can be rewarding, but it can also be hazardous. For all publicly traded stocks, one needs to find a licensed **stockbroker** to finalize the purchase or sale. Stockbrokers are not difficult to find, but they charge for their services. Some brokers provide rather elaborate investment counseling and advice; others simply execute buy and sell orders. The kind of broker you choose depends on how much you are willing to pay and on how much advice you need. Large, well-known brokers such as Merrill Lynch, E. F. Hutton, Dean Witter, and Bache have extensive research departments to help you avoid bad buys and select good ones.

The problem with depending heavily on brokerage firms for investment advice is that too many experts may spoil the forecast (just as too many cooks may spoil the soup). Because a large number of brokers are concentrating on learning everything they can about the companies on the major stock exchanges and then telling their clients everything they learned, there are few surprises. No one can really get the jump on anyone else. It becomes difficult to follow the age-old dictum "Buy low and sell high." In essence, many academic stock-market researchers have come to believe that selecting a large number of stocks at random will give as good a return as carefully selecting another set of stocks. This **random-walk theory** is based on the hypothesis that the current price of a stock already takes into account the present worth of a company and its future prospects as seen by the experts. In fact, according to this theory, the best strategy might be to buy and then hold a random selection of stocks for a long time. In this way one does not spend as much on sales commissions and should do as well as the market in general, so one can expect an 8 to 15 percent annual return on an investment over the long run.

EQUITY MUTUAL FUNDS

The idea that randomly selected stocks perform as well as rational, well-selected stocks is still not accepted by everyone. The presumption that the "experts" should outperform the individual investor is the idea behind **equity mutual funds**.* These mutual funds are investment companies that sell shares to individual investors and then pool this money to buy a range of carefully selected stocks that the mutual-fund managers believe will outperform the stock market in general. Because of the large number of investors in a given mutual fund, each one bears only a small part of the cost of hiring the best (highest-paid) financial advisors to run their investments. Mutual-fund managers do not readily accept the random-walk theory, because it strikes at the heart of one of their major selling points—expertise. Mutual funds can also limit the risk of loss to a small investor, because mutual funds generally spread their ownership, or diversify, in hundreds of corporations in different industries. Thus, mutual funds can avoid the small investor's dilemma of putting all of his or her eggs in one basket. If you like the idea of diversifying the risk but you don't believe that the high-paid investment advisors will be able to do better than the market average, you can buy an **index fund** that mirrors the composition of the 500 stocks in the Standard and Poor's Index (see Box 16-4).

The number of mutual funds that specialize in stocks grew from 259 in 1969 to 343 in 1979. But as

---

*Equity mutual funds invest in stocks (equities), whereas money-market mutual funds invest in bonds.

BOX 16-4
Making a Killing in the Market

Watching the stock market can be a fascinating avocation. Prices change daily, and the connection to world and national events is so real and yet so mysterious that watching the market has all the ingredients of a good spy novel. But can you earn a living at it?

The answer depends on your skill and your luck. Certainly, large fortunes have been made and lost in the market. But first you need to understand that "the stock market" is really composed of several markets in which stocks can be exchanged. The largest and most famous one in America is the New York Stock Exchange. Most large, well-known corporations trade their stock on this exchange. But there are other national exchanges, such as the American Exchange, and there are regional or local exchanges in which brokers can conduct stock sales without going through New York.

Because the overall health of the stock market is of considerable interest to investors, several averages have been developed to give a market overview. Two of the most frequently cited are the **Dow Jones Industrial Average** and the **Standard and Poor's Index.** The Dow Jones index monitors the progress of thirty U.S. corporations that are considered leaders in their fields. These are sometimes called **blue-chip stocks,** because they are supposed to be the best, although this is no guarantee of success. Only a few years ago Chrysler Corporation stock was in this exclusive average. The Standard and Poor's Index is a broader measure that includes the prices of 500 stocks. A rise in either average indicates that share prices of their stocks are increasing, on the average. And some experts take this as a sign of the general prosperity of other stocks. Whenever the market is rising, shareholders tend to be optimistic and are said to be **bullish.** When the market declines or is expected to decline, a pessimism settles over the experts and they are said to be **bearish.** Thus, a bull symbolizes an optimist, and a bear symbolizes a pessimist. In the figure, you can see waves of bullish and bearish behavior, as stock prices have risen and fallen in a wavelike pattern.

Making money in the market requires good timing as well as good stock selection. If you are really going to do well, you must have a feel for forecasting the ups and downs of the market. Contrary to the opinion of many speculators, no one has yet demonstrated a consistent ability to do this. Some people have made themselves rich and famous by correctly predicting a turn in the stock market. But in the long haul, the evidence seems to indicate that the additional expense in sales commissions for the average investor is not compensated by higher profits. The buy-and-hold strategy, in which one buys high-quality stocks and then holds on while the market averages follow a roller-coaster pattern, seems to promise greater returns.

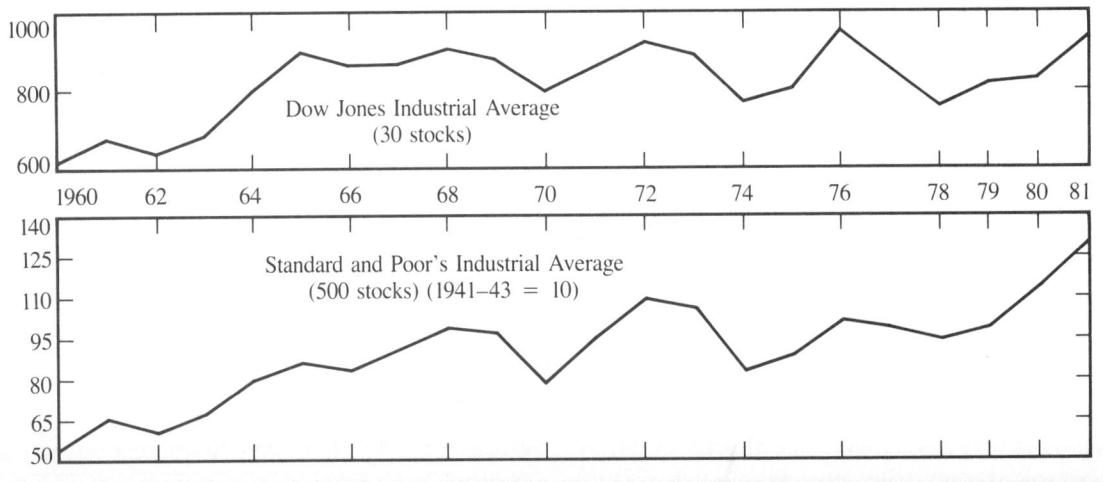

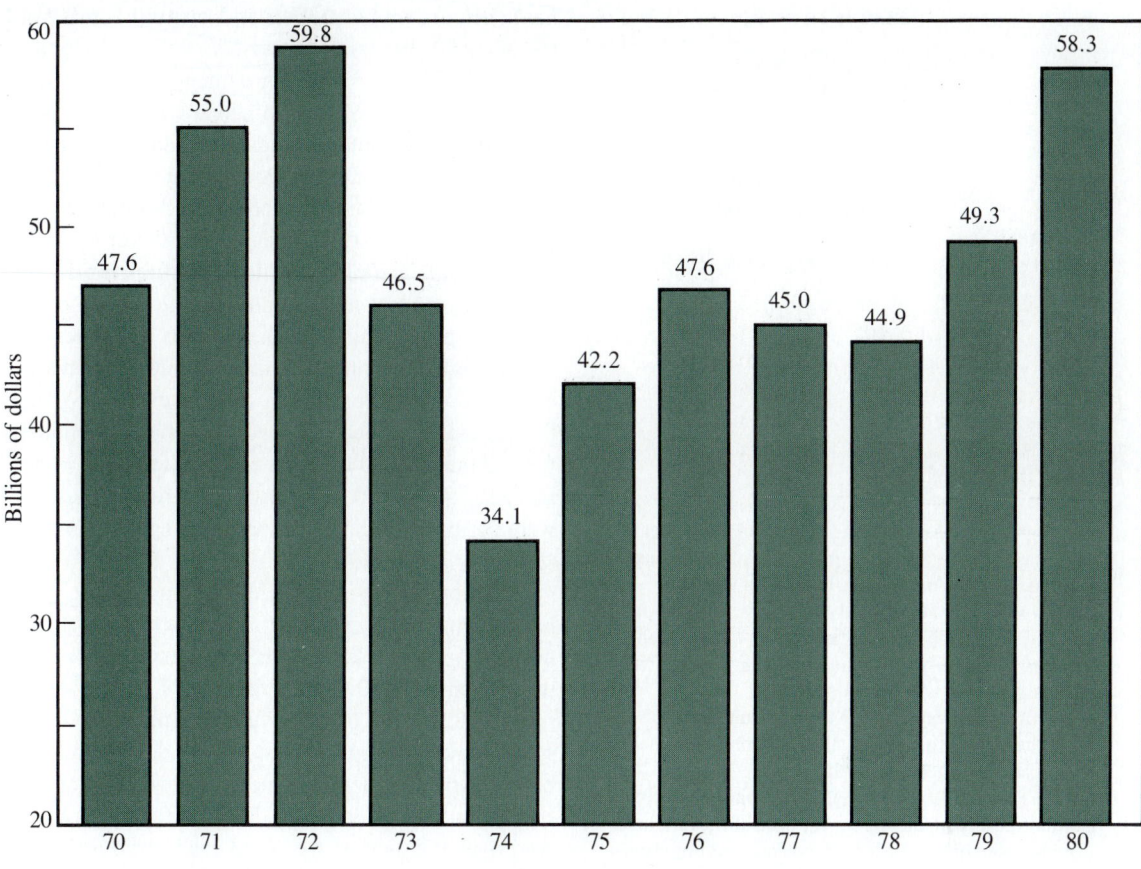

Figure 16-4. Assets of equity mutual funds, 1970–1980.

SOURCE: Investment Company Institute, *Mutual Fund Factbook* (Washington, D.C.: Investment Company Institute, 1980).

Figure 16-4 shows, the assets of these funds have fluctuated widely. Many are smaller today than at the beginning of the last decade. Investors seem reluctant to accept the idea that mutual funds offer a better way to invest. This is not for a lack of initiative on the part of the mutual funds. They have a variety of funds keyed to various investment targets and they use various sales tactics, but overall the industry has not grown.

Box 16-5 classifies and defines mutual funds by their investment objectives. Some funds, such as "aggressive" or "growth" oriented mutual funds, try to invest in stocks that offer the greatest potential for capital gains. These funds are not concerned with earning high dividends in the present. They want to see the value of their investment grow in the future. Aggressive funds take higher risks than growth funds. Other mutual funds, such as "income" funds, seek to maximize current income rather than to invest in stocks that will rise in price in the future and provide big capital gains. The stress on current income causes these funds to look for preferred stocks and bonds that are offering higher dividends and interest. The remaining categories of mutual funds try to balance the conflicting objectives of current income and long-term growth. Despite this variety of investment

> **BOX 16-5**
>
> ## Mutual Funds Classified by Investment Objective
>
> | Investment objective | Number of funds | | Assets (billions of dollars) | |
> |---|---|---|---|---|
> | | 1969 | 1979 | 1969 | 1979 |
> | Aggressive growth | 38 | 50 | $ 2.1 | $ 3.1 |
> | Growth | 105 | 142 | 15.8 | 13.0 |
> | Growth and income | 67 | 76 | 20.0 | 16.5 |
> | Balance | 25 | 21 | 6.8 | 3.4 |
> | Income | 24 | 54 | 3.6 | 4.5 |
> | | 259 | 343 | 48.3 | 40.3 |
>
> *Aggressive mutual fund.* A mutual fund that seeks maximum return through the use of investment techniques involving greater-than-ordinary risk.
>
> *Growth fund.* A mutual fund of which the primary investment objective is long-term capital gains. It invests principally in common stocks with growth potential.
>
> *Growth-and-income fund.* A mutual fund of which the aim is to provide for a degree of both income and long-term growth.
>
> *Balanced fund.* A mutual fund that has an investment policy of balancing its portfolio, generally by including bonds, preferred stocks, and common stocks.
>
> *Income fund.* A mutual fund of which the primary investment objective is current income rather than growth of capital. It usually invests in stocks and bonds that normally pay higher dividends and interest.

strategies and the increase in the number of mutual funds, equity mutual funds did not experience growth in the last decade.

Despite their wide variety of investment strategies, mutual funds have only two major organizational forms: closed-end and open-end. **Closed-end mutual funds,** which hold 10 percent of all funds, sell a fixed number of shares and then go about their business of getting the highest possible return for their shareholders. Closed-end shares are traded in the same way that common stocks of any other publicly held firm are traded. **Open-end mutual funds** hold the other 90 percent of the assets of all equity mutual funds. They issue shares on demand, and they will buy back any shares that someone wishes to sell. Some open-end mutual funds add a sales charge, called a **load,** whenever someone buys into the fund. Load mutual funds are usually sold through stock brokers or mutual-fund salespeople. Other open-end mutual funds are called **no-load mutual funds,** because they do not have a sales charge added to the purchase price. Shares in these funds are generally bought directly from the company, either by mail or by phone. The sales charge on a load fund averages 8.5 percent, and because load funds have not outperformed the no-load funds, their popularity has waned. In 1980, almost 70 percent of the industry's assets were in no-load funds compared to 10 percent in 1970 (*Business Week,* 1980).

Of the twenty mutual funds whose share values have grown most rapidly in recent years, most were no-load open-end funds. Their shares increased between 300 and 400 percent from 1977 to 1982 (*Barron's* 1982).* All of these funds outperformed the stock market averages. But do not be dazzled by these high returns. Remember, there are over 500 other equity mutual funds that did not perform this well. And over this period we could easily find a list of twenty common stocks that showed similar gains. The major advantages of investing in a mutual fund rather than directly in the stock market are the diversification and management services provided by the fund, not the chance for a big return. By buying into an investment portfolio that is managed by the experts, one is able to limit his or her risk and management costs, because one is leaving the task of watching the market to someone else. On the other hand, it is often difficult for large mutual funds to move quickly to take advantage of investment opportunities, whereas a small investor can get in, make a profit, and get out without encountering all of the inertia that seems part and parcel of a large firm. Thus, one can expect one's lower risk to be reflected in lower potential yields.

---

*Barron's provides a quarterly review of equity mutual fund performance and shows how much $10,000 invested in each fund five years ago, one year ago, and three months ago would be worth today.

Although real estate is often a good investment, you should thoroughly investigate any piece of property—and alternative investment opportunities—before putting your money in land.

REAL ESTATE

Will Rogers, a famous comedian of two generations ago, once offered this funny but true piece of investment advice: "Buy land. They ain't making any more of the stuff." The fact is that real estate can be a good and, in some cases, profitable investment, if one can accurately gauge the demand for land or buildings. People have to live and work somewhere, but real estate that is located in areas that people are migrating to is a better investment—the value of real estate increases because the demand for it is growing. Unless investors have special information that others do not about demand in a particular area, such as in a city in which a huge company is going to build its new plant, they have the same problem investing in real estate that they have in buying stocks or mutual funds.

Investing in unimproved land has other drawbacks as well. Vacant land, unlike financial securities, does not provide an annual return. There are no dividends or interest payments to offset the investment costs or the taxes incurred while awaiting a prospective rise in land values. For example, if you used $10,000 of your own money to buy a vacant lot and then you sold it three years later for $14,000, did you make a good investment? Well, it looks like a 40 percent profit at first ($4000 ÷ 10,000 = .40 = 40 percent). But don't forget the opportunity-cost concept. What was the next best alternative? If you had purchased a U.S. savings bond, you would not have earned such a return. However, United States Treasury notes often pay 12 percent interest. Compounded annually that comes to a 40.49 percent return over three years (1.12 × 1.12 × 1.12 = 1.4049). Taxes and real estate commissions further complicate the comparison, but as you can see, a simple increase in the value of your vacant land does *not* mean that you made a good investment.

The final characteristic to consider before you

Figure 16-5. Education and earnings.

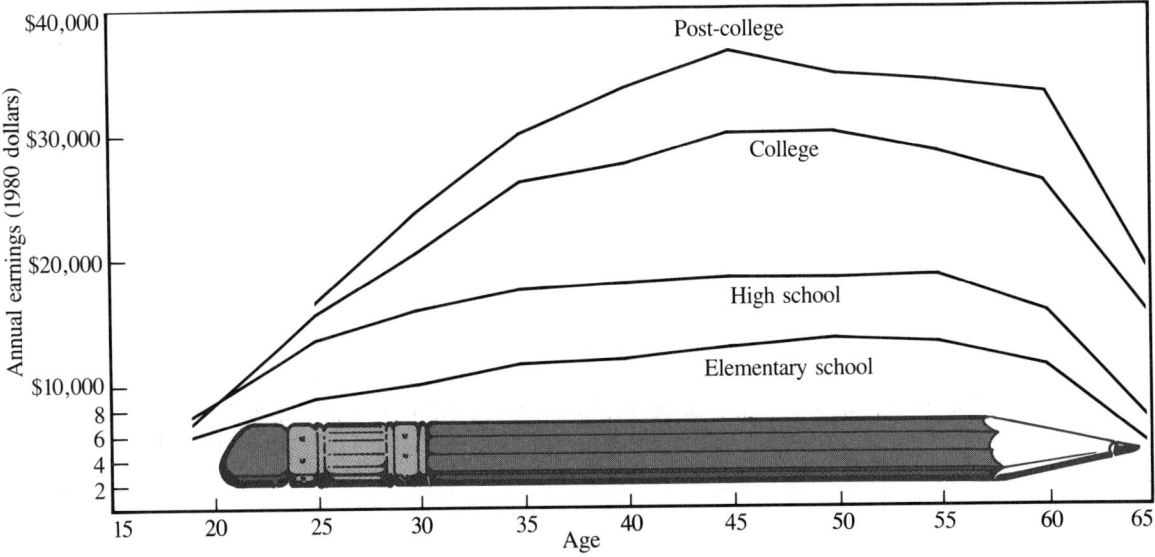

SOURCE: U.S. Bureau of the Census, "Money Income of Households, Families, and Persons in the United States," *Current Population Reports*, P-60 series (Washington, D.C.: U.S. Government Printing Office, 1982).

decide to invest in vacant land is liquidity. How easy is it to convert your ownership in that land into cash? Land is notoriously difficult to sell. If you are curious about this, simply call a real estate agent and mention that you are interested in undeveloped property. You will get a list that will take months to go through, and much of the land will have been on the market for years.

Of course, vacant land is not the only form of real estate investment. As we mentioned in Chapter 13, private housing has been shown to be an excellent investment. Owning your own home or condominium combines some nice tax advantages with long-term capital gain and short-term housing services. This kind of investment still suffers from some liquidity problems, but it is more liquid than other real estate ventures and certainly not as risky.

HUMAN CAPITAL

No discussion of alternative investments would be complete without mentioning one of the best investments available to everyone—oneself. It may seem odd to think of investing in yourself, but surely you and your parents have been doing just that. Your parents and you have been devoting resources to your education so that you will be a more productive member of society. In general, greater productivity leads to a higher income, which translates into a higher yield in investment terms. Of course, despite the fact that all of us are created equal, some have more natural ability than others, and the return per dollar of educational investment is higher for them. Economists estimate that the yield on an investment in a college education is between 8 and 12 percent. The most recent studies in this area have been closer to the lower end of this range than the upper end. Nevertheless, the returns on your education go far beyond simple monetary rewards. A college education provides psychological and life-enriching experiences that would be difficult and expensive to obtain elsewhere. And as Figure 16-5 shows, the average lifetime earnings of college graduates rise more rapidly and stay at higher levels than do the earnings of the less educated.

Table 16-2. A Comparison of the Strengths and Weaknesses of Various Investments

Investment	Average annual yield	Risk	Possibility of capital gain and long-term growth	Liquidity	Inflation hedge	Information, transaction, and management costs	Preferred tax status
Savings account	6%	None	None	High	Poor	None	None
Bank certificates of deposit	10–12%	Low	None	High	Moderate	None	Low
U.S. savings bonds	8½–9%	None	None	High	Poor	None	Low
U.S. Treasury bills	10–15%	None	Low	High	Moderate	Low	Low
Money-market funds	10–17%	Low	Low	High	Moderate	Low	None or high
Common stocks	0–20%	Moderate to high	Moderate to high	Moderate	Moderate	Moderate to high	Moderate
Mutual funds	0–12%	Moderate	Low to moderate	Moderate	Moderate	Moderate	Low
Municipal bonds	6–9%	Moderate	Low	Moderate	Poor	Moderate	High
Real estate							
unimproved land	0%	High	High	Low	High	High	Moderate
housing	10–12%	Moderate	High	Low	High	Moderate	High
College education	8–12%	Low	High	Low	Moderate	Moderate	Low
Cash	0%	Low	None	High	None	None	None

Of course, not all of the investment principles show a college education in such a favorable light. While there is not much risk, there is some. It is possible to get a college degree and not earn more than you would have without investing all that time and money. Liquidity is also very low, as anyone who has tried to turn his or her degree into cash is well aware. If you do earn a return on your educational investment, it is likely to be in the form of a slightly higher annual income than your less-educated friends rather than in a lump-sum payment. And there are few tax advantages associated directly with a college degree, although some courses, such as this one, may help you to use the tax laws to your advantage.

Comparing Various Investments

Table 16-2 presents the investments we have just discussed and compares their strengths and weaknesses in seven major categories. As you can see, there is no "perfect" investment. All involve some tradeoffs among goals. The investments that have the lowest risks are generally the ones that also have lower yields or fewer prospects for capital gains. Liquidity and hedging against inflation are two other characteristics that are subject to a major tradeoff. Investments that tend to be highly liquid also seem to provide poor or, at best, moderate protection against inflation. Some forms of investment entail high management and transaction costs, whereas others can be literally forgotten for long periods of time. Investing in common stocks is an example of the former, whereas buying a small savings certificate at a bank is an example of a "carefree" investment. Finally, the tax status of the return from an investment could be important in an overall investment strategy. As we stressed in Chapter 15, one can spend only after-tax dollars. For most investments, the major tax advantage comes when and if a long-term capital gain is earned. If one holds an asset for more than one year and then sells it at a profit, 60 percent of the gain is tax free, and the remaining 40 percent is taxed at a marginal rate. But other investments get their own tax breaks. For example, $100 in corporate dividends ($200 for a joint return) is exempt from income tax. And of course interest paid on U.S. bonds is tax exempt at the state and local level in the same way that the interest paid on most municipal bonds (and on money-market funds invested solely in those bonds) is exempt from federal income tax.

Given the variety of potential investments and their complementary, as well as conflicting, natures, you would be well advised to diversify your investment portfolio. This advice is very much like the proverb "Don't put all of your eggs in one basket." By diversifying investments, a person spreads the risk of losing everything in the event of a catastrophe. On the other hand, by spreading the risk, you also limit your gain if one guesses correctly about the future direction of the economy. This quandary strikes at the heart of investment strategy. How bold should you be? There is no pat answer for this, but your lifestyle and place in the life cycle both play a role. A young person with no dependents and with a lifetime of work opportunities ahead might be well advised to engage in investments that involve lower current yields and even moderate to high risks, as long as the potential for long-term growth and capital gains are significant. A retired couple should generally seek high yield investments that have little risk. Their concern is more with the immediate prospect of a return than with long-run capital gains and the risks associated with them. Middle-age investors in their peak earning years may be more concerned with tax advantages than other investors are. They will probably seek capital gains rather than interest income, because of the more favorable tax treatment. And liquidity may not be as important to them as to a retired person, because their employment is already providing cash flow.

These are only a few of the possible scenarios that could be developed to complement the varying needs of investors. The point is that no one knows your needs better than you do. And now that you have an idea of how the investment world works, you can begin making some plans, setting some goals, saving, and investing.

Summary

As we said at the beginning of this chapter, few areas are as confusing and yet as important to the average consumer as the world of investments and personal finance. In the first part of the chapter we tried to demystify the subject of investments by pointing out and defining some of the essential concepts that one should understand before making an investment decision. These concepts include yield, risk, liquidity, inflation hedge, transaction costs, and the tax implications of an investment. As we stressed earlier, there is no such thing as a perfect investment—one that will outperform all others on all of these criteria. Some investments are better at providing high yields than low risks. Others provide an inflation hedge, but at the cost of low liquidity. What you need to do is to gather enough information on a variety of investments so that you can accurately gauge the tradeoffs involved in choosing among them.

We also reviewed the major types of investments available to most consumers, from savings accounts to real estate, from the stock market to the money market. As we pointed out, financial markets are undergoing some revolutionary changes, partly as a response to an inflationary economy and partly because of economic legislation. The Depository Institutions Deregulation and Monetary Control Act of 1980, coupled with the Economic Recovery Tax Act of 1981, led to startling changes in investment opportunities and behavior. Despite the proliferation of new investment tools and the impending deregulation of interest rates, we have tried to provide an overall guide to the strengths and weaknesses of the major forms of investment.

Creating your own investment portfolio depends in large measure on your lifestyle and on your place in the life cycle. If you are a risk taker, the potential gains from investments in common stocks or real estate will probably outweigh the fear of loss, the lack of liquidity, and the information, transaction, and management costs that accompany such ventures. If security is more important and you have over $10,000 to invest, U.S. Treasury Bills offer a secure return and comparatively high yield. For the small-scale investor who wants more liquidity, money-market funds may prove to be a better investment. You may make these decisions yourself or you can hire someone else to make them for you. But in the final analysis, you must assume the responsibility for those decisions, because you will bear the consequences.

Neighborhood REVISITED

By this time, the tone of the conversation had risen a decibel or two, and the rest of the family had rejoined Joe and his grandmother. Some of the older family members began to nod their heads in agreement with Joe's grandmother. They too were skeptical of money-market funds that had offices hundreds or even thousands of miles away. They liked doing business with their local savings and loan association. So why should they change?

1. What is the current interest rate on a savings account at a thrift institution? How does this compare to the rate on a money-market account?

2. How much money can one person insure in a savings account? How much is insured in a money-market fund? Does this mean that money-market accounts are not safe?

3. If you were Joe, what arguments would you use to try to persuade Grandmother to shift her account into a money-market fund? Do you think you would be successful? Why or why not?

KEY TERMS

all-saver tax-exempt certificates
bearish
blue-chip stocks
bond
bullish
capital assets
capital gain
capital loss
certificate of deposit (CD)
closed-end mutual funds
common stock
compounding
dividend
face value
government securities
index fund

inflation hedges
interest
investments
investment portfolio
liquidity
load
mutual fund
money-market certificates of deposit
money-market mutual fund

negotiable order of withdrawal (NOW) accounts
municipal bonds
no-load mutual funds
open-end mutual funds
preferred stock
random-walk theory
risk
share of stock
stockbroker
stock split
Treasury bills (T-bills)
transaction costs
yield

QUESTIONS

1. What are the major purposes of saving? Give an example of each and estimate how long it would take you to satisfy each goal.

2. Explain why a high-risk investment has to offer a better-than-average return in order for people to invest in it.

3. What is the most liquid kind of investment? How would such an investment fare in times of high inflation? How would it do if average prices fell and deflation occurred?

4. What is a capital gain and how is it treated for income tax purposes? If you were in a high tax bracket, would you prefer an investment with a high yield, or one with large capital gains?

5. Why is there no such thing as a perfect investment? How is this related to creating an investment portfolio?

6. Briefly explain the advantages of investing in U.S. savings bonds. What are the disadvantages? Are they a good investment for you? Why?

7. What are the differences and similarities between T-bills, U.S. Treasury notes, and U.S. Treasury bonds? Call a local bank to find the current annual yields. Would they be a better investment for you than U.S. savings bonds? Explain.

8. What is a money-market mutual fund and how does it compare to an equity mutual fund? If you were going to invest in either a money-market or an equity fund, which one would you choose and why?

PROJECTS

1. Call or visit three financial institutions and ask for the annual yield on their interest-bearing checking accounts. Get their compounding, computing, and crediting policies. Compare the results and decide which one offers the highest return. Explain whether or not you would bank with them.

2. Call or write for information from a money-market mutual fund. You will get this information in a brochure called a "prospectus." Look over the prospectus. What is the mutual fund investing its funds in? Is the return higher than you could obtain at a bank? With a savings bond? With a T-bill?

3. This chapter discussed the up-and-down nature of the stock market. Get some information about the Dow Jones Industrial Average or the Standard and Poor's Index over the last year and graph it. Does it look like a roller coaster? Is there a definable trend? Has it outpaced inflation?

4. Call a local stockbroker and get some tips on the market. Follow these suggestions in the stock market to see whether they outperform the market averages. Select a dozen stocks at random and plot them. What does the random-walk theory predict?

READINGS AND REFERENCES

Eisenberg, Richard. "Money-Market Funds Go Tax Free." *Money,* November 1979.

Engel, Louis, and Wyckoff, Peter. *How to Buy Stocks.* New York: Bantam Books, 1977.

Federal Reserve Bank of San Francisco. "The Funds and Their Critics." *Weekly Letter,* March 20, 1981.

Gup, Benton E. *The Basics of Investing.* New York: John Wiley, 1979.

"In Spite of Low Yields, Savings Accounts Still Satisfy Many People." *Wall Street Journal,* April 15, 1981.

Investment Company Institute. *1980 Mutual Fund Fact Book.* Washington, D.C.: Investment Company Institute, published annually.

Morse, Richard L. D., and McDermott, Pat. "NOW Accounts: Cost and Benefits for Consumers." Kansas State University, March 1981.

Mueller, Eva, and Lean, Jane. "The Savings Account as a Source for Financing Large Expenditures." *Journal of Finance,* May 1967.

"Mutual Fund Performance." *Barron's,* May 10, 1982.

"Mutual Funds Resurge." *Business Week,* March 31, 1980.

Rukeyser, Louis. *How to Make Money in Wall Street.* New York: Doubleday, 1974.

"Savings Bonds—Do They Make Sense Now?" *Changing Times,* August 1980.

"Stockmarket Basics for Beginners." *Changing Times,* June 1981.

Thorsell, Richard L. *Investing On Your Own: How to Find Winning Stocks in Your Own Backyard.* New York: McGraw-Hill, 1979.

"Twenty-Five High Performance Mutual Funds." *Changing Times,* July 1980.

Weiss, Martin D. "What To Do With Your Savings." *Consumers Digest,* March/April 1981.

"Why Some Experts Say You Can't Beat the Stock Averages." *Changing Times,* May 1980.

Did You Know That...

- *there are two basic types of insurance policies: term policies that pay off only in case of death and cash-value policies that add a savings account to the death provision?*

- *insurance dividends on participating policies are nontaxable, because they are considered refunds of an overcharge?*

- *group life insurance is generally the least-expensive way to buy life insurance?*

- *insurance premiums for identical policies from two companies often vary by 100 percent and sometimes by as much as 400 percent?*

- *a study by the Federal Trade Commission showed that 20 percent of all new whole-life insurance policies were canceled by consumers in the first year and that even for those policies held for ten years, the average yield on the savings portion was less than 2 percent?*

- *Social Security automatically provides life insurance benefits based on one's contribution to the program?*

- *there is a straightforward way to calculate how much life insurance one needs to provide income for dependents that includes the value of Social Security benefits and inflation?*

- *by the time today's teenagers are ready to retire, the proportion of the United States population sixty-five and over will be twice as high as it is today? The number of people paying into Social Security per recipient will be 33 percent lower, and today's problems of funding Social Security and retirement will appear trivial by comparison.*

- *company pension plans are regulated and guaranteed under federal law, and employees' pensions cannot be taken away once they are "vested," which cannot take longer than 10 years?*

- *even if you have never written a will, your state already has one prepared for you?*

- *misinformation and poor decision-making lead most consumers to pay 50 percent more in funeral costs than they should, regardless of the type of funeral desired?*

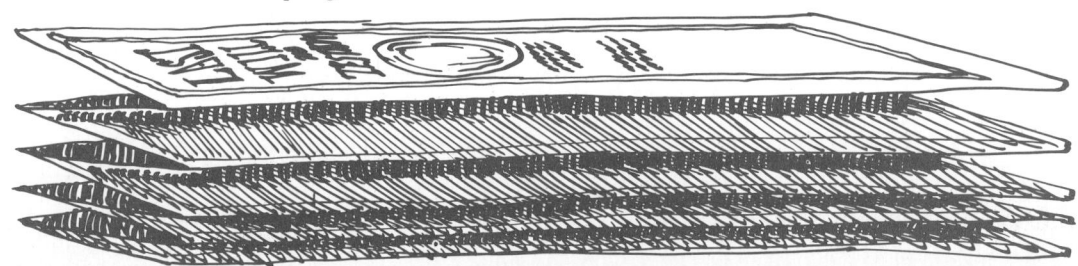

17 Planning for Your Future: Insurance, Retirement, and Beyond

Life Insurance
Retirement
Making a Will
Funeral and Burial Arrangements

Neighborhood CAPSULE
Providing for the Future

Fred and Marlene Barstow were just finishing dinner when the telephone rang. Reluctantly, Fred got up from the table and picked up the phone.

"Hello," the intruder's voice began. "May I speak to Fred Barstow?"

"This is Fred Barstow," Fred replied, trying to conceal the fact that his mouth was still partially full.

"Oh, hey, are you eating dinner?" the cheerful, anonymous voice went on. "I'm sorry. I'll call back later. I just had some information for you along with a road atlas, but don't let me interrupt your dinner. I'll call back."

By now Fred was a little puzzled and just a bit anxious. "What kind of information?" he asked.

"Well," the voice went on, "I know that you just bought a new home, and I'd like to show you how you can have that entire mortgage paid off in the event that something should happen to you. But I can't do it over the phone, so how about my coming over to your place around 8:00 tonight, and I'll explain the plan and give you a road atlas, too."

"Tonight?" Fred responded. "No, that's not a good idea. We're just not ready . . ."

"Don't worry about the mess," the voice interrupted. "Once your wife sees how important this is, she'll be grateful, believe me."

There was a slight pause in the conversation while Fred tried to force himself to stop digesting his food so he could think more clearly. However, the moment of silence passed quickly as the voice said, "O.K., I'll be over at 8. See you then."

When Fred returned to the table, he told his wife about the call, but he was too embarrassed to mention that he hadn't been able to refuse the caller's request, so he emphasized the free-gift aspect and said that there wasn't any obligation to buy.

At 8:00 sharp, Murray Aronson, the anonymous voice, arrived, attaché case in hand. By 8:15, the three of them were sitting around the dining room table poring over charts, graphs, and tables that all had one thing in common—they demonstrated beyond a shadow of a doubt that Fred Barstow did not have enough insurance. By 8:30, Fred and Marlene were convinced that they should buy mortgage insurance to pay off the house in the event of Fred's death. By 8:45, Murray had introduced the distinction between death insurance (term insurance) and life insurance (cash-value insurance).

"Just look at this policy. We call it our provider policy because it's intended for the breadwinner in the family. And it won't be very expensive because you're only thirty-five years old and in good health . . ." He paused for a moment to let the last phrase sink in. "You are in good health, aren't you Fred? Because we could have some real problems if you're not."

"No, I'm fine! Really," Fred said defensively. And the point had been made effectively.

"O.K." Murray went on. "Your premium on a $100,000 provider whole-life policy would be $1650 a year or $143.43 per month with the service charges for all the extra paperwork. And look at the advantages of this policy. The premium never goes up, even though your risk of death does go up as you get older. You are building a nice cash-value nest egg that you can borrow against at only 7 percent. Try to find that kind of rate at your local bank! And by the time you are sixty-five, you will have built up over $63,000 in guaranteed cash value, and you will only have put in, let's see now . . ."

He punched the numbers into his calculator slowly, for effect, as Fred and Marlene both peered over to see just how much they would be investing to get this $63,000 nest egg.

"Only $49,500! So you're getting all of your premiums back with interest *plus* $100,000 of life insurance from now until you're sixty-five."

492 Economic Decisions for Consumers

In the 1960s it was commonplace to hear the expression "this is the first day of the rest of your life." Well, you are now reading the first chapter of the rest of your life. All the information in this chapter is oriented toward helping you plan for your future. We begin with a discussion of life insurance, a subject that many consumers make poor decisions about because they are ignorant of its fundamentals. It is ironic that consumers are willing to spend more time shopping for a car than shopping for life insurance. A poor decision about an automobile is fairly easy to identify and not terribly expensive to correct. But an error in a life insurance decision can cost a consumer thousands of dollars, and it may not be discovered until the family has to pay the consequences, ten, twenty, or even thirty years after the policy is purchased. In our first major section, we will outline the principles behind life insurance and give you some insight into the kind and amount of life insurance that is right for you.

Life insurance can do more than provide death benefits to the survivors of an insured person. It can also provide retirement income. Our second major section looks at the retirement phase of the life cycle and goes beyond life insurance to compare various pension plans, from Social Security to Individual Retirement Accounts and Keogh plans. There has been a great deal of recent legislation in the area of retirement plans and pension funds, and a little familiarity with your rights can pay off as you plan for your future.

Making a will is an integral part of planning for your future and for the disposition of your worldly possessions. It may surprise you to know that you already have a will, even if you have never drawn one up for yourself. We will outline your current will and suggest how you can change it if you want to.

Finally, we turn to the ultimate consumer expenditure—a funeral. You will undoubtedly be involved in a number of funerals during your lifetime, and some knowledge about what is involved and how to handle it should prove helpful to you and to others who may depend on you for support during such troubled times.

Life Insurance

In 1980 alone, over 14 million new policyholders bought over $527 billion worth of new or additional life insurance coverage. Today, there are almost 150 million life insurance policyholders paying more than $30 billion annually for some type of coverage. Obviously, the life insurance industry must be offering the American consumer something in return for this tremendous outpouring of funds. But what are consumers getting in return? And are they paying too much?

Life insurance, like other types of insurance such as auto, home, and health, is an agreement on a consumer's part to give up a small, definite amount of income in the present—a **premium**—in order to be shielded from some uncertain but potentially greater loss in the future. It is a way of limiting risk. In the case of homeowner's insurance, the probability that the homeowner will make a claim is not certain. One could go through life without a fire or a theft and thus never invoke one's right to payment. With life insurance, on the other hand, death is always a possibility, and at some point it is a certainty. Insurance companies are well aware that the laws of immortality apply only in the afterlife. Thus, at some point they will have to pay off. If this is so, how can they afford to offer a large payment in the event of the death of a policyholder? The answer lies in the regularity of mortality.

Figure 17-1 illustrates this regularity for a population for which the average life expectancy at birth is seventy. As you can see, the risk of death drops dramatically during the first few years of life and rises steadily thereafter. If a company insures a large number of people across the age spectrum, it can spread this risk over a great number of policyholders. If hundreds of thousands of people are insured, the millions of dollars received in small premiums can allow the companies to pay large claims to families of the few unfortunate souls who die in any given year. In addition to taking advantage of this law of large numbers, insurance companies can adjust their charges to account for the particular age of the policyholder. For example, because sixty-year-old policyholders are twice as likely to die as fifty-year-old policyholders, the rates may be doubled to ensure that no age group subsidizes any other. Insurance employees who calculate these death probabilities are called **actuaries,** and they are good at what they do. They collect death probabilities based on the real-world behavior of death rates classified by age, sex,

Figure 17-1. Death rates at various ages.

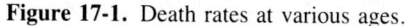

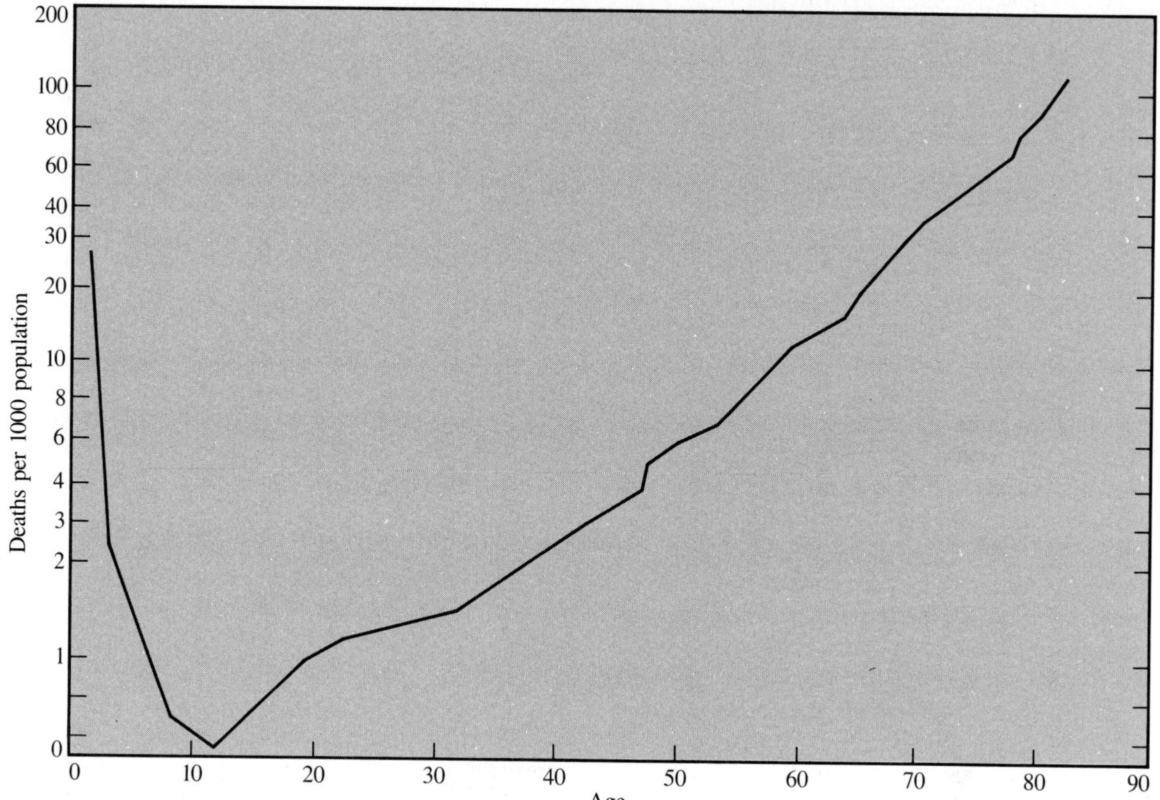

SOURCE: Based on United Nations, *Methods for Population Projections by Sex and Age*. (New York: United Nations, 1956).

health, and sometimes lifestyle (for example, smoker, nonsmoker, drinker, nondrinker). These characteristics are then used to determine the risk of death and the cost of insuring someone against this risk. All of this information is put into an **actuarial table,** which lists the probability that a person with certain characteristics will die in a given year.

In essence, then, life insurance can be viewed in much the same way as any other wager. The odds are established by the actuarial tables produced by insurance actuaries. Given the odds, the policyholder bets that he or she will die, and the insurance company pays off only when the policyholder is correct. Given this situation, it is little wonder that insurance companies often support antismoking campaigns, jog-a-thons, and other sporting events that encourage fitness and longevity. They have a genuine interest in keeping people alive and healthy.

TYPES OF INSURANCE COMPANIES

Insurance companies take one of two forms—they are either **stock insurance companies** or **mutual insurance companies.** Stock insurance companies have a structure that mirrors those of all modern publicly held corporations. They are owned by shareholders who expect dividends as a return on their investment. Over 90 percent of all life insurance companies are stockholder owned, and they account for about 50 percent of all life insurance in force. Mutual insurance companies compose a much smaller proportion of the industry, but they account for the other half of life insurance policies. These companies are technically owned and controlled by policyholders, who share in the profits of the company through dividends or reductions in their annual premiums. Insurance offered by mutual insurance companies is often called **participating life insurance,** because the policyholder gets to participate in voting for the company's board of directors and has the right to earn dividends on the policy. In reality, the voting power of any one policyholder is very slight, but the dividend rebate can be significant when one compares the relative costs of competing policies.

Because the dividend rate on a participating policy is never guaranteed by the insurance company, one does not know the exact amount of the annual rebate. However, in a study reported in the March 1980 issue of *Consumer Reports,* participating policies were shown to be less expensive than nonparticipating policies in about 75 percent of the cases studied. Nevertheless, if one prefers to limit one's risk, a nonparticipating policy for which the cost is fixed and guaranteed might be preferable to a participating policy in which there is no assurance of a refund. For example, the annual premium for a $100,000 life insurance policy for a thirty-five-year-old male might be $260 for a nonparticipating policy, but $320 for a participating one. If the participating policy has been paying a 25 percent dividend, its annual premium will be only $240—$20 cheaper than the other policy. Dividends are never guaranteed, however, and they could decline, making the nonparticipating policy a better buy. Before you select a participating policy, you should ask for the insurance company's dividend record over several years, not just the previous year (see Box 17-1).

FOUR WAYS TO BUY LIFE INSURANCE

Life insurance is sometimes classified by how it is sold. You can buy life insurance from an agent in your own home, through your employer, or from a retailer who has just sold you a new car on credit. Life insurance companies also distinguish between insurance policies on the basis of *how* you pay—that is,

---

BOX 17-1

Insurance Dividends: Benefits or Overcharge?

Insurance dividends are paid on participating life insurance policies, and they can significantly decrease the premium. These dividends are not taxable, because the Internal Revenue Service views them as a refund of an overcharge, not as a return on an investment. In effect, the insurance companies set the rates too high; thus the policyholder deserves a partial rebate on the premium.

The origins of insurance dividends go back to the nineteenth century, when mortality conditions were much more uncertain than they are today. An epidemic or a natural disaster could lead to huge, unforeseen losses, and even in good times, mortality estimates were subject to large errors. Because insurance companies needed a safety cushion in the event that they miscalculated, they inflated the premiums but promised to return the overcharge in the form of dividends.

With declining mortality rates, the cost of insuring people's lives has continued to fall. Thus, the premiums for participating policies have generally been cheaper than for nonparticipating policies. Partly because of this competitive pressure, some stock companies have begun to write participating policies that provide for dividends but do not give the policyholder a voice in the operation of the company. But because a policyholder's vote is so small, this difference is fairly slight. The real question to be weighed is whether a profit-maximizing stock company would issue as large a dividend as a mutual insurance company. On this point the experts are divided. Barry Kaye, author of *How to Save a Fortune on Your Life Insurance,* is skeptical of stock companies. He argues, "Consumers must remember that a stock company's first obligation is to its stockholders, who will receive most of the company's profits. This holds even for [those stock companies] offering 'participating,' dividend paying policies" (*Consumers Digest,* July/August 1981, p. 42). On the other hand, David Goodwin, author of *Stop Wasting Your Insurance Dollars,* wrote that " 'Participating' and 'low premium' are contradictory expressions in today's marketplace . . . If you want ownership of a life insurance company, buy stock in it. Buying a participating policy is not the wise way to seek profit or low costs" (*Consumers Digest,* November/December 1980, p. 31).

Figure 17-2. Life insurance policies (owned) by number and dollar value.

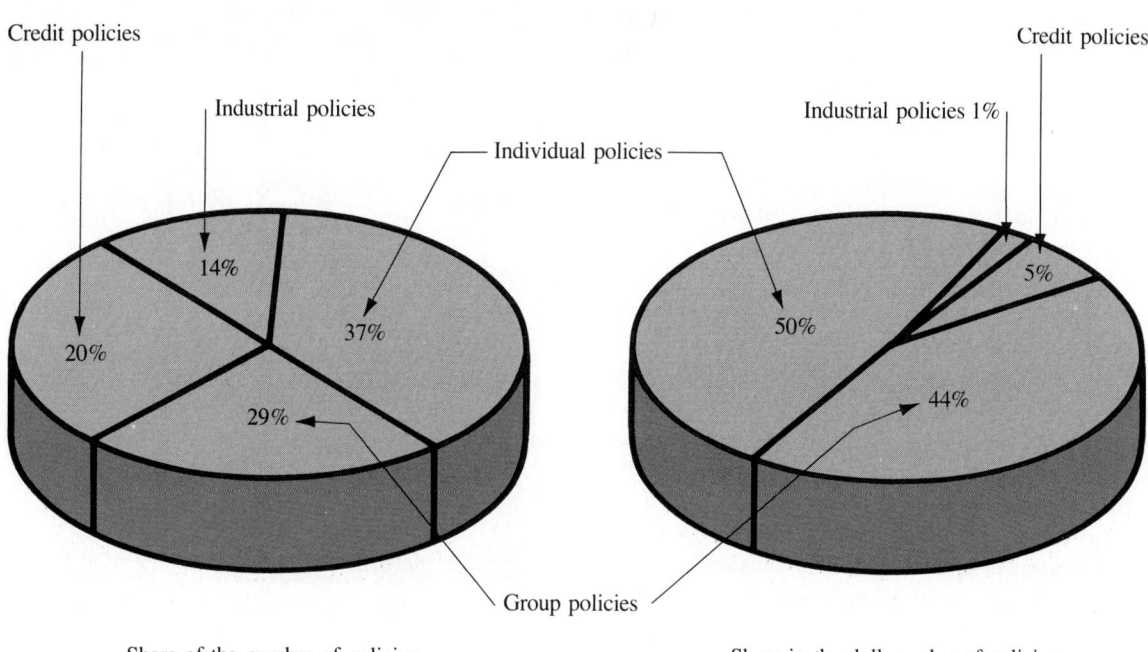

Share of the number of policies   Share in the dollar value of policies

SOURCE: Data from American Council of Life Insurance, *Life Insurance Factbook* (1981), p. 18.

whether you send in payments or an agent comes to collect them. The following sections describe four types of insurance: individual, group, credit, and industrial.

Individual Life Insurance. As Figure 17-2 shows, over one-third of all life insurance policies are purchased by individuals through an insurance agent, who issues a policy tailored to the particular needs of a consumer. Once the policy is written, the insured person is generally required to undergo a physical examination so that the insurance company can more accurately estimate its risk. The poorer the health of the insured person, the higher the insurance premium.

Group Life Insurance. Members of a particular association or people who share a common employer are often able to purchase life insurance as a group rather than on an individual basis. **Group life insurance** generally does not require a physical examination, because the group is large enough to allow premiums to be based on the life expectancies of people in that occupation or association. Often, there is no agent involved in the sale, and all correspondence is completed between the insurance company and the insured person. Because this type of insurance requires fewer intermediaries, it is often less expensive than individual life insurance, for which sales commissions have to be paid.

Another cost advantage is available to some consumers who belong to groups for which the life expectancy is better than average. College professors, for example, have exceptionally long lives and thus are often able to purchase group life insurance at lower rates than people in other occupations. Finally, because physical examinations are the exception rather than the rule, group insurance is a good buy for those in poor health.

Credit Life Insurance. As you can see in Figure 17-2, 21 percent of all insurance policies—6 percent of the value of all life insurance—are categorized as **credit life insurance.** These policies are written to ensure prompt payment of a loan in the event of the borrower's death. In essence, credit life insurance is really loan death insurance. It is standard procedure among banks and finance companies to try to persuade their loan customers to insure themselves for the amount of the loan. Because these policies are for small amounts of money and because no physical examinations or, generally, no adjustments for the life expectancy of the borrower are involved, these policies are usually quite expensive per dollar of insurance. This makes them a poor choice for the average customer.

If credit life insurance is not a good buy, why were there more than 84 million credit life insurance policies in force in 1980? Part of the reason probably lies in consumer ignorance. Many consumers do not know that these policies are *optional;* they cannot be a requirement of a loan. Second, these policies *appear* to be inexpensive because they increase the cost of a loan payment by only a few dollars. But if those dollars were spent on additional individual or group life insurance, they could buy more insurance coverage. However, consumer ignorance does not explain all behavior concerning credit insurance. Some consumers are willing to pay higher premiums for the peace of mind that credit insurance gives them. There is clearly a tradeoff here. Obtaining credit insurance is easy and quick. Getting additional insurance on an individual or group basis takes time, and although it is cheaper, some consumers value their time more than they value the dollar saving. Another reason for the relative importance of credit insurance is the policy of many credit unions to automatically give a credit insurance policy to members who borrow money. The cost of these policies is borne by the credit union itself, and it is used as an incentive for members to borrow there first.

Industrial Life Insurance. In 1900, when the United States life insurance industry was still in its infancy, the majority of insurance policies were industrial life policies. **Industrial life insurance** was sold on a door-to-door basis, largely to working-class Americans, who paid their premiums weekly to the agent who wrote the policy. They were fairly small policies, written for people whose death rates and incomes matched their dirty and dangerous jobs in early industrial America. As the insurance industry grew, individual and group life insurance policies quickly emerged as lower-cost alternatives to industrial life policies, premiums from which had to pay for the increasingly expensive weekly collection services and door-to-door sales techniques of the insurance agents. Nevertheless, these industrial policies and their descendants, more correctly described as **home-service life insurance policies,** continue to be purchased by a small but sizable number of consumers. Very few of these policies are issued for more than $2000. In 1980, the average policy was worth a little over $600.

Although group insurance usually reduces individual costs, some high-risk groups may have to pay high premiums or may even have trouble getting insured.

About the only positive attribute of these policies is the convenience of having a salesperson come to your door to collect the weekly or monthly premium. But as you can see from Figure 17-2, only about 1 percent of the value of all policies resides in home-service policies. These policies offer so little coverage and their overhead costs are so high that this category of insurance is practically useless for consumers.

As you may have realized by this point, the insurance industry has a vocabulary that could challenge even the investment counselor's for complexity. Individual life, group life, credit, and industrial life insurance may be distinguished from one another based on *how* they are sold. In the following section, we introduce insurance policies that can be distinguished from one another on the basis of *why* they are bought. These policies have different objectives and suit different consumer needs. Some policies provide protection only in the event of death. Others incorporate a savings component with the death benefits. And still others are more closely related to some of the investment strategies we discussed in Chapter 16. These investment-oriented policies may stress tax advantages, retirement provisions, growth potential, or a combination. But as we progress through the next few sections, you would do well to recall that there are only two major differences between these policies: one kind of policy pays off *only* in the case of death; the other kind of policy combines death insurance with a savings, or cash-value, component, so the policyholder can get money back if he or she lives.

TERM INSURANCE

Term insurance is the simplest form of life insurance. Under a **term insurance policy,** an individual's life is insured against death for a certain period of time, a term, which generally varies from one to five years. Term insurance also has a fixed price. Insurance agents frequently refer to term insurance as "death insurance" rather than "life insurance," because the policy pays off only in the event of the insured person's death. Thus, term insurance is similar to auto insurance (see Chapter 11) and health insurance (see Chapter 14)—it pays off only in the event of a loss. But unlike auto or health insurance, a term life insurance policy pays the full amount of the policy in one lump sum, provided of course that none of the provisions of the policy are violated. For example, some policies do not cover death during warfare or while one is pursuing a dangerous activity such as skydiving or mountain climbing. However, if the insured person does not die during the term of the policy, all payments made to the company remain there. If no death occurs, the person holding a term insurance policy is just like a consumer with an automobile insurance policy and no accidents. No one gets paid.

Level Term Insurance. A common form of term insurance is **level term insurance.** It provides a constant level of protection throughout the term of the life insurance contract. Figure 17-3(a) shows the protection benefit of level term insurance. An important clause to look for in any level term insurance contract is its renewability. **Renewable term insurance** differs from other term insurance in that it contains a clause that guarantees the insured person's right to renew the policy for another term, generally five years. Of course, as Figure 17-3(b) shows, the premium is higher because of the increased age of the insured person, but a physical examination is not required to continue the policy at the original death-benefit level. Most renewability clauses end at age sixty-five or seventy, but some companies agree to renew policies to age one hundred. But because the death rates rise dramatically as one gets older, so do the annual premiums.

Decreasing Term Insurance. Term insurance is generally the cheapest per $1000 of insurance because it provides only death protection; there is no cash value returned to a policyholder who survives. Figure 17-3(b) shows, however, that even the cost of maintaining a given term policy rises as an insured person ages. To counteract this rise in the cost of a policy, many companies offer **uniform decreasing term insurance.** Under this policy, the total cost to the policyholder remains constant from year to year, but the amount of insurance protection decreases by a constant amount each year to take into account the higher risk of death. Thus, each year, the same premium buys less coverage, as Figure 17-3(c) and (d) show. Another form of term insurance often taken out by homeowners when they buy a house is known as **mortgage term insurance.** Under this policy, insurance protection does not decrease at a uniform rate—see Figure 17-3(e) and (f). It remains high in the early years of the policy, when most of a home buyer's

Figure 17-3. Protection versus cost in various types of insurance.

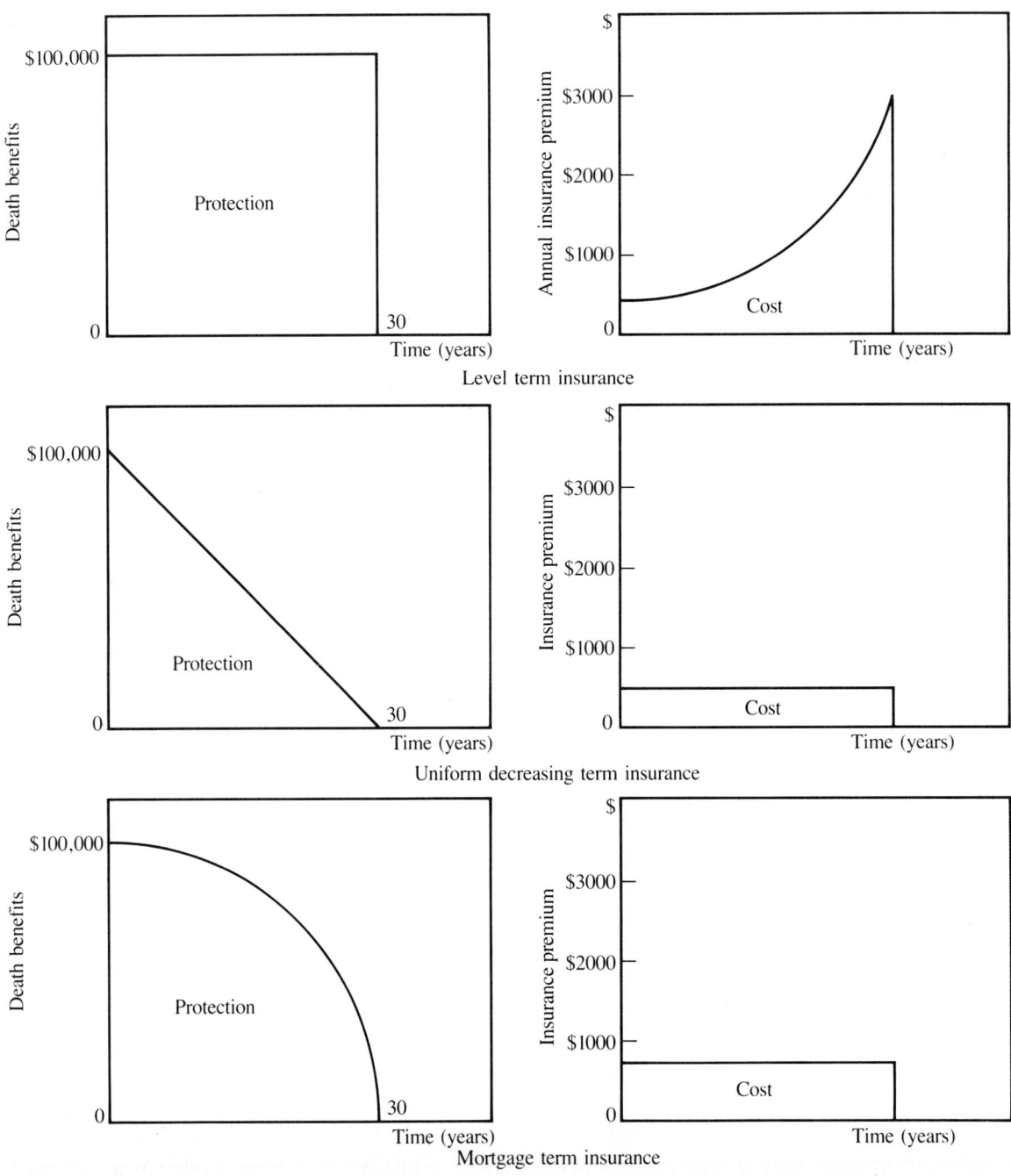

house payment goes to pay interest on the loan and does not reduce the mortgage principal by much. As the years pass, the mortgage payments reduce the indebtedness, so the amount owed to the bank remains about the same as the value of the insurance policy. In the event of death, the mortgage is paid off by such a policy.

Deposit Term Insurance. **Deposit term insurance** is based on the same concept as level term insurance, but the premium for the first year of the policy is significantly higher than for any other year. This "deposit," which may cost an extra $100 on a $10,000 policy, is returned with interest if the policyholder retains the policy for the full term—ten years. Sometimes, this plan is promoted as a double-your-money-back deal, because in ten years one gets twice the amount put on deposit. This amounts to a 7 percent rate compounded annually. However, if one allows the policy to lapse before the end of the term, one loses the entire deposit. Another drawback of deposit term insurance is that the policy rates are often more expensive than those of level term insurance. A study conducted by Harold Skipper Jr., associate professor of insurance at Georgia State University, showed that if the difference between an insurance company's rates on level term insurance and deposit term insurance were taken into account, the average rate of return on the deposit fell to 1.82 percent for twenty-five-year-olds and 0.44 percent for forty-five-year-olds (*Changing Times,* February 1981). With these kinds of returns, deposit term insurance is not a good investment.

The Cost of Term Insurance. The cost of a term insurance policy depends on a number of variables. The age and sex of the insured person, the amount and type of coverage, the cost of administering the policy, and the insurance company's actuarial rates are some of the more important ones. Even though death rates are fairly predictable, insurance-company premiums are not. It is common to find that some insurance companies charge twice as much as a competitor does for identical coverage. Some commentators have found price differences of more than 400 percent for similar policies (*Changing Times,* September 1981).

Such price differences can continue only if consumer information is limited and consumer decision making is impaired. In such an environment it is worthwhile for most consumers to spend additional time seeking information and practicing the principles of decision-making first presented in Chapter 2. According to Barry Kaye (1981), "Very simply, people are paying too much for life insurance because they won't stop, shop, and compare. Literally thousands of dollars can be saved through careful analysis of existing and new policies."

Term insurance is one of the most highly recommended forms of life insurance. Consumers Union, the nonprofit organization discussed in Chapter 5, has urged consumers to choose term insurance ever since its first study conducted in 1937. As stated in a recent article: "The case for term insurance rests on the assumption that people should buy as much insurance as they need to protect their families—and that most people can afford to do that only by buying term" (*Consumer Reports,* February/March 1980). In addition to being the cheapest insurance, term insurance has the advantage of offering especially low premiums to households headed by younger adults. Families in the early stage of their life cycle can be especially hard hit if they lose their major source of income. Term insurance matches the life-cycle needs of most families because it is least expensive in the early years and more expensive later, when a family has additional purchasing power and decreasing obligations to children. Nevertheless, millions of consumers continue to choose insurance plans that combine the death protection provisions with a savings option. You should understand cash-value policies before you decide to opt for term insurance.

CASH-VALUE INSURANCE POLICIES

There are a variety of **cash-value insurance policies,** but they all have some elements in common. In return for an annual premium that remains constant as long as the policy is in force, cash-value policies provide death insurance plus a savings account that increases in value throughout the life of the policy. If the policyholder dies while the policy is in force, only the death benefit is paid. In this case, a cash-value policy operates like a term policy. However, if the policy-

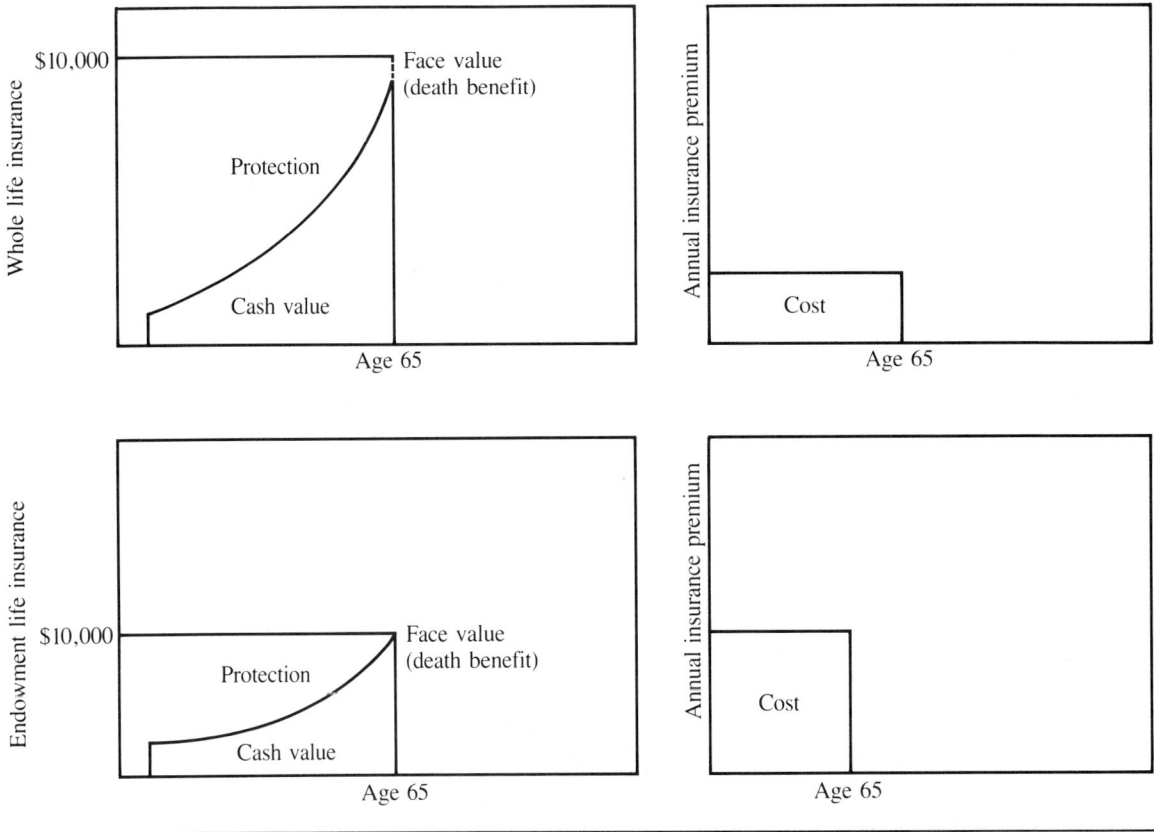

Figure 17-4. A comparison of two kinds of cash value policies. For policies of equal face value, premiums on whole life policies are less than those of endowment life policies, because the cash value of an endowment policy must equal its face value sooner.

holder survives, the savings portion (cash value) of the policy builds, and the policyholder can elect to borrow part of it, use it to pay the premium, convert it into a retirement income, or take it all in a lump sum.

Whole Life Insurance: A Savings Plus Plan. The most popular form of cash-value insurance is called **whole life insurance.** Like term insurance, a whole life insurance policy pays a stipulated amount—the "face value"—in the event of the death of the insured person. But unlike term insurance policies, the annual cost of a whole life policy remains constant, even though the risk of death increases as the policyholder ages. The premium remains constant because the build-up of the cash value helps to reduce the insurance company's risk in that the company never pays more than the face value of the policy. The cash-value provision is much like a savings account. During the life of the policy, part of the insurance premium is set aside and invested by the insurance company. This reserve increases over time and earns interest at a predetermined fixed rate. In essence, then, someone who buys a whole life policy is buying death insurance plus a savings account for a fixed yearly fee. As you might suspect, however, this fee is significantly higher than the cost of term insurance during the early years of the policy.

As Figure 17-4 shows, the cash-value, or savings, portion of a whole life policy generally does not begin for a few years. In the early years of the policy, administration costs and sales commissions take most of the funds not reserved for death benefits. (In fact, some observers have argued that one reason that life insurance salespeople are so eager to sell whole life policies is that the sales commission is nine times greater than that of comparable term insurance policies.) Given the heavy sales and administrative expenses during the early years of a policy, whole life insurance is an unrewarding way to save in the short term. And a recent Federal Trade Commission study (1979) showed that 20 percent of all new whole life policies were dropped in the first year, resulting in consumer losses of more than $200 million. Even policies held for ten years returned less than a 2 percent yield on the savings component of whole life insurance. And according to the FTC, 45 percent of whole life policyholders cancel within ten years and thus earn low and sometimes negative returns on the savings. Nevertheless, as you can see in Figure 17-4, the cash value does eventually rise because the insurance company is collecting more than it needs to insure against the risk of the policyholder's death. This surplus is also growing because it is earning nontaxable interest as long as it remains in the insurance policy.

The insured person can withdraw this savings by cashing in the policy and thereby eliminating the death-insurance provision, or he or she may continue paying the premium and borrow against the cash value at an interest rate that is generally well below the cost of credit elsewhere. However, the savings-account and death-insurance features do not pay off simultaneously. For example, in the event of the death of the insured person, the beneficiaries do not receive both the cash value of the policy and the face value of the insurance. Only the death-insurance provision applies in this case. And if any of the cash value was borrowed by the insured person, the face value is reduced by the amount of the loan plus interest owed.

Limited-Payment Life Insurance. Premiums on whole life policies continue until the death of the insured person or until the policy is cashed in. For **limited-payment life insurance** policies, the payments end after a certain number of years or when the insured person reaches a certain age. In insurance language, the policy is *fully paid up* after ten, twenty, or perhaps thirty years of paying premiums. Once the policy is paid for, it remains in force until the death of the insured person. Because the premium-paying period is shorter than those of other whole life policies, the annual cost is generally higher. If you are considering purchasing a whole life policy but want to limit your payments to a definite period of time, such as during your peak earning years, a limited-life policy may be the best plan. However, because this policy has higher premiums, you may not be able to purchase an adequate amount of protection.

Endowment Life Insurance. The savings element of whole life insurance is stressed in an **endowment life insurance** policy. This policy also provides some death benefits, but the real emphasis is on building a certain cash reserve in a given period of time, varying from ten to thirty years or until the policyholder reaches a specific age. At the end of the specific time period, the policy matures and the cash value, or ''endowment,'' equals the face value of the policy, as illustrated in Figure 17-4. The insured person can elect to receive the value of the endowment in a lump sum or in annual installments over an extended period of time.

An endowment policy is designed for consumers who want a definite sum of money or income at some future date to supplement or replace their earnings. This income is often combined with other retirement income to ensure a comfortable level of living after a household's paychecks have stopped. The necessity of providing for one's retirement years is clear, but it is not clear that an endowment policy is the best way to do this. Traditional savings programs and the more recent tax-sheltered retirement programs discussed later in this chapter can offer the same cash values at significantly lower costs.

Universal Life Insurance. The newest form of cash-value life insurance is **universal life insurance,** and it is similar to whole life insurance with these exceptions: the interest rate on the cash-value portion of the

Table 17-1. Death Benefits, Cash Values, and Accumulated Premiums from Universal Life Insurance*

End of policy year	December 31 of	(1) Cash value assuming hypothetical gross annual investment return equal to S&P 500 common stock index	(2) Cash value assuming hypothetical gross annual investment return of 6%	(3) Premiums accumulated at 5% interest per annum†
1	1948	150	153	707
2	1949	705	627	1,450
3	1950	1,502	1,124	2,229
4	1951	2,400	1,646	3,048
5	1952	3,392	2,236	3,908
6	1953	3,786	2,855	4,810
7	1954	6,479	3,503	5,758
8	1955	9,084	4,181	6,753
9	1956	10,100	4,889	7,798
10	1957	9,329	5,628	8,895
15	1962	19,247	9,786	15,260
20	1967	34,955	14,777	23,383
25	1972	48,867	20,671	33,751
30	1977	45,763	27,535	46,984
33 (age 65)	1980	73,988	32,150	56,619

*Based on a $50,000 policy with $673.50 annual premium issued to a 32-year-old woman on December 31, 1947.
†Presents the amount the annual premium would accumulate to if it were deposited in a savings account.

life insurance policy is variable, not fixed; the policyholder can withdraw funds directly from the cash value without going through the usual borrowing procedures; and the face value of the policy can be changed without rewriting the policy.

The key to universal life policies is their variable interest rate. Given the comparatively low (but guaranteed) interest rates that whole life policies have paid in the past, many consumers switched to term insurance for basic protection and invested the money they saved in something that would yield a higher return. As a result, many insurance companies have begun to offer cash-value life insurance for which the interest rate paid on the cash value is tied either to the insurance company's earnings on their investments or to some easily monitored rate, such as the return on government Treasury bills (see Chapter 16). Some companies also guarantee a minimum return on the cash value, in an effort to minimize the policyholder's risk in choosing a universal life policy over a whole life policy issued by the same company.

Because cash value can accumulate much more rapidly under a variable-rate plan, the amount of insurance protection and risk that the insurance company takes is lessened. As a result, the cost of the death-benefits package declines more rapidly than it does in whole life insurance. Insurance companies that offer universal life insurance deal with this pleasant problem in one of two ways. Either they automatically increase the death benefit, so that if the policyholder dies the policy pays more than its face value, or they agree, in the event of a policyholder's death, to add part of the cash value to the death benefit. Thus, universal life is the only kind of cash-value policy that offers to pay *both* the death benefit and part of the cash value.

Table 17-1 compares the growth in the cash values of (1) a universal life insurance policy for which the return is tied to the average performance of the stocks in the Standard and Poor's Index (discussed in Chapter 16), (2) a whole life policy with a 6 percent gross return, and (3) a savings account that yields 5 percent annually. The example assumes that the policyholder bought a $50,000 policy in 1947 at age thirty-two and paid an annual premium of $673.50 for thirty-three years until reaching the age of sixty-five. The stock market experienced some significant ups and downs over this period and the policy actually *lost* value between 1956 and 1957 and between 1972 and 1977. Meanwhile the cash value in a standard whole life policy rose predictably, and the savings account continued to accumulate interest on the principal and on the $673.50 in new deposits every year. Despite the ups and downs of the stock market, the universal life insurance policy, based on its movements, would have returned significantly more ($17,369) than a similar investment in a savings account, and it would have provided death insurance besides. It outpaced the standard whole life policy by even *more*—$41,838. However, the future returns on investments in the stock market are certainly not guaranteed. If the stock market does poorly over the next thirty years (or suffers a crash just as one's policy is about to mature), one would do better with a different insurance policy.

Another problem with universal life policies is in trying to compare the costs and expected returns of policies issued by competing insurers. In a way, it is more like choosing an investment option rather than a life insurance policy. It is difficult to gauge which company offers a better return, because there are no guarantees about who will pay the highest return on the cash-value surplus. It may be helpful to ask how the insurance company plans to compute its variable return. Will it be based solely on the stock market or on the return from government bonds, or will it be an average return from the insurance company's investments? You should also ask whether there is a guaranteed minimum return of your cash value. This kind of information can limit your risk.

WHICH FORM OF INSURANCE IS BEST FOR YOU?
Now that you understand the various types of insurance, you need to decide which one is best for you.

The answer depends on your lifestyle, your life-cycle needs, and your goals and values. No one, not even the most observant and dedicated insurance agent, can tell you what you need. You must decide this for yourself.

Table 17-2 describes the major types of life insurance policies. As you can see, all forms of life insurance have advantages as well as disadvantages. As our earlier discussion indicated, term insurance is clearly the best low-cost alternative, but it is also the most limited in terms of its range of uses. There is no element of forced saving, no sheltering of interest from taxes, no loan provision, and no way to get your money back except by dying, which is not a very inviting idea for most of us. All forms of cash-value insurance have more to offer than the narrowly defined term insurance policies, but they are all more expensive if the object is simply to purchase death insurance. If the objective is to set aside a cash reserve, the new universal life policies offer the greatest potential for yield, but as we learned in Chapter 16, higher yields are often associated with high risks, and most universal life policies are no exception. However, as the yields cited in the FTC study showed, other forms of cash-value life insurance have not been shown to be good investments if held for less than ten years. Consumers who purchase life insurance policies to help them save also pay the insurance companies for administration and investment counseling. These fees are especially important during the early years of an insurance policy; thus they reduce the yield more on policies cashed in early rather than on policies that mature.

An additional problem with all insurance policies is the impact of inflation. For example, a person may struggle for twenty years to pay the premium on a $50,000 limited-life policy and then discover that an annual inflation rate of 10 percent has reduced the real buying power of the policy to a little over $6000. Many insurance policyholders have discovered the ravages of inflation much too late to do anything about them. Remember, $50,000 twenty years from now is not going to give you the same protection that it does today. Before you agree to any policy, you ought to mentally invoke the "rule of 70" for calculating the effects of inflation (see Chapter 7). Ac-

Table 17-2. Types of Insurance Policies

Characteristics	Term	Whole life	Limited-payment life
Period of premium payment	Specific period of time, such as 5, 10, or 20 years.	For the entire life of insured person.	Stated period of 10, 15, 20, or 30 years, or to age 60 or 65.
When policy matures	Payment made to beneficiary if insured person dies within the term period. After term expires, coverage ends.	At death of insured person.	At death of insured person.
Advantages	Maximum protection at minimum cost for stated period of time. Usually may be converted to life or endowment policy without medical examination.	Provides lifetime protection at a constant rate. Investment-cash value may be used as income. Insured person may borrow money on the policy.	Premiums paid for limited time. Lifetime protection provided. Larger cash and loan values than whole life.
Suitable for	Persons with limited income who need a large amount of protection, especially temporary protection.	Persons who have small incomes and need a forced savings plan as well as long-term protection. Persons who want a policy with a cash and loan value.	Persons whose income is likely to decrease at a certain period and who can afford more than the cost of the whole life insurance policy.
Disadvantages	Premiums rise as the insured person ages. Lasts only for a few years and then must be renewed.	More expensive per $1000 of insurance than term policies. Inflation can reduce the real value of the policy.	More expensive than term or whole-life premiums. Inflation can reduce the real value of the policy.

cording to the rule of 70, you can determine how many years it will take for the value of a given sum of money to lose half of its buying power by dividing 70 by the inflation rate. Thus, if you expect a 10 percent inflation rate over the life of your insurance policy, the value of your death benefit (and cash value) will be cut in half every seven years (70 ÷ 10 = 7). So a $50,000 policy will have only $25,000 worth of buying power in seven years, $12,500 in fourteen years, and $6,250 in twenty-one years.

HOW MUCH LIFE INSURANCE DO YOU NEED?

In calculating how much life insurance to purchase,

medical bills, funeral expenses, estate taxes, and probate costs. If you have health insurance coverage and a written will and you do not want to leave this world with a funeral tribute rivaling the Shah of Iran's, the total for these expenses will probably not exceed $10,000. Long-run financial loss is the real reason for studying life insurance. Presumably, you are concerned that your death may cause some hardship on your family and you would like your insurance to provide some security for family members. We all realize that nothing can replace you, but you want to be sure that the assets you leave behind will be sufficient to meet your dependents' needs.

By narrowing our focus to the hardship that your death may cause to others, we are disregarding the investment aspect of insurance. But as the last few sections have demonstrated, life insurance has not been shown to be a good investment. On the other hand, death insurance can be a valuable and even a necessary adjunct to any consumer's budget. However, we should warn you that there is no magic formula for determining the amount of life insurance that a person should have. In some cases, it may be perfectly rational to have no life insurance at all. In order to put this problem into perspective, we will select a few typical lifestyles and then apply a simple analysis to delineate some guidelines for buying insurance.

Insurance and the Single Person. If you are a single parent caring for a child or if you are helping to support your parents or other dependents, then you should consider obtaining a sizable term life insurance policy. How large a policy depends on how much of a burden the loss of your income would place on these innocent bystanders. We will explore some guidelines for people with dependents in the next section. But if you are a single person with no dependents, is there any reason for you to have an insurance policy?

Insurance agents have an entire portfolio of reasons for convincing single people that they need insurance. One of the most frequently used arguments instills the fear of future uninsurability. "You may be healthy and a good risk now, but if you don't take advantage of your situation and buy insurance today, you may not be able to get it at a later date." The fear of deteriorating health is sometimes coupled with an

Endowment life	**Universal life**
Stated period of 10 15, 20, or 30 years, or to age 60 or 65.	Flexible, but premiums can be made over the entire life of the insured person.
At death of insured person or at the end of the period, if the insured person is still living.	At death of insured person.
Pays a definite sum of money at the end of the period. Gives insurance coverage while premiums are being paid.	Premium payments are flexible, both in timing and amount. Yield on cash value is variable and geared to market rates. Cash value can be withdrawn with no penalty. Can pay more than the face value at maturity.
Persons who want to save for children's educations for future years or prepare for retirement and still have insurance in the meantime.	Persons who are willing to try a new insurance approach and accept some risk with possibility of higher yield.
Does not pay as much interest as traditional savings accounts. Insured person pays insurance company for investment management. Inflation can reduce the buying power of the endowment.	Difficult to judge future return and cost of competing policies.

there are really only two elements that need to be weighed—the financial losses associated with the death and the assets that can be used to offset those losses. The financial losses can be separated into two parts—immediate and long-run. The immediate financial losses include all bills that are due shortly after the funeral. These might include uninsured offer of an insurance policy for which the premiums for the first few years can be paid on credit. Campus life insurance agents sometimes use this double whammy to sucker unsuspecting undergraduates into insurance policies that they may not need or even want. As you learned in Chapter 8, buying on credit means you must pay *more* in the long run. In addition, the premiums are likely to be higher for a campus policy than for one aimed at the general public. As far as the fear of deteriorating health, Consumers Union reported that only 3 percent of all life insurance applicants are rejected for any reason, and only 5 percent are charged extra because of health conditions (*Consumer Reports,* February 1980). Many insurance companies are willing to sell some coverage for which the buyer is not required to have a medical examination, unless the answers to certain questions on the insurance application indicate a need for a further check. For example, Equitable Life Assurance Society sells nonmedical policies of up to $100,000 to anyone under fifty, without a medical examination (*Changing Times,* September 1981). So unless you have a hereditary disease that will impair your insurability in the future, your current health status is not a good reason to seek life insurance.

Another argument that insurance agents use is that the younger consumer can lock into a low premium rate by buying early, before the risk of death (and the premiums) rises. Obviously, this locked-in premium applies only to cash-value insurance, because term insurance costs more every time it is renewed. But it is true that a twenty-five-year-old-man could buy a $10,000 whole life policy for a $129 annual premium, whereas the same policy might cost $175 at age thirty-five. But if the twenty-five-year-old policyholder doesn't need $10,000 worth of insurance over this period, why should he pay the insurance company $1,290 for the right to buy insurance at a later time when he *might* need it. If the $129 annual payment was put into an investment that yielded a 7 percent return compounded annually, it would have risen to almost $2000 in ten years. This more than compensates the policyholder for the additional $46 ($175 − $129) yearly cost that buying insurance at age thirty-five rather than age twenty-five entails.

Reducing economic hardship on others is about the only reason for single persons to buy life insurance. In some cases, the death of a young single person may put an undue strain on the finances of family or friends, either because of the costs associated with the funeral arrangements or because of outstanding debts that cannot be resolved by selling the assets of the estate. When a person's death could cause hardship to others, he or she often takes out a small term life insurance policy to lighten the economic burden. Of course, this decision depends on the values and goals of the consumer involved. And it should not be made unless adequate information is sought from other members of the family, as well as from insurance agents. After all, before you decide to minimize the financial strain that your demise might cause to your family, you ought to find out whether your parents or grandparents already have a policy on you. And before you agree to sign up for a new policy, you should do some comparison shopping among agents, because prices can easily vary by 100 percent.

Insurance for Those with Dependents. For a husband-wife household, especially one in which children are involved, or for a single-parent family, the death of an adult could bring real economic hardship in addition to psychological loss to other members of the family. The amount of life insurance in force should be in proportion to the degree of economic hardship that may be suffered.

Relating insurance needs to economic hardship can eliminate the rationale behind buying certain kinds of life insurance. For example, it makes little economic sense to insure the lives of children for any large amount. In crude terms, the absence of a child reduces the economic burden on a family. It does not increase the burden. Nevertheless, as Figure 17-5 shows, 15 percent of all individual life insurance policies in the United States in 1980 were issued to children under fifteen years of age. Why do consumers take out such policies? Part of the reason is simply

Figure 17-5. Distribution of individual life insurance purchases.

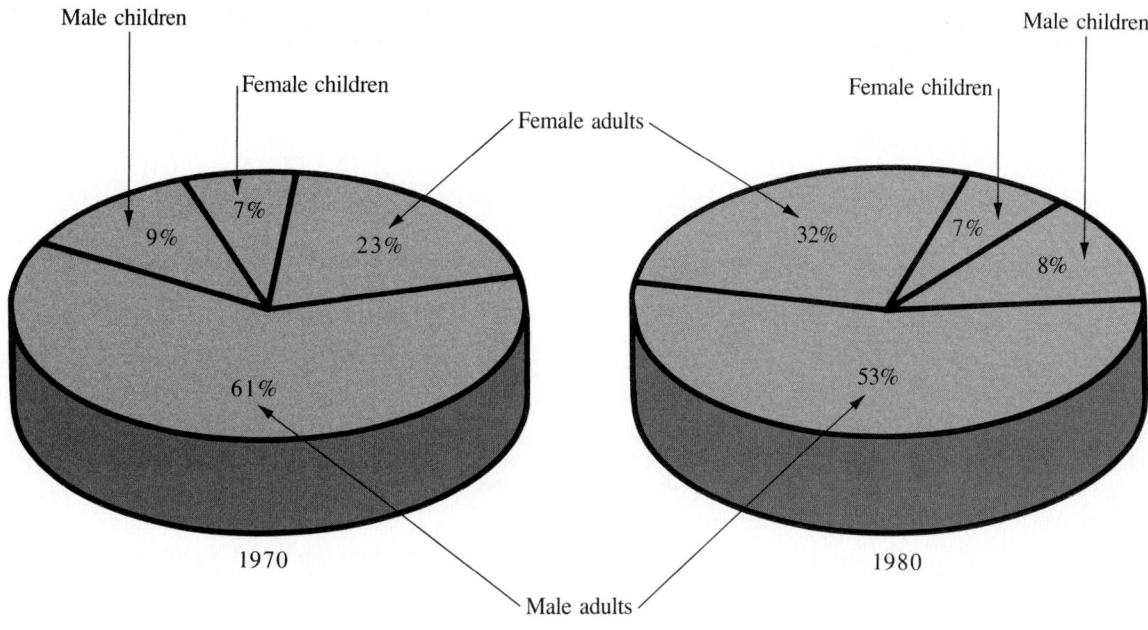

SOURCE: Data from American Council of Life Insurance, *Life Insurance Factbook, 1981* (Washington, D.C., 1981), p. 14.

to cover the small but real burden that goes with any death in the family. But insurance agents often encourage parents to take out larger policies with the argument that the policy is building some cash value or that if the child becomes uninsurable later for health reasons, this policy can remain in force without a medical exam. The first reason is not very compelling in that inflation quickly reduces the real value of a given amount of insurance and the interest rate is low on such policies. The fear of deteriorating health is even less important for a child than for a college student. And as we pointed out earlier, few people are ever denied life insurance for health reasons.

What about the traditional family in which the wife does not work outside the home? Does it make good sense to insure the homemaker? Although there is no direct income generated by a spouse who stays home to run the household, it is obvious that if the many services performed by him or her were to be purchased in the marketplace, the cost would be quite high. If the death of a spouse would result in additional family expenses for childcare, housecleaning, meal preparation, and the like, it would make sense to provide sufficient life insurance to supply these services.

Clearly, the most urgent need for life insurance exists when the family wage earner dies. Because about half of all married women are in the paid labor force and because their earnings account for over 25 percent of family income, life insurance policies for both husbands and their wives are often needed. As Figure 17-5 indicates, the growing importance of wives to family income has been reflected in their share of life insurance policies. In 1970, only 23 percent of all life insurance policies were written for women. By 1980 that share had risen to almost one-third. Families were responding to the growing importance of having two wage earners to maintain their levels of living by insuring them *both*.

The amount of life insurance one needs to re-

Table 17-3. What Social Security Survivors Get*

Average indexed yearly earnings	Surviving parent and one child†	Surviving parent and two children†	One surviving child†	Widow's or widower's benefit (starting at age 65)‡	Family maximum
$ 1,400	$183	$ 183	$122	$122	$ 183
2,400	265	265	132	177	262
4,800	361	361	180	241	361
6,600	433	482	216	289	482
8,400	505	613	252	337	613
10,200	577	707	288	385	707
12,000	649	771	324	433	771
14,400	737	860	369	492	860
16,200	771	900	386	514	900
18,000	805	939	402	537	939
20,400	850	992	425	567	992
22,200	884	1,031	442	589	1,031
22,900	897	1,046	448	598	1,046

*Monthly benefits, rounded to nearest dollar, payable at death, January–May 1980.

†Children receive benefits until they turn 18.

‡Widower or widow can elect reduced benefits at an earlier age. The benefits are reduced 17.1 percent from amount shown if begun at age 62, and 28.5 percent from amount shown if begun at age 60. A widow or widower receives no benefits between the time children reach majority and the age elected (60, 62, or 65).

SOURCE: "Life Insurance—A Special Two-Part Report," *Consumer Reports* (February 1980), p. 83.

place his or her share of the family income depends on the size of one's earnings and the number of years one plans to provide for. If you are a typical wage earner, you, like 90 percent of the labor force, are currently covered by Social Security. The abbreviation for this program is OASDHI, which stands for the Old Age, Survivors, Disability, and Health Insurance program. The S, or survivors program, is relevant here. Under this program, your spouse and dependents can expect to receive a monthly tax-free check from the government to supplement their income. The size of this income supplement varies, but in 1980, it ranged from $209.20 to $1130 a month for a family of three. The amount is indexed for inflation—it increases as the Consumer Price Index rises.

It is often difficult to determine just how much a family will receive from Social Security in the event of a wage earner's death. Life insurance agents have been known to ignore or grossly understate the size of these benefits, for obvious reasons. Consumers Union estimates that for a person who has consistently paid the maximum amount of Social Security taxes, the survivors' benefits equal an income stream worth more than $200,000 in term insurance. Table 17-3 presents the monthly income payable to various survivors of Social Security decedents. As you can see, these payments vary with income and family size.

How much income security should you provide beyond what Social Security supplies? To get a better idea of the additional insurance needed to offset the loss of income from your death, simply multiply your monthly take-home pay by .75 (75 percent). This should give you a rough idea of the monthly income loss that your family will need to absorb when your paycheck is no longer part of the family's budget. The reason we use .75 rather than 1.00 (100 percent) is that you consume a portion of the family's income, and this consumption will stop when you die. Once you arrive at the monthly income loss, subtract the monthly Social Security survivors' benefits to arrive at your net monthly loss. Multiply this figure by twelve to get the yearly income loss. Finally, multiply this yearly figure by the number of years you intend to provide for, and you have the total amount of your necessary insurance fund. The formula can be stated: (.75 × monthly take-home pay) − (monthly Social Security) × 12 × years of dependency = amount of insurance fund needed.

For example, suppose your annual income is $22,200 with a take-home pay of $1500 per month. Let us also assume that you are married and have an infant daughter. To provide for your family until your daughter graduates from college, twenty-one years from now, you would fill in the formula as follows (using Table 17-3 to calculate Social Security benefits):

[.75 × ($1500)] − ($884) × 12 × 21 = insurance fund
($1125 − $884) × 12 × 21 =
$241 × 12 × 21 =
$60,732 = insurance fund needed

Some insurance texts would tell you that this calculation overestimates the size of your insurance fund, because if this fund is invested, it could be earning interest that would provide additional income to the family. Thus, to ensure that your family can withdraw $241 per month for twenty-one years, you could actually set aside less than $60,732. In the first year after your death, for example, your insurance fund would earn over $3000 in interest, even from a secure investment such as U.S. Savings Bonds. However, what these experts neglect to include in their calculations is the rate of inflation. If the inflation rate exceeds the interest rate, your insurance fund will shrink in real purchasing power.

You may recall from Chapter 7 that inflation has shown a stubborn tendency to remain high. If the inflation rate exceeds the interest earned on your insurance fund, you will need to adjust your insurance fund upward. Of course, it is always possible to beat the inflation rate by investing shrewdly. However, as we mentioned in Chapter 16, this would entail an assumption of risk and a presumption of financial expertise—two elements your family may not be able

Spouses and families should not count on being able to live on Social Security's survival benefits.

or willing to acquire. Because insurance proceeds are by nature a family's nest egg, you probably wouldn't want a stockbroker to play stock-market roulette with them. This means accepting a lower interest rate in return for greater security. It is one of the tradeoffs that most of us understand and grudgingly accept.

If inflation remains a fact of life, we must adjust our insurance fund to account for it. Box 17-2 shows how to adjust for inflation under two different assumptions. Given the number of years the insurance fund is intended to provide for (column 1), the inflation rate will exceed the interest rate of secure savings by either 1 percent (column 2) or 2 percent (column 3). If we take the more pessimistic view, we will use column 3 and adjust our insurance fund by multiplying by the inflation factor. For example, for a $60,732 insurance fund, multiply by 1.51, because inflation is expected to exceed the interest rate by 2 percent every year for twenty-one years. The insurance fund must be $91,705 to account for inflation.

BOX 17-2
Adjusting Your Insurance Fund for Inflation

Years of dependency to be provided for	Inflation factor if inflation rate exceeds interest rate	
	1%	2%
1	1.01	1.02
2	1.02	1.04
3	1.03	1.06
4	1.04	1.08
5	1.05	1.10
6	1.06	1.13
7	1.07	1.15
8	1.08	1.17
9	1.09	1.19
10	1.10	1.22
11	1.12	1.24
12	1.13	1.27
13	1.14	1.29
14	1.15	1.32
15	1.16	1.34
16	1.17	1.37
17	1.18	1.40
18	1.20	1.43
19	1.21	1.46
20	1.22	1.48
21	1.23	1.51

Example

For someone with an annual income of $22,200 and a take-home pay of $1500 who wants to provide twenty-one years of protection for his or her family, the insurance fund should be $60,732.

insurance fund = (.75 × monthly take-home pay) − (monthly Social Security check) × 12 × (years of dependency)

insurance fund = (.75 × $1500)
  − $884 × 12 × 21
  = ($1125 − $884) × 12 × 21
  = 241 × 12 × 21
  = $60,732

Then adjust for inflation by assuming that inflation will exceed the return on your insurance fund by either an optimistic 1 percent or a pessimistic 2 percent. Thus:

insurance fund with inflation adjustment = insurance fund × inflation factor for years of dependency
= $60,732 × 1.51 = $91,705

SOURCE: Adapted from *Consumer Reports* (February 1980), p. 84.

Table 17-4. Comparison of the Cash-Value Savings Aspect of a Typical Whole Life Insurance Policy with a Premium of $1650 Annually and a Savings Account

Policy year	Insurance cash value	Savings account (5% annual returns)
5	$ 6,365	$ 9,544
10	15,156	21,724
15	25,521	37,271
20	37,487	57,113
25	51,067	82,436
30	63,441	107,647

THE COST OF LIFE INSURANCE

Once you have established how much life insurance you feel you need, the next question, one that is dear to most consumers' hearts, is: How much will this protection cost? The answer is not simple. Cost varies depending on age, employment, sex, and the type of policy, as well as the company one chooses to underwrite the policy. From our earlier discussion you already know that group policies are generally less expensive than individual life policies because the sales costs are lower. It is also true that term insurance is less expensive than whole life, because there is no forced savings plan included. And finally, we should note that paying your insurance premium on an annual rather than on a monthly or quarterly basis also reduces costs, because it is less expensive for the insurance company to administer.

Some insurance agents have been known to argue that insurance does not have to cost anything, if one buys the right kind of policy. These folks are often pushing orthodox whole life policies that incorporate the forced-savings feature we previously discussed. For example, a $100,000 whole life policy issued to a 35-year-old man might cost $1650 per year. If he continues to pay every year until he is sixty-five (thirty years later), his premiums would amount to $49,500 ($1650 × 30 years). But each year, the cash value continues to grow, as illustrated in Table 17-4. By the thirtieth year, the cash value is over $63,000, so if the policyholder wants to, he can cash the policy in and get a check for $63,441, that is,

Figure 17-6. Projected number and proportion of persons 65 and over in the U.S. population, 1980-2050.

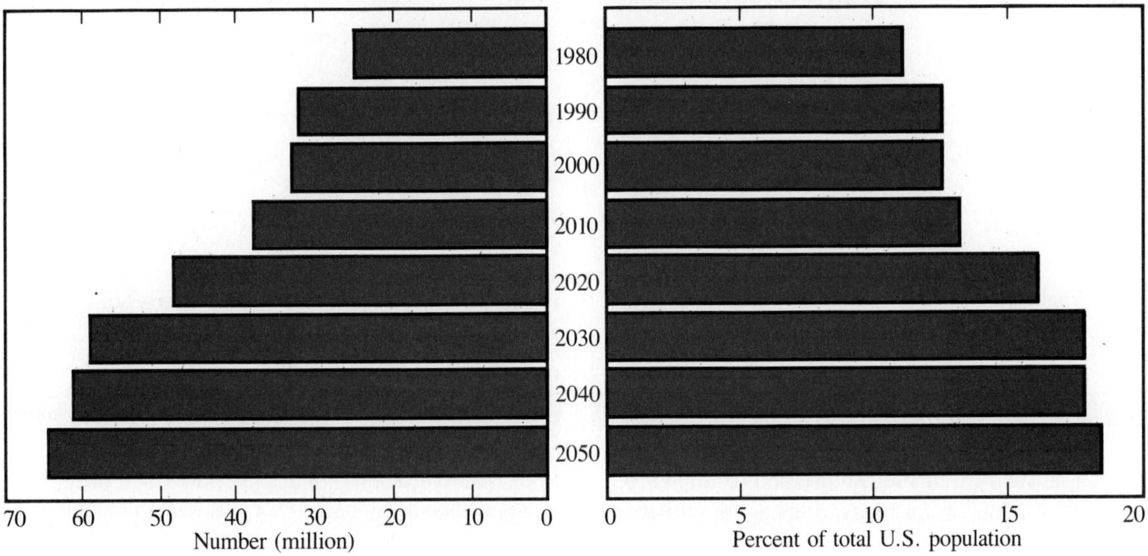

SOURCE: Leon F. Bouvier, "America's Baby Boom Generation: The Fateful Bulge," *Population Bulletin* (April 1980), p. 29.

$13,941 more than he paid over those years. So the cost, according to some insurance agents, would be *negative,* because the policyholder took out more than he paid in. But these agents are not considering the opportunity cost. As Table 17-4 shows, if this man had saved $1650 per year for thirty years in a savings account that paid only 5 percent interest, by age sixty-five he would have had over $107,000. So there is a *real* cost to the insurance—over $44,000 in lost interest.

You should realize by now that not all insurance policies are alike. But even policies that have identical death benefits and similar features often have widely different rates. In order to help consumers judge the real cost of competing policies, the National Association of Insurance Commissioners suggests that consumers use the **interest-adjusted cost index (IAC).** This index compares the net cost of each insurance policy by applying an adjustment for the opportunity cost of a policyholder's money (the interest rate) to the annual premium, cash value, and dividends, if there are any. This index can be computed for any number of years, but the twenty-year interest-adjusted cost index is the most common and useful. In twenty-nine states, insurance agents are legally required to furnish these data on request. But even if you are not in one of these states, it makes good sense to ask for the IAC index. And, as with all comparison shopping, you should compare policies from several companies before deciding to buy one.

Retirement

If you survive the hazards of mortality during your working lifetime, you will then launch what could be an equally uncertain period known as the retirement years. Americans generally consider sixty-five to be the age of retirement, although many people retire sooner and some choose to work well beyond that age. Figure 17-6 shows the number of Americans over sixty-five in the United States from 1980 to 2050. As you can see, this segment of our population is projected to rise from 25 million in 1980 to 31

Table 17-5. Work Credit Required to Qualify for Social Security

If you reach 62 in	Quarters you need	Years you need
1976	25	6¼
1977	26	6½
1978	27	6¾
1979	28	7
1981	30	7½
1983	32	8
1987	36	9
1991 or later	40	10

SOURCE: U.S. Department of Health and Human Services, *Your Social Security* (July 1980).

Table 17-6. Contribution Rate Schedule for Employees and Employers (each)

	Percent of covered earnings		
Years	For retirement, survivors, and disability insurance	For hospital insurance	Total
1981	5.35	1.30	6.65
1982–1984	5.40	1.30	6.70
1985	5.70	1.35	7.05
1986–1989	5.70	1.45	7.15
1990 and after	6.20	1.45	7.65

SOURCE: U.S. Department of Health and Human Services, *Social Security Information for Young Families* (Washington, D.C.: Government Printing Office, 1980).

million at the turn of the century and to almost 60 million by 2030, when today's teenagers will be retired. By then, almost 20 percent of our population will be over sixty-five.

The dramatic demographic changes of the last twenty years mean that society will have to provide for a much higher proportion of retired people in the not-so-distant future. The consumer who wants to avoid sudden bone-wrenching decisions late in life should begin planning for retirement in the present. Given the magnitude of the society-wide aging problem, you cannot expect government to bail you out or to absolve you from the responsibility of caring for yourself.

Besides adjusting to a new lifestyle when you quit work, your main concern will be whether you have enough income to maintain your level of living. In the following sections, we will review three major sources of retirement income: Social Security, company pensions, and personal pension plans.

SOCIAL SECURITY AND RETIREMENT INCOME

As we have seen, the Social Security program is a massive undertaking that has health, disability, and life insurance facets, but no part of the Social Security system is more important than the retirement income program. Of the 35 million people receiving some form of Social Security benefits today, over two-thirds receive income under the retirement provisions of Social Security.

Your Right to Social Security. The rules governing your right to Social Security retirement benefits are fairly straightforward. An individual's Social Security credit is measured in quarters—three-month periods of coverage, with a total of four quarters allowed for each year worked. In 1980, an employee or a self-employed person could earn one quarter of coverage for every three months in which he or she earned at least $290 that was subject to Social Security tax. The number of quarters needed to qualify for benefits depends on one's age. As Table 17-5 shows, the later one reaches the age of sixty-two, the more quarters one needs to qualify for benefits. If you retire in 1991, you will need forty quarters (ten years) of tax payments to qualify for retirement benefits.

The level of benefits one earns also depends on one's average yearly earnings. Those who have higher incomes pay more into the program, so they can expect to receive more when they retire. However, all of us pay the same tax rate, up to a maximum income. In 1982, the Social Security tax rate was 6.7 percent of an employee's income up to $31,800 (the taxable wage base). The employer had to match the employee's contribution, so the maximum annual payment into the fund could have equaled $4,261.20. Table 17-6 illustrates the projected rates from 1981

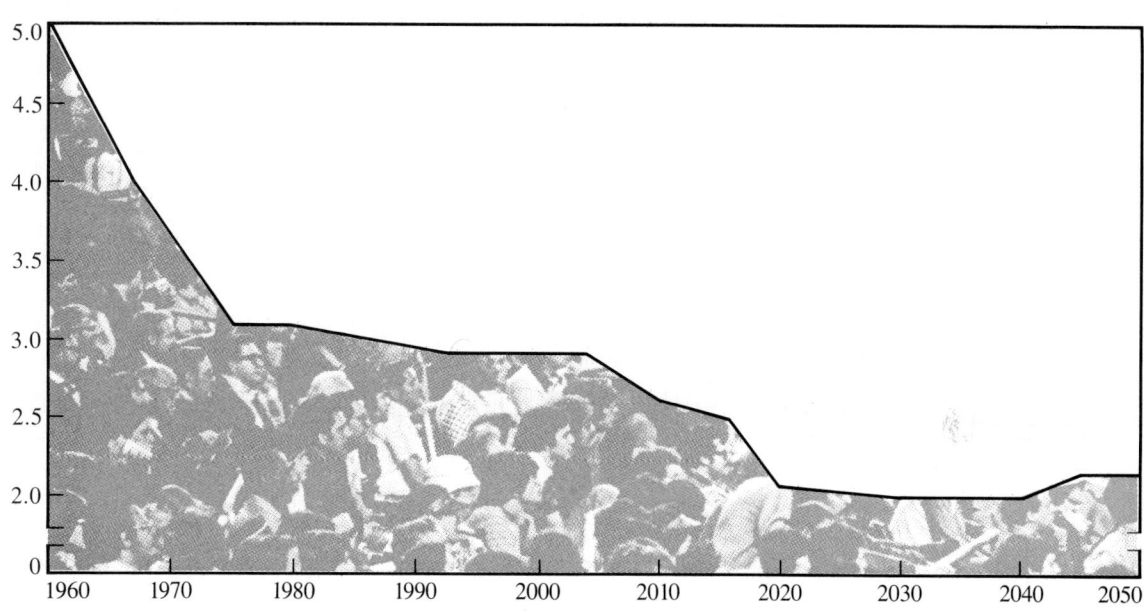

Figure 17-7. Number of persons paying Social Security taxes per beneficiary aged 65 and over: U.S., 1960–2050.

SOURCE: Leon F. Bouvier, "America's Baby Boom Generation: The Fateful Bulge," *Population Bulletin* (April 1980), p. 31.

through 1990. As you can see, part of the tax goes to pay for Medicare (see Chapter 14), but most of it is for the retirement part of the program.

Politics and Social Security. How much can you expect to receive as a result of your forced savings? This depends again on how much and how long you have been active in the program, in addition to when you retire. But it also depends on the willingness of political leaders to maintain the program. Social Security does not operate in the same way as a private investment fund. It does not take your money and invest it. Instead, the Social Security program takes tax money and distributes it to currently eligible participants. As a result, the program more closely resembles government transfer payments than life insurance endowment funds. Some critics of Social Security say that it operates like a pyramid in which new entrants supply cash flow so that previous participants get paid. This is not really a fair comparison, because the Social Security system, unlike fly-by-night pyramid schemes, has the support of the federal government behind it. In essence, it is our faith that the government will honor its commitment that ultimately supports the Social Security System.

Detractors of the system do have a good point, however, in that it is going to be more and more difficult to honor all of the commitments to those people currently enrolled in the system. As Figure 17-7 shows, the number of persons paying Social Security payroll taxes per beneficiary has been falling. In 1960, there were five people paying Social Security taxes for every one receiving benefits. By 1980, the ratio of payers to beneficiaries had fallen to almost 3 to 1. And by 2030 the ratio will be only 2 to 1. The 1960 to 1980 decline necessitated a large increase in the tax rate and in the taxable wage base. This decline was coupled with a plan to index benefits to inflation and to offer a comprehensive medical plan for the elderly. All three events resulted in a large tax increase on workers. It remains to be seen whether workers in the twenty-first century will allow such

Table 17-7. Examples of Monthly Social Security Retirement Payments for Workers Who Reach 62 Before 1979 (effective June 1980)

Benefits can be paid to a	$923 or less	$3,000	$4,000	$5,000	$6,000	$8,000	$10,000*
	\multicolumn{7}{c}{Average yearly earnings after 1950 covered by Social Security}						
Retired worker at 65	153.10	316.40	374.20	431.60	487.80	606.30	671.80
Retired worker at 62	122.50	253.20	297.80	345.30	390.30	485.10	537.50
Wife or husband at 65	76.60	158.20	186.10	215.80	243.90	303.20	335.90
Wife or husband at 62	57.50	118.70	139.60	161.90	233.00	227.40	252.00
Wife under 65 with one child in her care	76.60	167.40	263.80	364.70	406.80	454.80	503.80
Maximum family payment	229.70	483.80	636.00	793.30	894.60	1061.10	1175.60

*Maximum earnings covered by Social Security were lower in past years and must be included in figuring average earnings. This average determines the payment amount. Because of this, the amount shown in the last column generally won't be payable until future years. The maximum retirement benefit generally payable to a worker who is 65 in 1980 is $653.80 (effective June 1980).

increases to be placed on them or whether they will vote to restrict benefits or even abolish the program.*

Despite this somewhat pessimistic view, one may take heart in the fact that the first nation to institute a social insurance plan was Germany in the nineteenth century. It continued to pay its debts to pensioners in spite of being defeated in two world wars and suffering massive inflations. In addition, projected birth rates for the twenty-first century in the United States are so low that a switch in social expenditures from the young to the old can be made without decreasing expenditures per child. If there are fewer children, less tax revenue needs to be devoted to primary education, thus freeing resources to be given to the elderly. Because history indicates that societal obligations such as Social Security are seldom defaulted on and because the number of young people is projected to decline in the next century, the Social Security program should be able to muddle through.

If we accept the more optimistic outlook, how much retirement income can you expect to receive from Social Security? Table 17-7 gives some examples of the amounts of Social Security retirement

---

*In a recent public poll commissioned by the American Council of Life Insurance, 55 percent of the respondents said that they agree with the statement that Social Security will be unable to meet its financial responsibilities within ten years unless something is done. Of course, life insurance companies have never been supportive of Social Security because it does lessen demand for their product. Nevertheless, the poll indicates the current pessimism surrounding the Social Security system (*Changing Times,* May 1981).

payments made to qualified workers. The smallest payment in 1980 was $57.50 for the sixty-two-year-old spouse of a deceased worker who had earned barely enough to qualify for benefits. A worker who had consistently paid the maximum Social Security tax and retired at sixty-five would receive $653.80 in 1980. Future retirees at the top tax level will receive $671.80. If these workers have dependents, their checks can rise to a maximum of $1175.80 per month for the family as a whole. These payments are indexed to rise with inflation, and they are not subject to income tax.

Restrictions on Social Security. Contrary to what some people think, one does not become mentally or physically incapacitated at sixty-five. Many people choose to work beyond that age. For these people, Social Security offers two options. If they continue to work and choose to pay into the program, their benefits will increase by .25 percent for every month they work beyond age sixty-five. This amounts to an annual increase in benefits of 3 percent, and it can be continued until age seventy-two. Workers who retire at seventy-two get a bonus of over 20 percent more in retirement benefits than those who retire at age sixty-five. The second option is to begin receiving Social Security retirement benefits at age sixty-five, but to continue working. Because Social Security checks are intended to replace part of the lost earnings

The Social Security system is currently taking in less money than it is paying out, and the proportion of people receiving benefits compared to those paying into the system increases daily. For these and other reasons, many observers predict a demise for the system in the not-too-distant future.

occasioned by retirement, anyone who continues to work must pass what is called a **retirement test**—the maximum earnings that a Social Security retiree can receive without suffering any reduction in his or her Social Security check. In 1980, anyone retiring at age sixty-five could pass this test and suffer no reduction in his or her checks as long as the wages earned after retirement did not exceed $5000. If someone received wages in excess of $5000, his or her benefits were reduced by $1 for every $2 of earnings above the retirement-test limit. Thus, a retiree who earns $6000 a year in a parttime job will suffer a $500 reduction in Social Security payments.

The retirement-test doctrine has been quite controversial, although it is often misunderstood. In the first place, only wages are covered by the test. Income from interest on savings accounts, stock dividends, capital gains, inheritances, real estate income, royalties, or pensions are *not* included in the retirement test. Some people argue that excluding income from these sources biases the program against working-class people, who do not usually own large amounts of real estate or stock portfolios. As you might guess, one retired person could have thousands of dollars of income from these sources and still receive a full Social Security retirement check, whereas another person who takes a job and earns $6000 to help supplement Social Security checks will have his or her benefits reduced. The misunderstanding is in trying to determine how much Social Security income will be lost by continuing to work. There is no reduction until wage income *exceeds* the retirement test. And even then, the marginal tax rate is 50 percent, not 100 percent, as is often assumed. And for anyone over seventy, the retirement test is not applicable. One may earn as much as one likes without any reduction in benefits.

COMPANY PENSION PLANS

The Social Security program was never intended to

provide for all a person's retirement needs. When it was first introduced in 1935, it was seen as a supplement to other plans that could provide a minimal but important contribution to retirement. Since then, the program has expanded both in scope and benefits, but it still does not provide a complete retirement package. If you doubt this, look at Table 17-7 again and try to estimate how you would live if you had to depend on Social Security alone. Or interview some retired people and ask them whether Social Security by itself provides an adequate retirement income. The answer should not surprise you.

The inadequacy of the Social Security program requires people to have other sources of retirement income. One of the most common is a company pension plan provided by an employer. Such plans have been around for decades, but it wasn't until 1974, with the passage of the Employees Retirement Income Security Act (ERISA), that the federal government intervened in this vital and complex area. The problems with company pension plans prior to 1974 were in qualifications for receiving benefits and sufficient funding to guarantee payments to retired workers. Before 1974, it was possible for a long-time employee to be fired and thus not qualify for retirement benefits or for the company to go out of business and have the pension fund disappear with it. These abuses led Congress to pass ERISA, which set certain standards about employee participation and about the management of company retirement funds.

Under the rules established by ERISA, an employee is eligible to participate in the pension plan after one year of service, provided that he or she is at least twenty-five years old. Under most pension plans, both the employer and the employee make contributions to the retirement fund. The employee's contributions are treated like a savings account. If the employee is fired or quits, he or she can withdraw all of the employee contributions in the fund, but by doing so, he or she forfeits any contributions made by the employer. The employer's contributions are also regulated by ERISA. The question here is whether or not the employee has a right to any or all of these employer contributions. The process whereby an employee obtains a claim on the employer's contribution to the pension fund is called **vesting**. A vested right is a right that no one can take away. But one can give it up by quitting and taking one's money out of the pension plan. In plans in which employers make large contributions to the retirement fund, rules governing vesting can be important. It is possible for an employee to be fully vested or only partially vested, depending on whether all of the employer's contributions accrue to the benefit of the employee or only a portion remain with the employee if he or she changes employers.

If you get vested rights in a company pension plan, you will receive pension benefits based in part on your employer's contributions, even if you leave the company before retirement. But you have to leave your contributions in the pension fund. Nevertheless, vesting is an important right, and companies that offer pension plans must provide for full vesting after ten years of employment.

In addition to the problem of vesting, retired employees have sometimes been troubled by funds cutoffs caused by their former employer's mismanagement. Given the uncertainties of the marketplace, even an employee of a major company, such as Chrysler Corporation, would like some assurance that the retirement program will still be there even if the company is not. When Congress passed ERISA, it set up a two-pronged approach to this thorny problem. First, all pension funds must be placed under the management of a trustee whose function is to oversee the fund, not to be involved with other company affairs. This trustee can be an insurance firm, a bank, or another organization, but it must follow a federal guideline known as the **prudent man rule.** This rule states that trustees should invest the funds "with care, skill, prudence and diligence . . . that a prudent man acting in a like capacity and familiar with such matters would use." Essentially, this means that the trustees are to avoid speculative or high-risk investments that might result in a loss of the pension funds. In practice, this may lead to a lower return on the fund, because some high-risk investment opportunities must be forgone. On the other hand, there is less chance for a total collapse of the fund.

In the event of a financial calamity for a pension fund, ERISA established the nonprofit Pension Benefit Guarantee Corporation, which provides benefits to retired workers whose pension funds prove inadequate. This corporation is financed by compulsory insurance premiums that come from companies with retirement programs.

PERSONAL PENSION PLANS: IRA AND KEOGH

Not all companies offer their own retirement plans. Nor does everyone work for a company. To help people who do not have such plans provide for their retirement, Congress has created two strategies: **Individual Retirement Accounts (IRAs)** and **Keogh plans.** Both plans allow a person to make a tax-deductible contribution to a retirement fund in which the principal continues to grow tax free until it is withdrawn at retirement, but not before the employee reaches his or her fifty-ninth birthday. A retiree is able to postpone taxes while he or she is in a high tax bracket and then get this money back with interest when he or she is in a lower bracket.

Under the Individual Retirement Account (IRA), as amended by the Economic Recovery Tax Act of 1981, any employee can place up to $2000 annually ($2250 for a joint husband-wife account) into a special retirement fund. When the IRA was first established, it was only for employees whose employers had not already established a company pension plan for them to participate in. Under the 1981 Tax Act, even employees who are already enrolled in their companies' pension plans can put an additional $2000 ($2250 for a joint account) each year in an IRA. In fact, an employee who already has a company pension plan can simply add on to his or her plan at work, as long as the company allows it. This contribution is tax deductible, and the principal and the yield earned are not taxed until they are taken out. However, in order to fulfill all of the IRA conditions, you cannot withdraw any money before you are fifty-nine and a half years old and you must withdraw it all by the time you reach seventy and a half. If you take any money out of the fund before you reach fifty-nine and a half, you must pay a penalty to the Internal Revenue Service of 10 percent of the withdrawal. Until the 1981 Tax Act, one could have managed the fund however one liked. If, for example, you thought diamonds or gold would prove to be a better investment than corporate stocks or government bonds, you were free to put your IRA money into these investments. However, the 1981 Tax Act was partly motivated by the "supply-side" economics philosophy we discussed in Chapter 15. As a result, the Act specifically forbids IRA money to be put into what are known as "collectibles"—gold, diamonds, art, old coins, antiques, and other collectible forms of tangible property. Supply-siders stress the importance of stimulating output, of producing more. They see investments in diamonds, gold, and other collectibles as sterile investments that do not produce more goods and services or increase the productive power of an economy. Thus, IRA investments in collectibles are disallowed by the IRS, and they could be subject to penalties.

Self-employed people or those who have outside self-employment income in addition to the income from their regular jobs can take advantage of a different tax-deferred pension account called a Keogh plan. Under a Keogh plan, a self-employed person may contribute as much as 25 percent of his or her income, up to a maximum of $30,000 annually. There are no other major differences between an IRA and a Keogh account. The cutoff ages for beginning a withdrawal and for closing the account are basically the same, and the rules prohibiting investing in collectibles are identical.

Making a Will

The theme of this chapter is planning for the future, and barring any last-minute miracle cures for mortality, the future has to end with death. Although this is not a pleasant subject, it is one that everyone must face at some point. The spiritual aspects of this topic are not relevant to consumer economics, but the material implications are. One of the most important is the preparation of a will.

It may surprise you to learn that almost 70 percent of all Americans die without preparing a **will**—a legal document that tells the living how one would like to see one's estate disposed of after one's death. The first important advantage of drawing up a will, then, is the assurance that one's property will go to the people one wants to receive it. A second important feature of many wills is the part that names a guardian for children. Obviously, one's spouse will assume this role if he or she survives. But what happens if

> **BOX 17-3**
>
> **Your Last Will and Testament**
>
> You already have a will—a last will and testament drawn up by the state in which you live. If you have not made out a will of your own, you must operate under the will as drawn by the legislature of the state.
>
> Attorney James Leet furnished us with this will, which is based on California law.
>
> FIRST, I direct that the Probate Court consider for appointment as administrator of my estate one or more of the following persons, in the order named:
>
> 1. My spouse or some competent person whom he or she may request to have appointed.
> 2. My children.
> 3. My grandchildren.
> 4. My parents.
> 5. My brothers and sisters.
> 6. The next of kin entitled to a place in the estate.
> 7. The relatives who are entitled to succeed.
> 8. Public administrator.
> 9. Creditors.
> 10. Any legally competent person.
>
> SECOND, I direct that all of my debts be paid, including taxes, probate fees, administrator fees, and attorney fees. If necessary, the court shall order the sale of some of my assets in order to pay these debts.
>
> THIRD, with the remaining property, I direct that all property that I acquired during marriage, excepting gifts or inheritance, be transferred to my wife/husband.
>
> FOURTH, if only one child survives me, I direct that one-half of my property acquired before marriage or by gifts inherited during marriage be transferred to my spouse. If two or more children survive me, my spouse is to receive one-third instead of one-half of my property.
>
> FIFTH, I direct that the remaining portion of my property acquired before marriage or by gift or inheritance be transferred to my child or to my children.
>
> SIXTH, if my spouse does not survive me but my child or children do, I direct all my property to be transferred to my child or to my children equally.
>
> SEVENTH, if my spouse survives me but I have no living children, I direct that one-half of the property that I acquired before marriage by gift or inheritance be transferred to my spouse. I direct that the remaining half of this property be transferred to my parents if living and if not, to my brothers and sisters and their heirs.
>
> EIGHTH, if my spouse is the sole survivor of my family, including my children, parents, brothers, sisters, or their descendants, I direct that all my property go to my spouse.
>
> NINTH, if I am not survived by any of the persons mentioned in article Eight, I direct the court to search for my nearest blood relative and to divide my estate among my closest blood relatives.
>
> TENTH, if the probate court cannot locate any relative, I direct that all of my property be transferred to the state.

both the husband and the wife die? This event, although rare, should be prepared for. Third, a will can minimize the costs of transferring one's estate by clearly naming the beneficiaries and what they should receive. This can limit lawsuit costs caused by arguments among heirs. Fourth, a carefully prepared will can limit the tax liability of the heirs by taking advantage of the tax laws. Finally, writing a will allows one to name the person who is to be responsible for administering the will. This person, called an **executor** or an **executrix,** should be a responsible, concerned, and capable administrator, because he or she is the one who must gather all records, pay debts, and satisfy the court that everything is in order before the decedent's wishes can be carried out.

The legal process for establishing the validity of a will and ensuring that it is properly executed is called **probate.** The purpose of a probate proceeding is to ensure an orderly and fair transfer of ownership from the decedent to the heirs. Nevertheless, because creditors will have to be notified and given time to respond and because tax authorities also need time to issue their blessing (and take their share), probate can last for over a year. To limit the impact of this time loss on your heirs, you might consider placing some of your assets in **joint ownership.** This is most commonly done between husband and wife for possessions such as a house or a car. Any property held in joint ownership goes immediately to the surviving spouse without having to pass through the probate process.

Whether or not property is jointly owned, it will still be subject to estate tax, because under federal law it is assumed that all property held jointly belongs to the person who dies first. However, the 1981 Tax Act gave all surviving spouses an unlimited marital deduction so they will not have to pay estate taxes on anything they have inherited from their deceased husband or wife. In addition, according to the Act, by 1986 all estates of $600,000 or less will be exempt from federal tax. It is estimated that the new tax law will reduce the number of estates liable to federal taxation from 56,000 to 6,500 (*Wall Street Journal,* July 16, 1981).

It is generally a good idea to keep a will as simple as possible. Do not clutter it with interesting but irrelevant comments about the state of life or your opinions of relatives, friends, or how you would like to be buried. For these comments, a **letter of last instructions** should be drawn up. The whereabouts of this letter should be made known to your executor or executrix so that your final instructions can be carried out as efficiently as possible. The letter should contain information and instructions, as well as any personal messages. The information should include the location of your will, your insurance policies, and your bank accounts. Your instructions should include your desires concerning funeral and burial arrangements. We discuss this last point in the section that follows.

Funeral and Burial Arrangements

If you were to do a consumer survey and ask people to list the ten largest items they will purchase over a lifetime, very few would list a funeral. Nevertheless, this is a major purchase for almost everyone. According to the Federal Trade Commission, the average funeral service and burial in the United States costs over $3100. This is not very expensive when compared to housing costs, but it is almost three times the cost of delivering a child. Why does it cost more to leave the world than to enter it? And is there anything that consumers can do to limit the cost?

Part of the reason for the high cost of dying lies in the nature of the buying process itself. Consumers are simply not in the best frame of mind when they must find a final resting place for their relatives or close friends. The emotional trauma of death is sometimes used by unscrupulous funeral directors to raise the cost of this final expenditure. However, if you understand the funeral and burial process, you can do much to limit the expense for your own funeral, and you can also be of great help to others in their time of bereavement.

The first thing to recognize is that the funeral business is just that—a business. More than that, it is a *big* business. Consumers spend over $4 billion yearly to provide these services for their friends and relatives. As business people, funeral directors must tailor their services to meet public needs. But unlike many other firms, funeral homes often refuse to advertise their prices and sometimes offer more misinformation than information. Although laws can vary widely among states, certain rules clearly emerge:

1. No state requires embalming for all deceased persons, although most states allow funeral homes to embalm bodies without the permission of the next of kin. **Embalming**—treating a corpse with preservative preparations—does *not* prevent the body from eventual decomposition, but it does add between $50 and $150 to the cost of a funeral. Why is embalming the rule rather than the exception? According to one funeral-industry textbook, "without embalming, there would be little demand for beautiful caskets and protective vaults . . . and little need for mortuary service as we know it today" (*Consumer Reports,* August 1979).

2. No state requires a casket for **cremation**—the reduction of the body to ashes by fire. This is the least-expensive funeral process, yet many funeral parlors encourage the purchase of a casket even when cremation is desired.

3. No state requires an outer burial container—another expense that is often added to the funeral price. However, some cemeteries require such con-

tainers, which can be either concrete grave liners or full-fledged burial vaults. The cost can be as high as $1000 for a vault, which has little operational value.

Aside from these general rules, the funeral industry is a hodgepodge of large and small firms operating under confusing and sometimes conflicting laws. One way to limit your funeral expense is to join a **memorial society.** These are nonprofit groups with the major goal ''to obtain dignity, simplicity and economy in funeral arrangements by advance planning.'' Today there are over 160 memorial societies in the United States, with nearly one million members. For a $25 fee, most consumers can obtain a family membership that provides them with information about the costs and types of funerals available and the names of local funeral homes who cooperate with the society. Most of these societies are affiliated with the Continental Association of Funeral and Memorial Societies, which estimates that a consumer can typically save 50 percent in funeral costs, regardless of the type of funeral desired.

Summary

There are many types of decisions. Some have a relatively minor impact on your future, whereas others can have lasting consequences for yourself and your family. The topics covered in this chapter clearly fall into the latter category. The choices you make today concerning life insurance, retirement funds, and the final disposition of your estate may prove to be quite important in the not-so-distant future.

As we stressed in the first section of the chapter, a poorly conceived life insurance program could result in real hardship for people who depend on your income. Or it could result in your spending thousands of dollars more than you need to provide an adequate level of protection. But before you can make informed decisions about how much life insurance to buy or what kind of policy is best for you, you need to learn about the insurance industry itself. We explained that there are two kinds of insurance companies: stock companies and mutual insurance companies. Although mutual companies make up only 10 percent of the industry, they write over 50 percent of all policies. We also reviewed various ways you can buy insurance, the two most important of which are through an individual agent (individual life insurance) or through a plan covering a large number of people (group insurance). Then we covered the great debate over which kind of insurance is best for you: term or cash-value insurance. Term insurance is strictly death insurance, because it pays off only if the policyholder dies during the one- to five-year term of the policy. The cost of term insurance rises as one ages—gradually at first, but much more sharply in later years. The cost of cash-value insurance remains constant throughout the life of the policy, and part of the premium is put into a savings account to grow and be reclaimed if the policyholder lives. But, as we mentioned, cash-value insurance is an expensive way to buy death insurance, and the savings feature yields a low return, especially if the policy is cashed in during the first ten years. However, there are some new cash-value insurance plans on the market, such as universal life insurance, that offer higher returns but involve a greater risk. We concluded the insurance section with a formula for estimating how large your inflation-adjusted life insurance fund should be, given your income and responsibilities.

If you survive to retirement, as most Americans do, what can you expect in terms of income? As we demonstrated in the section on retirement, the twenty-first century is going to witness a dramatic increase in both the number and proportion of people sixty-five and older. Whether Social Security will continue to provide for the people on ''pension mountain'' will partly depend on political considerations, but there are ways to protect yourself through company and individual pension plans. All company pension plans are regulated and guaranteed by the Employees Retirement Income Security Act (ERISA). Even if your company does not have a retirement plan, you can set up an Individual Retirement Account (IRA) and make a $2000 tax-deductible contribution to the account each year. If you are self-employed, you can establish a Keogh account and make a tax-deductible contribution of 15 percent of your income, up to a maximum of $15,000 each year. But you cannot withdraw any money before you are fifty-nine and one half years old and all money must be taken out by age seventy and one half.

Preparing for your death is never pleasant, and

perhaps that is why almost 70 percent of all Americans die without preparing a will. Nevertheless, a well-written will and a letter of last instructions can lessen the burden on your dependents and assure you that your wishes will be carried out. But if you choose not to make up a will, the state has one prepared for you that may not be to your liking.

You can limit the expenses of a funeral by taking some time to understand the basic features of the ceremony and by making preparations in advance, whenever possible. If you are able to dispel some of the misinformation about funerals, you can be of significant help to others during this difficult time.

Neighborhood REVISITED

As Murray left with the signed insurance contracts and a check for six months' premiums, he was smiling. So were Fred and Marlene. They had reason to smile, or did they? Murray had seen their needs and provided a generous low-cost policy, and Fred and Marlene had a free road atlas and the peace of mind of knowing that for less than $200 per month their mortgage would be paid off and Marlene would get an additional $100,000 if Fred should die. And, of course, they would be building a $63,000 nest egg over the next thirty years in the hope that Fred and Marlene would retire together.

1. Did Fred and Marlene practice any of the decision-making steps that we have emphasized? Do you think they got a low-cost policy? Briefly outline the steps they should have taken in making a decision about purchasing insurance.

2. Are Fred and Marlene getting a good return on their investment? If inflation were to average 7 percent annually over the next thirty years, how much would $63,000 be worth in current dollars? (Hint: Use the rule of 70.)

3. If Fred were the only salaried worker in the family and if he and Marlene had a five-year-old child, how much should their insurance fund be if Fred's monthly take-home pay is $1200 and his Social Security benefits are figured on yearly earnings of $18,000? (See Table 17-3.) How much should the fund be if inflation is expected to rise 2 percent faster than the return on their fund for sixteen years of dependency?

KEY TERMS

actuarial table
actuaries
cash-value insurance policy
credit life insurance
cremation
decreasing term insurance
deposit term insurance
embalming
endowment life insurance
executor
executrix
group life insurance

home-service life insurance policies
Individual Retirement Account (IRA)
industrial life insurance
interest-adjusted cost index (IAC)
joint ownership
Keogh plans
letter of last instructions
level term insurance
limited payment life insurance
memorial society
mortgage term insurance
mutual insurance companies
participating life insurance

premium
probate
prudent man rule
renewable term insurance
retirement test
stock insurance companies
term insurance policy
uniform decreasing term insurance
universal life insurance
vesting
whole life insurance
will

QUESTIONS

1. What is the basic reason that consumers purchase insurance? Is it true that "you can never have too much insurance?" Explain.

2. What is a "participating life insurance policy" and how does it differ from a nonparticipating policy? Why are dividends on insurance policies nontaxable?

3. Compare and contrast the advantages and disadvantages of ordinary, group, credit, and industrial life insurance. Which types are most important to consumers today? Why?

4. Compare and contrast the characteristics of term insurance and cash-value insurance. Which generally has lower premiums per $1000 of face-value insurance? Is it always a better buy? Explain.

5. What are some arguments that a good insurance salesperson might make in trying to sell life insurance to a young, unmarried college student? Under what circumstances would these arguments be valid?

6. What is the insurance industry's reasoning behind selling life insurance for children? Does it make good economic sense to insure children?

7. Calculate your insurance fund using the formula in Box 17-2. How does it compare to the simple insurance-industry standard of multiplying one's annual income by seven?

8. What role does inflation play in calculating one's insurance fund and in determining both the amount and the kind of insurance to buy? If you could be certain that the inflation rate would be less than the interest rate paid on bank savings accounts, how would this change the amount of insurance you would buy?

9. The retirement provisions of the Social Security program have come under serious debate in the last decade. What are the major weaknesses of the program? What are its strengths? Do future recipients of the program's benefits have any cause for alarm?

10. What is the Social Security retirement test? Are all forms of income counted in this test? Do people lose their Social Security benefits if they fail this test?

11. What are IRA and Keogh plans? How do they differ and what are their major advantages?

12. What is a will? What are the advantages of having one? What happens if someone dies without a will?

13. Why are funerals so expensive? What can consumers do to limit funeral costs and still have the ceremony they prefer?

PROJECTS

1. Call three insurance agents and get their rates for a $25,000 term life insurance policy. Are their rates different? Which company offers the best price? Get similar information from these agents on a $25,000 whole life policy. Is the same company the lowest again?

2. Contact two mail-order insurance companies and get their rates on a $25,000 term policy and a $25,000 whole life policy. Are they less expensive than similar policies available locally?

3. Interview a friend or a relative who is contemplating retirement in the near future. What is his or her impression of the Social Security system? Given the person's lifetime earnings pattern, estimate the size of the Social Security retirement check that he or she can expect. (You can use Table 17-7 or more-recent information available at your local Social Security office.) Is this amount adequate for all his or her retirement needs? Should it be?

4. Investigate the pension plan of a local employer. What are the rules for qualifying for the pension plan? How long does it take for an employee to become fully vested?

5. Do a cost survey of two local funeral homes. Are these mortuaries willing to tell their prices over the phone? Do they have an itemized price list? Do they cooperate with your local memorial society?

6. Answer the questions based on the following situation:

The Altobelli family were gathered in the hospital outside room 1208 when the doctor walked out of the room and said, "I'm very sorry—we did all we could. Joe Altobelli has just died."

Joe's sister, Frances, burst into tears, and her husband, Frank, and her children tried to console her. Maryanne, the oldest daughter, took her mother by the hand and led her away. It had already been agreed by the other members of the family that she would be the one to take care of her mother in this hour of grief.

Frank turned to his son, Mike, and said, "Would you take care of the funeral arrangements, Mike? Your mother and I are Uncle Joe's only living relatives, and he wanted us to have him buried in St. Catherine's Cemetery in the family plot. Joe knew that he wouldn't get out of the hospital this time, given his age and all. And he didn't want to go out like a king. So let's just have a mass said and get this over with. I don't think your mother can take much more of this." And with that he went to join his wife and daughter.

Mike turned to his wife and said, "What do I do now? I've never arranged for a funeral before."
a. If you were in Mike's place, what would you do? What would be the most efficient way to gather information about the costs and the types of services available?
b. Given the desires expressed by Mike's father, would a burial vault be necessary? Why or why not?
c. If the Altobellis lived in a small town rather than in a large city, do you think their funeral costs would be higher? Why?
d. Do some states specifically require funeral directors to get permission to embalm the deceased? If the Altobellis do not live in one of these states, the funeral director will probably choose to perform the embalming. Is this because state law requires this?

REFERENCES AND READINGS

American Council of Life Insurance. *Life Insurance Fact Book.* Washington, D.C.: American Council of Life Insurance, published annually.

"Beating the High Cost of Probating a Will." *Changing Times,* May 1981.

Bouvier, Leon F. "America's Baby Boom Generation: The Fateful Bulge." *Population Bulletin,* April 1980.

"Credit Insurance: The Quiet Overcharge." *Consumer Reports,* July 1979.

Denenberg, Herbert S. *A Shopper's Guide to Life Insurance.* Washington, D.C.: Consumer News, 1974.

Federal Trade Commission. *Staff Report on Life Insurance Cost Disclosure.* Washington, D.C.: U.S. Government Printing Office, 1979.

"Funerals: The Memorial Society Alternative and the FTC's Halfhearted Reform." *Consumer Reports,* August 1979.

Goodwin, David. "Dividends: Benefits or Overcharge?" *Consumers Digest,* November/December 1980.

Harmer, Ruth Mulvey. *The High Cost of Dying.* New York: Collier-Macmillan, 1963.

Kaye, Barry. "Life Insurance: Don't Let the Cost Kill You!" *Consumers Digest,* July/August 1981.

"Keep Your IRA or Keogh Up to Date." *Changing Times,* September 1980.

"The Latest in Life Insurance with an Inflation Twist." *Changing Times,* August 1981.

"Life Insurance: A Special Two-Part Report." *Consumer Reports,* February 1980.

"The Push to Prune Social Security Benefits." *Changing Times,* May 1981.

Schulz, James H. *The Economics of Aging.* Belmont, Calif.: Wadsworth, 1976.

U.S. Department of Health and Human Services. *Social Security Information for Young Families.* Washington, D.C.: U.S. Government Printing Office, 1980.

U.S. Department of Health and Human Services. *Your Social Security.* Washington, D.C.: U.S. Government Printing Office, 1980.

U.S. Federal Trade Commission. "Life Insurance and Savings," *Facts for Consumers,* September 28, 1979.

U.S. Federal Trade Commission. *Life Insurance Cost Disclosure.* Washington, D.C.: U.S. Government Printing Office, 1979.

"What's New in Insurance?" *Changing Times,* February 1981.

Appendix I

Seeking Help for Consumer Problems

This list of common consumer problems includes the names of appropriate agencies to assist you. The addresses and phone numbers of federal agencies and state consumer offices are listed in Appendices II and III.

AREA	PROBLEM	AGENCY TO CONTACT
Advertising	***Deceptive or Misleading***	
	Companies involving interstate commerce	Federal Trade Commission
	Companies in your state	State Attorney General's Office
	U.S. Mail involvement	U.S. Postal Inspector U.S. Postal Service
	Prescription drug ads	Food and Drug Administration
	Other drug ads	Federal Trade Commission
	Automobiles	
	Credit contracts (Truth in Lending)	Federal Trade Commission
	New-car sticker price	Federal Bureau of Investigation
	Odometer alterations	State Highway Patrol
Consumer Information	General information; assistance in identifying the proper agency to help you	Federal Information Center
Communication	Radio and television broadcasting; mobile radio communications; interstate telephone and telegraph service	Federal Communications Commission
Credit	Deceptive, unlawful, or unfair financial practices; Truth in Lending, Fair Credit Reporting Act	Federal Trade Commission
	Unlawful practices of debt collection involving the mail	U.S. Postal Inspector
	Retail installment contract disclosure	State Attorney General's Office
	Credit bureaus (Insurance, obsolete credit ratings and reports)	Federal Trade Commission

Debt Collection Practices	Collection agencies Private investigators Insurance adjusters Patrol service Repossession and harassment within your state	State Consumer Affairs Office or State Attorney General
	Interstate	Federal Trade Commission
Door to Door Sales	Deceptive practices Matters regarding recession (within states)	State Attorney General's Office Consumer Fraud Unit
	Interstate companies	Federal Trade Commission
Finance Companies	Interstate and all Truth in Lending	Federal Trade Commission
Flammable Fabrics	Carpeting, draperies, interior furnishing, and apparel	Consumer Product Safety Commission
Foods, Drugs, Cosmetics, & Devices	Misbranding, contaminated foods, quality, labeling content, quack remedies, and drugs	Food and Drug Administration
	All foods, except meat and poultry	Food and Drug Administration
	Prescription and other drugs	(See "Advertising")
	Commercial weighing and measuring devices (scales, deceptive packaging and quantity labeling of consumer goods)	Department of Agriculture
Fraudulent Schemes	Bunco schemes and other similar schemes	Local Police Department BUNCO Squad
	Forgery	Local Police Department BUNCO-Forgery Division
Home Improvement	Licensed and unlicensed contractors, Failure to complete contracts, and deceptive business practices	State Consumer Affairs Office
	Fraudulent sales practices	Attorney General's Office Consumer Fraud Unit
	Interstate	Federal Trade Commission
Investment Fraud	Pyramid selling, chain schemes, franchises	Attorney General's Office Investment Fraud Unit
	Interstate	Federal Trade Commission
	U.S. mail involvement	U.S. Postal Inspector

Mail Order Complaints	Complaints, removal of names from "junk mail" lists	Consumer Relations Manager Direct Mail Advertising Association, Inc. 6 East 43rd Street New York, N.Y. 10017
Meat and Poultry	False grading markings, interstate mismarking, mislabeling and false advertising	Compliance and Evaluation Staff, U.S. Department of Agriculture
	Inspection of meat at retail level for poor quality, adulteration, mislabeling, discoloration	County Health Department
Mobile Homes	Sales or warranties	Federal Trade Commission
Moving	Rail, bus, or truck carriers (complaints include overcharges, late deliveries, late pickups)	Interstate Commerce Commission
Product Safety	Restricted to products for the home, school, farm, or recreation	Consumer Product Safety Commission
Toys	Dangerous	Consumer Product Safety Commission

Appendix II

Directory of Federal Consumer Agencies

This is a listing of federal agencies that help with consumer protection and regulation. Regional addresses and phone numbers have been included wherever possible.

Consumer Product Safety Commission

Washington, D.C. 20207
800-638-8326
800-492-8363 (in Maryland)
800-638-8333 (in Puerto Rico, Virgin Islands,
                 Alaska, Hawaii)

Regional Offices

800 Peachtree Street NE
Atlanta, Ga. 30308
404-881-2231

230 South Dearborn Street
Room 2945
Chicago, Ill. 60604
312-353-8260

1100 Commerce Street
Room 1C10
Dallas, Tex. 75242
214-767-0841

6 World Trade Center
Vesey Street
6th Floor
New York, N.Y. 10048
212-264-2266

U.S. Customs House
555 Battery Street
Room 416
San Francisco, Calif. 94111
415-556-1816

Federal Trade Commission

6th and Pennsylvania Avenues NW
Washington, D.C. 20580
202-523-3598

Regional Offices

1718 Peachtree Street NW
Room 1000
Atlanta, Ga. 30309
404-881-4836

150 Causeway Street
Room 1301
Boston, Mass. 02114
617-223-6621

55 East Monroe Street
Suite 1437
Chicago, Ill. 60603
312-353-4423

Mall Building
118 St. Clair Avenue
Suite 500
Cleveland, Ohio 44144
216-522-4207

2001 Bryan Street
Suite 2665
Dallas, Tex. 75201
214-767-0032

1405 Curtis Street
Suite 2900
Denver, Colo. 80202
303-837-2271

300 Ala Moana
Honolulu, Hawaii 96850
808-546-5685

Federal Building
11000 Wilshire Boulevard
Room 13209
Los Angeles, Calif. 90024
213-824-7575

2243-EB, Federal Building
26 Federal Plaza
New York, N.Y. 10007
212-264-1207

450 Golden Gate Avenue
Box 36005
San Francisco, Calif. 94102
415-556-1270

Federal Building
915 Second Avenue
28th Floor
Seattle, Wash. 98174
206-442-4655

Food and Drug Administration
5600 Fishers Lane
Rockville, Md. 20857
301-443-3170

District Consumer Affairs Offices

1182 W. Peachtree Street NW
Atlanta, Ga. 30309
404-881-3162

900 Madison Avenue
Baltimore, Md. 21201
301-962-4012

585 Commercial Street
Boston, Mass. 02109
617-223-1278

850 Third Avenue
Brooklyn, N.Y. 11232
212-965-5416

599 Delaware Avenue
Buffalo, N.Y. 14202
716-842-4478

433 West Van Buren Street
Chicago, Ill. 60607
312-353-7379

1141 Central Parkway
Cincinnati, Ohio 45202
513-684-3504

3032 Bryan Street
Dallas, Tex. 75204
214-767-0317

U.S. Customhouse
721 19th Street
Room 513
Denver, Colo. 80202
303-837-4915

1560 East Jefferson Avenue
Detroit, Mich. 48207
313-226-6260

20 Evergreen Place
East Orange, N.J. 07018
201-645-3023

1009 Cherry Street
Kansas City, Mo. 64106
816-374-5850

1521 West Pico Boulevard
Los Angeles, Calif. 90015
213-688-3776

240 Hennepin Avenue
Minneapolis, Minn. 55401
612-725-2121

297 Plus Park Boulevard
Nashville, Tenn. 37217
615-251-5851

4298 Elysian Fields Avenue
New Orleans, La. 70122
504-589-2401

P.O. Box 118
7200 Lake Ellenor Drive
Orlando, Fla. 32802
305-855-0900

2nd and Chestnut Streets
Room 1204
Philadelphia, Pa. 19106
215-597-8058

50 U.N. Plaza
San Francisco, Calif. 94102
415-556-0318

P.O. Box 4427, San Juan Station
San Juan, P.R. 00905

909 1st Avenue
Room 5003
Seattle, Wash. 98104
206-442-5304

Interstate Commerce Commission
12th Street and Constitution Avenue NW
Washington, D.C. 20423
202-275-7076

U.S. Department of Agriculture
Office of Information
Washington, D.C. 20205
202-447-2791

U.S. Postal Service
U.S. Postal Inspector
Washington, D.C. 20260
202-245-4144

Federal Information Center (FIC)

If you have questions about any program or agency in the federal government, you may want to call your nearest Federal Information Center (FIC). FIC staffs are prepared to help consumers find needed information or locate the right agency—usually federal, but sometimes state or local—to help with problems. Each city listed here has an FIC or a tieline—a toll-free local number connected to another FIC. Local listings (printed in italics) are tielines to the nearest FIC.

Alabama
Birmingham	205-322-8591
Mobile	*205-438-1421*

Arizona
Phoenix	602-261-3313
Tucson	*602-622-1511*

Arkansas
Little Rock	*501-378-6177*

California
Los Angeles	213-688-3800
Sacramento	916-440-3344
San Diego	714-293-6030
San Francisco	415-556-6600
San Jose	*408-275-7422*
Santa Ana	*714-836-2386*

Colorado
Colorado Springs	*303-471-9491*
Denver	303-837-3602
Pueblo	*303-544-9523*

Connecticut
Hartford	*203-527-2617*
New Haven	*203-624-4720*

District of Columbia
Washington	202-755-8660

Florida
Fort Lauderdale	*305-522-8531*
Jacksonville	*904-354-4756*
Miami	305-350-4155
Orlando	*305-422-1800*
St. Petersburg	813-893-3495
Tampa	*813-229-7911*
West Palm Beach	*305-833-7566*

Georgia
Atlanta	404-221-6891

Hawaii
Honolulu	808-546-8620

Illinois
Chicago	312-353-4242

Indiana
Gary/Hammond	*219-883-4110*
Indianapolis	317-269-7373

Iowa
Des Moines	*515-284-4448*
Other	800-532-1556

Kansas
Topeka	*913-295-2866*
Wichita	*316-263-6931*
Other	800-432-2934

Kentucky
Louisville	502-582-6261

Louisiana
New Orleans	504-589-6696

Maryland
Baltimore	301-962-4980

Massachusetts
Boston	617-223-7121

Michigan
Detroit	313-226-7016
Grand Rapids	*616-451-2628*

Minnesota
Minneapolis	612-725-2073

Missouri
Kansas City	816-374-2466
St. Joseph	*816-233-8206*
St. Louis	314-425-4106

Nebraska
Omaha	402-221-3353
Other	800-642-8383

New Jersey
Newark	201-645-3600
Paterson/Passaic	*201-523-0717*
Trenton	609-396-4400

New Mexico
Albuquerque	505-766-3091
Santa Fe	*505-983-7743*

New York
Albany	*518-463-4421*
Buffalo	*716-846-4010*
New York	212-264-4464
Rochester	*716-546-5075*
Syracuse	*315-476-8545*

North Carolina
Charlotte	*704-376-3600*

Ohio
Akron	*216-375-5638*
Cincinnati	513-684-2801
Cleveland	216-522-4040
Columbus	*614-221-1014*
Dayton	*513-223-7377*
Toledo	*419-241-3223*

Oklahoma
Oklahoma City	405-231-4868
Tulsa	*918-584-4193*

Oregon
Portland	503-221-2222

Pennsylvania
Allentown/Bethlehem	*215-821-7785*
Philadelphia	215-597-7042
Pittsburgh	412-644-3456
Scranton	*717-346-7081*

Rhode Island
Providence	*401-331-5565*

Tennessee
Chattanooga	*615-265-8231*
Memphis	901-521-3285
Nashville	*615-242-5056*

Texas
Austin	*512-472-5494*
Dallas	*214-767-8585*
Fort Worth	817-334-3624
Houston	713-226-5711
San Antonio	*512-224-4471*

Utah
Ogden	*801-399-1347*
Salt Lake City	801-524-5353

Virginia
Newport News	*804-244-0480*
Norfolk	804-441-3101
Richmond	*804-643-4928*
Roanoke	*703-982-8591*

Washington
Seattle	206-442-0570
Tacoma	*206-383-5230*

Wisconsin
Milwaukee	*414-271-2273*

Appendix III

Directory of State Consumer Agencies

This is a list of state consumer protection and assistance agencies. Their functions and responsibilities vary greatly from state to state, as do the services and information they provide. Some handle consumer complaints or refer you to the right place for help. Some regulate state industries or enforce state consumer laws. And many provide consumer education and information.

Alabama

Director
Governor's Office of Consumer Protection
138 Adams Avenue
Montgomery, Ala. 36130
205-832-5936, 800-392-5658

Alaska

Chief
Consumer Protection Section
Office of the Attorney General
420 L Street
Suite 100
Anchorage, Alas. 99501
907-279-0428

Arizona

Financial Fraud
207 State Capitol Building
Phoenix, Ariz. 85007
602-255-5763 (fraud only)

Arkansas

Deputy Attorney General
Consumer Protection Division
Justice Building
Little Rock, Ark. 72201
501-371-2341, 800-482-8982 (Arkansas only)

California

California Department of Consumer Affairs
1020 N Street
Sacramento, Calif. 95814
916-445-0660 (complaint mediation)
916-445-1254 (consumer information)
800-366-5131 (auto repair complaints, California only)

Colorado

Consumer Section
1525 Sherman Street
4th Floor
Denver, Colo. 80203
303-839-3611

Connecticut

Commissioner
Department of Consumer Protection
State Office Building
Hartford, Conn. 06115
203-566-4999, 800-842-2649 (Connecticut only)

Delaware

Director
Consumer Affairs Division
Department of Community Affairs and Economic Development
820 N. French Street
4th Floor
Wilmington, Del. 19801
302-571-3250

District of Columbia
Director
D.C. Office of Consumer Protection
1424 K Street NW
Washington, D.C. 20005
202-727-1158

Florida
Director
Division of Consumer Services
110 Mayo Building
Tallahassee, Fla. 32304
904-488-2221, 800-342-2176 (Florida only)

Georgia
Administrator
Governor's Office of Consumer Affairs
225 Peachtree Street NE
Suite 400
Atlanta, Ga. 30303
404-656-4900, 800-282-4900

Hawaii
Director of Consumer Protection
Office of the Governor
P.O. Box 3767
250 S. King Street
Honolulu, Hawaii 96811
800-548-2560 (administrative and legal office)
800-548-2540 (complaints)

Idaho
Deputy Attorney General
Consumer Protection Division
State Capitol
Boise, Id. 83720
208-384-2400, 800-632-5937

Illinois
Special Assistant to the Governor
Consumer Advocate Office
Office of the Governor
160 N. LaSalle Street
Room 2010
Chicago, Ill. 60601
312-793-2754

Indiana
Director
Consumer Protection Division
Office of Attorney General
215 State House
Indianapolis, Ind. 46204
317-633-6496 or 633-6276, 800-382-5516

Iowa
Assistant Attorney General in Charge
Consumer Protection Division
Office of Attorney General
1300 East Walnut
Des Moines, Iowa 50319
515-281-2956

Kansas
Assistant Attorney General
Consumer Protection Division
Office of Attorney General
Kansas Judicial Center
301 West 10th
2nd Floor
Topeka, Kan. 66612
913-296-3751

Kentucky
Assistant Deputy Attorney General
Consumer Protection Division
Executive Building
209 St. Clair Street
Frankfort, Ky. 40601
502-564-6607, 800-372-2960

Louisiana
Assistant Secretary
State Office of Consumer Protection
P.O. Box 44091,
Suite 1218
Capitol Station
Baton Rouge, La. 70804
504-925-4401, 800-272-9868

Maine
Deputy Superintendent
Bureau of Consumer Protection
State House Station 35
Augusta, Me. 04333
207-289-3731

Maryland
Chief
Consumer Protection Division
Office of Attorney General
131 East Redwood Street
Baltimore, Md. 21202
301-383-5344

Massachusetts

Secretary
Executive Office of Consumer Affairs
John W. McCormack Building
One Ashburton Place
Room 1411
Boston, Mass. 02108
617-727-7755

Michigan

Assistant Attorney General
Consumer Protection Division
690 Law Building
Lansing, Mich. 48913
517-373-1104

Minnesota

Director
Office of Consumer Services
7th and Roberts Streets
St. Paul, Minn. 55101
612-296-4512
612-296-2331 (complaints)

Mississippi

Chief
Consumer Protection Division
Office of Attorney General
P.O. Box 220
Justice Building
Jackson, Miss. 39205
601-354-7130

Missouri

Chief Counsel
Consumer Protection Division
Office of Attorney General
P.O. Box 899
Supreme Court Building
Jefferson City, Mo. 65102
314-751-3321

Montana

Administrator
Consumer Affairs Division
Department of Business Regulation
805 North Main Street
Helene, Mont. 59601
406-449-3163

Nebraska

Attorney General
Consumer Protection Division
State House
Lincoln, Neb. 68509
402-471-2682

Nevada

Deputy Attorney General
Consumer Affairs Division
2501 East Sahara Avenue
3rd Floor
Las Vegas, Nev. 89158
702-386-5293

New Hampshire

Chief
Consumer Protection, Antitrust Division
Office of Attorney General
State House Annex
Concord, N.H. 03301
603-271-3641

New Jersey

Director
Division of Consumer Affairs
Department of Law and Public Safety
1100 Raymond Boulevard
Room 504
Newark, N.J. 07102
201-648-4010

New Mexico

Director
Consumer and Economic Crime Division
Office of Attorney General
P.O. Box 1508
Santa Fe, N.M. 87501
505-827-5521

New York

Chairperson and Executive Director
Consumer Protection Board
99 Washington Avenue
Albany, N.Y. 12210
518-474-8583

North Carolina
Special Deputy Attorney General and
Division Head
Consumer Protection Division
P.O. Box 629
Justice Building
Raleigh, N.C. 27602
919-733-7741

North Dakota
Attorney General for the State of N. Dakota
State Capitol Building
Bismarck, N.D. 58505
701-224-2210

Ohio
Assistant Attorney General and Section Chief
Consumer Frauds and Crimes Section
30 East Broad Street
Columbus, Ohio 43215
614-466-8831

Oklahoma
Administrator
Department of Consumer Affairs
460 Jim Thorpe Building
Oklahoma City, Okla. 73105
405-521-3653

Oregon
Chief Counsel
Consumer Protection Division
Office of Attorney General
520 SW Yamhill Street
Portland, Oreg. 97204
503-229-5522

Pennsylvania
Acting Director
Bureau of Consumer Protection
301 Market Street
9th Floor
Harrisburg, Penn. 17101
717-787-9707

Puerto Rico
Department of Consumer Affairs
Minillas Governmental Center
P.O. Box 41059
Torre Norte Building
De Diego Avenue, Stop 22
Santurce, P.R. 00940
809-726-6090

Rhode Island
Administrator
Public Protection Consumer Unit
Department of Attorney General
56 Pine Street
Providence, R.I. 02903
401-277-3163

South Carolina
Administrator
Department of Consumer Affairs
2221 Devine Street
Columbia, S.C. 29211
803-758-2040, 800-922-1594

South Dakota
Assistant Attorney General
Division of Consumer Protection
Capitol Building
Pierre, S.D. 57501
605-773-3215

Tennessee
Director
Division of Consumer Affairs
Department of Agriculture
Ellington Agriculture Center
Box 40627, Melrose Station
Nashville, Tenn. 37204
615-741-1461, 800-342-8385

Texas
Assistant Attorney General
Consumer Protection and Antitrust Division
Office of Attorney General
P.O. Box 12548, Capitol Station
Austin, Tex. 78711
512-475-3288

Utah
Director
Division of Consumer Affairs
Utah Trade Commission
Department of Business Regulation
330 East Fourth Street
Salt Lake City, Ut. 84111
801-533-6441

Vermont

Chief
Assistant Attorney and Chief of Consumer Protection Division
State of Vermont
Office of Attorney General
109 State Street
Montpelier, Vt. 05602
802-828-3171, 800-642-5149

Virginia

Administrator and Director
State Office of Consumer Affairs
Department of Agriculture and Consumer Services
825 East Broad Street
Box 1163
Richmond, Va. 23209
804-786-2042,
800-552-9963 (regarding state agencies)

Washington

Assistant Attorney General and Chief
Consumer Protection and Antitrust Division
1366 Dexter Horton Building
Seattle, Wash. 98104
206-464-7744, 800-552-0700

West Virginia

Director
Consumer Protection Division, Office of Attorney General
3412 Stauton Avenue SE
Charleston, W.V. 25305
304-348-8986

Wisconsin

Assistant Attorney General
Office of Consumer Protection
Department of Justice
State Capitol
Madison, Wis. 53702
608-266-1852

Wyoming

Assistant Attorney General
123 Capitol Building
Cheyenne, Wy. 82002
307-777-7841

Glossary

A

ability-to-pay principle The principle of taxation that argues that those most able to pay taxes should subsidize those who are less able to pay.

acceleration clause A clause that requires a consumer to pay an entire debt in one lump sum if he or she fails to meet a single payment.

active solar systems Designs that take advantage of the sun's energy but require some moving parts, such as fans or pumps.

actuarial table A chart or list that shows the probability that a person with certain characteristics will have an accident or will die in a given year; used to calculate insurance premiums.

actuaries Persons who compute insurance premiums according to probabilities based on historical risks for various age groups.

adjustable mortgage loan (AML) *See* adjustable rate mortgage.

adjustable rate mortgage (ARM) A mortgage that allows the interest rate to rise and fall according to the supply and demand for money at a national level; sometimes called adjustable mortgage loan (AML).

adjusted balance method A method of computing finance charges in which creditors add finance charges only after subtracting all payments made during a billing period.

advocacy advertising Ads by a firm, an industry, or a special-interest group that seek to change public opinion on local or national issues.

age earning curve The gradual rise, leveling off, and perhaps reduction of income that occurs as a person ages.

all-savers tax-exempt certificate A time savings certificate available from most savings institutions for which the interest is exempt from federal income taxes.

amortization A payment plan that allows the mortgagor to gradually reduce the debt by monthly payments on the principal.

annual percentage rate (APR) The finance charge over a full year expressed as a percentage of the loan. The APR must reflect all the costs of the loan as required by the Truth in Lending Act.

appraisal A formal investigation of real property to estimate its value.

asset 1. Something of value that can be sold to repay debt. 2. In financial terms, all forms of property owned by a person or a business.

assumable loans Loans that transfer a mortgage and all its obligation from one person to another.

average cost The total cost of a product divided by the number of times it is used. The average cost includes all cost factors, such as purchase price, maintenance cost, depreciation, insurance costs, and energy costs.

average daily balance method A billing method in which the outstanding balance is computed daily. The daily balances are then totaled and the finance charge is based on this average.

average tax rate A tax rate that is computed by dividing the total tax owed by the total income earned.

B

bait and switch An illegal sales technique in which a merchant offers a product at a low price but then refuses to sell it and attempts to switch the consumer to a high-priced item.

bankruptcy A court action freeing a person of debt because of his or her inability to pay. Although most debts are discharged with this action, not all are dischargeable, and the assets of the debtor, with some exceptions, are turned over to the creditor in lieu of payment.

barter Direct exchange of goods or services that involves no money.

base year period A selected period of time used as a comparison for price changes in later years. Economists give the base period a value of 100 so that changes from that period can be more easily understood.

basic coverage Hospital, surgical, and physician insurance that covers simple medical needs.

Basic Four food groups A guide for wise food selection consisting of four food categories: milk and dairy foods, meat and other protein goods, fruits and vegetables, and bread and cereals.

bearish Describes pessimists who believe that the average prices of stocks are going to fall.

benefits-received principle The principle of taxation that argues that whoever receives government services should pay for them.

bill-consolidation loan A loan that combines several debts into one loan by providing the borrower with enough money to pay them off, with the new debt spread over a longer period of time.

binder *See* earnest agreement.

biomass Vegetable matter such as wood, crops, or animal wastes that can be burned to release energy.

blended (reconstituted) family A family created by the marriage of two formerly married individuals who both bring children to the second marriage.

blue-chip stocks Shares of stock in corporations that have demonstrated their financial dependability by paying good dividends and maintaining leadership positions in their respective industries.

bond A certificate of indebtedness that may be resold; an agreement whereby a borrower agrees to pay a fixed amount of interest each year for the right to use the bondholder's money. At the end of a specific time period, the borrower agrees to pay back the original debt.

bottom-up theory The theory that fashions filter up from the young, particularly from lower-income groups.

British thermal unit (Btu) The amount of energy needed to raise the temperature of 1 pound of water by 1 degree Fahrenheit. A burning kitchen match gives off about 1 Btu.

budget A tool used for money management; a spending plan.

bullish Describes optimists who feel that the stockmarket averages are going to rise.

buyer's guide window sticker A disclosure found on used cars that describes the warranty, if any.

buying process model A variation of the decision-making model; a step-by-step process that can be applied to the purchase of any consumer good.

C

calories Measurements of food energy, or heat, produced as a by-product of the utilization of food.

capital asset For federal income tax purposes, any property not used in business, including stocks, bonds, real estate, consumer durables, and jewelry.

capital gain The increase in the value of an investment from the time it is bought until it is sold. It is a long-term gain if one owns the investment for more than 1 year.

capital loss The decrease in the value of an investment from the time it is bought until it is sold. It is a long-term loss if one owns the investment for more than 1 year.

cash-value insurance policy A policy that provides death insurance plus a savings account that increases in value throughout the life of the policy.

caveat emptor Let the buyer beware, that is, the producer is under no obligation to the consumer after a purchase is made.

certificate of deposit (CD) An agreement between a financial institution and a depositor that the bank will pay a guaranteed rate of interest as long as the depositor promises to leave a certain sum of money in the bank for a specified time.

Chapter 7 (straight) bankruptcy. *See* bankruptcy.

Chapter 13 bankruptcy (wage-earner plan) A section of the Bankruptcy Act that restructures a consumer's debt without forcing a liquidation of all assets. Debts are not completely eliminated, and the debtor agrees to pay a regular sum each month to a court-appointed trustee.

characterizing ingredient The main ingredient of a food product, such as cherries in a cherry pie.

classics Styles that endure and that are accepted over a long period of time.

closed-end lease An agreement to pay a monthly rental fee for a set period of time, usually 12 to 24 months. At the end of the lease the product is returned to the lessor.

closed-end mutual funds Investment funds that sell a fixed number of shares.

closing The formal process by which ownership of real property transfers from seller to buyer.

closing costs Fees for services that effect the formal transfer of ownership of real property from seller to buyer.

co-insurance An insurance plan in which part of the loss is covered by the insured person. By agreeing to deduct some of the loss from the claim, the insured party can generally get a lower insurance rate.

collateral Anything of value pledged to assure loan repayment and subject to seizure on default.

collision insurance Insurance that covers the insured driver's car in the event of an accident.

coloring methods Processes used on textiles to create color or design on fabrics for clothing or household use.

commission A sum of money or a percentage of the selling price paid to an agent for his or her services.

common stock An investment in the ownership of a corporation that that entitles the stockholder to share in the profits of the firm and in the election of those who run the firm.

community hospital A nonfederal, short-term, general, or special hospital that provides care to the public, most often on a nonprofit basis.

comparative advertising An advertising strategy that compares the name-brand competitor(s) of the product being advertised.

compounding Paying interest on previous interest. The period of compounding can vary from a year to a day, with the shorter period producing a higher effective interest rate.

comprehensive insurance Insurance that protects the insured person's car against hazards other than collision with other automobiles. This generally includes protection against fire, theft, and vandalism, among others.

condominium An individual housing unit to which the owner holds title plus a proportionate interest in common areas.

conspicuous consumption Purchasing goods or services because of the status associated with them rather than for a specific need.

consumer cooperatives Organizations that attempt to lower prices for their members by pooling buying power and purchasing in bulk at the wholesale level.

consumer durable goods Items that provide satisfaction to their owners over a longer period of time and, due to high cost, are often purchased with installment credit.

consumer economics The study of personal decision making or maximizing well-being through rational economic choices.

consumer finance companies Financial institutions that specialize in small consumer loans.

Consumer Price Index (CPI) Statistics that measure changes in the retail cost of a given set of goods and services purchased by the typical urban consumer. The CPI is the official measure of the rate of inflation.

consumer sovereignty The doctrine that consumers hold ultimate power in determining what gets produced.

consumerism A movement for which the goal is to ensure that individuals who buy and use products and services get what they pay for—fair value.

contract of sale A contract that itemizes the terms and conditions of sale, usually of real estate; also called purchase contract.

conventional loans Fixed payment loans for which interest rates are established by the lender as a result of supply and demand in the national money market.

cooling-off provision A time period (3 business days under a Federal Commission ruling) during which a consumer is allowed to cancel a door-to-door installment sales contract.

cooperative A group of dwellings owned by a corporation of which the stockholders are residents of the building.

corrective advertising Informal advertising that a company must undertake when the Federal Trade Commission rules that the firm's past advertising was false and misleading.

cost of living adjustment (COLA) A clause in many labor contracts that provides automatic increases in wages whenever the Consumer Price Index rises (escalates); often called an escalator clause.

cost-push inflation A rise in the general level of prices caused by an increase in the cost of doing business.

creative financing Combining various mortgage instruments in order to sell real estate.

credit An arrangement to receive cash, goods, or services in the present in return for payment in the future.

credit bureau A firm that assembles credit information about consumers and then sells this information to other businesses.

credit history The record of how one has borrowed and repaid debts.

credit life insurance Life insurance issued through a lender to cover payment of a loan in the event of the death of the debtor.

credit union A cooperative financial institution that accepts deposits from and offers loans to only its members.

cremation The reduction of the body of a deceased person to ashes by fire.

custom A societal value that conditions an individual's behavior in a particular situation.

D

deceptive advertising Any attempt by a firm to consciously mislead a consumer. This may take the form of false claims, free goods, high pressure, contests, or bait-and-switch tactics.

decreasing term insurance A form of term insurance in which premiums remain constant but the face value decreases as the probability of death increases.

deductible The amount of covered expenses that must be paid by the insured person before benefits become payable by the insurer.

deductions Taxpayer expenditures that may be subtracted from earnings before calculating income tax.

default Failure to make monthly payments on schedule as promised.

deflation A decrease in the general level of prices.

Delaney Clause A section of the 1958 Food Additives Amendments that prohibits the use of any chemical linked to cancer in people or animals.

demand-pull inflation A rise in the general level of prices caused by an increase in total demand. This kind of inflation can be characterized as too much money chasing too few goods.

demography The science of vital and social statistics of a population, as of births, marriages, and deaths; the number of people of certain ages in a population.

deposit A set amount of money paid for security and to show good faith to obtain a service or a product; commonly required when renting equipment or an apartment or when buying a house.

deposit term insurance Similar to level term insurance, except that the premium for the first year is significantly higher than in subsequent years.

depreciation 1. A lessening of the value of a product due to age or use. 2. The decline in the market value of an asset.

diagnosis related groups (DRGs) A system of 383 categories that classifies all ailments and thus allows hospitals to charge a flat-rate fee per disorder rather than individual fees for each service provided in treating a disorder.

diminishing marginal utility An economic concept that states that the additional satisfaction a consumer gets from the last unit received will be less than the amount of satisfaction from the previous unit. For income, the utility of the last $1000 earned is assumed to be less than that of the previous $1000.

disability income insurance A form of health insurance that provides periodic payments to replace income when the insured person is unable to work as a result of illness, injury, or disease.

discount points A lump-sum payment to the lender to compensate the lender for offering a below-market interest rate.

discretionary income 1. buying power that does not have to be spent on basic, life-supporting goods or services. 2. The money that is left after fixed expenses have been paid and allotments have been made for basic necessities.

disposable income Take-home pay; the money available after deductions, such as taxes and Social Security; also called net income.

dividend A sum of money paid to shareholders of a corporation out of earnings.

down payment Cash paid at the time of purchase in installment or mortgage loans.

E

earnest agreement (binder) A written offer to buy real property at a given price.

earnest money A deposit to show one's intention to purchase real estate; also called a binder.

easements Rights to use land owned by another.

economic impact statement A statement in which the economic costs of a proposed regulation are measured against the prospective benefits.

economics The study of how societies and individuals cope with the problem of unlimited wants and limited resources.

embalming Temporarily keeping a dead body from decaying by treating it with various chemicals. Embalming does not prevent eventual decomposition.

emergency fund Money reserved to pay unexpected bills or living expenses during unemployment.

emotional advertising Ads with the major focus of persuading consumers to buy a product for psychological reasons such as guilt, fear, or snobbery.

endowment life insurance A form of whole life insurance that emphasizes the forced-savings feature so that the cash value of the policy builds rapidly.

energy The ability to work and overcome resistance.

energy conservation The practice of extending the useful life of the earth's energy resources through wise and efficient management.

energy efficiency rating (EER) A measure of the ability of an appliance to economize on the use of electricity; for a cooling appliance, it is calculated by dividing the unit's cooling output (measured in British thermal units) by the watts needed. The higher the EER, the less the unit costs to operate.

Engel's law The generalization that as a family's income rises, the proportion of its income spent on food declines.

enriched (fortified) Foods that have had small amounts of nutrients added to increase their nutritional level.

entitlement programs An umbrella term for social programs that provide transfer payments.

equity The dollar difference between the selling price and the mortgage payoff of real property.

escalator clause *See* cost of living adjustment.

escrow (impound) accounts Accounts used by lenders to hold funds in reserve to ensure future payment for recurring items such as real estate taxes and insurance premiums.

exclusions Items or conditions not included; typically found in insurance policies and income tax.

executor A man who is responsible for administering a will.

executrix A woman who is responsible for administering a will.

exemptions Specific amounts of money that are declared to be nontaxable.

expiration (use-by) date The date past which products do not perform their best and may not be safe.

express warranty A written guarantee from the manufacturer that itemizes the rights and responsibilities of both the consumer and the manufacturer regarding product repair or replacement.

extended families Three generations living together in the same house.

extended warranty plan A competitive device used by retailers to add extra time to the manufacturer's warranty period, the cost of which is borne by the retailer.

externalities *See* spillover effects.

F

fabric construction A method used to form textiles from fibers or yarns, most frequently weaving or knitting.

face value The amount of money a bond can be redeemed for at maturity. This amount is generally printed on the front (face) of the bond.

fad A short-lived fashion; often popular with smaller groups of people than adopt fashions.

family life cycle The identifiable stages that a family passes through, beginning with couples without children and progressing to the later years of retirement.

Fannie Mae *See* Federal National Mortgage Association.

fashion The prevailing or accepted style at a given time; the code language of status.

fashion cycle The stages through which an accepted style progresses from introduction to rejection.

Federal Housing Administration (FHA) The federal agency that offers mortgages at lower-than-prevailing fixed interest rates, with lower down payments, and with mortgage insurance by the federal government.

Federal National Mortgage Association (FNMA) One of two of the largest purchasers of mortgages from banks and savings and loan associations; commonly called Fannie Mae.

fiber content The basic ingredient of textiles. Fibers may be natural (cotton, wool) or manmade (rayon, nylon).

finance charge The dollar cost of a loan. This includes the charges of administering the loan as well as actual interest charges.

finishes Chemicals applied to textiles to improve durability, performance, or appearance.

fixed costs of driving Expenses, such as depreciation and insurance, that do not increase with vehicle usage; the costs of owning a motor vehicle.

fixed expenses Large, regular, and predictable expenses established by a contract or an agreement.

fixed-payment mortgage A type of mortgage that has an interest rate and payments that stay level for the lifetime of the loan; sometimes called a standard mortgage.

flat tax An income tax that takes the same percentage of your income no matter how much you earn. It is a type of proportional tax.

flexible expenses Daily living expenses that can be controlled by consumers, such as expenses for food, clothing, and entertainment.

Flexible Loan Insurance Program (FLIP) A fixed-interest-rate loan for which part or all of the down payment is kept in an interest-earning account and then withdrawn each month to supplement the borrower's payment.

floating-payment mortgage A mortgage for which a homeowner's payment may be flexible over the lifetime of the loan, such as with an adjustable rate mortgage or a Flexible Loan Insurance Program (FLIP).

food additive A substance added to food as a result of processing, production, or packaging.

foreclose To seize property and sell it to pay off a debt.

fossil fuels The remains (fossils) of dead plants and animals that can be burned to release energy. They generally come in the form of coal, natural gas, or oil.

fraud Deceit or trickery used to gain an unfair advantage.

free good Something that is so abundant that there is no cost to obtain it.

free-rider effect A situation in which nonpaying members of society obtain the fringe benefits of goods or services.

fringe benefits Nonsalary and thus nontaxable employer contributions to employees, for example, a fully paid employer-sponsored health plan.

full warranty A warranty that guaranties a consumer's right to full repair of a product in a timely manner at no cost to the consumer; may pay for incidental expenses incurred as a result of product breakdown.

G

generally recognized as safe (GRAS) Designates food additives that have been in use for a long time. Before 1968, many of these food additives had not been tested for safety.

generic drugs Non-brand-name drugs that contain the same ingredients as their better-known rivals. They are usually less expensive.

GNP deflator A price index that was created to measure the real value of all goods and services produced in the United States. It does not count the cost of imports and is not available monthly as is the Consumer Price Index, but it is broader in scope than the CPI and is generally preferred by economists.

goal A result toward which some effort is directed.

government securities Certificates of federal government debt, including savings bonds and Treasury bills, notes, and bonds.

graduated payment mortgage A fixed-interest-rate loan for which monthly payments are low at first but increase each year for a stated time period, often causing negative amortization.

gross income The total of wages or salary before deductions for income taxes, Social Security, and so forth.

group life insurance Insurance that is usually available from an employer; does not require a physical examination and often is less expensive than other forms of life insurance.

H

hazard insurance Insurance that is often required for a mortgage; protects the borrower and the lender against loss from fire, windstorm, or other natural disasters.

health A state of complete physical, mental, and social well-being, not merely the absence of distress or infirmity.

health foods An undefined and inherently deceptive term used to describe foods for special diets or foods used as nutrient supplements.

health insurance Insurance designed to help cover expenses arising from sickness or injury and in some cases to provide income during disability.

Health Maintenance Organization (HMO) An organization that provides comprehensive health-care services for a fixed payment.

Health System Agency (HSA) The local planning board that collects information and analyzes the health-care delivery system in a given area.

high-ball technique A sales strategy in which a salesperson deliberately overestimates the value of a potential buyer's old car in order to make a sale and then overcharges for the new car.

high nutrient density Describes foods that are high in nutrients and relatively low in calories.

home-service life insurance A small life insurance policy sold door-to-door that features a small amount of coverage and weekly or monthly premiums; descended from industrial life insurance.

hospital-expense insurance Insurance that provides specific benefits for daily room and board, routine nursing care, and other hospital services.

hospital indemnity coverage Insurance that pays a fixed amount of money (indemnity) directly to the patient for each day she or he spends in the hospital.

human capital Training or skills (mental or physical) that allow a person to perform services that he or she could not otherwise do.

hyperinflation Inflation characterized by rates that escalate to such high levels that money becomes almost valueless.

I

identity standard A product with standard, well-known ingredients that is not required to have a content label.

implied warranty An automatic guarantee by the producer that a product is usable and will not fall apart or break down under normal use.

implied warranty of habitability A warranty that requires rental units to conform to building, safety, and sanitation codes.

income brackets Divisions or levels of personal income used within the structure of a progressive tax system to determine tax obligation.

index fund An investment fund that mirrors the composition of the 500 stocks in the Standard and Poor Index.

indexes Measuring devices, such as the Consumer Price Index, used to follow the general level of prices.

Individual Retirement Accounts (IRAs) Retirement plans originally intended for employees whose employers did not have a company pension program, but expanded by the 1981 Tax Act to include all employees. Under an IRA an individual can place money into a retirement account and get a tax deduction of up to $2000 per year.

industrial-age values Values that support the "more is better" philosophy. Consumers with such values tend to view the earth's resources as inexhaustible and believe that technological solutions will allow economic growth to continue indefinitely.

industrial life insurance Life insurance issued in small amounts, usually less than $1000, with weekly or monthly premiums collected at the home by an insurance agent. Also known as home-service life insurance.

infant mortality rate The number of children who die before reaching their first birthday for each thousand born.

inferior goods Products or goods that are purchased less often by those with higher incomes than by those with lower incomes.

inflation A sustained rise in the average level of prices.

inflation hedge A purchase or investment that provides protection from loss caused by inflation.

inflationary expectations Belief by consumers that inflation will continue, causing them to purchase goods in the present rather than in the future.

informative advertisement An advertisement that provides the consumer with specific, understandable, and verifiable claims about a product or service.

informative legislation Laws and regulations that require manufacturers and/or businesses to supply consumers with specific product information.

installment (closed-end) credit Loans that are set up to be repaid in set amounts at constant intervals over a period of time.

institutional advertisement An advertisement that associates a product with ideas and institutions that are valued by a majority of the consuming public.

insurance An agreement whereby one party agrees to give up a small, definite amount of money in the present in order to be shielded from some uncertain but potentially greater loss in the future.

interest The income lenders earn for letting someone borrow their money.

interest-adjusted cost index (IAC) A method of comparing the relative costs of various insurance policies that takes the time-value cost of money into account.

investment A way of using current resources so that one will have a larger income in the future.

investment portfolio The mix of investments that an investor holds.

item pricing The practice of marking a price on a product or package as opposed to marking the price only on a store shelf.

J

joint ownership A form of partnership in which two or more people own the same property. In the event of the death of one of the owners, the survivor(s) retain ownership.

K

Keogh Plan A tax-deferred pension account for self-employed people.

kilocalorie The amount of heat energy needed to raise the temperature of 1 kilogram of water 1 degree Celsius.

L

labor income The wage or salary paid to an individual plus paid benefits such as pensions, medical and dental insurance, life insurance, paid vacation and sick days, and employers' Social Security contributions.

law of demand The law that states that consumers will buy more of a given product at lower prices than at higher prices.

lease A contract that conveys property to another for a specified time period for a specific fee.

legal clinic A group of lawyers who offer their services at reduced fees by using paraprofessionals and standardized forms, and by concentrating on common case types such as uncontested divorces and traffic citations.

leisure foregone The amount of time one gives up in order to work; time that is not now available for leisure.

leisure time Time not committed to income production or nonmarket home production.

lemon-aid Legislation such as the Magnuson-Moss Warranty Act of 1975 that is intended to help consumers who purchase new automobiles that are poorly built and need constant repairs.

letter of last instructions A document that conveys the wishes of a deceased person to the survivors. It is not a substitute for a will and can be informal as well as informational.

level of living The lifestyle and types of possessions that an individual income makes possible.

level term insurance Insurance that provides a constant level of protection throughout the life of the insurance contract.

liabilities 1. In financial terms, all bills or loans owed by a person or business. 2. Legal responsibilities to repay debts.

liability insurance Insurance that covers drivers for accidental damage to other persons and their property when drivers are judged to be at fault.

life cycle A series of identifiable stages of human growth that occur in a specific order.

life expectancy The number of additional years a person can expect to live given the current death rate; can be calculated for a person of any age.

limited-payment life insurance A form of whole life insurance on which premiums are payable for a fixed number of years.

limited warranty A written guarantee in which the costs for product repair are shared with the consumer.

liquidity The ease with which an investment can be turned into cash.

load A sales fee charged to investors in open-end mutual funds.

lobbyists People who try to influence the voting of legislators and encourage them to create certain legislation.

loopholes Special tax deductions that allow higher-income consumers to pay less in taxes.

low-ball technique A sales strategy in which a salesperson quotes a low price for a new car and later discovers a "mistake" was made or simply offers a low price on a trade-in.

low nutrient density Describes foods that are low in nutrients and high in calorie content.

lumen A measurement of light.

M

major medical-expense insurance Health insurance that pays the expense of major illness or injury; generally characterized by large benefit maximums and small deductible amounts.

malnutrition faulty or inadequate nutrition; too few or too many nutrients.

malpractice suits Lawsuits in which patients claim they have been harmed by a trained professional such as a doctor or a nurse because accepted medical procedures were not followed.

marginal cost The additional cost of using a good that one already owns. For example, the marginal cost of driving across town to see a friend is the cost of gasoline used on the trip.

marginal tax rate The percentage that taxes take of the last dollar earned.

market economy An economic system that relies on individual decisions (for example, of firms and households) to produce and distribute the resources of society.

marriage tax The increase in married couples' income taxes that results from a lower zero-bracket amount and a higher marginal tax rate.

Medicaid A joint federal-state program that provides health-care funding to low-income people.

Medicare The federal health insurance program that serves Americans aged 65 and over. It has two parts: hospital insurance that pays for inpatient care and medical insurance that helps pay for doctors' services, outpatient hospital services, and many other medical services not covered under standard policies.

memorial society A nonprofit organization of which the function is to reduce the costs of funerals through preplanning arrangements.

mental human capital Skills and abilities obtained primarily through the application of education.

merchandise acceptance curve The graphic representation of a typical fashion cycle.

mobile homes Factory-built units that are hauled to a semipermanent site, creating low-cost, minimum-upkeep housing alternatives.

modular homes Factory-manufactured living sections arranged in various ways on a permanent foundation on a building site.

monetarism A school of economic thought that argues that the size and growth of a nation's money supply is the chief determinant of inflation and output.

money management A system of planning for spending based on expected income; also called budgeting.

money-market certificates of deposit A 26-week investment with a minimum denomination of $10,000 and a cash penalty for early withdrawal.

money-market mutual fund An investment company of which the primary aim is to pool investors' money and buy high-yield bonds. The income on the bonds is then passed back to the investors.

month-to-month rental agreement A contract between a tenant and a landlord that identifies the amount of money charged to rent a living space for 1 month.

moped A vehicle that is a cross between a motorcycle and a bicycle. It is a small motorcycle with pedals, thus the name "mo-ped."

mortgage A claim against real property given by the buyer to the lender as security for money borrowed.

mortgage insurance 1. A form of decreasing term insurance that protects the borrower in that the decrease in the value of the policy is small during the early years and then rapid in later years when the mortgage is being paid off. 2. Insurance that protects the lender against loss by default of part of a mortgage, reducing the risk to the lender.

mortgage note A written agreement to repay a mortgage.

mortgage term insurance Insurance that pays off a home mortgage in the event of the death of the insured person.

municipal bonds Bonds issued (sold) by a state or local government agency. Interest on these bonds is exempt from federal taxes.

mutual fund An investment company that sells shares and uses the money to buy stocks and bonds.

mutual insurance companies Insurance companies whose policyholders participate in company ownership and profits.

N

National Consumer Cooperative Bank (NCC) A bank that is a major national source of credit, providing financial and technical assistance to existing and emerging consumer cooperatives.

natural food A food that contains no artificial preservatives, emulsifiers, or other additives.

necessities Goods or services that are essential to survival.

negative amortization Can occur in a floating payment mortgage when a mortgagor owes more money than was originally borrowed.

negotiable order of withdrawal (NOW) A checking account that pays interest.

net income Takehome pay; wage or salary minus deductions for income taxes, Social Security, retirement, and so forth; also called disposable income.

net worth The mathematical difference between assets and liabilities for a person or a business.

new home warranties Guarantees for materials, structure, and quality of workmanship that are now available from the National Association of Home Builders.

no-fault insurance An insurance system in which the injured parties collect from their own companies, regardless of who is at fault.

no-load mutual funds Mutual funds with no sales charge added to the purchase price.

nominal dollars Dollars measured by their face value, that is, not adjusted for inflation.

nonmarket home production Household tasks that include physical care for self, family, and possessions.

normal good A commodity that consumers buy more of as consumer incomes rise.

nuclear family A family that consists of husband, wife, plus dependent children, if any.

nurse-midwives Certified nurses who specialize in the care of pregnant women.

nutrients Substances contained in food that are essential for good health, specifically from six categories: carbohydrates, proteins, fats, vitamins, minerals, and water.

O

open-end (revolving) credit A line of credit that may be used repeatedly up to some specified limit. There is no preestablished payment schedule, although there often is a required monthly minimum payment. There is no definite period of time for repaying the entire loan.

open-end lease A conditional sales contract in which the consumer leases a car for a set period of time. At the end of the lease the consumer agrees to either buy the car outright or to pay the leasing company the difference between the actual market value of the car and the resale value that was stipulated in the original contract. If the resale value was overestimated, the consumer will have to make a large final payment.

open-end mutual funds Investment funds that issue shares on demand and that will buy back any shares that someone wishes to sell.

opportunity costs The value of whatever must be given up in order to get something else, that is, the value of all resources, including time.

ordinary life insurance *See* whole life insurance.

organic foods Foods grown without artificial fertilizers or chemical pesticides.

overregulation Government edicts for which the social costs are greater than their benefits.

P

Parkinson's Law A theory that states that the amount of time spent doing a job expands to fit the amount of time available.

participating life insurance An insurance policy that can pay a dividend or a rebate to the policyholder based on the earnings of the company and the size of the policy.

passive solar techniques Designs that take advantage of the sun's energy without using moving parts.

patient package inserts (PPIs) Short brochures that the FDA wanted pharmacists to give to consumers each time consumers purchased one of the ten most commonly prescribed drugs. These inserts were to be written in nontechnical language, and they described the purpose, the side effects, the risks, and the benefits of the drug. When President Reagan took office in 1981, this regulation was suspended indefinitely.

payback period The time it takes to recoup a dollar investment, in energy conservation devices, for example.

pesticides Chemicals that kill insects; used to prevent crop destruction.

photovoltaic cells (solar cells) Devices that convert the radiant energy from the sun directly into electrical energy.

physical human capital Skills and abilities that result primarily from strength and reflexes.

physican assistant A paramedic; an individual with medical training who can augment the health-care services of a doctor.

physician-expense insurance Insurance that helps pay doctors' fees for nonsurgical care in the hospital, home, or office, usually on a fixed-fee basis.

post-industrial-age values Beliefs that support a conservationist attitude toward the environment. Consumers with such values tend to view the earth's resources as exhaustible, and they stress a go-slow approach to tampering with the environment.

preferred stock A security that has some qualities of a corporate bond and some qualities of a common stock. Like a share of common stock it earns a return only if the firm earns a profit, but the size of this return is preset like the return on a bond. Like a bondholder, a preferred stockholder has no vote in corporate elections.

premium The amount paid for insurance of any type; can be paid in installments.

prepayment penalty A fee charged by the lender to the buyer for paying off a loan in advance, often as the result of selling property.

previous-balance method A billing method that charges interest on the full amount of the billing, regardless of payments made during the period.

principal The amount of a debt or investment minus the interest.

private (business) sector The part of the economy composed of private business; not paid for by public funds.

probate The legal process for establishing the validity of a will and for ensuring that it is carried out.

productivity A measure of output per unit of input. Most often this index refers to the value of production per worker.

progressive income tax 1. A system of taxation in which an increasing tax rate is levied on each successive amount of taxable income. 2. A tax that takes a larger fraction of income as income rises.

proportional taxation A system of taxation that takes a constant proportion of earnings regardless of one's income level.

protective legislation Regulations that force producers to alter the features or quality of their products or in some cases to discontinue production altogether.

prudent man rule The federal regulation that stipulates that managers of pension funds must invest the funds in a manner that shows both care and diligence.

psychic income Nonmonetary benefits of a job, such as feelings of satisfaction or pleasant working conditions.

public good A good or a service with significant social benefit that cannot be denied to people who are unable to pay for it. Public goods such as national defense, parks, and police and fire service are examples.

public sector The part of the economy composed of government services and paid for by public funds.

puffery Advertising that provides only mythical or unverifiable information. Its major goal is to persuade rather than to inform the consumer. Appeals on the basis of emotion, trust, institutions, rigged comparisons with the competition, or half-truths are all forms of puffery.

R

random-walk theory The hypothesis that no one can consistently outguess the stock market and make money by choosing the best stocks, because there is no secret information. Thus the best strategy for investing in the stock market is to choose a large number of randomly selected stocks and then hold on to them.

real dollars Nominal dollars adjusted for a change in their purchasing power over a specific period.

real estate broker Someone who has been licensed to sell real estate by the state as a result of passing a qualifying exam and as a result of job performance.

real income The number of goods and services one can purchase with labor income.

real property Land and everything permanently affixed to it.

recall The power to eliminate hazardous products from the marketplace.

recommended dietary allowances (RDAs) A recommendation of essential nutrient consumption for average, healthy people.

recreation Leisure time used to refresh the mind, the body, and the spirit.

recurring costs The costs of shelter, such as those for rent or loan payments, taxes, insurance, utilities, and maintenance, that occur on a monthly basis.

regressive taxation A system of taxation that takes a smaller proportion of one's earnings as income rises or, conversely, a larger proportion of one's earnings as income falls.

renegotiable-rate loan A mortgage for which the interest rate can be adjusted up or down, but only after a specified time.

renewable term insurance Term insurance that a policyholder can renew at the end of a specific period of time, generally 1 or 5 years, without giving evidence of insurability.

rent control Laws that regulate the conditions under which rent can be increased and what percent increase is allowable.

rental agreement An agreement that outlines the terms for renting living space, either from month to month or with a longer-term lease.

residual value The estimated resale value of a product, usually a car, at the end of the leasing period. This dollar value is always written into an open-end lease contract, and when the lease is over, the lessee guaranties that the lessor will receive this amount of money.

retailer A firm that sells directly to the consumer.

retirement test The maximum wage earnings that someone receiving a Social Security retirement check can receive before suffering a reduction in benefits.

retrofit A space-age term that describes increasing the energy efficiency of an existing system by installing improved components.

revolving credit (debt) A line of credit that may be used repeatedly up to a specified limit. There is no preestablished payment schedule and no specific period of time for repaying the entire loan; also called open-end credit.

ridesharing Car pooling as a means to energy conservation; car pooling by using a van provided for a fee and driven by members of the car pool.

risk The possibility of financial loss.

rule of 70 A simple way to discover how many years it will take for anything to double if it grows at a compound annual rate. Divide 70 by the annual rate to get the doubling time. For example, if prices are rising 7 percent annually, it will take 10 years (70 ÷ 7) for the price level to double.

rule of 78 A rule applied by creditors to one-year loans in order to determine the finance charge when the loans are paid off early.

R-values Measures of an insulation's ability to resist the flow of heat from a warmer area to a cooler one. The higher the R-value the greater the insulating power of a given material.

S

scarce resource A resource for which the demand exceeds the supply at a zero price.

seasonal energy efficiency rating (SEER) A rating found on appliances such as air conditioners that are used only part of the year. They are supplied to assist comparison shopping.

secret warranty Extended protection sometimes provided, but which is not made public, by a manufacturer when a particular problem habitually develops in a specific model beyond the limited warranty period.

secured loan A loan agreement containing a provision that if the debt is not paid in full, certain pledged property may be claimed by the lender as payment.

sell-by (pull) date A date stamped on grocery products that indicates when they should be removed from sale for best performance and safety.

service-benefit insurance Insurance that makes benefit payments to the hospital or doctor to pay in full for the specific hospital or medical service rendered.

service contract A contract that covers the repair and servicing of consumer durables for a specific time period and for a flat fee when the warranty runs out.

service flow The amount of usage that a consumer receives from the entire lifespan of a product.

share of stock A share that entitles the owner to an interest in the corporation and a share in its profits.

shared-appreciation mortgages (SAMs) A mortgage in which a lender provides a lower interest in return for sharing in the increased value of a home when it is eventually sold or refinanced.

shared-equity arrangements Arrangements in which an investor provides the down payment for a buyer who is responsible for the mortgage and other costs in exchange for a share of the increased value when the home is sold.

slack fill The practice of accepting empty space in a food container to allow for the product settling.

small claims court A court that handles disagreements between parties in which the sum involved is small, generally less than $1,500, and for which legal counsel is not necessary.

socialized medicine A term that generally means that a large fraction of all medical facilities are run by the government. In addition, most medical personnel are government employees who receive a salary and do not charge patients for treatment.

solar energy Direct sunlight or indirect forms of energy such as wind or falling water that are produced by the interaction of sunlight and the earth.

special-interest groups Groups of people who share an opinion on an issue as a result of their common business, profession, hobby, or so forth and who work to make their position accepted by legislators.

spillover effects (externalities) Unintended impacts of production or consumption on third parties.

standard of living The lifestyle and types of possessions one considers adequate for oneself and toward which one strives.

standard mortgage *See* fixed-payment mortgage.

standards Qualitative or quantitative measures of performance that offer individuals a guidepost by which to measure progress toward a goal.

stereotyping A subtle form of discrimination by which people with certain roles, ideas, or values are identified, thereby restricting their behavior both individually and as a group.

stock insurance companies Insurance companies owned by their stockbrokers.

stock split A corporate procedure that gives every common-stock shareholder additional shares based on the number of shares owned at a certain date.

stockbroker Someone licensed to buy or sell shares of stock.

straight life insurance *See* whole life insurance.

style A particular design or line having characteristics that do not change.

subsistence economy A society that barely produces enough of the basic goods and services to ensure the survival of its citizens.

sunk costs Expenditures of resources that cannot be reclaimed or salvaged; also called fixed costs.

sunset clause A rule that calls for the abolition of a government agency at the end of a specified period. This rule can also be applied to personal goals or values that may become counterproductive.

supply-side economics An economic theory that contends government should support policies designed to increase the productive capacity of the nation. More specifically, these policies often involve a reduction in tax rates and government regulation with the idea of stimulating work effort and private investment.

surgical-expense insurance Insurance that provides benefits for the cost of surgical procedures performed as a result of accident or illness.

T

take back a second An arrangement whereby a buyer makes a down payment on a house and assumes the responsibility of the seller's original loan and of a second loan that makes up the difference in the seller's equity and the selling price minus the down payment.

tax audit An investigation of one's tax records by a representative of the Internal Revenue Service.

tax avoidance Any legal technique used to lessen a person's tax liability.

tax credit A dollar reduction in a person's tax bill that is subtracted after he or she computes taxes.

tax evasion An illegal attempt to avoid paying taxes.

technology Society's pool of useful industrial knowledge that regulates the amount of production possible from a resource.

term insurance policy Life insurance payable to a beneficiary only if the insured person dies within a specified period. This is sometimes referred to as death insurance.

testimonial advertisement A positive recommendation about a good or service, often given by a famous person.

textiles Fabrics that are constructed out of fibers or yarns, generally by means of weaving or knitting.

therm The unit used to measure natural gas consumption in a home or business.

time costs The direct costs, in time, of a decision; more generally, opportunity cost.

title search A review of legal records and documents to determine whether there is a prior claim to real property.

tradeoff Another term for opportunity cost; what must be given up in order to get something else.

traditional economy An economic system that relies on customs (traditions) to produce and distribute a society's output.

transaction costs Expenses related to the actual buying or selling of an asset. These could include commissions, appraisal fees, and licenses.

transfer payment An unearned payment generally made to individuals for social reasons. It can be made in money form as are Welfare or Social Security checks or it can be an in-kind subsidy such as food stamps or public housing.

transitional-age values Beliefs that fall between the proeconomic growth values of industrial-age consumers and the conservationist beliefs of post-industrial consumers.

Treasury bills (T-bills) Government bonds issued for up to 1 year in denominations of $10,000 or more. These bonds pay the market rate of interest.

trickle-across (mass-market) theory A theory that suggests that a fashion can be accepted at all social levels simultaneously as a result of mass media; also called mass-market theory.

trickle-down theory A theory that suggests that a fashion is gradually accepted at progressively lower social levels.

truth to convey falsehood Describes an ad that tells the truth but makes a product or service appear to be decidedly better than its competitors.

U

ultrasuperior good A commodity for which demand rises by more than 1 percent for every percentage point increase in consumer incomes.

uniform decreasing term insurance Insurance that costs the same from year to year but offers less protection from year to year.

uninsured-motorist insurance Insurance that protects a policyholder and his or her family if they are injured by someone without insurance.

unit pricing Calculation of the price of a small unit of a food product, such as of 1 ounce or 1 gram; usually appears on a shelf tag.

universal life insurance Insurance that is similar to whole life insurance, except that the cash value is variable, the face value can be changed without rewriting the policy, and cash may be withdrawn directly.

Universal Product Code (UPC) A grid of lines and bars printed on a product that can be read by an electronic scanner and that indicate the type of product, the size, and the manufacturer.

unsecured loan A loan that requires only a consumer's promise to repay, so is generally offered at a higher interest rate than that of a secured loan.

usury laws Legal constraints on how much interest can be charged on a loan. These ceilings have a tendency to contract the amount of money available to borrowers and to restrict the number of people who qualify for loans.

V

value judgment An opinion that is an outgrowth of a learned belief.

values Strongly held, learned beliefs that tend to arouse strong emotional, physical, and intellectual responses when they are challenged.

values clarification The process of search and choice that helps one understand one's values.

variable costs Expenses that vary directly with the amount of driving; the costs of operating a motor vehicle.

variable-rate mortgage (VRM) A mortgage with an interest rate that can rise no more than 2½ percent over the term of the mortgage, with no limit on the decrease.

vesting The process by which an employee earns nonforfeitable rights over the employer's contributions into the employee's pension plan.

Veterans Administration (VA) loan guarantee A mortgage available to eligible veterans or veterans' widows at lower-than-prevailing fixed interest rates. Mortgage insurance is provided by the federal government.

vitamins and minerals Nutrients that we get from food that are necessary for normal growth and health.

W

wage garnishment A court order that instructs an employer to set aside a portion of a consumer's wages until a debt is paid off.

waiting period The time between the onset of an insured person's disability and the start of the policy's income-protection benefits.

warranty An assurance given by the seller that a product is in good working order and will provide good service for a period of time.

weights and measures standards Guidelines accepted as a basis for comparing the quantity or quality of consumer goods.

whole life insurance Life insurance that combines term insurance with a cash value or "forced savings" plan; sometimes called straight life insurance or ordinary life insurance.

wholesaler A firm that sells to other firms, not directly to consumers.

will A legal document that allows the transfer of an estate based on the wishes of the deceased person.

windfall profits A sudden undeserved increase in a firm's revenues with no change in costs.

wraparound mortgage A mortgage vehicle in which the seller loans the price of real property minus the down payment to the buyer, who in turn amortizes the loan directly to the seller. The seller retains the original mortgage obligation.

Y

yield The return on an investment.

Z

zero-based budgeting A concept under which all expenditures must be justified every year; no carryovers are allowed from the previous year.

zero-bracket amount (ZBA) The amount of income that a taxpayer may exclude from federal income tax instead of itemizing specific deductible expenditures.

Index

A

Ability-to-pay principle, 438
Acceleration clauses, 196
Active solar systems, 309
Actuarial table, 495
Actuaries, 494
Adjustable mortgage loan (AML), 383
Adjustable rate mortgage (ARM), 383
Adjusted balance method, 192
Advertising, 68–91
　benefits of, 86–89
　birth of, 72–73
　brand-name identification and, 87
　expenditures, 74–76
　major advertisers, 73–75
　types of, 76–86
Advocacy advertising, 85
Age, income and, 46
　credit and, 203
　health care and, 406
Age earning curve, 46
Age of high mass consumption, 6–8, 72
Aid to Families with Dependent Children (AFDC), 204
　Medicaid and, 407
ALA Auto and Travel Club, 324
All-savers tax-exempt certificates, 474
American Bankers Association, 473
American Bar Association (ABA), 87
American Chamber of Horrors (de Forest Lamb), 101–102
American Council of Life Insurance Institute, 412
American Medical Association (AMA), 87
　doctor printout profile, 405
American Trial Lawyers Association, 348
Amortization, 378
Annual Gas Mileage Guide (Environmental Protection Agency), 321
Annual percentage rate (APR), 188–191
　of financing a car, 322–324

Antitrust and Monopoly Subcommittee (Kefauver), 102
Apartments, 364
Appliances
　kilowatt-hour consumption of electric, 302
　shopping for, 244
Appraisal, 380
Argus Chart of Health Insurance, 419
Asset, 201–203
Assumable loans, 378
Atwan, Robert, 80
Auto CAPs, 339
Automobiles, 317–353
　comparison of new car models, 321
　costs of ownership and operation, 323–330
　energy costs of, 290–293
　insurance for, 342–349
　leasing, 332–334
　repair of, 337–342
　retrofitting, 293
　shopping for new, 330–332
　shopping for used, 334–337
　tuneup checklist, 292
Average cost
　of owning a car, 297
Average daily balance method, 192
Average tax rate, 439, 445–447

B

Bait and switch tactics, 85–86
Bankruptcy, 211–213
Banks, commercial
　as sources of credit, 196–197
Barter, 170
Basic Four food groups, 254
Basic insurance coverage, 419
Bates vs. *State Bar of Arizona*, 120
Bearish, defined, 480
Benefits-received principle, 438
Benham, Lee, 87
Bernard, Jessie, 62
Best's Insurance Reports, 347

Better Business Bureau (BBB), 111
Better Homes and Gardens, 89
Bicycles, 294–295
Bill collectors, 210
Bill consolidation loan, 185
Biomass, 311
Bird, Caroline, 42
Blended (reconstituted) families, 55
Blue Cross, 417–418
Blue Shield, 417–418
Bond, defined, 469
Bottom-up theory, 223
Boulding, Kenneth, 295
Brand names, quality control and, 87
British thermal units (Btu's), 310
Brooklyn College Consumer Education Classes, 416
Budgeting, 127–147
　buying-process model and, 225
　collective money management techniques, 143–144
　credit and, 188
　designing a budget, 133–136
　for household durables, 240–241
　housing and, 361–364
　need for, 130–131
　paying bills, 144–145
　the process of, 136–140
　for textiles, 230
Bullish, defined, 480
Bureau of Labor Statistics (BLS), 152, 155, 441
Burial arrangements, 521–522
Business, inflation and, 161–162
Buyer's guide window sticker, 335
Buying-process model, 223–224
　defined, 220
　for household durables, 239–246
　steps in, 224–228
　for textiles, 228–239

C

California Department of Insurance, 345
Calories, 252–253
Capital assets, 468

Capital gains, 459, 467
Capital loss, 467
Carcinogens, 268
Career decisions, 62–63
Cars, types of, 321. *See also* Automobiles
Carson, Rachel, 102
Case Against College, The (Bird), 42
Case, John, 162
Case goods, 243
Cash-value insurance, 501–505
Casualty losses, deductions for, 451
Caveat emptor, 98
Celebrity endorsements, 79
Center for Automotive Safety, 338
Certificates of deposit (CDs), 473
Changing Times, 89
Chapter 7 (straight) bankruptcy, 213
Chapter 13 bankruptcy (wage-earner plan), 213
Characterizing ingredient, 259
Charitable contributions, 451
Childcare, 62
  tax credit for, 453
Child Protection and Toy Safety Act, 109
Children, costs of, 55–56
  television advertising and, 81
Civil Rights Act of 1964, 46, 48
Civil Rights Act of 1968, 370
Claims Court, 455
Classics, defined, 221
Closed-end lease, 333
Closed-end mutual funds, 482
Closing (settlement), 386
  checklist, 388
  closing costs, 363
Clothing. *See* Textiles
Co-insurance, 343
Collateral, 196, 201–203
Collision insurance, 343
Coloring methods, 234
Commission, 375
Common stock, 478
Community hospitals, 411
Commuter Computer (California Department of Transportation), 298
Comparative advertising, 80
Competition, advertising and, 87
Compounding, 155, 472
Comprehensive insurance, 344–345
Condominium, 365
Confiscatory tax rates, 438

Conspicuous consumption, 22
Consumer action panels (CAPs), 119
  Auto CAPs, 339
Consumer agencies, directory of
  federal, 529–532
  state, 533–537
Consumer Bill of Rights (1962), 103
Consumer co-operative, 173–175
Consumer Credit Counselors Service, 210
Consumer Credit Protection Act, 103
  finance charges and, 188, 191
  Wage Garnishment Law, 211
Consumer decision-making model, 33–36
Consumer durable goods, 223–224
  where to buy, 226
Consumer economics, defined, 4–5
Consumer education, 4–5
Consumer finance companies, 198
Consumerism, defined, 6
  uses and abuses of, 107
Consumer Price Index (CPI), 152–155
  prices of clothing and, 230
Consumer problems, steps in
  voicing, 117, 123
  seeking help for, 526–528
Consumer Product Safety Commission (CPSC), 103, 105, 108–109, 529
  Reagan administration and, 123
  recalls and, 115
Consumer protection, 94–125
  food safety and, 100–102
  modern, 102–104
  in the 1980s, 123
  roots of in the United States, 101
  types and levels of, 106–115
Consumer publications, 115
Consumer Reports
  Buying Guide, 115, 336, 347
  household durables and, 242
  as an information source, 89
  rating of Volkswagens, 90, 102
Consumer rights, 116–123
Consumers
  benefits of being informed as, 98–99
  life cycles and, 38–67
  Presidential support for, 103–104
  rules for inflation-wise, 169–171
  values and, 23–27
Consumer's Digest, 89
Consumer Skills Test, 4
Consumer sovereignty, 31

Consumers' Research Magazine Annual Guide, 115
  household durables and, 242
  as an information source, 89
Consumer's Resource Handbook, 119
Consumers Union, 102, 115
  on life insurance, 501, 508
Consumption activity, defined, 4
Consumption patterns, 11–14
Contract of sale, 377
Convenience foods, 277
Conventional loans, 378
Cooling-off provision, 84
Cooperative housing, 364
Corrective advertising, 82
Cost-of-living adjustment (COLA), 164
Cost-push inflation, 157–158
"Crack the Codes," 265
Creative financing, 384
Credit, 179–215
  applying for, 200–203
  bankruptcy and, 211–213
  benefits of, 183–187
  correcting billing errors, 205
  costs of, 187–196
  denial of, 204–205
  language of, 197
  limits, 207–211
  overview of, 182–183
  sources of, 196–200
Credit bureau, 205
Credit cards
  advantages of, 187
  comparison of, 194–195
  reporting lost or stolen, 207
"Credit Cards: Auto Repair Protection" (FTC), 206
Credit counseling, 210
Credit history, 201
Credit life insurance, 498
Credit unions, 198
Cremation, 521
Customs, 30–31

D

Date of manufacture, 264
Debt. *See* Credit
Debt ceiling, 207–208, 209
Debt liquidation timetable, 208
Deceptive advertising, 82–86
Decision making, 6, 19–37
  automobiles and, 320–322
  benefits of, 21–22

contraints and restrictions on, 29–33
consumer model, 33–36
costs, of, 20–21
nutrition and, 273–279
in selecting housing, 361–391
See also Buying-process model
Decreasing term insurance, 499
Deductible, 344
Deductions, 499–451
Default, 378
Deflation, 156
de Forest Lamb, Ruth, 101–102
Delaney Clause, 268, 269
Demand-pull inflation, 156–157
Demography, income and, 46
Dental-expense insurance, 422
Department of Energy (DOE), 312
Department of Transportation (DOT), 322
 comparison of costs per mile of five types of cars, 325
 gasoline costs and, 325
Deposit, 364
Depository Institutions Deregulation and Monetary Control Act of 1980, 196, 199, 474
Deposit term insurance, 501
Depreciation
 of automobiles, 322
 of household durables, 241
Diagnosis related groups (DRGs), 413
Diamonds, as investments, 167
Diet. *See* Food
Diminishing marginal utility, 438
Disability income insurance, 421
Discount points, 380
Discretionary income, defined, 12, 136
Discrimination, income and, 48
 credit and, 203–204
 in housing, 370
Disposable income, 290
Ditlow, Clarence, 339
Divorce, 57–58
Donoghue's Money Fund Directory, 477
Dow Jones Industrial Average, 480
Down payment, 363
Drug interactions, 417
Drugs
 over-the-counter, 416
 prescription, 414–416
Duesenberry, James, 19

E

Earnest agreement (binder), 377
Earnest money, 377
Easements, 377
Economic impact statement, 106
Economic Recovery Tax Act of 1981, 444, 446, 466, 519
Economics, defined, 6
Edsels, Luckies, & Frigidaires (Atwan), 80
Education, costs and benefits of, 44
Educational expenses, deductions for, 451
"Effect of Advertising on the Price of Eyeglasses, The" (Benham), 87
Electric meter, reading, 301
Embalming, 521
Emergency fund, 133–136
 credit and, 186
Emotional advertisement, 80
Employees Retirement Income Security Act (ERISA), 518, 522
"Empty nest" stage, 56
Endowment life insurance, 503
Energy, 287
 future sources of, 311–312
Energy conservation, 282–315
 in the home, 303–310
 tips for, 304–305
Energy consumption
 for the home, 299–310
 for transportation, 289–299
 in the United States, 287–289
Energy Efficiency Ratings (EER), 109, 112
Energy efficiency ratio, 309–310
Energy Policy and Conservation Act, 243
Engel, Ernst, 8
Engel's law, 8
Entitlement programs, 436
Environmental Protection Agency (EPA), 109
 Annual Gas Mileage Guide, 321
 auto tuneups and, 292
 fuel economy and, 326–327
 pesticides and, 266–267
 Reagan administration and, 123
Equal Credit Opportunity Act, 103, 203–205
Equal Employment Opportunity Commission, 48
Equity, 359
Equity mutual funds, 479, 481

F

Escrow (impound) accounts, 388
Exclusions, 448–449
Executor (executrix), 520
Exemptions, 452
Expiration (use by) date, 264
Expressed warranties, 114, 338
Extended families, 52
Extended warranty plan, 340

F

Fabric construction, 233–234
Fabric finishes, 234
Face value, defined, 476
Facts for Consumers (FTC), 206
Fad, defined, 221
Fair Credit Billing Act, 205
 stopping payment for defective goods and services and, 206–207
Fair Credit Reporting Act, 103, 109, 205
Fair Debt Collection Practices Act, 109, 210
Fair Packaging and Labeling Act (FPLA) of 1966, 258
Family Circle, 89
Family life cycle. *See* Life cycles
Family patterns, 52–53
Family roles, 59–64
Fashion, 219
 influences on, 222–223
 style and fads and, 220–223
Fashion cycle, 222
Fashion dictators, 223
Federal and state agencies, consumer problems and, 119, 529–537
Federal Bankruptcy Code (Public Law 95–598), 212
Federal budget, 441–442
Federal Cigarette Labeling and Advertising Act of 1966, 103
Federal Communications Commission (FCC), advertising and, 77
Federal Department of Transportation, 297
Federal Deposit Insurance Corporation (FDIC), 471
Federal District Court, 455
Federal Fair Housing Law, 370
Federal Home Loan Bank Board, 381
 average of mortgage rates, 383
Federal Housing Administration (FHA), 380

Federal Information Center (FIC), 108, 119, 531
Federal National Mortgage Association (FNMA), 385
  Home Seller's Program, 386
Federal Savings and Loan Insurance Corporation (FSLIC), 471
Federal Trade Commission (FTC), 529
  advertising and, 77–78, 79, 82, 83
  buyer's guide window sticker and, 335
  creation of, 101
  credit laws and, 109–110
  door-to-door installment contracts and, 84
  energy efficiency ratings and, 309, 310
  enforcing Textile Labeling Act and, 230
  Fair Credit Billing Act and, 206
  Geritol case and, 107
  health foods and, 272
  Reagan administration and, 123
  study of advertising on cost of eyeglasses, 87
  whole life insurance and, 503
Federal Trade Commission Act, 101
  Wheeler-Lea amendment to, 102
Feminine Mystique, The (Friedan), 26
Fiber content, 230
  guide to, 231–232
Finance charges, 188–191
  methods of calculating, 191–192
Finance companies, 198
"First Meeting of Creditors, The," 212
Fixed expenses, 133
  of automobile ownership, 323–325
Fixed-payment mortgage, 378
Flammable Fabrics Act, 109
Flat tax, 440
Flexible expenses, 136
Flexible Loan Insurance Program (FLIP), 382
Flexner, Abraham, 408
Flexner Report, 408
Food, 249–281
  enriched (fortified), 257
  factors that affect choices of, 252–254
  health, 270–271
  natural, 271–272
  safety and quality of, 260–270
Food additives, 267–269
Food Additives Amendment, 268
Food and Drug Administration (FDA), 109, 530
  advertising and, 77, 82
  creation of, 102
  food contaminants and, 265
  generic drugs and, 415
  Reagan administration and, 123
Food and Nutrition Service (FNS), 110
Food, Drug, and Cosmetic Act (1938), 102, 268
Food labeling, 256–260
  codes for prices and dates, 262–264
  need for, 259–260
  nutritional, 257–258
Food safety, 100–102
  costs and benefits of, 269–270
  hazards to, 265
Food Safety and Quality Service (FSQS), 110
Forbes, Roy, 4
Forced savings, credit as, 185
Foreclosure, 380
Fossil fuels, 288
Fraud, 99
Free good, 20
Free-rider effect, 435
Free to Choose (Friedman), 105
Friedan, Betty, 26
Friedman, Milton
  proportional tax and, 440
  on regulation, 105
Friedman, Rose, 105
Fringe benefits, 164–165
Full warranty, 114
Funerals, 521–522
Future of Marriage, The (Bernard), 62

G

Galbraith, John Kenneth, 32
Gas meter, reading, 300–301
General Electric "Quick-Fix System," 245
Generally Recognized As Safe (GRAS) list, 268
Generic Drug Law (New York), 415
Generic drugs, 414–416
Generic (family) name, of fibers, 230
Geographic location, income and, 49
Geritol case, 82, 107
Goals, 27–28
  lifetime, 43
Good Housekeeping, 112
Goodwin, David, 496
Government
  health care and, 406
  inflation and, 160–161
Government regulation, 104–106
  federal protection, 108–111
  providing safety and, 106
  state and local protection, 111
Government securities, 475–477
Government services, 430–461
  an overview, 434–436
  providing, 434–435
  transferring income, 435–436
Graduated-payment mortgage, 381
Graduate Medical National Advisory Committee, 407–408
Great Expectations (Jones), 46
Gresham's Law, 157
Gross income, 132, 448
Gross National Product (GNP), 402, 437
Gross National Product Implicit Price Deflator (GNP deflator), 155
Group life insurance, 497

H

Harris, Marvin, 98
Hazard insurance, 388
Hazardous Substance Act, 109
Health
  defined, 398
  maintaining, 424–426
Health care, 395–429
  alternatives, 423–424
  cost of, 402–404
  deductions for, 449–451
  demand for, 404–407
  insurance, 416–422
  prescription drugs, 414–416
  supply of, 407–413
  in the United States, 398–402
Health foods, 270–271
Health insurance, private plans, 416–422
Health Maintenance Organization (HMO), 422–423
Health System Agency (HSA), 412–413

High-ball technique, 331
Highway Trust Fund, 297
Holmes, Oliver Wendell, 436
Home-service life insurance, 498
Hospital-expense insurance, 419
Hospital indemnity coverage, 419
Hospitals, 410–412
Household durables, 239–246
   shopping calendar for, 242
Households, types of, 53–57
Housework, 59–61
Housing, 354–393
   buying, 359–361, 374–389, 391
   decision making about, 361–391
   renting, 358–359
How to Get Control of Your Time and Your Life (Lakein), 43
How to Save a Fortune on Your Life Insurance (Kaye), 496
Human capital, 44, 484–485
Hyperinflation, 158

I

Identification, credit cards and, 187
Identity standard, 259
Implied warranties, 114
Implied warranty of fitness, 114
Implied warranty of habitability, 373
Implied warranty of merchantability, 114
Income
   budgeting and, 131–133
   expenses and, 184–185
   as a factor in consumption, 8
   factors that determine, 44–52
   health care and, 406
   types of, 42–44
Income brackets, 439
Income tax, 441–456
   calculations of, 447–453
   federal, 442–445
   understanding, 447
Index fund, 479
Individual life insurance, 497, 509
Individual Retirement Accounts (IRAs), 519
Industrial-age values, 23
Industrial life insurance, 498
Industrial Revolution, 58
Infant mortality rate, 401
Inferior goods, 8
Inflation, 149–177
   credit and, 186–187
   defined, 152
   fighting, 165–175

   history of, in recent times, 155–160
   life insurance and, 512
   measuring, 152–155
   productivity and, 158–160
   progressive income tax and, 446
   third-party payers and, 406
   types of, 156–158
   winners and losers during, 160–165
Inflationary expectations, 158
Inflation hedges, 468
Information
   advertising and, 86–87
   buying-process model and, 225–227
   obtaining product, 89–90
   See also Consumer publications
Informative advertising, 78
Informative legislation, 103
Insolvency, credit and, 187–188
Installment (closed-end) credit, 182
Institutional advertisement, 80
Insulation, 306–307
Insurance, 491–513
   of automobiles, 322, 342–349
   health care, 416–422
   See also Life insurance
"Intensity factor," 402
Interest
   deduction for, 451
   defined, 465–466
Interest-adjusted cost index (IAC), 513
Internal Revenue Service, 449, 453, 454, 455
   insurance dividends and, 496
International care labels, 233
International Fabricare Institute, 239
Interstate Commerce Commission (ICC), 390, 530
Investment portfolio, 471
Investments, 463–489
   comparing, 485–486
   inflation and, 159
   personal, to counter inflation, 165–167
   types of, 471–485
   vocabulary of, 466–470
Investment tradeoffs, 469–470
Item pricing, 262

J

Joint ownership, 521
Jones, Landon Y., 46
Jungle, The (Sinclair), 100

K

Kaye, Barry, 496, 501
Kefauver, Estes, 102
Kelly Blue Book Market Report, 331, 335
Kennedy, John F., 103
Keogh plans, 519
Kidder, Wesley J., 345
Kilocalories, 287
Kilowatt hours (kwh), 301–302

L

Labor income, 42
Laffer, Arthur, 444
Laffer Curve, 444
Lakein, Alan, 43
Landlord-tenant relations, 373–374
Law of demand, 11, 404
Lease, defined, 332
   types of, 333
Leasing
   automobiles, 332–334
   housing, 358, 372–373
Legal Aid Society, 121
Legal assistance, consumer problems and, 119–123
Leisure foregone, 44
Leisure time, 63
Lemon Aid, 339
Letter of last instructions, 521
Level term insurance, 499
Liability insurance, 342–343
Life cycles, 38–67
   defined, 41
   special problems in, 57–58
   types of households and, 53–57
Life expectancy, 398, 399
Life insurance, 494–495
   buying, 496–499
   cash-value, 501–505
   choosing, 505–512
   cost of, 512–513
   as a source of credit, 200
   term insurance, 499–501
Limited-payment life insurance, 503
Limited warranty, 114
Liquidity, 468
Load, defined, 482
Lobbyists, 172
Loopholes, 458
Low-ball technique, 331
Lumens, 308

M

Magna Carta, standardization of measures and, 99
Magnusson-Moss Warranty Act, 109, 112, 114, 337
Major medical-expense insurance, 420–421
Malnutrition, 251
Malpractice suits, 410
Manufacturers, consumer problems and, 119
Marginal cost of owning a car, 296
Marginal tax rate, 439, 445–447
Market economy, defined, 8
Marriage patterns, 52–53
Marriage tax, 450
Married-couple households, 54–57
Marx, Karl, 22
Mass transit, 295–297
Maynes, E. Scott, 6, 11
Meat, inspection and grading of, 260
Meatborne Hazard Control Center, 110
Mechanics, auto, 340–342
Medicaid, 398, 407
Medical insurance, for driving, 345
Medicare, 398, 406–407
Memorial society, 522
Mental human capital, 46
Merchandise acceptance curve, 222
 applied, 225
Micheletti, Julie, 413
Minarik, Joseph T., 164
Minerals, 272
Mobile homes, 365–366
Modular homes, 391
Monetarism, 157
Money, 89
Money, emotions and, 141–142
Money management. *See* Budgeting
Money-market mutual funds, 477
Month-to-month rental agreement, 371–373
Moore, John, 163
Mopeds, 295
Mortgage, 378
 fixed-payment, 378–381
 floating-payment, 381–386
Mortgage insurance, 380
Mortgage note, 378
Mortgage term insurance, 499
Motorcycles, 295

Moving, 389–391
 checklist for, 389
Muckraking, 101
Multiple Listing book, 375, 377
Municipal bonds, 469
Murphy's law, 133, 337
Mutual funds
 closed-end, 482
 equity, 479, 481
 money-market, 477
 open-end, 482
 See also Investments, Stock market
Mutual insurance companies, 495

N

Nader, Ralph, 102
National Assessment of Educational Progress (NAEP), 4
National Association of Furniture Manufacturers Seal of Integrity, 112
National Association of Home Builders, 368
National Automobile Dealer's Association (NADA), 331, 334
National Consumer Cooperative Bank, 175
National Credit Union Association (NCUA), 471
National Highway Traffic Safety Administration (NHTSA), 110
 auto repairs and, 337
 mopeds and, 295
 recalls and, 115
National Highway Traffic Safety hotline, 337
National Institute of Automotive Service Excellence (NIASE), 341
National Resource Center for Consumers of Legal Services, 120
Natural foods, 271–272
Necessities, 12
Negotiable order of withdrawal (NOW) account, 474
Net (disposable) income, 131
Net worth, 140–141
 assessment of, 208
New-home warranties, 368

New Jersey Hospital Cost Containment Plan, 413
New York Public Interest Research Group (NYPIRG), 416
No-fault insurance, 348
No-load mutual funds, 482
Nominal dollars, 154
Nonmarket home production, 44
Normal good, 8
Nuclear family, defined, 52
Nurse-midwives, 409–410
Nutrient density, 256
Nutrients, 251
Nutrition
 cost of, 272–279
 guides to, 254–256
Nutritive Values of Food (U.S. Government Printing Office), 255
Nystrom, Paul, 219

O

Oakley, Ann, 59
Occupational Outlook Handbook, 45
Occupational Safety and Health Administration (OSHA), 105
Octane ratings, 326
Odometer law, 335
Official Used Car Guide (NADA), 331, 335
Old Age, Survivors, Disability, and Health Insurance (OASDHI) program, 510
100,000,000 Guinea Pigs (Kallet and Schlink), 101
Open-end (revolving) credit, 191–196
Open-end lease, 333
Open-end mutual funds, 482
Opportunity costs, 9–10
 scarce resources and, 20–21
Organic food, 271–272
Organization for Economic Cooperation and Development (OECD), 437
Organization of Petroleum Exporting Countries (OPEC), 161
Overregulation, 106

P

Packard, Vernal S., 270
Pack (packaging) date, 264
Parents magazine, 112
Parkinson's law, 63

Participating life insurance, 496
Passages (Sheehy), 56
Passive solar technique, 308
Patient package inserts (PPIs), 417
Patterson, Patricia, 182
Pauling, Linus, 272
Pawnbrokers, 200
Payback period, 304–306
Payment adjustment period, 384
Pension Benefit Guarantee Corporation (ERISA), 518–519
Pension plans, 517–519
People Power: What Committees Are Doing to Counter Inflation, 173
Permanent Care Labeling Act of 1972, 233
Pesticides, 266–267
Photovoltaic cells, 311–312
Photovoltaics Division (Department of Energy), 312
Physical human capital, 46
Physician assistants, 408–409
Physician-expense insurance, 420
Physicians, 407–408
Poison Packaging Act, 109
Political contributions, 453
Politics, inflation and, 171–172
Porter, Sylvia, 210
Post-industrial-age values, 23, 90
Preferred stock, 477–478
Premium, defined, 494
Prepayment penalty, 378
Prescription drugs, 414–416
Previous balance method, 192
Price, as a factor in comsumption, 11
Principal, 378
Private (business) sector, 108
  consumer protection and, 111–115
Probate, 520
Progressive income tax, 160, 439
Proportional taxation, 439–440
Proposition 13, 359, 457
Protective legislation, 99, 103
Prudent man rule, 518
Psychic income, 42
Public assistance, 204
Public goods, 435
Public Highway Act of 1956, 297
Public Law 93-351, 175
Public Law 95-598, 212
Public sector, defined, 108
Puffery advertising, 79
Pure Food and Drug Act, 100, 101

R

Race, income and, 47–48
Random-walk theory, 479
Rate cap, 384
Reagan administration, federal consumer protection services and, 123
Real dollars, 154
Real estate, 483–484
Real estate brokers, 375
Real Estate Settlement Procedures Act (RESPA), 386
Real income, 49
Real property, 378
Recalls, 103, 115
Recordkeeping, credit cards and, 187
Recreation, 63
Recurring costs, 361
Refrigerator Safety Act, 109
Regressive taxation, 440–441
Relative price changes, 167
Renewable term insurance, 499
"Rental equivalence" measure of housing costs, 155
Rent control, 374
Renting, 358–359, 370–374, 390
Residential energy credit, 453
Residual value, 333
Retailers, 73
Retail outlets, as sources of credit, 198
Retaliatory eviction, 373
Retirement, 57, 64, 513–519
Retirement test, 517
Retrofit
  of automobiles, 293
  of the home, 304–306
Revenue, for state and local governments, 456
Ridesharing, 297–299
Risk, 467
Rostow, W. W., 6–7, 72
Ruggles, Richard, 154
Rule of 70, 155, 505–506
Rule of 78, 190
R-values, 307

S

Saccharin, 269
Salmonella, 266–267
Saving, 463–489
Savings accounts, 471–473
Savings and loan associations, 198
Scarce resource, 20

Schumacher, E. F., 22
Seals and ratings, 112, 113
Seasonal energy efficiency rating (SEER), 310
"Second" (irregular) goods, 225
Secret warranty, 338
Secured loan, 196
Securities and Exchange Commission (SEC), 77
Sell-by (pull) date, 264
Service benefit insurance, 419
Service contract, 245
  for automobiles, 340
Service flow, 241
Sex
  credit and, 203–204
  income and, 46–47
Shared-appreciation mortgages (SAMs), 384
Shared equity arrangements, 384
Share of stock, 477
Sheehy, Gail, 56
Shell Mileage Marathon, 291
Silent Spring, The (Carson), 102
Sinclair, Upton, 100
Single-family homes, 364
Single parents, 58
  childcare and, 62
Single-person households, 53–54
Skipper, Harold, Jr., 501
Slack fill, 259
Sloan, Frank, 408
Small claims court, 121–123
Small Is Beautiful: Economics As If People Mattered (Schumacher), 22
Smoking, 424–425
Socialized medicine, 423–424
Social Security, 510, 514–517
  politics and, 515–516
  restrictions on, 516–517
  rights to, 514–515
Social Security Act, 406
Solar energy, 308
Somers, Herman, 412
Special Assistant to the President for Consumer Affairs (1964), 103
Special-interest groups, 172
Spillover effects (externalities) of advertising, 89
Stages of Economic Growth, The (Rostow), 6–7
Stampfl, Ronald, 13, 158
  on values, 23–24
Standard and Poor's Index, 479, 480, 505

Standard and Poor's Register of Corporations, 119
Standard of living, 49
Standards, 28
State Health Planning Development Agency, 413
Statement of Affairs, 212
Stereotyping, 80
Stockbroker, 479
Stock insurance companies, 495
Stock market, 477–479
Stock split, 479
Stop Wasting Your Insurance Dollars (Goodwin), 496
Straight bankruptcy, 213
Style, 221
Sulfa drugs, 102
Sunk costs, 28–29
Sunset, 89
Sunset clause, 28
Supplemental Security Income (SSI), 407
Supply and demand, for occupations, 45–46
Supply-side economics, 444
Surgeon General's Advisory Committee on Television and Social Behavior, 25
Surgery, 411
Surgical-expense insurance, 419
Survey Research Center (University of Michigan), 182

T

Taste, as a factor in consumption, 10–11
Taxable income, 447, 452
Taxation, 430–461
  in developed nations, 437
  fairness of, 456–459
  of income, 441–456
  principles of, 438
  progressive, proportional, and regressive, 438–441
  property taxes, 457
Tax audit, 454–456
Tax avoidance, 453
Tax credits, 452–453
Tax evasion, 453
Tax Foundation, 437
Tax preparers, 453–454
Tax rate (estimated by income), 458
Technology, 159
Tele-law, 120

Term insurance, 499–501
Testimonial advertising, 79
Textile Labeling Law, 109
Textile product construction, 234–235
Textiles, 216
  buying-process for, 228–239
  clothing, 228–239
  household, 228
  shopping calendar for buying, 237
Thalidomide, 102–103
Theft losses, deductions for, 451
Therm, 301
Third-party payers, 405–406
Thomas' Register of Manufacturers, 119
Time, as a factor in consumption, 9–10
Time costs, 9–10
Time management, household tasks and, 61
Tires, 329
Title search, 386
Tobacco smoking, 424–425
Tom, Sally, 410
Tradeoffs, 20
Traditional economy, 7
Transaction costs, 468
Transfer payments, 435–436
Transitional-age values, 23
Transportation, 289–299
  automobiles, 290–293
  bicycles, 294–295
  mass transit, 295–297
  mopeds, 295
  motorcycles, 295
  ridesharing, 297–299
Treasury bills (T-bills), 476–477
Trickle-across (mass market) theory, 223
Trickle-down theory, 223
Truth-in-Lending Act, 103, 109
  lost or stolen credit cards and, 207
Truth to convey falsehood advertising, 81
Two-income households, 49–52
  childcare and, 62
"Typical consumer" endorsements, 79

U

Ultrasuperior goods, 8
Understanding Inflation (Case), 162

Underwriter's Laboratories (UL) seal, 112
Uniform Commercial Code, 114, 338
Uniform decreasing term insurance, 499
Uninsured-motorist insurance, 345
United States Tax Court, 455
Unit pricing, 262
Universal life insurance, 503–504
Universal Product Code (UPC), 262, 263
Unsafe at Any Speed (Nader), 102
Unsecured loan, 196
U.S. Cooperative Extension System, 111
U.S. Department of Agriculture (USDA), 110, 252, 530
  food consumption surveys, 272
  grading of beef, 260
  grading of eggs, 261
  grading of vegetables, 261
U.S. Department of Health and Human Services, 423
U.S. Office of Consumer Affairs, 173
U.S. Office of Education, 4
U.S. Postal Service, 531
  advertising and, 77
U.S. Public Health Service, 260
U.S. Recommended Dietary Allowances (RDAs), 254–255, 257–258
U.S. Savings Bonds, 476
  as investments, 160
"Usual, customary, and reasonable" (UCR), reimbursement system, 420
Usury laws, 193

V

Value judgment, 23
Values, 23–27
  clarifying, 26–27
  conflicts in, 26
  goals and, 27
  sources of, 24–26
Variable costs, of automobile ownership, 325–327
Veblen, Thorstein, 22
Veterans Administration (VA) loan guarantee, 380
Vitamins, 272

W

Wage-earner plan, 213
Wage garnishment, 210–211
Waiting period (insurance), 421
Warranties, 112–115
  for automobiles, 337–339
  new home, 368
Weidenbaum, Murray L., 104
Weights and measures standards, 99–100
Whole life insurance, 502–503
Wholesalers, 74
Wholesome Meat Act of 1967, 260
Wholesome Poultry Act of 1968, 260
Wiley, Harvey, 100
Wills, 519–521
Windfall profits, 161
Woman's Work (Oakley), 59
Work roles, 58–59
World Health Organization (WHO), 398
Wraparound mortgage, 384–385

Y

Yields, 446, 466–467
Your Federal Income Tax—For Individuals (Publication 17), 449

Z

Zero-based budgeting, 28
Zero-bracket amount (ZBA), 449
Zero risk, 106